AF607930

EARLY UKRAINIAN SETTLEMENTS IN CANADA, 1895–1900

THE CANADIAN CENTENNIAL SERIES

sponsored by the

Ukrainian Canadian Research Foundation

founded in 1957 by

Royal Canadian Legion Ukrainian Canadian

Veterans' Branches 360, Toronto, 522, Hamilton,

and 502, St. Catharines, Ontario

This study is the first in a series of cultural, historical, and sociological research projects of the Ukrainian Canadian Research Foundation.

EARLY UKRAINIAN SETTLEMENTS IN CANADA

1895-1900

Dr. Josef Oleskow's Role
in the Settlement of the
Canadian Northwest

by

VLADIMIR J. KAYE

Foreword by George W. Simpson

PUBLISHED FOR
THE UKRAINIAN CANADIAN RESEARCH FOUNDATION
BY UNIVERSITY OF TORONTO PRESS
1964

© UNIVERSITY OF TORONTO PRESS 1964
Printed in Canada
Reprinted in 2018
ISBN 978-1-4875-7727-8 (paper)

IN MEMORY OF THE PIONEERS

who by their courage and perseverance

helped to build the Canadian West

Foreword

BY GEORGE W. SIMPSON

THIS HISTORY of the beginnings of Ukrainian settlement in Canada is written by a Ukrainian Canadian scholar whose family traditions span centuries of Ukrainian history, and whose own experience covers both the Old World and the New. His is a completely documented story, one which adds new facts to the history of Canadian immigration. It is the most reliable and detailed source book for the study of early Ukrainian settlement in Western Canada which has yet appeared, or is likely to appear.

Dr. Vladimir J. Kaye (Kysilewsky) was born in 1896—at the very time of the emigration which he describes in his book—in the province of Galicia, then part of the Austro-Hungarian Empire. His family history has been traced back for some three hundred years. One of his ancestors is mentioned in the Cossack Army Register of 1648 as serving in the Poltava Regiment of Hetman Bohdan Khmelnitsky. Later, another member, a landowner in the Kiev area, joined Hetman Ivan Mazepa and served on his general staff. The Kysilewsky family was well known throughout the Ukraine. The last elected Mayor of Kiev before the abolition of self-government in 1836, Gregory I. Kysilewsky, who served as mayor in the years 1827–1834, was one of its distinguished members. A number of Dr. Kaye's relatives served in the Church. His father, the son of a clergyman, became a civil servant in the Austro-Hungarian Empire. His mother, Olena Simenovich, came from a literary family and herself had a notable career as a pioneer leader of the feminist movement in Galicia, the author of several books, the editor of two women's newspapers, and an assiduous worker in several Ukrainian women's organizations in Europe and overseas. In 1928 she was elected the first Ukrainian woman senator in the Polish Parliament. Twenty years later, she became President of the World Federation of Ukrainian

Women's Organizations. During her visit to the United States and Canada between the two World Wars, her work brought her into contact with women leaders elsewhere, notably with Jane Addams in Chicago, Margaret McWilliams, and Judge Emily Murphy.

Dr. Vladimir Kaye studied at the University of Vienna and at the Institute of Eastern European Studies, where he received his Ph.D. degree in 1924. He then went to Paris and eventually came to Canada. For two years, 1928–1930, he was the editor of a weekly Ukrainian newspaper published in Edmonton, the *Western News*. His newspaper activity brought him into contact with every phase of Canadian public life. He was particularly intrigued with the integration of ethnic groups into an evolving pattern of Canadian life. In 1931, Dr. Kaye went to England to pursue post-graduate studies at the School of Slavonic and East European Studies at the University of London. Here he worked under the direction of its outstanding scholars, Sir Bernard Pares, Professor Robert Seton-Watson, and Professor W. J. Rose. In London he also served in the position of Director of the Ukrainian Press Bureau. He was for many years a member of the Royal Institute of International Affairs in London, and was later accredited to the British Ministry of Information.

It was during his period in London that I first made Dr. Kaye's acquaintance and that I was impressed by the wealth of accurate information he possessed, as well as by his quiet, modest manner. In 1940 Dr. Kaye returned to Canada, and I became associated with him in 1941 when the Department of National War Services set up a special information branch to promote co-operation with Canadians of recent European origin. This branch was, incidentally, transformed after the war, in 1946, into a section under the Department of the Secretary of State, and in 1950 it became part of the newly-created Department of Citizenship and Immigration. Dr. Kaye's function in the original branch, and subsequently, was to act as liaison officer with ethnic groups and their press. Dr. Kaye was eminently qualified for this work, in that his knowledge of European languages was extensive, including even Yiddish, his academic studies were in history and ethnography, and his experience in Canada had already brought him into direct contact with many groups.

Dr. Kaye has made a significant contribution to the public service of his country in several areas. For twenty years Vladimir Kaye has laboured, in his official capacity, to create knowledge and understanding among all Canadians. He has not only consistently read and kept abreast of the Canadian foreign-language press, but he has undertaken the study of ethnic groups before and after their arrival in Canada. In 1950 he was appointed associate professor at the University of Ottawa, lecturing part-time at the School of Graduate Studies on problems of migration, ethnography, and the settlement of Slavic groups in Canada. It is safe to say that no one in this country has a more detailed knowledge of ethnic groups. His accumulated card catalogue of biographies and of ethnic groups and societies in itself represents a life's work.

It was natural that among all the ethnic groups Dr. Kaye should have had a special interest in the Ukrainian group to which he himself belongs. He soon became aware that much that was regarded as the group's history was superficial and based on stories which had been accepted and passed on without critical checking. He was determined that Ukrainians whose past history in Europe had been distorted, now in one direction and now in another, should have a judicious and firmly-established basis for the new chapter in their life which began with their emigration to Canada. As a former European scholar and now an active Canadian citizen, Dr. Kaye felt he had an obligation to both his past and his present loyalties.

In the preface to his study, Dr. Kaye tells something of the difficulties he experienced in tracing the history of the man who first gave direction to the Ukrainian emigration to Canada. Dr. Kaye's good fortune, coupled with his persistent endeavours, now gives us for the first time the full story of Josef Oleskow. Dr. Oleskow now comes into full and clear focus as a figure in Canadian history.

The writing of the history of the first Ukrainian settlements in Canada required an immense amount of work. Dr. Kaye spent endless hours examining existing records in the Public Archives of Canada—naturalization lists, immigration reports, homestead records, newspaper files, and other source materials. The list of names in the documents cited will constitute somewhat of a "Doomsday Book" record, especially for those Canadians who are the descendants of these first Ukrainian immigrants.

In his study of individuals and families, Dr. Kaye noted a fact which has been hitherto overlooked by most writers on Canadian immigration. It has been generally assumed that the Ukrainian immigrants belonged to a peasant class, for the most part poor and illiterate. While the majority of the Ukrainian immigrants were poor farmers in their native land, there were also a number of families among the early settlers who were of a class of small landholders descended from the ancient Ukrainian nobility that still cherished the old traditions of status, learning, and leadership.

Most Canadian historians associate the great immigration movement with the administration of Sir Wilfrid Laurier and the name of Clifford

Sifton. It is true that the mass movement did come in the period 1896 to 1911, and that it owed much to the energy of Sifton, but Dr. Kaye's study reveals that some of the important foundation work was done under the previous administration. The name of Sir Charles Tupper, among others, appears in connection with the early correspondence between the Department of the Interior and Dr. Oleskow. It is also most interesting to note the activity of the officials of the Department in this early period, and their methods in dealing with immigration matters.

This history and source book is a valuable addition to Canadian studies. It can be used for sociological and political, as well as for historical investigation. Most of all, it is a precious record for Canadians of Ukrainian origin, who will find in it an accurate account of the beginnings of a movement so fateful for them and for Canada.

It is to be hoped that Dr. Kaye will continue his arduous historical investigations of Ukrainian immigration, and that further works will be forthcoming from him to enrich Canadian history and to inspire Canadian scholars.

University of Saskatchewan

Preface

THIS STUDY is an attempt to fill in one of the gaps which still exist in the history of the settlement of the Canadian West. In the Foreword to his study entitled *The Ukrainians in Canada*, the late Gordon A. Davidson remarked: "In preparation of this article, I have been considerably surprised to find that only a meagre amount of published material is available on the subject. It is hoped that the attention of scholars, and especially Government Departments concerned with the matter, will be directed to research projects, to be engaged in both from the historical and the sociological viewpoints. . . ."[1] Davidson's observation offered food for thought. Serving with the Department of Citizenship and Immigration, which was concerned with ethnic problems and with encouraging research in historical and sociological fields, I became interested in the history of the settlement of various ethnic groups in Canada. I started to collect relevant material, shaping it in departmental surveys and monographs, such as "Canadians of Recent European Origin," "Canadians of Slovak Origin," "Canadians of Byelorussian Origin," and others. This led to the acceptance of the position of associate professor at the University of Ottawa, with ethnography, history of the settlement of Slavic groups in Canada, and problems of adjustment of immigrants and their acculturation as the subjects of my lectures. The two main Slavic groups in Canada were the Ukrainian and the Polish, and consequently the bulk of the material collected concerned these two bodies.

The seed of shaping the material into a documentary history of the beginnings of Ukrainian settlement in Canada was sown in my mind by Stephen Pawluk, a son of Ukrainian pioneer settlers in Alberta.[2] On his

[1]Gordon A. Davidson, *The Ukrainians in Canada: A Study in Canadian Immigration* (Montreal, 1947), 2.

[2]See the section "Biographies" for biographies of Stephen Pawluk's parents.

return from active service overseas in the World War II, Stephen Pawluk was instrumental, as a co-founder, in the establishment of Ukrainian Branch No. 360 of the Royal Canadian Legion in Toronto. This activity quickened his interest in the ecology of the Ukrainians in Canada, and he decided to devote all his energy to the encouragement and support of various research projects concerning the history of Ukrainian settlement, and the problems involved in it, such as integration and acculturation. My admiration for the originator of these ideas deepened, and I decided to support his efforts to the best of my ability. More than ten years of tedious searching for documentary material at last yielded tangible results. In 1959, an original copy of Dr. Josef Oleskow's rare booklet, *O emigratsii* / "About Emigration," published at Lviw in 1895, which describes his visit to Canada in 1895, was located. Of great assistance was the discovery in the Public Archives of Canada, among the papers dealing with immigration between 1895 and 1900, of the first letter written by Dr. Oleskow to Clifford Sifton, the Minister of the Interior, dated October 23, 1897. In that letter, Dr. Oleskow wrote: "Turning over my correspondence with your Department since 1895, you will get an exact view as to the origin of Galician immigration. I am its promoter and supporter in this country. . . ."[3]

The problem then was to find the correspondence referred to by Dr. Oleskow in his letter. It was not contained in the Sifton Papers, nor was Dr. Oleskow's name to be found in the catalogues or registers of the Public Archives of Canada. At the beginning of July, 1960, the missing link finally came to light. Four voluminous files of documents, containing Dr. Oleskow's original letters, memoranda, the correspondence of immigration officers and others—material as yet unknown to Canadian historians—were located.

The energetic and enthusiastic members of the Toronto and Hamilton Ukrainian Branches of the Royal Canadian Legion formed the Ukrainian Canadian Research Foundation, with Stephen Pawluk as its president, and work on the study went ahead at full speed. New material continually appeared and I was able to devote several hours daily to assembling it and to making copies of the many documents. During 1962 the work was intensified, and full time was devoted to it. This was made possible by the grant of a Senior Research Fellowship from the Canada Council. In the same year, an additional valuable source of material be-

[3]Public Archives of Canada, Sifton Papers, XXIX, 18680–18681, Dr. Josef Oleskow, Lemburg, Austria, to Sir Clifford Sifton, October 28, 1897. The Ukrainian transliteration of Dr. Oleskow's name is "Osyp Oleskiw." To avoid confusion, the Austrian spelling of the name, as used on all documents, has been retained throughout this study.

came available—backfiles of the Ukrainian weekly *Svoboda* / "Liberty," published in 1893 in Jersey City, N.J., later in Shamokin, Pa., and then in Mount Carmel, Pa. The paper contained reprints of articles published in Lviw that referred to Dr. Oleskow's activities, the formation of an emigrants' aid committee supporting Dr. Oleskow's emigration efforts, his letters to the press, as well as to articles by European and Canadian correspondents. From the content of these articles, we learn that Dr. Oleskow received his main support from the younger leaders of the Ukrainian community, while encountering severe criticism from the older, conservative circles who believed that emigration would weaken the Ukrainian element in Galicia and thus give the Poles the upper hand. Some Ukrainian members of the Provincial Diet also opposed Dr. Oleskow's emigration activities on the same grounds.

The assembling and shaping of the material was completed towards the end of 1962. Only a small number of the documents found could be utilized in the present study, but the remainder will be helpful for future work in this field. The study is based almost entirely on primary and documentary sources, its purpose being to provide students of the period 1895–1900 with factual material. It will also, I hope, assist in the attainment of a better understanding of the early Ukrainian agricultural immigration, commonly referred to in contemporary documents as the "Galician immigration," as well as make a modest contribution towards the history of the settlement of Manitoba and the Northwest Territories during the five years of the last decade of the past century. As the title indicates, this study is intended as a *documentary* history of the settlement of the Ukrainians in Canada, who during the years 1895–1900 formed the largest immigrant group arriving in the West. It is only through the study of contemporary reports, letters, and descriptions of events that the past becomes as real as the present in our eyes. These documents and letters were not written with a view to obtaining publicity, but were destined for the information of the persons to whom they were addressed. Their value is therefore greater than that of carefully-edited *Annual Reports*, although the latter also yield useful data and information.

The inclination to compare the Ukrainian economic immigration of 1895–1900 with the Irish immigration a few decades earlier still prevails in North America. Such a comparison, as Oscar Handlin points out, is an erroneous one: "Unlike the Irish immigration of the middle of the last century, it was not the evicted, starving paupers who emigrated from Galicia and Bukowina in the last decade of the past century. They were small land owners, who through division of inheritance came to the limit of making a living on their few acres and when they heard about 'free land' in Canada, started a movement which embraced practically the whole province and if it would have received encouragement and some guidance, would have probably doubled."[4]

Another misconception, that the "Galician immigration" of the period consisted wholly of small land-holders, should also be dispelled. A considerable proportion of the immigrants were peasants of means, and in their number was an admixture of the descendants of a very old, but in the course of centuries impoverished Ukrainian gentry, a fact that is not generally known. Although differing little from the surrounding peasantry, these latter jealously guarded their privileges of nobility and the consciousness that they had never been serfs of the lords of the manors. Their history reaches back centuries to the time of the Kingdom of Halych (Galicia), when their ancestors were granted privileged status in return for carrying out the arduous task of guarding the boundaries of the realm. When, in the fourteenth century, Poland occupied the Kingdom of Halych, it confirmed the noble status of these *boyars*, but because they resisted absorption by the Polish culture, they were denied public office and higher social standing, thus gradually becoming impoverished and yet growing in numbers. Hundreds of members of these numerous clans, with names such as Berezowskyi, Negrych, Genik, Arsenych, Romanchych, Sklepovich, Urbanski, Malkovich, Bachynskyi, Korchinskyi, and scores of others, came to Canada during the period dealt with in this study. To my surprise I noticed on the lists of settlers homesteaders who bore full titles of nobility. The names of the members of these clans are frequently encountered on the pages of this study.

It should be noted here that variations occur in the spelling of the names in this study. This arises out of inconsistencies in the methods of translation and transliteration from Ukrainian to English used in various documents; it would have been impractical to revise the original forms. Mistakes in spelling, punctuation, and grammar have been preserved throughout in recording original documents and letters. With regard to illustrations, all possible attempts were made to locate those who might hold copyrights on the photographs.

My thanks go to the veterans of Ukrainian descent who displayed unabating interest in this study and who were a constant source of encouragement to me. I would also like to thank Mr. T. J. Foran for his scrutiny of the manuscript and for the valuable observations he offered. To Mrs. Irene Kalyn I am indebted for the efficient typing of

[4]Oscar Handlin, *Boston's Immigrants: A Study in Acculturation* (Cambridge, Mass.: Harvard University Press, 1959), 45.

the manuscript. Her familiarity with the spelling of the names of original settlers, as well as her knowledge of the subject—she is herself a daughter of Ukrainian pioneers—were a valuable asset. I greatly appreciate the courtesy and boundless patience of the officers of the Department of Citizenship and Immigration, of its librarian, and of the officers of the Public Archives of Canada, who gave me all possible assistance during the preparation of this study. My particular gratitude also to Mr. John Gregorovich and Mr. Andrew Gregorovich for their assistance in the revision of the manuscript and my great thanks to Dr. R. M. Schoeffel of the University of Toronto Press for his painstaking editing of the manuscript.

My esteemed friend, Professor George W. Simpson, himself deeply interested in the subject, was kind enough to read the study, to discuss it, and to write the Foreword, for which I wish to express my sincere thanks.

The study of these documents—which contain descriptions of the founding of colonies, the establishment of homes on remote homesteads, the destruction of the meagre belongings of early settlers by prairie fires, and the joys of harvesting the first crop—revealed to me in its full scope the courage of these sturdy pioneers who faced almost insurmountable difficulties with patience and boundless perseverance that finally rewarded them with success. I developed a deep and sincere admiration for these homesteaders, the builders of the Canadian West, and to their memory I dedicate the fruits of my efforts.

V.J.K.

Ottawa, Ontario
January, 1964

Contents

Illustrations

BETWEEN PAGES 150 AND 151

Explanatory Notes

IN QUOTING documents contained in the files of the Public Archives of Canada, the following numbering system is used in the footnotes. The *first number* is the code number of the file of documents in the Public Archives, Department of the Interior (Immigration). Letters, telegrams, and cables from the Department of the Interior bear only this number. The *second number* is the current number that was stamped on all correspondence received by the Department of the Interior (Immigration). This correspondence was then sorted according to subject matter and placed in the appropriate files.

ABBREVIATIONS OF THE FILES OF THE PUBLIC ARCHIVES, DEPARTMENT OF THE INTERIOR (IMMIGRATION)

Code Number	*Subject*
1. Oles.	Professor Oleskow, Lemberg, Golembia Gasse 11A, Galicia, Austria. Austrian immigration to the Canadian North-West: 1895–1896.
2. Oles.	Professor Oleskow, Lemberg, Golembia Gasse 11A, Galicia, Austria. Austrian immigration to the Canadian North-West: 1896–1900.
3. Gal.	Galician immigrants from Austria: 1897–1898.
4. Gal.	Galician immigrants from Austria: 1898–1899.
5. Gal.	General file No. 3 Galicians: 1899.
6. Gal.	Galician immigrants: 1899–1904.
7. Dest.	Destitute conditions of immigrants in Western Canada. Applications for seed Grain: 1897–1905.
8. Rpts.	Reports re Galician and other colonies: 1896–1901.
9. Rpts.	Reports re Galician and other colonies in Western Canada: 1901–1904.

Code Number	*Subject*
10. Rpts.	Reports re Galician and other colonies in Western Canada: 1904–1906.
11. Lab.	Labour conditions: 1897–1908.
12. Med.	Dr. S. C. Corbett, Medical Officer in the Immigration Office in Winnipeg, Manitoba: 1898–1900.
13. H.C.	High Commissioner, London, General reports on immigration matters: 1898–1900.
14. Laws	Immigration laws of foreign countries: 1896–1905.
15. Laws	Immigration laws of foreign countries. General file. Austrian laws: 1895–1897.
16. Laws	Immigration laws of foreign countries: 1907–1909.
17. Rpts.	Reports on immigration operations from year to year: 1896–1904.
18. Imm.	Immigration, Dominion Lands Branch. Correspondence: 1896–1898.
19. Imm.	Immigration, Dominion Lands Branch. Correspondence: 1899–1904.

The Problem of the Ethnic Name

WHEN CANADA opened her gates to Central-European immigration in the 1900's, and the Ukrainians began to arrive in greater numbers, their very name was unfamiliar to the majority of Canadians. They were variously referred to in official reports as "Austrians," "Galicians," "Bukowinians," "Ruthenians," as well as "Little Russians," "Routhainians," and even "Gallatians." This varied nomenclature baffled even Professor Hurd, when he wrote his study of racial problems based on the census of 1931:

> The Ukrainian classification, again, includes four distinct stocks: The Bukowinian, Galician, Ruthenian and Ukrainian. But the problem here is not in the diverse elements within the group. The four peoples are separately classified and 96 per cent of them speak Slavic languages. The group thus comprises only closely allied biological strains—a circumstance which did not obtain with the Austrian or Russian. The difficulty is that the Ukrainian classification probably includes only a part of those who might properly be so classed. There were about 13,000 persons reported as of Austrian origin who spoke Ukrainian as the mother tongue, and it is probable that there were also some Ukrainians among the 21,000 so-called Polish who were reported as speaking Ukrainian as their mother tongue and among 4,500 Roumanians similarly reported.[1]

"Bukowinian" and "Galician" were politico-geographical designations applied generally to Ukrainians, whereas "Ruthenian" and "Ukrainian" were ethnic designations of the same group, which Professor Hurd apparently overlooked. Professor Ryder, who dealt with the same subject twenty years later, offered an apt answer to Professor Hurd's query:

> . . . Ukrainian immigrants have come to Canada from a large agricultural area in eastern Europe which, in terms of inter-war boundaries took in parts

[1]W. Burton Hurd, *Racial Origins and Nativity of the Canadian People: A study based on the Census of 1931 and supplementary data* (Ottawa: Dominion Bureau of Statistics, Monograph No. 4, 1937), 32.

of Roumania, Czechoslovakia, and Poland, as well as Russia. Prior to the First World War the Ukrainians were principally within the confines of the Austrian Empire, although now, of course, the Ukraine S.S.R. is part of the Soviet Union as well as being one of the United Nations. . . . It is not surprising, therefore, in view of the possibility of interpreting origin as ancestral nativity, that Ukrainians in very large numbers reported themselves in 1921 as Austrian . . . [but] we see a sharp decline in the inclusive heterogeneity of the Ukrainian language group between 1921 and 1931. This is attributable in the main to an abrupt shift of these people from reporting Austrian as their origin to reporting Ukrainian. . . . Despite an accrual, thanks to restatement by former Austrians, a new source of loss of members of the Ukrainian group arose in 1931, in the form of a defection of large numbers of the language group to the Polish origin, again presumably on ground of birthplace, this time using the definition of country of origin given in the Treaty of Versailles. Only part of this error has since been eradicated. . . . Thus the Ukrainian origin has clarified its ethnic identity with the succeeding censuses, but is still probably 10 percent too small.[2]

If the diverse nomenclature of the Ukrainian ethnic group caused confusion of opinion during the 1930's, it was a veritable enigma to Canadian officials during the 1890's. The Commissioner of Dominion Lands in Winnipeg wrote, in his yearly report in 1897:

A number of settlers from Austria, called Ruthenians, have come out recently. . . . They appear to be closely allied with Galicians, several parties of whom from time to time arrive here. They speak a language difficult to interpret, very few strangers having heard it.[3]

Cyril Genik, who became the Ruthenian Interpreter with the immigration office in Winnipeg in 1897, explained (rather vaguely) to the Commissioner of Immigration in Winnipeg, in January, 1899, who the Galicians were:

I have the honour to submit to you the report of Galician Immigration for 1898, commonly called Austrian Immigration.

These immigrants come out of two provinces of Austria, i.e. Galicia and Buckowina and they are composed of Slavs; they have a slight difference in their religious beliefs, namely, those from Galicia follow the tenets of the Roman-Greek Church, whilst those coming from Buckowina belong to the Greek-Orthodox faith.[4]

To an enquiry submitted in June, 1899, by Eduard Schultze, Austro-Hungarian Consul General in Montreal, as to the meaning of the term

[2]N. B. Ryder, "The Interpretation of Origin Statistics," *Canadian Journal of Economics and Political Science*, XXI, No. 4 (November, 1955), 474–475.

[3]Canada, Parliament, *Sessional Papers*, XXXI, No. 10, 1897; and *Annual Report* of the Department of the Interior for the year 1896: Immigration, Report No. 1, H. H. Smith, Commissioner of Dominion Lands, Winnipeg, January 19, 1897, 13.

[4]Canada, Parliament, *Sessional Papers*, XXXIII, No. 11, 1899. Report of Cyril Genik, Galician Interpreter, Winnipeg, January 9, 1899.

"Galician immigrants," the Deputy Minister of the Interior, James A. Smart, had to admit he was not quite sure:

> I have your letter of the 9th instant, and in reply beg to say that by the term "Galician Immigrants" is meant all persons who in Canada are recognized as *Galicians* and I presume would include those from Bukowina as well as from Galicia. I do not know what further explanation to give with regard to the people referred to.
>
> I do not understand that the term "Galicians" would include German immigrants from Austria or persons emigrating from Hungary.[5]

In a later report, submitted in 1901, the Commissioner of Immigration was more precise in defining "Galicians," stating that: "These people should be classed with the Ruthenians, though generally known as Galicians."[6] Cyril Genik added in the same report that: "Mostly all Ruthenians (or Little Russians) come from Austria (Galicia and Bukowina provinces). . . ."[7] It was not until much later that the Ukrainians found their proper niche in official statistics and correspondence. Professor Simpson sums up this lengthy process of clarification thus:

> In Canada, until the term "Ukrainian" was generally adopted, there was considerable confusion of names. The great majority of this ethnic group who came to Canada were from the Austrian province of Galicia. Most of them also belonged to the Greek Catholic Church. Sometimes they were called by Canadians "Galicians" and sometimes "Ruthenians," not only in popular speech but also in official reports and documents. Until 1910 the term "Ukrainian" was only occasionally used. . . .
>
> It was the great war and revolutionary events in Europe, with the adoption of the official names there which . . . quickly spread the term "Ukrainian" in common usage in this country. The amazing rapidity with which the term was adopted caused some confusion in Canadian minds and not a little stumbling in Canadian tongues. By 1920 the people directly concerned were insisting, usually with accompanying patient explanation, on being called "Ukrainian" by their fellow countrymen. By 1930 most people had accepted the term. By 1940 the victory was complete on both official and unofficial fronts with only rare isolated pockets of resistance still fighting for the lost cause of names fading into obsolescence.[8]

For further clarification it may perhaps be useful to add one or two observations. A stateless nation which becomes a minority within an alien body politic is invariably exposed to political, social, and economic

[5]5. Gal. June 6, 1899: James A. Smart, Deputy Minister, Department of the Interior, Ottawa, to Eduard Schultze, Imperial and Royal Consulate, Montreal.

[6]Canada, Parliament, *Sessional Papers*, XXXV, No. 10, 1901. Immigration, Report No. 1, Galicians and Bukowinians, 118.

[7]*Ibid.*, 130.

[8]George W. Simpson, "The Names 'Rus,' 'Russia,' 'Ukraine' and their historical backgound," *Slavistica*, No. 10 (1951) 17–18.

pressure aimed at the obliteration of its identity. Non-admission to public offices, denial of commissions in the armed forces, prohibition of the right to establish schools using a minority language for instruction, and difficulties in admission to educational institutions in general are the usual manifestations of official discrimination. This process can be carried even further by prohibiting the use of the language in print, changing the historical name of the minority people and of their country of origin, and using pressure to force them to change their religious affiliation and to identify themselves with the majority group.

Ukrainians within the Russian Empire were subjected to all of these pressures. The names "Ukraine" and "Ukrainian" were prohibited; Ukraine became "Little Russia," and the Ukrainian language a "Little Russian" dialect of the Russian language. The use of the Ukrainian language in schools was prohibited and the publication of newspapers and books other than poetry and the classics in the Ukrainian language was outlawed. Ukrainians in the Austrian Empire, in the provinces of Galicia and Bukowina, as well as in Hungary, were officially referred to as "Ruthenians." The Ukrainian language was not suppressed in Austria, although there did exist a certain degree of discrimination, in particular in Hungary.

The peasant masses in both politico-geographic areas, Galicia and Bukowina, had little national consciousness. For them geographic designation was tantamount to nationality. When, in the 1890's, Ukrainians made their appearance in Canada, they were referred to in official correspondence as "Austrians," later as "Galicians" and "Bukowinians" (in the ethnic meaning of the term), then as "Ruthenians," until finally the term "Ukrainian" replaced all other designations. In our study we propose to use the last four terms synonymously. During the period under consideration, the name "Galician" was the one generally used in official communications and documents.

PART I

DR. JOSEF OLESKOW

Chapter One

PRELIMINARIES LEADING TO DR. JOSEF OLESKOW'S VISIT TO CANADA IN 1895

I

ON APRIL 1, 1895, the Department of the Interior in Ottawa received a letter written in German by "Prof. Dr. Josef Oleskow, Lemberg, Golebia Gasse 11A, Galizien, Austria," dated March 16, 1895. The writer of the letter requested informative material about Canada and intimated the possibility of directing a mass migration of Ukrainian (Ruthenian) farmers to Canada:

> A great number of Galician agriculturists of Ruthenian (Slavic) nationality desire to quit their native country, due to over-population, subdivision of land holdings, heavy taxation, and unfavourable political conditions.
>
> The question therefore arises to find a country with ample good, free land for settlement, willing to accept thousands of farmers,—who although possessed of modest means, are diligent and thrifty—and to offer them the opportunity to attain a decent subsistence.
>
> The representatives of the Brazilian Government are conducting intensive propaganda with the aim of directing the flow of emigration towards Brazil, promising the immigrants, apart from a free homestead and some material assistance for the beginning, free transportation from Italy to Buenos Aires and to the place of settlement as well.
>
> The Committee of the prospective emigrant farmers has decided to make enquiries about the possibilities offered to agriculturists wishing to settle in Canada.
>
> As a plenipotentiary of this Committee, I would request you to be so kind as to send us the following information:
>
> 1. The last census of the population of Canada.
> 2. Information about free homesteads, their sizes in the different provinces (Manitoba, Ontario, Alberta, Saskatchewan, Assiniboia), and whether there is free land available for settlement in British Columbia, near the railway.

3. Whether the settlers, after one or two years on the land, having completed their agricultural occupations, would be able to obtain some paying employment, and if so, in what provinces.
4. Accurate maps indicating free homesteads where they are still available, and showing railway companies' land.
5. Accurate information about climatic conditions, about the sails, precipitations, forests, prices of draught animals, etc.

And finally, we would request further information about whether there could be made available reductions for travel for larger parties of immigrants, both on the boats and by rail.

If the comparison between conditions in Brazil and Canada is not overwhelmingly in favour of the first, we would prefer Canada (as the country of settlement) as it is a country with a stable form of government and safe living conditions.

The writer would come to Canada in order to survey places suitable for mass-settlement of emigrants.

Begging to be excused for not having the courage to use my inadequate knowledge of English to be able to write this letter,

I remain,

Very truly yours,

(Signed) J. OLESKOW

Please address any answer and enclosures to: Prof. Dr. Josef Oleskow, Lemberg, Golebia Gasse 11A, Austria, Galicia.[1]

Dr. Oleskow's letter created quite a stir in the Department of the Interior. The Superintendent of Immigration, L. M. Fortier, ordered a translation of the letter to be made and a copy of it forwarded to Sir Charles Tupper, the High Commissioner for Canada in London, suggesting that he get in touch with Dr. Oleskow. At the same time, Fortier left instructions for Mr. Poper, of his division, to prepare an acknowledgement of the letter and to gather together all the information on Canada requested by Dr. Oleskow:

Please acknowledge the receipt of this important letter. Say that it has been read with great interest, and that we are sending him publications which it is hoped will be found useful; also that a translation of his letter is being sent to Sir Charles Tupper, High Commissioner for Canada in London. Say that in the event of the writer deciding to come to Canada, the Department will endeavour to secure for him some privileges upon the railways, and will facilitate his seeing the country as thoroughly as possible, if he be good enough to write to us some little time in advance of his departure from Austria. Say that in the meantime it would be well for him to communicate with the High Commissioner, whose address is 17 Victoria

[1]1. Oles. March 16, 1895: Dr. Josef Oleskow, Lemberg, Austria, to the Department of the Interior, Ottawa. Translation from the German by Miss Mercer, Department of the Interior.

Street, London, S.W., England, in the event of his requiring any particulars in addition to those contained in the publications we are sending.

See about the books to be sent.

(Signed) L. M. FORTIER[2]

Dr. Oleskow's letter was duly acknowledged (in German), and he was informed that the Department of the Interior would be glad to arrange railway facilities for him if he decided to visit Canada. He was also requested to give ample advance notice about the date of his departure, so that arrangements could be made to facilitate his viewing the country.[3] The secretary forwarded to Dr. Oleskow the following material (the list is pencilled in on Fortier's memorandum): "Official Handbook; Tenant Farmer Delegates, Maps; Prof. Lory's and Prof. Wallace's References; Ritchie's pamphlet; Western World; Index Map; German pamphlet; Panoramic Commercial Views of Ottawa."[4]

Dr. Oleskow wanted to be certain that his request for information on Canada was met, and therefore he dispatched an identical letter to the Commissioner of Dominion Lands in Winnipeg, who forwarded it to Ottawa with the observation that: ". . . upon perusing it, it would appear to be a communication deserving very careful consideration."[5] The Secretary of the Department informed the Commissioner that: ". . . The Department is already in communication with Prof. Oleskow and an invitation to visit Canada was extended to him on 8th inst. . . . We supplied him with information on all points referred to in his letter. . . ."[6]

In a letter dated May 5, 1895, Dr. Oleskow acknowledged the receipt of the communication of April 8 from the Department of the Interior and of the material on Canada sent to his address in Lemberg:

In reply to your kind communication of April 8th, Ref. No. 21103, I have the honour to inform you that I shall leave Galicia during the first week of July of this year in order to visit Canada. I wish to thank you very much for the facilities promised on the part of Canadian authorities, without which it would have been a difficult task indeed to fulfil my task satisfactorily. I expect to spend 2 to 2½ months on the visit to Canada.

21. Oles. Memo, April 4, 1895: L. M. Fortier, Department of the Interior, Ottawa, to Mr. Poper of the same Department.

31. Oles. April 8, 1895: Lyndwode Pereira, Assistant Secretary, Department of the Interior, Ottawa, to Dr. Oleskow, Lemberg, Galicia.

41. Oles. April 10, 1895: List is signed "F.C.P." (Poper).

51. Oles. April 11, 1895: J. R. Burpé, Secretary, Commissioner of Dominion Lands, Winnipeg, to the Secretary, Department of the Interior, Ottawa.

61. Oles. April 19, 1895: Lyndwode Pereira, Ottawa, to the Secretary, Dominion Lands Board, Winnipeg.

I have already published some material against the trend to colonize Parana in Brazil, giving preference to emigration to Canada (I based my writings on material contained in pamphlets which are in my possession). The public is looking forward with keen attention to my intended inspection of conditions in Canada, the news of which already has spread in the country. I possess here as a writer on agricultural topics, as a professor of agriculture, and as a practical farmer at the same time, a certain confidence in rural circles. Therefore, a number of peasants intending to emigrate to Brazil have stopped their preparations, and I have already received a considerable number of letters requesting me to secure for the writers homesteads in Canada. Should there still be a sufficient number of homesteads available in Western Canada, economically well situated, not far from railway communications, in regions with adequate precipitation and without summer frosts, which would safeguard crops from destruction, Canada can be assured to receive a new influx of citizens from our country. Of course, if it is desired that the colonies should receive a steady flow [of new immigrants] they must be successful. The task of my visit will be to prepare the ground for this very purpose. I expect to be able to call on the Department sometime after the middle of July. . . .[7]

When this second communication from Dr. Oleskow was received, the Department of the Interior requested D. McNicoll, General Passenger Agent of the Canadian Pacific Railway Company in Montreal, to secure ". . . special privileges on railways, as well as facilitating his [Dr. Oleskow's] movements in other ways."[8] Mr McNicoll, on his part, assured the Department of the Interior that facilities would be extended to Dr. Oleskow as soon as definite advice as to what steamer he would arrive on was received.

The High Commissioner for Canada sent copies of correspondence relating to Dr. Oleskow to John Dyke, in charge of the Canadian Government Agency in Liverpool, England, for his information and opinion. John Dyke was rather cautious, and he warned the High Commissioner against any hasty actions:

With reference to the enclosed correspondence I have to inform you that there are undoubtedly numbers of people in Galicia desirous of emigrating. So much is shown by my own correspondence with that portion of the Continent, and no doubt it is owing to the pamphlets I have sent there that Professor Josef Oleskow has written to the Department. I have applications now for a large number of pamphlets in Polish, which I

[7]1. Oles./22085, May 5, 1895: Dr. Oleskow, Lemberg, Austria, to the Secretary, Department of the Interior, Ottawa. Letter written in German and translated into English by Miss Mercer of the Department.

[8]1. Oles. May 18, 1895: G. F. Sparks, for the Assistant Secretary, Department of the Interior, Ottawa, to D. McNicoll, General Passenger Agent, C.P.R. Company, Montreal.

believe is the prevailing language in Lemberg, one of the largest Jewish centres in Europe. It would be as well to ask Professor Oleskow if the people referred to are of the Jewish persuasion, and if they would remain agriculturists. At the same time we should make enquiries as to Professor Oleskow's position and standing; so many men have written in a similar strain and the results when they have been taken up have so often been unsatisfactory that great caution should be exercised.[9]

Dyke's suggestion was sound, and the High Commissioner instructed him to make the necessary enquiries on the European continent to find out as much as possible about Dr. Oleskow and whether his statements could be trusted.

Meanwhile Dr. Oleskow did as the Department of the Interior suggested. He wrote a letter to Sir Charles Tupper in London, informing him about his intended visit to Canada and suggesting that he would like to call on the High Commissioner to personally discuss details of the projected immigration of peasant settlers from Galicia to the Canadian Northwest:

I have been in communication with the Department of the Interior in Ottawa on matters connected with the emigration of farmers in Galicia, and am referred to your Honour for further information in connection with this subject.

The large emigration to Brazil which has been going from our country for several years is economically ruinous to the emigrants; I have accordingly, in company with a number of people of good intentions, worked up an active propaganda against Brazil, and have pointed to Canada as the country offering far and away more favourable conditions of settlement notwithstanding its severe winters. A number of farmers who desire to emigrate have postponed their departure until next spring, and are awaiting the results of my report on Canada.

I shall start from here early in July and propose to call on you in London and discuss personally with you the details of this question. I have perused all the printed matter which the Department of the Interior have sent me, as well as your very comprehensive and instructive paper in the *Scottish Geographical Magazine*, on the economic development of Canada.

I asked the Department of the Interior to forward to me the Census of Canada in which I hoped to find further particulars about the climate, productions, economic position of the country, etc., but this has not reached me yet.

I now have to ask you to kindly explain to me the meaning of the red colouring, and the shading of many township sections in the "Index showing the Townships in Manitoba."

[9]1. Oles./22312, April 18, 1895: John Dyke, Agent, Canada Government Agency, Liverpool, England, to J. G. Colmer, Secretary, High Commissioner for Canada, London.

I feel convinced that my journey will lead to an extensive movement thither of the farming community, a matter which will be a blessing to our much over-populated peasant holdings, and to Canada.

I am, etc.

(Signed) J. OLESKOW

P.S. Messrs Spiro and Co. of Hamburg seem to have obtained knowledge of my correspondence with the Department of the Interior, a matter I am quite unable to explain. They have written to me offering a free ocean ticket, and their support in securing free pass over the C.P.R. Of course I do not desire to make any use of an offer coming from a private firm of whose position in relation to the Colonization question I know nothing.[10]

John Dyke obtained information concerning Dr. Josef Oleskow which he communicated to the High Commissioner in London as follows:

I return herewith the letter of Professor Oleskow to hand with yours of the 10th instant, and also the correspondence previously forwarded. In answer to my enquiries I have this morning [i.e., May 13, 1895] received the following information:—

Josef Oleskow is a Ruthinian and of Greek Catholic religion, he is a Professor of Agriculture at the teachers' seminary in Lemberg, with a yearly salary of 1,300 florins [2½ florins = $1.00 approx.]. He is 34 years of age, married, and possesses a farm near Tarnopol, valued at about 12,000 florins and believed to be free of debt. He has a good reputation, and writes for some periodicals; is known to strongly oppose emigration to Brazil: the people he is interested in are supposed to be Polish and Ruthinian peasant farmers, not Jews.

With regard to the concluding paragraph in Professor Oleskow's letter to the High Commissioner I have learned that Messrs Allan Brothers received a copy of the correspondence—I believe from the C.P.R.—and they instructed Spiro and Co. to offer him facilities alluded to.[11]

A few days later, a second letter arrived from Dr. Oleskow addressed to the High Commissioner for Canada in London, giving among other things particulars about the "Prosvita" Society, which, according to Dr. Oleskow, was backing his campaign for emigration to Canada instead of to Brazil. The letter, written in German, was translated in London, and a copy of the translation sent to the Department of the Interior in Ottawa:

In matter of the emigration of Ruthenian Peasants from Galicia, Austria, to Canada.

[10] 1. Oles./22312, May 5, 1895: Dr. J. Oleskow, Lemberg, Austria, to the High Commissioner for Canada, London. Copy forwarded to the Department of the Interior, Ottawa. Translation from the German made in London.

[11] 1. Oles./22312, May 13, 1895: John Dyke, Agent, Liverpool, to J. G. Colmer, London.

I enclose one of the newspaper articles dealing with the emigration in which I attack the emigration of our farmers to Brazil, and advocate Canada. This treatise appeared in the Ruthenian supplement of the official organ *Hapogna zaconnes* [*Narodna chasopys*] ("People's Journal") and was reproduced in extenso a day later in two other Ruthenian and one Polish paper. This demonstrated that interest in Canada has already been awakened, and that emigration to Canada might be launched if it were feasible for me to obtain a clear picture of the . . . chances for the colonists in the course of my visit to Canada, which promises to be extremely advantageous.

I am now engaged in preparing a pamphlet, the object of which is to popularize the conditions of settlement in Canada, as far, of course, as this can be gathered from the printed matter sent to me. This brochure will appear as the authorized publication for the month of July of the "Proceedings" ["Prosvita"], one of the largest agricultural societies of the Ruthenian nation in Galicia, and in this way it will reach 12,000 members and in addition will be placed in every village reading room throughout the country.

With regard to my visit of investigation to Canada which I have mentioned in my letter to your Honour, I beg to state that I shall have to make an alteration in the date of departure, as I cannot leave before the 10th July.

Two peasant delegates of bodies of farmers who desire to emigrate have applied to me and have asked to be allowed to accompany my expedition, in order to be able to furnish to their friends verbally and in detail information as to the peculiarities of Canadian farm life. In the event of it being possible to obtain some assistance and travelling facilities for these persons, on their furnishing the necessary proof of their bona fides, I believe it would help forward this colonization question very considerably.[12]

The "Prosvita" Society was one of the leading Ukrainian educational societies in Galicia. From the letter cited and from subsequent letters of Dr. Oleskow, we know that he was closely associated with "Prosvita," as well as with the "committee of great respectability" mentioned by the Prime Minister of Austria in a letter to the British Ambassador in Vienna, in answer to an enquiry about Dr. Oleskow.[13] A brief description of the Society's history and aims is included here to give the reader a better understanding of Dr. Oleskow's interest in assisting farmers and of the role he played in the emigration movement.

The "Prosvita" Society was originally established in 1868 as a purely educational body with its headquarters in Lviw, the capital of Galicia. At its second convention, held on May 26, 1869, the aims of the

[12]1. Oles./22312, May 14, 1895: Dr. J. Oleskow, Lemberg, Austria, to the High Commissioner for Canada, London.

[13]1. Oles./25808, October 12, 1895: Count Casimir Badeni, Prime Minister of Austria, to Hon. W. Barrington, Ambassador of the United Kingdom, Vienna, Austria.

Society were broadened. Stress was placed on the education of peasant-farmers with the intention of assisting them in the improvement of their economic condition. This was to be done by the publication of educational manuals, lectures, and the like. During the years 1874–75 alone, the number of these popular educational booklets reached the formidable number of 281,850 copies, at that time a very high figure, considering the costs of publication and the high percentage of illiteracy among the villagers. To reach those who could not read or write, the "Prosvita" Society established village reading halls where the local priest, the teacher, or a better-educated peasant-farmer conducted regular reading sessions for those unable to read. During the 1890's the society increased its activities still more in the villages. Due to the unsatisfactory division of land holdings after the abolition of serfdom in 1848, the farmers were faced with economic ruin. High compensation payments to former landlords, taxes levied by the state, increased mortgaging of farm holdings, and the inability to find means of earning money created serious problems for the village population. It was estimated that during the decade 1873–1883 23,237 farm holdings in Galicia were seized for non-payment of taxes and debts. The value of the confiscated property was estimated at 23 million florins, whereas the debts burdening these holdings amounted only to 6,633,773 florins.

The "Prosvita" Society undertook to teach the peasants self-help, instructed them in how to start and manage village stores, established co-operatives, and offered legal and other advice. It also advocated temperance, or even complete abstinence from alcoholic beverages, as a means of saving money for the improvement of the farmers' holdings and for raising their moral standards. This brought the society into conflict not only with the Polish landlords, but with the state itself. The manors had for centuries enjoyed the so-called *ius propinandi*, the sole right to brew and sell liquor in their domains. When Austria took control of Galicia in 1772, the *ius propinandi* was only modified. The Austrian Government, which held a monopoly on the sale of alcoholic beverages, taxed the landlords for liquor produced. The landlords, in order to retain profits, increased the prices for alcohol and induced peasants to drink in their village taverns, which were almost invariably held by Jewish lessees, because according to custom noblemen could not engage in any trade. In 1878 there were 23,269 village public houses in Galicia, or one public house for every 233 persons. The consumption of hard liquor amounted to 26 litres per person per year. The "Prosvita" Society's temperance movement was viewed with hostility by the manor holders and regarded as an activity intended to injure governmental interests.

In 1895 "Prosvita" counted ten branches in various centres of the province, as well as a great number of reading halls in the villages with thousands of members. It regularly published educational manuals which served as correspondence courses for the members of these village reading halls. These manuals dealt with a variety of topics, as seen from titles such as: "About Grain Storage and about Village Stores" (1893), "About Village Co-operative Loan Societies and Savings Societies" (1894), and "About Free Lands," by Dr. Oleskow (1895). The Society also published guides on how to establish and conduct village stores, where to order mechandise, what goods to order, and other aspects of commerce. As a result of these efforts, 146 villages established their own stores as well as 124 Loan Societies and 60 Co-operative Granaries to assist members in case of crop failure and food shortage.

In the 1880's, when the emigration movement started, "Prosvita" stepped in to protect farmers from exploitation by various agents who invaded the country and lured land-hungry peasant-farmers to the "paradise on earth," Brazil. To counteract exploitation, it published Dr. Oleskow's booklet, "About Free lands," warning farmers against emigrating to Brazil, and advising them, should they decide to leave their native country, to choose Canada as their new home. Canada, it was pointed out, was a country which possessed a climate similar to their own, as well as an orderly government where immigrants were protected and not exploited. The settlers in Canada, Dr. Oleskow added, would receive free homesteads to start a new life on 160 acres of land. The "Prosvita" Society was supported by private means, and therefore it had no funds to finance the establishment of an office to aid emigrants, one which would assist villagers who wished to sell their property without loss, obtain loans to pay transportation to Canada before they sold their acres, procure travel documents without paying bribes, and buy steamship tickets directly from steamship lines' offices and not through sub-agents. The lack of assistance in these matters was to cause the emigrants much hardship when they ventured on their journey to their new homesteads in Canada.[14] This, then, was the organization which, with the support of well-wishing individuals

[14]For information on the "Prosvita" Society, see A. Kachor, *Rola "Prosvity" v ekonomichnomu rozvytku Zakhidnoi Ukrainy*/" 'Prosvita' in the Economic Development of Western Ukraine," UVAN Chronicle Series (Winnipeg: Ukrainian Free Academy of Sciences) No. 18 (1960).

loosely bound into an emigrants' aid society, was backing Dr. Oleskow in his efforts to put the emigration movement into orderly channels.

II

While preparations for the "expedition to Canada" were going on, Dr. Oleskow's booklet "About Free Lands" was published by the "Prosvita" Society as its July, 1895, issue and sent out to the numerous village reading halls across the province. The booklet contained thirty-eight pages, and was divided into three chapters with the headings, "Is your native soil unable to support you anymore?", "Only not to Brazil," and "Where should one turn?". In the first chapter, Dr. Oleskow depicted the economic situation of the Galician peasant-farmers, and quoted statistics on peasant incomes and expenditures. The statistics showed that an average peasant family consisted of five souls and possessed three hectares (seven and one-half acres) of land:

> We do not take into consideration that about one-sixth of peasant-owned land consists of village commons, we assume that all the land belonging to peasants, including hay meadows and unproductive pasture-land, is suitable for cultivation of highest grade of grain. The average yield in Galicia of wheat, rye, barley, oats, in the decade 1882–1891 was 750 kilograms of grain per hectare. If we count the price of peasant grain being 5 florins per 100 kg., then the gross value of production per hectare will amount to 37 florins and 50 kreuzers. It means that the value of the whole gross production of grain of a peasant family consisting of five persons amounted on the average during the last decade to 3 × 37.50 florins, or 112 florins and 50 kreuzer [2½ florins = a dollar]. But the farmer is not free to use all the fruits of his labour.
>
> He is obliged to leave 6 korets of grain for spring sowing, valued at 30 florins; taxes, renting of a team or feeding his own animals amounts on an average to 50 florins per year. The 32 florins and 50 kreuzers that are left, are one year's reward for the whole year's toil on the land, including interest on the value of the land, which he can use to meet his living expenses (feeding his family, procuring clothing, fuel, etc.). He could, if it were not necessary to meet debt payments, insurance, contributions towards the upkeep of the church and school buildings, repair of his own buildings, unforeseen expenses connected with accidents in the family (sickness, deaths, weddings), and many other expenses.
>
> How much is left to a farmer who works 5 morgs of land [1 morg = about ⅝ of an acre], i.e., to an average smallholder, for his living? Few florins per year, and if it happens that he has to meet several expenses at once, such as a tax for building a new church or school in the village, not only is nothing left to him, but he is plunged deeply into debt.[15]

[15]Dr. Josef Oleskow: *Pro vilni zemli*/"About Free Lands" (Lviw: "Prosvita" Society, 1895), 5–6.

Perhaps Dr. Oleskow painted too dark a picture, but, on the whole, he was not far from depicting true conditions. During the 1880's, the salvation of the Ukrainian villagers in Galicia was seasonal work in the United States:

> People migrated there for work, stayed a year or two and sometimes even longer, and sent their earnings home to improve their holdings, or brought the money they earned with them. In America they earned at an average of 2 florins and 50 kreuzer [one dollar] per day, and although living expenses there were higher, our frugal worker was able to save money. America did help us; many holdings were cleared of debts, and peasants gained capital necessary to improve their farms. But unfortunately, the possibilities of earning ceased there. After the Exhibition in Chicago in 1893 there came a depression which affected industries: factories were forced to close, the demand for coal the factories were using diminished, and the miners engaged in coal mining were laid off. Many of our emigrant workers had to return home. . . .[16]

The depression in the United States and the lack of ready cash at home were fertile ground for unscrupulous agents trying to induce farmers to sell their acres and emigrate to Brazil: "If somebody would ask me to define in one word what Brazil meant to our emigrants, I would answer: a grave. Not only a grave of all their hopes for the future, but literally The Grave. I am sure that everybody who reads and ponders the facts which I shall submit, will come to the same conclusion."[17] Dr. Oleskow was not exaggerating. Brazil was a grave for the early emigrants. The ruses employed by the agents to cheat the villagers into selling their holdings and embarking for Brazil defy description:

> To mention only [one:] the emigration agent Gargoletti, who in 1895 crossed practically the whole of Eastern Galicia on foot disguised as a peasant-farmer, pretending to be Archduke Rudolph. He appealed to the villagers to follow him to Brazil. In this deception of the naïve villagers he was assisted by the village inn-keepers who bought land from the duped peasant-farmers and shared tremendous gains with the swindler. The proof of the great confidence this swindler could arouse are the numerous letters written by the villagers to the Archduchess Stefanie from many parts of Galicia, in which they assured her that the Archduke, her husband, was not dead but alive, and was sending her greetings, and wishes them to follow him to Brazil. . . .[18]

Although the description of Brazilian horrors in Oleskow's booklet are blood-curdling, the accounts produced by contemporary eyewitnesses

[16]*Ibid.*, 7.

[17]*Ibid.*, 10.

[18]Sister Severyna, O.S.B.M., "Emigration in Ukrainian Literature," *Jubilee Book of the Ukrainian National Association* (Jersey City, New Jersey: *Svoboda* Press, 1934), 409 (In Ukrainian).

are still more horrifying. The first large party of immigrants to arrive in Brazil in 1895, ninety-five families in all, was directed to the State of Santa Catarina. They remained about two weeks at Lusina (Itaiopolis today) and then were sent to settle on government land, called shacres. One shacre was 1000 metres long and 250 metres wide, and formed a homestead, about 40 Galician morgs. The homesteads were practically all located in primeval forests (*sertones*) with savage Indians everywhere in the impenetrable thickets, and all kinds of wild beasts and snakes lurking in the wilderness. "When the settlers saw the green wall of impenetrable jungle with high *piniores*, *imbuias* hundreds of years old . . . they only gasped, wrung their hands in great sorrow, cried, and decried their misfortune. . . . Some lost all hope and just wandered aimlessly about. . . . Despair and hunger broke their spirits, morals deteriorated. . . ."[19] Here is a description of the beginnings of the Ukrainian settlement in the colony of Iracema, in 1895:

There was no bread to be obtained, hunger drove them mad. . . . The devil changed human beings into animals. Fathers started to sell their children to Brazilians. These Brazilians visited even more remote towns in large wagons to pick up children. Fathers brought the children to one place and Brazilians bought them. For healthy, good-looking children, they paid 25 milreis, for less attractive 20 or 10 milreis. . . .[20]

These were not the only misfortunes the settlers had to endure. The settlements were often attacked by Indians, and people were killed without warning:

On June 29, 1895, the morning of St. Peter and Paul's day, Indians unexpectedly attacked the home of Kateryniuk at Iracema, killed his 90-year-old mother, one son, Vincent Kateryniuk, and wounded another man with an arrow. . . . In 1898, another family was killed in the same place, a mother and her two sons. After the first attack, which resulted in the killing of several persons, the settlers notified the local authorities (*prefeitura*) at Itaiopolis. The *prefeitura* dispatched five police officers to investigate. They arrived, investigated the situation, and ordered a common grave to be dug to bury the victims. During the funeral, the Indians climbed the trees at the edge of the forest and watched the funeral from the distance. One policeman discharged his Winchester rifle in the direction of the Indians perched on trees, but whether he killed anybody was not known. The Indians disappeared from the trees. . . .

In 1895, the Indians also attacked the neighbouring colony of Moema or Noema, some 30 kilometres from Iracema. In the *rancho* of the settler

[19]Rev. Iryney Vihorynsky, O.S.B.M., *Ukrainski pereselentsi v Brazylii: Iracema v istorychnomu rozvytku v 1895–1958 rr.*/"Ukrainian Immigrants in Brazil: Iracema in the Historical Aspect of the Development of the Settlement during 1895–1958" (Iracema: The Basilian Fathers, 1958), 42.

[20]*Ibid.*, 48.

Koziura, they killed the wife of Charles Kisilewsky and his child. In the same house Koziura's three children were also killed. Both men were absent at the time, gone to buy provisions. . . .[21]

Similar descriptions of conditions in Brazil were related by Dr. Oleskow in his very popular booklet, "About Free Lands." He concludes his chapter on Brazil with the words: ". . . People die there like flies. As it appears, the climate for our people is deadly in those parts. . . . Such hell [as he described] is in the State of Parana, but today, I repeat, settlers are not admitted to that colony; people are sent to work on coffee plantations where the climate is still hotter and more unhealthy, and conditions are still worse in comparison with those in the colonies. Go to Brazil my man, because the passage to Brazil is free!"[22]

The third chapter of his booklet dealt mostly with Canada. In it, Oleskow described the country, its size, climate, people, and government, stressing the excellent schools, open to all without any discriminatory restriction:

> If someone finishes public school there, he is an educated person and may be elected to any office. . . . Post offices are in every village. It took a letter only 17 days to reach Lviw, although it was posted in the furthest corner of Canada.
>
> The climate varies in different parts of Canada; in the provinces where there is free land available, the climate is very much like that of our country, only the winters are as a rule more severe. But the cold is not as hard to bear as it is in Europe because the frost is always dry, although the thermometer may often show lower temperatures, sometimes much lower, than in our country. . . . There are all kinds of roads (in Canada) and much money is spent for their construction. . . . Railways are everywhere where settlements are situated. This is simply because railways are built first and people settle along the lines afterwards.[23]

Dr. Oleskow's accurate description of Canada, her climatic conditions, agriculture, industry, and government testifies to the fact that he had thoroughly studied the material received from Ottawa and London concerning Canada, as well as used other material procured locally. The booklet was intended mainly to serve as a guide for prospective emigrants wishing to settle in Canada. He devoted considerable space to the description of homesteads, explaining who was entitled to obtain a homestead and how long it took to receive title to the land. He also stressed who should emigrate to Canada and who should not:

> The whole country is divided into squares, sections of 640 acres each. A settler and his family, or a single man over 18 years of age, can obtain

[21]*Ibid.*, 56–57.
[22]Oleskow, *Pro vilni zemli*, 22. [23]*Ibid.*, 30.

a quarter of such a section. Each section has a number. Along the railway lines on both sides of them to a depth of 4 miles, odd-numbered sections belong to railway companies. In less-densely populated parts of the country they are sold at $3 per acre, with 10 years to complete the payments. Even-numbered sections belong to the government, and are given away as homesteads. . . .

The settler receives the patent of ownership after three years, provided he can prove that he was residing on the land at least 6 months each year, that he built a house, and that he has brought under cultivation a certain amount of land.

To become the owner of 113 morgs of land may seem to many a bliss hoped for only in a dream. There is little doubt that it can be achieved, if only the emigration is properly organized. But there are many conditions which have to be fulfilled first, and which may prevent many of our people from achieving that happiness. First of all, there is the great distance to travel; transportation alone would cost 150 florins per person. The Canadian Government as a rule does not assist passages; immigrants have to defray the costs of transportation from their own funds. The crossing of the ocean lasts one week, and travel by rail in Europe and in Canada takes about 5 days. Inexperienced people are not advised to venture alone. It is best to travel in groups under the guidance of an experienced person who knows the language, or who can at least speak German. . . .[24]

Dr. Oleskow further explained that people who did not possess enough money for the start, that is, enough to last them until the next harvest, should not emigrate:

In order to make a living on the land given to them, one should have enough money to be able to live after arrival until the next crop is garnered, to be able to buy a pair of oxen for the ploughing, as well as implements for husbandry, or at least enough ready money to be able to hire a neighbour of longer standing to do the ploughing. The first settlers who emigrate must also have a few hundred florins in cash for the upkeep of their families. Those who arrive after them may be able to manage with less money, working on arrival for wages with farmers who came before them, and later, when they have acquired some knowledge of the language, they can be hired by other farmers. After a year they will earn so much cash that they will be able to take out their own homestead.[25]

In Galicia, Dr. Oleskow continued, a smallholder might possess 5 morgs of land, worth 1000 florins ($400), but this did not provide sufficient income to live decently unless he had an opportunity to earn some additional money to supplement his income. Such chances did not, however, exist in Galicia, with the exception of the opportunity to work at starvation wages for the landlord. Therefore, reasoned Dr. Oleskow, people who possessed insufficient property to offer them a

[24] *Ibid.*, 32.
[25] *Ibid.*, 33.

living in their native country, but enough to start farming in Canada, should consider emigrating:

I repeat again, those who send people for colonization purposes abroad, i.e., for settlement on the land, without adequate means for a start when they arrive are either dishonest or outright crazy. Only a little thought would suffice to make one understand that a person without means cannot start farming barehanded. . . .

The best time to emigrate to Canada is in the early spring, because this will enable the settler to put in some potatoes and to sow some grain on his ploughed acres. Towards the summer, only those who intend to work during harvest time to earn some additional money to start farming should emigrate. *Nobody should venture to Canada in the late autumn or early winter*, because he will have difficulty in finding work and will have to spend his money, perhaps his last cent, to live through the winter. . . .[26]

After some additional information on the various provinces and districts of Canada, and the way of farming common there, Dr. Oleskow advises those who would like to emigrate to Canada to wait until his return from his trip of inspection. Immediately upon his return he promised to submit a detailed account of what he had seen in Canada:

Therefore, to assure success for the first future Ruthenian colonies, a Ruthenian delegation is preparing to go to Canada this summer, at harvest time, to view the country. It will consist of Dr. Oleskow, Professor of Agriculture at the Teachers' Seminary at Lviw, and two peasant-delegates, who will go as representatives of farmers and who intend afterwards to emigrate to Canada for settlement.

The purpose of this expedition is to pave the way for the first colonists, to advise them on the most inexpensive way of travel, to help them to select proper districts for settlement, where the settlers would have assurance of a safe future, and *to utilize all possible facilities the Government or the railway companies may offer to settlers who know how to apply for them.*

To the members of the expedition, or to be more correct, to its leader, Canada is not a strange country. He has thoroughly studied all available sources of information on that country, soil conditions, distribution of prairie land, wooded areas, park land, climate, farming conditions, industries, commerce, government, administration of the country, and conditions of settlement. All that has been studied, not only from informatory booklets written by the Government for the benefit of future settlers, but also from the *Statistical Year Book of Canada*, from many geographic and economic scientific publications about Canada, and from correspondence with Government authorities, as well as with Canadian colonists themselves. It is intended to view all these things with one's own eyes, to select the best places for settlement, and to find out particulars about local ways of farming, the amount of capital necessary for a start, in general, everything that would be important to know for a colonist's life.

[26]*Ibid.*, 34.

The peasant delegates will remain in Canada this year and will take up some work. The leader of the delegation will return home during the late autumn. The delegates will have the opportunity of investigating employment possibilities and will give a detailed account to their compatriots who sent them to Canada. Both peasant delegates have some knowledge of the German language. After a year, when they have earned some money, they will bring their families over to their homesteads. After the return of the leader of the delegation, a report on the visit will be published, in which all practical questions relating to Canada will be discussed in detail. . . .

The emigration for settlement is not intended to be a mass migration, but a carefully and thoroughly prepared movement. Only people who are in possession of property worth 1000 florins, or only slightly less, should contemplate emigrating. . . .

The first group of colonists will leave during the spring of 1896. Before that date nobody should try to emigrate, because if he ventures to go on his own, it is almost certain that he will be exploited by all kinds of agents, or he will settle blindly in some place where he may obtain a crop once in two or even in three years, or, not knowing the language, will be unable to obtain work.[27]

[27]*Ibid.*, 36–37.

Chapter Two

DR. OLESKOW'S VISIT TO CANADA
AUGUST–OCTOBER, 1895

I

DR. OLESKOW had expected to leave for Canada at the beginning of July but for some reason his departure was postponed three times. Finally a definite date was set, and he informed Sir Charles Tupper in London and the Department of the Interior in Ottawa that he and his companions were soon to sail:

To the Department of the Interior,
Ottawa, Canada.

I have the honour to inform the Department of my and my two companions' sailing from Liverpool at 1st August by *Sardinian* of Allan-Line. We beg to make the definite arrangements with respect to our journey through Canada as it is promised in letter of 1st June to the Office of the High Commissioner for Canada and in former letters.

I am,
Yours very respectfully,
PROF. DR. JOSEF OLESKOW
in Lemberg, Golebia Gasse 11A, Galicia, Austria.[1]

Before embarking for Canada, Dr. Oleskow stopped over in London, as arranged, for a conference with the High Commissioner for Canada, Sir Charles Tupper. He brought with him a letter of introduction from Spiro and Company of Hamburg, who presented Dr. Oleskow as a gentleman whose

. . . influence is omnipotent among these people [i.e., the Ukrainian peasants of Galicia], for whom he has worked out of pure humanity, and we would

[1]1. Oles./23312, No date, but written on or about July 9, and received in Ottawa on July 22, 1895: Dr. J. Oleskow, Lemberg, Austria, to the Department of the Interior, Ottawa. This is the first of Dr. Oleskow's letters written in English.

thank you to advise your people on the other side to treat the gentleman with utmost defference [*sic*] and attention. We may mention that Prof. Oleskow has toiled in the interest of his countrymen and supported emigration to Canada without remuneration or payment of any description and may worthily be treated and regarded as a guest of your Government. We therefore beg to renew our recommendation and request that special attention and courtesy be paid to him at all points he may touch on his journey.[21]

Dr. Oleskow remained in London two days and had a lengthy talk with the High Commissioner, in the course of which he explained the purpose of his visit to Canada and plans for the settlement of thousands of Ukrainian peasant-farmers in Western Canada, provided that conditions were found to be favourable. Sir Charles Tupper prepared a report on the talk, addressed it to the Minister of the Interior, and dispatched it with the same boat Dr. Oleskow was sailing on from Liverpool on August 1, 1895.

Dr. Oleskow arrived in Montreal on August 12. He was accompanied by only one companion, Iwan Dorundiak, a well-to-do peasant-farmer from the district of Kolomyja, who spoke passable German apart from his native Ukrainian. They spent one day in Montreal and arrived in Ottawa on August 13. The month of August was not a propitious time to visit the capital on business. Parliament was not sitting, the Minister of the Interior, T. Mayne Daly, was in Calgary on a business trip, and the Deputy Minister, A. M. Burgess, was on holiday in Shediac, New Brunswick. Dr. Oleskow was received by Acting Deputy Minister John R. Hall, and by L. M. Fortier, the Superintendent of Immigration. He presented his letters of introduction, one from John Dyke, the Government Agent in Liverpool, and the other from George Hannah of Allan Lines, Royal Mail Steamships, in Montreal. John Hall knew about the purpose of Dr. Oleskow's visit because the report prepared by the High Commisisoner in London arrived in Ottawa at the same time as the visitor. Sir Charles Tupper's report on Dr. Oleskow and his mission read as follows:

In continuation of my letter of the 11th ultimo on the subject of the proposed visit to Canada of Professor Josef Oleskow, of Lemberg, Galicia, for the purpose of enquiring into the suitability of the prairie regions for the settlement of his fellow countrymen belonging to the agricultural classes, I beg to say that Mr. Oleskow reported himself at this office on the 29th ultimo on his way, with a letter of introduction from Messrs. Spiro and Co., of Hamburg, copy of which I enclose for your information.

In the course of conversation Professor Oleskow explained to me the objects of his present visit. He is a Ruthinian of the Greek Catholic religion,

[21]1. Oles./23711, July 27, 1895: Spiro and Company, Hamburg, Germany, to the Secretary of the High Commissioner for Canada, London.

and his position as Professor of Agriculture at the Seminary in Lemberg, and also as a landowner, has brought him into very close contact with the problems arising out of the pressure of population on land in Galicia, leading to an excessive sub-division of holdings, and the impoverishment of the peasantry.

In his opinion emigration offers a substantial means of relief in the circumstances, but that it is above all important that the country or countries designated for that purpose should offer an abundance of free land, and conditions of soil and climate suitable for agriculture, so that the movement, once initiated, might continue without interruption under proper control and direction. For this reason therefore he has most vigorously opposed emigration to Brazil, which he considers from every point of view an unsuitable country, but whither numbers of Ruthinian peasants have emigrated. His reading and information have given him the impression that that Canada offers by far the best prospects for people in the position of his countrymen, and he is hopeful of being able to divert the present stream of emigration largely to the Dominion, provided the results of his enquiry are satisfactory.

Professor Oleskow wields a ready pen, and is well known for his contributions to the agricultural press in Galicia. It is the practice of the press in that part to issue every month a literary supplement, dealing with current subjects of interest to agriculturists, which is published in pamphlet form and supplied to subscribers. These supplements constitute largely the general reading of the peasantry, and they are probably perused by over 100,000 persons. In two of these pamphlets Professor Oleskow's writings on Brazil and Canada have been embodied—see enclosures—and his intention of visiting Canada made known for the purpose of prosecuting personal enquiry on the spot.

Professor Oleskow explained that he proposed to visit at the outset the various German speaking colonies, as the Galician peasantry are general bilingual, and can get on most easily with German settlers and understand their methods; that he would like to be provided with guides who understood German, as although he understood and spoke English fairly, he hardly felt able to conduct enquiry altogether without some help of that kind.

Provided the outlook were sufficiently encouraging his plan would be to advise at the outset the emigration of farmers with capital only, and to settle them in groups. The question of providing for labourers pure and simple would be thus largely avoided, and the element of weakness they form in any experimental scheme would be absent. He would advocate placing the settlers in village communities, a system to which they are accustomed, and which fosters village industries, spinning and weaving, basket making etc., in which they are adept, and which they generally prosecute during the winter. This would of course involve the granting of a reservation of land. I told Mr. Oleskow that a wise selection of the first parties in the sense he mentioned would greatly contribute towards the success of the emigration; that I had no doubt that the Department would be glad to facilitate his tour of inspection in every way, and the settlement of the emigrants that might come out on any plan which might be agreed upon and commended itself to your Department.

Professor Oleskow wished also to know whether the Government would be prepared to help in the matter of transportation, and in extending credit, if necessary, to the first settlers, in the event of their being harassed by failures of harvest at the outset, for although the settlers would have sufficient to start, the average means at their disposal would hardly be sufficient to withstand misfortunes of this character at so critical a time. I stated that I thought the Government would hardly feel able to give any promise of the kind, that the fares are extremely low, the railway rates to the North West comparing most favourably with the fares of the United States railways for similar distances into the Western interior: that the assistance rendered to the Mennonites had been given indirectly through their co-religionists already settled in Ontario, to whom the money was advanced and who became responsible for the repayment of the loan. I added that the best thing was to make sure of the solvent position of the first parties, and that the success of subsequent arrivals would be easily assured.

On the subject of his report I remarked that if it were favourable, and not too long, the Government might be prepared to share the cost of printing and circulating the same, but that I could not give any definite undertaking.

Mr. Oleskow replied that his report must in any case be published in the same form as his previous writings in view of his engagements towards his countrymen, and that it would not cost us anything, but that if his out of pocket expenses during his visit could be met he would be glad, as he was undertaking his journey on his own responsibility. I told him that was a matter which he should submit at Ottawa, but that I would also mention it when writing.

Mr. Oleskow will also explain to you the means he hopes to be able to adopt in order to retain control of the emigration movement towards Canada, in order to prevent any but the right class going out, and of these no excessive number at the same time.

Mr. Oleskow is sailing from Liverpool by the "Sardinian" to-day, and is accompanied by Mr. Dorundiak, a Ruthinian peasant farmer, who is acting as a delegate for his district. The Allan line and the Canadian Pacific Railway are affording both Mr. Oleskow and his companion travelling facilities out and home.[3]

The General Passenger Agent of the C.P.R. Company in Montreal had been informed about the date of sailing and the expected date of arrival in Canada of Dr. Oleskow and his companion, and about the fact that they would spend a few days in Ottawa, where ". . . arrangements will be made to show them the Experimental Farm, and other objects of interest."[4] A letter was dispatched to the Commissioner of

[3]1. Oles./23711, August 1, 1895: Sir Charles Tupper, High Commissioner for Canada, London, to the Minister of the Interior, Ottawa.

[4]1. Oles., August 5, 1895: Lyndwode Pereira, Assistant Secretary, Department of the Interior, Ottawa, to D. McNicoll, General Passenger Agent, C.P.R. Company, Montreal.

Dominion Lands in Winnipeg announcing Dr. Oleskow's arrival in Ottawa and his imminent departure for Winnipeg:

> Professor Oleskow is now in Canada, and it is likely that he will leave tomorrow [August 15] for Winnipeg. I am to ask you to bring to the commissioner's particular attention the enclosed copy of a letter from Sir Charles Tupper to the Minister dated the 1st instant, in this connection. No doubt the Commissioner will think it well to detail Mr. Carstens to accompany the Professor and his companion, and he will of course take such further action as may be necessary to facilitate the objects of these gentlemen.
>
> Accompanying Sir Charles Tupper's letter is a copy of one from Messrs. Spiro and Company of Hamburg, which is also enclosed for the Commissioner's perusal.[5]

In Ottawa Dr. Oleskow had two conferences with the Acting Deputy Minister and the Superintendent of Immigration, exploratory talks during the visit to the Experimental Farm, and an interview with the representative of the *Ottawa Journal.* With the Minister of the Interior out of town, Dr. Oleskow decided to prepare a memorandum which would contain his views, so that it could eventually be forwarded to the Minister for his information. The memorandum, although prepared in haste between talks and visits to "places of interest" (such as the Experimental Farm) contained a number of very interesting points, and gave a good idea of what Dr. Oleskow hoped to achieve. Although couched in very general terms, it contained basic ideas which, if they had been realized, would have reduced the difficulties encountered by subsequent immigrants who were to come to Canada without Oleskow's solicitation or assistance. It was written in German, since writing in English would probably have taken too long; it would also have been too difficult for Dr. Oleskow to express all the thoughts he wished to embody in a short memorandum. Miss N. Mercer of the Department of Immigration prepared the translation while Dr. Oleskow, accompanied by the Superintendent of Immigration, was visiting the Experimental Farm. The memorandum contained four points discussed in detail by Dr. Oleskow:

> In connection with the proposed emigration of the Galician peasant-proprietors of small holdings, the following interests must come under consideration:
>
> 1. The Canadian Government;
> 2. The Transportation Companies;
> 3. The Austrian Government; and
> 4. The Peasant-proprietor himself.

[5]1. Oles., August 14, 1895: Lyndwode Pereira, Ottawa, to the Secretary, Dominion Lands Board, Winnipeg.

1.

The Canadian Government has, I believe, an interest in giving to the land and soil, which lie useless, and only possess an imaginary value, an *actual value*, and thus increase the national wealth. Further, the Canadian Government is anxious that the settlers should be real farmers of such a class as to prosper under the climatic and agricultural conditions in Canada.

2.

The Transportation Companies strive to increase the passenger traffic without taking into consideration what kind of people they transport. The worst of it is that as regards the latter the Transportation Companies are obliged to make use of Agents and Sub-agents who deal dishonestly in the matter. Consequently, the movement develops unhealthily, and barbers, dancing-masters, and Jewish idlers ask for the free homesteads, which naturally they abandon later on. The emigration propaganda carried on in such a manner is completely discredited in Europe, particularly in Austria, where we had a great lawsuit against the Agents and Sub-agents of the Transportation Companies (almost entirely Jews) during which many deceptions which were practiced by these Sub-agents against the emigrants were discovered.

3.

On account of this it cannot be wondered at that European Governments oppose *every propaganda from the outside* and persecute them. On the other hand, it must be conceded that Austria does not possess any colonies or dependencies of her own, and that therefore the Government is obliged to let the surplus population go wherever it pleases. Thus in the last year a large number of the proprietors of small holdings have gone to Brazil.

4.

The position of the peasant-proprietors is, owing to the division of the holdings and the lack of the opportunities for making money, a very bad one. For want of employment all labourers turn to the large properties, and the supply is so great that the price of a day's work is in some places as low as 5 cents. This circumstance, which can be verified by statistical data, will suffice to make clear that the plan for the systematic emigration of several thousands of Galician farmers is in fact a very modest one. The price of land in Galicia is high, particularly for peasant holdings. There are districts where as much as $400 are paid for an acre of land, and $80 can be taken as a mean. Thus a peasant-proprietor of a small holding could realize enough from the sale of a few acres and his house to commence farming in Western Canada.

More suitable settlers for Western Canada could not be found than the Galician peasant-proprietors. The people have grown up in pursuit of agriculture; it forms their only occupation. They have modest requirements as to the necessities of life, which is to be valued in such circumstances; they will possess enough means, and will stand the climate of Canada better than any other nation (with the exception of the Russian) because the climatic conditions of Canada have much in common with those of Galicia. Thus, said emigration, if properly organized, would begin an epoch in the colonization of Canada, which hitherto has proceeded more slowly than the country really merits.

Taking for granted that the Canadian Government would thoroughly support the systematic yearly emigration of a few thousand farmers, I have thoroughly prepared such an emigration to Canada in our country, in Austria.

I conferred in respect to this with Government organizations, and particularly with the Governor of Galicia, Count Badeni, who is at present the most influential man in Austria, with the General Inspector of Agriculture in Galicia, with the Department of Agriculture (*mit den Organen des Ackerbauministeriums*), whose letters in this connection I can produce, and all these men thought well of my struggle against emigration to Brazil and of my intention to inspect Canada to divert emigration there. Of course, in the realization of this plan it would be necessary to work again to impress the Austrian Government favourably in this movement; this is possible if the emigration results are prompted not by outside factors but come from ourselves, as a result of necessity caused by prevailing conditions in our country.

As regards my position towards the peasant community, I owe the Department an explanation. The Peasant Community of Galicia was organized in several central organizations (*Vereine*) each of them having hundreds of branches all over the country. The aim of these societies was the enlightenment of the people and the furthering of national policy. Until a few years ago, I succeeded in also including in the activities of these societies the aim of furthering the material welfare of the peasants and bringing in agrarian policies. In these societies I became the intellectual director of these very branches (of activity), and one of the objects of my agrarian-political program consists of the furthering of emigration as a means of raising labourers' wages. The above-named societies have little means, but due to their excellent organization they exercise exceedingly great influence on the peasant community of Galicia; it may be said that they dominate it. In the monthly publications of these societies, which are read by some 100,000 peasants, I have published pamphlets on the subject of emigration, stressing Canada ahead of other countries, and announced my journey accompanied by a peasant delegate (who is now on his way to Winnipeg). The peasants, therefore, await with deepest interest the results of our exploratory inspection. If the report is favourable, the first contingents (of emigrants) will embark for Canada next spring.

The conditions for emigration to Canada cannot be considered satisfactory if the movement does not receive support from the Government. One should not deceive oneself. The people have a choice; the Brazilian Government offers entirely free ocean and railway transportation to the desired destinations; in Argentina, in better climatic conditions, land is to be had almost for nothing; the same holds true in Matabelle and Mashonaland, yes, even in South-east Russia the celebrated *black-earth* soil (the *tchernozem*) is sold for 20 roubles per *desiatina* (2½ acres), which, taken in connection with the unprecedented cheapness of transport on the Russian State Railways and the proximity of European markets, is very advantageous; there are only political reasons which drive the Germans from Russia.

Through the building of the Siberian-State-Railway [the Trans-Siberian Railway] a very formidable rival will arise in a few years for Canada. Taking everything into consideration, I do not know how I could justify my pleading for Canada in Austria if it were not supported on this side by the Canadian

Government. I believe, however, that in connection with our proposed emigration the Government could save the expense of intermediary agents to lead the propaganda, as it would receive without further anxiety a colony of real farmers, would be relieved from the duty of exercising control as to the class of emigrants as we should be able ourselves to choose a better class, and would select only real farmers, possessing some capital, without which it would be useless to send them to Canada to farm; for all these reasons the Government should not be afraid of making some sacrifices to further the movement.

If the Government concurs in the main idea which has been here developed, the emigration movement would have to be carried on in future in accordance with business principles.[6]

The day after Dr. Oleskow's departure for the West (August 16), John R. Hall sent a letter to the Minister of the Interior to inform him of Oleskow's visit to Ottawa. Dr. Oleskow's memorandum was enclosed in the letter to the Minister. It read:

Professor Oleskow, of whose intended visit we were advised by the High Commissioner in May last, arrived on the 13th instant, and after a preliminary discussion about his desire to promote the emigration from Galicia of the small peasant proprietors, he decided to put his views in writing, of which the enclosed is a translation made by Miss Mercer. While the translation was being made Mr. Fortier took the Professor out to the Experimental Farm with which he was very much impressed, and on their return we had a further conference aided by Miss Mercer as interpreter. The Professor speaks English fairly well, but does not catch on to spoken English readily.

You will see from the way he emphasizes the existence of competing fields that he thinks some assistance towards the transport of these people is necessary if we are to secure them. As to this I took particular pains to impress upon him the objections to assisted immigration; objections which are so potent that in the case of Father Lilge's Moravians we were obliged to adopt a plan of giving Father Lilge a sum of money nominally as a salary, but which he handed over to the Steamship Company. To do this for the Galicians would involve the expenditure of money which he understands could not be promised without your concurrence, and therefore the whole question of assistance to this scheme is in abeyance for the present. In the meantime having come so far and got railway passes he went on to the west yesterday and will see the Commissioner at Winnipeg. I have wired Mr. Smith to send Carstens with the Professor at our expense—this is all we are called upon to contribute so far, the Professor travelling at his own expense.

He says that the movement will be restricted to peasants possessing about, say, $350 to $400, some will have a good deal more, and that these people though distinctly of the agricultural class are what we would call out here

[6]1. Oles., August 16, 1895: Memorandum prepared in German by Dr. Oleskow during his stay in Ottawa, August 14, 1895. Miss Mercer, the translator, was not familiar with some of the expressions used by Dr. Oleskow, and corrections have been made in her translation where necessary.

handy men, some being competent carpenters or blacksmiths in addition to their agricultural qualifications. Their religion is a curious combination of Greek and Roman Catholicism.

The Professor fully understands the force of opposition to state aided immigration from the working classes who possess votes, and assented to my suggestion that he should avoid newspaper interviews. In Austria the opposition of the Government is only to be feared where they think an emigration movement is being promoted from without the Empire, and therefore the Professor is all the more willing to maintain secrecy on this point.

I have asked the Commissioner to keep track through Mr. Carstens of the Professor's movements and to try to arrange an interview after you return to the Territories or Winnipeg.[7]

A second copy of the translation of Oleskow's memorandum was sent to Deputy Minister Burgess at "Weldon House," Shediac, New Brunswick, for his information:

My dear Burgess,

Professor Oleskow has come and gone and I enclose a translation of the memorandum which he made while here, and also a copy of my letter to the Minister covering another copy of this translation.

These papers speak for themselves so I forward them to you without comment. This is a half day and I am in haste to catch the mail.

Yours sincerely, etc.

(Signed) JOHN R. HALL.[8]

In a telegram to H. H. Smith, Commissioner of Dominion Lands in Winnipeg, Hall requested: ". . . On return Minister North West try arrange meeting with Oleskow. His business important."[9]

Despite all the precautions that had been taken to avoid publicity, a reporter of the *Ottawa Journal* succeeded in obtaining an interview with Dr. Oleskow, and the paper published a news item on August 17 with the sensational headline:

IS SPYING US OUT

The Mission Of Prof. Oleskow Of Lemburg, Austria

He is Travelling Across Canada to Report to the Government of the Austrian Empire—Visit in Ottawa and Trip to the Experimental Farm.

Professor Oleskow, of Lemburg, Austria, was in the city for the past two days, staying at the Windsor, and left yesterday for Manitoba.

Mr. Oleskow is professor of Agriculture in the University of Lemburg, and along with a representative farmer from that country, has come to

[7]1. Oles., August 16, 1895: John R. Hall, Acting Deputy Minister, Department of the Interior, Ottawa, to T. Mayne Daly, Minister of the Interior.

[8]1. Oles./24243, August 17, 1895: John R. Hall, Ottawa, to A. M. Burgess, Deputy Minister of the Interior, Shediac, N.B.

[9]1. Oles./23819, Telegram, August 14, 1895: John R. Hall, Ottawa, to H. H. Smith, Commissioner of Dominion Lands, Winnipeg, Manitoba.

Canada to make a report to the Austrian government upon the Dominion as a field for emigrants from the congested districts of that part of Europe.

During their brief stay in Ottawa Mr. Oleskow and his travelling companion visited the Experimental Farm, along with Mr. Fortier, who has charge of the immigration branch of the department of interior. The visitors were very much impressed with what they saw at the farm. They had no idea that Canada was so advanced in agriculture, and they believe from what they have already seen that the Dominion would be a good place for intending emigrants from their country to come to.

Mr. Oleskow says that until very recently the government of Austria was opposed to emigration. Now they are beginning to see that there are certain congested districts (and the place from which Professor Oleskow comes is one of these), which would be benefited by emigration. At any rate, the people themselves have come to this conclusion, and about 50,000 emigrated to Brazil. The change to them proved disastrous. The Austrian government seeing that this has been the case and that a certain number of the people are bound to emigrate, has now determined to find out a better field for the surplus of their population to go to. It is with this view that Mr. Oleskow is here and for the same reason that he has gone to the Northwest. He will not only make a report upon the country himself but the representative farmer who is along with him will also make a report.

It is their intention if time will permit to go as far as the Pacific coast. They will go as far as Calgary at any rate. They will enquire fully into the agricultural capabilities of Manitoba and the Northwest, as they are of the opinion that it will be the best place to recommend to their people. Mr. Oleskow says that if his report is favorable, as he expects it will be, there are a large number of well-to-do farmers who will come from Austria to settle in Canada next spring.[10]

The newspaper reporter used his imagination when he stated that Dr. Oleskow came to Canada to make a report to the Austrian Government about the country as a possible field for emigrants. The Austrian Government did not encourage emigration, and Dr. Oleskow did not come to Canada to report back to it. As we have noted, Dr. Oleskow, supported by educational societies, was trying to assist members of the peasantry of Galicia and Bukowina who wished to emigrate by finding suitable places for their settlement.

II

Dr. Oleskow arrived in Winnipeg on Saturday, August 17, 1895, and was met at the station by Hugo Carstens, the German Interpreter with the Dominion Lands Office in Winnipeg, who was to accompany Dr. Oleskow on his trip to the Northwest and British Columbia. On Sunday, Dr. Oleskow expressed a wish to visit the few Ukrainian families living in Winnipeg, most of whom had come from the village of Nebyliw in the Kalush district of Galicia. Carstens was well acquainted with these

[10] *Ottawa Journal*, August 17, 1895.

newcomers and therefore he served as Dr. Oleskow's guide during the visits. In his booklet, *O emigratsii* / "About Emigration," published on his return from Canada the same year, Dr. Oleskow mentions this visit, discussing the financial situations of some of the families:

Some ten Ruthenian families, mainly from Nebyliw, live in Winnipeg. They have been there for three to four years and have already built houses for themselves. Employees of the Immigration hall know the place where they live. Our new arrivals may obtain certain information from these Ruthenians. They do not live too badly there; some of them are saving money in order to buy a farm, while others have become accustomed to the city life and intend to remain in Winnipeg. Their financial situation, as it was outlined to my companion Dorundiak, is as follows:

1. Vasyl Yatsiw arrived here in 1892, with $40 in his pocket (a dollar equals 2½ florins). He owns a house in Winnipeg worth $65, two cows, and has $120 in the bank. Last year he had $200.00 saved, but entered into a business partnership with a Jew and naturally lost his money.
2. Yurko Panishchak arrived without a cent to his name, but now owns a house worth $200, a cow, and has $120 in the bank.
3. Hnat Dmytryshyn, Luchka Kultchytskyi, and Iwan Barskyi, who arrived here in 1895, have $70 each in the bank.
4. Yurko Roshko, who emigrated in 1894, also has $70.
5. Dmytro Widynovych, who arrived here in 1893, had $40 upon his arrival and now has $400.
6. Yurko Paish sent home $120.

It is impossible to verify whether these figures are correct, and one must always keep in mind that everybody likes to boast about his possessions more than is justifiable in reality.[11]

On Monday, before leaving for Alberta, Dr. Oleskow had a conference with H. H. Smith, the Commissioner of Dominion Lands, who informed him that arrangements had been made to meet T. Mayne Daly, the Minister of the Interior, who was expected to be in Edmonton towards the end of the month. H. H. Smith had previously communicated with the Minister, who was on a tour in the West, and received a reply from him that he would be in Edmonton between August 26 and 28, and would be able to receive Dr. Oleskow then. The Commissioner confirmed receipt of the letter:

I have received your message informing that you will be in Edmonton from the 26th to the 28th this month, and that Professor Oleskow can have an interview with you there. . . . It seems to me from what Sir Charles says that the Professor's visit may be looked upon as one of considerable importance, and that if he is satisfied with the inquiries most important and valuable results may be anticipated.[12]

[11]Dr. Josef Oleskow, *O emigratsii*/"About Emigration" (Lviw: the Michael Kachkowskyi Society, December, 1895), 41.

[12]1. Oles./24733, August 21, 1895: H. H. Smith, Commissioner of Dominion Lands, Winnipeg, to T. Mayne Daly, Minister of the Interior, Calgary.

In Alberta, Dr. Oleskow, Iwan Dorundiak, and Hugo Carstens made a thorough survey of the lands available for settlement in the Edmonton area. Carstens later submitted a detailed report on the whole trip. Dr. Oleskow published his own observations in a cursory fashion without giving dates, and without mentioning his trip to British Columbia, his conferences with the Federal Minister of the Interior and with the Minister of Immigration for British Columbia, his spending a day in Banff on his return east, or his being the first Ukrainian to visit that summer resort.

The conference between T. Mayne Daly and Dr. Oleskow took place on Monday, August 26, 1895, in the "Hotel Edmonton." Dr. Oleskow came to the meeting armed with two introductions, one from Sir Charles Tupper and the other from the Austro-Hungarian Consul Eduard Schultze. Schultze's letter of introduction read thus:

IMPERIAL AND ROYAL AUSTRO-HUNGARIAN CONSULATE

Montreal August 12, 1895.

Sir,

This will serve to introduce to you

Dr. Josef Oleskow of the Province of Galicia, Austria, who comes to Canada in the interests of a philanthropic and patriotic Association, accompanied by a practical Farmer, to study the advantages offered by your Country to emigration of Farmers, who possess limited means, and to ascertain what such emigration will benefit these intending settlers.

Any assistance and facilities you can offer to encourage this important undertaking will meet with the approbation of the Galician organization, and greatly oblige me,

I have the honor to be, Sir

Faithfully yours,

(Signed) Ed. Schultze, Consul.[13]

Hon'ble
T. M. Daly,
Minister of the Interior
Ottawa.

The letter of introduction written by Sir Charles Tupper, the High Commissioner for Canada in London, was couched in more general terms:

Victoria Chambers,
17, Victoria Street,
London, S.W.
July 29, 1895.

Dear Mr. Daly,

Permit me to introduce to you the bearer of this letter Professor Josef Oleskow of Lemberg, Galicia, with whom your Department has been in

[13]1. Oles., August 12, 1895: Eduard Schultze, Imperial Royal Austro-Hungarian Consul, Montreal, to T. M. Daly, Ottawa.

communication with his proposed visit to Canada to enquire into the suitability of the prairie regions for the settlement of his countrymen belonging to the agricultural classes.

Professor Oleskow is sailing by the Allan Line Steamer "Sardinian" on Thursday next, and on his way through London to Liverpool has called upon me to explain the main points of his present mission. I have assured Dr. Oleskow that you will be much interested to discuss his plans with him and afford him all the facilities you can in seeing the country.

Professor Oleskow is accompanied by Mr. Dorundiak, a peasant Farmer Delegate from Galicia, who has been selected to report upon the conditions of western Canada from a working farmer's point of view.

Commending Professor Oleskow to your kind consideration,

I am,

Yours faithfully

(Signed) for Sir C. Tupper J. G. COLMER[14]

Hon. T. M. Daly,
Minister of the Interior,
Ottawa.

The conference mentioned in the letter lasted two hours, and T. Mayne Daly described it in a letter addressed to John R. Hall, the Acting Deputy Minister in Ottawa, the day of the meeting:

Edmonton, 27th August 1895.

Dear Mr. Hall,

I have met Professor Oleskow here (this evening) and have had a two hours' interview with him—Mr. Carstens acting as Interpreter. The Professor seems pleased with the country, and was most favourably impressed with the Austrian colony settled on the Stoney Plain, West of here, which he visited today and yesterday. He thinks if land similar to that at Stoney Plain, with like surroundings, could be got, it would be satisfactory to his people—the Farmer who is with him being personally impressed with the capabilities of the soil, etc. etc.

I have found, in the course of our conversation, that it is a *sine qua non* that aid in the nature of a bonus should be given to the settlers whom the Professor intends bringing out. He suggested himself that the assistance should be in the form of a bonus which we gave, up to two years ago—namely 10 dollars per head to each head of a family—and 10 dollars for the wife, and five dollars for children over 12 years of age. In addition to this he also said they would require an advance of money for preliminary expenses, such as the printing of his pamphlet, the establishment of an office, and the payment to clerks to receive applications from those who were desirous of emigration. When we reached that stage, I cross-examined him pretty closely; and must confess, I do not see exactly how we can best render the assistance desired otherwise than by way of a bonus, payable upon the settler making his homestead entry and actually settling upon the land. I explained this feature of our bonus system to the Professor, and he seemed quite satisfied, but I pointed out to him that if we made any advances to him for preliminary

141. Oles./24104, July 29, 1895: Sir Charles Tupper (per J. G. Colmer), High Commissioner for Canada, London, to T. Mayne Daly, Ottawa.

expenses we had no guarantee that we would get any return for such advances. It was suggested by me that, possibly, in this event this trouble might be overcome by the British Consul certifying to the responsibility of the Professor and his Committee. However, I informed him fully of the fact that it was impossible for me to give him any decided answer, or come to any definite arrangement with him, in the first place, that the Government had come to the conclusion the granting of bonuses to Emigrants, and that to re-establish this feature of emigration would be a matter of serious consideration; and, in the second place, that should the Government see fit to adopt any recommendation of mine in this direction I had not the money at my disposal at present to meet such an obligation—that I could only expend the money that had been already voted by Parliament—that the sum already voted was fully apportioned, and that it would be necessary for me, in order to provide for the bonusing of these emigrants to the number he expected to bring out, to have the sum required for this and preliminary expenses, voted by Parliament. I further added that it might be difficult under existing circumstances to prevail upon the Government to agree to the granting of Bonuses, or to the voting of such a large sum of money (say $10,000) for the purpose of encouraging the settlement of a class of people about whom we knew comparatively nothing.

I suggested, in conclusion, that when he reached Ottawa, on his return, he should put in writing the reasons for his coming out here, the object of the movement in Galicia, the conditions of these people there; the amount of capital which each family would be likely to bring out; the amount of assistance he would require; and, in fact, a full statement of his mission and aims; and that upon his leaving that statement with you I would bring the matter to the attention of my colleagues.

Further, I told him I did not expect to reach Ottawa until the end of September—probably not until the middle of October; and in that event it would be impossible for me to give him any answer before he leaves for home, which he expects to do on the 25th of September.

I may say to you for your information and that of the Deputy, when he returns, that I am rather favourably impressed with the Professor; but I would suggest that before committing ourselves in anyway we should ask Sir Charles Tupper to make enquiries through the nearest British Consul as to the ways and conditions of the people whom the Professor is encouraging to come out here, what his standing in the community is, and generally to make all such enquiries as would surround our action with every safeguard. Carstens may no doubt make his Report to Mr. Smith; but I think I have put as clearly as possible the nature of our interview.

I forgot to say that I am personally so impressed with the representations made that I would be prepared to submit the maker for the consideration of the Government; and in that event you might have a Memorandum to Council prepared setting out fully the facts; but possibly we might await this action until we hear from Sir Charles Tupper, with whom you might correspond at once.

I tried to impress upon the Professor the necessity of limiting the number of his emigrants for the first year: I suggested 100 families, aggregating 500 people. He seemed to be under the impression himself it would be well to bring out at the start 400 families, or say 2,000 people, and at the same time he seemed to think it necessary they should have an office man to drum up these people. All this creates enquiry in one's mind as to whether this is not one of these great schemes on the part of the promoters to make money. However, I shall be charitable to this man, and in the meantime make the closest investigation into all the facts.

Yours sincerely

(Signed) T. MAYNE DALY.

John R. Hall, Esq.
Acting Deputy Minister of the Interior.
I enclose letters received introducing the Professor.[15]

A copy of the Minister's letter was sent to the High Commissioner for Canada in London with the request ". . . that steps suggested by the Minister may be taken (to obtain information on Dr. Oleskow) and the result communicated to the Department, with the least possible delay."[16] Sir Charles Tupper complied with the request, passing it on to Joseph Chamberlain, the Secretary of State for Colonies, who, on his part, passed it on to the Foreign Office. W. Barrington, the British Ambassador in Vienna, was then instructed to approach the Austrian authorities and to request them to give such information as they might deem proper about Dr. Josef Oleskow of Lemberg.

Dr. Oleskow, completely unaware of the diplomatic activity he had caused, continued his tour of inspection of the open lands in the Fort Saskatchewan area. Together with Iwan Dorundiak and Hugo Carstens, he visited the country around Long Lake, Beaver Lake, Whitford Lake, Wetaskiwin. Finally, after six days on the move without change of horses, the group set out for Edmonton. After a brief visit to the Indian Reserve south of Edmonton, they left for Calgary, the parting point. Dr. Oleskow and Hugo Carstens headed for the Pacific coast, and Iwan Dorundiak travelled east with letters of recommendation to farmers in Balgonie and Grenfell.

Carstens, as instructed, submitted a detailed report about the trip to the Commissioner of Dominion Lands in Winnipeg. The Commissioner forwarded the report to the Department of the Interior in Ottawa, where the Superintendent of Immigration, L. M. Fortier, pencilled on it: "It would be well to shew Carsten's rep. to Minister before Prof. Oleskow comes in. . . ."[17] Carstens' report was dated September 20, 1895, and was received in Ottawa October 1, the day when Dr. Oleskow returned

[15]1. Oles./24104, August 27, 1895 (The Minister was mistaken, for according to Hugo Carstens the date was Monday, August 26): T. Mayne Daly, Edmonton, to John R. Hall, Ottawa.

[16]1. Oles., September 5, 1895: Lyndwode Pereira, Ottawa, to J. G. Colmer, Secretary, High Commissioner for Canada, London, England.

[17]1. Oles. Slip of paper attached to Hugo Carsten's report, signed "L.M.F." Date of Receipt of the report was October 1, 1895.

from the United States to Ottawa. It was a lengthy report which described each phase of the trip in detail:

Winnipeg, Man., September 20th, 1895.

Sir,

I have the honour to submit herewith my report of a trip through western Canada, taken in the interest of Immigration, by Dr. Josef Oleskow, Professor of Agriculture on the K.K. Teachers Seminary of Lemberg, Galicia, Austria, on which as per your instructions, I accompanied him as a guide and interpreter.

Leaving Winnipeg on Monday, August 19th last, we proceeded direct to Calgary, where we arrived the following Wednesday morning, there I introduced the Professor to Mr. Rowe, Agent Dominion Lands, and Mr. Pearce, Superintendent of the Mines, from whom we obtained much information regarding that district, and after obtaining, through the kindness of Mr. Superintendent Rowe, of the N.W.M.P., a team, we drove out to see Mr. Pearce's farm, and the "Old Government Farm" now owned by Mr. Hull, on both these farms some good results of irrigation are shewn, the fodder crop of timothy grass and oats being very heavy. Returning to Calgary by a circuitous route we saw some fine stock farms on some of which were heavy crops of grain being cut for fodder.

Leaving Calgary the next morning, August 22nd, we reached Edmonton that evening, calling next morning on Mr. Ruttan, Agent of Dominion Lands, who very kindly outlined a route for us in that district, here I also made enquiries regarding Police transportation, but found that owing to the expected arrival of the Premier, Sir Mackenzie Bowell, and the Hon. T. M. Daly, no police teams could be had, therefore I engaged a team from Mr. McCouly and left at noon for the Stoney Plains settlement, accompanied by the Professor and Mr. Dorndiack, the practical farmer who accompanied the Professor, reaching the German settlement in the evening, we stayed over night at the house of Frederick Goebel, S.E. 10-53-27 W. 4th M., the next day, Aug. 24th, we devoted to seeing the settlement, calling on a number of the settlers, there are about 150 families settled in this colony, mostly German Galicians, who removed to there from Dunmore four years ago, they have been very progressive and I am pleased to say everywhere we went there was evidence of satisfaction and content on the part of the settlers they being quite enthusiastic in their praise of the district.

Among the most satisfied I would like to mention Mr. G. Philipp Muller on the S.E.¼ 24-52-1, W. 5th M. who arrived 6 years ago in Winnipeg with only $55 and a family of 6 children, he also settled first at Dunmore from where he came 4 years ago to the Edmonton district with only a yoke of oxen and a plow, he and his oldest son now own, free of debt, 11 horses, 12 head of cattle, all the necessary machinery, including binder, and have 115 acres under crop, from which they expect to realize about $1000 in cash.

The crops throughout this settlement were excellent, and free from any damage of frost, and being rapidly cut.

The professor and the farmer were very much surprised and satisfied with what they saw and heard from the settlers, believing this to be an oasis, there however (are) no vacant lands in this district, but having been told further west there was supposed to be some more good land, we drove west next morning, Sunday August 25th, after exchanging our driver for one of the settlers acquainted with the roads. Leaving the South West corner of Township 52, Range 1, W. 5 M., we followed a trail running south-westerly through about 8 or 10 miles of solid timber coming out on the banks of the Saskatchewan, from where we followed two roads leading north-westerly to White Whale Lake [Whitevale Lake], the country here is very rolling with a good growth of grass, well adapted for stock but little for cultivation. Not being able to find another road we had to return that evening by the same road we came in and stayed again over night at the settlement, from where we returned the next morning to Edmonton in order to meet the Hon. Mr. Daly as per arrangement, where we arrived in the evening of August 26th.

After arrival on the train a meeting between the Hon. Mr. Daly and the Professor was arranged for that evening at the Hotel Edmonton. The main points discussed at this meeting were about as follows:—

The Professor said that up to his coming to Edmonton he had seen no part that would suit him for settlement, but after seeing Stoney Plains district, with its Austrian settlers, he was satisfied that if similar districts and climate could be found it would be of benefit to his people and to Canada to bring the people here.

That the settlers to be sent here were to be no Jews, but agriculturists with means, the minimum that each family would possess after landing on their homesteads in Cash to be $300. That these settlers would come out in colonies, and settle at once in colonies on land, at the head of each to be one of the intelligent, unselfish men, who will represent and direct the affairs of the settlers under a co-operative system.

And that in consideration of the fact that the settlers would need have to go long distances from railroad communication, to their great disadvantage, that the Canadian Government give these settlers the so-called settlers' bonus as given in previous years but now discontinued and that the Booking Agent would have nothing to do with the getting or inducting the settlers to come, that the Booking Agents' bonus be also given the settler.

That these bonuses be not given to the individual settler but in a lump sum for the benefit of the settlement in the erection of creameries or as might deem advisable.

But as there would necessarily be some expense in starting and maintaining this movement, for instance in printing reports, opening of office, clerks, and the securing of the people, that part of these bonuses be given to Professor or Committee and that also an advance would be required, the arrangement of which and the providing of security to the Government against loss the Professor had not thought out and must leave to Mr. Daly to think out.

That the number of settlers expected to be brought out the first year would the very least be 1000 families, and about the same number every following year if anything came of this movement.

Mr. Daly given his own experience and personal view recommended that only about 500 well chosen and picked families be sent out the first year to form a good nucleus of a settlement, but to this the professor could not agree as either large numbers or none would be sent, and besides all would be well picked families. Mr. Daly then informed the Professor that as this would mean an expenditure up to above the present Immigration grant, and besides would be departure from the usual way of paying bonuses to settlers, on proof of settlement and inasmuch as an advance of money was asked for, for which some guarantee had to be given the Government, no matter how much personally he might be in favour of the movement, he would have to lay the matter before his colleagues in the Government, and the better to enable him to lay the matter in the most favoured aspect before the Government he would ask the Professor to make his proposition in writing and either lay it before the Commissioner at Winnipeg or before the Department in Ottawa, and as soon as Mr. Daly would return to Ottawa, which would be about the following 15th October, he would lay the matter before the Government as favourably as possible and communicate the results at once to the Professor.

Before proceeding I might be permitted to say that the conversation at this meeting and what I could learn from the Professor, who is a Ruthenian (a Slavish tribe) and Greek Catholic, that I believe the people intended to be brought through this Agency besides Poles and perhaps some Germans, will chiefly be Ruthenians, who are generally speaking an agricultural people, of good physique, used to hardships, but rather slovenly in dress and habits. They number about 3,000,000, and live in Eastern Galicia, along the Carpathian Mountains.

On Tuesday, August 29th [Carstens meant Wednesday, August 28], after engaging Mr. J. E. Smith, an able Land Guide, as driver, we started in the afternoon for Fort Saskatchewan where we remained over night and bought provisions for our journey, leaving there the next morning we went to the Beaver Hills Settlement where there are also a large number of Galician-Germans settled in order to shew the Professor that these settlers had been equally as successful as those in Stoney Plains, he being somewhat prejudiced against the country East of Edmonton.

Here, too, we found the settlers well satisfied, the crops on an average were good and had been so during the 4 years that these people had been settled here, and although there might here be less of a rainfall, there was even less danger of frost than at Stoney Plains, after seeing some of the older settlers we went to a Ruthenian, named Anton Paisch, on S.E. 28-55-21 W. 4th M., a direct countryman of the Professor and the farmer accompanying us, this man had been two years on his land and came very poor, he had some nice stock and 25 acres cultivated and was well satisfied, here we saw some winter rye, fully 6 feet high, with ears measuring 7 inches. The only complaint made by the wife of this settler was very characteristic, that they had no Priest (Greek Catholic) and sinned too much in getting up late and not fasting enough, having too much to eat.

From here we followed the Victoria trail until Beaver Creek, passing through the Moravian settlement, from Beaver Creek we turned again north to Limestone Lake, where in Township 56, Range 19, W. 4th M. we found 16 families of Ruthenians (Bojkes) had lately settled. These people owned 16 horses, 20 oxen, and 40 head of other stock, with about 200 acres cultivated, they had little means when they came, and are making progress and are satisfied. Some were building better homes, and although a very primitive people with little to commence farming, I think they will make eventually good settlers.

Returning to the Victoria trail, we stayed over night at Edna P.O., the next morning, August 29th, we followed again the Victoria trail which here runs along an elevation, in places stony, with little timber, but making a fine sheep-raising country, until striking Long Lake, at the east of the Township 56, Range 18, between here and Egg or Whitford Lake the country becomes more bluffy with a light soil adapted for agriculture. Before reaching this Lake we left Victoria trail and went South East, passing by a few settlers on the west side of the Lake, these had raised some good crops and nothing had as yet been touched by frost, with the grain ready for cutting.

From here we went due south, reaching Beaver Lake in the evening, passing through some good land but chiefly adapted for stock raising, with no settlement. At Beaver Lake we called on the Agent, Mr. Kildahl, who shewed us a good sample of grain grown 16 miles east of there on Birch Creek, here there was quite a heavy frost that night, but some of the grain had already been cut, the next morning, August 30th, we followed a trail south-westerly, through a flat country with a fine growth of grass, passing on the west side of Lake Demay, the country again becomes bluffy and from here to Dried Meat the country is specially fine, reaching Stoney Creek, an arm of the Battle River, we went east, camping for the night on the N.W.¼ 14-46-20 W. 4 M. here there is also very little settlement, and the little grain grown was of good quality and so far free from frost. The next morning, August 31th, we went across prairie north east about 6 miles to an old trail running south east which we followed some distance going again south to Dried Meat Hill and from there a few miles east along Battle River, the land here within a radius of from 4 to 6 miles along and north of Dried Meat Lake and Battle River is exceptionally fine, well adapted for settlement, indeed this part of the country seemed to please the Professor and the farmer better than any other part we had seen.

From here we followed the Battle River West going to Wetaskiwin, arriving there in the evening, and drove the next day, Sunday, September 1st, to Edmonton having been 6 days out without change of horses.

The following Monday I went to see some of the settlers on the Indian Reserve south of Edmonton, these people had very heavy crops, which on account of too much growth were yet green and touched by frost, they had splendid buildings and are not disheartened.

On the morning of Tuesday, September 3rd, we left Edmonton for Calgary, arriving there in the evening, from here I gave Mr. Dorndiak, the farmer, letters of introduction to several settlers in the Balgonie and Grenfell districts which he intended to visit while the Professor and myself left that night for Vancouver, where he arrived without stoppage at 3 P.M. September 5th. After seeing the City we took next morning the Electric Car for New Westminster where we called upon the Agent, Mr. McKenzie, who gave us much information regarding lands within the Railway Belt. Returning to Vancouver by noon, we took the boat for Victoria, reaching there in the evening; the next morning, Saturday, September 7th, we called at the Provincial Buildings on Colonel Baker, Minister of Immigration, Mr. Marten, Commissioner of Lands, and Mr. Jessup, Provincial Immigration Agent.

We bore letters of recommendation to Colonel Baker from J. B. McKilligan of Victoria, with whom we travelled from Calgary, and who very kindly told us much of interest from B.C.

Colonel Baker received us very kindly, gave us every detail regarding their settlements and available land and offered facilities to inspect the latter, which on account of lack of time we had to decline.

In the afternoon we saw different points of interest, and also visited Esquimalt, the next morning, Sunday, September 8th, we took the train for Nanaimo, where we made enquiries about labour and saw two of the largest coal mines; from here we took, Monday morning, the boat for Vancouver, arriving there at noon, and leaving again at 2 o'clock for Sycamous Junction, where we made next morning connections for the Okanagan branch, reaching Vernon at 10 o'clock Tuesday, September 10th, that afternoon we took a drive through the Coldstream Valley a beautiful spot, where there are some very fine farms and ranches, here we also saw Lord Aberdeen's farm, with its orchards and hop-fields.

Wednesday morning we took the train for Okanagan Landing, where we had a look around and returned that afternoon by train to Sycamous Junction, from where we took the East Train next morning for Banff, remaining over one day, we left Banff Friday evening, September 13th, for Indian Head, where we arrived Saturday evening.

Next day, Sunday, we were, through the kindness of Major Bell, and Mr. Angus McKay, shewn about the Bell and Experimental farms, where the Professor received many facts regarding expenses and profits in grain raising.

Leaving Indian Head that evening we came direct to Winnipeg, and left from here again to noon Tuesday for Morris and Gretna, where we saw the Lowe Farm and others and also drove over some of the vacant lands east and west of the Red River, at Gretna I took Professor for short drive through part of the Mennonite Reserve and shewed him two of the best villages, Neubergthal and Somerfield.

The Professor was very much pleased with the look of the country here, especially with the location and the success of the Mennonites, who all spoke very favourably of the country; returning we reached Winnipeg again at noon Friday, September 20th.

From observations and what I could learn from the Professor, I believe he is on the whole very well satisfied with this trip and will recommend Manitoba and the North West Territories to his countrymen as a desirable field to immigrate to, if no hitch occurs in the arrangements between him and the Government.

We did perhaps not see as much of the Territories and Manitoba as might have been expected but on account of the limited time at the disposal of the Professor and other reasons we could not visit the Prince Albert, Yorkton, and other districts as had first been planned, but I can assure you the Professor has a fairly good idea of every district and is generally well posted and informed on the country.

I have the honour to be etc.

(Signed) Hugo Carstens

H. H. Smith Esq.
Commissioner Dominion Lands
Winnipeg.[18]

[18] 1. Oles./24687, September 20, 1895: Hugo Carstens, Winnipeg, to H. H. Smith, Winnipeg.

Carstens' description of Professor Oleskow's conference with the Minister of the Interior points to the two main problems Dr. Oleskow was anxious to settle: the location of suitable land for the settlement of Ukrainian peasant-farmers who wished to establish permanent homes in Canada, and the assurance of financial assistance during the initial period of settlement, in case of crop failure, or other disasters. To further ease the initial burdens of settlement, Dr. Oleskow suggested placing at the head of each colony one of the "intelligent, unselfish men," that Carstens referred to, to direct the affairs of the settlers under a co-operative system.

Dr. Oleskow arrived in Ottawa on October 1, and before his departure for Europe he was received, once more by the Minister of the Interior on October 3. The Acting Deputy Minister requested Oleskow to prepare a "statement of propositions relating to immigration" before calling on the Minister, and he complied with the request. Dr. Oleskow was pressed for time, and his statement was rather brief and somewhat vague in places, probably because he experienced some difficulty in explaining the points clearly in the English language. The statement was written on four pages of stationery from the "Windsor Hotel." No date or heading appeared but without doubt it was written on October 1:

Lower cereal prices, great distance from market and from railroads, no opportunity of earning money make the life of every new settler very hard as compared with that of old settlers.

Therefore I ask for Austrian settlers, coming in consequence of my activity in this matter (either direct from Austria or from Pennsylvania) a grant of $60 (in gold) pro each family or singel man taking up a homestead. The farmers will come organised in companys. Immediately after arriving on the (free or bought) homesteads receives the Company as many à $60, as they had members. The company warrants for the singel settlers.

Thus will the settler company have a capital to ground a institution like the agricultural syndicates—they will buy the articles of common use en gros, product on a co-operative way, establish creamerys, cheese factorys, build elevators, mills, etc.

If the Government were inclined to give such grants I am convinced, that the settlement would succeed, and I would in such case devote all my time and influence to carry on the emigration to Canada. I am sure the populating of Manitoba and the Northwest with the Austrian settlers (Christian, different nations, farmers), who have proved to be the very best kind of settlers (Grennfeld, Stoney Plains, Beaver Hills, etc.) would proceed quick and sure.

Another question is the directing of Austrian settlers *to* Canada and the steady and regular supporting of emigration in this direction.

There must be understood, that such pamphlets as the Government hitherto spreaded, are discredited in Europe, and the more the activity of transport agents. The very secret of succeeding in immigration matter is to support and aid the movement which comes from the interrested circles themselves. At least, what can be done, is a pamphlet written by me in proper manner, in which the people will have confidence, and in proper way (by national societys, and agricultural societys) distributed. For writing, printing expenses, and distribtuing of such a pamphlet I ask 2,000$.

But if the Government desires, that the emigration were steady, and that there is a controll upon the kind of settlers, there must be grounded a popular agency, backed by national and agricultural societys, which must have a capital at her (its) disposition to maintain the emigration movement, to smooth the obstacles, and to support the men, who would devote their time and power to this matter. In a former letter I have proposed to make that all on my own cost and account, asking as compensation every 12th homestead for me, but now I retire with the project and expect a project of the Government himself in this matter.

At rest, I think, the matter could be done in two manners:

1) To spend a larger sum of money to the above purposes, but it is very difficult to state the right amount and it *cannot* be given any guaranty for the use of money to emigration purposes.

2) I would take care of grounding a popular agency in Austria, which would receive 5$ pro each head of emigrants.[19]

Dr. Oleskow gave the statement to John Hall on Monday, October 2, and Hall dispatched it to the Minister the same day, reminding him about the appointment with the professor at noon the next day:

Ottawa, 2nd October, 1895.

Dear Mr. Daly,

Professor Oleskow has just handed me the annexed statement of his propositions. The principal one on which he lays stress is that at least $60.00 should be granted for each family, or single man, after taking up homestead to help them along, second, that he, the Professor, should be granted $2000 for writing, printing and distributing a pamphlet on Canada, and third, that he would open a popular agency in Austria "Which would receive $5 for each head of emigrants." I do not understand whether this $5 is expected from us or from the companies into which I gather from him the intended emigrants are to be banded.

You will recollect that you fixed 12 o'clock tomorrow for an interview with the Professor.

Yours faithfully

(Signed) J. R. HALL, Acting D.M.I.

The Hon. T. Mayne Daly,
Minister of the Interior.
Ottawa

P.S. 200 families or single men (to begin on) at $60–$120,000—it is useless to hope for vote of so much—J.R.H.[20]

[19] 1. Oles./24688, October 1, 1895: Statement by Dr. Oleskow prepared for the Minister of the Interior during his visit to Ottawa.

[20] 1. Oles./24688, October 2, 1895: J. R. Hall, to T. Mayne Daly, Ottawa.

The "former letter," mentioned by Oleskow in the seventh paragraph of his statement, did not reach the Minister until October 4, although it was written on September 22 in British Columbia. It contained interesting information concerning the attitude of the Prime Minister of Austro-Hungary towards emigration:

Canadian Pacific Railway
Steamship "Athabasca"
22nd September 1895.

Sir,

The chances of immigration of Austrian settlers improved as far as the Governor from Galicia, Count Badeni who was favourably disposed to my undertaking, became Austrian Premier and Minister of the Interior together. On my return home I want stop in Vienna and make to him a report upon the conditions of settlement in Canada. Therefore I must have your decision in this matter before my departure, all the more as I am pressed by letters from Austria to manifest my opinion about the chances of settlement in Canada, because the people became impatient and prepare themselves again to go to Brazil. I will be in Ottawa about October 1st on return from Pennsylvania, where I am invited by our people to visit them. I beg you, Sir, to give instruction to officers of your department, what they have me to say.

I must confess of my being disappointed as to the extent of free lands in Canada. In Manitoba is plenty of good land, but in the hands of speculators, who wait for future production citizens as for your victims. As to the N.W.T. I never thought, that the arid and semi-arid regions extend so far. How few there is of running water! Therefore all the places, suitable to growing cereals, situated along the rivers in a distance of two to three miles, and around these lakes which have any affluxes, are all taken up till to distance of fifty–sixty miles of the railroad. The settlement of these regions had stopped since two years notwithstanding of doing well of present settlers. In this case are "the satisfied settlers not the best immigration agents", because they see, that behind your backs, there is land suitable only to pasture, of which several hundred acres would be necessary to sustain one man! Notwithstanding I believe there is to find land in greater extention perhaps north of St. Albert, or between Yorkton and Prince Albert district, and therefore I will hold up my idea of populate the Northwest Canada's, but I would do it in my conscience under following conditions, which I am so free to propose to you. The our people (different nations) will be organized on a cooperative basis as companies of farmers, because the singel farmers would not succeed. These companies receive on the arrival on their grounds bonusses of at least 50–60$ per each homestead, taken up by a member of company. The company warrant, that the homestead, for which is paid bonuss, will not be abandoned, respective will be settled again. The bonusses will build a fundation store of an institution, which shall make easier the life of farmers. At first the institution which will be whole under controll of companies, will serve to common buying of such objects as seed, victuals, stoves, agricultural machines and tools etc. then to common purchase of products, to building of elevators, mills, establishing creameries, cheese factorys and other agricult. factorys, for improving of cattle breeding by buying of generous reproducteurs etc. It will by my care to convey through this organisation.

For the settlement of first year it would be very suitable to devote one of the Indian reserves, north west of Edmonton. One of these reserves is abandoned of Indians.

My present proposal to give bonusses pro taken up homestead, not pro soul seems to me more singel (plain) and expedient, all the more as children about 12 years are a help in the farmwork, and as this way does not include the paying for human beings, but for increasing of national wealth.

To bring about the emigration and to sustain it regularly there is indispensable, that somebody in Austria devotes his whole time, his power and his influence and I have made to you my proposition in a letter which you should to have received in Fort Saskatchewan. What I beg you at present, it is, to let me know through the officers of Department your decision *before* my departure, whatever it may be.

Yours very truly,

(Signed) DR. PROF. JOSEF OLESKOW.

I leave to Europe per "Parisian" of Allan Lines, sailing October 5th from Montreal.[21]

Dr. Oleskow's suggestion to grant a $60 bonus to each settled homestead family or single man and to use that money for the benefit of immigrant farmers to organize them into productive self-sustained communities with co-operative creameries, cheese factories, elevators, and the like, seemed to the officials of the Department of the Interior to border on the fantastic. Oleskow's planning, insofar as the West was concerned, was some thirty years ahead of its time.

Dr. Oleskow left Canada without receiving a definite reply to his proposals. The Acting Deputy Minister gave him only a written promise that an answer would be forwarded to him by mail:

I have the honour, by direction of the Minister of the Interior, to inform you that having heard your explanations of your plans for promoting immigration from Galicia to the North Western provinces of Canada, he will submit your proposals to his colleagues in the Government, and the decision which may be arrived at will be communicated to you by letter to your address in the course of a week or ten days.[22]

From the boat, on the day of his sailing from Montreal, Dr. Oleskow sent a hurried note (on "Allan Line" stationery) to the Acting Deputy Minister in Ottawa: "To obtain a more exact image of agricultural conditions Canadas I want to know, what rates pay the ranchowners for hiring public lands for pasture, I have heard, two cents per acre. Is it

[21]1. Oles./24719, September 22, 1895: Dr. Josef Oleskow, Canadian Pacific Railway, Steamship *Athabasca*, to the Minister of the Interior, Ottawa.

[22]1. Oles., October 3, 1895: John R. Hall, Ottawa, to Dr. Oleskow, The "Windsor Hotel," Ottawa.

true? Please inform me to that point. By this occasion I am as free to remember you my entreaty for Statistic Yearbook of Dominion."[23]

The Secretary of the Department of the Interior mailed Dr. Oleskow the information requested about grazing lands and asked the Department of Agriculture to forward the professor the *Statistical Yearbook* that he mentioned. A reply to his proposals was not given until much later: ". . . The Minister was not able himself to fully understand Professor Oleskow's scheme, and he felt that he would not be justified in coming to any definite conclusion until further information could be obtained either by personal investigation on the spot by Mr. Dyke, or by some such scheme as, he is glad to see, has been taken by the High Commissioner."[24]

III

On his return to Lviw, Dr. Oleskow reported on his visit to Canada at a conference of leading Ukrainians from the capital and various districts of the province, held on November 14, 1895, at Lviw. Among the participants at the conference who came from outside Lviw were: Dr. Longin Rozhankiwskyi, a barrister from Zolochiw; Paul Dumka, a peasant-poet from Kupchyntsi (elected a Member of the Provincial Diet in 1908); Cyril Genik-Berezowskyi, a school-teacher from Bereziw, district of Petchenizhyn; Iwan Radulak from Hlushkiw; Iwan Hoshovatiuk from Horodenka; Dr. Theophil Okunewskyi, a barrister from Horodenka (Member of Parliament in Vienna); the Reverend Iwan Maschak from Poputory; Mykhailo Lawryshko from Horodenka; Petro Rybitskyi from Nezvyska; Dr. Andriy Tchaikowskyi, a barrister from Berezhany and a well-known writer; and Stepan Harmatiy from Kuptchyntsi. From the city of Lviw there attended, among others: Dr. Iwan Franko, one of the founders of the Ukrainian Radical Party, a prominent poet and writer; Viacheslaw Budzynowskyi, the editor of the Ukrainian Radical Party's organ *Hromadskyi Holos* / the "Voice of the People," and author of numerous studies, such as "Peasant Properties," and "Agrarian Conditions in Galicia," as well as a writer of historical novels (elected Member of the Vienna Parliament in 1907); Dr. Andriy Kos, a barrister and public worker (Member of the Vienna Parliament 1900–1907); and Dr. Nykola Shukhewytch, a barrister.[25]

[23]I. Oles. Probably dated October 5, 1895: Dr. Oleskow, Allan Lines, Montreal, to John R. Hall, Ottawa.

[24]I. Oles., November 3, 1895: Lyndwode Pereira, Ottawa, to J. G. Colmer, London.

[25]*Svoboda*/"Liberty" (Shamokin, Pa.), No. 40, December 12, 1895. Reprint of an article published by the daily *Dilo*/"The Deed," Lviw, Galicia.

Dr. Oleskow pointed out to the group the advantages of settling in Canada for peasants wishing to emigrate. The conference unanimously decided to form a permanent Emigrants' Aid Committee to assist emigrating peasants and to protect them against exploitation. The chairman of the Emigrants' Aid Committee was Wasyl Nahirnyi, a leading economist and architect and the director and founder of the largest consumers' co-operative society, "Narodna Torhovla." Among the members of the Committee were Viacheslaw Budzynowskyi; Osyp Markow, the editor of the daily *Halychanyn* / "The Galician"; Dr. Kost Lewitskyi, a barrister from Lviw, future Member of the Parliament, President of the Ukrainian Parliamentary Club, and Prime Minister of the Western Ukrainian Republic during 1918–1919; Dr. Longin Rozhankiwskyi; Reverend Kachala from the Tarnopol district; Reverend Hirniak from the Lviw district; and Reverend Alexander Stefanovych of Lviw.[26]

[26]Announcement printed in No. 54 of *Halychanyn* (Lviw: April, 1896), and reprinted in *Svoboda*, No. 18, April 30, 1896.

Chapter Three

THE YEARS 1895–1897

I

THE IMPRESSION made by Dr. Oleskow on Sir Charles Tupper, the High Commissioner for Canada in London, and on T. Mayne Daly, the Minister of the Interior in Ottawa, was a favourable one. The information obtained by John Dyke, the Agent at Liverpool, was also of a kind to help Oleskow's case. In spite of these facts, however, he was still regarded as an "unknown factor," and the Minister of the Interior hesitated to undertake any commitments before receiving more definite information about Dr. Oleskow and the committee which was backing him, and whether Dr. Oleskow's claim to be able to organize a large scale emigration of peasant-farmers from Galicia to the Canadian West was not mere wishful thinking.

There were other reasons as well which deterred the Minister from bringing the matter up before the Cabinet or the House. Dr. Oleskow had formulated his statements vaguely, and he had not had the time or the opportunity to discuss fully some details of his project. Dr. Oleskow was aware of the difficulties the peasant-settlers would face during the initial period of their establishment in the new environment, and therefore his main concern was to secure for them at least modest financial assistance in the form of a grant, a bonus, or a long-term loan to give them a feeling of security and enable them to make a start. He had submitted a proposal that a grant of $50 to $60 per each family or single man taking up a homestead be given to settlers for a start, which, in addition to the money they would possess on arrival, would ward off the danger of privation and facilitate the establishment of their families on the homesteads. Although the amount asked for was modest in comparison with subsidies received by British, Jewish, or Mennonite immigrants from various benevolent organizations,[1] the Minister was hesitant to commit himself on this point. Additional funds would have been required which the Minister doubted could be obtained under existing circumstances. The House was also preoccupied with other matters. If such a concession were made to one group, it would create a precedent for other groups as well. Funds allotted for immigration purposes were less than modest and barely sufficed to cover current expenses, let alone additional spending. The High Commissioner in London referred to this fact in his yearly report to Ottawa: "Our activity during the year [1895] . . . has been somewhat curtailed by the smallness of the funds voted for immigration purposes. . . ."[2] Apart from a lack of funds, there existed at the time grave tension within the Cabinet itself, which finally led to the resignation of seven Cabinet Ministers and practically crippled the effective functioning of the governmental machine. Before he could bring Oleskow's proposals before the Cabinet, the Minister of the Interior needed reliable and full information on the person of Dr. Oleskow, together with a clear outline of his scheme. The Minister, of course, preferred not to commit the Department to any additional expenses.

On the day of Dr. Oleskow's departure from Ottawa (Friday, October 4, 1895), T. Mayne Daly cabled Sir Charles Tupper in London, requesting that John Dyke examine the emigration situation in person: "Professor Oleskow *Parisian.* Advise Dyke meet him and if possible accompany him home to investigate the scheme."[3] The High Commissioner acted on the Minister's instructions and sent this message to John Dyke:

> I am directed by the High Commissioner to quote for your information the following telegram received this morning from the Minister of the Interior: "Professor Oleskow *Parisian.* Advise Dyke meet him and if possible accompany him home to investigate scheme."

[1]A. Bodard, Agent in France and Belgium, reporting from Paris on October 15, 1895, to the High Commissioner for Canada in London, suggested that a loan be given to immigrant-settlers: "I think the number of good emigrants would increase constantly if there was in Canada some society to lend them $200 or $300 to settle on their land. The French and Belgian farmers who leave for Canada are worth generally from $400 to $600, but the cost of the voyage takes two-thirds of this when there is a large family to be transported, and they have not enough left to start on. Many good families are also too poor even to pay for their passage." (Canada, Department of the Interior, *Annual Report*, 1895, Part IV, Report No. 9, 44.)

[2]*Ibid.*, 9: Report of Sir Charles Tupper, High Commissioner for Canada, to Hon. T. Mayne Daly, Minister of the Interior, Ottawa, November 7, 1895.

[3]I. Oles./24710, October 4, 1895: Cable, T. Mayne Daly, Minister of the Interior, Ottawa, to Sir Charles Tupper, High Commissioner for Canada, London.

If you are able to meet Professor Oleskow and discuss the matter with him, and feel well enough to accompany him to Galicia, there will be no objection to your making the necessary arrangements.

If however, you do not feel quite strong enough to go to Galicia at present, you will be able to discuss the matter with the Professor now, and may possibly be able to arrange to go there in the course of a few weeks, after the High Commissioner has received some reply to the enquiries he is making through the Colonial Office.[4]

Dyke was recuperating from a prolonged illness and was not as yet fit to undertake a strenuous trip. But he met Dr. Oleskow when the S.S. *Parisian* called at Liverpool, had an interview with him, and reported afterwards to London: "Referring to your letter of the 5th inst., I have to inform you that Professor Oleskow landed late last night [October 14] and I had an interview with him this morning. He was in a great hurry, his leave of absence having expired, and he was proceeding direct to Vienna, en route for home. He stated that it would be utterly useless for me to accompany him, but he was expecting some communication from the Department and upon their receipt he would write me fully."[5]

A few days later, Dyke received the promised letter from Dr. Oleskow and forwarded it to London: "Referring to mine of the 15th instant, I have received a letter from Professor Oleskow of which the enclosed is a translation." The translation ran as follows:

I have nothing further to remark or to alter after my interview with and written representations to the Hon. Mr. Daly in reference to emigration.

You can only advise Mr. Daly to quickly make up his mind, or otherwise preparations may be advanced to drive emigration to U.S.A.

It would be advantageous if the Canadian Government would be decisive in their action, as the promotion of emigration on the part of agents is always followed closely by European Governments. Thus in our case the idea of emigration of a national and agricultural organization receiving no support may be fruitless.[6]

The High Commissioner forwarded the correspondence relating to Dr. Oleskow to the Minister of the Interior in Ottawa, adding that: ". . . I do not quite understand the position which Dr. Oleskow is taking in the matter, but I do not think we can do anything until I hear something more about him, and his position and standing, through the

[4] 1. Oles. October 5, 1895: J. G. Colmer, Secretary, Office of the High Commissioner for Canada, London, to John Dyke, Canada Government Agency, Liverpool.

[5] 1. Oles./25225, October 15, 1895: John Dyke, Liverpool, to J. G. Colmer, London.

[6] 1. Oles., October 22, 1895: John Dyke, Liverpool, to J. G. Colmer, London.

Foreign Office. They are making enquiries on the subject at my request and I hope very soon to receive a reply."[7]

Edward Wingfield, the secretary to the Secretary of State for the Colonies, informed the High Commissioner about the receipt of information on Dr. Oleskow from Her Majesty's Ambassador at Vienna and enclosed all copies of the correspondence connected with the enquiry:

> In reply to your letter of the 26th ultimo [September] I am directed by Mr. Secretary Chamberlain [Joseph Chamberlain, Secretary of State for the Colonies] to transmit to you a copy of a letter from the Foreign Office forwarding a despatch from Her Majesty's Ambassador at Vienna containing information with regard to Professor Oleskow and the proposed emigration to Canada of farmers from Galicia.[8]

It took nearly one month to procure the requested information, as it had to go through the "proper channels." Sir Charles Tupper wrote the request to the Secretary of State for the Colonies. Joseph Chamberlain forwarded it to the Secretary of State for Foreign Affairs, who submitted it to the Marquess of Salisbury, the Prime Minister of Great Britain. The Prime Minister then wrote a letter to the British Ambassador in Vienna, who submitted the request to the Prime Minister of the Austro-Hungarian Empire. In due course, Ambassador Barrington received a reply from the Austrian Prime Minister, and the reply went the same circuitous way back, until it finally reached the High Commissioner for Canada, and through him the Minister of the Interior in Ottawa.

The Prime Minister of the Austro-Hungarian Empire in 1895 (until 1897) was Count Casimir Badeni, a former Governor of Galicia who knew Dr. Oleskow personally, and who therefore was able to answer Ambassador Barrington without delay. In a letter dated October 12, 1895, and marked "personal," he wrote to Barrington:

> . . . As regards Professor Oleskow, he is a man of tried honesty and one who can be most confidentially recommended.
>
> He enjoys the support of a committee of great respectability in his effort to promote the emigration of Galician farmers.
>
> The majority of these people, concerning whom you have asked for information, are mere peasants only speaking Polish or Ruthenian and being often unable to read or write. For these men emigration is usually the last hope.
>
> In spite of this letter being private I must point out to you that the Austrian Government would never give its consent to the organization of

[7]1. Oles., October 24, 1895: Sir Charles Tupper, London, to T. Mayne Daly, Ottawa.

[8]1. Oles./25808, October 25, 1895: Edward Wingfield, Secretary to the Secretary of State for the Colonies, London, to Sir Charles Tupper, London.

an emigration of Galician subjects on a large scale, and that it [the Government] would certainly oppose any such intention. . . .[9]

This enquiry on the highest level elicited the desired information about the standing of Dr. Oleskow, but at the same time it alerted Austrian authorities to the possibility of an organized emigration movement to Canada, to which the Austrian Government, and particularly the large Polish land owners of Galicia, were strongly opposed, as it threatened to deprive them of cheap farm labour and disrupt their economy.

Edmund Monson of the British Embassy in Vienna communicated to the Prime Minister the contents of Count Badeni's letter to Ambassador Barrington:

My Lord—

With reference to the despatch of this series No. 26 which your Lordship addressed to Mr. Barrington respecting a scheme of emigration for Galician Farmers, I have the honour to report that I am informed that Dr. Oleskow, who appears to be in some sense its promoter, is Professor at a Teachers' Seminary in Lemberg, and that he is unconnected with any political party. He applied for several months leave in order to go to Canada, but his request was not granted by the School Council.

He enjoys an excellent reputation, and is aided in his efforts to facilitate emigration by a committee, but as your Lordship will see from the accompanying extract of a private letter, which the present Prime Minister Count Badeni, who till quite recently was Governor of Galicia, has been good enough to write to Mr. Barrington, the organization of any scheme involving emigration in large numbers from Galicia would not be permitted by the Austrian Government.

I have, etc.

(Signed) EDMUND MONSON[10]

Lord Salisbury in turn passed the letter on to the Secretary of State for Foreign Affairs, from whom it was forwarded to the Under-Secretary of State for the Colonies:

With reference to your letter of the 1st instant, I am directed by the Secretary of State for Foreign Affairs to transmit to you, to be laid before the Secretary of State for the Colonies, the accompanying despatch from Her Majesty's Ambassador at Vienna, on the subject of Professor Oleskow's scheme for the emigration of Galician farmers.

I am, etc.

(Signed) FRANCIS BERTIE, Foreign Office.

To the Under-Secretary of State,
Colonial Office, London.[11]

[9]1. Oles./25808, October 12, 1895: Count Casimir Badeni, Prime Minister of Austria, to W. Barrington, Ambassador of the United Kingdom, Vienna, Austria.

[10]1. Oles./25080, October 15, 1895: Edmund Monson, Embassy of the United Kingdom, Vienna, Austria, to the Marquess of Salisbury, London.

[11]1. Oles., October 22, 1895: Francis Bertie, Foreign Office, London, to the Under-secretary of State, Colonial Office, London.

The secretary to the Secretary of State for the Colonies forwarded the correspondence in question to Sir Charles Tupper. Tupper forwarded the whole file to the Minister of the Interior in Ottawa, November 1, 1895, with an accompanying letter in which he pointed out the difficulties that he foresaw regarding Dr. Oleskow's emigration plan:

Victoria Chambers, 17, Victoria Street,
London, S.W.,
1st Nov., 1895.

Dear Mr. Daly,

With reference to your letter of th 24th ult., in regard to Professor Oleskow, I now beg to send you a copy of a confidential letter from the Colonial Office, with its enclosures upon the subject.

You will see that I adopted your suggestion of making enquiries through Her Majesty's representative and that the result, so far as Professor Oleskow's position is concerned, is satisfactory. It would appear, however, that his efforts for the organization of emigration on a large scale will not meet with the approval of the Austrian Government.

I had hoped, in view of all the circumstances, that Her Majesty's Ambassador would have made inquiries through other than Government sources, upon the points raised in my letter, but we must accept the position as it now stands.

I have looked through the memorandum left by Professor Oleskow at Ottawa, of which a translation was enclosed with your letter of the 5th September, but it seems to me that his scheme is very far from definite.

I am rather afraid he requires more assistance in connection with his scheme than the Government would probably be prepared to give, and besides it is a question whether advantages could be offered in the case of emigrants from Galicia, without being extended to those from Germany and Scandinavia, who we are especially desirous of attracting.

Believe me, etc.

(Signed) Charles Tupper

The Hon. T. Mayne Daly,
Minister of the Interior, Ottawa.[12]

There was no longer any doubt in the mind of the Canadian officials as to Dr. Oleskow's integrity. But from Count Badeni's letter it also became very clear that the Austrian Government would never give its consent to the organization of an emigration movement of Galician farmers on a scale as large as Oleskow envisaged. Nevertheless, Dr. Oleskow was confident that the movement could be organized and carried out by means of his planned Emigrants' Aid Society. In order to be able to make the necessary arrangements, Dr. Oleskow pressed

[12]1. Oles., November 1, 1895: Sir Charles Tupper, London, to T. Mayne Daly, Ottawa.

for a decision on his proposals and plans, as promised by the Minister of the Interior on his departure from Canada:

Lemberg, 20 December 1895.

To the Honourable Mr. Mayne Daly,
Minister of Interior, Ottawa.

Sir,

Having not received the answer in concern of the emigration from Galicia and neighbouring countrys, promised in the letter from October 3rd 1895, signed by Mr. Hall, I am pressed by our people to ask, whether the Government is inclined to make something for promoting of the emigration from this country in the sense of my proposals, or in a manner choised by the Government itself. If I had had an answer, in any way satisfactory I could direct to Canada a lot of good settlers from these several thousands who in the last two months have gone to Brazil. Now has Canada received through the Jewish agents in Hamburg only a small number of refuse of settlers. I have till now more than *three hundred* familys, who will go in March on my advise either to Canada or to the U.S. If the Government does consider it good, to send some one of your people in London or Liverpool to make with us the terms for our emigrants and the emigration, we would be glad to receive him here.

Very respectfully,

(Signed) PROF. DR. JOSEF OLESKOW,
Golebia 11A, Lemberg, Austria.[13]

Dr. Oleskow was forwarded a non-committal reply by the Minister's private secretary, Mr. A. Chisholm: "Your letter of the 20th ultimo, addressed to the Hon. Mr. Daly respecting your scheme for promoting emigration to Canada, came duly to hand. I will see that your communication is handed to the Minister at once, and no doubt, you will hear from him shortly."[14]

Dr. Oleskow was unaware of the grave crisis that faced the Cabinet of Sir Mackenzie Bowell at the time, and which made it almost impossible for the Minister of the Interior to suggest an increase of expenditures for his department. After consultation with the Deputy Minister, the Minister instructed his secretary to write to Dr. Oleskow and request him to "state in the briefest terms" what he wished the Department to do:

The Minister is anxious at all time to do what he can to promote immigration of the very desirable character indicated in your letter, but in this case he is at a loss to know what is the next step to be taken, and he will be

[13]1. Oles./26492, December 20, 1895: Dr. Josef Oleskow, Lemberg, Austria, to T. Mayne Daly, Ottawa.

[14]1. Oles./26492, January 7, 1896: A. Chisholm, Private Secretary, Minister of the Interior, Ottawa, to Dr. Josef Oleskow, Lemberg.

glad if you will kindly write again and state in the briefest possible terms exactly what you would wish the Department to do, and what results we may look for if your proposition is accepted. The Minister is quite prepared to instruct Mr. John Dyke, our Agent in Liverpool to proceed to Lemberg if he is assured that this is necessary, and that good results are likely to accrue from Mr. Dyke's presence there.[15]

Dr. Oleskow replied that John Dyke was welcome to come to Lemberg, but that Dyke would not be able to accomplish very much, except to realize that the plan dealt with practical realities. Complying with the request to state in the briefest possible terms what he wished the Department to do, Oleskow replied[16] that he expected the Department (1) to grant assisted passages to his emigrants, (2) to grant a $50 bonus per homestead taken, or to secure loans "to the extent of $400 pro each homestead (at an interest not exceeding 6 per cent) as a mortgage on the homestead." Dr. Oleskow guaranteed that if this condition were granted, "Canada may have any number of settlers, even 10,000 per year." Apart from this, he also asked for £600 to establish an "agency" and to organize the emigration movement.

Time was passing quickly. Spring would soon arrive, and Dr. Oleskow was anxious to complete the arrangements for the first groups of settlers to sail for Canada. His booklet describing conditions in Canada and his visit to that country had already been published by the popular "M. Kachkowsky Society" as its December issue and sent out to village reading halls. Hundreds of letters began to arrive with requests for information, advice and assistance regarding emigration to Canada. The Minister was still not quite clear about what Dr. Oleskow wished the Department to do, and the professor was once again asked to clarify his propositions. It appears that Minister was mainly concerned to see that Dr. Oleskow's demand for assisted passages and bonuses for settlers were dropped, as the Department simply had no funds for such expenditures.

Another of Dr. Oleskow's concerns was to obtain free rail transportation from the port of entry to the final destination in the West, that is, to Winnipeg or to Edmonton. In this connection he corresponded with Archer Baker, European Traffic Agent of the Canadian Pacific Railway Company in London. As communication by mail proved unsatisfactory, Baker sent S. W. Coryn, a member of his staff, to see Dr. Oleskow in Lemberg and to make arrangements "by word of mouth." On Coryn's

[15]1. Oles., January 10, 1896: Lyndwode Pereira, Ottawa, to Dr. Josef Oleskow, Lemberg, Austria.

[16]1. Oles., January 27, 1896: Dr. Josef Oleskow, Lemberg, Austria, to the Department of the Interior, Ottawa.

return, Baker wrote to Sir Charles Tupper's secretary, informing him about the results of the negotiations:

I have yours of the 18th instant, enclosing the letter from Professor Oleskow. You will probably be aware of the correspondence and negotiations which have taken place between that gentleman, the Government and ourselves during past year, and that it was originally intended that Mr. Dyke should acompany the Professor to Austria last autumn on his return from Canada.

Mr. Coryn's visit to Lemberg was the outcome of several letters received from the Professor in which he wished to know exactly the lowest rates that could be furnished to the Farmers he hoped to be able to send out and I considered it better to let him have these terms by word of mouth.

As you know our railway rates have been materially reduced, particularly to points west of Winnipeg, within the last three months, and that this reduction has been more than offset by the increase in the ocean rates which we both of us feel to be both unfair and unwise. In order that no effort on our part might be wanting to facilitate Professor Oleskow's views I offered to carry the first two or three batches of his Farmers free so far as the Railway is concerned and made him this offer through Mr. Coryn. The latter had just returned from Lemberg but unfortunately he is now laid up with influenza so that I have not yet had his report, but as soon as I receive such report you shall have a copy of it with pleasure.

So far as I can gather the Professor seems to have made several propositions to the Government none of which have been accepted. His letter to you (which I retain for the moment) bears upon it somewhat the interpretation which you put on it, but before expressing a final opinion I should like to see Mr. Coryn when I will write to you again.[17]

A few weeks later, after he had fully recovered from the effects of an attack of influenza, Coryn produced his report and submitted it to Baker. The report describes Coryn's meeting with Professor Oleskow and contains several astute and shrewd observations on the professor and the emigration plans in general:

On arrival at Lemberg I went at once to see Professor Oleskow. I fear that the man is a good deal of a Visionary and what is really a very complicated and difficult matter, he imagines to be simple and easy. We have to contend against the Brazilian emigration; the Brazilian Government take the emigrants free from Genoa and support them on the land until they get their first crops. That alone is no small thing to fight against. He proposes nothing more or less than this: that we also take people for the first year in any numbers that present themselves, *free from Liverpool*; that we select suitable land for them in the North West, and pay to each family the sum of say $50 to tide them over the first few months. I explained to him that we were not actuated solely by philanthropy, and that on such terms as these we could get any number of the most desirable British emigrants, but he

[17]I. Oles./27327, January 20, 1896: Archer Baker, European Traffic Agent, C.P.R. Company, London, to J. G. Colmer, London.

considered that the superiority of the Galician emigrants would well repay us, as they were the best farmers in the world, accustomed to overcome great natural obstacles without grumbling, and would be sure to remain wherever they were put down. I asked him how he proposed to send people. He said he would buy tickets for them at the Railway Station in the ordinary manner and send them over Hamburg to Liverpool. I asked him if he was aware of the port regulations at Hamburg; he had not heard of them; he had not heard of anything.

He seems to imagine himself in his mind's eye, the salaried agent of the Canadian Government or of the Canadian Pacific, dispensing free tickets at his office door. I told him of course that so far as I was able to speak with any certainty at all, that the C.P.R. would not assent any such means of filling the country. In that case then could we not, he asked, advance to each emigrant the amount of his passage and allow this to remain as a charge upon the Land? I asked him what security there could be for any such debt? But the people it seems are so transparently honest that they would assuredly pay everything, and that if this is not sufficient security, he had a scheme whereby people were grouped in families of so many and the whole collectively made resonsible for the debts of each. I asked him if the $50 advance money would also be considered as debt. "Oh, no," he said, "that must be an absolute gift," and he seemed to think he was going a great way in regarding the passage money as a loan. I asked him what the Austrian Government thought of his proceedings; he said the Government had taken no notice until about six weeks ago, when he had been warned that his efforts were meeting with strong disapproval. He lamented that everything had not been got into working order before then, because he was afraid the Government would make a lot of trouble. I asked him if he was not afraid of being punished; he said that he did not think the Government would do more than deprive him of his Professorship, and I am afraid that he viewed this with equanimity in view of the great position he was going to get under the C.P.R. or the Government.

I asked him if the terms by which this emigration could be secured were *sine qua non*; he said that the $50 advance was absolutely a *sine qua non*, and that the advance passage money was almost so. I am afraid this makes his position a hopeless one; he admits that none of the people whom he has in mind have any money whatever, that if they can pay their fare to Liverpool it is all that they could do.

So long as the Professor is on the make, I really do not see what can be done, because in spite of the ignorance of emigration matters we know very well ourselves that the people must be booked by a properly concessioned agent, and that from such a country as Poland, all with their own regulations, it is quite impossible to smuggle emigration especially with people so deplorably poor as these people seem to be.

The Professor claims that when in Canada he was promised by Mr. Daly that the $50 advance money should be paid by the Government; that Mr. Daly then said that as a mere matter of form it was necessary for him to consult his colleagues, but that he would write me by the next mail; he begs me to go and see the Government in London to fix this matter up.

On the Sunday evening following my visit, he was advertised to lecture in the Public Hall on Canada; he showed me the announcement in the papers. He said he had received an intimation from the Officials that so long as he confined himself to an account of his trip, he would be allowed to continue, but if he advised or encouarged emigration, he would be stopped by the police. No doubt he is sowing a very good crop for the authorized agents to reap, but he himself will not, I fear, reap anything at all, unless it be the loss of his Professorship. His work will certainly not be lost, although it does not take an immediately tangible form. The agents in Hamburg who have also sub-agents in Austria, are watching what he does, and whenever the fruit is ripe it will drop into their mouth, which they will certainly keep open for the purpose.

Absolutely none of his emigrants will pay their passages and they must all be endowed on arrival. If we are willing to pay out all this money, we can get the people, but so we can from anywhere else on such terms. It is regrettable that he did not say this earlier, but he is not a practical man, he is living all the time in the future and the authorities are down upon him. As a side light on this situation—we were sitting in a café and Oleskow was accosted by a gentleman with whom he entered into long and warm discussion. He informed me afterwards that the gentleman in question was a member of the Provincial Parliament in Lemberg and of the Imperial Parliament in Vienna, that he was specially opposed to Canadian emigration, that he has done his best to talk him over but that he had told him that he would bring the matter up at the Polish Parliament and also, if necessary, at Vienna, in order to prevent any propaganda being made. The conversation being in a Slav language I did not myself understand it. All this seemed to amuse Oleskow. Whatever fruit there may be in Poland it will not be picked in a bunch but I do not doubt that during the Spring the authorised agents will get good pickings. But as for an emigration en mass with Oleskow at its head, it is out of the question.[18]

In his analysis of the situation, Coryn failed to discern Dr. Oleskow's aim, which was to drive a hard bargain so that as many advantages as possible would accrue to the peasants. This was very necessary if the peasants were to be protected from exploitation along the way and thus save their scarce funds for a start on their homesteads.

Coryn was correct, however, in his observation that the agents in Hamburg, with their sub-agents in Austria, were watching Oleskow's actions with interest, preparing to reap the harvest of his hard work. Coryn's prediction came true, and the agents frustrated Dr. Oleskow's hopes of building a well-organized emigration movement of selected farmers with adequate means and of preserving their funds and safeguarding them against exploitation, so as to give Canada a type of

[18]1. Oles./27327, February 10, 1896: S. W. Coryn, C.P.R. Office, London, to Archer Baker, London.

settler who would be sturdy, frugal, and devoted to the soil. The debate on emigration restrictions, which Coryn mentioned in connection with the conversation Dr. Oleskow had with a Member of the Galician Diet and of the Imperial Parliament in Vienna, did take place. The London *Times* of February 6, 1896, reported on the debate under the headline "Galician Emigration":

> The Select Committee of the Galician Diet appointed to investigate the emigration movement, the spread of which in that province has formed the subject of repeated discussion of late, has now placed a resolution before the Diet recommending that energetic measures should be adopted by the provincial authorities in conjunction with the Government to suppress those injurious influences which are calculated to increase the exodus. Furthermore, the Special Committee advises that the official corporations in those districts in which the emigration to Brazil is assuming greater proportions should be provided with the means necessary to check the evil effectually and that the attention of these local bodies should be drawn to the best methods of securing a remedy. The Government is also called upon to exercise the strictest possible control with regard to the proceedings of emigration agents, and to inflict the severest penalties in cases of malpractices or spoliation. Finally, an addition to the existing Penal Code with a view to prevent unauthorized instigation and encouragement to emigrate is considered desirable, and the appointment of special officials to be attached to the Austro-Hungarian Consulate at Genoa and to the Legation at Rio de Janeiro and competent to converse with the Galician emigrants in their own language is advised.
>
> During the discussion which subsequently took place in the Diet different opinions were expressed with respect to the expediency of the above resolution. One member pointed out that the movement was fully justified by the untoward agricultural conditions prevailing in the province and that it should be regulated, but not suppressed. The representative of the Government stated that at present no difficulties were placed in the way of intending emigrants provided they could prove to the satisfaction of the authorities that they were furnished with passages to Brazil. This, however, was frequently not the case, and in many instances it had happened that on their arrival at Genoa Galician peasants had been sent back to their homes at the expense of the State, as they had been found to be entirely without means to proceed further. The resolution of the Select Committee was finally adopted.[19]

Although the main attention in the debate was paid to emigration to Brazil, the proposed measures were to cover emigration in general. Several members of the Diet who were on the Committee which worked with Dr. Oleskow for the protection of emigrants expressed opinions in favour of modifying the resolution.

[19]London *Times*, February 6, 1896.

II

Coryn's reference to Dr. Oleskow as a "visionary" who imagined a very complicated and difficult matter to be quite simple cast doubt on whether the professor's promises of large-scale organization of farmer emigration from Galicia should be taken seriously by the Canadian Government. The Deputy Minister of the Interior enquired of the Vice-president of the Canadian Pacific Railway Company, T. G. Shaughenessy of Montreal, whether he had seen Coryn's report "with regard to the Professor Oleskow in Lemberg, who visited Canada last year, and who, as you know has an immigration scheme."[20] As can be seen from his reply, Shaughenessy concurred fully with Coryn's opinion:

> Referring to your letter of March 18th, in which you enquire whether I have seen a copy of Mr. Coryn's report after a personal visit to Lemberg in connection with Prof. Oleskow's immigration scheme. Yes, I have seen the report and am quite of the opinion that Professor Oleskow would be of no use as an Immigration Agent even though his case had not been prejudiced by the inquiry which was made of the Austrian Government as to his credentials.[21]

Almost the same day that Shaughenessy wrote his letter to the Deputy Minister, a letter from Dr. Oleskow arrived at the Department of the Interior that contained a message that changed the general opinion about his inability to organize an emigration movement to Canada:

> I am very sorry that my last writing of January 27th has been misunderstood.
>
> The Department is right in understanding that I have demanded 600 £ for arranging the emigration movement to Canada, and that my meaning is, that assisted passages would encourage the emigration movement but the Department is thoroughly wrong in understanding that I have demanded as a reward for my services $50 for every person. Instead of that I have written, that a grant of say $50 to each homesteader, or, the arranging of a loan to the extent of $400 to each homesteader would make it possible for many emigrants, who would arrive in Canada to take up the homesteads.
>
> That was the meaning of my letter.
>
> I have the honour to inform the Department that besides a small group of our emigrants I send a group of circa 30 families (farmers) to Canada who will leave Hamburg at April 11 or perhaps March 25th. They are booked by Spiro & Co.[22]

[20]1. Oles., March 18, 1896: A. M. Burgess, Deputy Minister of the Interior, Ottawa, to T. G. Shaughenessy, Vice-president, C.P.R. Company, Montreal.

[21]1. Oles., April 24, 1896: T. G. Shaughenessy, Montreal, to A. M. Burgess, Ottawa.

[22]1. Oles./27976, February 4, 1896: Dr. J. Oleskow, Lemberg, Austria, to the Department of the Interior, Ottawa.

Dr. Oleskow's emigration activity was initiated at an inauspicious time. The Cabinet crisis reached its peak at the very time the first group of Oleskow's emigrants was at sea. They arrived in Quebec on the evening of Tuesday, April 30, 1896, one week after the resignation of Sir Mackenzie Bowell. In his reconstruction of the Cabinet, Sir Charles Tupper, the former High Commissioner for Canada in London, who succeeded Sir Mackenzie Bowell as Prime Minister, dropped T. Mayne Daly, the Minister of the Interior, from the Cabinet. His place was taken by Sir Hugh John Macdonald, who had never met Dr. Oleskow.

The Deputy Minister instructed the Secretary to inform the Dominion Lands Office in Winnipeg about the expected arrival of Dr. Oleskow's settlers: "I am directed to request you to draw the Commissioner's particular attention to the letter and enclosures, copies of which are transmitted to you herewith. Special pains no doubt will be taken by the Commissioner to see that the families referred to are *well* [inserted in ink] received, and that every effort is made to have them settled to their satisfaction."[23] The Dominion Immigration Agent in Quebec had also been alerted about the arrival of Oleskow's peasant-settlers:

> I am directed to inform you that the Department has been advised that it is the intention of about fifty families of emigrants to leave Hamburg for Canada on the 11th instant. These people are Galicians, and have been induced to come to this country by Professor Oleskow of Lemberg, and it is desired that particular attention should be paid to them with a view to encouraging this class of emigration, if that is, it is found on the arrival of these people that they are up to our expectations.
>
> I am to request you on their arrival in Quebec to telegraph the Department, in order that we may send Mr. Akerlindh to meet them at Calumet and travel with them as far as Ottawa, or further, if thought desirable.[24]

The Deputy Minister also wrote a letter to T. G. Shaughenessy in Montreal. Shaughenessy, who was rather skeptical about Dr. Oleskow's ability to organize the emigration of a larger number of peasant-farmers to Canada, was informed of the anticipated arrivals and was asked to co-operate in receiving them: "I duly received your letter of the 24th ultimo—on the subject of Professor Oleskow. I have since, however, received a letter from Mr. Colmer, Secretary of the Office of the High Commisioner for Canada in London, stating that he has been advised by Professor Oleskow, that he is sending out 50 families who will leave Hamburg for Canada on the 11th instant, and I am giving instructions

[23] 1. Oles., April 1, 1896: Lyndwode Pereira, Ottawa, to the Secretary, Dominion Lands Board, Winnipeg.

[24] 1. Oles., April 1, 1896: Lyndwode Pereira, Ottawa, to P. Doyle, Dominion Immigration Agent, Quebec.

for the proper reception and placing of these people, in which no doubt the Department will have the hearty co-operation of the officials of your Company."[25]

On April 8, 1896, the Secretary of the High Commissioner's Office in London forwarded the list of Oleskow's emigrants to Ottawa and suggested how the Department of the Interior might aid them:

> With reference to my letter of the 18th ultimo, on the subject of Professor Oleskow's scheme, I now beg to send you lists I have received from the Canadian Pacific Railway of the persons who are going out to Canada from Galicia. You will notice that altogether there are about 29 families, equal to about 86 adults. There are six or seven young men apparently unattached to any family, and each of them has been included as a family in my enumeration.
>
> The party sails on the 11th inst. by the Hansa Line steamer, and goes direct to Quebec.
>
> In view of the importance of this matter, I think it would be well to have arrangements made by which the party can be received at Quebec and accompanied specially to Winnipeg. If they could there be taken hold of by a Committee consisting of a Government Agent, a C.P.R. Agent, and an agent of the Manitoba Government, and some supervision exercised over them until they are settled, I have no doubt they would appreciate it, and it would have a good effect on the Continent, as they would be sure to mention it in the letters they write to the friends they have left behind.[26]

D. McNicoll, the Passenger Traffic Manager of the C.P.R. Company in Montreal, had also received a list of passengers, which he forwarded to the Deputy Minister of the Interior in Ottawa with a letter informing the latter that the first immigrants would be transported to their destination without charge:

> Our European Traffic Agent has heard from Professor Oleskow, with the accompanying list of passengers, who, he anticipates, will leave Hamburg by the Hansa Line about 11th of this month. They will be accompanied by a relative of the Professor, of the same name, who speaks English. For your information, I may say that we are carrying them through free from Quebec to destination, as a trial case. The Professor particularly asks that our Land Commissioner and the "Government Officials" do their very best to locate the party. Some of them will want to take up land on arrival, and others will want to get employment.[27]

A cable from the High Commissioner's Office in London to the

25 1. Oles., April 1, 1896: A. M. Burgess, Ottawa, to T. G. Shaughenessy, Montreal. In the letter from Dr. Oleskow referred to here, the number of families is given as thirty.

26 1. Oles./28608, April 8, 1896: J. G. Colmer, London, to the Secretary, Department of the Interior, Ottawa.

27 1. Oles./28491, April 7, 1896: D. McNicoll, Passenger Traffic Manager, C.P.R. Company, Montreal, to A. M. Burgess, Ottawa.

Department of the Interior in Ottawa, dated April 9, 1896, announced: "Hundred Oleskow's Galicians sail Hansa Steamer 11th."[28] Finally, on April 30, 1896, the Hansa Line interpreter from Montreal, Ignatius Roth, wired Ottawa: "Father Point, Quebec, 'Christiania' passed here 4 A.M."[29] The lively exchange of telegrams continued, all in anticipation of the arrival of "Oleskow's Galicians." The S.S. *Christiania* arrived in Quebec late in the evening of April 30, 1896, and on May 1, Mr. P. Doyle, the Government Immigration Agent in Quebec, wired to Ottawa: "Oleskow party one hundred seven leave by regular train tonight—Anderson to Montreal with them."[30] On May 2, John Hoolahan, the Government Immigration Agent in Montreal, wired the following news to Alfred Akerlindh, the interpreter who was to accompany them to Ottawa: "*Christiania's* passengers will leave St. Martin Jct. by special about 8 A.M."[31]

After the departure of the S.S. *Christiania* passengers for Montreal and the West, Doyle forwarded the ship's list of the arrivals to the Department of the Interior with a brief report:

> I beg respectfully to report the arrival here yesterday [May 1] of the S. S. "Christiania" from Hamburg with 4 cabin and 288 steerage passengers. I enclose herewith a list of 107 Galician immigrants destined for Winnipeg sent out by Professor Oleskow of Lemberg in charge of his brother. The party left in time this morning for the Winnipeg train from there. Mr. Anderson accompanied them as far as Montreal.
>
> List of Galician Emigrants forwarded by Professor Oleskow of Lemberg, p. S.S. "Christiania" from Hamburg arrived at Quebec 1st May 1896:

Name	Age	Capital
Lucian Keryk (Kyryk)	Aged 38 years	Capital $400
Melania Keryk	35	
3 children aged 8, 6 years and 9 months.		
Josef Procinsky	36	$400
Daria (Dokia) Procinsky	22	
2 children 8, 7		
Leon Procinsky	33	$300
Eva Procinsky	21	
3 children 6, 3, and 9 months.		
Ivan Lakusta Andreja	50	$800
Katharine Andreja	43	
Anna Andreja	18	
Ivas (Tanas) Andreja	13	
2 children aged 11, 3.		

[28]1. Oles./28485, April 9, 1896: Cable from the Office of the High Commissioner for Canada, London, to the Department of the Interior, Ottawa.

[29]1. Oles./28957, April 30, 1896: Ignatius Roth (Hansa Line), Father Point, Quebec, to Alfred Akerlindh, Government Interpreter, Ottawa, who was to meet the passengers and accompany them to Ottawa.

[30]1. Oles./29006, May 1, 1896: Telegram from P. Doyle, Quebec, P.Q., to John R. Hall, Secretary, Department of the Interior, Ottawa.

[31]1. Oles., May 2, 1896: Telegram from John Hoolahan, Montreal, to Alfred Akerlindh, Ottawa.

Ivan Halkow	48	$700
Anna Halkow	38	
4 children aged 11, 9, 7, 3.		
Anton Tesluk	41	$250
Anna Tesluk	38	
Maria Tesluk	15	
Anastasia Tesluk	13	
5 children, aged 11, 10, 8, 5, and 6 months.		
Nicholas Stecyk	33	$200
Maria Stecyk	31	
2 children aged 5 y. and 1 month.		
Ivan Lakusta Theodora	39	
Konstantin Nemyrski	51	$600
Maria Nemyrski	32	
Magelal (Maria Magdalena) Nemyrski	64	
Basil Nemyrski	17	
2 children 11, 7 years.		
Joseph Dziwenka	37	$300
Magdelena Dziwenka	37	
Tatiana Danylek (Danylcek)	24	$100 (both of them)
Gregor Semsrad (Semograd)	33	
Anton Sawka	41	$400
Rosalia Sawka	33	
Olga Sawka	13	
Ignatz Samborsky	24	$50 (both of them together)
Paul Kobersky	37	
Basil Piskliwets	41	$500
Pelagia Piskliwets	22	
2 children aged 11 and 10 years.		
Alex Czorny	31	$400
Maria Czorny	29	
2 children aged 4 years and 11 months.		
Peter Rozkosz	50	$250
Kaska Rozkosz	35	
1 child 6 years.		
Theodor Rudyk	45	$400
Maria Rudyk	44	
1 child, infant.		
Ivan Fantowiski (Fantowski-Jadlowski)	aged 40	$100
Ivan Danczuk	55	$200
Maria Danczuk	42	
Tekla Danczuk	20	
4 children aged 12, 8, 6 and an infant aged 6 months.		
Demko Maciloski (Maciborski)	44	$250
Adolphine Maciloski	33	
Michal Maciloski	14	
5 children 10, 8, 6, 3 years and infant 9 months.		
Ivan Hawrylenko	45	$250
Anna Hawrylenko	42	
5 children aged 12, 10, 6, 3 years and one infant.		
Teodor Nemyrski	26	$100
Teodor Fur	28	$200
		$7,250

32 men
23 women
52 children

107 souls

Party left per C.P.R. Regular Train 10 P.M. for Winnipeg, in charge of Mr. Wladimir Oleskow who accompanied them from Hamburg.
Quebec 1st May, 1896.[32]

The three passenger lists sent to Ottawa differed slightly from one other. The list Dr. Oleskow forwarded to Archer Baker, the European Traffic Agent of the Canadian Pacific Railway Company in London, was prepared before the boat sailed on April 11 and contained the names of several persons who were left behind:

Alex Kis	Aged 39	Capital $200
Pelagia Kis	28	
Teodor Adamczyk	24	$ 50
Gregor Wasylyszyn	37	
Adalbert Kotula	36	
Anna Kotula	34	
Gregor Andruchow	52	$100
Anna Andruchow	47	
Peter Andruchow	24	
Basil Andruchow	17	

Dr. Oleskow explained this discrepancy in his letter of April 10, written to Archer Baker:

The whole party of settlers—to whom you so kind as to grant free transportation left Lemberg for Hamburg for Canada on April 7th. Only

Gregor Wasylyszyn booked by Spiro & Co.	No. 263
Simeon Andrejko	264
Atanas Andrejko and family	265
Alexan. Kis	325

are detained and come with the next steamer. I suppose they will not lose the free transportation on the C.P.R.

I have decided to send the whole party to Edmonton district, and I please therefore to order that they receive free transportation till Edmonton. The party is conducted by Mr. Wladimir Oleskow a gentleman who speaks English and with whom you can communicate. . . .[33]

The list that Mr. McNicoll forwarded to the Deputy Minister on April 7, 1896, also contained the names of the children not included on the list forwarded by Doyle.

[32] I. Oles./29027, May 2, 1896: P. Doyle, Quebec, P.Q., to the Secretary, Department of the Interior, Ottawa. The names in parentheses are the correct spellings, as checked with the Naturalization Records.

[33] I. Oles./28830, April 10, 1896: Dr. Josef Oleskow, Lemberg, to Archer Baker, London.

III

The arrival of Dr. Oleskow's party was heralded by the press. The *Manitoba Morning Press* announced in its issue of May 1, 1896:

AUSTRIANS COMING

Mr. H. E. Carstens has returned from Wetaskiwin, where he went on behalf of the Dominion immigration department to inquire into the condition of the settlers. Spring farm work is well advanced in Alberta; the weather has been favourable and is bright and warm. Mr. Carstens leaves to-day for the east to meet Prof. Oleskow's party of Austrian immigrants, who are expected in the city in few days. Mr. Carstens conducted the professor through the west when that gentleman was here inspecting last fall.[34]

Dr. Oleskow, for his part, wrote to T. Mayne Daly about the sailing of the first party of emigrants dispatched by him. His letter arrived in Ottawa on May 5, when the Minister had already resigned and Sir Hugh J. Macdonald had taken over the portfolio of the Interior. Dr. Oleskow's letter was therefore received by the Deputy Minister:

On April 11th a party of 30 families left Hamburg by "Christiania" (Hansa Line) with the aim to settle down in Canadian Northwest. I let them book by Messrs. Spiro & Co. The party is conducted by Wladimir Oleskow, a english speaking gentleman who will conduct them to Winnipeg or further, if necessary, and return.

No one of this party or of many families who are gone apart is forwarded by any agent in German sea ports; no one of your emigration-pamphlets has been used to encourage this people to Canada and this party has nothing common [i.e., has any connection] with these people from Nebylow, Galicia, who have visited their countrymen in Edna, Ft. Saskatchewan last autumn.[35]

He further requested that his group of settlers be divided into two parties, and outlined his thoughts on their establishment:

One should settle near Edmonton and to this end, I beg if this is in any way possible, to grant to this party a corresponding part of Indian Reserve near Edmonton [name illegible, but undoubtedly he refers to the Indian Reserve south of Edmonton, abandoned by Indians, that he visited Septem-

[34]*Manitoba Morning Free Press,* Winnipeg, Friday, May 1, 1896.

[35]Dr. Oleskow is referring to the two peasant delegates from Nebyliw who were induced to visit Canada by a self-styled agent (Dr. Oleskow calls him a "crook"), who "to enhance his importance . . . refers to himself as the 'vice-president,' but the unfortunate 'vice-president' (he may even be sweeping streets, for what I know), cannot even write well!" Dr. Oleskow mentions this agent approaches his victims with a promise that he will procure from the government "certain papers which need not be procured at all, as they are made out by government employees without cost." (Oleskow, *O emigratsii*/"About Emigration," 64.)

ber 2, 1895]. On this place will the people be satisfied, what should have in future the best influence on further immigration. . . .

The another party of about 8 families and singel (but married) men, who will bring their families later, should settle in Lake Dauphin District and form a nucleous of a great colony there. Perhaps would do for this end the township XXVI range 23, but I was not myself there.[36]

In this letter Dr. Oleskow also suggested that, in view of the intensification of the propaganda for emigration to Brazil, he should be given more support by the Canadian Government to stem the tide. It would be of advantage to Canada to receive:

. . . this very good sort of settlers, agriculturists with sufficient means, with no exaggerated national ambition because to different nations belonging and having no independent political existence, would become very soon truly Canadians, and the Government had no other care as to bring among them a certain amount of people of english blood. . . .

If you reflect on an immigration from this country on a large scale, will you order one official of England to meet with me on the Europe continent, and impower him to make the terms in the sense of my proposals in the *last* letter addressed to Mr. Lyndwode [Lyndwode Pereira, Assistant Secretary of the Department of the Interior].

Mr. Pereira, in acknowledging the letter, assured Dr. Oleskow that his letter would be given careful consideration:

The Hon. Mr. Daly, who was Minister of the Interior when you were in Canada has since retired from the office, but before going back to his home in the Northwest he proposes making a trip to Europe, with the special view of examining into the general question of our immigration interests and a copy of your letter will be placed in his hands and he may possibly be able to meet you and hold the discussion you invite, and which no doubt will lead to a satisfactory understanding between the Department and yourself.

I am to add that the immigrants you refer to have duly arrived, and we have made very careful arrangements for their reception and settlement. I am to convey to you the sincere thanks of the Department for your kind efforts which have been productive of such excellent results, and I am to say that you will be further communicated with on the subject when the reports of our officers now engaged in looking after immigrants come to hand.[37]

The efforts of Dr. Oleskow and of the "committee of great respectability," as the Prime Minister of Austria had termed the group which

[36] 1. Oles./29051, April 18, 1896: Dr. J. Oleskow, Lemberg, Austria, to T. Mayne Daly, Minister of the Interior, Ottawa.

[37] 1. Oles., May 7, 1896: Lyndwode Pereira, Ottawa, to Dr. J. Oleskow, Lemberg, Austria. The proposed meeting did not take place, due to the dissolution of Parliament and the following general elections of June 23, 1896, which resulted in the defeat of the Conservative administration.

supported him, bore striking results. The two booklets written by Dr. Oleskow and published by the popular educational societies, the public lectures he delivered on his return from Canada, and his articles that appeared in the press turned the tide of Galician emigration away from Brazil to Canada. Canada became the principal topic of discussion in village communities, and the offer to supply information about this new land and to assist in arranging emigration to it received wide response, not only from the peasants, but also from the "intellectuals": "I am very pleased to learn [Dr. Oleskow wrote in his booklet "About Emigration"] that some of our intellectuals, i.e., people experienced in the ways of the world, also intend to go to Canada in the spring and will serve as guides to our peasants, who would otherwise be surely robbed by agents on the way. I shall provide these intelligent people with most vital information and will show on the map the places, where the peasants ought to settle now. I shall tell them a number of practical details, without which it would be difficult for them to get along, but on which I cannot enlarge in this small booklet."[38] Not only individuals but whole delegations from villages began to arrive at Lviw to seek the promised advice and information.[39]

With the growth of interest in Canada on the part of broader masses of the population, there arose expenditures which Dr. Oleskow and the committee supporting him had to bear and for which no ready funds were available. The request made by Dr. Oleskow to the Minister of the Interior to grant him the sum of £600 for current expenses, such as printing of pamphlets, the establishment of an emigration "agency," and the payment of railway fares of guides who were conducting groups of emigrants from Galicia to the ports of embarkation in order to prevent the inexperienced peasants from falling victim to hucksters did not meet with the expected response. Oleskow pressed for a decision in this regard, and his brother Wladimir brought the matter up with the Commissioner of Dominion Lands in Winnipeg. H. H. Smith mentioned this lack of funds in a letter of introduction he gave Wladimir Oleskow to the Deputy Minister in Ottawa:

> This will introduce to you Professor [Smith was in error in using this title] Oleskow who is on his way back to Europe after having safely brought out a large party of Galicians. He has pointed out to me that great difficulties

[38]Oleskow, *O emigratsii*, 64.

[39]Joseph Kohut of Stuartburn mentions in his memoirs the delegation which, after reading Oleskow's booklet, went from the village of Synkiw to Lviw to consult him about Canada. This led to mass migration from that village, and the establishment in the Stuartburn district of a settlement which bears the name of their original village. See Josef Kohut, *Moi spomyny*/"My Memoirs," 6.

and opposition have to be overcome in this matter, and as this is but a trial party and beginning of what he believes to be a large movement to this country, his brother, Dr. Oleskow, desires some recognition from the Government of Canada, possibly in the shape of assistance to open an Intelligence Office, the details of which Dr. Oleskow would arrange through correspondence. It seems to me that the Professor's request is not an unreasonable one, and I shall be glad if you can see your way clear to accede to it.[40]

Dr. Oleskow could not establish a steamship agency in Lviw because the Austrian authorities would not permit it, but he hoped to be able to open an "intelligence office," as he called it—a sort of emigrants' aid service and information office—where prospective emigrants could receive all necessary general information and assistance in procuring railway tickets, without resorting to the eager "help" of various agents. To procure steamship transportation for prospective emigrants, Dr. Oleskow turned to authorized steamship agents in Hamburg, thus saving the emigrants extra expenses claimed by sub-agents for "services." He bought the tickets for the first group of emigrants through Spiro and Company of Hamburg, who, aware of the financial position of Professor Oleskow and of the committee supporting him, offered him the regular commission on steamship tickets and on bonuses, which the firm was otherwise obliged to pay sub-agents. The steamship companies and their agents kept a close watch on Dr. Oleskow's attempts to divert the flow of emigrants from Brazil to Canada. His efforts began to bear fruit, and the steamship companies made ready to garner the benefits of receiving thousands of passengers bound for Canada without any effort or solicitation on their part or on that of their agents. The steamship agents were also paid a bonus by the Canadian Government for every bona fide settler.

The arrival in Canada of the first group of Oleskow's agriculturists, many of them with substantial initial capital, accompanied by an experienced, English-speaking guide, convinced the immigration authorities in Ottawa that Dr. Oleskow was not merely making empty promises. The Department of the Interior decided to compensate Dr. Oleskow for his efforts. The High Commissioner for Canada, Sir Donald A. Smith, was instructed: ". . . to remit Dr. Oleskow £100 in consideration of the work he has already performed on behalf of the colonization of the Canadian Northwest."[41] The Deputy Minister of the Interior also wrote a letter to Sir William Van Horne, the President of the C.P.R. Company in Montreal, informing him of this decision to make payment

[40]1. Oles., May 11, 1896: H. H. Smith, Winnipeg, to A. M. Burgess, Ottawa.
[41]1. Oles., May 16, 1896: Lyndwode Pereira, Ottawa, to J. G. Colmer, London.

to Oleskow: "I understand that Mr. Daly advised you of our intention to send Professor Oleskow £100, in consideration of his services in sending us the recent batch of 107 Galician immigrants and I write this to say that the Secretary of the High Commissioner's office in London was instructed on the 16th instant to make the payment in question to Professor Oleskow."[42] Sir William not only expressed his pleasure that the Department decided to recognize Dr. Oleskow's efforts, but also made a prophecy about long-term immigration which, as time has shown, proved to be correct: "I am very glad that Professor Oleskow's efforts have had such prompt recognition at the hands of your Department, for I believe that the securing of this first batch of Galician immigrants will lead to a great many more from that direction, and they seem to be very desirable people."[43]

Dr. Oleskow, ignorant of the decision of the Department of the Interior to remit him the sum of £100 wrote to the High Commissioner in London again, on April 30, 1896, about the urgent need for funds to meet the expenses of preparing emigration to Canada and of counteracting propaganda spread by Brazilian agents:

> . . . Till now depends the movement of our agriculturists to Canada exclusively on my efforts, so that I may say I have acted as a true Canadian patriot. But with my own means cannot the effect be a grand one, because the Brazilian interests are supported here with considerable capital. Nevertheless I state once more, the little sum of say £600 in my hands would suffice to lay the foundation for regular monthly expedition of some 100 families agriculturists with necessary means to make a start on a homestead in Canada. A guide to every expedition would prevent the diverting of parties in the seaports from Canada to some other land.
>
> Should you now conceive the extraordinary importance of Austrian emigration for populating of Canadian North-West, then I am ready to meet with your representative somewhere on the Continent, say in Frankfort on Main, and talk the matter over.[44]

This letter arrived in London after Sir Charles Tupper had already left for Canada to take over the premiership on Sir Mackenzie Bowell's resignation. While awaiting a favourable decision concerning his request, Dr. Oleskow busily prepared for further movements of emigrants to Canada. Envisaging a rapid growth of colonies in Manitoba and the

[42] 1. Oles., May 22, 1896: A. M. Burgess, Ottawa, to Sir William Van Horne, President, C.P.R. Company, Montreal.

[43] 1. Oles., May 24, 1896: Sir William Van Horne, Montreal, to A. M. Burgess, Ottawa.

[44] 1. Oles./29254, April 30, 1896: Dr. J. Oleskow, Lemberg, Austria, to the High Commissioner for Canada, London.

Northwest, particularly of those in the vicinity of Edmonton, to which he had directed his first batch of settlers, he was concerned about their proper establishment and economic security. To prevent the emigrants from being exploited on their way by dishonest money-changers, self-styled agents, and other swindlers, Dr. Oleskow hoped to add to each group of emigrants an experienced person who would act as a guide during the long journey and who would be able to speak at least sufficient German to make himself understood. Oleskow was also concerned that the settlers should be given a proper start on the land, making them economically independent by encouraging home industries, in which field the Ukrainian peasants were quite adept, and by establishing creameries and cheese factories. In this connection, he wrote the Department of the Interior for relevant literature so that he might be better informed about the possibilities of establishing these kinds of industries. He submitted plans outlining how the settlers could be assisted and instructed in the new ways of farming, and he urged that credit should be extended to them to buy cows, build homes, and become economically independent.

The necessity for the establishment of schools for the children of the settlers, as well as for the building of churches and the organization of religious communities to serve the spiritual needs of the settlers was stressed by Dr. Oleskow. He undertook to assist the settlers even in this matter by trying to find a young Ukrainian Catholic clergyman who would be willing to emigrate to Canada and to devote his life and energy to the religious service of the settlers on remote homesteads. Dr. Oleskow thought that this role might be filled by the Reverend Ostap Nizhankowskyi, who, in 1896, was an instructor of choral singing at the Teachers' Seminary where he himself was a professor of agriculture. Whether, as a composer of some note and an outstanding choir conductor, Father Nizhankowskyi was well suited or not to become a missionary priest to lead pioneer life on a homestead and to attend to the spiritual needs of pioneer settlers scattered over a vast, often roadless area, did not seem to occur to Oleskow.

Well aware that the new immigrants would be unable to support a priest, Dr. Oleskow hoped to obtain for him a small stipend from the Canadian Government, at least for the duration of the first year, until the settlers could harvest their second crop and improve their financial position. He also suggested that the priest might himself take out a homestead, to which he would be entitled as a settler, and thus help to increase his income and make a living. On the subject of obtaining support for a clergyman and of the other religious needs of the settlers,

Dr. Oleskow wrote the following letter to Sir Hugh Macdonald, the Minister of the Interior:

Lemberg, May 16, 1896.

To the Honourable Sir
H. J. Macdonald,
Minister of the Interior,
Ottawa.

Sir,

The Austrian greek catholic settlers in the Canadian Northwest, which are located in near Ft. Saskatchewan in Edna, in Neudorf near Grenfell, and dispersed through Manitoba are devoid of every possibility to accomplish their religious needs, as there is not one priest of this religion in Canada. The last transport of Austrian emigrants, conducted by Mr. Wladimir Oleskow, who landed in Quebec on May 1st by the steamer "Christiania" does also belong to this religion.

In interest of all these people and in interest of further immigration, it is necessary to take care for a greec-catholic priest.

As there has declared his decision for accomplishing of the services of one minister the greec catholic people in Canada the Rever. Ostap Nizankowski, so I please to inform me in which measure would the Government contribute for the sustentation of the first greec catholic priest in Canada. The Government is expected besides the usually grant of lands to destine for this first gr. cath. priest a certain salary, as the beginning farmers will be unable to give a sufficient sustentation for their minister. Rever. Nizankowski would sail for Canada in the July and reside where the last, above mentioned party of emigrants will settle down.

As all greek catholic clergymen are married so is Rever. Nizankowski too. He has a wife and an enfant. He is 35 years old and is high appreciated in this country because of his good spiritual and wordly quality. He is an eminent composer too.

If the Department wished some information as to the greek catholic religion, I think, Rever. W. Mercer, Ottawa Metcalf Str. would perhaps able to give them.

Yours truly,

(Signed) PROF. JOSEF OLESKOW,
Golembia Gasse 11A, Lemberg, Austria, Europe.[45]

The answer that Dr. Oleskow received from Lyndwode Pereira, Assistant Secretary of the Department of the Interior, was not very encouraging:

It is regretted very much that the Government of Canada has no fund at its disposal out of which a stipend could be paid to this gentleman as a Priest, and all that we can do under the circumstances is to send a copy of your letter to the Commissioner of Dominion Lands at Winnipeg and to request him to have the goodness to bring it to the attention of the authorities of the Roman Catholic Church with a view to ascertaining whether they can

[45] 1. Oles./29537, May 16, 1896: Dr. J. Oleskow, Lemberg, Austria, to H. J. Macdonald, Minister of the Interior, Ottawa.

do anything in the matter as no doubt they will be interested in looking after the spiritual welfare of your immigrants.[46]

The question of a clergyman for Ukrainian settlers which Dr. Oleskow raised was considered seriously in the Department, and since they were uncertain whether the Roman Catholic authorities would bear the costs of supporting a Ukrainian (Greek) Catholic clergyman, other solutions were sought. The Superintendent of Immigration made the following proposal to the Deputy Minister about aiding the priest that Dr. Oleskow had mentioned: "Perhaps you will authorise a further letter to be sent to Professor Oleskow in re 29537, stating that if the Rev. Ostap Nizankowski brings out a party of immigrants we will be prepared to give him, say $100 on account of his own expenses, and will also make application to the Canadian Pacific Railway Company to grant him either free, or greatly reduced transportation from seaboard to Edmonton. [The Deputy Minister pencilled on the memo: 'Approved tell the C.P.R. what we propose.']"[47] Mr. Burgess accepted this suggestion and instructed that Dr. Oleskow be informed of this development. The letter to Dr. Oleskow on the subject was delayed and was not mailed until June 22, 1896:

> I am further to say [wrote Mr. Pereira] with reference to the subject of your letter of the 16th of May, last, that although as explained in my letter of the 2nd instant, we have no fund out of which a stipend could be paid to the Revd. Ostap Nizankowski as a Priest we will be prepared to make a payment to him of say $100.00 on account of his own expenses in coming to Canada if he brings out a party of immigrants with him, and we will also in that event endeavour to arrange with the Canadian Pacific Railway authorities to grant him and his wife free, or greatly reduced, transportation from the Seaboard to Edmonton. I am to add that a copy of this letter is being sent to Mr. J. G. Colmer, Secretary of the High Commissioner's Office in London, in order that he may take action in accordance with its tenor on being satisfied that M. Nizankowski is coming out with a party of your Galician settlers.[48]

The departure to Canada of Reverend Ostap Nizhankowskyi (Nizankowski) planned for July, 1896, did not materialize. His name is not mentioned in subsequent letters written by Dr. Oleskow.

Dr. Oleskow, while concerned about the spiritual needs of the settlers, did not forget their material requirements. He submitted several

[46]1. Oles., June 2, 1896: Lyndwode Pereira, Ottawa, to Dr. J. Oleskow, Lemberg, Austria.

[47]1. Oles., Memo, June 4, 1896: L. M. Fortier, Superintendent of Immigration, Department of the Interior, Ottawa, to A. M. Burgess, Ottawa.

[48]2. Oles., June 22, 1896: Lyndwode Pereira, Ottawa, to Dr. J. Oleskow, Lemberg, Austria.

plans to R. A. Ruttan, the Dominion Land and Immigration Agent in Edmonton describing how the settlers could best be helped to establish themselves satisfactorily on homesteads and how they could most profitably use their modest financial resources to develop their economy. Ruttan was quite impressed by Dr. Oleskow's ideas and passed them on to the Commissioner of Dominion Lands in Winnipeg:

> Referring to your letter of the 2nd inst. (May, 1896) 330281, it may possibly be necessary, if the Austrians come here, to employ someone familiar with the country and survey system to locate them. I do not think that Mr. Carstens is qualified for the work and dare say that his energies will be fully engaged in looking after the transport arrangements and essential purchases of the party. I enclose copy of a letter reecived from Professor Oleskow in regard to these people.
>
> His suggestion that families with little children should have houses erected for them is a very good one. You will appreciate the advantage to the immigrants if you will take into account his position on reaching his destination here, ignorant perhaps of our language, certainly knowing little about our laws, system of survey etc. He would have difficulty enough to contend with if it were possible to take him, his family and outfit, direct to a quarter Section 25, 35, or 50 miles distant upon which he would find a house say 16 × 18 feet with half-attic or loft and a bit of cellar. All he would have to do would be put in his stove and feel at home. A stable should also be built of the same size as the house, these two buildings would cost about $100.
>
> This is in the line of the Professor's suggestion. I think if you will put the question to him he will assure you that if 50 of these houses or 100 of them are erected during next Autumn or Winter in the outskirts of settlement he can guarantee that as many families, having the necessary means will undertake to purchase them and pay cash.
>
> I would not recommend their erection upon each quarter section but upon alternate quarter sections. You would find perhaps that a settler having $100 cash in addition to his entry fee wishing to bring alongside him a friend who could not do more than pay the fee and whom he would house for the first year until he could put up a house upon his own place. The objection that will be urged to this proposal is the old one which derives everything that may be burlesqued under the stigma of "paternalism."
>
> But the Cavillers talk too fast. In one sense they are right enough in saying that the country will settle "rapidly enough" if left alone—severely alone—so it will, slowly. What the present state of Canadian Commerce requires is not the gradual slow settlement of the West but a rapid settlement; an increase of population that will afford a market for Eastern manufactures.
>
> If we can get useful Settlers such as the Professor has in view by building houses for them and not otherwise, I see no objection to building the houses, there seems to be little risk in building them even if we had to sell them on time: $20 a year or even less payment so long as we absolutely decline to go to a greater expense than $100. on any quarter section. This amount,

properly expended, will suffice to erect the buildings which are indispensable to new arrivals. The question of water supply is important in some districts but we could avoid localities in which this difficulty is experienced, you often hear it is said that there is no use sending folk into our North West whilst the freight rates are so high. They are high and occasionally absurdly high, unreasonably high and oppressive—obstructing progress and in a thousand ways militating against the country the sparse population and the Railway Company. The Railway Company will discover in due time how far it is in its own interest to reduce charges and the settlers will thereupon find relief—but the Railway Co. is not to be hurried. Meanwhile as to the argument of the people who advocate a check to settlement rather than its encouragement, they forget or have not yet realized that one of the most serious hardships of the settler who is now in the North West is his comparative isolation. If you add to his numbers you permit him to operate a creamery, a school etc. where it was impossible formerly to do this and benefit him in every aspect and relation to life.

If Agriculture in Canada is paying industry and I believe it is, we want to push it and help it in every way—not putting to the task half a man to each square mile but 10 or 20 men. Folk who argue otherwise seem to me to have curiously failed in their estimate of the situation.

If you approve of this house building scheme men could be found here in August or September to undertake Contracts for say 100 of them on the outskirts of settlement—in localities which I might myself choose. It would be safe undertaking for the Government and very moderate care would be necessary to prevent spoliation of the buildings prior to their occupation by the homesteaders.[49]

The Commissioner confirmed receipt of Ruttan's letter and informed him that "the scheme to erect small buildings on alternative quarter-sections for Austrian immigrants who are expected to arrive under the auspices of Professor Oleskow" would be drawn to the attention of the Minister. In forwarding Ruttan's report to the Deputy Minister in Ottawa, the Commissioner added a comment about more encouragement for Dr. Oleskow in the future: "In view of the very satisfactory nature of this communication, I would suggest the advisability, when the vote for immigration for the coming fiscal year has been obtained, to consider what encouragement can be offered to the Professor to continue his efforts on behalf of promoting immigration of his countrymen to the North-West."[50] But Commissioner Smith's suggestion arrived too late. Parliament was dissolved a few weeks after his letter reached Ottawa, and, in the elections which followed, the Government of Sir Charles Tupper was not returned to power.

[49]1. Oles./29572, May 6, 1896: R. A. Ruttan, Dominion Lands and Immigration Agent, Edmonton, to H. H. Smith, Winnipeg.

[50]2. Oles./29746, June 1, 1896: H. H. Smith, Winnipeg, to A. M. Burgess, Ottawa.

The location of Dr. Oleskow's settlers in the Fort Saskatchewan district proceeded satisfactorily, and R. A. Ruttan reported favourably to the Commissioner in Winnipeg: "They are good settlers and I should like to see more of them. Their frugality modest ambition and industry fit them to meet in the best way the difficulties this remote locality presents. They are all of the Greek Church (Russian) and it would be an excellent thing if Professor Oleskow could send out one or two priests with the next batch of Emigrants."[51] By June 1, 1896, eighteen families were placed on homesteads and they all "made entry," Ruttan reported:

> I am glad to report that the new arrivals are favourably impressed by their reception and greatly pleased with the land that has been selected for them, and with their prospect. With the assistance of the Guide and Interpreter they made very good bargains for the oxen, horses, machinery and general outfit purchased.
>
> Several others are yet to make entry but desired time to examine the land further. I would suggest that Professor Oleskow be asked to interest himself in sending a priest of the Russian Church to settle in this Colony. This is a highly important matter to the Colonists and should receive early attention.
>
> I would also recommend that the Professor should be furnished from our Agricultural Department with full particulars of the cost of a Creamery plant and the method of working it, and that he be asked to enjoin upon his Countrymen the desirabliness of establishment of a Creamery as early as possible after they obtain the cattle necessary to its support.
>
> Professor Oleskow would do wisely to explain fully the advantage to these people, in their remote situation, of engaging chiefly in stock raising and dairy work. It is furthermore of importance that those of them who can spin and use a hand loom should be encouraged to bring their implements with them and to prosecute here these most useful branches of home industry.
>
> It would be of great assistance in the education of these people if you could have an edition of "The Settlers Guide" issued in the Russian language [Ruttan probably meant in the Ukrainian language], leaving out the reference to the "Two Miles Radius System" and giving more fully the provisions of the Territories Exemption Ordinance and the ordinance relating to Statute Labor and Fire Districts. Indeed if this pamphlet was issued in the French, German, Russian and Scandinavian tongues its liberal dissemination amongst the peoples would have an excellent effect. The Timber Regulations should however be more fully quoted showing the cost to the Settler of timber other than his free allowance and informing him clearly of the penalties by trespassers.
>
> The importance of this recommendation becomes apparent to any one who attempts to realize the miserable helplessness of these foreigners, who, ignorant of our language, have no means of informing themselves as to our laws and fall easy prey to any malicious or designing individual who may

[51]1. Oles./29771, June 6, 1896: R. A. Ruttan, Edmonton, to the Commissioner of Dominion Lands, Winnipeg.

seek to set them astray. Their chief difficulties and discouragements arise very often from their absolute ignorance of our laws and regulations.[52]

On Ruttan's suggestion, the Secretary of the Department of the Interior wrote to the Department of Agriculture requesting that manuals on creameries and cheese factories be sent to the settlers in the Fort Saskatchewan region and to Dr. Oleskow in Austria:

> I am directed to inform you that an important movement of immigrants from Galicia to our Northwest is now in progress, under the auspices of Professor Josef Oleskow, who occupies the chair of Agriculture in the University of Lemberg, his address in full being as follows: Professor Josef Oleskow, Lemberg, Golembia G. 11 A., Galicia, Austria. 125 of these immigrants have recently settled in the vicinity of Edmonton, and the Agent of Dominion Lands there, who speaks very highly of them, recommends us to ascertain on their behalf the probable cost of establishing a creamery for them in their settlement and full particulars as to the working of it, etc. If you have any printed matter on the subject which we could send to the settlers themselves and to Professor Oleskow, will you have the kindness to forward a supply to the Immigration Branch.[53]

The Department of Agriculture obliged and forwarded to the Immigration Branch twenty-five copies of a bulletin entitled "Cheese Factories and Creameries," of which five copies were mailed to Dr. Oleskow.

IV

Sir Donald A. Smith, who succeeded Tupper as High Commissioner for Canada in London in the spring of 1896, was instructed by the Department of the Interior to remit £100 to Dr. Oleskow "for services rendered," in having directed to Canada thirty families of settlers. The High Commissioner hoped to save the Government the extra expense of paying bonuses to seaport agents for something that they did not in fact do. He therefore wrote a letter to Spiro and Company in Hamburg, without first consulting Ottawa. ". . . The High Commissioner thought it advisable to communicate with Messrs. Spiro & Co. of Hamburg, pointing out to them that as the party was entirely organized by Professor Oleskow, and as presumably they had neither expense nor trouble in the matter, beyond issuing the tickets (on which of course they would get the usual Steamship commissions) they would he hoped in the circumstances be good enough to allow the Government bonus to

[52]2. Oles./29810, June 1, 1896: R. A. Ruttan, Edmonton, to the Secretary, Department of the Interior, Ottawa.

[53]2. Oles., June 10, 1896: Lyndwode Pereira, Ottawa, to the Secretary, Department of Agriculture, Ottawa.

be paid to Professor instead of them."[54] Spiro and Company's reply was sharp, bordering indeed on rudeness, and they categorically objected to the High Commissioner's interference in the Company's affairs:

> . . . It seems to us out of the way that the Government should wish to control the relation of the steamship agents to their sub-agents, and might ponder which of these different factors has the greater or smaller merit in the organization of the business. We, on our part, must decline in the politest but also in the most positive manner, to accept advice from anyone, how we are to compensate our agents for services rendered to us. The Government might have sufficient confidence in us to know that we do not need any guidance, and we believe also that the Government should give more consideration to what we have done during a period of 30 years in the interest of the colonization of Canada, than appears from your favour of the 5th.
>
> As for the special case of Dr. Oleskow we beg to note that this gentleman is in relation to us as an agent and that in loyalty all his letters to the Government should be referred to us.
>
> We must deny any claim of this gentleman for direct payment of bonuses for the "Christiania" passengers, with still greater reason as in order to bring about the engagement of the passengers, we paid this gentleman besides the highest commissions on the ocean fares, also the Government bonuses even *before* the shipping of the passengers.
>
> The Government will see by this statement that *we* only are entitled to receive the bonuses and we beg you to see that the cheque for the amount due is sent as promptly as possible.[55]

The £100 that the Department of the Interior intended to remit to Dr. Oleskow had been held back, although, as the Deputy Minister stated, it was to be a renumeration "in consideration of the work he had already performed on behalf of the colonization of the Canadian Northwest," and not as a bonus usually paid to steamship agents. No further correspondence has been found on this matter, and it is logical to assume that Spiro and Company was paid the full bonus.

Two years later, Smith once again met with difficulty by dealing independently with immigration matters. At that time he visited Hamburg to address the steamship agents and the visit almost ended in his arrest by the German police authorities for violating German law. Shortly after this unfortunate incident, Clifford Sifton appointed W. T. R. Preston, a senior officer of the Department, to act as Inspector of Canadian Immigration Agencies in Europe, with headquarters in London.

Dr. Oleskow, anticipating a substantial increase in the number of emigrants from Galicia and Bukowina to Canada during the 1897

[54]2. Oles./30075, June 15, 1896: J. G. Colmer, London, to the Secretary of the Interior, Ottawa.

[55]2. Oles., June 10, 1896: Spiro and Company, Hamburg, to the Secretary, Office of the High Commissioner for Canada, London.

season, approached the Commissioner of Dominion Lands in Winnipeg with the request to reserve until the end of 1897 Township 28, Ranges 22 and 23 West of 1.M., for colonists who would arrive in Canada in the course of the year. According to information he obtained from official publications and from the settlers with whom he was in close touch, the Dauphin region was particularly suited for settlement by the farmers: "To this purpose I beg to reserve for the settlers going under my auspices the township 28 Range 22 and 23. Under the condition that any claim to the singular sections of homesteads unless really settled will be abolished (relinquished) I oblige me [i.e., 'I undertake'] to fill till end 1897, all homesteads in these two townships available for settlement. I beg to take all steps necessary for fulfilling of this my request as early as possible and to affirm me of acceptance of my project, so as I am able to direct the August expedition straight to Lake Dauphin District."[56] Dr. Oleskow also referred in this letter to the inadvisability of publishing a pamphlet on Canada in Polish with the purpose of encouraging immigration:

> . . . I am informed that the Gov. authorities are about to publish a pamphlet in Polish with the purpose to encourage the immigration. That would be just the thing I can assure you to spoil my whole action in favour of Canada. The immediate result of such pamphlet printed abroad would be a warning of the press and of the Government against the land which induces the immigrants in such manner, such pamphlets are total discredits here. I wonder the Canada Government is not yet aware of this fact and does spend much money thoroughly successless instead of supporting through the press the public opinion in favour of Canada in these lands themselves from which goes the emigration.

The Commissioner's secretary, informed Dr. Oleskow that the Commissioner's office had no authority to reserve land for future colonists, but that the request would be referred to Ottawa:

> . . . With reference to your desire to have reserved for your Colonists until the end of the year 1897, Township 28, Ranges 22 and 23 W., I beg to say that the Commissioner has no power to grant this, but he is forwarding a copy of this correspondence to Ottawa, with a request that you may be advised with as little delay as possible as to the action which can be taken in this direction. I am also asking the special attention of the authorities to the remarks which you made as to the inadvisability of issuing any pamphlets in the Polish language, and you will no doubt be communicated with from Ottawa on this point.[57]

[56]2. Oles./30307, June 7, 1896: Dr. J. Oleskow, Lemberg, Austria, to the Commissioner of Dominion Lands, Winnipeg.

[57]2. Oles./30307, July 3, 1896: J. R. Burpé, Secretary, Dominion Lands Office, Winnipeg, to Dr. J. Oleskow, Lemberg, Austria.

The matter of the reservation of the two townships was discussed in the Department in Ottawa, and the Deputy Minister decided that the request could not be granted. Dr. Oleskow was then informed of this decision:

It is observed that in your letter of the 7th of June, last, to the Commissioner of Dominion Lands at Winnipeg, you requested that two Townships, namely, 28 in Ranges 22 and 23, West of the 1st Meridian, might be reserved for your settlers until the end of 1897. It is regretted, however, that it is not possible to meet your wishes in this regard as a good deal of homesteading is going on in the neighbourhood in which the above mentioned Townships are situated, and the reservation of such a large area for so long a period would be certain to lead to discontent and complaints on the part of other settlers—I am, however, to again assure you that your people will have no difficulty in securing suitable locations on their arrival and that the officers of the Department will help them in every possible way to this end.[58]

Dr. Oleskow, in answering the Commissioner's letter of July 3, drew his attention to a "weak point" in the emigration procedure that he felt the Commissioner could help to eliminate:

I am in receipt of your letter of July 3rd, in which you say that "a very satisfactory report as to parties of emigrants sent by me, has been received from the Agent at Edmonton who speaks very highly of their industry and frugality." The C.P.R. officials join as I gather from the Canadian Gazette (from August 13th) in the opinion that "these people make excellent agriculturists."

I knew it, before I have inagurated the emigration of Galicians to Canada, that the peasants from here will make the very best sort of settlers in Canada, but I am very pleased that the Canadian officials have it so soon recognized.

There is one weak point in the emigration process whose improvement lies, I suppose, in power of the Office of the Commissioner of the Dominion Lands.

As there are till now no steps taken by the Canadian Government towards organization of this emigration movement, which I have proposed,—so come these people to Winnipeg without a determined place of settlement. They can neither English nor German, and fall in the hands of Austrian Jews or some depraved individuals who act in the interest of private land owners, persuade these people that there are in Canada no free homesteads, and endeavour to purchase wet, improper to culture grounds. So search the people for good, free lands, for months, and write here to Austria, that there is no free land apt to cultivation in Canada. Several families who were so deceived by agents returned here. This radical situation can be improved by an organization of the emigration, by which every emigrant says already here where he will settle, but in the meantime should be in Winnipeg in emigration house, appointed an Intelligence Officer, who speaks not only English and German but Slavic languages too. And this official should be

[58]2. Oles., August 12, 1896: Lyndwode Pereira, Ottawa, to Dr. J. Oleskow, Lemberg, Austria.

a known man from this country, to whom would have the emigrants a confidence. I would take care for finding such a man if the Canadian Government will create the basis for an organized emigration in this country —must be the number of officers in emigration house in every case increased.[59]

For the "intelligence officer" whom he mentions, Dr. Oleskow had in mind Charles (Cyril) Genik-Berezowsky, who in the summer of the same year was the leader of one of Dr. Oleskow's groups of settlers.

The Commissioner's office, in reply to Oleskow's letter, observed that it was impossible to prevent emigrants from disregarding the advice of immigration officers and buying land from agents if they so desired:

With regard to your complaint that immigrants are approached by Agents having lands to sell on their own account, I am to explain that it is next to impossible to prevent this, and it remains for the newcomers to refuse the offers that are made to them. Our officials take every opportunity of warning them against these attempts, and to impress upon them the advantages of free homesteading, and if in spite of this they deliberately decide to purchase land, the Department cannot be held responsible. I might explain to you that we had a good deal of trouble with certain settlers who came out, presumably from your locality, from this very reason. They were taken charge of by our officials and several excellent locations in different parts of the Province pointed out to them, but in consequence of their listening to the advice of strangers, they became unsettled, and finally purchased land not far from the City instead of going further away and obtaining each a quarter-section of land, possibly better suited to their needs.

It would be much better if, in the future, the people you send out here were to decide beforehand as to their locations, so as to avoid staying in Winnipeg, and with the experience gained by yourself and your brother in your visit to this country the Commissioner does not see that there should be any serious difficulty in the way of adopting this course. It would probably, however, entail certain correspondence beforehand, but this might easily be arranged, and the difficulty which you now point to would thus be avoided.

The Commissioner noted what you say with regard to the appointment of an Interpreter. This is a matter with which he has no power to deal, but attention of the Minister will be drawn to it. . . .

In conclusion, I am to say that the Commissioner is desirous of, as far as possible, meeting your wishes and will do all in his power to encourage immigration of a class of people who he has no doubt will make excellent settlers.[60]

As he promised, the Commissioner approached the Department of the

[59]2. Oles./31296, August 27, 1896: Dr. J. Oleskow, Lemberg, Austria, to the Commissioner of Dominion Lands, Winnipeg.

[60]2. Oles./31296, September 12, 1896: E. H. Taylor, Office of the Commissioner of Dominion Lands, Winnipeg, to Dr. J. Oleskow, Lemberg, Austria.

Interior in Ottawa and requested permission to engage Charles Genik as an interpreter for the Immigration Hall:

Referring to my letter to Professor Oleskow, of Galicia, in Austria, dated the 12th instant, a copy of which was forwarded for your information, the Commissioner directs me to say that some little inconvenience is experienced in handling the Ruthenians owing to their language not being understood by our officials. There is one of Professor Oleskow's settlers, however, of the name of Charles (Cyril) Genik who has, from time to time been employed as Interpreter, and the Commissioner would like to be authorized to engage him at a fair renumeration as occasion for his services occurs. [The phrase "which is not likely to be often" is pencilled in here.]

Will you be good enough to submit this point and let the Commissioner have a decision as early as may be convenient.[61]

The Commissioner, as it turned out, erred in one respect—Genik would, in future, be kept much busier than he anticipated. In due course, the permission to engage Genik as an interpreter was granted: "I am directed to say in answer to your letter of the 16th instant . . . that the proposal to employ Charles Genik as Interpreter as occasion requires, is approved, and that the necessary arrangements in this relation are left to the Commissioner to make at his discretion."[62] Dr. Oleskow was not informed about this appointment, however, until November 17 of the same year.

As Oleskow had predicted, the flow of immigrants from Galicia steadily increased, and he considered it essential to have the movement organized efficiently on both sides of the Atlantic, for the benefit of both the immigrants and the Canadian Government. To this end, he worked out an elaborate plan and submitted it to the Department of the Interior for approval. This plan was based on the hope that he would be able to secure "the concession for the *sole* agency in this country (Galicia) under certain restrictions." The provincial authorities in Galicia had informed the professor that this was possible. Dr. Oleskow and his Committee enjoyed the backing of a number of Ruthenian members of the Galician Diet (some of whom were members of the Committee), but the final decision nevertheless rested with the *Reichstag* in Vienna. Oleskow was not aware that the Prime Minister of Austria, Count Casimir Badeni, had stated in a private letter to Ambassador Barrington that the Austrian Government would never give its consent to the organization of an emigration of Galician subjects on a large scale, and

[61]2. Oles./31306, September 16, 1896: E. H. Taylor, Winnipeg, to the Secretary, Department of the Interior, Ottawa.

[62]2. Oles., September 22, 1896: Lyndwode Pereira, Ottawa, to the Secretary, Office of Dominion Lands Board, Winnipeg.

that it would indeed certainly oppose such an intention. Dr. Oleskow also underestimated the influence of the powerful steamship companies who would look with disfavour upon the granting of a concession to open an emigration office to a person who was outside their direct control. The steamship companies and their agents looked upon Dr. Oleskow's activities with toleration as long as the results of his work brought commissions and bonuses with little direct effort on their part. But were he to try to act independently, to bypass the agents, he would certainly meet powerful opposition.

Oleskow's plans were received in Ottawa in September, 1896, two months before Clifford Sifton took charge of the Department of the Interior. Radical changes were already planned in the organization of the Department; key personalities were to be replaced, new offices to be formed, and new immigration policies to be instituted. The incoming Minister was determined to overhaul the whole machinery of the Department, starting with attending to the "arrears." It was to take him approximately two years to deal completely with the accumulation of these "arrears" in the Department.[63] There was, therefore, scant hope that Oleskow's plans could be decided upon before a general plan of action had been worked out. Discouraged by what he thought was indecision on the part of the Department, Dr. Oleskow discontinued his emigration activities for some time, leaving the field to the busy sub-agents of steamship companies. These men were of course delighted to find the ground already prepared for them, and not being overly selective about the type of emigrants who approached them, they booked everyone who could pay passage. Whether or not an emigrant had sufficient money left for a start in Canada was of no consequence to them.

The plan for the organization of the emigration from Galicia that Dr. Oleskow submitted for approval and action to the Department of the Interior was an elaborate one, as is evident from the following letter to the Department of the Interior, September 6, 1896:

> I take for known my journey through Canada in 1895 in order to investigate whether there is suitable land for Austrian settlers. In consequence I have inaugurated a movement of our emigrants to the Canadian Northwest. The movement commenced by sending a party of settlers, conducted by Mr. Wlad. Oleskow, which are in this spring settled in Edmonton district. The party was followed by severals more who are settled in Beausejours and Brokenhead (18 families) in Dominion City Twp. 2. Rge 6 & 7 East (16

[63]John W. Dafoe, *Clifford Sifton in Relation to his Times* (Toronto: The Macmillan Co., 1931), 134.

families), 20 families were induced by Roman Cathol. priests in Winnipeg to buy by them land in extent of 10 to 30 acres, and circa 10 families purchased land to 120–160 acres in St. Andrews, Springfield Twp. 12 Rge 6 East. A great party leaved Hamburg by S. S. Christiania in the first days of August.

These parties let I book by seaport-agents Spiro & Co., Karlsberg, Morawetz in Hamburg.

The colony Beaver Hills (Edmonton District) alone is now numbering over 600 souls (see the Canadian Gazette, August 13th), and there were by my visit in 1895 only 12 families. These people make in the opinion of the local Government authorities and the C.P.R. officials (see Canad. Gaz. Aug. 13th) excellent agriculturists. I enclose here an extract of a letter from the Office of the Commiss. of Dominion Lands to me, in which is praised ther industry and frugality. From the political point of view, I think, that it is only favourable for Canada, that the majority of emigrants, the Ruthenians (an old culturell but depressed nation) have since many centuries no own political existence, and therefore no national ambitions, and will become so sooner than other nations true Canadian patriots. By hitherto results, accomplished exclusively through my own efforts and means, it is sufficiently proved, I think, that if I had devoted all my time and influence to this question, and if I were firmly and steadily backed by the Canad. Governm. the results would be magnificent. The Canad. Northwest would be soon filled up with settlers of different Austrian nations. Indeed the question of settlement of the Northwest would be simply solved.

What is to be done?

The answer is: To *organise* the movement of emigrants. To organise it in this country, en route and in Canada in a system, under one direction. The Department knows by experience, that the inducing of settlers from any country, for inst. from England is very expensive and has a limited success. The secret of success is: To secure emigrants in the country, where emigration arises spontaneously and where emigration lies in the interest of the people themselves. Such a country is at present Austria, where there have gone from the province Galicia only, last year about 30,000 for Brazil. That is a number, in which one could select (with means in hand) the best element for settlers.

The emigration in any direction cannot arise and be maintained to any extent, unless there is here, in this country, one man of authority, in whom the emigrants have confidence and our Government authorities too; who gives the bail (the surety), that the emigrants will find in the country he recommends, good conditions of living. This I have done till now for Canada. The seaport-agents could write hundreds of letters, and hundreds of pamphlets from abroad, could be distributed, among the people, but such things are so discredited here, that nobody believes even the assurances of agents, that there are *free* homesteads in Canada, unless the people hear from me the confirmation of this fact.

The first step of organization of emigration to Canada is therefore, that I devote myself wholly to this work, and I am ready to do this, if the Department will acknowledge all points of organization, proposed here as good and expedient,—will help me to accomplish this scheme of emigration, and so will me enable to take upon me the responsibility for welfare of emigrants.

The Government in this country have decided to give me the concession for the *sole* emigration agency in this country (Galicia) under certain restrictions, for which will have the agency under my direction practically the monopoly for issuing of tickets for railways and ocean passage to the emigrants. The emigrants will be gathered in parties and conducted by experienced travellers to embarkation. For the real services by embarkation will be the selected seaport-agents paid through me.

So would the diverting of emigrants in the direction of Canada, and the care of their safety in the way entirely rest upon me. But in Canada itself there must be made some preparation in order to handle the emigration of say thousend families yearly, which I plan.

The sentence "The contented settler is the best immigration agent", has grown to a maxim in Canada. I shall add: One disappointed settler, one who made a failure, destroys to intending emigrants the good impression of a hundred contented settlers. If we are about to maintain a numerous immigration, we must take care, that there are no disappointed settlers. At present, that is not so. The people, who are not specially instructed by me, are booked by agents simply to Winnipeg. They understand neither english nor german, they cannot come therefore to an understanding with government officers and become victims of jews and some depraved individuals from this Country. They are even told, that there are no free homesteads in Canada, and the private agents endeavour to sell to emigrants private lands under hard conditions (terms), and often unfit for cultivation. After being led from one place to another similar the people gain the conviction, that Canada in general is a bad land. Discouraged returned even some of such people home, being unable to find free lands, suitable for cultivation. I consider it to be unfortunate for the development of emigration movement that one party is settled at Brokenhead, from where many settlers fled, having made a failure and have abandoned their homesteads in previous years. This fact is known here, by people returned from Manitoba. A failure is also, that 20 families were induced by Roman Catholic priests to buy from them lands at the high price of 6$ pro acre. Besides of that, that the dwarf farms of 10 till 30 acres in Manitoba must be regarded as a economical nonsens, will in this country very displease the fact that the *Greec* Catholic settlers have in Manitoba fallen in moral and material dependence from Roman Catholic priests. The difference between these two religions is very great, even the liturgy is not in latin language as with Roman Catholic, but in a Slav. language, and in this country are these two Churches in a state of struggle.

So is the assurance in your esteemed of August 12th 1896 file 21103 Immigr. "that our people will have no difficulty in securing suitable locations on their arrival" unfortunately refuted by real facts unknown to the Department.

Here experience teaches, what to do:

I) There must be established in Winnipeg one intelligence officer more, who speaks not only english and german but also the Slavic languages. This officer must be known in this country as a honest, reliable man, that the people have confidence in him. I could recommend the proper gentleman for this post.

II) Let not every settler be an explorer, who loses time in searching for land, and makes unevitably the observation, that all the best land, which pleases him is already taken up, (With thousands of emigrants what a disorder it would be!), but let me make preparation, that every settler has in advance a destined place for settlement. You cannot imagine in Canada, what effect on intending emigrants it would have, if I could here in this country, not only give them the railway tickets for such and such station, but also the number of his homestead. This feeling of surety, that he does not go in blindly, but that he has a destined homestead, selected by his friends, means to the intending settler far more, than all other considerations. The land, which in this way will organise the immigration will beat all other competitors for settlers.

To this aim, I beg:

a). To reserve for a short time certain townships, selected direct by me, or by settlers, or by government authorities, that I may direct to them *parties* of emigrants as nucleus of further colonies. As first step in this matter, I repeat my asking: To reserve the Townships in Lake Dauphin Dstr. 26, Rges 21, 22, and 23 W. of the 1st Mer. for my settlers at least till August 1897.

b). I beg further: To decide in principle and assure me that every application to the Dep. of Inter. or to the Land Comm. signed here, before me, by intending settlers, asking that their friends or specially commissions of old settlers from here, may be authorized to make entries in advance on their behalf—will be *favourably received.* Please to send me kindly to this aim a proper formular of such application and instruction as to this.

c). I beg: To decide in principle and assure me, that every request to the Minister of Interior of emigrants from here, for granting them a *whole* year's grace, (after paying of fee) in which to perfect their entries may be favourably received. There is sufficient cause for such a request, because all emigrants, which I shall send, are agriculturists, and owners of small holdings, which they must have ample time to sell advantageously. The settlement of previous point *b*) will give them surety, that selling here, they have already a new home in Canada. A proper formular for this request, please to add to the response to me.

d). I beg to give me full information as to the particulars of the advances of money from persons or Companies under the provisions of the Dominion Lands Act, upon the security of the homesteads.

The credit is extremely important for such settlers, as the majority of ours, I think, it is no real drawback, when the settler is not rich. A rich settler will be dissatisfied with conditions, which can give to him the Northwest at present, the poorer will be content and satisfied. But there must be created the conditions of the development of his husbandry. I intend to give foundation to that, by calling into life among our settlers "The Cooperative Farming Companies."

The sphere of the action of such Companies will be:

1. To give credit to a proper extent to single settler.
2. Common purchase (en gros) of articles needed on farms, and

common sale of agricultural products, building of own elevators, mills, establishing of creameries, cheese factories, and in general acting as do the agricultural syndicates in France, or similar institutions in Germany and with us.

3. To promote the immigration with aim, to get in arriving settlers, purchasers of agricultural products (seed, cattle, etc.) in this way, that the Co-operative Companies, for months before the arrival of a settler, but after making entry on his behalf (see *b*, *c*) will with his concord and on his account plough for him 10 acres of land. A settler, who comes to his homestead in spring, will in such way have ploughed 10 acres of land already before winter. Every agriculturist knows, what a advantage this is. This ensures a crop in the first year to the settler. He gains a year by this measure.

To get cheap credit on easy terms, it is necessary, that the Cooper. Companies can offer to the creditors the absolute safety of their capitals. To this aim, will the members, who belong to one Company be security one for another (*solidarische Haftung*), and the engagements of the Companies will be secured as mortgage on the homesteads of members, up to 600$ each. (The farmers from this country pay their debts very promptly and exactly.)

So I beg: To decide in principle, that any person or Company, who shall be willing to lend money to the planned "Cooper. Farming Co's." will always receive the authority to lend upon the security of the homesteads of members by mediation of the Company.

I am so free, to beg to send me kindly the "Dominion Statutes" in order to outline the project of the mentioned Coop. Co's. in accordance to Dominion Laws.

To gain the financial basis to accomplishment of the plan of this immigration on large scale, I think, it would be simplest, when the Canad. Government would determine the number of souls, in accordance to his means (say 4-5,000 souls) and to lay aside the sum, which was in previous years spent for immigration of such a number (in hands of agents, for printing of pamphlets, useless here, and so on). This sum were to be paid in instalments in my hands, as the immigration from this country will proceed. And it would be better spent, than in previous years, because besides of insuring a great immigration of industrious agriculturists, it would be partly used by me to the welfare and success of settlers, these future Canadian citizens.

In any case an advance of 500–600 £ would be necessary for preparatory expenses and to enable me to abandon my present position, as a professor of agriculture in services of Austrian Government, and enter in the services of the Canadian Government as an organisator of Austrian colonies in the Northwest.

The bonusses were to be paid to my hands, and I would pay the seaport-agents for their real services.[64]

Lyndewode Pereira, Assistant Secretary of the Department of the Interior, acknowledged Dr. Oleskow's letter, assuring him that it would

[64] 2. Oles./31442, September 6, 1896: Dr. J. Oleskow, Lemberg, Austria, to the Department of the Interior, Ottawa.

be brought to the Minister's attention: "As soon as opportunity presents itself, your proposals will be brought forward, and will, I am to assure you, receive the consideration which their undoubted importance demands."[65] On the Deputy Minister's instructions, the Assistant Secretary forwarded a copy of Dr. Oleskow's letter to D. McNicoll, Passenger Traffic Manager of the C.P.R. Company at Montreal, for his information and opinion, and in due course received a reply. McNicoll had very important information for Burgess: S. W. Coryn, the European Representative of the C.P.R. Company, had again visited the continent, met Professor Oleskow, and talked at length with him. The observant and cautiously critical Coryn had considerably modified his opinion about Dr. Oleskow in his second report, McNicoll informed the Deputy Minister:

With reference to the Assistant Secretary's letter, 21103 Imm. of 28th. September, in reply to mine of the 18th. September with regard to Mr. Oleskow.

I read with much interest the correspondence, and had been hoping since its receipt on my return from the west, to have had an opportunity of going to Ottawa and talking the subject over with you. As I am not likely to be there, however, for a week or two, I think I had better write you, and I trust that you will not look upon my letter as in any way interfering. I thought that you might like to have the information that I have on the subject.

As I think I mentioned in a previous letter, our European representative has been travelling through Austria, and met Prof. Oleskow and had a long conversation with him. I think that there is but little doubt but what Spiro & Co. the ticket agents at Hamburg, have been paying Prof. Oleskow a sub-agent's commission, the Professor not having a concession from his Government, and being therefore unable to ticket himself.

Mr. Coryn, our representative, advises me that Professor Oleskow this past season has done an immense amount of travelling, has answered innumerable letters, and spent considerable money in the interest of immigration, and the sub-agent's commission which he may have received from Spiro & Co. would not in any way compensate him, or reward him for practically giving up his profession. The Professor has applied to the Austrian Government for a concession, which would enable him to do the ticketing direct, without the assistance of Spiro & Co., and the indications look good for him obtaining same.

Karlsberg, a semi-partner of Spiro & Co., I understand, undertook to take a party of Galicians out, independent of Oleskow, possibly with the idea on the part of the steamship agents of seeing whether they could not handle this business independent of the Professor, and I believe the police interfered and the party were turned over to Oleskow, and came out under his charge.

[65]2. Oles., October 1, 1896: Lyndwode Pereira, Ottawa, to Dr. J. Oleskow, Lemberg, Austria.

Spiro & Co. are agents of very high standing, and have it in their power to influence business time and again to Canada or from Canada, and having paid money out to Oleskow, I do not think that they should have their understood and promised commission deducted.

Undoubtedly the Professor has done good work. He is not a wealthy man who can afford to indulge in expensive philanthropy, and I think that he is a man who should be strongly encouraged. Of course as a paid agent temporary or permanent of the Canadian Government, it is hard to say how the Austrian Government may then look upon him, but at the present time he evidently meets with favour, and should they grant him the concession he applies for, it would indicate that they approve of his action.

There seems to be two elements in his section of the country at the present time, one Polish and the other Galician, which are pulling against each other on the emigration feature, the Poles pulling for Brazil and the others, with Oleskow at their head, pulling for Canada.

I thought that I had better give you this information, my opinion being that we should not make enemies of either Spiro or Oleskow, and that it would help you very largely in settling the question as to the payments.

Of course, as you know, there was no commission on the rail transportation of these passengers this season, from the fact that we carried them free.[66]

The generally high opinion about Dr. Oleskow's abilities as an organizer and as a person possessing the confidence of the peasant masses was shared by the President of the Ruthenian National Association in the United States, John Glowa, and the publishers of *Svoboda*, the only Ukrainian-language newspaper on the American continent. In a letter to the Department of the Interior, referring to advertisements in *Svoboda* to encourage emigration of Ukrainians in the United States to Canada, Glowa stated:

According to your wish expressed in the letter of the 17th of June File 29567 (advertising) was inserted several times in our paper "Liberty," our people of Pennsylvania and other regions of the United States hesitate to go there until a more numerous and organized emigration of their countrymen from the Austrian Province, Galicia, will settle; among whom our people are willing to settle.

In consideration thereof, it might be of great importance in this cause, if the Department of the Interior could come to an agreement with Prof. Josef Oleskow, Dr., 11A Golembia, Lemberg, Austria. The latter gentleman has directed this year the immigration of our people and upon whom depends the initiative of the immigration as well as the continual emigration of our people from Austria.[67]

The Department was aware of the facts pointed out by Mr. Glowa,

[66]2. Oles./31809, October 14, 1896: D. McNicoll, Montreal, to A. M. Burgess, Ottawa.

[67]2. Oles., Original on File 29597, October 24, 1896: John Glowa, President, Ruthenian National Association, Excelsior, Pennsylvania, to the Secretary, Department of the Interior, Ottawa.

and it endeavoured to come to some working arrangement with Dr. Oleskow, heeding those of his suggestions that it was felt could be fulfilled. One of Oleskow's greatest concerns, as we have seen, was the appointment of a Ukrainian-speaking interpreter in Winnipeg to assist new arrivals who spoke neither English or German. Apparently he was not yet aware that such an appointment had already been contemplated, for he wrote again, on October 7, 1896, to the Department of the Interior on this matter:

. . . In my last memorial concerning the immigration matters, I have urged the necessity of appointment of an intelligence officer in Winnipeg, who speaks the languages of different Slavic nations from Austria (Ruthenian, polish, bohemian, moravian, slovakian, etc.). As there is in Winnipeg already a certain Mr. Charles Genik who would willingly occupy this position, and whom I know as an intelligent, reliable gentleman, so I please, to appoint him in Winnipeg as intelligence officer for Slavic nations. . . .[68]

The Department's reply assured the professor that his advice had been followed: "I am directed to inform you [wrote the Secretary of the Department] that in accordance with the suggestion you were kind enough to make to the Department in your letter of the 7th ultimo, authority has been sent to the Commissioner of Dominion Lands at Winnipeg to employ Mr. Charles Genik, as occasion may require, in the capacity of an interpreter."[69]

Oleskow's letter of September 6, 1896, containing a detailed outline of his suggestions and plans for the emigration to Canada, was referred to the High Commissioner in London with instructions to contact Dr. Oleskow and to try to clarify some of the uncertain points. Sir Donald Smith's secretary wrote to Dr. Oleskow on October 7, referring to the points still in question:

. . . In the course of the correspondence you have mentioned that you are prepared to take this position but you do not say precisely upon what terms as regards (*a*) salary, and (*b*) allowances to cover all expenses, you would be prepared to undertake the appointment. It is true you speak of £500 or £600, but it is not quite clear whether you intend this to include salary, and all expenses; and it is necessary before the matter can be properly considered, that the Government should know precisely what you would want for salary, and what amount in addition would be necessary to cover the other expenses.[70]

[68]2. Oles./31858, October 7, 1896: Dr. J. Oleskow, Lemberg, Austria, to the Department of the Interior, Ottawa.

[69]2. Oles., November 17, 1896: Lyndwode Pereira, Ottawa, to Dr. J. Oleskow, Lemberg, Austria.

[70]2. Oles./32288, October 7, 1896: J. G. Colmer, London, to Dr. J. Oleskow, Lemberg, Austria.

After a month's delay, Dr. Oleskow answered the High Commissioner's office at length:

I saw, from what you have written in your letter of October 7th, that the circumstances in this country are too strange to you as to be right understood. Against my information of the state of things here you oppose your informations and I fear there is difficult to come to one agreement in this way. This is the reason I have delayed the reply.

There are to face two cases. Either I shall have the concession, or I shall have it not. It is already decided by the Provincial Government (Galicia, Bukowina) to give to me the concession with the aim to control and regulate the emigration movement, as the Provincial Government are convinced that the emigration here could hardly be suppressed. But the final decision depends from the Central Government in Vienna, and it is possible that the Central Government shall have another opinion.

Should however the Central Government partake the opinion of the Provincial Government, then having the unlimited confidence of the peasantry in this country, and the support of the Government, I shall *ipso facto* wholly control the movement. The emigrants will go there where I shall them advise to go. No one shall directly deal with seaport agents. What you write of impossibility "to delegate such extensive power to any one person," that is to leave to me all arrangements of emigration—will be without subject (*gegenstandslos*).

If I do not receive the concession I cannot deal with emigration matters in the matter of business. But I cannot too let the people go to Canada (that is to country which I have recommended) being unable to protect them en route, to secure them the future and to organize the emigration movement. So remains to me either to stop the movement, or secure me the influence on the emigration—without concession. With means in hand there could be yet secured a regular influx of desirable settlers (agriculturists with some means) in number mentioned in my last letter. Then I would act in character of the Vice-president of the "Ruthenian Commercial Geographical Society," a humane society which remained till now inactive, but which I shall make active if necessary.[71]

Dr. Oleskow suggested further that the Canadian Government should discontinue the payment of bonuses to seaport-agents for emigrants from Galicia and Bukowina, as it was he who controlled the flow of emigrants, and not the seaport-agents. The bonus could be used for the benefit of the emigrants themselves:

As to the particulars you wish to have explained, I may say that I require no salary at all. The £500 to £600 I consider necessary for preparatory expenses and this sum must be risked in any case before I have the concession even. It should be readily understood that without such a bail of confidence from the Canadian Government, I cannot have the spirit to

[71]2. Oles./32535, November 9, 1896: Dr. J. Oleskow, Lemberg, Austria, to the High Commissioner for Canada, London.

abandon my present position and to devote me wholly to the work which so lightly can be misinterpreted. In this sum is included the deposit of money as assurance for the concession, but should this sum exceed £100, I must the surplus require from the Canadian Government. The rest would be used for discreet expenses, as the holding up the opinion of the press in favour of Canada, etc. the pamphlets for correspondents in all parts of country, etc. and for office. The bonuses will be used in favour of emigrants.

Sir Donald Smith kept the European Traffic Agent of the C.P.R. Company in London, Archer Baker, informed about the exchange of correspondence with Dr. Oleskow, and invited his opinion on the situation. Baker, on returning copies of the correspondence to Smith, made the following observations:

I return herewith copies of correspondence which has passed between yourself and Professor Oleskow in connection with his proposed scheme for the promotion of Emigration from Galicia.

It seems to me that at the outset it is absolutely necessary to know whether the Professor can procure from the Imperial Government at Vienna the licence he requires. The second paragraph of his letter would point to uncertainty on his part in regard thereto.

There can be no doubt that if he can, as he says, get the support of the Government and has the unlimited confidence of the peasantry in his country, he ought to be able to accomplish a good deal, but as you have pointed out to him, he will be powerless unless he obtains an Agency for one of the various S.S. Companies doing business on the Continent and it is doubtful to me whether any of the S.S. Lines interested in Continental business will delegate to the Professor the full authority which he desires and which he seems to think necessary to the accomplishment of his scheme.

In this connection, however, it might be worth while to see what the three St. Lawrence Lines would do. If they could be convinced of the Professor's ability to secure a large emigration from his country they might (I do not say could) be able to put him in the position which he desires.

You know as well as I do the system under which Continental emigration is worked and that even if the S.S. Companies were willing to do so it is not allowed by the Government regulations in the various countries that the Inland Agents should issue the Railway ticket.

He must issue a through ticket or contract from the place of departure to destination, this ticket being dealt with at the port of embarkation in the respective manners prescribed by the various S.S. Companies.

The Professor indicates in his letter that his continuing to direct emigration to Canada would not altogether depend upon his obtaining the licence in question.

If he obtains the concession he wants then of course he would be entitled to the bonus and Railway Commission as the S.S. Companies' Agent. If he does not, however, I think it would be well to consider whether a direct arrangement could not be made between himself and the Government which would enable him to obtain the $5 bonus.

Provided that you are satisfied of the Professor's ability to carry out his ideas is there any reason why the Government should not appoint him as Emigration Commissioner for Austria-Hungary and pay to him the bonus he asks on such passengers as he can satisfy the Government he has been instrumental in securing.

He sweeps away a good many difficulties when he tells you that he requires no salary.

In short I would recommend that the Government *should satisfy themselves as to his bona fides* in such a way as may seem best to them and that this being done the amount asked by him, say $2,500, would not be unwisely expended. This is what I would do myself were I dealing with the matter but I think he should make it more clear why he requires this money before he gets the concession; it does not seem to me that £400 would pay him to relinquish his position as Professor with no permanent contract behind it.

How would it be to say to him that provided he gets the concession from the Government enabling him to deal with passenger business from his territory and obtains the S.S. Agencies which of course we all would endeavour to get for him, the Government should then put up the money necessary as security in connection with his licence and give him £400 ($2,000) to enable him to commence the work in which he seems to take so much interest.

I think it would be a good idea that he should be induced to come over here and discuss the matter with you. I myself should be very pleased to meet him and give any assistance in my power.[72]

While this correspondence was being carried on, Dr. Oleskow became thoroughly discouraged with the continuous procrastination of the Department of the Interior regarding a decision on his proposals. On December 9, 1896, he wrote to the Department of the Interior in Ottawa expressing his feelings on this question:

. . . If there are among these immigrants many of an undesirable sort, namely such without necessary means, so is this a consequence of the behaviour of the Canadian Government against my endeavours to organise and regulate a movement of settlers with necessary means to start with. Such a work requires material sacrifice, and is entirely different from the agitation of seaport-agents which in this country can only awake a rush of paupers to Canada. I commenced the work on my means in spring 1896: in due sense by sending out an organised party of settlers of desirable sort under conduct of my brother, and I have patronised several consequent small parties. But as I saw, that the Government does not take any serious steps towards securing of such a emigration and has shown no signs of will to support my efforts, so I have retired in a more passive position and remain in this position till now.[73]

[72]2. Oles./32536, November 24, 1896: Archer Baker, London, to the High Commissioner for Canada, London.

[73]2. Oles./32880, December 9, 1896: Dr. J. Oleskow, Lemberg, Austria, to the Secretary, Department of the Interior, Ottawa.

The reference Dr. Oleskow makes in this letter to undesirable immigrants refers to the complaint voiced by the Department of the Interior about the arrival in Canada late in the season of a considerable number of Ruthenian immigrants with very limited, or even no means, so that they immediately became a burden to the Canadian Government which had to support them. These destitute immigrants had been sent by steamship agents, without Dr. Oleskow's consent or approval: ". . . I regard the sending of emigrants without sufficient means as quite pernicious even for the people themselves. But you cannot expect, that the seaport agents, which of course have only their material interests in sight, should reckon with this." The year 1896 drew to a close with Oleskow still awaiting a decision on his proposals, submitted in September to the Department of the Interior in Ottawa.

In his yearly report to the Commissioner of Dominion Lands in Winnipeg, dated October 31, 1896, Hugo Carstens, the German Interpreter summed up the year's progress with regard to the new settlers:

Ruthenians

As already mentioned a large increase has been in the number of Ruthenians; in former years only a few of these people came here and there, and only one colony had been formed of them in Alberta.

This large increase is I think chiefly due to the efforts of Dr. Oleskow, who visited this country in the interests of immigration during the months of August and September, 1895, when I had the pleasure of accompanying him on an extended tour through Manitoba, North-West and British Columbia.

On his return Dr. Oleskow published in a pamphlet, issued by a society for promotion of knowledge, a full report of his trip and impressions, recommending to his people the Canadian North-west as a suitable country for Ruthenians to settle in, and also sought to turn the stream of emigration from its former course to Brazil, to Manitoba and the Canadian West.

In this effort he has been very successful as upward of one hundred families, in all 630 persons, have settled, principally in Manitoba and Alberta during the past season.[74]

V

The Provincial Government of Galicia decided to grant to a person known for his integrity a concession to establish an emigration agency in order to protect the emigrating peasantry from exploitation by the numerous agents preying on the ignorance and credulity of the peasants. Dr. Oleskow was recommended as the most suitable person to head

[74]Canada, Department of the Interior, *Annual Report*, 1896, Part IV, Report No. 7, October 31, 1896, 118–122. Hugo Carstens, Dominion Immigration Office, Winnipeg, to H. H. Smith, Winnipeg.

such an agency. But the final decision rested with the Imperial Government in Vienna, and Dr. Oleskow awaited the outcome of the debate on emigration which would decide whether such a concession would be granted or not.

In 1895 the Polish Members of the *Reichsrath* from Galicia, Dr. Pininski, Dr. Rutowski, Dr. Wielowieyski, and others, moved that:

> The High [Upper] House pass a resolution requesting: (*a*) the permanent Criminal Commission to prepare and present an Act making it a criminal offence to offer any inducement to emigrate or to carry on an unauthorized emigration business: (*b*) Inviting the Government to pass an Act enlarging and making more stringent the Criminal Law against usury making special provision for protection of the agricultural population of the Kingdom of Galicia: (*c*) inviting the Government to draft a law for the organization of emigration business: sections (*a*) and (*b*) to be submitted to the Permanent Criminal Law Commissions and section (*c*) to the Political Economy Commission.[75]

A Special Criminal Commission was formed in 1896 and was sitting when the matter of granting the concession to Dr. Oleskow to conduct an Emigration Agency came up in the Provincial Diet and was referred to Vienna for a decision. Dr. Oleskow was known to most of the Members of Parliament from Galicia, including the former governor of the province, Count Casimir Badeni, who had become the Prime Minister of Austro-Hungary in 1895. There was no doubt as to the integrity of Dr. Oleskow, but the reference made to him as "promoter of a scheme of emigration of Galician Farmers to Canada" by the British Ambassador to the Prime Minister of Austria aroused apprehension. The Prime Minister, alerted by this enquiry, instructed the Austro-Hungarian Consul in Montreal to find out what encouragement was given to Dr. Oleskow by the Canadian Government to induce agriculturists from Galicia to emigrate to Canada.

Eduard Schultze, the Austro-Hungarian Consul, wrote to Deputy Minister A. M. Burgess, November 13, 1896, requesting information about inducements that the Canadian Government had offered to settlers:

> . . . I am led to believe that the aforesaid Professor Oleskow has received some special encouragement from your good government for the formation of an Austro-Hungarian colony in the North West and I therefore have the

[75]15. Laws/63708, Austria, Parliament, Session XI, 1895, 1351 der Beilagen zu den stenogr. Protokollen des Abgeordnetenhauses. "Antrag der Abgeorneten Pininski, Rutowski, Wielowieyski und Genossen." The quoted translation was prepared at the time by the Office of the High Commissioner for Canada in London.

honor to also request you to kindly inform me what inducements have been made to the settlers. I might add that my Government although acknowledging the inability to stem the tide of immigration feels the humane duty to direct the tide to such countries whose social-political and climatic conditions are the most favourable for intending settlers. For this reason my Government had to discourage and practically prohibit immigration to Brazil and is now asking me for a full report about Canada.[76]

The Department of the Interior answered the Consul's queries about the settlers, but omitted any reference to the one which referred to Dr. Oleskow. The Consul thanked him for the reply and repeated his request for information about encouragement extended to Dr. Oleskow personally:

. . . However one point of my letter of the 13th ult. No. 396/96 is left unanswered, namely if Professor Oleskow has received any special encouragement from your Government perhaps in the shape of advances for stock and implements and I therefore have the honor to request possible further information on this point.[77]

There are no records on file to show whether or not Schultze's request was complied with. His insistence on information concerning Dr. Oleskow would suggest, however, that the Austrian authorities desired to find out whether Dr. Oleskow had committed any infringement of emigration laws, such as that of offering inducement to emigration of Austrian subjects. The Bill on that subject was going through the readings in the Vienna Parliament at the time of the request, and it became law on January 21, 1897. The law read as follows:

LAW OF JANUARY 21, 1897 relating to criminal regulations in reference to emigration matters.

With the consent of both Houses of the *Reichsrath*, I order as follows:

Para. 1

Anyone carrying on, or taking part in, an emigration business without official permission, or who, having the permission, acts contrary to existing regulations, is liable to imprisonment of from eight days to six months. The district courts have the jurisdiction for trial and punishment.

Para. 2

Anyone who misleads other persons by false statements or by other deception inducing them to emigrate is liable to imprisonment with hard labour for from six months to two years, to which may be added a fine up to 2000 florins.

[76]2. Oles./32217, November 13, 1896: Eduard Schultze, Imperial Royal Austro-Hungarian Consul, Montreal, to A. M. Burgess, Ottawa.

[77]2. Oles./32866, December 23, 1896: Eduard Schultze, Montreal, to the Secretary, Department of the Interior, Ottawa.

In aggravating circumstances the imprisonment may be increased to three years and the fine to 4000 florins.

Para. 3

The Ministers of Justice and of the Interior are to have charge of the execution of the Law.

Vienna, January 21, 1897.

FRANCIS JOSEPH, m.p.

BADENI m.p.

GLEISPACH m.p.[78]

Apparently Dr. Oleskow was not violating the law, however, because when spring approached he resumed his emigration activities, assisting and advising those who desired to emigrate to Canada. He also found a better response in Ottawa because the new Minister of the Interior was personally interested in fostering immigration, and especially in settling Manitoba and the Northwest with experienced farmers. Clifford Sifton invited his former colleague in the Manitoba Cabinet, James A. Smart, to take over the post of Deputy Minister. Like Sifton, Smart was a lawyer. He possessed great administrative abilities and was keenly interested in the promotion of immigration. With the view of intensifying and properly organizing the settlement of the West, a new office, that of Commissioner of Immigration, was created and W. F. McCreary, who was Mayor of Winnipeg in 1897, was put in charge. Unfortunately, Dr. Oleskow had not met any of these officers personally, and they were not familiar with the plans and activities, that he had presented to the Department of the Interior for approval. Thus it took several months before they familiarized themselves with the role that Oleskow played in the initiation of the emigration of Ukrainian farmers to Canada.

Oleskow followed the events in Canada keenly, and, encouraged by the new trend in immigration policy, decided to renew his own activities. He wrote to the Department of the Interior on March 24, 1897, informing the Government that he was preparing to send more settlers:

It is known, that the immigration of Austrian settlers inaugurated in a correct manner by a organised party in spring 1896 (which only included more enlightened people and in possession of sufficient means to start with a husbandry) degenerated in late autumn and in winter in a rush of paupers, devoid of all means. The reason of this was the reserve with which the Canadian Government authorities met all my informations and suggestions in this matter. So I remained passiv, and the seaport-agents had a free field for their action. As the people who have something to loose dare not risk

[78]15. Laws/647133, "No. 27: Gesetz vom 21. Jaenner 1897, womit straftrechtliche Bestimmungen in Bezug auf das Betreiben der Auswanderungsgeschaefte erlassen werden."

to go to Canada without consulting me so could Canada not have any other immigration, as the immigration of unenlightened paupers.

In this spring I am directing once more a party of emigrants of better sort to Canada. I let them book by Spiro & Co. for Arcadia, the Hansa Line steamer, leaving Hamburg on April 10th. It were very instructive for the Canadian Government to compare this time the emigrants booked by Spiro with those by other agents.[79]

The S.S. *Arcadia*, a slow old boat with steam engines and sails, brought 648 Ukrainian settlers to Quebec. It was followed closely by the S.S. *Scotia* with 435 settlers who landed at Halifax.

The Deputy Minister, in a letter to the High Commissioner in London, noted especially the difference between Oleskow's settlers and those who were induced by steamship agents to emigrate:

I am in receipt of your letter of the 29th ultimo [April, 1896], addressed to Mr. Sifton, enclosing one from Mr. Colmer with reference to the party of Galician immigrants who sailed by the "Arcadia". With regard to these people I would point out that the party referred to have been sent out by Professor Oleskow who has been doing some work amongst the better classes in Austro-Hungary. He advised the Department that these immigrants were possessed of means and had decided before leaving Austria to go to the Dauphin District where they have friends residing.

A party arrived in Halifax by the "Scotia" on the 30th ultimo numbering between four and five hundred. On enquiry I learned that these immigrants were sent out by Steamship Agents and were possessed of no means whatever and were of a much inferior class to those amongst whom Professor Oleskow is working. It seems to me necessary that some action should be taken to prevent the sending out of pauper immigrants, and in this connection I would suggest, if it is at all possible, that you should communicate with some of the continental agents and find out who is responsible for forwarding these people. It is quite possible that Professor Oleskow could give you some information on the subject.[80]

The High Commissioner then promised the Deputy Minister that he would be in touch with Dr. Oleskow about the settlers sent out by agents:

It gives me pleasure to acknowledge your letter of the 4th instant, having reference to Galicians sent out by Professor Oleskow, and to other immigrants represented as having been forwarded by Steamship Agents, these latter being of a much inferior class to those whom Professor Oleskow was instrumental in procuring. Communication will at once be had with Professor Oleskow on the subject. He appears to have been doing a very

[79]2. Oles./36560, March 3, 1897: Dr. J. Oleskow, Lemberg, Austria, to the Department of the Interior, Ottawa.

[80]2. Oles./37076, May 4, 1897: James A. Smart, Deputy Minister, Department of the Interior, Ottawa, to Sir Donald A. Smith, High Commissioner for Canada, London.

good work in sending excellent class of settlers to Canada, and I think we cannot do wrong in encouraging him to continue in the same course. In my former communications to your Department you will see I have had occasion to speak very favourably of Professor Oleskow.[81]

Sir Donald Smith does not appear to have had clear and definite opinions with regard to emigration matters. He was easily swayed, even by rumours, as is reflected in his correspondence with Ottawa. In April, 1897, when on a visit to Canada, he received a communication from J. G. Colmer in London to the effect that: "A gentleman from the North West whom I saw yesterday [April 13] spoke to me in very high terms of the Galician settlers. He told me that even if they arrived without money they seem to make good progress, and that he knows of many cases among them where in the course of a couple of years they have been able to place themselves in comfortable circumstances. . . ."[82] Sir Donald then forwarded this letter to the Minister of the Interior, adding a comment that clearly revealed his support for the Galician immigration: "We must set ourselves in one way or another to get as many good immigrants as possible from the Continent of Europe, and none I believe have turned out better in our North West than the Galician settlers."[83] A few months later, a Mr. Seeman called on Smith in London and expressed an adverse opinion about the Galician settlers. The High Commissioner was anxious at that time to dissociate himself from the suspicion that he was in favour of them, a fact which is evident in this letter which he wrote to Clifford Sifton:

My dear Sifton—

I had an interview a few days ago with Mr. R. Seeman, whose name will be known to you as the owner of land along the line of the Manitoba and North Western Railway.

Among other matters Mr. Seeman mentioned the question of the emigration of the Galicians, which as a general rule he does not approve of, not considering the people to be suitable for Western Canada.

He stated that an impression prevails in your Department that I am responsible for most of this emigration that has taken place. I informed Mr. Seeman, however, that while, in the first instance, I encouraged Professor Oleskow to show his bona fides and his capacity for carrying out his suggestions, which resulted in the emigration of many desirable families, I have had nothing directly to do with the large parties which have left Galicia during the present year, and even at the end of 1896, under the auspices of various Continental Steam Agents.

[81]2. Oles./38345, May 22, 1897: Sir Donald A. Smith, London, to James A. Smart, Ottawa.

[82]2. Oles./37076, April 24, 1897: J. G. Colmer, London, to Sir Donald A. Smith, Hudson's Bay Co., Montreal.

[83]2. Oles./37076, April 24, 1897: Sir Donald A. Smith, Hudson's Bay Co., Montreal, to Hon. Clifford Sifton, Ottawa.

You will be aware that in the course of the last year, I have written a good many letters to your Department on the subject, urging the necessity of regulating this movement, and in this connection I would refer to a letter I wrote Mr. Smart on the subject on May 25th last, in which allusion was also made to my letters to the Department of the 20th and 25th of November 1897. [This date should be "1896."]

It will be within your knowledge also that a letter was sent to me from the Department, under date 15th June, 1897, in which it was stated that the matter of Professor Oleskow's work, and the subject generally of Galician emigrants, was under your consideration, and that you hoped to be able to communicate something to me on the subject at an early date.

You will be aware that I have for some time been waiting to hear from you with regard to your views on the matter of Continental emigration generally, and that until I do so it is difficult for me to move energetically in the matter.

Yours faithfully

(Signed) DONALD A. SMITH.[84]

The letter addressed to the Minister was answered in his absence by James A. Smart, who tended to disagree strongly with Smith on the matter of the Galician settlers:

I am in receipt of your letter of the 11th instant, addressed to Mr. Sifton, and in his absence desire to reply with reference to Galician Immigration.

I am not personally acquainted with Mr. Seeman but have seen his name figuring in connection with immigration work for sometime. I do not know what ground he has for making the statements he has made with reference to the Galicians, but I presume that they are simply an expression of his personal opinion. I may say, however, that many persons I have met would appear to be disposed to differ with Mr. Seeman as to the encouragement of Galician immigration or the adaptability of these people as settlers for our North Western country. There is no doubt that many of the Galicians who were sent out to Canada had little or no means, and in a few instances did not seem inclined to help themselves to make a start, as would be expected of persons going into a new country, but, from what I can gather, I feel perfectly satisfied that the great bulk of these people are a desirable class and in a few years will show by results that they are equal to almost any nationality as successful agriculturists.

I do not know that, even if the impression does prevail that you have personally taken an interest in the immigration of these people, there is any reason for you to regret having done so, because the Galicians have, so far at all events, shewn themselves to be possessed of qualities which will ultimately make successful settlers. We are not, therefore, disposed to discourage further immigration but rather to put forth increased effort to assist it by reasonable endeavour. I am inclined to think Prof. Oleskow ought to be shewn that his work has been appreciated, because so far as I am aware he has sent only those of the better class to this country.

I will ask Mr. Schultze, the Consul General for Austria, to kindly forward

84. Gal./45531, October 11, 1897: Sir Donald A. Smith, London, to Clifford Sifton, Ottawa.

you a copy of his report on his visit to the various Galician Colonies in the North West. Some two or three months ago he visited all the colonies in Manitoba and the North West Territories with the intention of making a report on the condition in which he found these settlers and also as to their prospects, and I think a report from him would probably give as fair a statement of the condition of affairs as it would be possible to get, because he visited practically every little settlement and could form a better opinion of the conditions of these people than any person who might casually pass through the country.

In the meantime I am sending you a copy of a letter received from Mr. Schultze, which will show you that his views do not coincide with those of Mr. Seeman on the subject of Galician immigration.[85]

Deputy Minister Smart's opinion of the suitability of Ukrainian agriculturists as settlers in the Canadian Northwest was shared by the Minister as well. The arrival of thousands of Ukrainian settlers during the 1897 season convinced him of Dr. Oleskow's ability to organize, and although not all of the settlers who came to Canada were sent directly by him, Oleskow was undoubtedly responsible for initiating the movement. For two years Dr. Oleskow fostered emigration at his own expense, and, as the C.P.R. Company's representative, S. W. Coryn, who visited Dr. Oleskow in 1896, pointed out, the professor had done an immense amount of travelling, had answered innumerable letters, and spent considerable of his own money in the interest of immigration.

It took some time for the Minister to become acquainted with the details of the immigration problems of his department, but when the positions were filled and the new machine began to function, the Minister was ready to act. He held consultations with his senior officers, went to Winnipeg, and after a lengthy conference held on November 26 at the Manitoba Hotel with W. F. McCreary, the Commissioner wired the Deputy Minister in Ottawa to contact Professor Oleskow: "The Minister wishes you to cable Professor Oleskow, Lemberg, to come out with a view of assuming control of Galician immigration. Say his expenses will be borne by the Government."[86] The Deputy Minister then cabled, in the name of the Minister, the High Commissioner in London as follows: "Wire Professor Oleskow, Lemberg, asking if convenient to come to Ottawa to arrange Galician immigration. His expenses will be paid."[87]

Lord Strathcona complied with the instructions received from Ottawa. Dr. Oleskow, as his letters intimate, was determined, despite frustrating

[85]3. Gal., October 30, 1897: James A. Smart, Ottawa, to Sir Donald A. Smith, London.

[86]2. Oles., Telegram, November 27, 1897: William F. McCreary, Commissioner of Immigration, Winnipeg, to James A. Smart, Ottawa.

[87]2. Oles./46792, Cable, Clifford Sifton, Ottawa, to the High Commissioner for Canada, London.

delays on the part of the Government in answering his proposals and requests, to continue to promote emigration to Canada. He wrote to the Commissioner of Immigration in Winnipeg, on October 17, once again pointing out that the Government could spare itself much difficulty with new immigrants if he were given more authority and aid:

> From the reports which I receive from more intelligent settlers in each colony, I am quite well informed as to the state of things concerning the situation of Galician settlers in Canada. Indeed, to command such an immigration as is gone this year, required a great deal of energy, activity and ability from the Canadian Government authorities. On the other side, I cannot help to tell, that all the troubles you had, could be dispensed with, if the Canadian Government had listened to my suggestions. Instead of paupers, Canada could have immigrants with sufficient means to start on a farm, who would be here by me instructed as to the manner of cultivating lands in the Northwest as to the danger which awaits them (prairie fires, etc.) as to the laws of your country, as to this, how they should arrange their journey and to spend in seaports a great deal of money unnecessary, what they could bring with them to Canada.[88]

Oleskow also expressed fear that the emigration to Canada would diminish considerably in 1898, if no positive action on the part of the Canadian Government were taken:

> Don't rely upon the seaport agents, they do not speak the language of emigrants, have no confidence with the people, and cannot make no propaganda in favour of Canada, because they would there arrested upon arrival. In 1897 they turned to their account the situation which I created, and their whole merit was that this or other of them had the chance, that his address fell in the hand of intending emigrants. It is now the highest term to refresh the propaganda in favour of Canada through new pamphlets, through papers in the Gazettes and above all through speeches on public meetings among the agricultural classes, unless with the emigration in this direction ceases at all. It were a pity if the work, such successfully commenced by me, should collapse. I will give in next year several thousands of settlers, if the Government will decide to follow my suggestion, which I have the honour to lay before them.
>
> Your project, to send two representatives from Canada with the aim to give instructions to intending emigrants, does not reckon with the actual state of things here. The emissars of a foreign country acting in favour of that country, would be quite sure arrested at their first step. And besides that, I can, what is wanted, far better fulfill as the emissars could do.
>
> Only the journey of Rever. Dmytrow's could be of some use, as far as he would be not suspected to be a representative of Canada.
>
> On the other side, your arrangement to prepare a book, shewing all the Galician settlers, where they are located, and to send this book to me, is, indeed of great value for regulating of emigration. This book should be supplemented every month. In this book should noted to locality too in

[88]2. Oles./46814, October 17, 1897: Dr. J. Oleskow, Lemberg, Austria, to W. F. McCreary, Winnipeg.

Galician [Ukrainian] from which the emigrant came, I would here reprint the list of country's, and send by mail to the localities, from which the emigrants originate. You live too far from here in order to conceive that the centre of gravity of emigration from Galicia in Galicia lies, and that with the agreement of two factors, f.i. of Government respective you with me; the third factor f.i. the seaport agents are of no consequence.

You fear, they can the people avert to any other country? Well, I give to each party a versed conductor and there is no peril. If I had to give any important suggestion in this question, there would be that. The Canadian Government should have in Hamburg a asyl (an emigration house) for their emigrants. We should have our own steamship agency in Hamburg, connected with Canadian Emigration house. . . .

The Commissioner of Immigration sent a copy of Dr. Oleskow's letter to the Deputy Minister in Ottawa and informed him at the same time about the discussion he had had with the Minister in Winnipeg:

In discussing the question of Galician immigration for next year with the Minister at the Manitoba Hotel yesterday [November 26, 1897], I produced a copy of a letter received by me from Dr. Joseph Oleskow, another copy of which I beg to enclose.

I also told the Minister that I had discussed the matter with Mr. L. A. Hamilton of the C.P.R., and that he desired a conference between the three of us on the subject, as it is most important at the present time to see that the emigration from that country next year is somewhat filtered out before the people are allowed to start.

There are many questions to be considered. In the first place, none but those accustomed to farming, and physically strong should be sent. In the second place, they should have some means, $50 at least, or have friends who would be willing to assist them. Then again, they should not leave Hamburg without their baggage. It is invariably the case that when a man leaves his baggage behind him, he does not receive it until several months after, or, if it does arrive, it is in badly broken condition, with large extra charges against it.

Now it seems that by the law in Germany, they are only allowed to carry 50 lbs., of baggage. These people should be instructed what kind of baggage to take. They bring over here many useless articles, such as pieces of wood hewn out for a child's cradle, and this in itself would weigh almost 50 lbs., and there are many other articles of this sort which are absolutely useless, at least, the same things could be got here, or things to serve the same purpose, for a nominal sum. Then again, we find large bags of bread laying here at the station with very heavy charges against them.

All these matters, and many others of this kind could be discussed.

I suggested to the Minister that we should either bring out Professor Oleskow, or send Mr. Genik, or some other man, to Austria. He adopted the former course, consequently at his request I sent you the telegram as hereunder—

"Minister wishes you to cable Professor Oleskow, Lemberg to come out with a view of assuming control of Galician immigration. Say his expenses will be borne by Government."

I understand that Professor Oleskow is at present engaged as a teacher in a school at Lemberg, at a salary of 1600 gulden, which would be about $600 of our money. In your cable I think it would be well to state that you would give an engagement, if necessary, for one or two years, at an advance on this price, and he could come out, discuss the matter, and return at once, either accompanied by some farmer from Austria who had succeeded here, or he could go alone. He has, of course, considerable influence with the Austrian Government, has a fair knowledge of the English language, and is well educated, and I think would be able to do good work.

Please keep me advised as to what you are doing in this matter.[89]

Dr. Oleskow, in answer to the wire sent by Lord Strathcona informed him that it would be impossible for him to proceed to Ottawa but that, if necessary, he could come to London to discuss immigration problems. He also mailed the High Commissioner a more detailed explanation of the situation that prevented him from coming to Canada, and proposed a date for a meeting in London:

I wired to-day answering to the telegram of the High Commissioner and cablegram of the Minister of the Interior, that I am not able to proceed to Ottawa, as this would involve my absence here during four weeks. This being irreconcilable with my present position as Professor in one of the Government schools, I must quit my position, a leave of absence shall I not obtain.

But I could easily arrange to leave to London for a couple of days, between December 18th and January (1898) 10th. There I could meet with representatives of the Canadian Government and perhaps of the C.P.R. and give suggestion, how to prevent the imminent danger of ceasing the Galician immigration in the future, and secure a better sort of emigrant than in 1897. In Galicia they are preparing one emigration to Russia on the one side, and a great action with aid of the Government in favour of parcellation of properties of gentry among the peasants on the other.

You have to destine the term when I have to leave for London, I expect my expenses will be paid.[90]

The High Commissioner forwarded Dr. Oleskow's letter to Clifford Sifton for advice on how to proceed: "This telegram [Dr. Oleskow's reply] was repeated to you, and I asked whether I should see Professor Oleskow, discuss the (matter) with him and report to you. No further communication has, however, reached me on the subject up to the time of writing. You will find enclosed, a copy of the letter from Professor Oleskow which reached me this morning [December 4, 1897]."[91] Lord Strathcona's letter was written on December 4, and the Deputy Minister

[89]2. Oles./46814, November 27, 1897: W. F. McCreary, Winnipeg, to James A. Smart, Ottawa.

[90]2. Oles./47927, November 30, 1897: Dr. J. Oleskow, Lemberg, Austria, to the Secretary, Office of the High Commissioner for Canada, London.

[91]2. Oles./47927, December 4, 1897: Lord Strathcona, London, to Clifford Sifton, Ottawa.

sent his letter with instructions to the High Commissioner on December 8—the two letters crossed each other in the mails.

Mr. Smart's letter to Lord Strathcona urged that Oleskow be brought to London and that any necessary arrangements with regard to encouraging emigration to Canada be made with the professor at that time:

My Lord—

Referring to your cable of the 30th ultimo in which you state that Professor Oleskow telegraphs that he cannot come to Ottawa, but will go to London, I beg to say that I cabled you yesterday to have him proceed to London, for the purpose of arranging with you regarding his work among the Austro-Hungarians. I would understand from the Professor's letter that he is desirous of engaging more actively than ever in the interests of Canadian Immigration among Austro-Hungarians who are likely to emigrate, and the Minister directs me to say that he will be glad to have you make any definite arrangement with him in this connection you may wish—including his full services if necessary—so as to secure his services until the end of next summer, or at least until the end of the immigration season, or upon any other basis that may occur to you as being advisable. It would be well for you to cable the expenses incurred in securing his services for the year, and the Minister will be pleased to reply immediately advising you as to the matter.[92]

Dr. Oleskow was therefore to arrive in London for consultations during the first week of the new year. After two years of waiting he would at last receive a reply to the propositions which T. Mayne Daly had promised to consider in October of 1895.

To sum up, the year 1897 showed an unprecedented increase in Ukrainian emigration to Canada. The Dominion Government Immigration Agent in Montreal, John Hoolahan, in his yearly report to the Department of the Interior on December 31, 1897, outlined the progress that had been made over the year and struck a note of optimism about the future for both the settlers and their new country:

GALICIAN IMMIGRANTS

Several parties of Galician immigrants to the number of some six thousand persons, passed through the city during the year en route for Manitoba and the North West. Each party was accompanied by a special Government interpreter, who furnished a means of communication between these people, the public, and the railway officials. They were from the Austro-Hungarian monarchy, almost all farmers. They appeared to have money with them, and there is every reason to expect that they will prove a desirable addition to the population of the country of their adoption.[93]

[92]2. Oles./47308, December 8, 1897: James A. Smart, Ottawa, to Lord Strathcona, London.

[93]Canada, Department of the Interior, *Annual Report*, 1897, Part IV, Report No. 4, 145: John Hoolahan, Montreal.

Chapter Four

THE YEARS 1898–1900

I

DURING THE YEARS 1898–1900, Dr. Oleskow acted as the Canadian immigration representative for Austrian Galicia. To protect his position as an Austrian civil servant, his appointment was not announced officially. The granting of the concession to establish an Emigration Agency, for which the Emigrants' Aid Committee and Dr. Oleskow applied, was still under consideration, but there were indications that the influential "Polish Club" of the Chamber of Deputies in Vienna, consisting of about one hundred members, mostly landed gentry from Galicia, would oppose any relaxation of existing emigration restrictions; the tendency was rather to stiffen emigration regulations. In 1895, thirty-nine Polish Members of the Chamber of Deputies submitted a petition to constitute a Criminal Commission which would be charged with the preparation of a bill that would make it a criminal offence to offer inducement to emigration. The Commission was actually formed, and the bill presented and passed in 1896.

The landlords opposed emigration because it threatened to diminish the peasant labour reserve and thereby to cause an increase in wages for agricultural labour. On the other hand, the landlords were unable to prevent individuals from emigrating because Austrian law guaranteed personal liberty to its subjects. If a person wished to emigrate, he was free to do so, provided that he procured a legal passport from the district governor and fulfilled the military service requirements—but procuring a passport was not always a simple matter. In spite of the numerous restrictions and police supervision, many sub-agents of steamship companies invaded villages and towns in various disguises—as peddlars and journeymen, for example—to reap what Dr. Oleskow, the "Prosvita" Society, and other welfare committees had sown.

In preparation for their departure, prospective emigrants had to sell their possessions in order to obtain the money necessary for their passage and for a start in the new land. Prospective buyers, usually their own fellow-villagers, seldom had the necessary ready cash to purchase their neighbours' belongings. They were therefore obliged to borrow money, usually from the local Jewish innkeeper or the Polish lord of the manor, paying interest rates reported to be as high as 250 per cent in some cases. As cash was difficult to obtain, land was sold for a fraction of its actual value. Dr. Oleskow described the terrible situation that existed among the Ukrainian peasants as the seaport-agents encouraged the craze to emigrate to Brazil: "People driven to despair by misery, sell their land here and there no longer for half of its value, but for a third or even a quarter of what it is worth in order to gain at least hope of getting to that Parana in Brazil. . . ."[1]

The temptation to take advantage of the ignorance of the peasant-emigrants was irresistible. Their limitless patience, their reluctance to complain, and their inability to protect themselves all played into the hands of their exploiters. Constant warnings voiced by Dr. Oleskow, the Emigrants' Aid Committee, and the societies that supported him reached many, but when an agent appeared at the villagers' door and assured them that he could arrange everything for them, they were quick to place their trust in him. The ingenuity employed by these agents to swindle the villagers was matched only by the hopeless credulity of the victims. The high degree of illiteracy among the peasants was taken advantage of by the agents who cheated them in every way, even by selling them worthless steamship advertising cards in lieu of steamship tickets.

The illiteracy of the peasant-farmers was not of their own making or desire. The teaching of village children was prevented for a long time by restrictions adopted by the nobility, who formed the majority of the Members of the Provincial Diet, and who objected to the education of the peasant-farmer class. Even the Dean of Cracow University, who was also a Member of the Provincial Diet, voiced the opinion that public schools in rural districts should be limited to four grades rather than to six, and that peasant children should be taught only to read and write. In this way, he claimed, the task of the teachers would be considerably eased.

[1]Dr. Josef Oleskow, *O emigratsii*/"About Emigration" (Lviw: "Publications of the Michael Kachkowskyi Society," No. 241, 1895), 1.

Michal Bobrzynski, a Polish historian, Vice-president of the Provincial Board of Education for eleven years, and Governor of Galicia during 1908–1911, was equally opposed to the education of village children because, he held, education would awaken in them aspirations to rise above the social station into which they had been born. He cautioned the teachers in rural schools to remember that the education of peasant children should be kept at a minimum to prevent them from qualifying for entrance to the *Gymnasium*, and so from gaining a higher education.[2]

Overcharging for steamship tickets was an accepted practice of the sub-agents. Double price was usually demanded—and received—by the agents for tickets for young men of military age because of the "risks involved," in that the young men had to be smuggled out of the country. Emigrants were cheated in the exchange of money, overcharged on prices for meals on the journey, sometimes compelled to remain for weeks in seaports "waiting for the boat" and to pay exorbitant prices for their board and lodging. Even on arrival in Canada, where special care was taken to protect the immigrants from exploitation, they did not escape being cheated. In May, 1897, the Dominion Immigration Officer in Montreal reported that "exhorbitant prices [were] charged Galician immigrants for food on landing from steamers 'Scotia' and 'Arcadia'."[3] A year later, W. F. McCreary, Commissioner of Immigration in Winnipeg, complained to the Superintendent of Immigration in Ottawa about the exploitation of new arrivals and suggested ways to prevent it:

> I have the Secretary's letter of the 13th instant [April 13, 1898], advising me that 931 Galicians had left Hamburg per S.S. "Bulgaria" for Halifax on the 10th destined for the West, and I am to-day despatching my Galician interpreter, Mr. Genik, to Montreal, for the purpose of meeting them.
>
> I think you are already aware of the difficulties we have at this point with such large number as this. They get off here without having any destination in view, and are immediately met by a lot of Poles, Jews, and even Canadians, who try to take all the money they have from them for useless goods, and persuade them to give every resistance possible to our efforts to locate them [i.e., to settle them on homesteads]. This became so serious last spring that we had to call in the Police, and if possible, I want to avoid this condition of affairs this year, I believe by taking these people off at Montreal and keeping them in the sheds for one or two days, ascertaining what money

[2]*Encyclopedia of Ukraine* (Paris-New York: Shevchenko Scientific Society, 1955), II, 141. See also Henry J. T. Dutkiewicz, "Main Aspects of the Polish Peasant Immigration to North America from Austrian Poland Between the Years 1863 and 1910." (Master's thesis, University of Ottawa, 1958). Dutkiewicz quotes Alexander Swiętochowski, *Historia Chłopów Polskich w Zarysie* (Lwów, Poznan, 1928).

[3]2. Oles., May, 1897: A note without date, marked "See File 37210 Imm."

they have and also where they have friends, if any, that they can then be put into the cars with their destination clearly before them, and given tickets to the point to which they decide to go. . . .[4]

Much advantage was taken of the immigrants during the long journey from their native villages to their destination in Canada. A vivid description of some of the abuses is presented in a report submitted to the United States Immigration Commission by an American woman investigator who, posing as an immigrant from Galicia, made the journey from Cracow to New York. She described her experiences at the border station at Myslowitz, Galicia, as follows:

Food and provisions are to be had only at the canteen. The keeper was intoxicated the evening of our arrival, as were the watchman and porters during the entire time. Though the price list on the walls contained fruits and other desirable foods, the stock at the canteen consisted mostly of drinks, beer and various wines and whiskies in small bottles. There were also tobaccos, some bread and sausage. The travelers ate such provisions as they still had from home. Sunday morning we tried to get either some coffee or tea. The canteen keeper was either still or again drunk and there was nothing to be had of him but liquors, and, moreover, his manner was most objectionable. The officers who again appeared to relieve newly arrived emigrants of their tickets declined to release us to go to the adjoining depot for some breakfast. Their reply was that there was a canteen to supply all an emigrant's needs. Finally, after 9 o'clock, the wife of the canteen keeper appeared and she consented to get us some coffee. By ordering it immediately we were able to have some dinner at noon. This consisted of soup, boiled beef, potato salad, and bread. The price charged us was 25 cents. Later a higher price was asked of others. This, of course, was exorbitant and far beyond the means of the average emigrant. Besides, not less than the full meal could be had, and this must be ordered a half day in advance. Prices, too, were constantly wavering, and getting correct change was all mere luck. German, Russian, and Polish were all spoken in the canteen, and German, Russian and Austrian money all accepted. Ignorance of some one of these languages or coins was affected in order to defraud. A Russian laid a half mark on the counter and ordered a glass of beer. He drank it and waited for change. Receiving none, he asked for it. The waiter pretended he had been given only the price of the beer. In other instances he argued that the coin given him had not the supposed value, or returned too little change. More often he insisted on explaining in a language unknown to the emigrant. There was constant argument at the bar about overcharges, and watching the transactions there for some three hours I saw that most of the complaints were well founded. In a few instances where the emigrant insisted and was about to prove his point beyond dispute he was turned over to the drunken canteen keeper, who talked so loudly and so without reason that no argument availed.

It was not only difficult, but practically impossible to get any food, while

[4]4 Gal./58001, April 22, 1898: W. F. McCreary, Commissioner of Immigration, Winnipeg, to Frank Pedley, Superintendent of Immigration, Department of the Interior, Ottawa.

beer and whiskey tempted the hungry and the thirsty. Needless to say many of the emigrants drank more or less, not only in Myslowitz but later in the train. Liquor was the one thing with which a person could supply himself for the journey.[5]

Finally, after a twenty-hour journey in an overcrowded train, in which even standing room was at a premium, the emigrants arrived at the seaport. There they went through various examinations:

. . . A physician looked into each one's eyes. Another officer measured each one, noted his description and birthplace. Another officer put the usual questions as to age, kind of employment, address of friends in America and Europe, and amount of money at hand. To him were also given such papers as each had to indicate that his passage was paid or partly paid. . . .

When the officers returned, the names of all those, having engaged in the steerage of the ——— were called off and an interpreter was told to inform us that the steerage passengers had gone on board just before noon; that we had either to wait ten days for the steamer ——— or pay the difference, 30 marks, and go third class on the ———. This news caused great dismay to all. Waiting meant not only weariness and loss of time, but considerable expense for board and lodging. The payment of an additional 30 marks was impossible for some, for others it meant the paying out of their last coin, and how was one to get to his destination? What could he show in money in America, or how telegraph his friends there? And there was no longer time to get money from home by telegraph. Many of those from Eastern Galicia and Slavonia had already had to make unexpected additional payments along the way after thinking that their transportation to New York had all been paid to the agent at home. . . .

The exploitation, which started the very day the prospective emigrants decided to sell their land to procure money for the journey, did not cease even after their arrival in Canada, and it left most of them practically destitute.

It was Dr. Oleskow's constant endeavour to protect emigrants against such losses in order that they should not arrive in Canada penniless. The Austrian Government passed laws aimed at the protection of emigrants, but these measures proved inadequate. Private individuals and welfare societies lacked the necessary funds to make their assistance effective, for such assistance involved travelling across the province, answering innumerable letters, helping in the sale of land, aiding in the purchase of steamship tickets directly from agents in Hamburg, and often conducting groups of emigrants to seaports, in some cases even to Canada. They had to compete with steamship companies' sub-agents, supplied with ample funds which they used to further their aims, including even the bribing of government officials. The case of two agents, Jacob Klausner and Simon Herz, who operated at the border station

[5]Edith Abbott, *Immigration: Select Documents and Case Records* (Chicago: University of Chicago Press, 1925), 88–89.

at Oswiecim, became notorious. During the 1890's these unscrupulous men charged exorbitant prices for steamship tickets, cheated the emigrants in the exchange of their money, staged fake "doctor's" examinations (with fees charged), and perpetrated many other betrayals of trust. They worked with impunity, having bribed the customs guard at Oswiecim, the police, the station master, and even the district governor himself.[6] Dr. Oleskow hoped to be able to counteract these and other abuses and to protect the emigrating peasants by obtaining a concession to establish an emigration agency which would if not end then at least curtail the malpractices of the sub-agents. Dr. Oleskow, the "Ruthenian Popular Society" ("Prosvita"), and the Emigrants' Aid Committee hoped to obtain funds from the Canadian Government to run such an agency, since the whole emigration movement they sponsored was directed towards Canada as the ideal country for the settlement of Ukrainian agriculturists.

Because he was unable to obtain a leave of absence from his post, Dr. Oleskow suggested meeting the Canadian High Commissioner, Lord Strathcona, in London. He arrived in London at the beginning of January, 1898, and during his stay he had a series of conferences with the High Commissioner, leading to the formulation of a preliminary agreement subject to approval by the Minister of the Interior in Ottawa. On January 4, after the first conference with Dr. Oleskow, Lord Strathcona cabled Clifford Sifton in Ottawa regarding a decision on expenses:

> Oleskow here says £500 to £600 necessary on engagement for preliminary expenses, printing pamphlets, advertising, distribution, to cover all other expenses. Prepared accept commission equal half that now paid shipping agents for adults, stipulated arrangements for three years, as must give up present position, but willing accept for one year on understanding that if work satisfactory will continue for another and third year on same terms, less preliminary expenses. Probable emigration each year 5,000 souls or about 3,000 adults. Think agents might perhaps be induced accept reduced commission, but in any case can we accept Oleskow's terms which he wishes regarded confidential? Cable today. Oleskow waiting reply, leaving to-morrow night.[7]

The Minister cabled the following reply to Lord Strathcona: "Oleskow's offer accepted. You should endeavour to arrange for reduction in Continental steamship bonuses. Present rate considered high. Am writing.—SIFTON."[8]

[6]Leopold Caro, *Wychodztwo Polskie*/"Polish Emigration" (Kraków, 1911).

[7]2. Oles./48728, Cable, January 4, 1898: Lord Strathcona, London, to Clifford Sifton, Ottawa.

[8]2. Oles./48727, Cable, January 6, 1898: Clifford Sifton, Ottawa, to Lord Strathcona, London.

The High Commissioner mailed a copy of the memorandum and preliminary agreement that he had concluded with Dr. Oleskow to the Minister. The agreement ran as follows:

Professor Oleskow is prepared to take up the work of promoting the emigration of desirable and suitable persons of the Agricultural classes, from Galicia to Canada, on the following terms:

1. That for the first year, sum of from £500 to £600 be paid to him, on his engagement, to cover preliminary expenses. This amount will include the cost of the preparation of a pamphlet, its printing and distribution; any advertising that may be necessary; and the assistance he may have to engage for carrying on the work in Galicia.

2. Professor Oleskow will be willing to accept in addition, one half the Commission that would, in ordinary circumstances, be paid to the Steamship Agents, upon any emigrants secured by him to settle in Manitoba or the North West Territories. Professor Oleskow understands that the commission is only payable upon adults of 18 years or over—no commission being payable upon children under the age of 18. This additional payment is to cover Prof. Oleskow's remuneration, the expenses of the guides he proposes to send with each party of emigrants, and in fact all other expenses in connection with the work, including the travelling expenses of Professor Oleskow to and from Canada, a journey which he thinks, in order to carry on the work properly, he will have to make once or twice a year.

3. Professor Oleskow stipulates that the arrangement should be made for a period of at least three years. At the same time, he is willing to make it for this year only—with the understanding that it will be continued, if the Government are satisfied with the work, for 1899, and again at the end of that year, for 1900, on the same conditions.

4. In the event of the arrangement being continued for a second and for a third year, it is understood that the remuneration to cover all the expenses of Professor Oleskow in connection with the emigration to Canada, will be the $2.50 bonus upon each adult whom he may send out—it being understood that the payment of the £500 to £600 for preliminary expenses is only to be made for the present year.

5. This memorandum will be submitted to the Canadian Government, and the matter will also be brought before the Steamship Agents to see whether an arrangement can be made on the lines suggested. Professor Oleskow stipulates that the Steamship Agents should not be made aware of any arrangements that may be made between the Government and himself.[9]

The Minister of the Interior ratified the agreement between Dr. Oleskow and the Canadian Government. In acknowledging the receipt of the copy of the memorandum, the Deputy Minister, Jas. A. Smart, suggested to the High Commissioner that "with respect to the continental bonuses I think that this is a matter that you will have to arrange in the

92. Oles./50442, January 4, 1898: Memorandum of the High Commissioner for Canada, London, on a conversation with Dr. Oleskow. Enclosed in the High Commissioner's letter of January 8, 1898, to Clifford Sifton, Ottawa.

way that will seem to you to be the best. There is no doubt that the bonuses heretofore paid, that is upon each ticket, is exceedingly high and ought to be reduced but I quite agree with your suggestion that it would not be well, even if we were to have to pay it for some time yet, to antagonize the various steamship agents who are possibly more encouraged by this year's operations than of those of any previous year. . . ."[10]

A few days after his return to Galicia, Dr. Oleskow wrote to the High Commissioner in London, probably on consultation with his committee, requesting that the High Commissioner "take favourable consideration" and forward to Ottawa the request that full bonus be allowed for all settlers from Galicia, regardless of whether their transportation was arranged by him or booked directly through steamship companies. Having no concession to sell steamship tickets, he lacked control over the emigrating individuals. They might have decided to go to Canada after having listened to this talk, or having read his articles in the press, or his booklets in their village library, but they might have bought steamship tickets through the agents without notifying or informing Dr. Oleskow about it. Dr. Oleskow's letter was answered by J. G. Colmer, who pointed out to him, in the High Commissioner's name, that it would be desirable if he would abide by the original agreement:

> The High Commissioner would prefer not to depart from this arrangement. In fact, it was upon this understanding that the Government agreed to your propositions. The same arrangement would apply to any emigrants booked direct by the Hamburg-American steamship Co. on the same understanding—that they were emigrating as the direct result of your influence and efforts.
>
> Of course, if you become a Steamship Agent, there is no necessity for the Government to have any special arrangement with you at all. In those circumstances you would be entitled to the ordinary bonus paid to such agents, which, of course, is subject to alteration from time to time; but it would hardly be possible in these circumstances for the Government to make you an advance for preliminary expenses.[11]

Dr. Oleskow thought that if he went personally to Hamburg and discussed the matter with the Steamship Companies' Agents, he might settle the matter of bonus payments satisfactorily: " . . . I beg to delay any negotiation with the Steamship Agents in Hamburg, concerning

[10]2. Oles./50442, January 25, 1898: James A. Smart, Deputy Minister, Department of the Interior, Ottawa, to Lord Strathcona, London.

[11]2. Oles./54721, January 21, 1898: J. G. Colmer, London, to Dr. J. Oleskow, Lemberg, Austria.

the Government bonuses, until my proposed journey to that place. I leave for Hamburg on January 28th, and will try to arrange the matter to satisfaction of all interested parties. Thence I shall make a trip to London to inform you as to result of the arrangement in Hamburg, and give some additional information as to this matter on the whole. . . ."[12] Unforeseen events prevented Dr. Oleskow from going to Hamburg on the arranged date. A "great meeting of delegates of National Ruthenian Societies" was called for February 7, which he was obliged to attend:

> . . . On February 7th, there is a great meeting of delegates of those Societies, so I cannot leave Lemberg and I beg to remit the £500 as quick as possible in the way mentioned in your letter of January 19th. There should be no indication of the Government as sender. There is no time to deal as to the amount of bonuses just now; the matter remains at present at the basis we agreed, and quoted in the memorandum. As to the emigrants, which will book themselves directly and immediately by the Steamship Companies, and for whom I claimed the whole bonus, we can agree later on.
>
> The pamphlet is already written; I wait for the money to edit it; I consider now necessary to issue a regular Gazette.[13]

The High Commissioner intended to visit the Continent during February 1898, and made arrangements to meet Dr. Oleskow and have a talk with him. Lord Strathcona informed the Minister of the Interior on February 18, 1898 of his intention: " . . . I hope to visit the Continent in the course of next week, and after doing so will write to you with my recommendations in the matter of the bonus that is being paid to continental Steamship Agents."[14] On his return from the Continent, the High Commissioner reported to the Minister the results of his interview with Dr. Oleskow, whom he met in Vienna:

> During my recent visit to the Continent I had an opportunity of seeing Professor Oleskow in Vienna. He tells me that his work has been somewhat interfered with by unfavourable reports that have been published in Austrian papers from some of the Galician settlers in Manitoba and the North West. He has, however, adopted the best means of counteracting the erroneous impressions thus created by publishing other letters of a favourable character. I told him that he should supply me with newspaper cuttings containing any important information about Canada, so that you may be advised of what is being done.
>
> Professor Oleskow added, that owing to a new law in Austria, emigration

[12]2. Oles./54721, January 20, 1898: Dr. J. Oleskow, Lemberg, to the Secretary, Office of the High Commissioner for Canada, London.

[13]2. Oles., January 29, 1898: Dr. J. Oleskow, Lemberg, to J. G. Colmer, London.

[14]2. Oles./54721, February 18, 1898: Lord Strathcona, London, to the Minister of the Interior, Ottawa.

work will be conducted under greater difficulties than it has been in the past. The Austrian Government does not favour the appointment of agents for emigration work, and the principal steamship agents in Hamburg have to conduct their business by correspondence, or surreptitiously through agents who are nominally engaged in other work, such as peddling various articles of common use throughout the country. At the same time, however, Professor Oleskow states that his application for a licence is now before the Galician Government for consideration. He adds that if he is successful it will enable him to book passengers, and to be more or less independent of the shipping agents, who now practically control the business from Hamburg. In that event he trusts to make arrangements with the Hamburg-American Steamship Company for booking the passengers direct through them. This is very important, because the German Government will not allow the Galician emigrants to enter Germany on their way to Hamburg, or other ports, unless upon a guarantee, either from the Steamship Company, or from a responsible agent, that the persons will not be allowed, in any circumstances, to become a charge upon the German community. . . .

In answer to my enquiry Professor Oleskow stated he thought as many Galicians would go to Canada this year as last, but that he believed they would be of a better quality than many of those who went out last year. He added that a proportion of those who emigrated last year were booked by Steamship Agents, who were not careful enough of the class of people who were sent out. What he, the Professor, wishes to avoid, is the booking of people who have only enough to pay for their passages—that is the smallest kind of landholders in Galicia. The classes he desires to reach are those who would have from $800 to $1000 or more after arrival in Manitoba or the North West. He states that some of the Agents have been circulating unfounded statements as to the advantages offered in Canada to emigrants, in the shape of free houses, cattle, etc. This he claims has led to the emigration of persons without much means, who have subsequently complained through the press. Professor Oleskow could not however, give the names of any agents who had given publicity to such statements.

In view of the attention the matter is attracting just now in the press, Professor Oleskow has not thought it advisable to print any special pamphlet on Canada, but is circulating in the country, and through his correspondents, Austrian newspapers which contain letters speaking favourably of the prospects of settlers in the Dominion.[152]

The publication of a pamphlet on Canada was only postponed and not abandoned, because on March 24 Dr. Oleskow wrote to the High Commissioner in London a request for illustrations to be included in a new pamphlet: " . . . I want for little book about Canada which I intend to issue, the 'cliches' (wood-cuts or other) of the characteristical and striking views of Canada. Please to select and send me them if this is possible. Please too to send me your recent books, pamphlets, maps of Canada, etc., that I may myself select from them the neces-

152. Oles./56676, March 23, 1898: Lord Strathcona, London, to Clifford Sifton, Ottawa.

sary views, if you regard it proper."[16] J. G. Colmer, the Secretary of the Office of the High Commissioner in London, reported to Ottawa that Dr. Oleskow's request had been answered: "A complete set of our illustrations are being sent to Prof. Oleskow."[17]

In a letter to the Minister of the Interior, Dr. Oleskow informed him about the formation of a co-operative loan society to enable prospective emigrants to obtain a fair price (in cash) for their land. Their fellow villagers who wished to buy the land would be able to obtain loans from the society at fair interest rates, without the need to resort to usurers. As readily available capital was scarce in Galicia, Dr. Oleskow decided to approach the High Commissioner in London with a request to interest British capital in investing in the loan society. The money invested would be fully guaranteed, he assured the Commissioner. Dr. Oleskow also suggested to the Minister that a "Superintendent of Galician Emigration" be appointed in Ottawa to deal with the Galician immigration that would soon reach considerable proportions:

> The wise decision of your Honour by agreement with me to prop the Galician immigration on the National Ruthenian organization, which, adopted under my influence the emigration to *Canada* as a point of national policy, is crowned with the best results.
>
> The number of emigrants exceeds that of 1896, and the percentage of people with sufficient means to start with a farm is greater too.
>
> The approximative item derived from the reports from the branches of the National Ruthenian organization, acting in favour of Canada, showed till April 15th 147 families of Canadian emigrants from counties: Czerniowce, Storozynce, Kocman, and Wyznica in Bukowina—and Borszczow, Brzezany, Brody, Czortkow, *Jaroslaw*, Przemysl, Sokal, Sniatyn and Zaleszczyki in Galicia. But after 15th April the movement grew considerably, diffusing upon the counties Husiatyn, Buczacz, Tarnopol and Skalat, so that in the spring season Canada will gain in sum about 3,000 immigrants.
>
> The practice in this season has shown most clearly, that in *our* emigration the successful work can be achieved only by parting of work in such manner, that the upholding of emigration movement to a distinct country is done by national organization apart from issuing of tickets and apart of all, what looks to be a business. So we choosed to leave off all booking of passengers or even enlistening of the names, number of family-members, their age, etc. because that would look businesslike, and would hurt the confidence of people in our work and in the country we recommend. Now is that confidence so strong, that in spite of greatest efforts of some seaport-agents to turn the emigration to another country, all emigration goes to Canada. As a prove I send you one letter written by Missler, steamship agent in Bremen, endeavouring to induce emigrants to Argentina and detest Canada. The same

[16]2. Oles./57142, March 24, 1898: Dr. J. Oleskow, Lemberg, to the High Commissioner for Canada, London.

[17]2. Oles./57142, March 23, 1898: J. G. Colmer, London, to the Department of the Interior, Ottawa.

agent must book *to Canada* in the end of April 300 families from Husiatyn-county, who insisted to be carried to Canada, confidential recommended by us.*

As the steamship agents do not have any influence either as to the figure of emigrants nor the more as to the decision of emigrants where to emigrate, so is the bonus paid by the Government to steamship agents an useless expense, and it were better to revoke the bonus for the steamship agents, and after paying the agreed half-bonus to me as representative of national organization of Ruthenians for sustaining of Canadian immigration, turn the other half of the bonus as assistance for poor settlers.

According to the nature of work we do in favour of Canada, its generality, we claim (the agreed) half bonus for *all* emigrants from this country, and I shall not prepare a detailed list of Canadian emigrants as this would hurt the confidence in Canada with our people, not to say that, that such a writing down of names, age etc. by the dependencies of national organization, would comprometre this organization in the eyes of our Government. The amount of Galician emigrants I reckon about 6000 in 1898. To enable the richer ones, willing to emigrate, to find purchasers of their properties I formed a Loan Association under the name: "Zaszczyta Zemli" on the Austrian law from 9 April 1873. No. 70., of whom I am Director. This Association lends money to the peasants buying farms from emigrants *upon the mortgage till half value* of their property and is in itself the most sure business as according to the above law all associates answer above to the creditors with their shares and a amount double to the share. If I succeed to find for this Association credit in England (in this country is capital exceedingly scarce), the emigration of richer peasants would rise *very* high. I write in this matter to His Lordship, the High Commissioner, begging him to endorse me in finding credit in England for our Loan Association.

I wonder how the Canadian Government will smooth all the troubles inevitable coming with the increasing emigration of masses of foreign people, whose mode of living, character, resources and possibilities are unknown to you. Your European dependencies are even more ignorant as to all these questions, as the Government authorities in Canada, because they do not come in any contact with the people at all. So I dare instantly counsel, you should early procure an official for the Department in Ottawa, an superintendent of Galician emigration, who would fill the gap between the Canadian Government and Galician Settlers. That would spare you many unnecessary expenses, unadvisable dispositions, would help the people to find themselves their way in new conditions, and accelerate the assimilation of these immigrants.

I hope your Honour will duly appreciate the importance of this matter. Even in the chosing of a proper person for this post, there would be no difficulty as there is Reverent Nestor Dmytriw, the Ruthenian priest, well acquainted with Canadian colonies, who, I guess, would willingly accept this post.

I am, etc.

*Missler is in connection with Morawetz, Hamburg, and it is probably, that he will cede those passengers to Morawetz.[18]

[18]2. Oles., May 10, 1898: Dr. Josef Oleskow, Lemberg, Austria, to Clifford Sifton, Ottawa.

Dr. Oleskow's suggestions were communicated to the High Commissioner for Canada in London by Deputy Minister Smart. He was inclined to accept some of them, and he so informed Lord Strathcona:

> I have the honor to enclose you herewith a copy of a letter received a few days ago from Professor Oleskow, of Lemberg, having reference to the Galician immigration. On referring to previous correspondence with regard to the arrangements entered into with Professor Oleskow and our subsequent correspondence with reference to the bonus paid to steamship agents, the latter of which remain in force as formerly, I am inclined to think that the bonus paid for the Galician settlers is now somewhat larger that it is possible to continue paying. You were rather inclined to the opinion that it would be very bad policy during last spring to curtail the amount of bonus paid to steamship companies as it might have a very detrimental effect on emigration from Europe, in which view the Department concurred, but it now appears from the letter which I enclose that this bonus is paid to steamship agents without regard to their influencing emigration at all. In fact their influence, if they have any, is used rather against Canada, but from the force of circumstances and the fact that the Galicians have already made some progress in Canada it seems impossible for them to turn the tide to any other country as they appear to desire to do. I think, therefore this matter ought to be taken up and dealt with in a way which would relieve the Government from having to pay such a very large bonus on account of these immigrants and I would be glad to have your opinion by cable as soon as you have given the matter consideration, especially in the light of your recent visit to Hamburg.
>
> I may add that arrangements will be made at once in the direction of having an official who will have more complete charge of the Galician immigrants. Considerable difficulty has arisen lately in placing these people in the various districts of the North West. They seem determined to decide for themselves as to where they should locate, while the Government agents are only anxious to locate them where they think they can make the best progress. You are of course aware that the Reverend Nestor Dmytrow [Dmytriw], a Ruthenian priest, is now in the employ of the Department inducing emigration from the United States to Canada, and it is thought that Professor Oleskow's suggestion in this respect may be carried into force and Dmytrow removed from the United States to look after the details of location and other interest in connection with this particular nationality.[19]

As Dr. Oleskow intimated in his letter to the Minister, he dispatched a letter to the High Commissioner for Canada in London, requesting him "to indicate the way and if possible to make preparatory steps" to obtain British capital for the loan society he headed:

> Although there is greater percentage of people with sufficient means among the emigrants this year, so please to notice, that such a desirable immigration is so long impossible on a greater scale, as there are not taken measures enabling this sort of people to leave the country. In every village find these

[19]2. Oles., Noted on 2614 Immigration, June 2, 1898: James A. Smart, Ottawa, to the High Commissioner for Canada, London.

emigrants who own only three to four acres of land, neighbours with so much cash as to buy such very small patches of land. But the peasants who own ten to twenty acres or more, and who could realise for their property, according to existing prices, several thousand florins, although very much of them are in the same grade willing to emigrate as the former, do not find cash enough with their neighbours as is necessary for buying up of their land. To remove this impediment is to inaugurate the most desirable immigration on a large scale. We have founded here a Loan Association under the name "Zaszczyta Zemli", on the Austrian law from 9 April 1873, No. 70 R.G.B. (*Gesetz ueber Erwerb- und Wirtschaftsgenossenschaften*). This association is already registered and licenced by authorities. I am acting Director of it. This association will lend money on a reasonable percentage to peasants, who wish to enlarge and round their properties, by purchasing of properties from the emigrants. So will in this country arise greater properties on which rational husbandry is possible, and at once to the emigration of richer peasants, supplied with greater means, will be given a mighty push.

According to law answer the Associates to the creditor not only with their shares, but above with an amount equal to the shares.

The Associate cannot withdraw unless after a year's notice.

The loans will be given only on mortgage in the amount not exceeding the half of value of the property of debtor. The debtors themselves submit themselves to the rigor of the Para. 3 of Austrian Notarial Law (*Notarial Gesetz*) empowering the Association to immediate execution of a debtor [i.e., the sale of his possessions at auction] who does not fulfil his engagement. So is the security of capital given by a creditor the imaginable greatest, and the Association is willing to pay to the creditors 4½ per cent or even if there were foreign capital on this per cent not obtainable even 5 per cent. In this country is the capital exceedingly scarce, and on the other side the limits of emigration would be pushed only by capital, or will have to disposition for helping the peasants to buy properties from richer peasants. In interest of development of emigration and of improving the quality of immigrants I dare to beg you to indicate the way and if possible to make preparatory steps that our Association may be supplied with English capital on the above terms. In this point lies the factor of Canadian immigration. . . .[20]

The High Commissioner did not approach financial circles in London to interest them in the investment of capital in a loan society formed in Galicia. Mr. Colmer of the High Commissioner's office informed Dr. Oleskow of this fact: "I am directed to acknowledge your letter of the 10th instant and the enclosures, all of which the High Commissioner has perused with much interest. The suggestion you make has been very carefully considered, but the High Commissioner is afraid he cannot advise you as to the best means of procuring British capital for a Company such as that in which you are interested."[21] This was a great

[20]2. Oles./60332, May 10, 1898: Dr. Josef Oleskow, Lemberg, Austria, to Lord Strathcona, London.

[21]2. Oles./60322, May 20, 1898: J. G. Colmer, London, to Dr. J. Oleskow, Lemberg, Austria.

disappointment to Dr. Oleskow and to the associate members of the loan society. With the very limited capital at their disposal only a very small number of loans could be made.

Another important question interested Dr. Oleskow, that of bonuses paid to steamship agents. The Minister was inclined to agree with Dr. Oleskow that the payment of bonuses to steamship agents for emigrants from Galicia was a waste of money, because the agents were by no means responsible for the emigration of prospective settlers from that country. He therefore instructed the Deputy Minister to send the following cable to London: "Referring to my letter second instant Minister thinks well to withdraw all bonuses to steamship agents at Hamburg until further arrangements can be made."[22] The Deputy Minister also informed the High Commissioner in London that the services of Father Dmytriw had been obtained: "Father Dmytrow has now been engaged permanently to look after these people and we will have less difficulty in settling them than heretofore as no doubt he will exercise a strong influence over them and be able to show them that it is to their own interest to follow the suggestions of the Government in the matter of location."[23] On receipt of the cable from the Deputy Minister, the High Commissioner informed the steamship agents about the decision of the Department of the Interior to discontinue paying bonuses for immigrants from Galicia. He then advised the Minister of his actions:

> Instructions had been issued to the Steamship companies and to the Steamship Agents, telling them that from the date of the issue of our circular, no further commissions will be paid on Galician emigrants. At the same time I have given instructions that the country of origin of other emigrants on whom bonuses are claimed must be shewn on the forms, and every care taken to prevent Galician emigrants being included under any other designation. . . .[24]

For several months there was no communication to the High Commissioner's office from Dr. Oleskow. Lord Strathcona, wondering about the cause of the professor's silence, instructed J. G. Colmer to enquire from the Superintendent of Immigration in Ottawa whether the Department of the Interior had received any correspondence from him: "We have heard nothing from this gentleman for many months past. It may be that he has communicated direct with the Department of the Interior."[25] A few days after this communication, the High Commis-

[22]2. Oles., June 18, 1898: James A. Smart, Ottawa, to Lord Strathcona, London.

[23]*Ibid.*

[24]2. Oles./60332, July 15, 1898; Lord Strathcona, London, to Clifford Sifton, Ottawa.

[25]2. Oles./69594, November 10. 1898: The High Commissioner for Canada, London, to Clifford Sifton, Ottawa.

sioner received the explanation of the prolonged silence from Dr. Oleskow himself:

In consequence of the anti-Jewish uproar, was during this year proclaimed upon Galicia, an ecceptional state (*ein Ausnahmszustand*). Many constitutional rights were suspended, among them the secrecy of correspondence (*Briefgeheimnis*). By this occasion introduced the Government severe measures against all oppositional parties. In such circumstances I had not answered your letters, which I have duly received. To correspond with abroad with the suspended secrecy of correspondence was not only exceedingly dangerous for correspondents but our cause could be lost for ever.

Notwithstanding, the work went on, and had not suffered very much, thanks to the national organization and the zeal of the people devoted to me. Of course their influence upon the people desiring to leave their land was practiced through press only in general, the rest of the work being done oral through my adherents. In such circumstances it was impossible for me to prepare a list of names of those influenced by us, a work which were suspicious even in a normal state and quite impossible in an *Ausnahmszustand* ["state of emergency"]. This very work, the preparing of list, which I never undertake in future too.

The cost of the whole work amounted to £750, so that I still owe to the employed in this work throughout this country £250. I beg before all to transmit this sum £250 under the form of a check of the Credit Lyonnais to the K.K. priv. Oesterreichische Credit-Anstalt fuer Handel und Gewerbe in Wien. As a recompensation for the agreed bonusses I propose £200 (beside those of £250) a sum, which I think very modest, both in regard to the greatness of organized work here the risk and to the advantage of your country. This sum must serve me as a basis of future work too.

As for the future the system of bonuses pro person is impracticable. The notice of discontinuance of paying bonusses to the Booking Agents of the S.S. Cos. I met with satisfaction. This step was one upon which I insisted from the beginning. This money was uselessly thrown away. The determining of direction in which people emigrate must be allotted to us here, not to the S.S. agents excepting some paupers.

But now is the latest time to say me expressly which is the immigration policy of your Government for the next years. Do not they wish the Galician immigrants at all? or do they wish them but only the better class? possessed of sufficient means? For us here, there is no difficulty of diverting the stream of immigrants to another country, say for Siberia for instance. But in the other case if you wish settlers, only richer ones, then is the case far more difficult, and cannot be satisfactorily settled by paper and word alone. I had already for several times the occasion to indicate the way the only way which can lead to the aim.

I will once more submit for your inspection the relative circumstances. The emigrants from Galicia are all proprietors of small holdings; the capital which they bring with them originates from the sale of their cottage garden and field. The field in Galicia is on an average worth about £13 per acre, the cottage with garden £20. The most candidates to emigration belong to the class of peasants holding three or four acres, because they can realize from sale of their property an amount sufficient to reach America, and because they find no difficulty in disposing of such small areas of land as 3 or 4 acres among the remaining peasants of the village. The owners of 10, 20, and more acres are in the same degree as the smaller ones desirous to emigrate, because the circumstances both political and economical in which they live are very difficult. But there is in the whole village no cash necessary for buying up a property of twenty or so acres from an emigrant. This very same state of things is in every village with quite rare exceptions. For buying up a property of 3 or 4 acres there is in every village sufficient cash in possession of peasants, but not for a considerable greater property. This is the reason why the emigrants who come across the Ocean come there as paupers. They had mostly no more money than was necessary to pay their passage. If there be here in Galicia a financial institution strong enough to meet the requirements of credit to those peasants remaining in land, who wish to buy up land from emigrating richer peasants than would make the "gros" of emigrants consist of settlers with 1000, 2000 and even more.

The soil belonging to the richer peasants is always in better cultivation and so would the buyers having choice between the soil from greater farmers and that of poorer buy up the first. So must remain in land the smaller proprietors and could emigrate the greater ones. I have done this step, indispensable for a better emigration. I have founded a Company for trade with soil, we have got licence from the Government, and we have begun to act. I am the chief director of the Company with name "Zaszczyta zemli". Of course we act with very small capital and years are necessary before this Company could act on a large scale. But you should comprehend the exceedingly great importance of such an institution for emigration of *good sort* which is for every new land the nervus of life, and so for Canada. Please to communicate with His Lordship the High Commissioner the state of things, in Galicia. It is the same as in Ireland about 1840, mutatis mutandis, of course. About 1840 there was in Ireland circa 8 millions habitants who were in the very same economical position as the Galicians with Bukowina has now just about 8 millions. The present population of Ireland is less than 5 millions, the rest emigrated. This is the very moment where in Galicia a similar movement arises. The opening of free passage to Brazil has in one year drawn more than 50,000 of whom more than a third died from yellow fever. If this terrible event has not stopped the emigration, so is evidently that the emigration is indispensable.

There is some 2 or 3 millions decidedly too much in Galicia. Year after year could many thousands emigrate without any sign as there is in Galicia above the average yearly increase in population of 60,000 souls, (1880–1890). Please to contemplate now how meritorious were it against your father-land to bring together a yearly emigration of say 20,000 people of good style. To this is necessary that a powerful financial institution devotes its capital for this business. The residence of this institution should be in London. It should act on both sides, in Galicia and in Canada, in Galicia by lending money to our Company "Zaszczyta zemli" which will lend money to those buying the land from emigrants upon mortgage of both their own property and of new purchased land. As the "Zaszczyta zemli" is a Company founded on Austrian law, "Gesetz ueber Erwerbs and Wirtschaftsgenossenschaften vom 9 April 1873 . . ." and by virtue of their own statutes is entitled to act only among their own members who are all responsible with their property for engagements of the Company so is the capital lended to "Zaszczyta Zemli" absolutely sure. Who will lend money for buying land with us enters as a member to the Company. We could pay to those lending us the capital 5 to 6%. In Canada should the mentioned financial institution act through lending money to those Galician settlers who have taken up land and built a cottage but had not the sufficient capital to develop the husbandry. With permission of the Canadian Government could this loan be mortgaged on the homesteads.

This is the only way in which the question of settlement in Canada could be satisfactory solved once and for ever. And I dare to expect his Lordship will seriously consider my suggestion. As to the bonuses I think it were best to annul the personal bonuses and establish bonuses in per cent of imported capital by the emigrants.[26]

On the High Commissioner's instructions, J. G. Colmer forwarded a copy of Dr. Oleskow's letter to the Department of the Interior in Ottawa, and observed that the High Commissioner did not think it possible to form such a company as the professor suggested in his letter, but he asked the Minister for advice: ". . . The High Commissioner is afraid it will not be possible to do much in the way of forming such a Company, but he will be glad to have the views of Minister on the subject for his guidance."[27] As there are no further records on this subject, it may be assumed that Lord Strathcona's views prevailed.

The year 1898 drew to a close. With the approach of winter, the immigration movement from the continent almost ceased, and the Department of the Interior closed its books for the year. The Commissioner of Immigration in Winnipeg concluded his yearly report to the Superintendent of Immigration in Ottawa on a note of optimism:

In conclusion I may state that all things point to a new era of progress. Our scheme of immigration has now developed into a system whose operations are similar to those of a well-contrived machine, and whose object is the introduction into Canada of approved agriculturists from the best countries to fill up the yet unoccupied lands of Western Canada, and to give openings to innumerable commercial, industrial and professional employments which without an increased agricultural population could have no existence.[28]

The overwhelming majority of agriculturists referred to in the McCreary

[26]2. Oles./70728, November 17, 1898: Dr. J. Oleskow, Lemberg, Austria, to the High Commissioner for Canada, London.

[27]2. Oles./70728, December 12, 1898: J. G. Colmer, London, to the Superintendent of Immigration, Ottawa.

[28]Canada, Department of the Interior, *Annual Report*, 1898, Part II, Report No. 1, 219: W. F. McCreary, Winnipeg, to the Superintendent of Immigration, Ottawa.

report were Ukrainian settlers from Galicia and Bukowina. The Imperial and Royal Austro-Hungarian Consul in Montreal devoted a special reference to them in his report, dated December 20, 1898:

> The influx into Canada recorded last year of Austro-Hungarians, more especially Galicians and Bukowinians, has kept up at the same large proportions during the present year and it is most gratifying that all reports coming from Manitoba and the North-West Territories, where most of them go, speak uniformly laudably of their thrifty and industrious habits and show the rapid progress of the various settlements.
>
> Considering that nearly 10,000 of these people arrived in Canada during the last two years, the percentage of those who have been obliged to look for Government assistance is exceedingly small and must, in nearly all cases, be ascribed partly to the difficulty of cultivating the soil in some parts of their settlement and partly to the existing prejudice of the older settlers in some places against these people in the matter of giving them employment, as wherever they have been given a fair chance they have invariably come with great credit. Of course their foreign language, habits and dress have created this prejudice against them, but the better they become known the more their worth is found out and acknowledged. They are born farmers and readily adapt themselves to Canadian climate and habits, and more than other nationalities, have learned quickly to assimilate themselves. As proof of this, the desire of these people to have their children educated in English schools may be cited.[29]

By the beginning of 1899 there were indications that the numbers of Ukrainian immigrants from the Austrian provinces of Galicia and Bukowina would surpass the figure of the previous year. To what extent this was due to Dr. Oleskow's activities would be difficult to estimate, as the movement was now beginning to assume the aspects of a spontaneous chain reaction. But undoubtedly the movement was stimulated by Dr. Oleskow's writings in the local press, his correspondence with individuals, and the activities of the Emigration Committee, as well as of the "Prosvita" Society's representatives across the country. Of great assistance in all these activities were Dr. Oleskow's close connections with the Ukrainian Members of the Provincial Diet and of the Imperial Parliament in Vienna who opposed the large landowners' proposal for total prohibition of emigration of peasants. In his letters, Dr. Oleskow mentions Dr. Theophil Okunewskyi and Professor Alexander Barwinskyi, who frequently raised questions on emigration matters in the Provincial diet and in the House of Representatives (*Abgeordnetenhaus*) in Vienna. Professor Barwinskyi, although not always in agreement with Dr. Oleskow's views, was his senior colleague at the Teachers' Seminary at Lviw. He was a Member of the Provincial Diet after 1894,

[29]*Ibid.*, "Report of the Imperial and Royal Austro-Hungarian Consul," Eduard Schultze, Montreal, December 20, 1898, 197.

and a Member of the House of Representatives in Vienna from 1891. Professor Barwinskyi was also an active member of the "Prosvita" Society and its vice-president from 1889 to 1895. In 1917 Barwinskyi was called by Emperor Charles I to the Upper House (*Herrenhaus*), and during the short-lived West-Ukrainian Republic he was Minister of Education and Religious Affairs.[30]

Dr. Oleskow's unorthodox and in some instances even radical approaches to many questions—such as the emancipation of the Ukrainian peasant-farmers, the raising of their economic status, their independence from the big landowners, instruction in maintaining their human dignity and refusing to bend before sundry petty officials—were viewed with suspicion by the land-owning nobility. In his writings, Dr. Oleskow called upon Ukrainian peasants in Galicia to follow the American example: "There are no noblemen in America. There are no officials to whom one has to bow," he wrote, and castigated the contemporary Ukrainian "intelligentsia" who "have not succeeded in forming a healthy solid class, which would eliminate the fatal caste differences. They have partly remained peasants and slaves themselves, and partly have followed the example of the nobility in their relationship with peasants. . . . Rural intelligentsia are bringing up their children according to the same Mongol etiquette as peasant women do. Is it not true that the poor children are taught to kiss the hands of all and sundry? . . ."[31]

Despite these unorthodox ideas, Dr. Oleskow was left unmolested, even when he was quite openly praising immigration to Canada as a solution for the land-hungry peasants who wished to better their lot. He had excellent ideas on how best to assist the emigrating peasants and tried to put these into operation, but circumstances and the reluctance of the Canadian authorities of that time to create precedents frustrated most of his plans. The costs of the emigration activity conducted by Dr. Oleskow during 1895–1897 were borne mostly by himself, as the Canadian officials who visited him at that time observed. Only after Clifford Sifton became acquainted with Dr. Oleskow's activities in 1898 was he reimbursed for his expenditures.

The movement of emigrants from Galicia during 1899 started in the early spring. In February the Commissioner of Immigration in Winnipeg, W. F. McCreary, wired to Ottawa that "32 Galicians arrived in one day" without warning having been given to him.[32] C. W. Badgley of the Department of the Interior reported in his memorandum of February

[30] *Encyclopedia of Ukraine*, II, 93. [31] Dr. J. Oleskow, *O emigratsii*, 12.

[32] 5. Gal./75732, Telegram, February 27, 1899: W. F. McCreary, Winnipeg, to Frank Pedley, Ottawa.

28, 1899, that "four Hamburg-America Liners will land in Halifax in April and May. Passengers will be mostly Galicians and Hungarians."[33] On March 23, 1899, Dr. Oleskow wrote to the High Commissioner's Office in London:

> The immigration movement in direction to Canada is in no way smaller than in previous year, and I think to be right in saying, that in the whole the quantity of immigrants is improving.
>
> As the balance of my accounts takes up a (great) deal of time in Ottawa, I am obliged to beg his Lordship, the High Commissioner for a advance of £200 to cover the outstanding debts I owe to people employed in this work.[34]

In response to this request, the Minister of the Interior instructed the High Commissioner in London to pay Dr. Oleskow £250.[35] When transmitting the money to Dr. Oleskow, J. G. Colmer informed him that W. T. R. Preston, Inspector of Emigration Agencies was preparing to visit the continent in the near future and would be glad to meet him to discuss immigration matters: "Mr. W. T. R. Preston, the Inspector of Emigration Agencies, is now in London and proposes shortly to visit the Continent. He would like to see you, and I shall be glad to be informed if it would be convenient for you to meet him some time towards the middle or end of the month [April] and what place would be convenient."[36]

W. T. R. Preston, the newly appointed Inspector of Emigration Agencies, was making an exploratory tour of continental countries together with Professor James Mavor of the University of Toronto, who was also in the service of the Department of the Interior. Preston's visit was to be conducted "with the view of cautiously studying the question in each country, but, necessarily, not with the intention of inciting emigration lest by so doing I should place myself under the notice of the authorities. . . ."[37] An able journalist and writer before he was called to join the Immigration Branch of the Department, Preston was formerly the Librarian of the Ontario Parliamentary Library. He was already in his fifties when, in 1899, Clifford Sifton appointed him to

[33]5. Gal., Memorandum, February 28, 1899: C. W. Badgley, Ottawa.

[34]2. Oles./79419, March 3, 1899: Dr. Josef Oleskow, Lemberg, Austria, to the High Commissioner for Canada, London.

[35]2. Oles., Cable, March 29, 1899: Department of the Interior, Ottawa, to the High Commissioner for Canada, London.

[36]2. Oles./79419, April 5, 1899: J. G. Colmer, London, to Dr. J. Oleskow, Lemberg, Austria.

[37]Canada, Parliament, *Sessional Papers*, XXXIV, No. 10, 1900, Part II, Paper No. 13, Report No. 2, 14: W. T. R. Preston, Inspector of Agencies in Europe, to Lord Strathcona and Mount Royal, London.

his new post, much against the liking of Lord Strathcona. In his book, *The Life and Times of Lord Strathcona*, Preston comments on his appointment:

When Sir Donald A. Smith [who later became Lord Strathcona and Mount Royal] was appointed High Commissioner for Canada in London, in 1896 . . . it was thought that something would be done of a practical character in regard to emigration, but he too settled down to the ordinary official *status quo.* As the result of correspondence with Sir Donald A. Smith, Mr. Sifton proposed that a Canadian official should be sent to London to take charge of emigration work. Sir Donald in reply thought that a minor clerk with a small salary would answer the requirements. But the Minister decided that a much more responsible official was necessary. . . .[38]

Preston was therefore sent to London and, in order to become better acquainted with the emigration problems on the continent, he proposed to undertake an extensive tour, covering Russia, Finland, Norway, Sweden, Denmark, Germany, Austria, Hungary, Holland, Belgium, and France, during which he also intended to meet Dr. Oleskow to learn more about his activities and to arrange the details of the professor's remuneration, which were becoming complicated. Preston also intended to "inquire into the manner of life of this people [the Ukrainians in Galicia] in their native country, in view of the fact that from this province there has been, during the past three or four years such an extensive movement to Canada."[39]

Dr. Oleskow suggested May 20 as the most convenient date for meeting Preston. Receiving no communication to the contrary from London, he proceeded on that date to Vienna, called at the hotel at which Preston was to stop over, and failing to find him, wrote to London, enquiring about Mr. Preston and commenting on the situation in Galicia:

Under the address of Mr. Colmer I wrote that the sole term I could meet with Mr. Preston in Vienna was May 20th. To this letter I received no answer. Presuming that the answer failed to reach me, I proceeded to Vienna and called at Hotel Erzherzog Karl, which was designed as place for meeting, but there was no notice from Mr. Preston. So I take the occasion to write from here as I am in Galicia not sure that the secrecy of corerspondence will be kept. I sent also from here today the receipt for $250.

Before all I must explain the present state of things in the country. The movement in this Spring made very much alarm with the higher classes of this country, especially with the Polish land-gentry, who pursues regardless only their own interests and uses the public authority to that aim. The

[38]W. T. R. Preston, *The Life and Times of Lord Strathcona* (London, 1914), 237.

[39]Canada, Parliament, *Sessional Papers,* XXXIV, No. 10, Paper No. 13, Report No. 2, 16.

present governor is a Polish landlord too, and is quite hostile to the emigration movement. The governing party penetrates with zeal and passion, where is the secret hand, which governs the movement to Dominion as they know from hundreds of circulars of the Steamship Agents which fall in the hands of Provincial Authorities that the agitation from this source was this year very much stronger to Argentina and Brazil than to Dominion.

This awakened sharp opposition of the governing party and in consequence of the authorities against the movement to Dominion obliges to a greater caution because an indiscretion say in correspondence could lead to reveal the source of the movement and even to a small diplomatic conflict. On the other hand, the correspondence safe, the specifying of results on behalf of bonusses is nearly dispensable, and nobody from abroad can me give some advice to do better work as I do. The second reason for which the Canadian Immigration is endangered is strengthened endeavour of Polish democratic party to build a colonisation society, with aim to divert emigration to South America. But they have not confidence with peasants and rule not the ways which lead to the peasants.

The most imminent danger for the movement to Dominion the danger in re itself, is the completion of the Transsiberian Railway. In two or three years when this railway will be constructed, with their immense low tariffs, so that the emigrants will reach the Nasiri Land, on the Pacific Coast at a third of the expense, which he must spend to reach the Northwest, there can be no talk of emigration to Canada. If the Dominion will neglect these two or three years the source of Galician emigration can be regarded as dried up. Make use of these years.

Freed of danger to be comprometted by an indiscreet correspondence, I can in the same ways as till now hold up and develop the movement to the Dominion, because the ways to the peasants which I command, so long as I myself do not reveal them are unaccessible to governing party. The more, although it is far more difficult than could be initiated the movement of Polish peasants of West Galicia which has chance to endure even after the completion of Transsiberian Railway, because the irreconcilable hostility between Russians and Poles.

The account of the agreed bonusses for the expired period I please to settle according to the well-meaning of your Lordship and of the Government. This is sure the same scheme as to the Steamship Agents is in my case inadmissible my work is of quite other nature.[40]

The meeting proposed for May 20 was not given up, however, merely postponed. A month later, on Monday, June 19, 1899, W. T. R. Preston and Professor James Mavor met Dr. Oleskow at Cracow and held a three-hour conference with him. Preston later reported the results of the conference to the High Commissioner in London, as well as to the Deputy Minister in Ottawa:

It is not improbable that this mail will also bring you from Professor Mavor an account of our interview with Professor Oleskow at Cracow on

[40]2. Oles./83363, May 20, 1899: Dr. J. Oleskow, Vienna, Austria, to the High Commissioner for Canada, London.

Monday, the 19th instant [June, 1899]. We were together about three hours, therefore all I will be able to give you will be a short summary of what transpired.

Oleskow, as might be expected, claims all the credit for the exodus from Galicia, and he told us the means he had adopted to bring Canada to the favourable notice of the population, i.e. personal work by his confidential agents; leaflets or pamphlets judiciously distributed; and occasional reference to Canada in his lectures; and by newspaper articles. He had not any of the printed matter with him. He stated that the work now is much more difficult than it was, inasmuch as the present Governor is strongly opposed to emigration, whereas his predecessor looked with favour upon moderate exodus.

We told him about the withdrawal of the bonus on Galicians since the 1st of June as far as the Steamship agents were concerned, and he told us that, in his estimation, this was all right as they had done nothing, and the movement was entirely due to his efforts. He frankly admitted that many of those who had gone to Canada were not possessed of sufficient means to readily get on their feet there, and we pointed out that such persons could not be numbered among the "desirable class of emigrants" to whom reference was made in the memorandum of his agreement with the London office. . . .[41]

Preston stated further in his report that Dr. Oleskow would be willing to receive "much less than £500 and [to] give a receipt in full for any obligation the Government may be under in connection with his work." After receiving the reports from Preston and Mavor, the Deputy Minister prepared a memorandum for the Superintendent of Immigration, specifying the arrangements made with Dr. Oleskow and also suggesting a solution to the bonus payment problem, which was not properly and clearly set out in the agreement concluded with Dr. Oleskow:

Referring to the arrangement with Professor Oleskow, I would suggest that the High Commisisoner be written to and asked to procure from Prof. Oleskow a statement of the expenditure of the £500 advanced to him a year ago, which was to have been spent in the publication of a pamphlet, and in printing and advertising in connection with the emigration from Austria. The arrangement to pay him ten shillings (or say $2.50) for each adult over 18 years of age can hardly be calculated on the immigration which came to Canada last year, there being in all about 5,500 persons who emigrated from Austria. It would be safe to say that most of these came of their own accord, that is, they followed friends who came to Canada a year or two previous. I would consider that Prof. Oleskow would possibly be entitled —if the matter could be probed to the bottom and made clear, which it evidently cannot now as he himself says that it would be very difficult for him to settle on the actual number of emigrants he sent out—to a commission on 1,000 persons. This would give him $2,500. On account of this he has

[41]2. Oles./85836, June 23, 1899: W. T. R. Preston, London, to James A. Smart, Ottawa.

been paid already £250, which was sent to him in April last, and as I understand he is willing to accept £200 in full settlement of this matter I think, on receipt of a satisfactory account for the expenditures of last year, that a cheque ought to issue to him for the amount referred to, namely £200, to close out any claim that he may have.

The question of the 1899 immigration can hardly be settled at present until most of the immigration for the year is over and reports have been received from our Agents.[42]

To inform the Minister about the beginnings of the immigration to Canada of the Ukrainian peasant-settlers, the Immigration Branch prepared a brief summary:

Correspondence appears to have been opened by Professor Oleskow, Professor of Agriculture in the University of Lemberg, Austria, by letter of 16th March, 1895, addressed to the Minister of the Interior, with reference to the emigration from Galicia of the Ruthenic (Slavonic) nationality on account of the excessive population.

Professor Oleskow's mission was apparently philanthropic and patriotic and with a desire of assisting these people, many thousands having already emigrated to Brazil from Galicia.

The matter was afterwards referred to the High Commissioner, who opened correspondence with Professor Oleskow with the result that in the autumn of that year (1895) Professor Oleskow visited Canada with letters from the High Commissioner, Sir Charles Tupper. He was accompanied by a Galician and was given every facility to make an examination of the resources of the North West country, the German interpreter from Winnipeg going through the country with him.

At Edmonton he met the Hon. T. M. Daly, then Minister of the Interior, with whom he conversed and, from Mr. Daly's letter to Mr. Hall on the subject, evidently impressed with the importance of taking up this work.

The proposition made by Professor Oleskow in connection with German immigration was to grant him a subvention of £600 for establishing an agency at Lemberg, to provide (1) for assisted passages, and (2) bonuses of $50 per homestead, or securing loans to the extent of $600 for each homestead at interest not exceeding 6%.

On the 11th April, 1896, Professor Oleskow appears to have sent forward a party of settlers, about 107 souls, without waiting for a definite arrangement, through Spiro & Company, Steamship Agents at Hamburg.

The question of steamship bonuses did not enter into the arrangements with Professor Oleskow at all, it apparently being clearly understood that the Government had no hesitation in paying the £1 per ticket, which system of bonus had been in operation since 1882.

The only point, up to this time, was as to granting assisted passages and a bonus of $50 per family to assist the settlers in locating.

It appears from the correspondence that at this time the Minister who

42. Oles./86572, Memorandum, July 22, 1899: James A. Smart, Ottawa, to Frank Pedley, Ottawa.

had undertaken to deal with his matter retired from office and nothing definite was arranged as to the movement of these people.[43]

II

It was arranged during the June, 1899, visit that Preston would visit Galicia again, sometime in July or August, as Dr. Oleskow suggested, because at that time the school year would be over, and the professor would be free to spend more time with Preston. Arrangements had to be changed again, however, as Preston was able to visit Galicia only late in the autumn. The discussions with Dr. Oleskow resulted in the professor's acceptance of the final arrangements proposed by Preston on behalf of the Canadian Government, thus terminating the agreement for 1898.

Preston prepared a detailed, general report on his European tour, which was included in the yearly report of the Department of the Interior (Immigration) for the year 1899. In order not to endanger Dr. Oleskow's position, his name is not mentioned in this report. The report touches on points of emigration policy and dwells on practices of certain booking agents who learned that "it necessitated less expense to try to secure the privilege of booking emigrants at the port of embarkation, and thus secure the bonus, than to work the fields from whence the emigrants hailed,"[44] a fact about which Dr. Oleskow constantly complained. Particularly interesting is Preston's description of the Ukrainian villages, the peasants, their dwellings and schools, their habits and appearance:

> On the occasion of my late trip to south eastern Europe, I embraced the opportunity, while in that locality, to visit several villages in the province of Galicia, (Austro-)Hungary, for the purpose of inquiring into the manner of life of this people in their native country, in view of the fact that from this province there has been, during the past three or four years, such an extensive movement to Canada. By driving out from such centres as Cracow, Lemberg and Tarnopol, I was given an opportunity of visiting, among other places, the villages of Berozwisca (Berezowiska?), Ostrow, Bucniow, Zboiska, Gryzbowice (Grzybowice), Dublang (Dublany) and Malechoir (?). To see one such peasant community is practically to understand the mode of living in all. In Galicia, as in peasant life in every country in Europe, and similar conditions appear to prevail all the way through the Caucasian district in Asia, the people gather together in villages or communities separated only by a few kilometres. These communities are very frequently situated

[43]2. Oles./88635, Memorandum, July 5, 1899: Department of the Interior.

[44]Canada, Parliament, *Sessional Papers*, XXXIV, No. 10, 1900, Part II, Paper No. 13, Report No. 2, 16–19: W. T. R. Preston to Lord Strathcona, London.

along the great thoroughfares. Their agricultural holdings, unless they are unusually prosperous, probably average ten or twelve acres, but it is a rare occurrence for their possession to be in one location; that is, the aggregated area of rentings is in three or more places. Very rarely is a fence seen in hundreds of miles, the holdings being simply staked out at the corners. In the cultivation of their respective locations not even the width necessary to the furrow of a plough is wasted, so that a fertile valley looks like a vast farm under one management. The care given the cultivation of each plot may be better understood by the statement that the crops may be seen at any stage of growth, and I had an opportunity of passing through this locality this summer, and in so far as the most careful observation could reveal, not a sign of a noxious weed met the eye. In the fertile valleys of Galicia land is very valuable and rents are extremely high, therefore, the peasant population must be thrifty and careful if they want to eke out more than a bare existence. With good crops and good farming they can manage to make some provision for the future. The peasant houses or huts everywhere are identically the same type. Timber is scarce and costly, and only sufficient is used to support the thatched roof. The walls are made of specially prepared or puddled clay, and built with as much care as would have to be given to layers of brick and mortar. . . . One cannot avoid admiring the care and labour expended in that direction to make their habitation attractive. In very few cases did I observe a failure to whiten the outside of the cottages, and in not a single instance did I find cattle or fowl sheds annexed to the living apartments. What might be termed the barnyards were very limited, and the people of the village were, as might be inferred, living closely together. Yet there was evidence of order and cleanliness that could not escape observation. Each community had a common well, and it was invariably placed and guarded against surface drainage. Around the outskirts of many of the communities was to be seen a particularly ramshackle kind of building, which I found out upon entering to be the tavern. Here animals and men were given an opportunity of mingling under the same roof, and in the same compartment. A glance was sufficient to lead to the conclusion that business in such a place was far from prosperous, and that the people in the neighbourhood were not afflicted with appetites for strong drink. These places were invariably in the hands of Polish Jews. In marked contrast with the tavern was the village school-house, which, next to the church, was always the most extensive and best looking building in the community—large, airy, neat and clean. I glanced into one and, but for the quaintness of the costumes, might have imagined myself looking at the children of a rural school in some newly opened section of my own country. The law is strictly enforced in Galicia in respect to compulsory education, the children from six to fourteen years of age must attend school continuously. The effect of this is seen in the gymnasium or higher schools in the centres of population like Cracow, Lemberg, and Tarnopol, where, among the brightest pupils are the children of the peasants. And it was also pointed out to me, as an evidence that in the peasant life of the country there are latent aspirations, that sons of peasants occupy many positions in official life. In this way they are working themselves above the class to which they belonged in childhood. In respect to the general health of the people there was every evidence of it being good. As to vaccinations, it will be satisfactory to your lordship to learn that every year the state or provincial authorities have every community visited officially by medical health officers, and the additions to the population are vaccinated. This is absolutely compulsory.

I am fully aware that the Galician whom I have seen here, neat and tidy in his attire, although somewhat quaint to the Anglo-Saxon-eyes, cheerful in his demeanour, and deferential to a marked degree, does not bear a strong resemblance to the Galician whom I have seen arrive in Canada, haggard, and tired after four weeks' travel by land and sea. But I have seen his home, the village whence he has come, the farm and land that he has cultivated, and I have no difficulty in arriving to the conclusion that, given a chance in our country, amid its free institutions, he will quickly become Anglicized, and, through his natural thrift and industry, will develop in a few years into a citizen of whom the most sensitive Canadian will not be ashamed.

Lord Strathcona forwarded both of Preston's reports to the Minister of the Interior in Ottawa and added his own comments on the settlement with Dr. Oleskow: "In my judgement, the basis of the proposed settlement of our accounts with Professor Oleskow is equitable; and I do not think 2000 dollars is an excessive payment for the work of the last two years."[45] The letter addressed to the Minister was acknowledged by the Deputy Minister, James A. Smart:

I have your letter of the 1st instant (December, 1899), addressed to the Minister of the Interior, enclosing a copy of Mr. Preston's report with regard to emigration work on the Continent. I am inclined to think that the arrangement he has made with Professor Oleskow is as satisfactory as could be under the circumstances, and as I understand that this closes out everything between him and the Department I presume that it is just as well that the matter should be settled at once. You are, therefore, authorized to make a final settlement of the matter for the amount named, namely £400.[46]

Several months later, the accountant of the Department of the Interior, Charles H. Beddoe, presented for the Deputy Minister's information a statement showing the payments made to Dr. Oleskow in the course of the two years:

Re Prof. Oleskow

Nothing was paid to Professor Oleskow during 1895–96. In May 1896, Department instructed the High Commissioner to pay him £100 in consideration of the work he had performed on behalf of Immigration. This payment was not made as Messrs. Spiro & Co. of Hamburg informed the High Commissioner that they had already paid him all he was entitled to for commission on ocean fares of his party and Government bonus.

[45]2. Oles./86087, December 1, 1899: Lord Strathcona, London, to Clifford Sifton, Ottawa.

[46]2. Oles./86087, December 12, 1899: James A. Smart, Ottawa, to Lord Strathcona, London.

The following are the only payments made to him by the Department:

Date	*Service*	*Amount*
1898		
Jan. 5.	Expenses to London re Galicians	$118.50
Feb. 14.	Expenses, printing pamphlets, advertising and other expenses	2435.77
Apl. 1.	Expenses to Vienna	27.98
1899		
Apl. 6.	On account of Continental Emigration	1216.67
1900		
July 19	Services re Continental Emigration	1946.67
	Total	$5745.59

No details of expenditure have been furnished.

Respectfully submitted
(Signed) CHAS. H. BEDDOE
Accountant.[47]

With his appointment as Director of the Teachers' Seminary at Sokal, and with the death of his wife, Dr. Oleskow's activities in the field of emigration slowed down and finally ceased altogether. Soon afterwards he fell gravely ill and died, October 18, 1903, in the forty-third year of his life. For a few years after his death his name was still vividly remembered by the Ukrainian settlers in Canada. Gradually, however it slipped into oblivion, and today very few Canadians have ever heard of Dr. Josef Oleskow. He nevertheless deserves at least a modest niche among the builders of the Canadian West for having initiated and for five years vigorously and successfully propagated the emigration of Ukrainian settlers to Canada, an ethnic group which today numbers half a million persons, and whose sons, grandsons, and even great-grandsons can be found in every walk of Canadian life.

[47]2. Oles., August 17, 1900: Memorandum re Dr. Oleskow by Chas. H. Beddoe, Accountant, Department of the Interior, Ottawa, for the Deputy Minister.

PART II

UKRAINIAN SETTLEMENTS IN WESTERN CANADA

Chapter Five

STUARTBURN

I

C. S. PRODAN, the Agricultural Representative of the Manitoba Department of Agriculture gave the following description of the Stuartburn region when he visited it thirty-five years after its settlement by Ukrainians:

> Stuartburn lies in a plain which stretches east of Emerson, on the Roseau river along the United States-Canada border. The Ukrainians settled Townships 1, 2, and partly 3, ranges 5, 6, 7, 8, and 9. Today [1931] these settlements bear the names of their respective post offices: Tolstoi (which was called Oleskow before), Stuartburn, Gardenton, Vita, Arbakka, Zhoda, Senkiw, Rosa and Caliento.
>
> The soil in this region is predominantly light with patches of black earth and clay. There are also stony patches with granite and limestone predominating. Because this terrain is mostly flat and the banks of the Roseau River—sometimes called Rosa River—are rather low in places, swampy conditions occur. Vegetables thrive in this region exceptionally well. Potatoes grow large and clean. Onions reach a three-inch size, and the so-called potato-onions thrive so well that they are produced here for seed purposes, supplying the whole of Western Canada. When Western Canada is unable to absorb the commercial crop of this onion, it is shipped to New York where there is a great demand for it. Cucumbers and melons grow very well without artificial prompting in seedbeds and hothouses. From cereals, buckwheat, rye, oats, barley and wheat are grown with great success. Fruit ripens here better than in any other part of Manitoba where the Ukrainians settled. . . .[1]

Stuartburn, or to be more precise, Township 2, Ranges 6 and 7 East of the First Meridian, is the oldest Ukrainian colony in Manitoba. The

[1]C.S.P. (Prodan), "Okolytsia Stuartburn"/"The Stuartburn Settlement," *Providnyk*/"The Leader" Almanac (Winnipeg: St. Raphael's Ukrainian Immigrant Welfare Association of Canada, 1931), 35–41.

first families settled on homesteads there in August, 1896. That group of first settlers, consisting of some ninety-four persons, families with children and several single men, came to Canada under the auspices of Dr. Josef Oleskow of Lviw. It was the third family group that he had assisted in emigrating to Canada.[2]

Dr. Oleskow's booklets "About Free Lands" and "About Emigration," published in 1895, were read to thousands of peasant-farmers in village reading halls throughout the land. One of these booklets came to the newly established library of the "Prosvita" reading hall in the village of Synkiw in the district of Zalishchyky, Galicia. The contents were eagerly discussed by the villagers who were anxious to find out more information about Canada. Dr. Oleskow's name and the "Prosvita" society's endorsement were sufficient guarantee of the reliability of the information. "The villagers chose two delegates to go to Lviw to see Professor Oleskow personally and to obtain additional information about Canada. On the return of these two delegates, Wasyl Stefura and Jacob Shelyp, preparations for the departure of the first families began."[3] Dr. Oleskow not only gave them exhaustive information and advice about Canada, but also assisted in making arrangements for the journey with as little financial loss as possible. He arranged for a competent leader to acompany the group and to be its spokesman during the long journey, as well as to be of help in Canada.

The ten families from Synkiw were joined by the family of Wasyl Zahara from the village of Bridok of the district of Zastavna in the neighbouring province of Bukowina, by several families from the village of Bereziw of the district of Kolomyja (at that time district of Pechenizhyn), as well as by Peter and Joseph Majkowsky from the vicinity of the town of Hvozdets, Peter Majkowsky was a former reeve of one of the villages and was personally known to Dr. Oleskow. His family remained in Galicia to await word from him before emigrating. In Hamburg they were joined by the family of Michael Stasyshyn (or Stashyn, as he called himself later in Canada), from the village of Solone in the district of Zalishchyky. This family was originally induced to emigrate to Brazil, but after it encountered the "Canadian" group in Hamburg, it changed its mind and decided to proceed to Canada. The leader of the whole group was the thirty-nine-year-old school teacher

[2]2. Oles./367554, August 27, 1896: J. G. Burpé, Secretary, Office of the Commissioner of Dominion Lands, Winnipeg, to the Secretary, Department of the Interior, Ottawa.

[3]Joseph Kohut, *Narys istorii Ukrainskoi Katolytskoi Tserkvy Sv. Troitsi v Stuartburn, Manitoba: Moi spomyny/* "A Sketch of the History of the Ukrainian Catholic Church of the Holy Trinity in Stuartburn, Manitoba: My Memoirs" (Yorkton, Saskatchewan, 1958), 6.

from the village of Bereziw, Cyril (Charles) Genik Berezowsky, also well known to Dr. Oleskow. Genik was going to Canada for permanent settlement with his wife and his four children. Mykhailo Stashyn indicates Genik's industry and spirit when he writes of him: "He did not remain idle on the boat, but was diligently studying English from a book."[4]

The Hamburg-America liner *Sicilia*, on which the emigrants travelled, left Hamburg during the first part of July, 1896, and landed in Quebec on July 22. The emigrants continued their journey without interruption to Winnipeg, arriving there on July 25. In the Immigration Hall they met several other Ukrainian families who had arrived in Canada a few weeks earlier. These families, taken originally to Whitemouth for settlement, had returned to Winnipeg because they did not like the Whitemouth region. Several families which were not without means were induced to buy land in St. Norbert, near Winnipeg, but the rest preferred to wait until suitable homesteads were found for them. The two groups joined forces, and Cyril Genik, with a good command of German and some knowledge of English, acted as their spokesman and interpreter.

After careful consultation, southern Manitoba was selected as a suitable area for exploration. The Commissioner of Dominion Lands assigned John W. Wendelbo, the Scandinavian Interpreter, who spoke German, to act as a guide, with Genik to assist him. It was not practical for the whole group to search for settlement locations, and therefore it was decided to select six trusted men to accompany Wendelbo to southern Manitoba and act as spokesmen for the whole group. Once suitable locations had been found, the delegates would return to Winnipeg and describe the land to the whole group. After the locations had been approved, those families wishing to settle would proceed to them.

John W. Wendelbo and the six delegates chosen to accompany him left Winnipeg on Friday, July 31, 1896, and headed south. About a week later, they returned to Winnipeg, and Wendelbo reported on the trip:

> I proceeded on Friday morning July 31th in charge on three delegates selected by the families above mentioned, and three delegates selected by a party of newly arrived Austrians.
>
> In order to show the delegates, how their former Neighbors the Mennonites had prospered in this country, we traveled through a few of their settlements east of Niverville, and at the end of our first days journey, reached the beautiful little Mennonite Village Steinback about 38 miles south of this city. I may here mention that the delegates were very much surprised and pleased with what they had seen.
>
> Saturday Aug. 1th. we proceeded east and south into Tsps 5 and 6. Range 7 East, hoping to find enough suitable land for a small colony, my

[4]Stashyn, Mykhailo, "Moi spohady za sorok lit zhyttia v Kanadi"/"My Memoirs of Forty Years in Canada," *Illustrated Calendar of the "Ukrainian Voice"* (Winnipeg: 1938), 76.

desire being to locate them as near as possible to the Mennonites, where Stock, Food, and other necessities, required for a new settler could be had on very reasonable conditions, and where employment is plenty nearly any time of the year.

Although a few families would do well at any time to make that district their home, and would in time be able to find fairly suitable land to settle on, yet I found the land not well suited for so large a Colony as the one whose delegates I had in charge.

Owing to the total absence of any roads in this eastern district in order to reach a point some 20 miles south of 5–7 East where more suitable land I knew could be found, we were obliged to return to Steinback, and from there the following day south west through a number of Mennonite villages to St. Malo. From there 10 miles due south to the Roseau River.

On Monday Aug. 3rd we followed the north east bank of the River untill we reached Tsp 2 Range 6 East, where we found the land very satisfactory, mixed with Poplar groves, scrubby Prairie, and Meadow lands, and anough vacant Homesteads for about 35 or 40 families, the delegates in my company expressed themselves very much pleased and satisfied with the land.

We being then about 70 miles from Winnipeg, with a load of in all eight persons, two days were necessarely consumed in returning to the city. After returning and the delegates having had time to discribe the district we had visited, 26 heads of families at once dicided to make settlement, and the Colony has now been named Ruthanea.

It has now been dicided that the whole party of 24 or 25 families will proceed by train to Dominion City, on Tuesday morning Aug. 11th, and from there by Wagons to take possession, by each head of the family selecting and making entry for his quarter section of land.[5]

In the Immigration Hall, excitement was great. Talk was of nothing but the impending departure, and even those who had hesitated before joined the group, so that twenty-seven families were ready to go to the "promised land," which they decided to call "Ruthenia." Some apprehension was felt, however, because of the season of the year; the settlers worried about not being able to plant potatoes or other vegetables in time to have supplies for the winter. On Tuesday, August 11, 1896, the whole party, consisting of twenty-seven families and several single men, led by John W. Wendelbo and assisted by Cyril Genik, set out on the historical trek that ended in the founding of one of the largest Ukrainian colonies in Manitoba. One of the participants in that memorable expedition was Mykhailo Stashyn, then a boy of eight, who described the story of the settlement in his memoirs some forty years later:

After two weeks' stay in Winnipeg, we were taken to Stuartburn some sixty miles south of Winnipeg. We were brought to the big farm of a man who was raising stock, and he allowed us to use his stables as our temporary

[5]18. Imm./371399, August 8, 1896: John W. Wendelbo, Dominion Immigration Office, Winnipeg, to H. H. Smith, Commissioner of Dominion Lands, Winnipeg.

dwellings. We slept indoors, but all housework was done outdoors. There the laundry was washed, the bread was baked, the meals were cooked, and we, the children, played near our mothers. Our fathers went to select homesteads with the surveyors and to cut the lanes, because all land was covered with bush.

As soon as a homestead was measured, one of the heads of the families registered it in his name. All wanted to have as much wood on their land as possible. And that was because in the old country everybody was fed up with having to pay—or to work hard for the landlord in lieu of pay—for the privilege of obtaining some wood.

Everybody was asking the agent to allot homesteads as near as possible to each other. All wished to be with their friends, because being in a strange country, among strange people, whose language they could not understand, made them feel very lonely. In order to satisfy their wishes even C.P.R. sections were thrown open for the settlement of homesteaders. Some people divided their farms in two, saying that 160 acres was too much for them to work. . . .

Charles Genik entered his homestead not far from us. He was doing well. He was employed as an interpreter and was well paid for it.

Our father brought approximately $50 with him. Immediately on arrival he bought a cow so as to have milk for the children. . . . He paid $22 for her. She was a very good cow, and gave enough milk to supply seven families.

After some time we moved onto our homestead in the bush to live. The cow used to go into the woods to graze and when milking time approached she came home on her own. It would seem that she was good and gracious to us, for we would have never been able to find her if we had had to look for her in the woods.

There were no roads worthy of that name, only trails. But even they had to be marked off with sticks, and we cut notches on trees so as not to lose our way to the next neighbour. In those days people were very friendly to each other. Visitors were received with open arms and accorded open-hearted hospitality. They assisted each other in every way. This helped us to endure the hardships of pioneering and to overcome homesickness.

The time came to build the house as winter was approaching. But how does one build a house? Nykola Genik stood us in good stead. He hailed from the Carpathian Mountains and knew how to build shacks. He helped us put up our house. It wasn't much of a house. A ditch three feet deep was dug, and two poles in each end of the ditch were put in, with a log across. Long poplar poles were then leaned to on the log and covered with sod. The end walls were plastered with clay. In one a pane of glass 10″ × 10″ was put in, and in the other a door made from hewn poplar planks. It was a memorable day when we moved into our own house. There was great rejoicing and great delight.

The banks of the walls served us as beds. An old ink bottle was used as a lamp to light the house in the evenings. The fuel did not cost much. The lamp consumed only one quart of kerosene during the whole winter. We made wicks from threads.

We also accepted lodgers into our house. Many people arrived later than we did and had no time to build houses. Seventeen persons lived in our house for a time. . . . I remember, we had a great amount of snow during the first winter. . . . We ran short of money and supplies before spring arrived, the same as other settlers. But we were able to manage somehow. Usually those who had some flour to spare, loaned it to those who were short. And thus we we carried on, waiting for the spring.

One day, during the winter, an Englishman came to our place, clad in a fur coat, with the fur on the outside, asked some questions, and tried to explain something, but nobody could understand him or guess what he wanted. He looked in every corner of the house, counted all of us, left a note and went away. The next day another Englishman came. He also started to tell us something, but again we didn't understand what he wanted. We guessed that perhaps he was asking for the note the other man left. He took the note and brought us seven sacks of flour and with his hands intimated that it was for making bread.

We were now well supplied with bread, and there was no lack of meat either. There were plenty of rabbits. Father made a big trap from twigs, 4′ × 6′, and caught them in the trap. Sometimes several were caught in one night. We ate the meat and made socks from their skins.

In the spring, the Indians showed us some roots, called "Seneca." They dug those roots and sold them in stores. We started to do the same. In those days the stores paid thirteen cents for a pound of dry roots. This became our source of income. . . .[6]

The experiences that Stashyn's family went through were almost identical with those of the rest of the settlers. John W. Wendelbo's account, written only a few days after the establishment of the settlement, provides some particulars which Stashyn, who wrote his memoirs forty years after the event, could hardly have known or remembered:

In accordance with your instructions, I proceeded on August 11 with a party of 27 heads of families in all about 100 souls, to Dominion City, and from there by teams 17 miles east, near Stuartburn P.O. where Mr. Dodge, Manager on a Stock Farm, kindly consented to permit them the use of his large outbuildings for shelter, until they were inabled to errect houses of their own.

From Wednesday morning Aug. 12th to Wednesday Aug 19th, I was very busy ingaged, locating each settler on his respective quarter section of land, and I beg to mention that when the work of locating was compleeted, the land was found to be very satisfactory to all parties, we having been obliged to set aside, after careful inspection some few quarter sections of second class land, my desire being to select for the first settlers, only the very best Homestead land to be found, and at the time of my diparture, all expressed themselves well satisfied with the district and their location, assuring me that a considerable number of their freinds and countrymen would surely join them in the near future, trusting that the Department would kindly give them the odd numbered sections as Homestead.

[6]Stashyn, "Moi spohady," 76–77.

Although some nine or ten families of this party had very limited means wherewith to settle on land, yet I am confident, that they will manage to live much better in the country than they could in the City, where expencess are greater and compitition for employment much keener. I may mention, that as soon as they have arrected shelters for their families, a number of them have been promised employment on Thresingmashines intending to work near Dominion City.

The Routainers with few exception seems to be possessed of but a limited education, but are in every way a very industrious class of settlers, who will be able to start on a farm with much less capital than most people, they having been practical farmers on a very small scale in Galitzien, and find 160 acres of land a very large farm. At home they have been well accustomed to house industry, handling Flax from its seed until a garment is completed out of its fibers, and such garments, sublemented in winter by home manufactured Sheep skin Coats seems to constitute their principal wearing apperal, the raw cow hide after a home taning is made into a crude feet gear.

Mr. Cyril, or Charles Genik, a Garman speaking Routainian, has during the trip been a great service to me as interpreter, without him I would have been intirely unable to communicate with these people.

On behalf of this colony, I very respectfully beg to recommend, that all odd numbered sections not now disposed of, in Tsps 2, Range 6 and 7, east may be granted as Homesteads to these people and their freinds, whom I am sure will in a very short time make this settlement a very prosperous community.[7]

To his report, Wendelbo appended a list of the first settlers and their locations. Although some of the names are misspelled, they are easily recognized and form the record of the original pioneer families of the Ukrainian colony of Stuartburn. The names in brackets have been compared with Hugo Carstens' list submitted in February 1897, the Naturalization Records, and information obtained from Joseph Kohut, the son of the original settler, Nicholas Kohut of Stuartburn. The families of three settlers were to arrive shortly.

Name of Settler		Sec.	Tsp.	Rge.	East of 1.M.	No. of Souls
Ivan Prygroski (Ivan Prygrocki)	SE¼	22	2	6	E	5
Nykolai Kahut (Nicola Kohut)	NE¼	22	2	6	E	1
Onofry Smuk (Onufry Smuk)	NW¼	22	2	6	E	4
Josef Bzowy	SW¼	28	2	6	E	4
Iwan Storoszuk (Ivan Storoszczuk)	NW¼	28	2	6	E	2
Jan Tomeszewski (Ivan Tomaszewski)	NE¼	28	2	6	E	4
Simon Salamandyk (Semen Salamandyk)	SE¼	28	2	6	E	6
Nikol Wyseczynski (Nicola Wysoczynski)	NW¼	14	2	6	E	1

[7]18. Imm./372274, August 21, 1896: John W. Wendelbo, Winnipeg, to H. H. Smith, Winnipeg.

Name of Settler		Sec.	Tsp.	Rge.	East of 1.M.	No. of Souls
Wasyl Stefura	SW¼	14	2	6	E	4
Jakob Szelep (Jacob Szelyp)	SE¼	14	2	6	E	1
Iwan Negrycz	NE¼	14	2	6	E	1
Charles Genik (Cyril Genik)	NW¼	16	2	6	E	6
Wasyl Zahara	NW¼	2	2	6	E	6
Fedor Horobec	NE¼	10	2	6	E	3
Maksym Stasyszn	SE¼	10	2	6	E	3
Michael Prytoski (Michael Prygrocki)	NW¼	12	2	6	E	5
Itasz Prokopczuk (Ilasz Prokopczuk)	NE¼	12	2	6	E	6
Fedor Pidhirny	SW¼	24	2	6	E	5
Fedor Dymianyk	NW¼	24	2	6	E	3
Wasyl Salamandyk	SE¼	24	2	6	E	3
Ivan Salamandyk	NE¼	24	2	6	E	1
Hehory Prygroski (Hryhory Prygrocki)	SE¼	30	2	6	E	5
Nikol Prygroski (Nicola Prygrocki)	NE¼	30	2	6	E	1
Peter Majkowski	NW¼	20	2	6	E	1
Nikol Majkowski	NE¼	20	2	6	E	1
Sawka Perun	SW¼	30	2	6	E	5
Peter Strurbicki (Peter Strubicki)	NW¼	30	2	6	E	7
						94

The majority of settlers came from the villages of Synkiw and Bereziw. Nicola Kohut, Josef Bzowy, Onufry Smuk, Iwan Storoszczuk, Semen Salamandyk, Wasyl Salamandyk, Iwan Salamandyk, Wasyl Stefura, and Josef Szelyp came from Synkiw, while Iwan Negrycz, Iwan and Michael Hryhory, Nicola Prygrocki, and Cyril Genik came from Bereziw. Individual families were from other villages, mostly from the southern districts of Galicia. The family of Maksym Stasyszyn came from the village of Solone, in the Zalishchyky district, the family of Wasyl Zahara came from the village of Bridok in the Zastawna district, in the province of Bukowina. Peter and Nykola Majkowskyi hailed from a village near the town of Hvozdets.

II

During his inspection of the land for settlement, Wendelbo observed that most of the markings between the individual quarter-sections had become obliterated and that there was some danger the homesteaders would erect their buildings in the wrong places if the markings were not replaced. The Commissioner therefore thought it advisable to send along a qualified Dominion Lands Officer to check the boundaries and to replace those markings which were lost, before the entries were made.

This officer, Joseph Turenne, was also authorized to collect entry fees for homesteads, and he made this report on new entries:

> I left St. Boniface on the 10th (August) and drove to Dominion City where I arrived at noon next day and met the party. I took Mr. Wendelbo with me and, followed by all the Austrian families, we reached Stuartburn the same night.
>
> Early next morning I was at work and as there was no sign of any lines I began cutting a new one, starting from the mound of the South West corner of the South West quarter of Section 20, Township 2, Range 6, East, going North. I have been obliged to chain the most of the lines to find all the mounds which I have the pleasure to report having found and put new marked posts in every one of them. I located twenty eight heads of families of whom seventeen made their entries on the spot, as authorised by you verbally to do; the rest had not enough money to pay the entry fee and they request that the land they have chosen be reserved for them for a few weeks. They all seem to be satisfied with the land.[8]

The weather remained favourable, and the settlers immediately began clearing plots for shelters and gardens. Some found temporary employment in the neighbourhood.

They were still occupied with building their homes and cutting and storing hay for the winter when new settlers began to arrive in the colony. The Commissioner of Dominion Lands was much perturbed about these late arrivals. The majority of them did not bring sufficient money to carry them through the winter, and, with the harvest practically over, there was little chance to obtain work with farmers. A serious difficulty facing the newly-arrived settlers was the fact that it would soon be too late in the season to start building houses. Another important problem was the task of locating the newcomers. They insisted on being given homesteads near their relatives and fellow villagers, but most of the even-numbered sections of Township 2, Range 6, were already occupied. Anticipating the arrival of new immigrants, Wendelbo had suggested to the Commissioner in August that he apply to Ottawa for the release of the odd-numbered sections. This would not only make room for new arrivals, but it would also enable them to be close to their relatives and friends. Commissioner Smith forwarded Wendelbo's recommendation to Ottawa with his own request that the release of the sections be given immediate attention: "I beg to hand you herewith copies of reports by Mr. Wendelbo, dated the 8th and 21st instant, with regard to the settlement of a number of Austrian immigrants in Townships 2,

[8]18. Imm./411031, August 25, 1896: Joseph Turenne, Clerk, Dominion Lands, Winnipeg, to the Commissioner of Dominion Lands, Winnipeg.

Ranges 6 and 7, East, and would direct especial attention to the last paragraph of Mr. Wendelbo's report of the 21st instant, in which he recommends that if possible the odd-numbered sections in the townships mentioned be made available for homestead entry. Will you advise the Commissioner at your early convenience whether these lands can be thrown open to entry.[9]

Thousands of acres of land in Townships 1 and 2, Ranges 6 and 7, east of Dominion City, were at one time apparently taken as homesteads or pre-empted with small downpayments. Few of them were, however, ever occupied, worked, or paid for in full; instead, they were left standing idle. Land-hungry settlers were knocking at every door to have these acres released for settlement. They even wrote to Dr. Oleskow in Lviw, describing the situation in Stuartburn and requesting him to intercede on their behalf with the authorities in Ottawa for the release of the odd-numbered sections for entry as homesteads. The settlers thought that the odd-numbered sections were "railway land." This information was most probably supplied by Cyril Genik, who was in constant communication with Dr. Oleskow, and who acted as the spokesman for the settlers. On the receipt of their request, Dr. Oleskow wrote the following letter to the Department of the Interior, requesting the opening of the "railway lands":

> The Galician settlers in Stuartburn Man. Twn. 2, Rge 6 and partly 7 and 5 East of the 1st Merid. beg instantly the Department of Interior through me, in order of establishing a community with their own clergyman, that the Railway Lands in Twn. 2 Rge. 5, 6, 7, East of 1st Mer. may be exchanged and opened as free homesteads to the friends of the above settlers, who live still in Galicia, but wish to settle in Manitoba near their friends.[10]

The Deputy Minister acknowledged Dr. Oleskow's letter and assured him that his communication would be "submitted."

The Commissioner in Winnipeg then urged Ottawa to comply with Dr. Oleskow's request, pointing out that ". . . many quarter sections in these townships were taken up as homesteads years ago, but on account of the comparatively inferior quality of these lands with others which were then available, most of these entries were abandoned, and in a few cases reports were obtained from the Homestead Inspector, though the larger number of entries were cancelled by voluntary abandonment." Therefore, the odd-numbered sections which were not occupied or were

[9] 18. Imm./371399, August 25, 1896: The Secretary, Dominion Lands Commission, Winnipeg, to the Secretary, Department of the Interior, Ottawa.

[10] 18. Imm./416736, November 29, 1896: Dr. Josef Oleskow, Lemberg, Austria, to the Department of the Interior, Ottawa.

abandoned long ago could be thrown open for settlement. He continued on the matter of the cancellation of the original time sales:

In my letter of the 1st September, a request was made that the odd-numbered sections in these Townships might be also made available for entry, as numbers of these settlers are still arriving and more are expected. Will you kindly have this matter considered.

There appear to be a number of old Time Sales in both these Townships, in connection with which the Local Agent reports that only a small amount has been paid. The Commissioner would be glad if steps could be taken with a view to cancelling these sales, so that the lands thereby may also be rendered available.[11]

In answer to the Commissioner's letter of September 9, 1896, the Department of the Interior wrote:

In reply I am directed to inform you that according to the books of the Department all the odd-numbered sections in these two Townships are entered as time sales, some having been patented, but the majority of them being liable to cancellation for non-payment. A list is now being prepared of all cases where payments are in default, and the Deputy Minister will take the judgement of the Acting Minister [Hon. R. W. Scott, M.P.] as to what should be done in the premises. I am further to state that in the meantime these lands cannot be made available for the Austrian immigrants immediately.[12]

The delays in reaching a decision were caused to a great extent by changes which occurred as a direct result of a change in government. The new Minister of the Interior, Clifford Sifton, was asked to make a decision on the question before he had time to become acquainted with the work of his department, and before he assumed his duties. The Commissioner of Dominion Lands in Winnipeg, H. H. Smith, reluctant to make decisions in budgetary matters, despatched a letter marked "private and urgent" to the Minister while the latter was still in Brandon:

I regret the necessity of troubling you at this time with official matters, but there is a subject which appears so urgent that I feel it is desirable the facts should be reported to you without delay.

During the past season considerable number of Ruthenians from Austria have arrived here. Most of these people are reported to have some small capital, but a few of them have arrived here entirely without means. When the first of these settlers arrived there was considerable difficulty in finding suitable locations for them; they had some idea of purchasing lands and a visit was also made to Brokenhead and Whitemouth for the purpose of examining lands available for homesteads in these localities. Finally they

[11]18. Imm./371721, October 23, 1896: The Secretary of the Commissioner of Dominion Lands, Winnipeg, to the Secretary, Department of the Interior, Ottawa.

[12]18. Imm./377335, October 23, 1896; Lyndwode Pereira, Assistant Secretary, Department of the Interior, Ottawa, to the Secretary, Dominion Lands, Winnipeg.

settled in Township 2, Ranges 6 and 7 East, about 40 miles east of Dominion City. [This distance should have been cited as eighteen miles.] In this settlement there are now 36 families embracing 132 souls. Of these there are 8 or 9 families at present in destitute circumstances, who are said to be indeed without the means of subsistance. It would, therefore, seem absolutely necessary to provide some assistance, at least in the way of food. . . . I may say that should you recommend the supply of provisions, the cost in each case might be charged against the homestead, and the amount required to be paid at all events before certificate of recommendation for patent be issued.

There have been some later arrivals of settlers of the same nationality, and we have at present in the Immigration Hall here 35 families, numbering about 150 souls. The most of these also have some means, though there are a few with almost nothing, and it is very difficult to know what is best to be done with them. The attention of the Department has already been called to the matter, copy of letter attached, and I have pointed out the undesirability of this class of immigrants being brought to the country at this season of the year. Meanwhile I have been obliged to furnish some of those in the Hall with flour and potatoes to keep them from absolute want. I am told the men are strong, used to a wooded country, and are good choppers. I am, therefore endeavouring to find employment for them in Winter camps, cutting wood, railway ties, etc., but as they are new to this country, I fear their wages may not be much more than sufficient to provide for their own wants, and there remains the difficulty of providing for their families.

I need hardly add that everything possible will be done to meet the case, and I shall be glad to receive your views in regard to the matter. It may be considered, at all events with reference to those who have already taken up land, that the Local Government should assist, but as these people have so recently arrived in the country, I am doubtful whether it can be called upon to bear any expense.[13]

The Commissioner enclosed a list of 9 families of Stuartburn settlers needing immediate assistance. The loan would be a repayable one, he stated, with a lien on the homestead, and not an outright gift of the government. The names of the nine heads of the families needing assistance were listed thus:

1. Iwan Prygrocki—SE¼ 22–Tp.2–Rge.6 E; 3 children, 5 souls settled August 21, 96, had $10. cash, has no stock, did not cultivate any land but built a log house.

2. Wasyl Stafura (Stefura)—SW¼ 14–Tp.2–Rge 6 E; 2 children, 4 souls, settled August 21, 1896, without means, has no stock, no land cultivated, built a log cabin.

3. Maksym Stasyszyn—SE¼ 10–Tp.2–Rge 6 E; 2 children, 4 souls, arrived August 21, 1896; had $60 capital; has 1 cow and one ox; no land cultivated; has built a log cabin.

4. Ilasz Prokopczuk—NE¼ 12–Tp.2–Rge 6 E; 4 children, six souls, arrived

[13]18. Imm./378361, November 20, 1896: The Commissioner of Dominion Lands, Winnipeg, to Clifford Sifton, Minister of the Interior, Brandon.

August 21, 1896; with $30 cash; has one cow and calf; no land cultivated; has no house.

5. Fedor Pidhirny—SW¼ 24–Tp.2–Rge 6 E; 3 children, 5 souls; had $10 cash; has no stock and no land cultivated; the family shares house with Fedor Dymianyk's family.

6. Fedor Dymianyk—NW¼ 24–Tp.2–Rge 6 E; 1 child; 3 souls; no means; no stock, no land cultivated; shares cabin with Pidhirny.

7. Sawka Perun—SW¼ 30–Tp.2–Rge 7 E; 3 children; 5 souls; arrived August 21, 96; no means; no stock, no acres cultivated; built a log house.

8. Peter Strubicki—NW¼ 30–Tp.2–Rge 7 E; 5 children, 7 souls; had $10 on arrival; no stock and land cultivated; built a log house.

9. Wasyl Hawryluk—SE¼ 28–Tp. 2–Rge 6 E; 4 children, 6 souls; arrived September 26, 1896; without means has no stock, did not cultivate any acres and has no house.[14]

In forwarding this list also to the Deputy Minister, on November 12, 1896, the Commissioner added that "the destitute Ruthenians at Dominion City would appear to have been sent out by Prof. Oleskow."[15] This communication undoubtedly prompted the Deputy Minister, A. M. Burgess, to dispatch to Dr. Oleskow a rather sharp letter with the list of destitute immigrants enclosed:

I am directed to transmit to you the enclosed schedule of Ruthenian settlers in the neighbourhood of Dominion City, in the Province of Manitoba, who are reported to be in a state of great poverty. This information is sent to you as we gather from your letter, dated the 6th of September last, that the persons referred to were amongst those you were instrumental in sending to this country. It is observed that these nine settlers, all of whom have families, arrived in Manitoba without the necessary means to make a start in that Province. Several other parties of Austrian immigrants have arrived, who are in a destitute condition, but apparently are not traceable to your influence. We are in great difficulty with regard to these people and it is sincerely hoped that no more of them will be induced to come forward, that is to say, none who are without the necessary means to take care of themselves, and even where this is the case, it is undesirable that they should arrive in Canada at a date so close to the beginning of the winter.[16]

III

The news about destitute Ukrainian immigrants arriving in Winnipeg and the necessity to support them at Government expense was picked up quickly by those opposed to "foreign immigration," and probably

[14]2. Oles./32246, November 12, 1896: Memorandum, Commissioner of Dominion Lands, Winnipeg.

[15]Note attached to the memorandum of November 12, 1896.

[16]2. Oles., November 24, 1896: Lyndwode Pereira, Ottawa, to Dr. Josef Oleskow, Lemberg, Austria.

still more opposed to the new Government in power. The *Daily Nor'Wester* of December 23, 1896, published this sensational news item about destitute immigrants, with biting comments on the immigrants and immigration agents:

UNDESIRABLE IMMIGRANTS

Parties of Galician immigrants continue to arrive in Winnipeg. If our foreign immigration agents cannot send us a better class of immigrants than these it is almost time to consider whether we might not dispense with immigration agents altogether. The southern Slavs are probably the least promising of all the material that could be selected for nation building. . . . There is a class of immigration which retards rather than promotes progress. The uncleanly and illiterate are an evil rather than a good. . . . Many of them have also arrived in such a destitute condition that the Government has had to support them. It is bad enough if these people come to us of their own accord; but it is monstrous that we should be paying agents to induce them to come.[17]

Pressure was also brought to bear from other quarters regarding immigration policy. There appeared in Winnipeg a "Committee of the Foreign Immigration Association" which claimed to consist of "Germans, Poles, Russians, and Ruthenians." The committee held a

. . . special meeting and had a conversation in which way to bring immigrants in this province, as the Immigration work was neglected in the past; it was brought in a large number of Immigrants in the last fall and Winter without money so that the City have to help them in keeping them of starving. The reason of it was that a certain man of Galicia Prof. Olesskoff of Lemberg, was there in Summer 95. and after he had returned he sent the poorest class of immigrants into this country; and last Summer he send his Assistant Carol Genik who said that he is appointed as Govt. Interpreter.

If the Government would not do something in this matter, we will get hundreds of this kind of immigrants in the Spring and the City have to suffer them.[18]

The group forwarded a petition to the Commissioner of Dominion Lands under the signature of Joseph Edinger, a member of the committee.

In order to obtain reliable information about conditions prevailing in the Stuartburn colony, the Commissioner sent Hugo Carstens to the colony, with instructions to make the necessary arrangements for the supply of provisions to families needing assistance and to submit a general report on the colony. Carstens was to accompany Dr. S. J. Elkin, the Health Officer of Franklin Municipality, sent to inspect the Stuartburn colony as a result of rumours that smallpox infection was brought in by outsiders.

[17]*Daily Nor'Wester*, Winnipeg, Wednesday, December 23, 1896.
[18]2. Oles./34818, February 24, 1897: Joseph Edinger, Winnipeg, Committee of the Foreign Immigration Association.

Carstens visited the colony December 1–3, 1896. His report gave a fair picture of conditions three months after the establishment of the colony:

I have the honour to report that I visited from the 1st to the 3rd Instance incl. in company with Dr. Elkin of Emerson, Health Officer of the Municipality of Franklin, the settlement of Ruthenians east of Dominion City, located in the townships 2 Range 6 & 7 East. There are at present in all 152 souls, 31 families and 7 men, 5 of the latter having their families in Galicia, in the settlement, of these 16 families containing 74 souls, have no land as yet, but are living with friends.

The first 19 families settled here the latter part of August, 4 families in October and 8 families in November last.

21 families had no stock whatever, but 10 families own together 34 head of stock: 6 oxen, 15 cows and 13 calves, one yoke of oxen is owned jointly by three families having each a third interest.

The settlers have in all erected 13 small log houses (the largest one is 16 × 18) in which live 141 people, 2 families 11 souls have rented a farm house on the SE 2–6 E.

I found most of the settlers busy adding additions to their houses for the better accommodations of their new overcrowded families.

The annexed list gives the particulars of each family, also as to the means they now possess, those marked thus (X) have been provisioned with two sacks of flour and 1 sack of cornmeal each, which is supposed to keep them in provisions one month, those marked thus X are also in need of monthly rations from the first of January next until such time as the men will be able to earn support of their families.

There are 18 men, heads of families, who are willing to go to work at anything, but who cannot very well hire out by the year on account of their families, but there are 8 young men and 3 young girls who could accept employment by the year, but all these people are so very poorly provided with clothing, wholly inadequate against our severe winter, that for this reason I could not advise them to walk across country to Rosenfeld, where otherwise 5 men could have found employment with the Mennonites.

The people seem to me on the whole very frugal and industrious, and would get along well in this country, if they only had some means to start farming with, but with few exceptions they came here with nothing or almost nothing, and having come late in the season, and being so very poorly provided with suitable clothing, they are in poor position to earn sufficient to provide for their families during this winter.

The Township in which this colony is located appears to me to be somewhat low, and as there seems to be no drainage, I am afraid that at least a portion of the land settled upon will be flooded in the spring, but hope there will be sufficient dry land for small gardens, which will be all these people can put in next year, as they have no implements or teams wherewith to put in a crop.

While at Dominion City my attention was called to the necessity of a small immigration building being erected by the Government at that point for the accommodation of the new arrivals and also for the convenience of those already settled there.

The settlers come into Dominion City for their supplies on foot, having no teams, and living about 25 miles away they must of necessity remain over night, in the summer time they can sleep outside or in barns, but in winter time this is not possible and the citizens do not wish to take them into their homes.

The health of the settlers was excellent and none had to be vaccinated.

The following are prices of flour & cornmeal quoted me by the two storekeepers of Dominion City:

Agnew & Co.
delivered in the settlement to each individual settler
flour XXXX .... $1.15 per sack
corn meal .... $1.90 per sack
Morkill & Scott
at their store in Dominion City
flour XXXX .... $1.35 per sack
cornmeal .... $1.65 per sack

Both grades of flour are the same, from Emerson mill. John C. Ginn of Dominion City and John Ramsey of Stuartburn offer to deliver goods from Dominion City to these settlers at 15 cents per hundred. James Simpson of Dominion City wants 20 cents per hundred delivering goods.[19]

To this report is attached a list of all Ukrainian settlers of the Stuartburn colony as of December, 1896, with the description of their locations and "particulars of each family":

1. Konstantin Stefanowietz (Stefanowicz)—SE¼ 20–2–6E, 2 souls, family in Austria, has fair house & 1 cow, is O.K. has $188.

2. Peter Majkowski—NW¼ 20–2–6E, family in Austria, no building, lives with the above, has 1 cow & means. O.K.

3. Hryhor Prygrocki—SE¼ 30–2–6E, 6 souls, has fair buildings, 2 oxen, 1 cow & 2 calves, had $420.00, is O.K.

4. Iwan Negrycz—NE¼–14–2–6E, single lives with the above. O.K.

5. Iwan Prygrocki—SE¼–22–2–6E, 5 souls, settled in Aug. 96, very poor hovel 12 × 6, no means, no provisions, man says suffers from rheumatism, may be lazy, needs provisions badly, children all small, no stock, bad water, needs 3 sacks of flour per month, supplied for December. (X)

6. Wasyl Stefura—SW¼–14–2–6E, 4 souls, no house, lives with Fedor Horobec on NE¼–10–2–6E, no stock, no means, needs provisions, good active man, willing to go to work, supplied for December. (X)

7. Fedor Horobec—NE¼–10–2–6E, 3 souls, has small house & stable, good well & water, owns 1 cow, 2 calves & ½ interest in yoke of oxen, had $120.00 when settling, is O.K.

8. Maks Stasyszyn—SE¼–10–2–6E, 4 souls, has poor house, is building, good water, has 1 cow & ½ interest in yoke of oxen, has no means, needs assistance, supplied for December. (X)

---

[19] 18. Imm./380647, December 7, 1896: Hugo Carstens, German Interpreter, to H. H. Smith, Commissioner of Dominion Lands, Winnipeg.

Dr. Josef Oleskow

Cyril Genik

Corner Jasper Avenue and Grieson Street, Edmonton, 1902
(*Alberta Government Photo, Ernest Brown Collection*)

Ukrainian peasant-settlers from Bukowina *en route* to Edna–Star, Alberta, 1897
(*Public Archives of Canada*)

A future citizen newly arrived in Canada (*Alberta Government Photo, Ernest Brown Collection*)

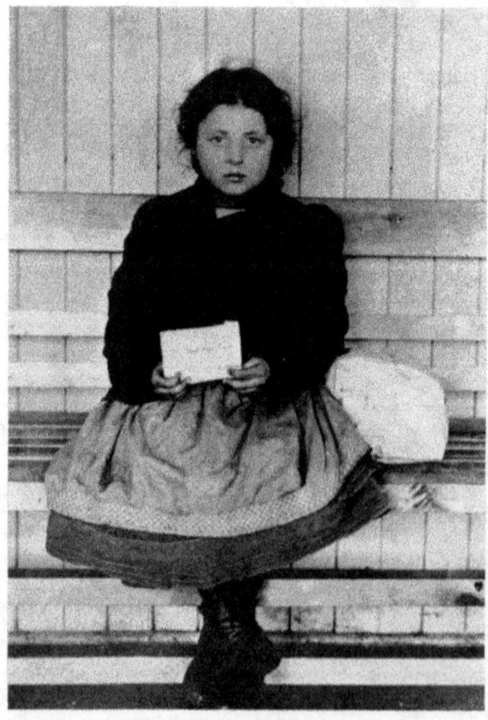

Another young Ukrainian immigrant, 1905 (*Public Archives of Canada*)

Reverend Nestor Dmytriw, 1895
(*Photo courtesy* Svoboda)

Theodore Nemirsky (1869–1946), Land Guide and first postmaster of Wostok, Alberta, N.W.T.
(*Courtesy of the Nemirsky family*)

Hugo Emil Carstens, 1912
(*Public Archives of Canada*)

Ukrainian hay market at Edmonton, 1903
(*Alberta Government Photo, Ernest Brown Collection*)

Wasyl and Wasylyna Zahara (*seated*) and Sanda and Maria Sandul (*standing*),
Stuartburn, 1920
(*Photo courtesy John Panchuk*)

416736

Lemberg, November 29th 1896

DEPT OF THE INTERIOR RECEIVED DEC 14 1896 OTTAWA

To the Department of Interior

in Ottawa

The Galician settlers in Stuartburn Man. Twn. 2 Rge 6 and partly 7 and 5 East of the 1st Meri. beg instantly the Department of Interior through me in order of establishing of a community with their own clergyman, that the Railway Lands in Twn 2 Rge 5, 6, 7 East of the 1st Mer. may be exchanged and opened as free homesteads to the friends of the above settlers, who live still in Galicia, but wish to settle in Manitoba near their friends.

Yours very respectfully

Prof. Dr. Josef Oleskow

Golembia G. 11A

Lemberg Austria Europe

Letter from Dr. Oleskow to the Department of the Interior, November 29, 1896 (*Public Archives of Canada*)

M. S.

Ottawa. 24th Jany. 1897

Mr. Langford for the minister WH 1/2/97

Dft. appd WH

Sir,

I have the honour to acknowledge receipt of your letter of the 29th November, written on behalf of Galician Settlers in Stuartburn, Manitoba, and asking that the railway lands referred to by you, namely in Township 2, Ranges 5, 6, and 7, East of the 1st meridian, may be secured for the purpose of providing free homesteads for friends of the above settlers still in Galicia who wish to settle in Manitoba.

I am to inform you that your communication will be submitted/

Prof. Josef Oleskow,
Glembia G. 11 A
Lemberg. Gallicia, Austria, Europe

Draft of the reply to Dr. Oleskow's letter of November 29, 1896
(*Public Archives of Canada*)

The Department of ~~Agriculture,~~ Interior No.

Service Immigration
Subhead Interpreting

To Cyril Genik Dr.
Lusted street 111
P. O. Address

1896 9-10 12-13 19-20 November	To 6 days interpreting for Ruthenian immigrants a $2.00 O.K. [illegible]	$ 12

I certify that the above account is correct; ~~that the articles therein enumerated were necessary for, and have been or will be applied to~~ and that the prices paid were just and reasonable.

Cyrill Genik

F. 77
Imm. No. 77

Received Winnipeg this 12 day of January 1897

the sum of twelve dollars and — cents, in full payment of the above account.

Cyrill Genik

Receipt for the first pay received by Cyril Genik as an interpreter, January 12, 1897 (*Public Archives of Canada*)

The first house built by Peter Smuk, Senkiw, Manitoba, 1905

The second house of a Ukrainian pioneer settler
(*Archives of Saskatchewan*)

Ukrainian settlers threshing, Stuartburn, about 1900
(*Public Archives of Canada*)

Main Street, Fort Saskatchewan, Alberta, 1898
(*Alberta Government Photo, Ernest Brown Collection*)

Ukrainian Catholic church, Tolstoi, Manitoba, 1898–1903

Ukrainian Greek Orthodox church, Gardenton, Manitoba, built in 1897
(*Photo courtesy Maria Tanchak*)

Dauphin Manitoba, with grain elevators and mills, 1902
(*Public Archives of Canada*)

Henry Hall Smith, Commissioner of Dominion Lands, Winnipeg, 1885–1897 (*Public Archives of Canada*)

T. Mayne Daly, Minister of the Interior, 1892–1896 (*Public Archives of Canada*)

Major A. H. Griesbach, Commander of G Division, N.W.M.P., Fort Saskatchewan, Alberta (*Alberta Government Photo, Ernest Brown Collection*)

James A. Smart, Deputy Minister of the Interior, 1897–1904 (*Public Archives of Canada*)

Corporal George D. Butler, N.W.M.P. (*Alberta Government Photo, Ernest Brown Collection*)

William F. McCreary, Commissioner of Immigration, Winnipeg, 1897–1900 (*Public Archives of Canada*)

Sir Charles Tupper, High Commissioner for Canada, London, 1883–87, 1888–96 (*Public Archives of Canada*)

C. W. Sutter, Agent of the Dominion Lands Office, Edmonton (*Alberta Government Photo, Ernest Brown Collection*)

Sir Clifford Sifton, Minister of the Interior, 1896–1905 (*Public Archives of Canada*)

Sir William C. Van Horne, President of the C.P.R., 1888–1910 (*Public Archives of Canada*)

William T. R. Preston, Inspector of Canadian Immigration Agencies in Europe, 1899–1902 (*Public Archives of Canada*)

Sir Donald A. Smith, High Commissioner for Canada, London, 1896–1914 (*Public Archives of Canada*)

9. A. Jaremowietz (Jaremowicz)—no land, lives with the above, 4 souls, has now $120, settled in November, is O.K.

10. Wasyl Zahara—NW¼ 2–2–6E, 6 souls, has fair house, is building, owns 1 cow, 1 calf, & ½ interest in yoke of oxen, good well & water, had $200.00 but says spent all means, has 4 families living with him in same house, is O.K.

11. Andrej Glowatsky—no land, 4 souls, settled in Nov., lives with the above, has about $45.00, is O.K.

12. Iwan Sandul—no land, 4 souls, settled Nov., lives with the above, has about $50.00, is O.K.

13. Iwan Mukanyk—no land, 4 souls, settled in Nov., lives with W. Zahara, has about $45.00, is O.K.

14. Michael Zahara—no land, 4 souls, settled in Nov., lives with W. Zahara, has about $220.00, is O.K.

15. Michael Sokolowsky—SE¼–36–2–6E, 6 souls, settled in Oct., lives on SE¼ 2–2–6E, no house, no stock, had no money when settling, oldest boy 26 years, earned $50.00, has now 5 sacks of flour left, head of family old, needs some assistance in January. X

16. Joseph Kuchinsky—SW¼–36–2–6E, 5 souls, settled in Oct., lives on SE¼–2–2–6E, no house, no stock, had $80.00 when settling, claims to have no money, has 3 sacks of flour, oldest boy 19 years, needs assistance. X

17. Ilasz Prokopczak—NW¼–12–2–6E, 6 souls, settled in Aug. 96, lives with Jacob Szelep in 14–2 6E, no house, owns 1 cow & 1 calf, had only $37.00, old man, oldest boy 17 years, no means, needs provisions, supplied for December. (X)

18. Jacob Szelep—SE¼ 14–2–6E, family in Austria, has a house, 2 cows & 1 calf, is O.K.

19. Fedor Pidherny (Pidhirnyj)—SW¼ 24–2–6E, 5 souls, settled in Aug. 96, had $20.00, has house 12 × 12, no stock, worked on threashing machine but got no pay, has now no provisions, needs provisions, supplied for December. (X)

20. Fedor Dymianyk—NW¼–24–2–6E, 3 souls, settled in Aug. 1896, had $20.00, no house, no stock, lives with the above, earned $12.00, all expended, has 1 sack of flour, needs assistance, provided for December. (X)

21. Wasyl Salamandyk—SE¼ 24–2–6E, 3 souls, settled in Aug. 96, had $20.00, has no house, stock, means & only ½ sack of flour, old man 56 years old, daughter of 14 years, needs assistance. X

22. Michael Michanuk (Michael Michaniuk)—no land, no house, no stock, 5 souls, settled in October 1896, had 25 cents only, worked out and earned $80.00 with which he repaid his debts, children small, needs assistance. X

23. Peter Strubicki (Petro Strumbicki)—NW¼ 30–2–7E, 8 souls, small house, children all small, no stock, no nothing, needs clothing and assistance very badly, supplied for December. (X)

24. Michael Cysmystruk—no land, 5 souls, settled in October 96, lives with No. 23, had no means, earned $22. on Railway, has nothing, children small, 9, 5, and 3 years, needs assistance bad. X

25. Sawka Perun—SW¼ 30–2–7E, 5 souls, small house, has no stock, settled Aug. 96, had no money, worked out but received no pay, needs provisions & clothing, supplied for December. (X)

26. Iwan Sokolyk—no land, arrived in Novbr., 4 souls, had $8.00, has now 1.50 & ¼ sack of flour, enough for one week, needs assistance badly, has one foot frozen. X

27. Matij Probizansky—no land, arrived in November, 3 souls, has $30.00, needs assistance, for the present is O.K.

28. Konst. Didiuk—no land, arrived in Oct., 6 souls, worked on M. & NW Ry. claims to have earned only $3.50, has now no means & only 1 sack of flour, lives with No. 25, needs assistance. X

29. Josef Bzowy—SW¼ 28–2–6E, 4 souls, has house 12 × 14, & 1 cow, had $80.00, all expended, has 2 sacks of flour, may need a little assistance.

30. Nikol Kohut—NE¼ 22–2–6E, family in Austria, was burned out, has no clothing, lives with No. 29.

31. Anufry Smuk—NW¼ 22–2–6E, family in Austria, is O.K.

32. Iwan Storoszczuk—NW¼ 28–2 6E, no children, no house, no stock, lives with No. 29, has $6.00 & 2½ sacks of flour. X

33. Fedor Saranczuk—no land, arrived in Novbr. last, 7 souls, head of family 54 years old, has $20.00 & 1 sack of flour, enough to live for two months, needs assistance in February, lives with No. 29. X

34. Simon Salamandyk—SE¼ 28–2–6E, arrived in Aug. 96, fair house & stable, 3 cows, 2 oxen & 2 steers, wagon, plow, etc. was burned out once, 4 children, is O.K.

35. Wasyl Hawryluk—no land, arrived in Oct. 6 souls, children all small, had only $5.00, has nothing, lives with No. 34, needs assistance, supplied for December. (X)

36. Jan Tomaszewsky—NE¼ 28–2–6E, in Aug. 96, 4 souls, has house, 1 cow & calf & 2 steers, had $130.00 is O.K.

37. Oparko (Ozarko) Niwransky—no land, arrived in Oct. 96, 6 souls, has $90.00, is O.K. lives with No. 36.

Note: 31 families & 7 men, in all 152 souls, comprise the settlement, these have 13 houses, and own 32 head of cattle. 20 families (97 souls) need assistance in provisions to keep them through the winter, and are indicated by X, those who have been supplied for the month of December are marked thus (X). 16 families have no land as yet.

(Signed) HUGO CARSTENS

The estimated cost of supplying Ruthenian settlers east of Dominion City with provisions (until April, 1897) is estimated at $341.55.

IV

The settlers were so busy establishing themselves on their homesteads that they neglected to notify the Austrian Consul in Montreal about their whereabouts, or, more likely, they did not consider it necessary to continue maintaining connections with the Austrian authorities because they had decided to make Canada their permanent home. But the Austrian authorities were of a different opinion. The Minister for Foreign Affairs (and Prime Minister of Austro-Hungary) wrote to Schultze in Montreal that he was desirous to learn the fate of "Oleskow's settlers," and also to find out what connection existed between the

Canadian Department of the Interior and Dr. Oleskow. On November 13, 1896 Schultze dispatched a long letter to the Deputy Minister of the Interior in Ottawa enquiring about the settlers:

I have the honor to inform you that I am directed by the Imperial and Royal Austro-Hungarian Minister of Foreign Affairs in Vienna to enquire into the position and present welfare of a party of Austrian immigrants who are supposed to have settled in the North West and formed a colony there. The founder of this colony is Professor Oleskow and the party in which my Government is specially interested consists of 25 farmers who having sold their lands in Galicia, Austria, left there about the 20th of July last under the leadership of Johann Dorundiak. Among this party are the former reeve of Kolomyjaer named Majkowski and also a Cyril Genik Berezowski from Berezow, both rather prominent men in their former circle, and as no news whatever had been received since from either, my Government has desired me to ascertain their present whereabouts and further to report about their present condition and doings. I therefore have the honor to request you kindly give me at your early convenience all the information regarding these two men, in particularly the whole party in general, which you may be able to furnish, or to kindly give me the proper address to whom I should apply for such information.[20]

The busy Ukrainian homesteaders in Stuartburn never suspected that the Imperial and Royal Austro-Hungarian Minister for Foreign Affairs would personally enquire about their well-being, and particularly about the whereabouts of Cyril Genik Berezowski and Peter Majkowski, "both rather prominent men in their former circle." As for Johann Dorundiak, who was supposed to have been the leader of the group, his name was not on the list of S.S. *Sicilia* passengers, which suggests that he stayed behind. Dorundiak, a well-to-do farmer from the district of Kolomyja, had accompanied Professor Oleskow on his visit to Canada during the late summer of 1895.

The Department of the Interior forwarded the copy of the letter from Austro-Hungarian Consul in Montreal to the Commissioner of Dominion Lands in Winnipeg, asking him to prepare a report containing the information asked for with regard to Oleskow's colonists. The Commissioner charged Hugo Carstens with the task of supplying the necessary information. Carstens duly reported:

. . . Regarding the party of Immigrants referred to, numbering 64 souls, was met by me at Rat Portage, Ontario, and that they reached Winnipeg on the 25th of July last, where they were temporarily made comfortable at the Dominion Immigration Building, after a rest of a few days, 3 delegates, selected by this party, were furnished with free transportation and an officer

20. Oles./32217, November 13, 1896: Eduard Schultze, Imperial and Royal Austro-Hungarian Consul, Montreal, to A. M. Burgess, Deputy Minister of the Interior, Ottawa.

of this Department [John W. Wendelbo] as guide, to select a suitable location, if possible, near the settled portions of Manitoba where free homesteads were available. The delegates selected the district east of Dominion City in the Municipality of Franklin, about 70 miles south east of the city of Winnipeg, in Township 2, Range 6, East of the 1st Mer. . . . .The two men in this party especially enquired about have both taken a free grant in this settlement, Mr. Peter Majkowski has taken and is residing upon N.W.¼ of the Section 20 in Township 2, Range 6, East, his present address is Stuartburn P.O., Man. As far as I know he is well satisfied with the change and will bring his family next spring. The other gentleman, Mr. Cyril Genik, has entered the N.W. 16-2-6 East, but resides for the Winter at 111 Lusted Street, in this city to enable him to send his children to the City Schools. . . .[21]

A copy of Carstens' report was forwarded to the Austro-Hungarian Consul in Montreal, together with various pamhlets describing Canada and the opportunities for settlers, in the hope that ". . . this will afford you the desired information with regard to the particular emigrants on whose behalf the Imperial and Royal Austro-Hungarian Minister for Foreign Affairs made enquiry, and on the general subject of the advantages of Canada as a field of colonization."[22]

V

Despite severe winter conditions, activity in the Stuartburn colony never abated. The number of settlers passed the 150 mark, and there were indications that with the opening of spring navigation their numbers might easily double. The settlement began to acquire the aspects of a community. The establishment of rural schools was discussed, as well as the idea of building a church, with the hope that some day it would be possible to have a priest to attend to their spiritual needs, and they wrote about these matters to Dr. Oleskow in Lemberg.

One dominant and most pressing problem occupied the minds of the whole community, namely, how to obtain more land for settlement, in anticipation of the arrival of their friends and relatives. This question also concerned the Commissioner of Dominion Lands in Winnipeg, who repeatedly and persistently urged Ottawa to issue an order to release odd-numbered sections, thus making them available for homestead entries. In his memorandum of December 8, 1896, he reiterated his request to free the lands:

The lands in Townships referred to (i.e., odd-numbered sections in

[21]2. Oles./32524, November 25, 1896: Hugo Carstens, Winnipeg, to H. H. Smith, Winnipeg.

[22]2. Oles., December 17, 1896: Lyndwode Pereira, Ottawa, to Eduard Schultze, Montreal.

Tp. 2 Rge. 6 & 7) were mostly taken up either under homestead entry or by purchase many years ago, but were abandoned for the probable reason there were then more desirable locations to be secured. The Homestead entries have practically all been cancelled, and steps are being taken to cancel sales. As it is probable other settlers of the same nationality will arrive, it would seem very desirable that all the lands in this locality should be made available for settlement by these people, and it was recommended that the odd-numbered Sections in these Townships should be thrown open.[23]

But the Commissioner was still uncertain what policy the new Minister intended to adopt, and what action he desired should be taken: "The Deputy Minister [A. M. Burgess] has suggested that from the views expressed of late by the Minister in his public speeches with regard to the question of alternative Sections, he may not be in accord with the proposal made and consequently the matter is at present held in abeyance."[24]

The qualms of the Commissioner proved to be unfounded. The Minister fully approved the release of additional land for the benefit of Ukrainian settlers in the Stuartburn colony, but the release had to be carried out in accord with legal rules and regulations in order to safeguard the future occupants from possible legal entanglements. On December 22, the Secretary of the Department of the Interior, directed by the Deputy Minister, informed the Commissioner of Dominion Lands in Winnipeg: ". . . in the matter of the settlement by Austrian immigrants of certain lands in Manitoba, I am now directed to enclose you herewith a schedule of sales of certain lands East of the 1st Meridian, which sales have been cancelled in the books here. A separate letter in each case has been written to the Agent of Dominion Lands at Winnipeg advising him of this action, and instructing him to note the same in his books. He was told, however, that he is not to dispose of any of the lands in question until further instructed by this office."[25]

With this letter was enclosed "The Schedule of Time Sales Cancelled by the Head Office." Some of those whose claims were cancelled had registered for several sections—for instance, James Sinclair opted for four sections, and Henry Mandeville, William Beech, and others also had whole sections in their names. They had failed to fulfil conditions of sale or of homestead requirements, thus forfeiting their claims. Gradually more and more sales were cancelled and made ready for release, but for the time being the ruling was that "no disposition [is] to be made

[23] 18. Imm., December 8, 1896: Memorandum from the Dominion Lands Commission, Winnipeg, to the Department of the Interior, Ottawa.

[24] *Ibid.*

[25] 18. Imm./381608, December 22, 1896: Lyndwode Pereira, Ottawa, to the Secretary, Dominion Lands Board, Winnipeg.

until definite decision has been arrived at with regard to these odd numbered sections."[26]

Anticipating a positive decision, the settlers who were waiting for the release of homesteads occupied the odd-numbered sections, so as not to miss the spring sowing, and subsequently they informed the newly-appointed Commissioner of Immigration in Winnipeg, W. F. McCreary, of their action. McCreary in turn informed the Agent of Dominion Lands, E. F. Stephenson:

The following Austrian immigrants have informed this office that they have settled upon lands set opposite their names, and that they will make entry as soon as they are permitted to do so:

Mich Prygwsky (Mykhailo Prygrocki)	NE¼	19	2	6E
Anton Janmowicz (Anton Jaremowicz)	NE	9	2	6E
Maty Probizanski	SE¼	9	2	6E
Stefan Sasanczuk (Stefan Saranczuk)	NW¼	27	2	6E
Michal Stotoszicuk (M. Storoszczuk)	NE	27	2	6E
Iwan Salamandyk	SW	27	2	6E
Iwan Sokoluk (Iwan (Sokolyk)	SE¼	23	2	6E
Michal Zahara	NW¼	12	2	6E[27]

. . . The following four persons notified us that they have settled on Section 1, Township 2, Range 6 East:

Elasz Prokoszuk (Ilasz Prokopchuk)	NE¼	1	2	6E
Fodor Makonyk (Fedor Mukanyk)	SW¼	1	2	6E
Andryorsz Glowvicky (Andrej Golowacki)	NW¼	1	2	6E
Michal Kaminskyz (Michael Kaminsky)	NW¼	17	2	7E

These people have to some extent been promised that the odd sections suitable for settlement would be opened for homesteads and are very impatiently waiting the time when you will be able to permit them to make entry.[28]

Stephenson, a very conscientious official, was concerned about these irregularities and enquired of the Commissioner of Dominion Lands ". . . whether it is expected that these lands will be made available for *homesteading* in the near future, as you will observe that the Commissioner (of Immigration) states they are impatiently awaiting the time when they will be allowed to make entry."[29] The Commissioner of Dominion Lands then requested the Department of the Interior in Ottawa "to give the matter early attention," because

. . . the Austrian settlers in Township 2, Ranges 6 and 7 East are urging

[26]18. Imm./136441, February 19, 1897: Lyndwode Pereira, Ottawa, to the Secretary, Dominion Lands Board, Winnipeg.

[27]18. Imm./Ref. No. 433, April 5, 1897: W. F. McCreary, Winnipeg, to Agent, Dominion Lands, Winnipeg.

[28]18. Imm./Ref. No. 532, April 22, 1897: W. F. McCreary, Winnipeg, to E. F. Stephenson, Agent, Dominion Lands, Winnipeg.

[29]18. Imm./Ref. No. 95619, April 22, 1897: E. F. Stephenson, Agent, Dominion Lands, Winnipeg, to the Commissioner of Dominion Lands, Winnipeg.

that a decision be made as to opening for entry the odd-numbered Sections therein. Of course, these lands being East of the Red River are not within any Railway Company's grant [as Dr. Oleskow presumed in his letter of November 29, 1896], and the Commissioner thinks it very desirable that some steps should be taken immediately to arrive at a decision. It is especially important at this season of the year, and I may say that it is reported by Mr. McCreary, Immigration Commissioner, that a number of these Austrian settlers have already located on odd-sections. Will you please give the matter early attention.[30]

The settlers of Stuartburn, not certain that their appeals had been receiving the desired attention, themselves composed a petition (written in Ukrainian and translated into English) and transmitted it to the Commissioner of Immigration:

There are here of us 20 families who have not yet got land to work because none of us know what Section is open for homesteading and without a Surveyor we cannot find out for ourselves. We beg, therefore, that someone may soon be sent out by the Government who would be empowered to accept our entries.

(Signed) THE INHABITANTS OF STUARTBURN.[31]

The attitude of the Department of the Interior was sympathetic to the requests of the settlers at every turn. There was no doubt that the Minister would try to surmount the obstacles which still stood in the way of release of the land for settlement. The Secretary of the Department,[32] passing the Commissioner's note to the Deputy Minister, added:

I submit herewith Mr. McCreary's application to have the odd-numbered sections in Township 2, Ranges 6 and 7 East opened to settlement. It has been our practice for some time to open the odd sections East of the Meridian and if the Minister wishes to do so in this case the annexed report to Council will be sufficient.

P.S. Please see the Order in Council of the 12th December last, marked, in the case of Tp. 13 and 14, Ranges 7 and 8 East.[33]

He enclosed the draft of a "Report to the Governor General in Council" for the release of certain lands, should the Minister ask for it. The matter suffered some delay because the Minister travelled to the West and was not expected to return to Ottawa before the first week of May,

[30] 18. Imm./371399, April 30, 1897: The Secretary, Dominion Lands, Winnipeg, to the Secretary, Department of the Interior, Ottawa.

[31] 18. Imm., April 21, 1897: The inhabitants of Stuartburn, to the Commissioner of Immigration, Winnipeg.

[32] The Secretary was John R. Hall. He was Acting Deputy Minister of the Interior during Dr. Oleskow's visit in 1895, and Secretary of the Department of the Interior, 1896–97.

[33] 18. Imm., Memo, April 4, 1897, from "J.R.H." (Hall), Secretary, Department of the Interior, Ottawa, to James A Smart, Deputy Minister of the Interior, Ottawa.

1897. While in Winnipeg, the Minister discussed matters with the Commissioner of Immigration, and as a result of these discussions, he dispatched a telegram to the Deputy Minister in Ottawa, asking that a draft of the recommendation be prepared:

Secretary's letter to McCreary File 410595 re opening odd-numbered sections for homestead entry. Have recommendation prepared and submitted to me immediately on my return.—CLIFFORD SIFTON.[34]

The draft of the recommendation, prepared by the secretary, was waiting for Sifton on his return. The Commissioner of Immigration, on his part, sent a confirmation of the telegram to the Deputy Minister by mail and added necessary information about the immigrants and the land in question:

Referring to the conversation I had to-day with the Minister, in reference to opening certain odd-numbered Sections for homestead entry, the Minister wired you as follows this morning. [See text of preceding telegram.]

He expressed a desire that in addition I should write you on the subject, in order that it might be fresh in his memory and could be attended to at once on his arrival.

As a file is kept for each set of Townships, I will write more particularly in reference to what is known as the Ruthenian or Galician, Colony in Townships 1 and 2, Ranges 6 and 7, East being a settlement established some time last Fall, at or near the Post Office of Stuartburn.

As you have already advised me, a large number of Galicians are on their way here, and some already have not yet got places. There are, however, in these four Townships quite a number of odd-numbered Sections owned by the Government, as far as we know, that would make good homesteads were they made open for entry. There are, of course, some scrub and poplar bluffs on them, but these Galicians like farms of that kind; in fact, they do not care to go to open prairies.

Our Galician Interpreter has received a long letter from them, dated the 21st instant, the gist of which, translated into English I send you.

In addition to these twenty families now there waiting for entry, I intend sending down a large number of this expected contingent and locate them in that district, so that it is most important that these people should be settled at once in order that they may put in something in the way of potatoes and other vegetables this year, otherwise, there is no doubt they will be a charge upon the Government next winter.

Now, I do not think, from what the Minister said, there is any likelihood of this request not being granted, except the possibility that the lands may have been included in the Land Grant to the South-Eastern Railroad.

If, upon receipt of this letter you look the question up at once and ascertain that they have not been included in that Land Grant, then the chances are that they will be open for homestead, and I want you to wire me to that effect. If you do not, I will have to take the responsibility of either removing

[34]18. Imm., April 30, 1897: Telegram, Clifford Sifton, Winnipeg, to James A. Smart, Deputy Minister, Ottawa.

these people from that district or sending down a Forest Ranger to shew them the lands, and let them go and squat. I have arranged with the Department here that the moment I have authority for taking their entries, or for squatting on the land, with power afterwards to make entry, I shall send down an interpreter from this office, along with the Forest Ranger, and each party shall be placed on his land properly.

I should have your wire to this effect not later than Wednesday morning, so that I will tell my Interpreter in this office to write those people to-day that I will send some word to them by Wednesday's train.[35]

A few days later the Deputy Minister informed Commissioner McCreary that he was attending to the matter and that a positive decision was expected to be reached in a very short time:

Referring to your letter of the 30th ultimo with regard to the opening of the odd-numbered sections east of the Red River for homestead entry, I beg to say that I have carried out the Minister's instruction and no doubt this matter will be attended to without further delay, Mr. Sifton having returned to the Capital yesterday. You will be further advised in this connection so that you will not need to delay taking advantage of the new order as soon as it is issued, and you will probably be able to settle a great many people on these lands.[36]

The eagerly awaited release of the odd-numbered sections in Township 2, Ranges 6 and 7 East, was within grasp. On May 5, 1897, Mr. Smart wired Mr. McCreary: "Odd sections in township two ranges six and seven east available; in township one same ranges sales not yet cancelled; many of them will be at once."[37] And, concerned about the well being of the settlers, the Deputy Minister added: "Is it not rather wet? Be careful in settling Galicians. Understand they are a good lot."

On receipt of this telegram, Commissioner McCreary decided to go to Stuartburn personally to satisfy himself about the suitability of the released sections for settlement and to verify whether the Deputy Minister's apprehensions were justified.

I am in receipt of your favour of the 4th, with reference to the opening of odd-numbered Sections east of the Red River, for homesteading, and also your telegram of the 5th instant, saying that the odd-numbered Sections in Township 2, Ranges 6 and 7, East, are available, and in Township 1 the sales are not yet cancelled, but many of them will be at once.

Shortly after the receipt of this I took a delegation of 46 of these people out through that country in order that I might satisfy myself at to its desirability as a field for the settlement of not only these at present here, but those

[35] 18. Imm./975. April 30, 1897: W. F. McCreary, Winnipeg, to James A. Smart, Ottawa.

[36] 18. Imm., May 4, 1897: James A. Smart, Ottawa, to W. F. McCreary, Winnipeg.

[37] 18. Imm., May 5, 1897: Telegram, James A. Smart, Ottawa, to W. F. McCreary, Winnipeg.

who may arrive in the future. I found Township 1 Range 6 a very fair Township, all except the south-east corner which was somehow wet. I was told before going that the Big Slough ran all across the South end, but I believe that the Slough is chiefly south of the International Boundary.

These Galicians are a peculiar people; they will not accept as a gift 160 acres of what we should consider the best land in Manitoba, that is first class wheat growing prairies land; what they particularly want is wood, and they care but little whether the land is heavy soil or light gravel; but each man must have some wood on his place. This Township has got some very nice timber bluffs, and also some meadows suitable for hay, but in a great many sections there are stones. They do not object to stones, however, if they have sufficient for small crop. In my opinion it will be many years before they will go extensively into grain raising. I think from ten to twenty-five acres will be the outside cultivated by any one of these people for the next ten years, with the exception possibly of one or two out of a thousand settlers who may have a considerable amount of money, and to go into farming extensively; but the man with $100, which is the average amount any of them possesses who have any means at all, will not go extensively into grain raising.

From advices received this morning, and from a letter I received from Professor Oleskow, it is quite evident we are going to have a large number of these immigrants, and I would advise you to cancel all those sales in Township 1, Range 5; Township 1, Range 6; Township 2, Range 5; Township 2, Range 6; Township 1, Range 7; and Township 2, Range 7. I understand there are still a number of uncancelled sales in all those Townships, and I think we should be able to place 1,000 or 2,000 people in that colony if we had all those lands available. Of course, in opening up the odd-numbered Sections you would have to be careful that a lot of speculators do not again enter for them, as I found some of the settlers in that district were all wanting more land. One man, for instance, the Postmaster Mr. Ramsay, who had already homesteaded twice or three times, and also pre-empted both for himself, his sons and his son-in-law, acquiring over 1,000 acres in that way from the Government, wanted still another half-section, that is Section 19, Township 2, Range 6, and when I talked rather sharply to him I was surprised to find that all the land he had under cultivation out of this vast extent of territory was about eight acres, although a resident for ten years. Now, people of this kind should not be allowed to tie up a lot of land in that way, and there are many other quarter-sections in the same district about which I will write you again. You had better advise me from time to time as to when each sale has been cancelled, and its number, and so forth.[38]

Having had previous experience with land speculators, Commissioner McCreary wanted to take all possible precautions to prevent the repetition of their encroachments in this area newly opened for settlement:

I enclose for you copy of a list I took from the Assessment Roll in that district, which may assist you in the cancellation of these homesteads and sales. I might say that it would be just as well that these lands should not

[38]3. Gal./37564, May 14, 1897: W.F. McCreary, Winnipeg, to James A. Smart, Ottawa.

be made open for entry at the Land Office here, because if this is done there is no doubt speculators down in that district will at once apply in order, if possible, to shut out the Galicians. I think the better plan is for our men in this office, when a party arrives, to take them down; have them select their various quarter-sections, and if they are in a position to make entry, write your department and have you give special instructions that these particular entries should be allowed. You must bear in mind that there is a very strong aversion on the part of English-speaking people to allowing those Galicians to come into their districts, and I have got to devise all sorts of means to circumvent their actions.

Commissioner McCreary's preparations for the settlement of larger numbers of Ukrainians in the Stuartburn district were made just in time. Even while he was writing his letter to the Deputy Minister, the latter received a cable from London about more Ukrainian immigrants on their way to Canada.[39] The S.S. *Prussia* was carrying 672 Ukrainian settlers; the S.S. *Arabia*, with "539 mostly Galicians" had left Hamburg on May 8 and other ships were on their way. The cancellation of time sales and the opening of more land for settlement in the Stuartburn district became a pressing necessity. To obtain releases of time sales, an Order in Council was required; but before such an order could be issued, it was necessary to clear all legal obstacles, which could only be accomplished by the lawyers and the courts. Even then there would still remain some conditions which could challenge full title to the homesteads. It would take a number of years to clear the titles—the Commissioner of Dominion Lands explained the procedure involved:

There is a tangle in connection with the titles of some Galicians in the Stuartburn, Man. district. Some of these lands homesteaded by the Galicians were originally time sales, and the parties who originally purchased the lands made transfers by Quit Claim Deed and otherwise, which instruments are registered in the Registry Offices. These time sales were subsequently cancelled, and the Galician settlers were given homestead entries for the lands. Upon compliance with the provisions of the Act the Galician settlers secured patents, but when they go to mortgage the land they find that the prior conveyances registered form clouds upon the title. They have been told that the Government would see that the clouds were removed from the title.

It will be necessary to have a list of the cases made out in which settlers have been allowed to homestead time sales in that district. A search should then be made in the Registry Office to ascertain in what cases there are clouds upon the title. A Solicitor should be instructed to do this and afterwards instructed to take proceedings, at the expense of the Department but in the name of the patentees, to remove the clouds upon the titles by petition under the Real Property Act. When searches have been made and the information procured, the Department of Justice should be asked to take

[39]3. Gal./37432, May 12, 1897: Cable, High Commissioner for Canada, London, to the Minister of the Interior, Ottawa.

the necessary proceedings as above specified, Mr. T. L. Metcalfe [member of a law firm] of Winnipeg, to do the legal work.[40]

The removal of the "clouds" was outlined as follows by the solicitors and barristers Perdue and Rothwell of Winnipeg, who, together with Mr. Metcalfe, handled most of the cases of clearing the titles of Galician settlers in Stuartburn:

While our Mr. Perdue was in Ottawa he and Mr. T. L. Metcalfe mentioned to the Law Clerk of the Department and also to the Hon. Sifton what would be necessary to be done in connection with the removal of the clouds on the titles to the lands referred to in the letter from the Department dated 20th February, 1903. As they explained, the only quick and effectual way of removing the clouds from the titles is by applying the Certificates of Title under the provisions of the Real Property Act. We understand that there are some 200 quarter sections in the condition mentioned, that is to say, clouded by the registration of deeds from persons who had purchased from the Government some twenty years ago. It will be necessary that a separate application should be made for each quarter-section. In addition to the fees charged upon each application by the Solicitors conducting the matter there will also be actual disbursements amounting on each application to from $12. to $18. Considerable of these disbursements are occasioned by the charges made by the Land Titles Office and as suggested to the Department the advisability of requesting the Local Government to limit their charges under the circumstances. We understand that correspondence will take place with the Local Government with the view to having the fees in the Land Titles Office reduced in respect to the application in question.

The writer and Mr. Metcalfe also consulted with the Deputy Minister of Justice as to the advisability of fixing a straight charge to cover the Solicitors' fee for each application. The sum of $12.00 for the work connected with each application was discussed as a fair charge on the part of the Solicitors in view of the large number of applications. An itemized bill according to the tariff would considerably exceed that amount. We mention these matters now so that the Department may be in a position to include a sufficient sum in the Estimates to cover the expense.

In the meantime we are preparing applications for the patentees and taking steps to have a number of the parcels brought under the operation of the Act and the clouds removed. On consulting with the District Registrar he infoms us that he requires a letter from the Department shewing the cancellation in each case and also the facts upon which such cancellation was based. We shall prepare a draft letter and forward it.

It was understood, also, that we should be furnished with a list of the persons to whom patents of portions of said land have been issued or who have been recommended for patent. We shall have to go to Emerson and search the titles to all the parcels in the list to find out which of them are clouded. Some of them are likely clear. An extra charge will have to be made to cover this.[41]

[40]19. Imm./754716, January 28, 1903: Memorandum from the Commissioner of Dominion Lands, Ottawa, to J. G. Burpé, Ottawa.

[41]19. Imm./765753, March 12, 1903: Perdue & Rothwell, Solicitors, Winnipeg, to the Secretary, Department of the Interior, Ottawa.

The difficulties which darkened the titles of Stuartburn settlers were gradually removed. One "cloud" remained, though, which no legal efforts were able to clear, and with which the Department of Agriculture had to cope. This was the plague of mosquitos which bred in milliards in the lower parts of the Roseau River district and made the life of man and beast an agony, as Stashyn described in his memoirs: "There were such masses of them that they obstructed the view to work. If one wished to do some work outside, it was necessary to wear a face net, like the one beekeepers wear. Gloves had to be worn too. But in spite of all these precautions they still found ways to bite you. They once attacked our father so badly, in spite of the heavy sheepskin coat he was wearing for protection, that his neck and throat were badly swollen and his face and ears were a shapeless mass."[42]

VI

With the approach of spring came the great feast of the Resurrection. For the settlers in Stuartburn it was the first spring in Canada and the first Easter in the New Land. They learned that Father Nestor Dmytriw had just arrived from Buffalo, the first Ukrainian priest to visit Canada.[43] He was not unknown to the settlers, as he was the editor of *Svoboda*, the Ukrainian-language newspaper published weekly at Mount Carmel, Pennsylvania, which the Ukrainian settlers had read almost from the day of their arrival in Canada. They invited Father Dmytriw to come to Stuartburn for Easter Sunday, but he was unable to accept the invitation since he had already made arrangements to visit Edna, Alberta, the oldest Ukrainian settlement in Canada. He suggested, therefore, that he come to Stuartburn on Palm Sunday, April 17, 1897.

The Canadian Government made Father Dmytriw an immigration officer and interpreter to assist the newly appointed Commissioner of Immigration in Winnipeg, who was short of interpreters. The appointment gave Father Dmytriw an opportunity to attend to the spiritual needs of Ukrainian settlers across the country, who were still unable to support a priest from their own funds. Father Dmytriw visited Stuartburn April 16–19, 1897, and later described his visit in *Svoboda*, as well as in his "Travel Reminiscences," published in booklet form:

> Stuartburn is the largest Ukrainian colony in Manitoba. It is located in the southern part of the province, 9 miles north of North Dakota. . . . I set out to visit the colony on April 16, 1897, leaving Winnipeg at 8 A.M. In the same coach, travelling with me, was also a Ukrainian family from the district of

[42]Stashyn, "Moi spohady," 79.

[43]Nestor Dmytriw, *Kanadiyska Rus: Podorozhni spomyny*/"Canadian Ruthenia: Reminiscences of Travels" (Mount Carmel, Pa.: *Svoboda* Publishers, 1897), 3.

Borshchiw, with two settlers from Stuartburn who walked the 54 miles all the way to Winnipeg to meet their fellow-country-men. . . . The two citizens from Stuartburn [of eight months standing] looked quite presentable. They discussed current events, debated, joked about Galician misery, and talked about the future which lies ahead of them in Canada. The new immigrant from Galicia listened attentively with his mouth open, his wife clad in dirty old country clothes was dozing with a child in her arms. . . .[44]

In the course of the conversation, Father Dmytriw learned that the new immigrant was illiterate because the Austrian authorities had not established a school in their village (and many other villages) until as late as 1884, when he was already too old to attend. Father Dmytriw was shocked at the existence of such conditions in Europe and at the unfortunate consequence that so many middle-aged people were left illiterate. With these thoughts on his mind, he arrived in Dominion City. He describes his travels through that region thus:

The postmaster of Stuartburn [L. G. Ramsey] put me on his wagon, I settled down comfortably on the flour bags he was taking to Stuartburn for distribution among our needy settlers, and we started leisurely on the twenty-mile ride. The Englishman was whistling and humming tunes all the way, the horses were trotting at a comfortable pace, and I was chilled to the bone because a northern wind brought cold air from icy regions. Finally, towards evening, we arrived at our destination and I put up at the hospitable home of Peter Majkowski. . . . The next morning I went to visit some of the farms. The first farm I visited belonged to a former farm manager (*econom*), who was of Armenian origin. He built a small temporary shack, a temporary pen, which he erected last autumn, and everything looked temporary indeed. The next farm I visited belonged to a better-off Ukrainian peasant. His house was roomy, like a house of a well-to-do peasant in Galicia—solid farm buildings, in the farm yard a sixty-dollar wagon, ploughs, in the stables four oxen, two cows, and one calf. Behind the house stretched a well-tilled field, and further away, a well-kept wood. It was a pleasure to look at such a farm. This man brought with him $500 in cash, and together with his three sons they are efficiently managing their farm. I am sure that in some five years he will be able to put to shame even old established English and German farmers, not to mention the French. [Although Father Dymtriw does not mention the name of the farmer, it would seem the farm belonged to Hryhor Prygrocki, SE¼ 30-2-6E, whom Hugo Carstens mentions in his report of December 6, 1896, as having "$420.00, fair buildings, 2 oxen, 1 cow & 2 calves . . ."].

The next farm belonged to a poorer man. He met with a misfortune during the winter. His cow and calf died, which was a tragic blow to him and still a greater one to his children who were now deprived of the cow's milk. In the house of this farmer, as in many other houses, I saw beside the iron kitchen stove, a Galician bread oven, a pot-bellied monster, occupying half of the whole living room. When summer comes, I was told, the monster is put outside.

[44]*Ibid.*, 26–28.

Not far away there stood a small house of a poor settler who arrived in Winnipeg with only four cents to his name. He even showed me these four cents and said that he will keep them until he dies. "These were—dear Father—the last drops of my blood," said the poor man. This unfortunate peasant was robbed in Galicia by everybody, beginning with the District Governor and ending with Moshe, the village inn-keeper, who most brazenly demanded the repayment of some debt, threatening to wire police authorities at Lviw to stop him from leaving the country if he did not pay. The poor peasant, frightened to death, paid everybody what was demanded, only to get away. During the journey he was cheated again by everybody, and when finally he arrived in Winnipeg from Borshchiw, all there was left of his eight hundred gold florins was four cents. It was indeed the last drop of his blood. He was able to earn a little money in Canada, and what he earned helped him to settle on the holy earth. He received nice rolling acres—you could hardly see the boundary of his farm—but how could he start working them? Should he begin to fell poplar trees with his head? But the good man did not despair. He cut some logs during the bitterly cold winter weather and built himself a little house. A modest house, a poor house it was, but nevertheless it was his house, and he does not lose hope and faith in the future. "At least my children will have it better," he said.

Yes, the children will have it better, that I firmly believe. The children are a soothing hope, sweet comfort for the bedraggled and poverty-stricken parents. Indeed, it is comforting to see the progress their children have already made. Older boys and girls serve with well-to-do farmers, where they acquire wisdom, polish, and are able to help their parents, and in some cases even support them entirely. The younger ones go to school and their progress astounds even English neighbours. I met girls who were already able to converse quite freely in English. The children are our future and are already exercising a beneficial influence over their parents. . . .

Father Dmytriw's visit was a memorable event in the life of the settlers. Not only was he the first Ukrainian priest to visit Stuartburn and to attend to the settlers' spiritual needs since they had left Galicia, but his visit came on Palm Sunday, one of the greatest feasts of the year:

The same evening [Saturday, April 17] the settlers erected a cross and an altar in the nearby grove, rejoicing that on Sunday they would participate in the celebration of the great feast of the Blessing of Palms. Unfortunately the celebration under the cross didn't materialize. During the night a terrible storm blew up, with lightning and thunder, and in the morning heavy snow fell, driven by bitterly cold wind. During the stormy night I saw an awe-inspiring prairie fire some miles away. Fire can be a cruel enemy of the farmer, especially when it occurs during the summer. Never before did I experience such dreadfully cold weather as on that memorable Sunday. The icy wind almost paralysed me. It was almost impossible to keep warm. We reached the store where I was to celebrate Holy Mass all shivering.[45] Eighty-seven persons went to confession. Many could not come due to the bad weather.

[45]Kohut, *Narys istorii*, 7: "Father Dmytriw, unable to celebrate Holy Mass under the cross, celebrated it in the store of a Frenchman in Stuartburn, about one mile from the place where the cross was erected."

The Stuartburn colony consists of 45 families, 175 souls all told. The first 24 families settled here on August 19, 1896. They were joined in the autumn and during the winter by other families. Still more families are on their way intending to settle in the colony. The majority of the settlers came from the districts of Zalishchyky, Borshchiw, Kolomyla, (the province of) Bukowina, and one family from the district of Towmach. . . .

The soil (in Stuartburn) is generally good, stony in places, but the stones were brought in in their time from somewhere else, and therefore they are on the surface only. The hay meadows are excellent; there is plenty of arable land, and an abundance of wood. In the bush I have seen wild plum trees, sour cherry trees, and even grape vines. All kinds of vegetables can be raised here. Of the cereals, wheat, oats, barley, and other kinds, as well as potatoes, can be grown. The country is particularly suitable for cattle-raising. Being only nine miles from North Dakota, people can go there to work during harvest time and may earn from $40 to $60. There are plenty of prosperous farmers in the vicinity who need help and they pay good wages. For instance, last summer a boy of 15 was earning $16 per month. . . .

During Father Dmytriw's visit, plans for building a church for the colony and a house for the parish priest were also discussed:

Of course, he should be a married priest, an experienced husbandsman, energetic and understanding, who would serve as an example for the people. A celibate priest wouldn't be able to live in these unpenetrable woods and prairies.

The Government is giving 40 acres of land to the church, and the priest may obtain *ad personam* an additional 160 acres. I am trying in every colony I visit, to select proper parcels of land (for the Church) and to complete the necessary formalities connected with it.

On Monday, April 17,[46] early in the morning, I left for Dominion City and having arrived there at noon, I met two Ukrainian families who came from Winnipeg with the intention of settling at Stuartburn. A very cold wind was blowing. The women and children were sitting on their bags near the freight shed waiting for their men who went to look for teams and wagons (to take them to Stuartburn). . . .[47]

Many of the immigrants who came late in the season without sufficient cash were experiencing great difficulties during the winter. To prevent them from suffering privation, the Government helped out with flour and cornmeal which was distributed to the settlers by the immigration agents, one of whom was Hugo Carstens. In this regard, Father Dmytriw was told the following amusing humorous story about Hugo Carstens, which the priest accepted at face value: "For the destitute settlers the Government was supplying flour during the winter, and the official who brought the flour and distributed it (among the needy) was immigration

[46]Apparently a printing error. It should read April 19.
[47]Dmytriw, *Kanadiyska Rus*, 56.

officer Carstens. Some of the more ignorant peasants even today, are ready to swear that he is (the Archduke) Rudolph, they even wrote letters to him, addressing them to His Highness (Archduke) Rudolph. . . ."

VII

When the waters receded and the soil became reasonably dry in the spring, feverish activity set in. Land was broken, houses were built, and piles of stones were removed from garden patches to make room for seeding and planting vegetables. Men left the colony to earn cash that was badly needed to buy cows, implements, and supplies for their families, especially since there was a shortage of seed grain and potatoes in Stuartburn. The settlement was spreading beyond Ranges 6 and 7 of Township 2, reaching out into Ranges 5 and 4 of Township 1. Often this incursion into new domains was made without previous consultation with the authorities. New arrivals simply occupied empty quarter-sections as squatters, hoping that the substantial improvements they undertook, the houses they built, and the crops they raised would in the long run help them to obtain homestead grants for the land they occupied.

The release for settlement of the odd-numbered sections, which was obtained after the completion of all formalities, was a great boon to the settlers. It helped relieve the congestion reported by the immigration officers who visited the colony during the winter months. Late arrivals, unable to erect their own shelters for the winter, had to stay with friends, often ten or more persons in a one-room house built only a few months before. In the shack his parents built, Stashyn relates in his memoirs, seventeen persons spent their first winter in Canada. Such overcrowding and the necessarily primitive living conditions offered fertile ground for the various sicknesses, which broke out in Stuartburn in the spring of 1897. Several cases of scarlet fever were reported, and as soon as this became known to the Commissioner of Immigration, he dispatched Dr. James Patterson, of the Provincial Health Board to survey the situation in Stuartburn and to render the necessary medical help where required. The few scarlet fever cases were isolated, and the Commissioner, to prevent the spreading of the disease, resorted to some radical precautions, concerning which he wrote to the Deputy Minister in Ottawa on June 12, 1897:

> Mr. Wendelbo (the Scandinavian Officer) just returned from Stuartburn and I beg to enclose herewith a copy of the report he makes to me. As the Scarlet Fever frequently turns into Diphtheria, I have given him instructions to go down again on Monday [June 14], taking the strongest dis-infectant

possible, together with a pump for spraying their sheepskin coats, and so forth. All the articles that can be boiled, of course, can be dis-infected in that way, and for this purpose I am sending down a large cauldron. I am also sending down 50 more bushels of potatoes, it was found utterly impossible to purchase potatoes down there at any price, though we scoured the country-side; and even went so far as to authorize him to pay 75 cents per bushel for some. However, it is not too late yet, and he now has a man ploughing small patches on the various farms they will be able to seed a few potatoes, turnips and so forth until the end of this month. I am also sending off 20 sacks more flour, some cornmeal, together with a few axes and spades which are absolutely necessary for the last party who went out there. . . .

Wendelbo does not say how the settlers felt (or looked) after the disinfecting operation was completed. The Commissioner was aware that with several scarlet fever cases in the colony more frequent medical inspection would be advisable to prevent the disease from spreading. Sending Dr. Patterson to Stuartburn from Winnipeg might not always be possible, Commissioner McCreary wrote, but "if I find it necessary I will again send Dr. Patterson down to the Stuartburn Settlement, as the only man we can use down there is one Atkinson who while he is a regular doctor, I believe, from Toronto, has not practised for a number of years, having married a squaw and settled somewhere near Stuartburn. Still, I believe, he is pretty clever, but very lazy, and if I can utilize his services to save expense I will do so. On Wendelbo's return, however, should the disease shew signs of an epidemic, I will at once send out Dr. Patterson, as it would not do to have it spread in the colony."[48] The patients were put up in a "hospital," improvised from tents, to prevent further infection: "I was very fortunate in having procured tents for these people which will have to be destroyed, though having bought them second-hand they only cost $15 each. I sent two to Stuartburn."[49] Apparently the disease did not develop into epidemic proportions as there were no further reports on the Stuartburn scarlet fever cases.

The boats that arrived in Quebec and Halifax with ever-increasing frequency, brought thousands of new Ukrainian settlers to the West. In February the S.S. *Labrador* arrived with 140 settlers and in March the S.S. *Scotsman* came with 42 immigrants, but the large flow started in May. The S.S. *Arcadia* landed in Quebec on May 2 with 633 Ukrainian immigrants. She was followed by the S.S. *Scotia*, which arrived on May 3 with 435, the S.S. *Prussia* with 672, the S.S. *Arabia* with 558 Galicians

[48]3. Gal./39087, June 12, 1897: W. F. McCreary, Winnipeg, to James A. Smart, Ottawa.

[49]*Ibid.*

bound for Manitoba, the S.S. *Armenia* with 717 Ukrainian immigrants on board, the S.S. *Hispania*, and other boats. The Immigration Hall in Winnipeg became overcrowded, and the Commissioner worked overtime trying to settle as many immigrants on the land as soon as possible. "I have just returned last night from Dominion City," Commissioner McCreary wrote to the Deputy Minister in Ottawa on June 11th, "having been four days looking over that country with a view to settling some eighty families of these Galicians. I found Township 1, Range 6, a very good township, and will be able to locate them in portions of 1–7 portions 2–7, portions of 2–6, and quite a large portion 1–6."[50] This task kept McCreary quite busy, and on July 2, 1897, he wrote again to the Deputy Minister to inform him about the progress of the Manitoba settlers: "It has been so long since you have heard anything from me on the subject of the Galicians, that I presume you will now have to come to the conclusion that they are all dead. I wish to disabuse your mind of this idea, however, as I assure you they are still pretty lively corpses, or at least most of them, although unfortunately, a few of them have died from Scarlet Fever and other causes."[51]

Mr. Sifton took a personal interest in all immigration matters and on June 26, 1897, he took Commissioner McCreary with him to meet the trains bringing the Ukrainian immigrants West. "I may say that I accompanied the Minister last Saturday night [June 26] on his trip east and personally met the consignment who arrived per Steamers 'Hispania' and 'Armenia' a few days before. We discovered about five cases of Scarlet Fever on the two trains. I came on with the first train and brought Doctor Inglis and Corbett with me as far as Rat Portage. They then got off and waited for the second train and brought it through. . . ."[52] Forty-three families of the newly arrived immigrants were bound for Stuartburn, and Commissioner McCreary was busy making arrangements for their settlement:

I have sent Mr. Wendelbo out with the new colony to Stuartburn. He will likely be there about eight or ten days, as it will be more difficult with these people on account of there being no timber on the lands to which he has taken them, and it will be necessary to put sod houses, and as there is very little sod there, I am afraid, he will have trouble in getting them proper shelter. I sent out some flour and cornmeal, with instructions to Mr. Wendelbo, as well as to Mr. Speers, I may say, to give two or three sacks

[50]2. Oles./37455, June 11, 1897: W. F. McCreary, Winnipeg, to James A. Smart, Ottawa.

[51]3. Gal./39703, July 2, 1897: W. F. McCreary, Winnipeg, to James A. Smart, Ottawa.

[52]*Ibid.*, 1.

of flour to each family who had no means, and to sell the balance to those who had means at the actual price at which we purchased it. I do not think we will be much out in the long run, as most of those to whom we supplied the flour formerly will go out to work and we will hold the price as we have it to them out of their wages. The greatest expense will be hauling them and their baggage the long distances from the Station to their farms. However, if we allow them to come in without any money, then we have simply got to put up until we get them producing.[53]

The Commissioner complained that he had considerable difficulty finding interpreters able to produce intelligent reports in English, who at the same time had a good command of Ukrainian:

I have great difficulty in getting good Interpreters, that is, men who can speak their language and are able to write a report to me in English, in fact, it is almost impossible, and much goes on in consequence of which I cannot advise you, and you will kindly overlook the fact that I do not write you as frequently on some of these subjects as I should, as, to tell you the truth, I cannot keep up with my work. Although yesterday was a holiday, I do not think I ever put in a harder day's work. I came to my office at 8 o'clock in the morning, took fifteen minutes for my lunch and went home again as half past eight without dinner, as tired as I ever was in my life. This morning I arrived here at 7 o'clock. Amidst a downpoor of rain we succeeded in getting 43 families, about 200 souls, loaded on their train, together with all their baggage, as well as the flour and cornmeal spoken of, when I got them off at 8.30. . . .[54]

Full of hope and expectation, the families travelled the distance to Dominion City by train, and the eighteen to twenty miles from there to Stuartburn by wagon. During the late summer, the colony was visited by Eduard Schultze, the Austro-Hungarian Consul. Ignatius Roth of the Montreal offices of the Hamburg-America Packet Company acted as his interpreter. On his return to Winnipeg, Roth sent this report to his superior in Montreal about the situation in Stuartburn:

I have now returned from a Colony called Stuartburn situated 20 miles from Dominion City, where there [are] 180 Galician and Bukovina families. I find that the people are doing fairly well, all have good houses and gardens, also cattle with the exception of a few Bukovina families, who reached the Colony this year without any means whatsoever. Almost all the men are out harvesting and earning from $20 to $25 per month and board, some getting $1.50 a day. I visited all those that can write and do the writing for others, and explained to them the necessity of their writing home to their friends and relatives that this country is good and there is plenty of room here for more. In answer I was told that it is their wish to have their friends come out here and leave Galicia "that bad country" as soon as possible. It is really wonderful what progress these people are

[53]*Ibid.*, 4.

[54]*Ibid.*, 5.

making and what fine houses they have built with only an axe. Mr. Schultze is delighted and is doing well.[55]

While acting as an interpreter for the Austro-Hungarian Consul, Roth obviously did not let the opportunity slip by to spread a little propaganda for Canada as well as for his steamship company.

VIII

The years 1897 and 1898 were probably the busiest and at the same time the hardest for the growing Stuartburn community. In the summer of 1898, the Commissioner of Immigration sent Leon Roy, the French Interpreter to the Stuartburn colony to locate twenty new families on the land and to present a brief report on the colony in general. Roy's report about conditions at Stuartburn read as follows:

In accordance with your instructions, on the 8th of August (1898) I proceeded to Stuartburn settlement, and when there I located twenty families on land as per list herewith attached. I have visited one hundred and forty Galician settlers, and find that the number of acres they have broken

(i.e., new land broken) are	39½
Under wheat	47½
Under oats	24
Under barley	30
Rye	2½
Under vegetables	77
Number of milk cows	128
Number of young cattle, working oxen and horses	234
Number of poultry	1084

These 146 families have cheap, but very comfortable houses. Their building improvements on each place are worth at an average about $50.00. Plenty of hay put for their stock. The growing crop is good, and seems well put in, except the potatoes that are poor. Plenty of work to be had in the neighborhood of the settlement, and they ought to be able to make enough to support themselves during the coming winter.[56]

Commissioner McCreary, on forwarding Roy's report to Ottawa, added a personal opinion about the cost of aiding the new arrivals: "When you consider that most of those people were of the very poorest class; I think the showing is a very fair one and as they are getting more constant employment this year we are in hopes that notwithstanding the large number of new arrivals this summer, a large percentage of those with-

[55]3. Gal./45576, September 5, 1897: Ignatius Roth, Interpreter of the Hamburg-American Packet Company, writing from Winnipeg on a trip to Western Canada with the Austro-Hungarian consul, Eduard Schultze, to James Thom, Manager, Hamburg-America Packet Company office in Montreal.

[56]8. Rpts./65335, August 26, 1898: Leon Roy, French Interpreter, Winnipeg, to the Commissioner of Immigration, Winnipeg.

out means, the expenditure for assistance . . . will be much smaller than last winter."[57]

In his report to the Commissioner of Immigration, Roy also enclosed a description of every quarter-section on which the 146 families were settled. From that description, it can be seen that many of the families who were receiving assistance from the Government during the winter of 1896–97 were on the road to comparative well-being in 1898. Jacob Szelyp, for instance, had one acre under wheat, one acre under oats, half an acre under barley, and half an acre under roots and vegetables by 1898. He also owned three oxen, two cows, two calves, and fifteen hens. Wasyl Zahara, the first settler from Bukowina, had three acres under wheat, one acre under oats, one under barley, one under rye, one under roots and vegetables, and owned three oxen, one cow, two calves, and fourteen hens.[58] The late arrivals had no land broken. At the most, they managed to put in some roots in small half-acre plots, and to buy a cow to have milk for their children.

The number of children in the colony was quite high, and parents were concerned about their education. Those who lived within walking distance of the town sent their children to the Stuartburn public school, but the majority of the settlers lived too far from the town, and therefore there arose a demand to establish one or more rural schools which would be within reach of the settlers. The problem of erecting a church for the community also came to the fore. When Father Dmytriw visited the settlement in April, 1897, the number of settlers was still too small to warrant the erection of a church and the upkeep of a resident priest. But towards the end of 1898 there were nearly 150 families in the district, a sufficient number to form a modest congregation. The settlers elected a committee and entrusted it with the task of beginning to build a church. Michael Dumanski of NW¼ 15-2-6E donated 1½ acres of land two miles east of the town, and the post office of Stuartburn and the members of the community undertook to donate a certain number of working days during the year for the construction of the church. Nicholas Kohut and Gregory Prygrocki were chosen to direct the construction work. Timber was cut, a plan worked out, and construction of the church begun. By 1899 the foundation was laid, and fourteen-foot-high walls were erected. It took two more years to finish the church.[59]

[57]8. Rpts./65335, August 27, 1898: W. F. McCreary, Winnipeg, to Frank Pedley, Superintendent of Immigration, Ottawa.

[58]8. Rpts./65335, August 8, 1898: Report presented by Mr. Roy. Many names on his list are misspelled.

[59]Kohut, *Narys istorii,* 8.

The school problem was also tackled with vigour by the community: "In spite of all the hardships the settlers were going through to make a bare living, these pioneers did not neglect the education of their children. When there was a school in the vicinity (as in Stuartburn) the youngsters were immediately sent to attend it. Looking over the Stuartburn school registers, we see that the ages of pupils ranged from 10 to 21 years. Among them were married women attending grades one, two or three. Under the year 1898 we encounter the names of Joseph Kulachkowski, Anna Wachna, the Saranchuks and many others. . . ."[60] The settlers decided to approach the Provincial authorities with the request to establish and build schools in their rural communities. Theodosy Wachna, Ivan Probizanski, and several other leading settlers signed a letter to Commissioner McCreary, whom they knew to be their friend and champion, with the request that he support their petition to local authorities. "We hoped," related Theodosy Wachna, "that [the Government] will build schools for us, as was done in the old country. But the authorities declined our request, advising us to turn to the Franklin Municipality. We applied to the Municipality but were turned down. We pressed our demand but without any results whatever. Finally, discouraged, we decided to break away from Franklin Municipality. We succeeded in that, but were burdened with a debt amounting to $13,000. We appealed to London against this decision but without success. We had to start organizing the municipality burdened with an initial debt which, in time was reduced by $1,500 but still left $11,500 to be paid."[61]

The new Stuartburn Municipality was organized in February of 1902. Theodosy Wachna was elected its first Municipal Secretary, having to overcome considerable difficulties, such as the opposition of the Municipal Commission, before receiving the confirmation of this election. At the suggestion of a school teacher, a post office was opened and named "Oleskow P.O." In 1905 it was moved to the railway point of Tolstoi and took the name "Tolstoi."[62] In the same year that the municipality was formed, three rural schools were established in the district, the settlers themselves erecting school buildings from timber logs. In the course of three years, nine schools were built, with the names "Lukivci," "Purple Bank," "Koroliwka," "Shevchenko," "Arbakka," "Bukowina" (now "Lord Roberts"), "Franko," "Becket," and "Kupchenko." C. W. Speers, the General Colonization Agent, who visited the Ukrainian colonies in 1898, stressed, in his report to the Superintendent of Immi-

60Prodan, "Okolytsia Stuartburn," Interview with Theodosy Wachna, 38.
61*Ibid.*, 39.
62*Ibid.*, 40.

gration in Ottawa, the need to assist the immigrants with the establishment of schools: "The establishment of schools among these people is a very important matter, which I trust will receive attention in the proper quarters. The people are very anxious to learn our language and ways, and this is particularly the case with Galicians who have even adopted Canadian dress and discarded their traditional costume. They will soon become absorbed in our Canadian nationality and being people of good physique, and good complection, moral, industrious, and frugal, they should be acceptable as immigrants. . . ."[63]

The number of Ukrainian settlers in the Stuartburn district at the end of 1900 was estimated at 3,000.[64] The majority of the families lived on homesteads or on farms acquired by purchase. A few families still squatted on Government land, and a number of Ukrainians moved to Stuartburn town to engage in various trades. At the request of the Department of the Interior in Ottawa, the Agent of Dominion Lands in Winnipeg prepared a list of homestead holders of the Stuartburn colony, together with their names and locations, which gave a comprehensible picture of the spread of the colony:

I beg to acknowledge your letter of the 12th instant (February, 1901) File 610676 and say in reply that I presume what is required is a list of all lands taken up under homestead entry by Galicians, in what is known as the Stuartburn Colony, and which comprises Townships 1, 2, and 3, in Ranges 5, 6, & 7, East. In the schedule which will be found enclosed, we have carefully gone through the Township Register for Galician entries in Townships 1, 2, and 3, Range 4, East, and although sometimes it is a little difficult to know precisely which are German and which are Galician settlers, the assistance of Mr. Cyril Genik, Galician Interpreter at the Immigration Hall, has been obtained and the schedule will, I think, be found to be very nearly a complete list of all Galicians who have entered for land in that vicinity. There may be a few squatters who have not yet made homestead entry, but care was taken in the fall of 1899 and 1900 to issue notices to all who were reported from the Dominion Immigration Commissioner's office, as located on land, requiring them to come forward and make entry. This notice was complied with in the great majority of cases and it seems likely that the number of squatters in that settlement is very limited. . . .[65]

[63]Canada, Parliament, *Sessional Papers*, 1898, XXXIII, Paper 13, No. 7, 233–235: Report of C. W. Speers, General Colonization Agent, Winnipeg, to the Superintendent of Immigration, Ottawa, January 9, 1899.

[64]6. Gal./139859, February 1, 1901: J. Obed. Smith, Commissioner of Immigration, Winnipeg, to the Department of the Interior, Ottawa.

[65]19. Imm./133943, February 22, 1901: E. H. Taylor, for the Agent, Dominion Lands, Winnipeg, to the Secretary, Department of the Interior, Ottawa.

STATEMENT SHOWING LANDS HOMESTEADED BY GALICIAN SETTLERS IN THE NEIGHBOURHOOD OF STUARTBURN, MANITOBA

PART	SEC.	TP.	RGE.	NAME	PART	SEC.	TP.	RGE.	NAME
NE¼	13	1	4E	Stefan Krajnyk	SE¼	34	1	5E	Kost Manoly
NW¼	1	1	5E	Michal Paciorka					(Mandzij)
SE¼	1	1	5E	Fedor Jaremij	SW¼	34	1	5E	Simeon Rudkowsky
SE¼	2	1	5E	Stefan Wiwsianyk	NE¼	35	1	5E	Nykola Mandzij
NE¼	2	1	5E	Dmytro Glowachuk	SE¼	35	1	5E	Ignach Bednar
SW¼	3	1	5E	Dmytro Kozak	SW¼	35	1	5E	Tomko Drewniak
NE¼	1	1	5E	Andrij Myroniw	NE¼	35	1	5E	Joseph Antoshkiw
SW¼	1	1	5E	Fedor Olijnyk	NW¼	35	1	5E	Andrij Baran
SE¼	5	1	5E	Joseph Oleinizak	NW¼	36	1	5E	Michal Lepiszczak
				(Olienchuk)	NE¼	36	1	5E	Onofry Rekrut
NE¼	9	1	5E	Iwan Kozuk	SW¼	36	1	5E	Kazimir Drewniak
SW¼	12	1	5E	John Tkachyk	SE¼	36	1	5E	Michel Jaremij
SE¼	12	1	5E	Wasyl Tkachyk	NE¼	1	1	6E	Konstantin Predij
NW¼	13	1	5E	Matij Tkachyk	SE¼	1	1	6E	Andrij Kossowan
NE¼	13	1	5E	Dmytro Tkachyk	NE¼	2	1	6E	Dmytro Horychka
SW¼	13	1	5E	Onufrij Tkachyk	SE¼	24	1	5E	Iwan Zaporozan
SE¼	13	1	5E	Jacob Prociuk	NE¼	24	1	5E	Jakim Kozak
NE¼	14	1	5E	Petro Tkachyk	NW¼	24	1	5E	Hrynko Darchuk
SW¼	14	1	5E	Dmytro Lenyk	NE¼	24	1	5E	Teodosij Ktytor
SE¼	14	1	5E	Fedor Lozowyj	SE¼	25	1	5E	Iwan Holojda
NE¼	15	1	5E	Dmytro Bojko	NE¼	26	1	5E	Wincenty Mazur
SW¼	15	1	5E	Semen Sopiwnyk	NE¼	27	1	5E	Fedor Woloshyn
NW¼	15	1	5E	Michal Sawczuk	NE¼	5	1	6E	Michailo Onysko
NW¼	19	1	5E	Prokip Storoschuk	NW¼	5	1	6E	Kirylo Kossowan
NE¼	20	1	5E	Iwan Szerban	SE¼	5	1	6E	Iwan Pafriuk
SW¼	20	1	5E	Iwan Tofan	SW¼	5	1	6E	Wasyl Kossowan
SW¼	21	1	5E	Andrij Danylejko	NE¼	6	1	6E	Wasyl Kokol
NW¼	21	1	5E	Andrij Glowachuk	SW¼	6	1	6E	Andrij Tymofijchuk
NE¼	21	1	5E	Wasyl Prokopchuk	NW¼	9	1	6E	Iwan Magas
SE¼	21	1	5E	Andrij Wiwsianyk	SE¼	9	1	6E	Petro Zyha
SW¼	22	1	5E	Hnat Galushka	SW¼	9	1	6E	Nykola Sawka
NE¼	23	1	5E	Iwan Darchuk	NE¼	10	1	6E	Kost Kossowan
SE¼	23	1	5E	Andro Komarnisky	SW¼	10	1	6E	Arkadij Zyha
SW¼	23	1	5E	Michal Schendel	SE¼	10	1	6E	Petro Kossowan
NW¼	23	1	5E	Michal Darchuk	NW¼	10	1	6E	Michal Zeha
SE¼	3	1	5E	Tanasy Kozak	NW¼	12	1	6E	Dmytro Bojda
SW¼	4	1	5E	Leo Grabowski	SE¼	12	1	6E	Wasyl Semeniuk
SW¼	27	1	5E	Oleksa Jaremij	NE¼	12	1	6E	Gawrilo Semeniuk
SE¼	27	1	5E	Hrynko Drewniak	NE¼	13	1	6E	Teodore Baduk
NW¼	27	1	5E	Petro Antonijchuk	SW¼	13	1	6E	Oleksa Kossowan
NE¼	30	1	5E	Iwan Bialyj	NW¼	13	1	6E	Mykolaj Kossowan
SE¼	31	1	5E	Jarema Wiwchar	SE¼	13	1	6E	Iwan Kossowan
NE¼	31	1	5E	Janko Nedohan	S½—				
NW¼	31	1	5E	Igance Nedohan	NW¼	14	1	6E	Semen Lelyk
SW¼	31	1	5E	Mykyta Ottawa	SE¼	2	1	6E	Wasyl Boychuk
SE¼	33	1	5E	Iwan Olenyk (Olynuk)	SW¼	2	1	6E	Nykola Shypot
SW¼	33	1	5E	Petro Waselyszyn	NW¼	3	1	6E	Gregoire Kossowan
NE¼	33	1	5E	Stefan Romaniuk	SE¼	3	1	6E	Oleksa Shypot
NW¼	33	1	5E	Jakob Arseniy	SW¼	3	1	6E	Pentely Shepit

PART	SEC.	TP.	RGE.	NAME
NW¼	4	1	6E	Wasyl Maly (Maley)
SE¼	4	1	6E	Kost Dubniak
NW¼	17	1	6E	Fedor Molynek
				(Malynyk)
SW¼	17	1	6E	Wasyl Kindzierski
SE¼	17	1	6E	Nykola Salomon
NE¼	18	1	6E	Iwan Hudyma
NW¼	18	1	6E	Semen Saranchuk
NE¼	19	1	6E	Tanasko Kostyniuk
SW¼	19	1	6E	Todor Glowacki
NW¼	19	1	6E	Iwan Wiwchar
SE¼	10	1	6E	Iwan Kostyniuk
SE¼	20	1	6E	Yakem Kowaliuk
NE¼	20	1	6E	Petro Hudyma
SW¼	20	1	6E	Iwan Kowaluk
NW¼	20	1	6E	Michal Zahara
NW¼	21	1	6E	Nikolaj Rozka
				(Roshko)
SW¼	21	1	6E	George Shydlowski
SE¼	21	1	6E	Jakob Zahara
NE¼	21	1	6E	Todor Orlecki
NE¼	22	1	6E	Dmytrash Pauluk
SE¼	22	1	6E	Simion Korol
NW¼	22	1	6E	Aksentyj Dmytruk
SW¼	22	1	6E	Onofrij Tyran (Tyron)
N½—				
NW¼	14	1	6E	Petro Duleniak
SW¼	14	1	6E	Nekola Goszuliak
NE¼	14	1	6E	Wasyl Goszuliak
SW¼	15	1	6E	Achtemij Stefiuk
NW¼	15	1	6E	Danylo Posztar
SE¼	15	1	6E	Iwan Zyha
NE¼	15	1	6E	Dmytro Kosowan
NE¼	16	1	6E	Petro Dzaman
SW¼	16	1	6E	Aksenia Kosowan
				(widow)
SE¼	16	1	6E	Metro Shewchuk
NE¼	17	1	6E	Petro Salamon
NE¼	28	1	6E	Iwan Bojczuk
SE¼	28	1	6E	Domna Serediuk
SW¼	28	1	6E	Wasyl Shewchuk
Pt.				
NW¼	28	1	6E	Andrij Glowacki
NE¼	30	1	6E	Michalo Wiwsianyk
SE¼	30	1	6E	Wasyl Czornopyski
NW¼	30	1	6E	Elash Kossowan
SW¼	30	1	6E	Onufrij Hryhorasz
SW¼	31	1	6E	Ivon Bojda
SE¼	31	1	6E	Andrij Halicki
NE¼	32	1	6E	Todor Maksymchuk
SW¼	32	1	6E	Nikola Djoba
N½—				
NE¼	33	1	6E	Maksym Malicki
S½—				
NE¼	33	1	6E	Iwan Towstowaryk
NW¼	33	1	6E	Wasyl Chornopyski
SE¼	33	1	6E	Dmytrash Olijnyk
SW¼	33	1	6E	Dmytrash Dutchak
SE¼	23	1	6E	Iwan Marchuk
NW¼	24	1	6E	Wasyl Sidor
NE¼	24	1	6E	Iwan Odokychuk
SW¼	24	1	6E	Nikol Sidor
SW¼	25	1	6E	Semen Badiuk
NE¼	25	1	6E	Iwan Tkadiuk
				(Badiuk)
SE¼	25	1	6E	George Tkachuk
NE¼	26	1	6E	Iwan Denyshchuk
NW¼	27	1	6E	Dmytro Korol
SE¼	27	1	6E	Sandyk Mekelij
NE¼	27	1	6E	Petro Shkwarchuk
NE¼	2	2	5E	Hrynko Poloz
NW¼	2	2	5E	Michal Panisiak
SE¼	2	2	5E	Hrynko Shmyr
SW¼	2	2	5E	Wasyl Gushczak
SE¼	3	2	5E	Ilo German
NE¼	3	2	5E	Iwan Nykolajishyn
SE¼	4	2	5E	Tomko Federczuk
SE¼	5	2	5E	Danylo Struzowski
NE¼	10	2	5E	Olesko Tkaczuk
L.S. 7 & 8 of				
SE¼	10	2	5E	Fedor Czubej
NE¼	12	2	5E	Fedor Horobec
NW¼	12	2	5E	Iwan German
SW¼	12	2	5E	John Jaremovich
NW¼	13	2	5E	Stefan Horbul
SE¼	13	2	5E	Michal Kaminski
NE¼	13	2	5E	Dymian Horbul
SW¼	13	2	5E	Michal Horbul
NE¼	34	1	6E	Wasyl Roshka
SE¼	34	1	6E	Iwan Hrynyk
N½—				
NW¼	34	1	6E	Gawrylo Kantymir
S½—				
NW¼	34	1	6E	Ivon Woroniuk
SE¼	35	1	6E	Achtemij Miszczanczuk
L.S. 3 & 4 of				
SW	35	1	6E	John Golecki
L.S. 5 & 6 of				
SW	35	1	6E	Jan Szczygelski
SE¼	19	1	7E	Iwan Tkachuk
NE¼	19	1	7E	Iwan Kowaliuk
SE¼	32	1	7E	Jakiw Niwranski
NE¼	32	1	7E	Dmytro Niwranski
NE¼	1	2	5E	Josef Bzowy
NW¼	1	2	5E	Stach Lepeshchak
SW¼	1	2	5E	Marcin Lepishchuk

PART	SEC.	TP.	RGE.	NAME
SE¼	1	2	5E	Jan Narzarewicz
NW¼	2	2	6E	Wasyl Zahara
NE¼	2	2	6E	Michajlo Zahara
SW¼	5	2	6E	Iwan Machnij
SE¼	5	2	6E	Symen Tyran (Tyron)
NE¼	6	2	6E	Jan Kulaczkowski
NW¼	6	2	6E	Wasyl Bzowyj
SE¼	6	2	6E	Iwan Zaporozan
SW¼	6	2	6E	Andrij Skrypnyk
SE¼	7	2	6E	Andrij Keweryga
SW¼	7	2	6E	Ilo Zaporozan
NW¼	8	2	6E	Nykola Humeniuk
SW¼	8	2	6E	Michal Pauluk
E½ of E½	9	2	6E	Makij Probizanski
NE¼	22	2	5E	Stefan Kosman
SE¼	23	2	5E	Kost Machnij
NW¼	23	2	5E	Jakiw Pawlowski
SW¼	25	2	5E	Petro Lesiuk
SE¼	25	2	5E	Nykolaj Poliszczuk
NE¼	25	2	5E	Nykyfor Klym
NE¼	33	2	5E	Hryhor Goy
NW¼	33	2	5E	Hrycko Panchyshin
SE¼	33	2	5E	Nykola Didyjchuk
SW¼	33	2	5E	Iwan Sirman
SE¼	36	2	5E	Wasyl Sirman
NW¼	1	2	6E	Andrij Balan
NE¼	1	2	6E	Elash Prokopchuk
SW¼	1	2	6E	Todor Mukanyk
SE¼	1	2	6E	Hnat Dykun
NE¼	18	2	6E	Nikol Pryhrocki
NE¼	20	2	6E	Josef Majkowski
NW¼	20	2	6E	Peter Majkowski
SE¼	20	2	6E	Konstanty Stefanowicz
NW¼	22	2	6E	Onufry Smuk
NE¼	22	2	6E	Nykol Kohut
SE¼	22	2	6E	John Pshygrocki
SE¼	23	2	6E	Iwan Sokolyk
NW¼	23	2	6E	Iwan Koshman
NE¼	23	2	6E	Todor Saranchuk
SW¼	23	2	6E	Iwan Probizanski
SE¼	24	2	6E	Wasyl Salamandyk
NE¼	24	2	6E	Hryc Bugera
W½ of E½	9	2	6E	Anton Jaremowicz
SE¼	10	2	6E	Maksym Stasyszyn
SW¼	12	2	6E	John Blonski
SE¼	12	2	6E	Josef Solomon
NE¼	12	2	6E	Jan Gonkowski
NW¼	12	2	6E	Wasyl Storoszczuk
SE¼	13	2	6E	John Karpinski
SW¼	13	2	6E	Nykola Kyryluk
NE¼	13	2	6E	Jakiw Bojko
SW¼	14	2	6E	Wasyl Stefura
NW¼	14	2	6E	Mikolaj Wysoczynski
SE¼	14	2	6E	Jakob Szelep
NE¼	14	2	6E	Hrycko Storoshchuk
SE¼	15	2	6E	Dmytro Kolodrubski
NW¼	15	2	6E	Michal Dumanski
SW¼	15	2	6E	Semen Maksymchuk
NE¼	15	2	6E	Nazarko Panchuk
NE¼	16	2	6E	Austin H. Griffith
L.S. 2 of SE	17	2	6E	Paulo Tymchuk
E½ of SE	17	2	6E	Wasyl Fostij
SW¼	17	2	6E	Nykola Keweryga
SW¼	33	2	6E	Jakiw Mandziuk
SE¼	33	2	6E	Dmytro Kohut
NE¼	34	2	6E	Iwan Sokyrka
NW¼	34	2	6E	Wasyl Maruszczak
SE¼	34	2	6E	Petro Skrynski
SW¼	34	2	6E	Stefan Zolobaniuk
SE¼	36	2	6E	Michal Sokolowski
NW¼	36	2	6E	Stefan Lapchuk
SW¼	24	2	6E	Fedor Pidhirnyj
NW¼	24	2	6E	Theodor Dymianyk
NE¼	26	2	6E	Wasyl Stecko
SW¼	27	2	6E	Simon Pidhirnyj
SE¼	27	2	6E	Petro Marushchuk
NW¼	27	2	6E	Stefan Saranczuk
NE¼	28	2	6E	Jan Tomaszewski
SE¼	28	2	6E	Semen Salamandyk
NW¼	28	2	6E	Iwan Storoszczuk
SW¼	28	2	6E	George Chubej
NW¼	29	2	6E	Jurko Sirman
NE¼	29	2	6E	Timko Paskaryk
SE¼	29	2	6E	Hryhoryj Prygrocki
SE¼	31	2	6E	Theodosy Wachna
SW¼	31	2	6E	Iwan Pistenchuk
SW¼	32	2	6E	Helio Cohote (Kohut)
SE¼	32	2	6E	Ivther Cohote
NW¼	32	2	6E	Hryc Paskaryk
NE¼	32	2	6E	Iwan Salamandyk
NW¼	33	2	6E	Iwan Kohut
NE¼	18	2	7E	Michal Michaniuk
SW¼	18	2	7E	Iwan Zahara
NW¼	18	2	7E	Hnat Iwonchyk
SW¼	19	2	7E	Ozarko Niwranski
NW¼	19	2	7E	Kost Diduck
SE¼	19	2	7E	Iwan Andrejiw
SE¼	20	2	7E	Michael Belinskie
SW¼	20	2	7E	Nykola Cysmistruk
SW¼	36	2	6E	Emil Sokolowski
NE¼	36	2	6E	Iwan Ambrosychuk
NW¼	5	2	7E	Iwan Sandul

PART	SEC.	TP.	RGE.	NAME
NE¼	5	2	7E	Prokop Druzyk
SW¼	5	2	7E	George Kifiak
SE¼	5	2	7E	Petro Sandul
NE¼	6	2	7E	Michel Arsenij
NW¼	6	2	7E	Gawrylo Storoshchuk
SW¼	6	2	7E	Petro Kosteniuk
SE¼	6	2	7E	John Watling
NE¼	7	2	7E	Stefan Mukanyk
NW¼	7	2	7E	John Baraniecki
SE¼	7	2	7E	Tanasko Jacyshyn
SW¼	7	2	7E	Dmytro Bugera
NE¼	9	2	7E	Anton Rymar
SE¼	9	2	7E	Demko Tkach
NW¼	14	2	7E	Iwan Podolski
NE¼	14	2	7E	Phylyp Podolski
SE¼	14	2	7E	Hrynko Podolski
SW¼	14	2	7E	Stefan Krawec
SE¼	16(?)	2	7E	Paulo Fedorowich
SW¼	16	2	7E	Nikola Bilinski
NW¼	16	2	7E	Michal Kamenski
SE¼	17	2	7E	Tomasz Wolf
SW¼	17	2	7E	Karol Wolf
NW¼	20	2	7E	Wasyl Hawryluk
NE¼	20	2	7E	John Prokopchuk
SW¼	21	2	7E	Petro Halasik
SE¼	21	2	7E	Onofry Chornyj
NW¼	21	2	7E	Iwan Iwanicki
SE¼	21	2	7E	Iwan Tochak
NW¼	23	2	7E	Semen Kolisnyk
NE¼	23	2	7E	Dyonizy Krawec
NW¼	27	2	7E	Wasyl Podolski
NW¼	30	2	7E	Petro Strumbicki
SW¼	30	2	7E	Sawka Perun
SE¼	30	2	7E	Mykola Smuk
NW¼	31	2	7E	Iwan Kolodrubski
NE¼	33	2	7E	Andrij Bodnarchuk
SE¼	33	2	7E	Karol Herman
SE¼	2	3	5E	Mykola Chubej
NW¼	2	3	5E	Joseph Samborski
NW¼	9	3	5E	Maksym Smuk
SE¼	10	3	5E	Joseph Nawolsky
SW¼	10	3	5E	Wasyl Tanchak
S½—				
SE¼	13	3	5E	Iwan Wychnenka
N½—				
NE¼	6	3	6E	Iwan Taras
SE¼	7	3	6E	Dmytro Wachna

The list prepared by E. H. Taylor, with the assistance of Cyril Genik (which explains the relatively small number of misspelled names), contained the names of 337 homestead holders, and was based on 1900 entries. From the locations of the homesteads, it is evident that the settlers were concentrated in Township 1, Range 6E (99 homesteads), Township 1, Range 5E (66 homesteads), Township 2, Range 6E (81 homesteads), and Township 2, Range 7E (46 homesteads). There was a noticeable tendency to spread northwards and eastwards. At the beginning of the new century, Stuartburn was a rapidly expanding young community, one soon to play a lively part in the economic and political life of the province.

Chapter Six

DAUPHIN

I

IT WAS Dr. Oleskow who, in the spring of 1896, suggested to the Canadian Immigration authorities that a Ukrainian colony be established in the Lake Dauphin district. While looking for a suitable place of settlement to which he could direct his first group of settlers, his choice fell on the Lake Dauphin region. According to the information that he had collected, it was a good farming area with rich soil, an abundance of meadow land and woods—an advantage especially valued by Ukrainian settlers—as well as sufficient yearly precipitation. He wrote to the High Commissioner for Canada in London for additional information and announced that he had a party of settlers ready to proceed to Canada:

> I am sending a party of settlers, about 30 families, who will leave Hamburg at April 11th (1896) for Canada through Messrs Spiro & Co. . . .
> This party I will direct to Lake Dauphin District, but as I have not personally visited that District, please to inform me whether there is enough space, especially on the south shores of the Valley River for a greater number of Settlers. The failure of this first expedition would close for ever the flow of emigrants from this country.[1]

The High Commissioner communicated the contents of Dr. Oleskow's letter to Ottawa and requested of the Department of the Interior: "Will you enable me to answer the enquiry relating to homesteads in the Dauphin District?"[2] The Deputy Minister of the Interior, on receipt of the communication about the sailing of the Galician group, asked

[1]1. Oles., March 12, 1896: Dr. J. Oleskow, Lemberg, Austria, to the High Commissioner for Canada, London.

[2]1. Oles./28151, March 18, 1896: J. G. Colmer, Office of the High Commissionner for Canada, London, to the Secretary, Department of the Interior, Ottawa.

the Superintendent of Immigration to notify the Commissioner in Winnipeg "and any other officers who ought to know of the date when this party is expected, so as to provide for their reception and distribution. . . ."[3] At the same time, Deputy Minister Burgess also asked the Dominion Lands Office to inform him about the district in which Dr. Oleskow wished his settlers to be located. W. M. Goodeve of the Lands Office replied to this request:

> You ask for information as to sufficiency of vacant land on the south side of the Valley River in the Lake Dauphin District upon which to locate a number of Galicians. I find on perusal of the books in the vicinity mentioned that there are not a great many vacant lands in the locality, but you will observe by list attached to this fyle, that in townships 24, 25, 26 and 27, in Range 21 West of the 1st Meridian, there are numbers of sections close to each other which are available. These lands are vacant according to the last return from the Agency dated the 23rd ultimo.[4]

The Commissioner of Dominion Lands in Winnipeg, on his part, forwarded to Ottawa the "diagram of the land in the Lake Dauphin District which according to records was available for homestead entry in the neighbourhood in which Professor Oleskow desired to establish his colony."

On further investigation, it was found that communications in the Valley River district were disrupted due to spring floods, and that the area was therefore almost inaccessible. It was decided to look for some other suitable location which would be equally acceptable to Oleskow's party, already on the way to Canada. The Commissioner of Lands in Winnipeg wired Ottawa on April 21 concerning a new location and possible employment: "After consulting C.P.R. & Stephenson [Inspector of Crown Timber Agencies, Winnipeg] propose locate Oleskow's party in Township 12 & 13, R.11 East along Whitemouth River if you authorize notifying permit holders land withdrawn. Stephenson says timber remaining is of no commercial value. By locating there already winter employment obtainable in lumber camp."[5] Deputy Minister Burgess consulted the Registers and wired in reply: "Re Oleskow party. No objection if present permittees consent, and entries reserve the right to Crown to issue permits to cut timber. Am afraid permittees have right to occupy land as well as take off timber."[6] The Lands

[3]Oles., April 10, 1896: Deputy Minister of the Interior, Memorandum to L. M. Fortier, Superintendent of Immigration, Ottawa.

[4]1. Oles., Memorandum, April 11, 1896: W. M. Goodeve, Department of the Interior, to A. M. Burgess, Deputy Minister Department of the Interior, Ottawa.

[5]1. Oles./28758, Telegram, April 22, 1896: H. H. Smith, Commissioner, Dominion Lands, Winnipeg, to A. M. Burgess, Ottawa.

[6]1. Oles., Telegram, April 23, 1896: A. M. Burgess, Ottawa, to H. H. Smith, Winnipeg.

Commissioner in Winnipeg, H. H. Smith, undertook to obtain the required releases, as well as to secure employment for those who might need it and to build a road extension to the locations. He reported to Ottawa on his progress regarding these matters:

On consultation with the Land Commissioner of the Canadian Pacific Railway Company, and with the Local Agent here, it was thought preferable to locate the Oleskow settlers on land North of Whitemouth rather than in the Lake Dauphin country, as in the latter case a journey of some 60 miles would be necessary over roads, which at this season of the year would be almost impassable in consequence of the large rainfall which has been experienced this spring.

The land along the Whitemouth River is reported to be of good quality, and a Colonization road has been built by the Provincial Government for some 10 miles North of Whitemouth and on inquiry of Department of Agriculture here, it is stated that no difficulty is anticipated in arranging the extend of this road further for the convenience of these settlers, if it is found necessary during next summer.

As already reported, the proposed location of these settlers would admit of their finding ready employment in cordwood camps during the winter season, and Mr. Stephenson proposed to visit Whitemouth on Monday next, and employ a resident settler to visit and report on the quality of land.[7]

On receipt of this communication, a letter was dispatched to the High Commissioner in London informing him about the arrangements made for the immigrants soon to arrive:

The Commissioner of Dominion Lands [in Winnipeg] appears to have made excellent arrangements to settle these people near Whitemouth, East of Winnipeg. It is thought by the local Government authorities, our own Commissioner and Land Commissioner of the Canadian Pacific Railway Company, that no better location can be found for them. The lands are excellent, they will have plenty timber for building purposes, and they will be able in that neighbourhood to find ready employment in the cord-wood camps during the winter season. An arrangement has been made to allow two of the party to stop off at Whitemouth on their way to Winnipeg, and to carefully examine the proposed location of the colony, after which they can rejoin the compatriots at Winnipeg, who will then be better able to come to a decision as to what they will do.[8]

The S.S. *Christiania*'s passengers, one hundred and seven persons in all, arrived in Quebec on May 1, 1896. Dr. Oleskow, informed about the difficulties of locating the party in the Lake Dauphin district, requested that the party be directed to Edmonton instead of to White-

[7]Oles./28891, April 25, 1896: E. H. Taylor, Office of the Commissioner of Dominion Lands, Winnipeg, to the Secretary, Department of the Interior, Ottawa.

[8]1. Oles., April 28, 1896: Lyndwode Pereira, Assistant Secretary, Department of the Interior, Ottawa, to J. G. Colmer, London.

mouth. The Commissioner of Dominion Lands, who had made the arrangements for settlement at Whitemouth, suggested that Ottawa try to convince Dr. Oleskow that in view of conditions in the Lake Dauphin area and the difficulty of finding employment in Edmonton, Whitemouth would be the best place to settle the party. In any case, Hugo Carstens, the German interpreter, would meet the party, and on their way to Winnipeg they would all be given the opportunity to inspect the Whitemouth locality. They themselves should decide whether they would wish to remain in Whitemouth or proceed to Edmonton. Enclosing E. F. Stephenson's report, the Commissioner communicated these opinions to Ottawa:

I beg to enclose copy of a report from the Crown Timber Agent as to the result of his visit to Whitemouth in connection with the proposed location there of Oleskow's immigrants which it will be observed fully bears out the favourable impression which had been formed as to the quality of the lands. In a telegram just received from Mr. McNicoll by Mr. Hamilton, it is learned that the former fully concur as to the desirability of this course, and has given instructions to impress his views on Mr. Oleskow.

Mr. Hamilton is strongly of opinion that it would be unwise at the present time to locate these immigrants in the Edmonton district, where urgent applications to be provided with work have been recently received from some foreign settlers, whose means are insufficient to maintain them on their land until it begins to yield them some returns.

Professor Oleskow proposes that while the families with young children should go to Edmonton, the single men and those with families nearly grown up should be placed in the Dauphin district, but it would be physical impossibility to carry out the latter proposal at the present time, as inspector Cox reports that the roads are now impassable in his district owing to repeated snow and rain storms, and since the date of his report a continuous rain of 60 hours duration has occurred.

The offer made by Mr. McKinley to employ these immigrants cutting cordwood ensures them a revenue next winter and they can procure the material for their buildings without expense from their own land. Mr. McNicoll has given instructions that the whole party will have an opportunity to inspect their proposed location, and if they are dissatisfied, the original plan can be carried out without expense to them. The Local Agent at Edmonton has been advised of their coming, and asked to look out for a suitable location.

Mr. Carstens left yesterday to meet the party and advise them of the details of the Whitemouth project, and you will be fully advised of the decision arrived at as to their destination.[9]

The party arrived, and after visiting the Whitemouth River country,

[9]1. Oles./29064, May 2, 1896: E. H. Taylor, for the Secretary, Dominion Lands Office, Winnipeg, to the Secretary, Department of the Interior, Ottawa.

the members decided against it. On May 7, the Commissioner's office informed Ottawa of the decision to move on to Edmonton:

> Carstens returned last night (May 6th) to Winnipeg with members of Professor Oleskow's party, with whom he had been inspecting lands in the vicinity of the Whitemouth River, upon which it was proposed to locate them.
>
> After careful examination they decided not to settle there considering that the land was too full of brush and stumps to be successfully cultivated. They have accordingly decided to proceed to Edmonton and endeavour to find homesteads in the vicinity of their countrymen who have already taken up land there.
>
> Three of the party proposed going to the Lake Dauphin District, but in the present condition of the roads which makes travelling almost impossible, the Commissioner has thought that they had better all keep together, and this arrangement will, therefore, be carried out.
>
> It has been learned with regret that certain Germans have been endeavouring to unsettle these people in their determination to remain in this country, and for this reason it is thought advisable to hurry them West without any delay, and they are to leave by this evening's train. This will necessitate their remaining over a day in Calgary, but this will be preferable to their being allowed to listen to the stories that have been poured into their ears in Winnipeg. . . .[10]

Eighteen families and nine single men proceeded to Edmonton, and three families chose to settle in Beausejour, Manitoba. Later Dr. Oleskow set down in a letter to the High Commissioner for Canada the reasons why he objected to settling his party in the Whitemouth River area. After thanking the High Commissioner for the information about vacant lands in the Dauphin District, he described his misgivings about Whitemouth:

> As to the proposed location of my first party in Manitoba near Whitemouth . . . I cannot suppress my fears as to the choice of this place. I read in "Description of the Province of Manitoba," published under the authority of Hon. T. M. Daly, page 137, that on the township near Whitemouth Rge XI, Township 11, "nearly all is swamp. The soil is of second and third quality," and so is the township 12 Rge XI.
>
> I am informed by our emigrants who lived several years in Manitoba, that many people who have taken up the homesteads in similar positions (in Brokenhead) have lost all their fortune and have abandoned the houses and improved lands. Such an error of the local Government authorities would be really fatal for the cause of immigration from Austria, which is at present the most important source of emigrants in European continent. But I hope the information of the Surveyors Pearce and Fitzgerald which I have above

[10]1. Oles./29253, May 7, 1896: E. H. Taylor, for the Secretary, Commissioner of Dominion Lands, Winnipeg, to the Secretary, Department of the Interior, Ottawa.

mentioned, is not particular enough. For the rest it is possible that the party will yet follow my advice and settle down in Edmonton District or in Lake Dauphin District for instance in Rge 23, Township 28, or some other in this district.

I learn from the "Canadian Gazette" that Mr. Daly will sail on May 16th for England to make a thorough investigation of the immigration agencies of Canada on European centres. I would like to discuss the immigration scheme with Mr. Daly and with High Commissioner office representatives; and I would proceed even for London if there were in sight any practical result of this conference. . . .[11]

Thus, the attempt to start a settlement in the Dauphin district in the spring of 1896 with the settlers of the first family group sent to Canada by Dr. Oleskow under the leadership of his brother Wladimir did not materialize. Other groups of immigrants followed in rapid succession. One party, that arrived on June 27, consisted of nine families; two families went to Edmonton, one to Dominion City, and some bought land in St. Norbert and Springfield. The Dauphin district was not mentioned in reports on these settlers. More Ukrainian immigrants arrived in July, and all of them settled in Stuartburn.

Of the group which arrived on August 21, eight families and five single men proceeded to Edmonton, and others went to Dauphin, according to J. R. Burpé, the Secretary of the Dominion Land Office in Winnipeg.[12] According to the records, several families who arrived during the late summer and autumn of 1896 also went, on Dr. Oleskow's recommendation, to settle in the Dauphin region. They took homesteads in Township 26, Range 20, W.P.M., in the Valley River District. Among the first settlers in the Dauphin region was Basil Ksionzik from the village of Zawale, in the district of Terebowla, who, as soon as he had

[11]1. Oles./29757, May 15, 1896: Dr. J. Oleskow, Lemberg, Austria, to the High Commissioner for Canada, London. Dr. Oleskow is referring to the publication *Description of the Province of Manitoba*, published in 1893 under the authority of the Minister of the Interior, T. Mayne Daly.

[12]2. Oles./30995, August 28, 1896: J. R. Burpé, Secretary, Dominion Lands, Winnipeg, to the Secretary, Department of the Interior, Ottawa. Burpé does not give the names of the three men who left for the Lake Dauphin district to select land whom he mentions in his report, but we know that one of them was Basil Ksionzik, who, writing to *Svoboda*, April, 1897, related: "In August of the past year, several of us families came to Canada from Galicia, and when we arrived in Winnipeg, we discussed which would be the best place for us to settle. Some decided to proceed to Edmonton where they had relatives, but others decided to go where I went. When I was preparing to leave the old country, I called on Dr. Oleskow to seek his advice, and he recommended that I settle in the Lake Dauphin region. Therefore, taking two companions with me, I set out to look over the region. . . ." They arrived at the Drifting River Valley, liked the district, and took homesteads there. (*Svoboda*, No. 16, April 15, 1897.)

established himself, sent Dr. Oleskow a description of the district and confirmed the possibility of the establishment of a larger Ukrainian colony in this region. Dr. Oleskow put Ksionzik in touch with Father Nestor Dmytriw in Mount Carmel, Pennsylvania. In the spring of 1897, Father Dmytriw came to Canada, and after visiting the Stuartburn colony on Palm Sunday and the Edna colony on Easter Sunday, he arranged to visit the budding Dauphin colony with Basil Ksionzik.

In his booklet published later that year, *Kanadiyska Rus—Podorozni spomyny / Canadian Ruthenia—Travel Reminiscences,*" Father Dmytriw described his arduous visit to the first Ukrainian settlement in the Dauphin district. The date of his visit is not given, but indications are that it was early in the spring of 1897, since Basil Ksionzik, in a report to *Svoboda,* mentions April 12 in this connection. The priest arrived at Dauphin after a slow train ride from Portage la Prairie and stopped over at the immigration shed to spend the night with newly arrived immigrants. The account of his travels on the following day vividly portrays the difficulties that faced the settlers:

> Early in the afternoon I hired a team of horses and headed for our colony on the Drifting River, sixteen miles from the Valley River rail station; the settlers called their colony Trembowla.
>
> The valley was spread out wide before my eyes. The white houses of the settlers, each a mile apart, could be seen from afar. Near the houses were roughly-built stables that looked like potato bins; the cattle and horses waded in snow and water pools, scratching for dry grass like the reindeer of the north. . . . Forlorn and deep in thought, I finally reached the Valley River. It was impossible to proceed further by wagon. The river, which during the summer is reduced to a trickle, could not be crossed by wagon now. After some consideration I saw no other alternative but to continue my journey on foot, the colony being still some six miles away. On the other side of the river I came to a farm of an Englishman and hired a wagon and a team of horses. We drove three hours through bush and glens and finally reached the homestead of a young English farmer who lived alone in a small shack. The track ended behind his house. The wagon could not penetrate the bush. Again there was no other choice than to proceed on foot. The sun was beginning to set, and its cold parting rays glistened on large snow patches and reflected in the pools of water. For more than an hour I picked my way through dense bush and deep dry grass in a country where probably only hunting Indians ever walked. Darkness was falling. I became alarmed. I experienced the fear of a lonely human being who was like a small worm amidst invincible silent nature, a fear that engulfs one who faces the dark night in the heart of the primeval forest or the steppes.[13]

[13]Nestor Dmytriw, *Kanadiyska Rus: Podorozhni spomyny*/"Canadian Ruthenia: Travel Reminiscences" (Mount Carmel, Pennsylvania: *Svoboda* Publishers, 1897), 56.

After wandering in the bush for some time, Father Dmytriw came across a track which led to the homestead of a young Scotsman who helped him to reach the first homestead of the Ukrainian settlement:

> I finally reached my destination [the home of Basil Ksionzik]. The place was in a beautiful setting, especially in the bright moonlight. A stream wound between gently-wooded banks. Behind the stream, on its higher shore, stood the house. . . . In front of the house there was a wagon which apparently also served as a temporary pantry, with pots and pans stored under the box and one of the pots covered with the weekly *Svoboda.* A fairly large stable housed two cows, two oxen, and two calves; in the yard stood two plows—the beginnings of husbandry. In the house similar order reigned. I made myself at home, took off my soaking-wet shoes to dry, and after a friendly chat with my hosts, I went to bed and fell sound asleep in no time. On Sunday morning I was awakened by the loud crowing of a rooster under my bed. . . .
>
> The settlers were already assembling in front of the house. There are fifteen families, seventy-eight souls in the colony at present, and most of them now filled the yard. . . .

The majority of the settlers of the Trembowla colony had arrived in the early winter, or around Christmas (of 1896): "The families originated in the districts of Borshchiw, Chortkiw, Buchach, and Terebowla. When I visited the colony they owned five oxen, two cows, and two calves. Two oxen, two cows, and two calves were owned by one family. . . . What remained for the rest of the families? Three oxen and one wagon. . . ."

Father Dmytriw's visit was a festive occasion, the first visit of a priest of their denomination, and people cried openly when they heard the first words of the Holy Mass: "During the sermon I myself could restrain tears only with difficulty, remembering the reasons which drove us across the seas, into the snows and forests to seek a better future for our children. After Mass I baptized a small Ukrainian Canadian, and then we proceeded to the Cross of Liberty erected on the hill overlooking the river. The settlers made the cross out of poplar wood to commemorate the liberty which they attained in 1896. . . ." Father Dmytriw does not mention the names of the settlers in the Dauphin district in his booklet. Some of them are found, however, in the records of the Registration Branch of the Government. The report of the General Colonization Agent, C. W. Speers, presented in 1899, provides interesting details that supplement Father Dmytriw's account of the settlement. According to Speer's statement, the Ukrainian colony in the Dauphin region consisted, in 1896, of only eight families, and not of fifteen, as Father Dmytriw states in his booklet. The following are the names of seven of these families, as found in the Naturalization Register:

Name	
Ksionzyk, Basil, Farmer, Valley River, Man.	Naturalized October 25, 1899
Paulitzki, Joseph, Farmer, Valley River, Man.	Naturalized October 25, 1899
Perchaluk, Petro, Farmer, Valley River, Man.	Naturalized November 29, 1899
Perchaluk, Petro J., Farmer, Valley River, Man.	Naturalized November 29, 1899
Niplanski, John, Farmer, Valley River, Man.	Naturalized November 29, 1899
Sytnyk, John, Farmer, Valley River, Man.	Naturalized November 25, 1899
Gereluk, Jan, Farmer, Valley River, Man.	Naturalized November 25, 1899

Mr. Speers visited the colony in March, 1899, and submitted a report which contains more detailed information about the history of this settlement. His remarks about these pioneer settlers and the details concerning their locations and personal effects present a good picture of the Dauphin colony:

In pursuance of instructions, I have the honor to submit to you a report of inspection of the Galician Colony in the Dauphin District situated in townships 26, 27, 28, and 29 in ranges 19, 20, 21 and 22, also in Township 23 in range 20, the base of the Riding Mountain.

Owing to the great depth of snow, and the condition of the road, as well as the fact, that in many places there is only a path from one settler to the other, it was difficult to go over the settlement as thoroughly as I desired to do. Accompanied by Paul Wood, I visited first the Drifting River Colony ten miles west of Valley River. *These are the first Galician settlers that went into the Lake Dauphin district comprising about eight families* [My italics] and settling there in the fall of 1896. The country they possess is timber country and is only open where fires have run and destroyed the timber, and this is covered with a light scrub. The land is slightly undulating and is watered both by the Valley and the Drifting rivers.

Permit me to say, that my idea of checking up these eight families was to see what progress they had made during the four years since their advent, and compare and contrast that with other Galician settlers in other portions of western Canada. Certainly the conditions are different, and the process of clearing and bringing land up to state of cultivation is slower and more expensive than in an open country where there are no obstacles. However, I must say that there is not the progress and the advancement made by these people that I have observed among their nationality in other districts.

I will submit for your information the names of these settlers and their effects:

Joseph Bastchak—NE¼ 20, Tp. 26. Rge. 20. W.P.M.

Seven souls; 1 ox, 1 cow, 1 calf—$100; wagon and plow and sleigh—$80; 8 acres cleared—$30; 40 bus. wheat, 300 bus. potatoes—$130; Two children working out. Building, house and stable. Started with capital of $80.00 in 1896.

Basil Ksionzik—NE¼ 19, T. 26, Rge. 20. W.P.M.

Seven souls; House and stables—$150; 10 head of cattle—$275; Wagon and plow—$90; Mower, rake, sleigh and harrow—$110; Five acres plowed—$25; 500 bus. potatoes, 40 bus. of wheat—$200. Splendid garden. Started with capital of $500.00 in 1896. Runs a small store.

Joseph Paulitzki—SE¼, Tp. 26, Rge. 20. W.P.M.

Six souls; House and stable—$100; Two cows—$70; 200 bus. of potatoes and 40 bus. of wheat—$100; Two acres cleared—$10; Started with no capital in 1896.

John Gereluk—NW¼ 20, Tp. 26, Rge. 20, W.P.M.

Four souls; House and stable—$100; Two oxen and two cows—$160; Ten tons of hay—$30; Sleigh—$30. One acre ploughed—$5; 200 bus. of potatoes. Started with no capital in 1896.

Ivan Setnik (*Sytnyk*)—NE¼ 18, Tp. 26, Rge. 20. W.P.M.

Eight souls; House and stable—$100; 2 oxen and 2 cows—$150; Wagon—$80; 100 bus. of potatoes—$40; One acre broken—$5; Boy and girl working out. Started with no capital in 1896.

John Niplanski—Three souls; House and stable—$75; Cow and calf—$40; 200 bus. of potatoes; 10 tons of hay—$40; 1½ acres plowed. Has been kept back owing to sickness. McKenzie & Mann contractors owe him for 21 days work.

Petro Perchaluk—SW¼ 30, Tp. 26, Rge. 20, W.P.M.

Seven souls; House and stable—$100. One cow—$35; 150 bus. of potatoes—$50; One acre plowed—$5; Started with no capital.

The above are the pioneer Galicians of the Dauphin district, I may add, that they are a thrifty contented people. Although I have not gone very fully into detail, I notice that each settler has a goodly number of chickens about their stables. They are evidently going into mixed farming, and are making a good living, although the amount each settler has under cultivation does not appear large.[14]

For purposes of comparison, here are the particulars regarding three of these original settlers contained in a report presented three years later, in April, 1902:[15]

Bastchak, Joseph—Valley River, Man.

Number of family—10; Date of arrival—1896; Capital on arrival—$400; Land now owned—320 acres; Acres under cultivation—32; Present value of land—$2,500; Cattle owned—6; Swine—3; Implements—All machinery. Total value—*$3,479.*

Ksionzek, Basil—Valley River, Man.

Number of family—7; Date of arrival—1896; Capital on arrival—$700; Land owned now 320 acres; Acres under cultivation—32; Present value of Land—$2,500; Cattle owned—15; Swine—5; Implements: wagon, sleighs, 2 plows, harrow, binder, mower, rake. Total value—*$3,984.*

Gereluk, Jan—Valley River, Man.

Number of family—5; Date of arrival—1896; Capital on arrival $8; Land owned—160 acres; Acres under cultivation—18; Present value of land—$2,000; Cattle owned—6, Swine—2; Implements—All machinery. Total value—*$2,732.*

As is evident from the two reports, the settlers in the Dauphin region who settled on homesteads in 1896 had made substantial progress by 1902.

II

In the spring of 1897, new Ukrainian immigrants began to arrive in the West. A considerable number of them went to the Dauphin district for settlement, probably induced to go there by Dr. Oleskow, for he wrote

[14]8. Rpts./78733, March 27, 1899: C. W. Speers, General Colonization Agent, Portage la Prairie, to Frank Pedley, Superintendent of Immigration, Ottawa.
[15]17. Rpts./198189, April 9, 1902.

to the Department of the Interior, in March, 1897, about a new group that he was sending to Canada:

> . . . In this spring I am directing once more a party of emigrants of better sort to Canada. I let them book by Spiro & Co. for "Arcadia", the Hansa Line steamer, leaving Hamburg on April 10th. It were very instructive for the Canadian Government to compare this time the emigrants booked by Spiro with those by other agents.
>
> This party will settle in Lake Dauphin District Man., and it is in interest of sound development of immigration, that these very immigrants are received with some special attention. I beg namely that 1) for this party were timely provided a shelter in Lake Dauphin. 2) to hire at the cost of Government the services of Mr. Basil Ksionzek, farmer in Trembowla, p.o. Rigby, Lake Dauphin District, that he may help the settlers in finding suitable location and to be their interpreter in Land office.[16]

The Deputy Minister followed Professor Oleskow's suggestions, and on April 20 the following instructions were sent to the Commissioner of Immigration in Winnipeg about securing the help of Mr. Ksionzik:

> I am directed to inform you that on the 10th instant a party of Austrian immigrants will leave Hamburg for Canada [This should read "left Hamburg"]. These people are sent out by Professor Oleskow, and are of an entirely different class from those whom you have had in charge recently. Professor Oleskow asks that the services of Mr. Basil Ksionzick, of Trembowla, Rigby P.O., Lake Dauphin District, be secured with a view of helping the intending settlers to select locations, and I am to request that you will communicate with Mr. Ksionzick in advance, telling him that the Department will defray his expenses and give him a small allowance for any work he does in this direction. Upon being advised of the date on which these immigrants will arrive in Canada, Mr. Akerlindh, or some other officer of the Department, will be placed in charge of the party and see them through.
>
> The Deputy Minister would be glad if upon the arrival of the settlers in Winnipeg you would communicate with Professor Oleskow, giving him your views as to their prospects. He is willing to do good work for Canada, and from his letter there is no doubt that he is in no way responsible for the undesirable [i.e., destitute] immigrants who have come from his native country recently.[17]

Mr. Smart also sent a lengthy reply to Professor Oleskow, in which he added this paragraph about preparations being made to meet the latest group of immigrants:

> With reference to the party which you are sending on the 10th of April, I may say that every care will be taken to receive them kindly and help them to settle on lands. The Government has now at Winnipeg a Commissioner of Immigration who is specially in charge of the reception, care and locating

16. Oles., March 24, 1897: Dr. J. Oleskow, Lemberg, Austria, to the Department of the Interior, Ottawa.

17. Oles./36560, April 20, 1897: Lyndwode Pereira, Ottawa, to W. F. McCreary, Winnipeg.

immigrants, and I am sure your people will be very pleased with the work that he will be willing to do to help them. I will instruct one of our officers to meet the steamer on her arrival on this side. I should add that the Government has now an Immigration Hall in Dauphin with a competent person in charge, and until locations are decided upon this building can be occupied by your people. We will also gladly avail ourselves of the services of Mr. Basil Ksionzick, of Trembowla, in the manner suggested in your letter. . .[18]

After twelve days had passed since the departure of the *Arcadia* from Hamburg, the Deputy Minister sent a memorandum to the Superintendent of Immigration, requesting news of the ship: "Have you had any word of Prof. Oleskow's party yet?—J.A.S., D.M.I."[19] But no word came. Another week passed, and on April 28 the Deputy Minister wired additional instructions to the Commissioner in Winnipeg about meeting the party: "Departmental letter twentieth, Austria immigrants. Arrange immediately with Ksionzick meet them Fort William as Akerlindh cannot go beyond that point. Six hundred forty eight in the party. Arrival Quebec not yet telegraphed. Will wire you when to expect. RUSH [In pencil]."[20]

The Commissioner of Immigration acknowledged the letter of April 20 from the Deputy Minister and informed the Department of the steps taken to receive the *Arcadia* passengers:

I am in receipt of your favour of the 20th instant, informing me that on the 10th instant a party of Austrians will leave Hamburg for Canada, which might indicate that they will leave on the 10th of next month. However, from the copy of your letter attached which you had mailed to Mr. Doyle [Immigration Agent in Quebec, P.Q.] you state that they have left on the 10th.

Now, from this I would suppose that this Steamer must be a slow one, as in the ordinary course these people should be here now. You are aware, of course, that 435 Galicians sailed on the 15th by S.S. "Scotia" which would make a total of 1,081 people, all of whom, if the Steamers were nearly of equal speed, should be here about the same time.

This is a large number to handle at once, and unfortunately I had advices from Edmonton last Sunday that Measles had broken out in the Sheds among the last party that went up, there being eight cases developed. . . . We can accommodate about 300 to 500 here; as many more in Brandon; 75 at Portage la Prairie, and 75 at Dauphin, and, of course, any destined for Edmonton we could place in the Calgary sheds.

[18]2. Oles./36560, April 20, 1897: James A. Smart, Deputy Minister, Department of the Interior, Ottawa, to Dr. J. Oleskow, Lemberg, Austria.

[19]2. Oles., April 22, 1897: Memorandum from "J.A.S." (Smart) to L. M. Fortier, Ottawa.

[20]2. Oles., Telegram, April 28, 1897: James A. Smart, Ottawa, to W. F. McCreary, Winnipeg.

My object in knowing all I can in reference to them is to enable me to send one or two interpreters down the line to meet them at Port Arthur, so that before they arrive here, that is, should they all arrive in one day, it will be possible to send those going to Edmonton straight along to the Calgary sheds, and despatch the others to the various points nearest their ultimate destination.

I have to-day communicated with the Caretaker of the Dauphin Sheds, Mr. Mouat, instructing him to send out and bring in Mr. Basil Ksionzik, of Rigby P.O., who will assist in looking after those who intend settling in that district.

In accordance with your request, I will in a few days, make quite a long report upon the Galician immigrants to Professor Oleskow. . . .[21]

On the same day, Commissioner McCreary wrote a separate letter to the Deputy Minister, replying to his telegram, and giving additional information about how he planned to handle the large number of immigrants:

I am in receipt of your telegram of the 28th instant, and also of your Departmental letter of the 20th, referring to Austrian immigrants, and asking me to arrange immediately with Ksionzick to meet them at Fort William as Akerlindh cannot go beyond that point. I wired the Caretaker at Dauphin to send a messenger out to Trambola, Rigby P.O., for the purpose of bringing in Ksionzick, and expect him to reach this city next Sunday, and will send him down with my Interpreter here, Mr. Genik, to take charge of the party, as it will likely take two trains to transport this number of people. I shall probably accompany the interpreters to Port Arthur myself,[22] as I should like to decide before they arrive here what number I shall keep in those Sheds and those I shall send on either to Brandon or Calgary. As to the latter, we will not bring them out of the trains at all, or, at least if we do we will just allow them to stay in the Station until the train is cleaned up, and will not bring them over to the Sheds, so that it will be well that this division shall be made before they arrive at this point, and the plan I have formed is this:—

I shall have a number of blank tickets given to the interpreter, and when a man is going to Edmonton, I will have him write his name and "Edmonton" on the ticket, and hand it to him to be produced at the Station here, so that we can sort them out by this means. There is no doubt it will take considerable work to handle this number, together with the 435 coming by the "Scotia", but I think my plans are now laid in such a way that we will get along without much difficulty.[23]

[21]2. Oles./36912, April 28, 1897: W. F. McCreary, Winnipeg, to the Secretary of the Department of the Interior, Ottawa.

[22]McCreary's expectations and plans did not materialize. The arrival of the *Scotia* and *Arcadia* passengers on the same day kept him occupied in Winnipeg, and Ksionzik was busy in Dauphin helping Paul Wood locate the great number of settlers sent to the Dauphin district from Winnipeg.

[23]2. Oles./36988, April 29, 1897: W. F. McCreary, Winnipeg, to James A. Smart, Ottawa.

The accountant of the Department of the Interior was notified about the arrangement with Mr. Basil Ksionzick, and all details then appeared to be in order. Finally, after days of waiting, the Superintendent of Immigration in Ottawa received the long overdue message from the Immigration Agent in Quebec, dated May 1, 1897, informing him of the arrival of the ship: "Arcadia passed Father Point five P.M. Due here six A.M. tomorrow."[24]

III

Commissioner McCreary was correct in suspecting that the steamer was a slow one. The S.S. *Arcadia* was not only slow, she was of ancient vintage as well. The voyage of the *Arcadia* is vividly described by Dmytro Romanchych, who came to Canada with his father and sisters and settled in the Dauphin district, becoming one of the pioneers of the Vermillion River colony. Romanchych described the start of the voyage in his memoirs:

> After a short wait in Hamburg, one and a half thousand Ukrainian emigrants were loaded into an very old but not very large ship, the *Arcadia*. It was a boat that had steam engines as well as sails which were hoisted when a favourable wind was blowing. Under the top deck there were about a dozen passenger cabins where the "city-coated gentlemen" travelled. Under the second deck were the galleys and the dining room. Below water level, under the third and fourth decks, there were no cabins, only one big space with rows of iron bedsteads, three or four storeys high. In the lower beds the women and children slept, and in the upper beds, the men and boys. If one wished to reach the upper storey, an iron ladder had to be used.
>
> We stopped over at Antwerp, in Belgium, where the boat took on ballast, hundreds of barrels with cement. We stayed at Antwerp for five days. Nobody was permitted to leave the boat, and only Bodrug and Negrych [Iwan Bodrug and Iwan Negrych, both teachers] managed somehow to get off the boat and view the city. On the boat it was unbearably hot, and below deck an unbearable stench made breathing difficult.

After five days of unexplained delay at Antwerp, the boat was on its way once again. Conditions aboard ship were extremely poor, and the voyage was an ordeal for all concerned:

> Probably no Ukrainian emigrant ever experienced such a dreadful ocean crossing as we did on our *Arcadia*. When we left the English Channel and entered the open sea, the weather was beautiful for the first few days. The sun was shining all day, the sea was calm, and it was a pleasure to travel. Above our heads flew loudly-shrieking flocks of seagulls, and in the water whole herds of dolphins accompanied our ship as if they had never seen a boat before.

24. Oles., Telegram, May 1, 1897: P. Doyle, Immigration Agent, Quebec, P.Q., to L. M. Fortier, Ottawa.

When about half-way across the Atlantic, the weather suddenly changed one evening and a storm broke out, a real hurricane accompanied by a deluge of rain. In no time the sea was transformed into high mountains with white tops. One moment we were on top of these foaming mountains and the next we were thrown into what seemed a bottomless abyss. . . . The ballast shifted, and our boat began to list to one side. . . . People were holding on tightly to their iron bedsteads, and many started to pray, and until all became seasick. The seamen apparently anticipated the storm, because they herded us all below deck and closed the hatches. Passengers who had been warned about seasickness before they started the voyage were also told that garlic, onions, whiskey, and Hoffmann's drops were good remedies against seasickness. People were not overly stingy with these remedies, and they partook of them as much as they could stand. As a result of them, such terrible smells developed below deck during the storm that even the stewards who ventured in became sick. They swore and cursed, but as they did it in German, which few people understood, it had little effect.

The storm lasted three days without a break, and somehow we survived it without great losses. Only two persons died, an old man and a child. On the fourth day the storm stopped as suddenly as it had started. People breathed in relief and all went to sleep exhausted. Suddenly, during the night, a loud blast and a shock which rattled our iron bedsteads woke us up. People were asking, frightened, "What happened?" Those who could, hurried to the top deck, and were amazed to learn that the boat was surrounded by ice. The crew was patching up a hole below, pumps were throbbing, and our boat was trying to free itself from the icy embrace by moving backwards and forwards. The siren was blowing all the time to prevent eventual collision with some other boat, because it was foggy and one could hardly see a few yards ahead.

We remained ice-bound until morning. The boat was imprisoned by the ice and could not move. The captain ordered all passengers on deck, and we obeyed the order. Bodrug interpreted the captain's commands. We were ordered, when the whistle blew, to run from one side of the boat to the other as fast as we could, and back again. We repeated this manoeuvre many times. The boat began to sway, broke the ice which was surrounding it, and began to move forward slowly. Our baggage, which was stored below, became soaking wet during that storm, and we suffered great losses.

We wrestled with the ice floes for three days, and only on the fourth day we reached the open sea, which was as calm and smooth as a mirror. After another two and a half days of sailing against the wind on the St. Lawrence, we finally reached Quebec and Canada. We had been at sea twenty-one days. . . .[25]

The voyage had lasted more than a month from the day that the settlers left their villages until they landed in Quebec on May 2, 1897.

[25]Dmytro Romanchych, "Ukrainski kolonii v okruzi Dauphin, Manitoba"/ "Ukrainian Colonies in the Dauphin, Manitoba, District," *Memorial Book of The Ukrainian National Home Association In Winnipeg*, 1949, 511–512.

After staying in vermin-infested immigration halls, travelling steerage amid filth and stench, the immigrants, weary, dirty, and haggard, longed to "stretch their legs," to leave the boat and train and feel the firm earth underfoot again. Alfred Akerlindh, the Scandinavian Interpreter and Immigration Officer who was sent from Ottawa to accompany the *Arcadia* passengers part of the way, reported on his return concerning the number of the immigrants:

> Here in Ottawa, I waited for and met the second party ex S.S. *Arcadia*, which arrived here early in the morning of the 3rd of May and left after an hour's stay here. The party were contained in ten cars making a long and heavy train and rather difficult to handle for one agent. I counted the number as far as I could, there were 152 men 138 women and 343 children making a total of 633 souls, there might be a slight difference between these figures and the actual numbers caused by the constant roving about in the cars of the people and by me being obliged to stop the count for a minute or more at some station where we stopped, and where it was necessary to watch that no one got off the cars or got left behind. These people have the fashion that no matter how much you tell them and warn them, they always insist upon being on the platform of the cars and at all places where the train makes the least stop, they are bound to be out in all directions making it very difficult for the agent to guard them. . . .[26]

The trip west went off smoothly, with only a slight accident which, Akerlindh was glad to report, had no undesirable consequences:

> A narrow escape from an accident took however place on this journey in spite of my constant watch and repeated warnings to the people in that a little girl aged about ten fell from the train near Onaping station and I was not aware of the fact until about three miles away from the place being busy in the other end of the train. I stopped the train and ordered it to back up slowly and after a little while we met the little girl walking on the track not hurt the least not having received even a scratch from her fall, this chiefly accounted for by the slow rate of travel, 15 miles an hour, going up heavy grade.

Akerlindh was critical of the filthy condition and the "unclean habits of these people," but he managed to bring the whole train safely to Fort William where the people had a good rest and the cars were thoroughly cleaned before being taken over by Cyril Genik and John Wendelbo, the interpreters who were to conduct the train to Winnipeg.

The passengers from the S.S. *Scotia* and S.S. *Arcadia* arrived in Winnipeg almost at the same time, and Commissioner McCreary reported to Ottawa on their condition: "The whole party of 1100 came in within six hours of each other, and you may depend upon it it was no easy

[26]2. Oles./37225, May 8, 1897: Alfred Akerlindh, Government Immigration Officer, Ottawa, to L. M. Fortier, Ottawa.

task to manage them. However, they were all well fed and were apparently happy; no sickness prevailed, and I think they were fairly well satisfied. 475 of them left by special train last night for Dauphin, and the balance are still here, but I expect to despatch them to-day and to-morrow. I will write more soon as I get a moment to spare."[27] A few days later, the caretaker of the Dauphin Immigration Shed, Agent J. N. Mouat, reported to the Commissioner in Winnipeg about the large party of prospective settlers which arrived at Dauphin in a special train:

> . . . Re the Galicians, I got the tents prepared for them as directed but as there was not sufficient room even then Mr. Burrows wired for another which was sent per next train, some thirteen families moved up to the valley by this same train I went up and with the assistance of Mr. Paul Wood got the tent up there and between that and empty cars got them under cover. It was a big mistake of them moving there as we are out of touch with them. A number have been down here since and complain about the scarcity of surveyed lands they are ready and willing to work and eager to get the seeds etc. into ground that they have brought with them. B. Borrows has gone to the end of the track to-night in their interests. It is a big contract to get them all settled satisfactorily, but will do our best for them under the circumstances. We should have three or four guides to take them out in batches and keep them on the move. Some in their ignorance have gone out without information as to locations, whether entered for or not, Ksionzick should be down here soon probably to-morrow with a number whom he has been looking after, as also Mr. Woods, and they are well prepared for working the land with spades, hoes, and even plows which they have brought with them from their own country, the great drawback as I said before is the unsurveyed lands, and this cannot be seen to too soon. . . . Mr. Woods tells me that between Lake Dauphin and Lake Winnipeg there is a lot of good land for settlers that is in Townships 26 and 27, Ranges 16 and 17. . . . I am afraid it will be almost impossible to get the names of all those Galicians as the names are almost unpronounceable but will get as many as possible correctly from their old passports which they have with them. The names of those returning for Dominion City will be wired you to-morrow.[28]

IV

Every new transport of immigrants arriving in Halifax or Quebec during the spring and summer of 1897 invariably also brought a large number of settlers who gave Dauphin as their destination. The S.S. *Prussia*, which arrived in Halifax on May 22, had 672 Ukrainian settlers on board, many of whom were heading for Dauphin. Akerlindh, sent from

[27]3. Gal., May 6, 1897: W. F. McCreary, Winnipeg, to the Deputy Minister of the Interior, Ottawa.

[28]3. Gal./37611, May 10, 1897: J. N. Mouat, Caretaker, Immigration Shed, Dauphin, to W. F. McCreary, Winnipeg.

Ottawa to meet and conduct the new arrivals part of the way, wired this information about them to Ottawa: "Left Halifax three P.M. [May 23, 1897] 195 men, 169 women, 311 children. Majority Dauphin. Funds fair, 92 families over fifty dollars mark, 47 under. Total brought —14,275 dollars. Montreal Monday night."[29] Of this group, thirty-nine families gave the settlement of Trembowla near Rigby as their destination,[30] the place where their countryman Basil Ksionzik was locating families on homesteads.

If the weary immigrants thought that their ordeal was now over, they were very much mistaken. There were more obstacles to be overcome before they would reach the place that was to become their and their children's home. Dauphin was situated on the line owned by the Lake Manitoba Railway and Canal Company, which was not in as strong a financial position as the Canadian Pacific Railway Company. It refused to transport immigrants to Dauphin unless they paid the extra fare from Portage la Prairie to Dauphin, amounting to $1.20 per person. The majority of the settlers vigorously protested against this extra expense, claiming that they had already paid all that was due for transportation to the place of settlement, and that they did not intend to spend any more money for this purpose. The Superintendent of the Lake Manitoba Railway and Canal Company, Mr. D. B. Hanna, sent the Commissioner of Immigration the list of ninety-three passengers who refused (or were unable) to pay the fare and enclosed a bill for $111.60, the cost of this transportation, asking for reimbursement.[31]

Commissioner McCreary was considerably annoyed with the obstacles raised by the railway company and he wrote to the Deputy Minister, requesting a decision on the matter:

> As you probably are aware, the Canadian Pacific Railway Company have been in the habit of hauling these people to all points on their lines free of charge, but the Manitoba and North Western, as well as the Dauphin lines have tried to charge one cent per mile rate over their roads. The people strenuously object to pay more for their fares; and you cannot blame the people so much as the agents who forward them.
>
> I told Mr. Hanna he would likely have trouble with these parties, and with the first consignment he did have considerable, having to stop them in the bush some miles out of town, and forward an engine to procure help and Interpreters. I believe, however, with the first contingent he collected

293. Gal./37732, Telegram, May 23, 1897: Alfred Akerlindh, Moncton, N.B., to L. M. Fortier, Ottawa.

303. Gal./37808, Telegram, May 25, 1897: Alfred Akerlindh, Ottawa, to W. F. McCreary, Winnipeg.

313. Gal./38814, June 12, 1897: D.B. Hanna, Superintendent, The Lake Manitoba Railway and Canal Company, Winnipeg, to W. F. McCreary, Winnipeg.

most of the fares. This later contingent, however, of some 400 to 500 people I pleaded with him not to charge them, as I feared he would have difficulty; however, he collected about sixty five of the fares, leaving some ninety-three who still refused to pay. The conductor held all their baggage on the arrival of the train in Dauphin, and would not deliver it to them. That was a week ago last Saturday night. The weather turned cold and these people were without flour or blankets and threatened to tear down the Freight Sheds and create other riots. The Caretaker wired me, and I left my bed and went down to Mr. Hanna's house, and after talking the matter over in a rather excited manner he finally agreed to release this baggage on condition that I would become good for the fares, which I had to do, as it would no doubt have created a considerable uproar to have allowed these people to commit any riotous acts.

The bill of $111.60 is for the fares of these people, and I want you to advise me whether or not this should be paid from here, or a cheque sent from Ottawa. I may say that I also guaranteed the fares as far as Yorkton to the Manitoba and North-Western Road to Mr. Baker, as this included a large number of those whom I had difficulty with in the Shed. . . .[32]

The Deputy Minister wrote a rather strong letter to Hanna, protesting against this added expense to the settlers:

The Commissioner of Immigration, Winnipeg, has referred to me the account rendered by your Company amounting to $111.60, being ninety three fares of Galician immigrants on your Line. I am distinctly of the opinion, however, that this is an account which the Department should not be called upon to pay. We are expending large sums every year in promoting immigration and in the case of these poor people, who have come to Canada without any direct solicitation on our part, we have incurred additional expenses in forwarding them to their destinations and getting them settled on lands, advancing them seed, and in some instances cattle, etc., and we think that the Transportation Companies, and especially those directly interested in the settlement of particular districts, as your own Company is, should shew a greater willingness to co-operate with the Government in work of this kind and that, considering the permanent benefit which your company will derive from the presence of these people in the neighbourhood to which you have transported them there. I may add that the Canadian Pacific Railway Company evidently take this view of the matter, and that if we cannot get parties of this class carried free on other Lines, we will be compelled to turn them over to the C.P.R. Company, and send them to neighbourhoods on their main or branch lines. . . .[33]

Reluctantly, with one eye on the possibility of losing settlers in the area served by the Lake Manitoba Railway and Canal Company, Superintendent Hanna relinquished his company's claim for the payment of

[32]3. Gal./38814, June 9, 1897: W. F. McCreary, Winnipeg, to James A. Smart, Ottawa.

[33]3. Gal./38814, June 14, 1897: James A. Smart, Ottawa, to D. B. Hanna, Winnipeg.

$111.60, but at the same time he informed the Deputy Minister that the company would insist on collecting fares from future parties: "I discussed the question with the Minister during his recent visit here; and although I have arranged to cancel the bill, it is understood we are not prevented from collecting nominal fares from further parties which we may subsequently locate tributary to our road. . . . With regard to future parties, I think all trouble would be avoided if the European agents were instructed to raise the through rate to such an amount as would admit of the Can. Pac. allowing us say one cent per mile per passenger over fifteen years of age. . . ."[34]

When most of the obstacles of the journey were finally overcome, the region rapidly began to fill with settlers. They spread mainly in a north-westerly direction, occupying homesteads in Townships 26, 27, 28, and 29, Ranges 19, 20, 21, and 22. One group of settlers, consisting mainly of Ukrainian highlanders (*Hutsuly*), attracted by the Riding Mountains, which reminded them of their native Carpathian Mountains, became squatters in Township 23, Range 20, which was a timber reserve not open for homesteading. This group experienced great difficulty afterwards in having the land released for homestead entry. Nicholas Hryhorczuk, one of the pioneers of the Ethelbert colony, who later represented the Ethelbert constituency in the Manitoba Legislature for twenty-two years, described the beginnings of the Ukrainian colony in Ethelbert thus:

> The first Ukrainian pioneer-settler in this region was George (Yurko) Syrotiuk, who hailed from the District of Kolomyja in Galicia. He came to Dauphin in 1896—it was the terminal of the rail line at that time—and after looking around, he went some 35 miles north, selected a homestead there, and paid the entry fee. He wrote letters to his native village inviting his relatives to join him in Canada, because, as he said, Canada offered great opportunities for the settlement of Ukrainian smallholders.
>
> In the spring of the next year (1897) there arrived in Dauphin hundreds of Ukrainian peasant-settlers from the District of Kolomyja. They spread in all directions, looking for suitable land to settle upon. Some have hired teams of horses and driven 35 miles north of Dauphin, taking out homesteads in that region, which is about 12 miles distant from what is today the town of Gilbert Plains. Others joined Wasyl Syrotiuk (brother of George) and settled in the vicinity of Ethelbert. About 10 families took homesteads there at that time (1897).[35]

[34]3. Gal./39826, July 5, 1897: D. B. Hanna, Winnipeg, to James A. Smart, Ottawa.

[35]N. Hryhorczuk, "Ukrainska kolonia Ethelbert, Manitoba"/"The Ukrainian Colony of Ethelbert, Manitoba," *Memorial Book of The Ukrainian National Home Association In Winnipeg*, 1949, 489–493.

In the spring of 1899 C. W. Speers, the General Colonization Agent of the Department of the Interior, inspected the Ukrainian settlements in the Dauphin district and submitted a report to the Superintendent of Immigration in Ottawa which gives a very comprehensive picture of the colony two years after its establishment:

. . . Generally speaking the Dauphin District possesses every natural advantage for the Galician settler. I would submit a short description of the land, based largely from my observation of external appearances the growth on the surface as well as the information I could glean from all sources pertaining to the different townships. In townships 26, 27, 28 and 29 in range 22, the land is gently undulating to the west, and is thickly wooded with timber, and where burnt is covered with poplar scrub. The soil is a good depth and it is well watered. In township 29 range 21, known as the Fork River settlement, the land looks excellent along the rivers, but I am afraid it is stoney away from the river bed. It is covered with light timber and poplar scrub and possesses a great many desirable bluffs of evergreen that affords excellent building timber. Townships 26, 27 and 28 Range 21, is mostly of a poorer quality. There are many ridges, and I would judge from appearances the flats are low and sour. There are a number of good hay meadows. This district is watered by several creeks. There are a number of Canadians and English speaking settlers in this township. Township 26 range 20 is well watered by the Drifting River and Valley River. This is a very good settlement; the land is of excellent quality. This was the first settlement occupied by the Galician people. Township 26 range 19 the land is somewhat light, covered with light scrub and interspersed with small hay meadows. There are only a few Galicians in this settlement. There are some available homesteads here. Townships 29 range 19 and 20 is fair land with a generous supply of hay. Township 28 in ranges 19 and 20 possesses a good deal of swamp land; there are a good many bluffs of evergreen in the western portion and some very good hay meadows. A portion of this is watered by the Mink and Fishing Creeks. This is thickly settled with Galicians.

Township 29 in ranges 19 and 20 is partly surveyed; very fair land. In township 23 Range 20 on the Riding Mountains are about 55 Galician squatters. This is on the east side of the Vermillion River and was within the permanent timber reservation. . . .

I may say that these Galicians have done considerable improvements, and that the timber in that district that they possess has been destroyed by fires. Doubtless the Department is aware of the fact that for reasons of their own they are not desirous that these entries should be completed, but I beg to say that the land is useless for any purpose other than colonization. I beg to draw your attention to the fact that there is a portion of country on the east side of Vermillion River adjacent to the present Galician colony where the timber has been destroyed by fire that would make good land for settlement.

I beg to report, as I have hitherto reported on other Galician colonies, the great necessity of establishing schools among these people. There is no public school among these people and they themselves are anxious to procure them. The municipal authorities are likely to form new districts shortly, one at Sifton, one at Drifting River.

I would suggest that the Provincial authorities appoint uncertificated persons to do the first good work of teachers among these colonists.

I may say that there is no church, nor place of worship among these colonists, but the Missionaries of the Roman faith are endeavouring to give some attention to this work and three thousand feet of lumber has been shipped to Sifton to be used for building a church. The Galician settlers subscribed $28.00, Bishop Langevin subscribed $50.00, but the people are very much divided, and a very large majority said they would withdraw their subscription if the money was not appropriated in building a church of the Greek orthodox faith.

There has been large sums of money earned by these people on the construction work of the Lake Manitoba & Canal Co.'s railway, and this has been of very great assistance to these new settlers. They are all in a fair way of progressing rapidly, and I think it can be safely said that they will make first class settlers in time.

I beg to call your attention to a number of districts that are especially adapted for Galician or other European colonization. Townships 25 to 30 in ranges 28 and 29, along the Provincial boundary west in Manitoba, and would be east of the present Galician colony at Saltcoats and Yorkton, and south east of the Doukhobor colony at Thunder Hills. There would be about ten townships in this block, and it possesses from what I can learn very natural advantages for colonization purposes. There are a few English speaking settlers in the southern portion of it, townships 25 and 26.

I would also call your attention to another block of land situated in Townships 20 and 21 in range 24 and township 21 in Range 25 and township 22 in range 26 comprising five townships. This land is situated north of Rossburn, near the Birtle valley and should be an excellent place for Galician colonization, Mr. D. B. Hanna and Mr. T. A. Burrows have called my attention to a very desirable district situated in the vicinity of Glenella and Glencairn, comprising townships 18, 19 and 20 in ranges 11, 12, 13 and 14. There is a very considerable amount of desirable land available in these townships.

I submit to you a Provincial map of Manitoba. The present settlement of Galicians are marked in red, the land desirable for future Galician colonization marked in blue squares. The land desirable for survey for future colonization dashed along the rivers with blue lead pencil. The districts to which I refer, I think it necessary that I should drive through and inspect and submit you a detailed report of the natural advantages they possess and their desirability for the incoming settlers. Of course, this would have to be accomplished after the snow had disappeared. With the advent of so many European settlers it is essential, that we should have some adequate knowledge of the best districts and be in a position to place them according to your wishes without incurring any loss of time, as well as this would be valuable information for the Department.

I observed when in Dauphin, a great influx of people already commencing to move into the Swan River country, and in conversation with Mr. Herchmer, the Land Agent, Mr. Thomas Young, the Homestead Inspector, Mr.

Paul Wood, our agent, they are of one opinion that all the available land for homestead purposes should be thrown open, and that the further survey of more land should be effected as soon as it was possible. I promised to submit these matters for your consideration.

I beg to refer to another matter—Some of the Galician settlers claim that in writing letters to Austria to their friends their mail is intercepted, possibly by the Military authorities of Austria who may wish to stop the issue of more pass-ports. Should it be possible for Edwin R. Schultz, Austrian Counsel [Eduard Schultze, the Austrian Consul] at Montreal, to nominate somebody in Austria, who would be responsible for the safe delivery of these letters.

I beg to submit with this report a book showing each Galician settler in the Dauphin district and his location.[36] The map I submit will show the different districts to which I have referred. It is my intention, at an early date, to submit to you a book showing the names of the Galician settlers, and their location in the Fish Creek colony and Rossburn colony and also more particularly along this line with a great many settlers and their effects and locations pertaining to the large colony of Galicians at Edmonton.

I might remark that the Galicians in Dauphin are very contented and in a very satisfactory condition. There are features of interest in the report, that may require your attention, the large number of settlers that have not obtained entry, the advisability of throwing open for homestead entry all lands that are surveyed and available, the necessity of the further survey of more lands owing to the great influx of people, and the necessity of an early inspection of the different districts that I have pointed out for future colonization.[37]

Speers described the Dauphin region as he saw it in March, 1899. A few months later, however, in October of the same year, a disastrous prairie fire struck Townships 26, 27, 28, and 29, Ranges 19, 20, 21, and 22, and many of those whom Speers described as "contented and in very satisfactory condition," lost most of their possessions, including their houses and other buildings, and had to be assisted with food and clothing to survive the approaching winter.

V

The Vermillion River colony in Township 23, Range 20 W.1.M. was established in May of 1897. It was within the timber reserve and therefore not open for homesteading, but the settlers who squatted hoped that if they improved their holdings and put in a request to the proper authorities they would be able to obtain homestead entries for the sections they occupied.

[36]The list of Ukrainian settlers prepared by C. W. Speers is given at the end of the chapter on Dauphin.

[37]8. Rpts./78733, March 27, 1899: C. W. Speers, Portage la Prairie, to Frank Pedley, Ottawa: a ten-page report, including a list of the original settlers of the Drifting River colony.

Those settlers who took out homesteads in townships open for settlement in other parts of the Dauphin district had no difficulty in obtaining entry. But the forty-odd families who settled in the Riding Mountain Timber Reserve had to wait many trying years before they could legalize their positions, enter their holdings as homesteads, and finally obtain title to their farms. Dmytro Romanchych wrote this description of the beginnings of their settlement:

> We arrived in Dauphin on May 6th, 1897 [i.e., less than one week after their landing in Quebec, May 1]. The little town was just beginning to grow. We were put up in tents near the station and the next morning, having left the women and children in the tents, we started on foot to look for places available for settlement, north and west of Dauphin, because the land nearer to town was already taken by English and Scottish immigrants who arrived before us. Our guide was Paul Wood, the local Immigration Agent, who knew the country well. And we, having Bodrug and Yurko (George) Syrotiuk (who hailed from the village of Balyntsi) as interpreters, were able to receive detailed information from Wood, everything that was important for us to know. Wood was of Swiss origin and spoke German well.
>
> I, being a lad of twenty, was given the task of carrying the heavy bags with provisions for our group of prospectors, while they went ahead with spades and axes, occasionally testing the quality of the soil and cutting a path through underbrush. We made about thirty miles during the first day, going in a northwesterly direction, inspecting the land which was covered with dense bush, some meadows, and in places with forests. We passed the place where the projected terminal of the railway line was to be established and called Sifton after Clifford Sifton, Minister of the Interior in Ottawa.[38] Some ten miles beyond Sifton we stopped for the night in the middle of the woods. . . . The next day our party went further in a northwesterly direction and halted in the bush not far from the place where the Ukrainian village of Ethelbert is today.[39] We found good black soil there and spent several days looking over the district.[40]

Several members of the party selected homesteads about seven miles

[38]Sifton, a Manitoba community in Dauphin Rural Municipality, sixteen miles northwest of Dauphin on the C.N.R. line. The first settlers, English and Ukrainian, came into the area in the late 1890's. The railway reached the district in 1896. The present population in predominantly of Ukrainian and Polish origin. Sifton is a small, highly industrialized centre with woollen mills and wood-products factories. Its schools are part of the large Dauphin-Ochre River School District formed in 1947. (*Encyclopedia Canadiana*, IX, 307.)

[39]Ethelbert, Manitoba, a village thirty-two miles northwest of Dauphin on the C.N.R. line to Swan River. It is said to have been named after Ethel Berta, a daughter of Sir William Mackenzie, the president of the Canadian Northern Railway. The first settlers arrived in 1897—from Ontario, Manitoba, the United States, and central Europe—two years before the railway reached the area. One of the early Ukrainian settlements in the province was in the surrounding rural municipality where the population is now 90 per cent Ukrainian in origin. (*Encyclopedia Canadiana*, IV, 50.)

[40]Dmytro Romanchych, "Ukrainski kolonii," 514–516.

south of Ethelbert and remained there to erect shelters for their families. The rest of the group went further until they reached Drifting River near Venlaw. Iwan Negrych—a cousin of the teacher Iwan Negrych—his brother Wasyl (the two had fifteen small children between them), Jacob Genik and his two sons, Nicholas Podlasecky, the large family of the Hryhorczuks, and others entered homesteads here. About thirteen families from the Carpathian Mountains decided to look for a place further south, where there were mountains to remind them of their homeland. "We went straight in the southwesterly direction from Dauphin, because we were attracted by the hills which reminded us of our native Carpathian Mountains. Although Paul Wood did caution us not to settle there because that part of the district was a timber reserve, not open for homesteading, we nevertheless insisted on going to investigate. We reached the foothills and found the soil to be first class black earth, and there was little timber left, for it was burnt out as far as Vermillion River, some time ago." The prospective settlers concluded that where there was no timber left, the land could not be truly considered to be a timber reserve, and, that if they applied to the authorities the sections would most likely be released for homestead entries. They therefore decided to squat, and the agent who accompanied them and marked the quarter-sections promised to make the necessary recommendations. About forty families settled in the region. In a personal interview, Romanchych gave these further particulars about the settlers:

> The majority of the families who settled in that township on the timber reserve, were *Hutsuly* (Highlanders) originating in the three Bereziw villages (Lower, Middle, and Upper Bereziw) in the district of Pechenizhyn (later Kolomya) in Austrian Galicia. They were descendants of the ancient free Ukrainian gentry, who retained their privileges of the nobility. In mode of living and in wealth they did not differ from the surrounding peasantry. There were also a few families from other highland villages, from Bania Bereziwska, Liucza (the Lysyshyn family), and also a few families from the lowlands, from the village of Hleszczawa, in the district of Terebowla (or Trembowla), in particular. We chose to settle in that part of the district because the mountains, woods, streams, and meadows very much resembled our native Carpathian scenery.[41]

Two months after the establishment of the colony, on August 17, 1897, Paul Wood, the Land Guide, reported to the Agent of Dominion Lands in Dauphin in reply to a request for particulars about this settlement:

> In reply of recent date re Tp. 23 Rge 20, I beg to state that I found the land nearly all burnt off and void of timber with the exception of the S.E.

[41]Personal interview with Dmytro Romanchych held in Grimsby, Ontario, October 8, 1961.

and S.W. portion. The Northern boundary is considerably broken by hay meadows, there are also a few green bluffs in this portion left by the fire. The Southern portion of the Township towards the W. and E. contains green timber, for the greater part thin and scraggy.

Following is a list of the names of the squatters thereon with their locations:

Sec.		
15	Stephan Urbanovitch	N.E.¼
16	Dimetro Genik (Dmytro Genik)	N.W.¼
16	Ivan Genik	N.E.¼
17	Ivan Slezowk (Ivan Slozuk)	S.E.¼
17	Michael Ilenitski (Michael Ilnitski)	N.E.¼
21	Ivan Leseshen (Ivan Lysyshyn)	S.E.¼
21	Anton Genik	N.E.¼
22	Vaseil Semtchitz (Vasyl Symchych)	S.E.¼
22	Nichola Genik	N.E. S.W.
22	Dimetro Malkovitch (Dmytro Malkovich)	N.W.¼
22	Feodor Teremba von Klopovich (Sklepowich)	N.E.¼
23	Josef Romantchitz (Joseph Romanchych)	N.W.¼
23	Petro Cemtchitz (Petro Symchych)	S.W.¼
26	Dimetro Romantchouk (Dmytro Romanchych)	S.W.¼
26	Petro Mellashowski (Petro Matlashewsky)	N.W.¼
27	Anton Milianski (Anton Milowski)	S.E.¼
27	Simon Fitchitz (Semen Ficych)	S.W.¼
28	Nichola Fitchitz (Nykola Ficych)	S.E.¼
28	Michel Fitchitz (Michael Ficych)	S.W.¼
28	Vaseil Podoun (Vasyl Pidodworny)	N.W.¼
28	Ivan Boschak (Ivan Bosiak)	N.W.¼
27	Petro Podedvoien (Petro Pididworny)	N.E.¼
27	Matoi Koumka (Matwij Kumka)	N.W.¼
29	Fedko Boschak (Fedko Bosiak)	N.E.¼
30	Koubaian Thesen (Kuba Yanchyshyna, widow)	S.E.¼
30	Stephan Pelouski (Stefan Palanski)	
30	Michael Michailetski	
30	Vincente Jankievitch	
30	Danilo Rabiuk (Danylo Hrabliuk) N.E.¼—Sec. 19. Tp. 23, Rg. 20. W. (1902)	
30	Michel Dmetrouk	

The above six men were locating on [Section] 30 at the time of my visit and expressed their willingness to take eighty acres each.

Sec.		
31	Michel Kut	N.E.¼
31	Antoin Dribnetski	N.W.¼
31	Hilias Skakoun	S.E.¼
31	Josef Dribnitski	S.W.¼
32	Paulo Tratch	S.E.¼
32	Ignatz Skakoun	S.W.¼
32	Michel Boiko	N.W.¼
33	Petro Boiko	N.E.¼

Some settler of British extraction has [made] improvements on the N.E.¼, house, stable and hay in the stack. He was absent at the time of my visit, I was told he located here some five years ago.

Sec.		
33	Feodor Squareck (Fedir Shkwarok)	N.W.¼
33	Ivan Boran (Ivan Baran)	S.W.¼
33	Katrina Urbaniska (Kateryna Urbanska)	S.E.¼

This latter is a widow, her husband having died during their stay in the immigrant shed in Dauphin.

Sec.		
34	Michael Koshowski	S.E.¼
34	Michel Leichkov (Michael Leskiw)	S.W.¼
34	Samko Magalas	N.E.¼
34	Stephan Kochowski	N.W.¼
35	Tomko Tabaka	S.W.¼
35	Michel Tchornig (Tchornyj)	N.W.¼

I beg to request that the whole of this Township be thrown open for settlement. Every quarter at present occupied could accommodate one more settler, the land for the greater part being first class. New arrivals could thus be located quickly and easily.[42]

F. R. Herchmer, the Agent of Dominion Lands in Dauphin, sent Wood's report to the Commissioner of Immigration in Winnipeg, as well as to E. F. Stephenson, Inspector of Crown Timber Agencies in Winnipeg, for further action on the recommendations made by Wood, but nothing transpired for a whole year. During that time, the Ukrainian colonies in the Dauphin region were growing with such rapidity that the Deputy Minister decided to transfer Forest Ranger Thomas Young from Winnipeg to Dauphin to deal with problems of settlement of the arriving immigrants. Mr. Smart informed Stephenson: "In view of the growing demand for land in the Dauphin District, it has been decided to have Mr. Thomas Young, Forest Ranger, of your agency, transferred to Dauphin to do homestead inspection work in that district during the coming summer months."[43] A few weeks later, on June 18, 1898, Young produced his first report "on the Galician squatters" and forwarded it to the Inspector of Crown Timber Agencies in Winnipeg:

I have the honor to report as follows on the Galician squatters in Township 23 Range 20 W. referred to in your letter No. 96636.

I have made a careful inspection of every quarter section occupied as well as examining all that portion of the township that has been subdivided.

I found that no other settlers but Galicians have squatted in this township. Of the Galicians there are forty-five families located on about as many quarter sections and they have improved their holdings in every case, to a creditable extent by clearing the land, building houses & stables planting gardens also some grain and hemp.

[42] 18. Imm./440271, August 17, 1897: Paul Wood, Dominion Land Guide, Dauphin, to the Agent of Dominion Lands, Dauphin.

[43] 18. Imm., May 30, 1898: James A. Smart, Ottawa, to E. F. Stephenson, Inspector of Crown Timber Agencies, Winnipeg.

Sections 15, 16, 17, 21, 22, 23, 26, 27, 28, 32, 33, 34, and 35 were burned over few years ago and are at present a brulé with a thick undergrowth of young poplar, while sections 18, 19, 20, 29, 30 and 31 are covered with green poplar bush. A number of green bluffs are to be found in the burned district.

I think it was unfortunate that these parties were allowed to locate in this reserve as it will result in the entire destruction of the green-timber on their holdings but as they have been permitted to remain in possession for over one year (in most cases) and have exhausted their means in improving the land and supporting their families, I cannot do other than recommend that they be given their holdings.

I have found them very industrious and although poor, they are well satisfied with their prospects if this difficulty is settled.

If it is found necessary to remove these people to another location the question of compensation for their year's work and the matter of supporting them will in my opinion have to be considered.

Complications appear in two cases viz. in S.E. and N.W. of 22. Following your instructions I proceeded to take sworn testimony as to the facts but found the parties interested willing to swear to anything so I have considered it best not to complicate matters further, by taking from them false affidavits, but to recommend a division of the land held. This recommendation is based on information received by me from every source available.

I therefore recommend that the legal subdivisions 13 & 14 of section 22 be given to Dmytro Melkovich [Dmytro Malkovich] and 11 and 12 to Anton Genik. Also that subdivision 8 of section 22 be added to the fractional part of S.W. 23 and given to Wasyl Symchez [Symchych], leaving subdivision 12 & 7 to Stefan Yrbanovick [Stefan Urbanovitch].

I append to this a list of names with lands squatted on, giving all information obtainable also a map of the district.[44]

As may be gathered from Young's intimation, the colony, although only a year old, already had some boundary and ownership disputes, although none of the parties were legal owners of the land. Young's list of names is the first description of the pioneer settlers of the Vermillion River colony. Most of the names were misspelled and the correct spellings are given in parentheses:

LIST OF SETTLERS WITH PARTICULARS

TOWNSHIP 23—RANGE 20

N.E.¼ Sec. 16	Iwan Genik—house 16 × 18, has 2 cattle, stable 14 × 16, well 7 ft. cultivates 1 acre, settled June 1897.
N.W.¼ Sec. 16	Dmytro Genik—house 16 × 18, family of 4, well 7 feet, cultivates 1 acre, settled June 1897.
S.W.¼ Sec. 18	Michael Livecki (Michael Ilnicki)—house 18 × 20, family of 7, has 2 cattle, cultivates 1 acre, settled in June 1897.

[44]18. Imm./480870, June 18, 1898: Thomas Young, Forest Ranger, Dauphin, to E. F. Stephenson, Winnipeg.

S.E.¼ Sec. 18 Iwan Slozuk (Iwan Slezuk)—house 16 × 20, family of 9, stable 16 × 16, well 9 feet, has 2 cattle, cultivates 1 acre, settled in July 1897.

N.W.¼ Sec. 19 Michale Tinkavick (Michael Jankiewicz)—house 16 × 24, has 1 cow, stable 12 × 18, cultivates 1½ acres, family of 7, settled in October 1897.

N.E.¼ Sec. 19 Danylo Zrobucz (Danylo Hrabliuk)—house 16 × 24, 1 cow, stable 14 × 18, cultivates 1 acre, well 6 ft, family of 4, settled in October 1897.

S.E.¼ Sec. 20 Frank Noliak[45]—house 16 × 20, stable 12 × 14, well 9 ft. settled in October 1897.

N.E.¼ & N.W.¼ Sec. 20 sons of Frank Noliak of S.E. 20. claim these.

S.E.¼ Sec. 21 Iwan Lasyszyn (Iwan Lysyszin)—house 14 × 26, has 3 cattle, stable 14 × 16, well 7 ft. cultivates 1 acre, family of 5, settled in June 1897.

N.E.¼ Sec. 22 Fedor Sklepovich—house 14 × 18, has 2 cattle, stable 14 × 18, cultivates 1½ acre, well 8 ft., family of 7, settled in June, 1897.

S.W.¼ Sec. 22 Mykola Genik—house 16 × 18, has 2 cattle, stable 12 × 15, cultivates 2 acres, well 5 ft., family of 4, settled in June, 1897.

S.E.¼ Sec. 22 Steban Yrbanovich (Stepan Urbanowicz)—house 12 × 16 of poles and sod, cultivates 5 acres, has a family of 7, settled in June, 1897.

Walsal Samchych (Wasyl Symchych)—claims this quarter.

N.E.¼ Sec. 22 Dmytro Molkovich (Dmytro Malkovych)[46]—house 10 × 16, stable 10 × 17, well 8 ft., family of 3, cultivates 4 acres, has 2 cattle, settled on land June 4, 1897.

N.W.¼ Sec. 22 Anton Genik—house 14 × 16, has a family of 7, cultivates 3 acres, settled early in June, 1897.

SW.¼ Sec. 23 Wasyl Samchycz (Wasyl Symchych)[47]—house 16 × 20, cultivates 2 acres, has 3 cattle, well 8 ft., family of 5, settled in June 1897.

N.W.¼ Sec. 23 Juz Romanczycz—house 16 × 20, cultivates 2 acres, stable 16 × 16, has 2 cows and 1 horse, well 9 ft., family of 5, settled in June 1897.

S.W.¼ Sec. 26 Dmytro Romanczych—Lives with his father on N.W.¼ 23, cultivates ½ acre.

---

[45]Frank Nolak is not mentioned on later lists. The Canadian Registration Branch contains the following information about Wasyl Nolak, probably one of his sons: *Name*: Nolak, Wasyl; *Residence*: Pleasant Home, Man.; *Occupation*: Farmer; *Former residence*: Serafynci, Austria; *Nationality*: Austrian; *Date naturalization granted*: 23.12.1903; *Where granted*: Winnipeg; *Name of court*: King's Bench; *Number of return*: 135.

[46]The daughter of D. Malkovych married C. S. Prodan, the first graduate of Ukrainian descent of an agricultural college.

[47]Reverend S. P. Symchych of Vancouver, a former Ukrainian Greek Orthodox Chaplain with the services overseas, is the son of Wasyl Symchych.

N.W.¼ Sec. 26 Petoro Matlashoski (Petro Mellashowski)/Krasucki Matlaszewski—house 16 × 20, has 2 cattle, stable 12 × 12, cultivates 3 acres, well 9 ft., family of 7, settled in 1897.

N.E.¼ Sec. 27 Matwij Kumka—house 16 × 20, stable 16 × 20, cultivates 5 acres, well 9 ft., settled in June 1897, family of 5.

S.E.¼ Sec. 27 Tomey Prygrocski—house 16 × 20, has 1 cow, stable 16 × 18, cultivates 2 acres, family of 4, settled in June 1897.

S.W.¼ Sec. 27 Samani Fisacsh (Semen Ficych)—house 16 × 18, stable 12 × 14, cultivates 4 acres, settled in June 1897.

N.W.¼ Sec. 27 Peter Pidworsne (Petro Pidodworny)—house 20 × 24, stable 16 × 20, cultivates 7 acres, well 6 ft., has 1 horse, 2 cows, family of 6.

N.E.¼ Sec. 28 Nisail Pidowornie (Wasyl Pidodworny)—house 16 × 18, cultivates 3 acres, stable 16 × 20, has 3 cattle, well 6 ft., family of 9, settled in June 1897.

S.E.¼ and
S.W.¼ Sec. 28 sons of Samani Fisacsh (Semen Ficych)[48]—of S.W.¼ Sec. 27. Some brush cut and log heaps made. No other improvement.

N.W.¼ Sec. 28 John Bushak (Ivan Bosiak)—house 16 × 18, has 2 horses, 2 cows, stable 12 × 12, settled in June 1897, cultivates 2 acres, family of 8.

S.E.¼ Sec. 30 Yiakub Ainchyshyn (Jacob Janchyshyn)—house 16 × 24, has 2 cattle, stable 12 × 12, cultivates 1 acre, has family of 8, settled in October 1897.

N.W.¼ Sec. 30 Michael Dimitriuk (Dmytruk)—house 12 × 18, well, cultivates 1 acre, family of 4, settled in October 1897.

S.W.¼ Sec. 30 Michael Michalieske (Michael Michailetsky)—house 16 × 18, stable 12 × 16, has 2 cattle, cultivates 1 acre, family of 7, settled in October 1897.

N.E.¼ Sec. 31 Michael Myke (Michael Kut)—house 16 × 18, stable 14 × 16, has 1 cow, well 7 ft., cultivates 1 acre, family of 7, settled in August 1897.

S.E.¼ Sec. 31 Elko Skakoon (Ilko Skakun)—house 14 × 18, cultivates 1 acre, Father of the S.W. 32.

S.W.¼ Sec. 32 Ignace Skakoon—house 16 × 20, has one cow, stable 12 × 14, cultivates 2 acres, well 9 ft., family of 5, settled in August, 1897.

N.W.¼ Sec. 32 Peter Boikal (Michael Boiko)—house 15 × 18, cultivates 1 acre, stable 12 × 14, well 5 ft., family of 2, settled in August 1897.

S.E.¼ Sec. 32 Pulla Trach (Paulo Tratch)—house 16 × 18, cultivates 2 acres, stable 12 × 16, has 1 ox, 1 cow, family of 5, settled in August 1897.

S.E.¼ Sec. 33 Kataryna Urbanska—house 16 × 16 unfinished, well, cultivates 5 acres, family of 6, settled in November 1897.

S.W.¼ Sec. 33 John Basan (Iwan Baran)—house 16 × 18, cultivates 2 acres, stable 16 × 16, has 1 cow, well, family of 4, settled in June 1897.

---

[48]Semen Ficych's sons were Nykola, Michael, and George.

N.W.¼ Sec. 33 Lazor Szkwarok (son Daniel)—house 14 × 18, cultivates 2 acres, stable 16 × 18, has 3 cattle, well 8 ft., family of 5, settled in August, 1897.

S.E.¼ Sect. 34 Michael Coshoski (Michael Koshowsky)[49]—house 16 × 24, cultivates 5 acres, stable 12 × 12, well 6 ft., family of 5, settled in June 1897.

N.E.¼ Sec. 34 Sam Mogulesk (Semen Magalas)—house 16 × 20, cultivates 4 acres, well 4 ft., family of 4, settled June 1897.

S.W.¼ Sec. 34. Michael Laskive (Michael Leskiw, sons: Semen and Ivan)—house 16 × 20, cultivates 6 acres, stable 12 × 16, has 2 cattle, well 9 ft., family of 6, settled in June 1897.

S.W.¼ Sec. 35 Tom Tabaka—house 16 × 20, cultivates 4 acres, stable 16 × 18, has 2 cows, well 18 ft., family of 7, settled in June 1897.

N.W.¼ Sec. 35 Michael Chorne (Michael Chornyj)—house 16 × 16, cultivates 4 acres, stable 14 × 20, has 2 cows, well 4 ft., family of 4, settled in June 1897.[50]

Young's report gives a general picture of the pioneer colony on the Vermillion River (Vermillion is spelled on later maps with one "l"), showing the progress the settlers made in one year. Subsequent reports submitted by Paul Wood in 1900, and the list submitted by the settlers themselves in 1901, give further indications of the progress made by the homesteaders from year to year. The list submitted by the settlers contains additional information, such as the ages of the heads of families and the amount of money brought with them to Canada. Whereas the statement about ages is probably correct, that concerning money may be slightly at variance with actual fact. There was a tendency, as the years passed and wealth was acquired, either to overstate the amount of money brought in—so as to appear more respectable—or to state "arrived without funds," so as to gain the prestige of having done exceptionally well despite the odds. On the average, however, the statements are correct.

VI

Mr. Stephenson forwarded Young's report to Ottawa so that the Federal Government would be able to decide on the matter: "Referring to your letter . . . concerning the squatters (principally Galicians) in Township 23, Range 20, West of the 1st Meridian, I now beg to enclose a report by Mr. Forest Ranger Young, after his inspection. Mr. Young appears to have gone into the matter fully and his report seems to

[49]Dr. Peter Kay of Edmonton, Alberta, is the son of Michael Koshowsky.

[50]The list is an enclosure in Thomas Young's report of June 18, 1898, quoted previously.

cover the whole ground and will doubtless enable the Department to deal with this case satisfactorily."[51]

To disentangle this very involved problem, Deputy Minister Smart decided to take matters into his own hands. He enquired with the Land Office about the legal position of the land involved and gained this reply: "Tp. 23—Rg. 20—W 1.—This Tp. is within tract in dispute between Lake Dauphin Branch of C.P.R. & Lake Man. Ry & Canal Co.—It is also within the Riding Mountain Timber Reserve."[52] Smart wrote a letter to T. A. Burrows, M.P.P.,[53] connected with the Lake Manitoba Railway & Canal Company, and pleaded for the settlers. He suggested that the company should accept other lands in exchange for the sections occupied in the Timber Reserve by Ukrainian squatters:

> It would appear that some time in the summer of last year a party of Galicians were located by a guide named Off, of whose authority nothing is known here, on lands in Township 23, Range 20, West of the 1st Meridian. This Township, as you probably are aware, is within the Riding Mountain Timber Reserve, and also within the tract in dispute between your company and the Lake Dauphin Branch of the Canadian Pacific Railway Company. Forest Ranger Young, who was instructed to make an inspection of this Township, reports under date 18th ultimo that there are some forty-five families of Galicians located on about as many quarter-sections and that they have improved their holdings in every case to a creditable extent, by clearing the land, building houses and stables, planting gardens, &c. They have of course located indiscriminately on both odd and even sections, and the question which now presents itself is as to what action should be taken in the premises. It was no doubt unfortunate that they were allowed to locate on the Reserve, but as they have gone on with their improvements undisturbed since over a year, and were no doubt misled by some unauthorized agent in locating upon these lands, I think it would be a serious hardship to them today to have them removed. I am of opinion that it is a case where your Company should accept other lands in exchange for those occupied by these people, but before taking any action I would be glad to hear from you as you no doubt understand the situation.[54]

Burrows replied after some delay, on September 3, 1898, and presented additional background information about this land:

> *Re: Twp 23 R. 20 West.*—On the 30th of July you wrote me the enclosed letter. I fully expected to have seen you and discussed the matter when in Ottawa.

[51] 18. Imm./480870, July 2, 1898: E. F. Stephenson, Winnipeg, to the Secretary, Department of the Interior, Ottawa.

[52] 18. Imm., July 9, 1898: Memorandum, W. M. Goodeve, to J. A. Coté, Ottawa.

[53] For a brief biography of T. A. Burrows, see the section, "Biographies."

[54] 18. Imm./488883, July 30, 1898: James A. Smart, Ottawa, to T. A. Burrows, Winnipeg.

The circumstances under which the Galicians settled on this Township are as follows: a large party of these people were camped at the town of Dauphin for quite a while awaiting the procuring of land on which to settle. Some of them had found that the land in this Township west of the Vermillion river was good land and that the fire had cleared all the bush off and left it in a favourable condition for starting farming operations. Michael Off is a German settler whose services had been temporarily obtained as Interpreter by the Emmigration Dept. here—and through him as well as through other Interpreter Mr. Steinhard I explained several times to the Galicians whom I addressed at meetings at their Camps, that notwithstanding the fact that this land was free from timber now, still they would not be allowed to go on it as it was a permanent Timber Reserve. They could not find other land to suit them at that time and were bound to go on this, so I recommended that the portion of this township lying west of the Vermillion river should be subdivided and that these men be given entries; this was done, and Mr. Off went up with the Galicians and tried to locate them on even sections. They were told not to go on the odd sections, but it appears they have not done as directed.

This Township is situated on the L.M.R. land grant, and also in the area of the C.P.R. land grant. I understand that the Minister of Justice has decided that the C.P.R. claim has priority. If such is the case you had better write L. A. Hamilton in regard to this matter. Speaking for our own Company, I would say that we would be willing to take other lands of equal value.[55]

Matters became still more complicated when the squatters, anxious to speed up a decision on the land situation, sent repeated appeals to the Government, which Cyril Genik translated and the Commissioner of Immigration forwarded to Ottawa. A year passed, but no decision was reached. The Commissioner of Immigration pressed for a favourable decision, as further delays might adversely affect the growing, thrifty community. He requested the Dominion Land Agent in Dauphin to prepare a detailed report on the squatters, which he intended to forward to Ottawa for action. F. R. Herchmer entrusted Wood with preparing the report and making a detailed list of settlers. The list that was prepared reveals that there were only slight changes in the distribution of settlers. Herchmer sent this report and list on to Commissioner McCreary:

In accordance with your letter of the 20th inst. I have secured a report from Paul Wood as to how the Galician Squatters in Tp. 23 R. 20 W. came to be located within the Timber Reserve, these facts as reported by him are so far as I know correct, and are, I understand, well known to the Department, I am as suggested by you, sending a copy of this to the Commissioner at Ottawa, with copy of Mr. Wood's report.

[55]18. Imm./488883, September 3, 1898: T. A. Burrows, Dauphin, to James A. Smart, Ottawa.

The list of names with Mr. Wood's prior report has already gone to Ottawa, and a copy to you. I am, etc.

(Signed) F. R. HERCHMER, Agent, Dominion Lands.[56]

Paul Wood's report, dated Sifton, Man. April 26, 1900:

I am in receipt of a communication from the Agent of Dom. Lands at Dauphin in which he advises me that you wish for a report as to the settlement of Galicians on the Riding Mountain in T. 23 R. 20 & 21—W.

These people as you are aware arrived in the Country during the Spring of 1897, after hunting land some considerable time in the Sifton & Fork River Districts, decided they would not locate there, stating that the land did not suit them. A number of them returned to Dauphin where by some means or other they were informed of land in the Riding Mountain, and proceeded to Squat, in the above named Townships 23–20 without regard to lines or sections.

A large number of these people stayed around the Town for a considerable time refusing to locate elsewhere but in the Riding Mountain, although repeatedly warned they could not obtain any rights there, by Mr. Herchmer, Mr. Mouat, myself and others. They however continued settling on these lands squatting anywhere, finally representation having been made to the department by some party or parties in Dauphin, Mr. A. J. McPherson of Dauphin was sent I understand at the instance of Mr. T. A. Burrows M.P.P. to run lines for these people in these townships. Mr. McPherson's son having been taken dangerously ill, Mr. McPherson returned to Dauphin and Mr. M. Off took his place, I understand that the services of both these gentlemen were paid by the Department. Subsequently as you are aware Mr. Martin was sent to subdivide these lands exactly. In 1899 several more families settled on these lands.

I am, etc. (Signed) PAUL WOOD.[57]

Enclosed is the copy of the list of settlers, dated April 23, 1900:

In answer to yours of recent date instructing me to report as to Galicians settled within the Permanent Timber Reserve south of Dauphin, I beg to submit a list of these settlers and their locations as follows:

(*N.B.*—residents are marked "*S.*" and new residents "*N.R.*") In some instances new residents have improved the lands and are out working for wages, in some few instances claim has been laid to a certain quarter section by a new resident but he has made no improvements.

Tp. 23—Rge.20 W.

N.E.¼ Sec. 18	Michel Ilnitski *S.*
S.E.¼	Iwan Sléjouk *S.*
S.W.¼	Anton Genik *S.*
N.W.¼	Filko Genik *S.*
N.E.¼ Sec. 16	Iwan Genik *S.*
S.W.¼	Nicola Koustrak *S.* (Nat. Reg.—Nichola Kusztra)
N.W.¼	Michael Duda

[56]19. Imm./564629, April 30, 1900: F. R. Herchmer, Agent, Dominion Lands, Dauphin, to W. F. McCreary, Winnipeg.

[57]19. Imm./564629, April 26, 1900: Paul Wood, Dominion Land Guide. Sifton, Manitoba, to W. F. McCreary, Winnipeg.

N.E.¼ Sec. 14 Michael Krasoutski *N.R.*
N.W.¼ Petro Gudz *N.R.*

N.W.¼ Sec. 23 Josef Romantchitz (Nat. Reg.—Josef Romanczycz) *S.*
N.W.¼ Wasyl Semtchitz *S* (Wasyl Symchych)

N.E.¼ Sec. 28 Wasyl Pidedworni *S.*
S.E.¼ Semen Fitchitch *S.* (Semen Ficych)
S.W.¼ Nicola Fitchitch *N.R.*
N.W.¼ Iwan Boschak *S.* (Iwan Bosiak)

N.E.¼ Sec 27 Matvi Koumka *S.* (Matwij Kumka)
S.E.¼ Antosh Milianski *S.*
S.W.¼ Wasyl Schelski *S.* (Wasyl Smylski)
N.W.¼ Petro Podedworni *S.* (Petro Pidodworny)

S.W.¼ Sec. 26 Petro Romantchitz *S.* (Dmytro Romanczycz)
N.W.¼ Petro Krasoutski *S.* (Petro Krasutski)

S.W.¼ Sec. 35 Tomka Tabaka (Tomko Tabaka, father of Adamko T., 15 ys.) *S.*
N.W.¼ Michael Tchorné *S.* (Michael Czorny)

N.E.¼ Sec. 34 Sauko Megalas (Semen Magalas) *S.*
S.E.¼ Michael Kochowski *S.* (Koshowski)
S.W.¼ Michael Mouliar *S.*
N.W.¼ Improvements made by Tomka Tabaka who intends shortly abandoning his present location for this.

N.E.¼ Sec. 33 Blasko Tabaka *S.*
S.E.¼ Katerina Urbanska *S.* (widow, husband died in Dauphin)
S.W.¼ Iwan Baran *S.*
N.W.¼ Fedj Squareck *S.* (Fedir Szkwarok)

N.E.¼ Sec. 22 Feodor Sklepovitch *S.*
S.E.¼ Stefan Urbanovitch *S.*
S.W.¼ Nicola Genik *S.*
N.W.¼ Dmétro Malkovitch *S.*

N.E.¼ Sec. 21 Dmetre Podedworni (Dmytro Podedworny) *N.R.*
S.E.¼ Iwan Leseschen *S.* (Iwan Lysyszyn)
S.W.¼ Iwan Miller *N.R.* (also claimed by Iwan Sklepowitch)

N.W.¼ Sec. 21 Iwan Schmelski *N.R.* (Iwan Smylski)
N.W.¼ Sec. 19 Anton Jankiewitch *N.R.*
S.E.¼ Adolph Jankiewitch *S.*
N.E.¼ Danelo Hrabliuk *S.*
S.W.¼ Jatzko Jankiewitch *S.*

N.E.¼ Sec. 32 Petro Boitchuk *S.*
S.E.¼ Paulo Tratch Welsevitski *S.*
N.W.¼ Michael Boitchuk *S.* (Boyko)
S.W.¼ Hilko Skakoun (Ilko Skakun) *N.R.*

N.E.¼ Sec. 20 Nicola Pochowski *N.R.* (Nicola Puchalski)
S.E.¼ Anton Pochowski *N.R.*
S.W.¼ Frantz Pochowski *S.*
N.W.¼ Jatzko Pochowski *N.R.*

N.E.¼ Sec. 30 Michael Dmétruk *S.* (Metruk)
S.E.¼ widow Yancheshena *S.*
S.W.¼ Michael Michaeletski *S.*
N.W.¼ Iwan Presuruka *S.*

N.E.¼ Sec. 31	Jatzko Kochowski *S.*
S.E.¼	Ignatz Skakoun *S.* (Ignace Skakun)
S.W.¼	Wasyl Pochowski *S.* (Koshowski)
N.W.¼	Nicola Osé *S.* (Nycola Huzy)
N.E.¼ Sec. 36	Jan Nikourash *S.*
S.E.¼	Michael Malowski *S.*
S.W.¼	Jatzko Tabaka *S.*
N.W.¼	Jantoch Kochowski *S.* (Koshowski)
Tp. 23—Rge. 21 W.	
N.E.¼ Sec. 24	Jatzko Loubinietski *S.*
S.E.¼	Nicola Letartski *S.*
S.W.¼	Marian Loubinietski *S.*
N.W.¼	Uilko Loubinietski *N.R.*
N.E.¼ Sec. 14	Dmetro Loubinietski *S.*
S.E.¼	Nicola Gabilievitch *S.*
S.W.¼	Michael Horetchka *S.*
N.W.¼	Maxim Squareck *S.*
Sec. 22	Petro Bornuk *S.*
	Iwan Bornuk *S.*
	Paulo Duch *S.*
	Lucas Duch *S.*

(above section not visited)[58]

In October of 1900, the Dominion Lands Office in Ottawa, after receiving all of this pertinent information, finally released the even-numbered sections, which were Dominion-owned, for entry by the squatters who occupied them. This was a great relief for many families—but the odd-numbered sections were still in question, for they were not only within the timber reserve but within the railway grant as well. The release of these sections was a much more complicated affair. Correspondence between the various branches of the Department of the Interior, as well as between the Department and the Land Offices of the railway companies, went on constantly, but no solution was as yet found.

With the economic improvement of the settlers, life in the colony became truly organized. The settlers built a school, engaged a teacher, started to erect a church, and planned to organize a district, as soon as the rest of the settlers ceased to be squatters. On February 3, 1901, a joint petition to the Department of the Interior in Ottawa was composed and dispatched to Ottawa by the settlers:

We have been located in the month of May 1897 by the Dominion Immigration Agent from Dauphin at Tp 23–Rg 20—It was not a track found of the lines where we came up so that Local Agent located us on Government and C.P.R. lands. Then in November 1897 these lands have got surveid and in October 1900 the settlers living on Homestates land have got the permission from Government to make entrys for this land. But

[58] 19. Imm./563232, April 23, 1900: Paul Wood, Dominion Land Guide, Minnedosa, Manitoba, to the Secretary, Department of the Interior, Ottawa.

we are living on the C.P.R. Co. lands since that same time, and we have built a good house and stables and give You a list how many money we spent here and how menny we have cleared and broken land (each of us) and we have a school building up for purpose of our children and we paid whol our taxes to the Dauphin Municipality.

Now we are writing to ask you for permission to make entry's for thise lands. You will grant such permission as we are very anxious to gain permission of thise lands, when we have spent so much time and money on it—as we are Your Obedient servants,

1. Joseph Romanczycz N.W.¼ 23—Tp. 23 Rge 20 W. Money brought from Galicia $430.00; Acres broken 15; 1 house, 3 stables.
2. Wasyl Symczych S.W.¼ 23—Tp. 23 Rge 20 W. Money brought from Galicia $400.00; Acres broken 7; 1 house, 3 stables.
3. Anton Milewski S.E.¼ 27—Tp. 23 Rge 20 W. Money brought from Galicia $160.00; Acres broken 10; 2 houses, 3 stables.
4. Matwij Kumka N.E.¼ 27—Tp. 23 Rge 20 W. Money brought from Galicia $102.00; Acres broken 12; 1 house, 3 stables.
5. Petro Pododwornyj N.W.¼ 27—Tp. 23 Rge 20. Money brought from Galicia $400.00; Acres broken 30; 2 houses, 2 stables.
6. Michael Czornyj N.W.¼ 35—Tp. 23 Rge 20 W. Money brought from Galicia $140.00; Acres broken 8; 2 houses, 3 stables.
7. Katharina Urbanska S.E.¼ 33—Tp. 23 Rge 20 W. Money brought from Galicia $200.00; Acres broken 8; 1 house, 1 stable.
8. Iwan Baran S.W.¼ 33—Tp. 23 Rge 20 W. Money brought from Galicia $200.00; Acres broken 7; 1 house, 2 stables.
9. Lazarous Szkwarok N.W.¼ 33—Tp. 23 Rge 20 W. Money brought from Galicia $300.00; Acres broken 8; 1 house, 2 stables.
10. Ignacy Skakun S.E.¼ 31—Tp. 23 Rge 20 W. Money brought from Galicia $115.00; Acres broken 6; 1 house, 2 stables.
11. Iwan Lesyszyn S.E.¼ 21—Tp. 23 Rge 20 W. Money brought from Galicia $220.00; Acres broken 5, 1 house, 1 stable.
12. Dmytro Romanczycz S.W.¼ 26—Tp. 23 Rge 20 W. Money brought from Galicia $80.00; Acres broken 8; 1 house, 1 stable.
13. Petro Krasucki N.W.¼ 26—Tp. 23 Rge 20 W. Money brought from Galicia $160.00; Acres broken 8, 1 house, 1 stable.
14. Daniel Hrabiuk N.E.¼ 19—Tp. 23 Rge 20 W. Money brought from Galicia $105.00; Acres broken 5; 1 house, 1 stable.
15. Adolph Jankewicz S.E.¼ 19—Tp. 23 Rge 20 W. Money brought from Galicia $80.00; Acres broken 3; 1 house, 1 stable.
16. Jack Jankewicz N.W.¼ 19—Tp. 23 Rge 20 W. Money brought from Galicia $110.00; Acres broken—; house—, stable—.
17. Anton Jankewicz S.W.¼ 19—Tp. 23 Rge 20 W. Money brought from Galicia $50.00; Acres broken—; house—, stable—.[59]

A month later, March 10, 1901, the settlers prepared a second petition and addressed it to Thomas Young, the Homestead Inspector in

[59] 19. Imm./614610, February 3, 1901: Seventeen petitioners from Dauphin to the Secretary, Department of the Interior, Ottawa.

Dauphin, who forwarded it to the Commissioner of Immigration in Winnipeg. This petition contained additional particulars about many of the settlers who signed the first petition:

March 10, 1901.

Thomas Young, Esq.
Homestead Inspector
Dauphin, Man.

Dear Sir,

These men want speak to you about themselves and the rest of men (Galician families) who are living in Tp. 23, Rg. 20 on the C.P.R. Co. lands. Here is 12 families who came to Dauphin in the month of May 1897. Mr. J. A. McPherson was the first man who brought them down to this Township and started to run the first line, saying, that here is no Company's lands at all. He says, he had the authority from Mr. W. F. McCreary, Commr. of Immgrn., to do that. After Mr. J. A. McPherson left us here, it was another man (German, his name is unknown to us) who had been running the lines and locating us. We dont know who he had the authority from to do that.

Mr. Moat local Agent came down for 5 or 6 times to see us in summer time 1897, and every time he told us not to get off of C.P.R. Co. lands. Mr. Paul Wood, local agent, told us for the first three years not to get off, we will get these lands for homesteads. In November 1897 the surveyor found us living at the places and did not tell us a word.

In 1899 you have been down to see us, when we asked you could we live on the C.P.R. Co. lands, without having any trouble afterwards. You told us to live on and work as many as we can, we will get them for homesteads.

We have sent a petition to Government asking for permission to make entries for these lands, but we never got reply. In February 4, 1901, we sent another petition for this same thing, but we did not get reply yet, and we dont know what could be done with us.

The Englishmen are coming to us saying—we must get off here, because *they are going on to buy the C.P.R. lands which we are living on.*

We are coming to ask you, what could we do not when we spent so much time and money on these lands—

Following is a list of us—

Township 3
Range 20 W.

Wasyl Symchych S.W. 23—house 3 stables; 4 acres broken; wife and 4 children; 7 head of cattle; Religion: Greek Catholic; Money from Galicia—$240; Age—50.

Joseph Romanczycz N.W.¼ Sec. 23—house 3 stables; 10 acres broken; 3 children; 8 head of cattle; Religion: Greek Catholic; Money from Galicia—$500; Age—60.

Anton Maloski S.E.¼ Sec. 27—house and 4 stables; 10 acres broken; wife and 3 children; 5 head of cattle; Religion—Roman Catholic; Money from Galicia—$160; Age—34.

Matwij Kumka N.W.¼ Sec. 27—house & 3 stables; acres broken 12; wife and 4 children; Religion: Greek Catholic; 5 head of cattle; Money from Galicia—$100; Age—50.

Petro Podedworny N.W. ¼ Sec. 27—house & 2 stables; 20 acres broken; wife & 5 children; 4 head of cattle; Religion: Greek Catholic; Money from Galicia—$300; Age—48.

Michael Czorny N.W.¼ Sec. 35—house & 4 stables; 10 acres broken; wife & 4 children; 5 head of cattle; Religion: Greek Catholic; Money from Galicia—$150; Age—48.

Catherina Urbanska S.E.¼ Sec. 33—house & stable; 6 acres broken; widow with 4 children; 2 head of cattle; Religion: Greek Catholic; Money from Galicia—$160; Age—50.

John Baran N.W. ¼ Sec. 33—house & 3 stables; 10 acres broken; wife & 3 children; 9 head of cattle; Religion: Greek Catholic; Money from Galicia—$250; Age—55.

Lazar Szkwarok—S.W.¼ Sec. 33—house & 2 stables; 4 acres broken; wife & 2 children; 3 head of cattle; Religion: Greek Catholic; Money from Galicia—$300; Age—30.

Blasko Tabaka N.E.¼ Sec. 33—

(Ignace) Skakun S.E.¼ 31—house & 2 stables; 4 acres broken; wife & 3 children; 8 head of cattle; Religion: Greek Catholic; Money from Galicia—$150; Age—60.

John Lesyszyn S.E.¼ Sec. 21—house & 3 stables; 8 acres broken; 3 head of cattle; wife & 3 children; Religion: Greek Catholic; Money from Galicia—$260; Age—44.

The 13th man in this colony is Petro Krasucki (Matlaszewski) who is living since the same time on N.W. 26—23—20 and he is going to ask Government to have his ¼ section to change for any one of vacant ¼ of section of C.P.R. land in this Township. Petro Krasucki (Matlaszewski) *X* his mark—house & 2 stables, 8 acres broken, 4 head of cattle; Religion—Greek Catholic; Money from Galicia—$160.

Dmytro Romanczycz S.W. 26—23—20.[60]

Thomas Young, the Homestead Inspector from Dauphin, received the petition of the squatters and forwarded it to the Commissioner of Immigration in Winnipeg with his own request to "do what you can" to obtain homestead entries for the settlers. In his accompanying letter, he wrote:

I enclose a copy of a letter I have received from certain Galicians who were placed by Government Agents in Tp 23 Rg 20 in May 1897. This township was then within the Riding Mt. permanent timber reserve and unsurveyed.

These people were allowed to go in to this land and squatted on odd and even unnumbered sections and Mr. Paul Wood and myself were requested to report on the matter in 1898 with the view of having them removed off the reserve.

I think it was on strength of these reports that the Government decided to have this portion of the township subdivided and thrown out of the reserve and opened for entry.

[60]19. Imm./621566, March 10, 1901: Thirteen petitioners from Tp. 23, Rge. 20, W., to Thomas Young, Homestead Inspector, Dauphin, Man. Translation from the Ukrainian by Cyril Genik.

Those who had squatted found themselves on odd numbered sections and who now write have not been considered and are in danger of being left at the mercy of English purchasers.

Knowing that these people have not themselves to blame for their present position I submit these facts to you and would request that if you consider them bona fide squatters who had entered on this land in ignorance before survey, that you do what you can to obtain for them homestead entries for the holdings which have been granted to other similar squatters.[61]

To lend additional weight to the petition which they sent to Ottawa, the squatters wrote a "reminder" a month later:

The Secretary of the Department of the Interior—Ottawa.

February the 4th 1901 we sent out to You a petition, from Dauphin P.O. asking you for to get permission to make entrys for C.P.R. Lands in Tp. 23. Rg. 20 West of the First Meridian; and we wait impatient for Your worthy reply.

Kindly please, send it by return the mail and obliged Yours obedient servants,

SETTLERS OF THE GALICIAN COLONY OF RIDING MOUNTAINS,
Address: Matwij Kumka, P.O. Dauphin, Man.[62]

The feverish activity on the part of the settlers was prompted by the danger of the sale of C.P.R. Company's sections to "English people," possibly even land speculators attracted by the rapid development of the Dauphin region and a possible rise in the value of the land. The Department of the Interior was genuinely interested in legalizing the position of these squatters, since the matter was beginning to acquire unwanted publicity. The Commissioner of Dominion Lands in Ottawa sent a memorandum to Frank Clayton of his office, asking him to find out particulars about the sections in question:

Memorandum:—Mr. Clayton

Will you please let me know if the odd-sections in Township 23, Range 20, West, North of Vermillion River, have been transferred to the Canadian Pacific Railway Company. They were squatted on some two or three years ago by Galicians who have made extensive improvements, and it appears that there is no other way out of the difficulty but to grant them entries if at all possible.

The sections squatted are 21, 23, 27, 31, 33 and 35.

Kindly return file at your convenience.

(Signed) J. G. TURIFF,
Commissioner.[63]

[61]19. Imm./621566, March 12, 1901: Thomas Young, Dauphin, to the Commissioner of Immigration, Winnipeg.

[62]19. Imm./621864, March 14, 1901: Matwij Kumka, Dauphin P.O., to the Secretary, Department of the Interior, Ottawa.

[63]19. Imm./April 9, 1901: Memorandum from J. G. Turiff, Commissioner of Dominion Lands, Ottawa, to Frank Clayton, Office of Dominion Lands, Ottawa.

Mr. Clayton's reply was not very encouraging: "The lands mentioned in your Memorandum are reserved for the Lake Dauphin Branch of the C.P.R. Although not yet transferred or scheduled to the Company, they cannot be disposed of without the consent of the Company. It is possible, that if you made application to the Company pointing out the circumstances, they might be induced to accept other land in lieu of these sections."[64] The Secretary of the Department of the Interior did not lose time in following Clayton's and Commissioner Turiff's advice, and he wrote the following letter to the Lands Commissioner of the Canadian Pacific Railway Company in Winnipeg, explaining the situation and requesting the Company to accept other lands:

> I am to inform you that owing to some misunderstanding, which is regretted, certain Galician settlers have been located since 1898 upon odd numbered sections in Township 23, Range 20, West. They appear to have begun operations in earnest and are very anxious to obtain the lands in question so as to be near their friends who have lands in the locality. The Commissioner desires to know whether under the somewhat special circumstances your Company would be willing to release to the Crown the odd numbered sections in Township 23, Range 20, West lying North of the Vermillion River. The sections referred to are 21, 23, 27, 31, 33 & 35, and to accept in lieu thereof an equal area of Dominion Lands at the disposal of the Department.[65]

The Lands Commissioner of the C.P.R. company waited six months to answer the letter from the office of the Commissioner of Immigration. In the meantime, the Minister of the Interior, Clifford Sifton, himself became involved in this complicated problem. Sifton received a letter from Mr. John Nicholson of Dauphin, who pointed out the urgency of the situation:

> Dear Sir—
>
> I trust you will excuse the liberty I take in writing you on a matter in which I am not directly interested but *is* (as it seems to me) of public interest.
>
> I have recently been engaged as Census Enumerator in the Galician Settlement Tp. 23, Rge 20, and I found in the one Township over 270 in actual residence not counting the absentees, and I was greatly impressed by the signs of progress (notwithstanding enormous difficulties) which they have made, but my object more particularly is to draw your attention to the fact, that there are a number of them, who are Squatters on C.P.R. Lands; many of them having gone in there before the land was surveyed and they have recently been notified by the Co. that they must either buy or get

[64]19. Imm., April 10, 1901: Frank Clayton, Ottawa, to J. G. Turiff, Ottawa.

[65]19. Imm., April 15, 1901: P. G. Keyes, Secretary, the Commissioner of Immigration, Ottawa, to Fred Griffin, Lands Commissioner, Canadian Pacific Railway Company, Winnipeg.

off the land. They are not in a position to buy, and hence are very much depressed and discouraged, and to my mind it would amount to little less than a public scandal now to enforce their removal after the work they have done, and comfortable houses they have built.

A school has been built by private subscription chiefly I believe by the Presbyterians of Winnipeg and a Teacher is being paid by the same body for 4 years, and I found about 20 or 25 children already in attendance, and making most wonderful progress, although the school had only been open about 45 days when I was there.

I think the sooner something is done to relieve the minds of these Squatters the better it will be, for some of them are so discouraged that they have suspended their operations, and the buildings they are putting up are remaining unfinished.

If they were removed no English speaking people would think of going in there as all the homesteads are taken up entirely by Galicians.

Hoping you will pardon the liberty I have taken in writing you on this matter and that you may see your way clear to do something to relieve the situation.

I am, Dear Sir,

Yours very obedient,

(Signed) J. NICHOLSON.[66]

The Minister responded by sending the letter on to Commissioner Turiff with this note attached: "Attached is a letter from Mr. John Nicholson at Dauphin. The matter to which he refers is one which should receive the immediate attention of the Department. I think you had better attend to it personally."[67] Mr. Turiff sent a detailed reply to Mr. Nicholson, explaining that he could make no definite statement about when the lands in question might be made available:

I beg to acknowledge the receipt of your favour of the 6th instant (May, 1901), addressed to the Minister, in reference to the odd sections squatted on by Galician settlers in Township 23, Range 20. At the time these squatters went on this land it was part of the permanent timber reserve and they should not have gone there. Subsequently, we had them withdrawn from the reserve and made the even sections available for homestead entry, the odd sections not belonging to the Government, having been set aside for the C.P.R. Company, but on the strength of the reports we received from the officers of the Department sometime ago we have entered into correspondence with the Railway Company and are endeavouring to secure the release of those odd sections that are squatted on. I do not know whether we will succeed or not, but we will use our best efforts to make these lands available.

There is this to bear in mind—that when settlers go on unsurveyed lands and locate, they do it at their own risks, and if this land should be

66 19. Imm./632902, May 6, 1901: John Nicholson, Dauphin, to Clifford Sifton, Ottawa.

67 19. Imm./632902, May 6, 1901: Clifford Sifton, Ottawa, to J. G. Turiff, Ottawa.

made available for them it lays the Department open to the charge that we are granting these settlers privileges which are not granted to English-speaking settlers.

Until we get a reply from the Railway Company I am not in a position to say definitely that the lands can be made available.[68]

The school mentioned by John Nicholson in his letter to Clifford Sifton, was built by the Ukrainian settlers in the Vermillion River colony, and was established in 1900. Romanchych describes its beginnings in his memoirs:

During the first years of our immigrant life one problem in particular gave us great concern, namely, that our children might grow up illiterate. The province was unable to build schools fast enough and to supply a sufficient number of teachers to satisfy the fast-growing colonies formed by the various nationalities arriving from Europe who rapidly filled the open spaces of the new province of Manitoba. Even if we could have put up some kind of a school building, what English teacher would have been willing to live among us (in this wilderness) and share our misery? Iwan Bodrug [a school-teacher who arrived with the *Arcadia* group of immigrants in May, 1897] rendered us good service. He was attending a theology course at the Manitoba College and visited our colony as a student in 1900. He arranged for a meeting of the farmers of our colony and addressed us in a wise and sincere way.

"You will soon prosper on these lands"—he said—"and in time you may even become rich, but your children will grow up in this wilderness without education and will be looked upon with contempt and live in degradation among cultured Canadians. You must, therefore, start building a school for your children without delay. True, all of you are very poor and at present unable to maintain a school or to support a teacher, but I have some advice ready, which you can take or leave, as you please."

We were all curious to hear what advice he had to offer, and we asked him to tell it to us.

"I suggest," said Bodrug, "that you go into the bush and cut suitable timber, haul it to a place which you think would be best suited and convenient to erect a school for your children, and start building. I, on my part, shall see to it that you obtain a loan to buy the material necessary for outfitting the school. The head of the Home Missions of the Presbyterian Church assured me that the Mission will loan our immigrants, from its missionary funds, the money necessary for the completion of a school building, and it will also pay the teacher's salary until such time as the province takes over the school, and will also assist the communities in paying the teachers. If you start immediately, I shall procure the money for you to buy shingles, boards for the floor, windows, doors, and school equipment. If you erect the building before the winter sets in, I, as a professional teacher shall come and teach your children."

The community gladly accepted Bodrug's proposition, and two months later the school was opened—probably the first among the Ukrainian settlers in Canada. A similar school was established seven miles south of

[68]19. Imm., May 21, 1901: J. G. Turiff, Ottawa, to John Nicholson, Dauphin.

Ethelbert, where Bodrug's school mate, Iwan Negrych, became the first teacher. [Negrych died in 1946.][69]

Attempts to establish schools for the children of the Ukrainian settlers in this region were made even earlier. In the autumn of 1898, James A. Smart, the Deputy Minister of the Interior, visited Manitoba and paid a call on the ambitious settlement of Dauphin to inspect the newly built immigration shed, and to learn on the spot the prospects of this new rural community. The settlers approached the Deputy Minister with requests, as a former Minister in the Manitoba Cabinet, to obtain schools for their children. He promised to do his best to comply with their wishes.

At the same time the Archbishop of St. Boniface, Monsignor Adélard Langevin, was also trying to arrange for schools for the Dauphin colony. He directed a personal letter to Dr. Blakely, the Secretary of the Manitoba Board of Education, informing him that Inspector Télesphore Rochon would call on him to discuss the question of erecting school buildings for the Ukrainian settlers in the Dauphin district:

Allow me to inform you that Mr. Télesphore Rochon, inspector, has been asked to approach you about the organization of school districts and the erection of school houses in the Dauphin Region for the Galicians. These people are Catholics (Greek or Ruthenian rite) and consequently they are under my jurisdiction. The Rev. Father Page of Esterhaz, and the Rev. Father Culavi[70] of St. Mary's Church, Winnipeg, are instructed with their spiritual care, and both will give Mr. Rochon a helping hand to organize the new school districts.

I am glad to hear that the Federal Government, represented by Mr. Smart, take interest in the educational welfare of these excellent settlers. They are laborious and thrifty, and one of their countrymen, a young priest who came from Galicia to visit them and those of Dominion City, Stone-Wall and Edmonton, told me that they were perfectly satisfied and on the way to comfort.

Evidently, Catholic school teachers should be given them and I have already found two young men who know English fairly well and who talk fluently German and Polish—*Unicuique suum.*

I invoke this "motto" in the present circumstances because I see by the newspapers that somebody has already tried to harvest in our own field.

Trusting in your spirit of fair play, I have the honour to be, dear Doctor,

Yours very truly,

(Signed) MSGR. LANGEVIN, O.M.I.
Arch. of St. Boniface.[71]

[69]Dmytro Romanchych, "Ukrainski kolonii," 516.

[70]Reverend Albert (Wojciech) Kulawy, O.M.I., of Polish origin, who studied theology in Ottawa and was called, in April of 1898, by Archbishop Langevin to serve the Polish and other Slavic Catholics as a parish priest in Winnipeg.

[71]PAC File 497408, November 24, 1898: Msgr. Adélard Langevin, O.M.I., Archbishop of St. Boniface, Manitoba, to Dr. Blakely, Secretary of the Manitoba Board of Education, Winnipeg.

A copy of this letter was forwarded by the Archbishop's secretary to the Deputy Minister of the Interior in Ottawa. From Mr. Smart's reply we learn that he had already made arrangements to establish at least a temporary school for the children of Ukrainian settlers in the Dauphin region:

I am in receipt of your letter of the the 24th instant (November, 1898) enclosing copy of one addressed to Dr. Blakely with reference to the establishment of schools amongst the Galicians.

In reply I beg to say that while at Dauphin recently the question of the education of the children of the Galician settlers faced itself upon my attention and by way of experiment I agreed to allow Mr. Paul Wood, the Interpreter and Agent of this Department amongst the Galicians for that District, to act as teacher for a few months, provided the Local Government would supply sufficient funds for the school. I am not yet fully aware what Local Government's intention is, but I am informed that the matter is under consideration. As I was obliged to leave Winnipeg before it was finally settled I left the details so far as this Department is concerned in the hands of the Commissioner of Immigration to carry out.

I may add that the Lake Manitoba Railway & Canal company very generously placed at the disposal of the people their Station at Sifton, which is, I think, admirably adapted for a school house and living quarters for the teacher and his wife. So far as my action was concerned I may say that it was simply prompted by the desire to experiment with a nationality which I think will show within few months their desire to acquire every advantage in the way of education for their children and will be only too eager to assist the Department by having their children attend school during the few months the experiment is in operation. The arrangement was only temporary one as of course, the Department could not allow its officer to act permanently in the capacity of a teacher as his services will be otherwise required when the spring opens.[72]

No records have been found as to whether or not the temporary school arrangement at Sifton actually functioned. But the schools established by the settlers themselves with the assistance of the Home Mission of the Presbyterian Church were in operation, and many of the later Ukrainian professional men, the sons of the pioneers, acquired their basic education in these rural establishments.

In October, 1901, a reply finally came from the head office of the C.P.R. Company in Montreal to the letter sent by the Department of the Interior on April 15, 1901, about the squatters' land:

Referring to your letter of the 15th April last to Mr. Griffin, our Land Commissioner, File 410595-2, relating to certain odd numbered sections in Township 23, Range 20 West, settled upon by Galicians, I beg to state that the Company will relinquish their claim to the said lands on the under-

[72]PAC File 49708, November 30, 1898: James A. Smart, Ottawa, to Arthur Boleveau, Private Secretary to the Archbishop of St. Boniface, St. Boniface.

taking that we may select even numbered sections of equal value in lieu thereof. I will have a selection made and submit the same to you as soon as possible.

I am, etc.

(Signed) C. DRINKWATER,
Assistant to the President.[73]

This letter was most welcome news for the harassed squatters on the timber reserve in the Riding Mountains. The Department of the Interior informed the Agent of Dominion Lands in Minnedosa without delay. The error made in addressing the communication to Minnedosa instead of Dauphin created a great deal of confusion. The letter authorized the agent to contact the settlers concerning their entries:

Referring to the Galician settlers who squatted upon certain odd-numbered sections in Township 23, Range 20, West, I am to inform you that the Canadian Pacific Railway have consented to relinquish their claim to sections 21, 23, 27, 31, 33 and 35 in said Township, with the privilege of accepting an equal area of available Dominion Lands in lieu thereof. You may, therefore, communicate with the settlers referred to so that they may make the necessary entries without delay.[74]

If the Department of the Interior thought that the matter had now been brought to a satisfactory solution, it was greatly mistaken. There arose such confusion in connection with the exchange of land that many more months passed until, after the exchange of innumerable memoranda, notes, and letters, the affair was successfully concluded. The squatters waited for the release of the land for homestead entry. The Commissioner of Immigration in Winnipeg became impatient and wrote to the Superintendent of Immigration in Ottawa, July 23, 1902, reminding the Department that action had not yet been taken concerning these centres: "Some years ago Galician families were settled by officers of the department upon sections 15, 17, 21, 27, 31, 33 and part of 35 all in township 23 Range 20 W. of the 1st M. but they have not yet been granted homestead entries upon these odd numbered sections, they have all improved their farms and I think are now fully entitled to receive their entries for this land."[75] At last the long overdue release (with some reservations) arrived. The Commissioner of Immigration in Winnipeg was informed of this fact on August 27, 1902:

[73]19. Imm./657561, October 11, 1901: C. Drinkwater, Assistant to the President. The Canadian Pacific Railway Company, Montreal, to P. G. Keyes, Ottawa.

[74]19. Imm., October 17, 1901: Lyndwode Pereira, Ottawa, to the Agent of Dominion Lands, Minnedosa.

[75]19. Imm./Ref. No. 61, Winnipeg, Man. July 23, 1902: J. Obed. Smith, Winnipeg, to Frank Pedley, Ottawa.

Replying to your letter of the 23rd ultimo, Reference 61, addressed to the Superintendent of Immigration, with regard to certain Galician families settled by officers of this Department on sections 15, 17, 19, 21, 27, 31, 33 and part of 35 in 23-20 W. 1st M. I am directed to say that entries should be granted to all squatters who were located by officers of the Department in the portion of the township now surveyed, that is the part north of the river, but the portion south of the river is unsurveyed and within the Riding Mountain Timber Reserve, and all persons who squat on odd-numbered sections or on timber reserves should be notified that they will not get entries, a copy of this letter is being sent to the Agent in Dauphin for his information and instruction.[76]

The squatters finally became homesteaders, although it still took some months before they were able to receive their patents. For example, Joseph Romanczycz (N.W.¼ Sec. 23, Tp. 23, Rge. 20) was issued his patent (No. 755075) on April 16, 1903, after six full years of waiting. His dream of settling in the Riding Mountains because they reminded him of his native Carpathian Mountains had come true.

VII

While the settlers of the Vermillion colony were occupied with the long-drawn-out struggle to obtain homestead entries for the land on which they squatted, the settlers in other parts of the Dauphin district were busy with improvements on their farms. Although the first two years were usually taken up by outside work to earn money needed to buy implements, stock, and food for the family, the wives and children of the settlers remained on the homestead to tend the gardens, improve the dwellings, and take care of the cattle, if they possessed any. The progress of the settlers was not spectacular, but it was steady and encouraging. Suddenly, however, in the late autumn of 1899, a disastrous prairie fire swept a large area of the Dauphin district and destroyed not only most of the settlers' crops and hay, but in many cases all their buildings and personal belongings as well. Among those who suffered the most were the more recent homesteaders who had not yet had time to clear away the underbrush and break the acres around their dwellings, which would have helped to save their buildings. The Sifton area was particularly heavily hit and many who were burnt out would have faced starvation had assistance not been given. This fire was one of the major disasters which struck the still very young colony, and it caused many hardships and dealt a considerable set-back to the economic establishment of the settlers who were affected by it.

[76]19. Imm., August 27, 1902: P. G. Keyes, Ottawa, to J. Obed. Smith, Winnipeg.

The misfortune also brought to light some misconceptions regarding the status of the Ukrainian settlers in Manitoba, whom the Provincial Government regarded as "wards of the Dominion Government," and to whom they therefore did not extend the aid proffered to settlers of other ethnic origins who suffered losses during the same fire. James Sutherland, the Acting Minister of the Interior, received a letter in May, 1900, from D. J. McMillan, a farmer in Neepawa, Manitoba, in which he drew the Minister's attention to the Ukrainian settlers' suffering as a result of the fire, and the refusal of the Provincial Government to come to their assistance. He appealed to the Dominion Government to lend these people some aid:

You are probably aware of the destructive fires that passed over the Dauphin Country in this Province last fall and as a result many lost everything. The Gallacians were among the number and while the English speaking people who suffered received aid from the Prov'l Gov't the Gallacians have received no aid at all. I wrote to Hon. J. A. Davidson—Minister of Ag. & Immigration—who informed me that the Gallacians were the wards of the Dom'n Gov't this matter was left to them to deal with. It is really too bad that this has been neglected as many of them are in destitute circumstances. I have one of them in my employ at present, a splendid man who was working for me last fall and who lost everything—house & clothes, 30 hens, hay, wheat & barley from 4 acres, stove broken in the fire, etc.

I trust the Gov't will do something; the man (I mentioned) is truthful so I can vouch for what I say, I am a Farmer myself and know something of hardships in Manitoba. Hoping to hear from you, I remain,

Respectfully yours,

(Signed) D. J. McMillan

P.S. I trust this matter will receive your careful consideration. For the truthfulness of what I say would refer you to Dr. Roche, M.P. but don't *think* I am a Tory. . . .[77]

The matter was passed to the Deputy Minister to deal with, and he was surprised at the attitude taken by the Manitoba Government. Mr. Smart wrote as follows to Mr. McMillan, promising to look into the affair carefully:

I am in receipt of your letter of the 18th instant (1900) having reference to the great loss sustained by the Galician settlers in the Dauphin country last year in consequence of the destructive fires which passed over that district, and in which you suggest that the Government should do something to relieve the distress amongst these people in consequence. In reply I beg to say that I am quite amazed at the statement which you attribute to the Minister of Agriculture and Immigration at Winnipeg and from which it appears that he would undertake to distribute relief amongst a certain class

77. Dest./116353, May 18, 1900: D. J. McMillan, Neepawa, Manitoba, to James Sutherland, Acting Minister of the Interior, Ottawa.

of settlers in the country and deliberately ignore another class, saying that the Galicians are "wards" of the Government. I may say that the Galicians are "wards" of no Government and I think statistics will show that the settlement of Galicians in the North-West Territories contain men of different spirit from what is generally expected of persons who are wards of a Government. They are an independent, hard-working, law-abiding people, and if the Government of the Province undertakes to relieve any distress from destructive fires or otherwise, it seems to me that they cannot fairly discriminate against any particular class of the community. I will be very glad, however, to look this matter up and to ascertain in what condition these people have been left and if it is possible to arrange to relieve them in any way. . . .

P.S. I would be glad if you would send me the letter Mr. Davidson wrote you. I would like to see exactly what position the Provincial Government is proposed to take with regard to matters of this kind.[78]

The Deputy Minister also wrote a letter to the Commissioner of Immigration in Winnipeg informing him about the contents of McMillan's letter and requesting Mr. McCreary to inform him of the people's problems and their needs: "I do not know what you have done in connection with this matter or what report you have with regard to the losses sustained by these people, but I am informed that the Provincial Government undertook to relieve some of the distress in that country but did not include the Galicians in their deeds of charity. Would you kindly let me know what the conditions and necessities of the people are. I may add that I think the losses sustained by these people is, no doubt, the reason for their looking for railway work during the present year. . . ."[79]

Commissioner McCreary was well informed about the situation in Dauphin, but his attention was focussed not only on assistance for the distressed but on economy in Government expenditure as well. With the latter point in mind, he was inclined to minimize the extent of the distress and to intimate that it should be the duty of relatives and neighbours to help the victims in the first place. He also regretted that the Deputy Minister did not forward him the copy of McMillan's letter:

. . . as I am not aware of such condition of affairs existing. The day after the fire occured last fall I went up to Swan River and on the way through met Paul Wood, a week even before McKellar got there. Having learned at Sifton that there had been eleven houses burned, I instructed Wood to provide immediate relief to those who might require it, and to send me a detailed report. He did that, and I will send you a copy of same.

[78]7. Dest./116353, May 28, 1900: James A. Smart, Ottawa, to D. J. McMillan, Neepawa.

[79]7. Dest., May 28, 1900: James A. Smart, Ottawa, to W. F. McCreary, Winnipeg.

I have now advised Paul Wood again to visit the district and ascertain if any relief is necessary. I believe, however, Mr. McMillan has exaggerated the matter. When you tell these people they have to pay an advance with interest, they generally find means of getting it from their neighbours without having to do this in cash.[80]

McMillan forwarded Mr. Davidson's letter to the Deputy Minister, as requested, and the latter acknowledged it, adding that ". . . I still do not see how the Local Government can take the position they have taken with regard to these settlers, or how they can discriminate between one settler and another. The Galicians are no more the wards of the Government, of course, than any other class of the community. . . ."[81] Commissioner McCreary was now instructed to deal with the whole question of distress and to send a report to Ottawa describing the situation. He forwarded to the Deputy Minister a copy of Wood's report submitted immediately after the fire occurred. Wood's report, dated October 23, 1899, gave detailed information about damage to the settlers' possessions:

I beg to send you the enclosed report re Galicians burnt out in the Dauphin district. I made enquiries about settlers in the Riding Mountain and as near as I could find little or no damage was done by fire in this settlement, so I did not go there.

A great many as you will see have lost their hay, in most cases all of it. Ten families were entirely burnt out, loosing buildings and contents, though in one case I cannot vouch for this (Ssuks . . .? Tp. 29, Rg. 19) as I noted it from hearsay without going to verify the report.[82]

My trip took five days on foot, and by train, and three days with team. In one or two instances settlers have cut feed still fairly green in the bottom, which with some bran & chop will bring the cattle through the winter, the heavy snow however which immediately followed the fires did not allow of this being general. Many of the men were working, and the women were not able to fight the fire.

Naturally the later settlers have suffered more than the earlier ones, Basil Kouzieuzik [Ksionzik] told me that fire brands jumped 300 yds at his place [N.E.¼ Sec. 19, Tp. 26, Rge 20W.] leaving his wheat stacks but firing his neighbour Gereluk's [N.W.¼ Sec. 20, Tp. 26, Rge 20W].

There then follows the list of burnt out settlers. Unfortunately Wood was not very careful in spelling the settlers' names, and therefore it was difficult to trace them in some instances:

[80]7. Dest./116746, June 2, 1900: W. F. McCreary, Winnipeg, to James A. Smart, Ottawa. McCreary refers in his report to Hugh McKellar, Provincial Clerk of the Department of Agriculture and Immigration.

[81]7. Dest., June 8, 1900: James A. Smart, Ottawa, to D. J. McMillan, Neepawa.

[82]Probably Andrij Stefaniuk, a squatter on SE¼ 10-Tp. 29-Rge. 19.

BURNT OUT ENTIRELY (INCLUDING HAY)

Tp. 28. R. 19.
Nicolai Chunitski (Nicolai Czernecki)—owns 9 head of cattle.
Paulo Soppel (Paulo Sopil)—owns 3 head of cattle.

Tp. 29. R. 19.
Jaukee . . . ? said to have lost goods to the amount of $300.00—owns 1 head of cattle.

Tp. 27. R. 20.
Fedjko Peyelo (Fedko Bujeko)
Dalbert Skulmouski (Adalbert Skulmowski)—owns 3 head of cattle.
Gnat Kouvaltchuk (Hnat Kowalczuk)—lost house, two stables, 3 loads of wheat, vegetables, 20 b. potatoes, owns 7 cattle.
Prokip Zazulek (Prokip Zazuliak)—owns 2 head of cattle.

Tp. 27. R. 19.
Nicolai Pauloski (Nicola Pawlowski)—owns 2 head of cattle.
Nicolai Koulka (Kawulka ?)—owns 1 head of cattle.

Tp. 28. R. 22.
Lucien Merka (Luke Merko) 1899 immigrant—owns 2 head of cattle.

Tp. 29. R. 22.
Demetro Nechouski (?)—owns 2 head of cattle.
Suton Kulchetski

Tp. 28. R. 22.
Iwan Perepelouk (Iwan Perepeluk) wheat stack and hay—owns 2 head of cattle.

Tp. 27. R. 20.
Hilko Boitchuk 5 loads of wheat burnt—owns 4 head of cattle.
Iwan Varove (Iwan Warowy) 15 tons of hay burnt—owns 2 horses, 4 head of cattle.
Wasyl Pouliak (Wasyl Puliak)—owns 3 head of cattle.
Joseph Kovaluk 5 tons of hay burnt—owns 3 head of cattle.
Iwan Fedjuk (Iwan Fediuk)—owns 3 head of cattle.

Tp. 27. R. 20.
Fedjko Holame (Fedjko Holomej)—owns 1 head of cattle.
Jan Grocholski—stable & 1 calf burnt—owns 2 head of cattle.
Michel Houpalo—owns 4 head of cattle.
Sauko Houtzel (Sawko Hutzal) 12 tons of hay burnt—owns 4 head of cattle. (above was working out at Hamiota—19 days—but left for home when he heard of fire in Dauphin District).

Tp. 26. R. 20.
Fedjko Kouvaltchuk (Fedko Kowalchuk)—owns 2 head of cattle.
Jan Gerlak (Jan Gereluk) one acre wheat burnt
Basil Kouzieuzik (Basil Ksionzik) 2 tons of hay burnt, 123 yards rail fence.
Josef Paulitzke (Josef Pawlicki)—owns 4 head of cattle.

Tp. 26. R. 21.
Wasyl Waseleutchuk (Wasyl Wasylenchuk)—owns 5 head of cattle.

Tp. 27. R. 22.
Wasyl Negrycz—owns 4 head of cattle.
Gmetro Baron (Dmytro Baran) 9 tons hay burnt—owns 5 head of cattle.
Micheta Thebliuk (Mykyta Hrabliuk). [Should be listed on Tp. 26, Rge. 20.]

Tp. 25. R. 20.
Paulo Tratch—owns 1 head of cattle.
Micheta Chomiak—owns 2 head of cattle.

Tp. 28. R. 22.
Nichola Musig (Nicola Muzyka)—owns 2 head of cattle.
Semen Buchko—owns 3 head of cattle.

Tp. 26. R. 22.
Jacob Genik 2 horses—owns 8 head of cattle.

N.B.—In cases where amount of hay burnt is specified, more or less was spared by fire, in the other cases it was all burnt. Nearly all the above named worked during the summer on R.R. construction or with farmers and have a little money, hay however is locally very scarce and consequently dear.

(Signed) PAUL WOOD.[83]

On November 3, Wood sent additional information on this situation, and he gave an indication of the difficulties which faced the victims of the fire:

With regard to hay, a great many settlers have recut frozen hay and others have procured small quantities from neighbours. As the frozen hay is very poor feed alone, and will barely pull stock through, may I suggest that if found necessary later on, you authorise me to supply some bran and shorts in certain cases.

When in Dauphin yesterday I heard that several settlers in the Riding Mountain had been burnt out, I have taken steps to procure the names and details and will furnish you with them next week.

Some of the stock around here has already been sold by the Galicians, but not many.

In the several cases I reported to you under the heading "burnt out entirely," only three families lost their clothing, they have since rebought some clothes, but when the cold weather comes they will probably feel the want of their sheepskins and blankets. I will watch all the different cases and report to you later.[84]

Some relief was given to destitute settlers in the spring of 1900, as most of them were in great need before the crop could be harvested. Five heads of families received a few sacks of flour, cornmeal, and bran. In his report of June 8, 1900, Wood mentions to the Commissioner that: "As I had been enjoined economy by you, I certainly did not press any relief on any of them, several certainly were hard up but I know of no case of actual destitution amongst them as a result of the fires, either in the fall or at the present. . . ."[85] The reason why so few settlers actually applied for relief was that even for the smallest assistance a lien

[83]7. Dest./117170, October 23, 1899: Paul Wood, Sifton, to W. F. McCreary, Winnipeg.

[84]7. Dest./117170, November 3, 1899: Paul Wood, Sifton, to W. F. McCreary, Winnipeg.

[85]7. Dest./118369, June 8, 1900: Paul Wood, Sifton, to W. F. McCreary, Winnipeg.

on their homestead was demanded and taken. The settlers preferred to borrow money from friends or from other persons, who did not burden their land with mortgages or liens and who did not set a deadline for repayment. Many settlers borrowed money from the local storekeeper:

> Since last writing you re financial standing and general condition of the Galicians near Sifton (i.e., the townships immediately surrounding) I have had a long conversation with Mr. John Kennedy, storekeeper here. It appears from what Mr. Kennedy says that the apparently comparatively comfortable condition of a great many of them is the result of credit obtained from him during the past year. He states that a large proportion owe him sum from $5,00 up, in some few cases reaching the sum of $50.00. He however states that he is quite sure of collecting every cent providing they procure work. I will also interview the store-keeper at Ethelbert and Valley River and let you know what they say.[86]

An improvement in the existing situation could hardly be expected before harvest time. Although destitution persisted, Commissioner McCreary was determined to exercise stringent economy at all costs, as he informed the Deputy Minister in Ottawa: "Mr. Genik, who has just returned from Yorkton, tells me that the people must be assisted, and the reports from Dauphin and Ethelbert are along the same lines. Rest assured, I will give no more assistance than will barely prevent sensational reports in the press of a condition of starvation."[87]

Another year passed. Time began to heal the scars of the initial battles with nature and adverse conditions. By 1901 the Ukrainian colony in the Dauphin district, including Sifton and Ethelbert, numbered 5,500 persons, and was still growing.[88] When C. W. Speers, the Dominion Colonization Agent, reported in January, 1904, to the Deputy Minister on his trip through the Ukrainian settlement, he remarked on the progress that had been made by the settlers and paid them a high compliment indeed: "Having driven from Strathclair right through the Riding Mountains to Gilbert Plains and Dauphin Districts. . . . The Galician settlers are making a marked progress, they have plenty of stock, good buildings and are in a position, many of them, to remain at home, and look after their own interest, instead of going out to work as has been their custom. On the north side of the Mountain at the Vermillion River and Gilbert Plains the same can be said of these people. They are among our very best settlers."[89]

[86]7. Dest., June 11, 1900: Paul Wood, Sifton, to W. F. McCreary, Winnipeg.

[87]7. Dest./123434, August 6, 1900: W. F. McCreary, Winnipeg, to the Deputy Minister of the Interior, Ottawa.

[88]9. Rpts., February 1, 1901: J. Obed. Smith, Commissioner of Immigration, Winnipeg, to the Secretary, Department of the Interior, Ottawa.

[89]9. Rpts., January 15, 1904: C. W. Speers, Winnipeg, to W. D. Scott, Ottawa.

Chapter Seven

PLEASANT HOME

THE NUCLEUS of the Ukrainian colony of Pleasant Home in Manitoba was established in June, 1897, in Township 17, Range 3, East of the 1st Meridian. The colony expanded rapidly and before a decade had passed, it spread over Townships 17, 18, 19, 20, and 21, Ranges 1 to 4, E.1.M., splitting into a number of populous, thriving rural communities, such as Pleasant Home, Komarno, Melnica, Jaroslaw, and many others. The establishment of school districts followed almost immediately after the settlement had taken on permanent aspects. They were given the names of rivers, towns, and villages in the places where the settlers originated in Europe. Thus the school built on N.E.¼ Sec. 35, Tp. 17, Rge. 3, E.1.M. was called Prut after a river; that on S.E.¼ Sec. 20, Tp. 18, Rge. 2, E.1.M. was named Zbruch also after a river; that on S.W.¼ Sec. 13, Tp. 17, Rge. 3, E.1.M. bore the name of the town of Melnica; and the school on N.W.¼ Sec. 12, Tp. 18, Rge. 2, E.1.M. was called Stry after the town of the same name in Galicia.

The Commissioner of Immigration in Winnipeg, reporting to the Deputy Minister of the Interior in Ottawa on June 25, 1897, described the location and establishment of the Pleasant Home colony in detail:

Some days ago I wrote you that I had despatched a colony of eleven families of Galicians to settle in the Pleasant Home District north of Stonewall. All those parties came in this morning to make entries for these places, well satisfied with the district.

I immediately sent up to the Land Office and got a list of all the vacant lands in Townships 17 and 18, Ranges 1 to 4 East, and made out Township diagrams shewing these vacant lands. These I have submitted to the Minister this morning, and made a request that the odd-numbered Sections, as well as the even, be thrown open for homesteading in order that I may fill up these six Townships, or at least nearly 8 Townships, with Galicians. As far as I can learn from the Land Office reports, they stand about as follows—

Township 17, Range 1, East—can all be opened for homesteads except the S.½ of 23, and W.½ of 35, which have been patented.

Township 17, Range 2, East—can all be opened for homesteading except the S.½ of 20; all of 3, 3 quarters of 2; part of 1; all of 12; 3 quarters of 10; part of 13, 14—and part of 24.

Township 17, Range 3, East—nearly one half the Township is still vacant; of the balance some has been given to the Provincial Government, and some patented.

Township 17, Range 4, East—some of it is patented, the most of it is vacant.

Township 18, Range 1, East—is all vacant.

Township 18, Range 2, East—is all vacant.

In regard to Township 18, in Ranges 3 and 4, East, I find that this is known as an Icelandic Reserve, having been some years ago reserved for the settlement of Icelanders who were supposed to locate there. I understand a few have located along the Lake, but the Townships are largely unsettled, and you will no doubt have there in the books which have recently been forwarded from the Land Commissioner's Office here, a list of the lands actually taken up. I do not think this land should be retained vacant any longer, as a reserve, if these people are not going to settle on it, and I see no reason why, after a proper notice being given to these Icelanders in that district, that the whole Reserve should not be cancelled.

I may say that I do not think much time should be wasted. Now, what I want you to do is, immediately upon the Minister's return, have an Order-in-Council passed, setting aside all the odd-numbered Sections in these Townships for homesteading, also cancelling this Reserve, in so far as it applies to all lands not yet entered for; and even-numbered Sections.

I also want you to send me a list of any Time Sales that there are in any of these Townships, and I understand that there are some not yet paid up; they should also be cancelled at once.

In speaking with Mr. Jackson, M.P.P., last night he told me that it might be necessary to run a small ditch a few miles through these Townships to make it a first class settlement, and as some of the poorer of these Galicians may require a little help, I will later on report upon the advisability and practicability of constructing this ditch. In the meantime, kindly attend to the Orders-in-Council and wire me.[1]

In order not to delay the settlement, Commissioner McCreary wired the Deputy Minister in Ottawa on the same day: "If the Minister concurs is there anything to prevent odd numbered sections as well as even in townships seventeen and eighteen ranges one & four east being thrown open for homesteading? Answer at once."[2] The reply to McCreary's telegram was prompt, arriving the next day:

Of township 17, range 1 east, all available excepting south half 23, and west half 35 and School and Hudson Bay sections.

[1]18. Imm./431311, June 25, 1897: W. F. McCreary, Commissioner of Immigration, Winnipeg, to James A. Smart, Deputy Minister of the Interior, Ottawa.

[2]18. Imm./431167, Telegram, June 25, 1897: W. F. McCreary, Winnipeg, to James A. Smart, Ottawa.

Township 18, range 1 east—Timber Reserve.

Of township 17, range 2 east, all available excepting east half and south west 1; east half and north west 2; all 3; west half north east 10; south east 12, south east 13 and all 14; south half 20; north east 24 and School and Hudson Bay sections.

Township 18, range 2 east—Timber Reserve.

In township 17, range 3 the following available: all 2; east half 5, east half 9, all 12, south half 14, all 15, south east 20, all 23, 24, 25, 27, 28, north east and south west 30, all 31, 32, 33, 34, 35 & 36.

In township 18, range 3 east all available excepting all 4, 9, 10, 13, 14, 15, 23 and 24, and School and Hudson Bay sections.

In township 17, range 4 east the following are available: all 1, 4, 6, west half 10; all 16, 18, 19, 20; west half 22; all 25; south half 27, all 28, 30, 31, 32, 33, south east 34.

In township 18, range 4 east the following are available: north half 4; all 5, 6, 7, north east 9, south west 9, south west 10, east half and south west 16, north half and south west 17, all 18, south half and north west 19, north half and south east 20, south west 30, north half 31.

The odd sections in the foregoing are all reserved in our book for the Winnipeg Great Northern.[3]

Although most of the land in the region was open for settlement, there were certain reservations to which the Deputy Minister pointed in his letter dated July 8, 1897, addressed to the Commissioner of Immigration in Winnipeg: "Referring to my letter of the 30th ultimo confirming telegram to you respecting the lands in Townships 17 and 18, Ranges 1, 2, 3, and 4, East of the 1st Meridian, I beg to state that you will understand that the odd-numbered sections will be in the same position as regards settlement as those north of Township 30 in the Dauphin District, that is, that no entries can be given therefor for at least a year and one-half but any squatters settling on the lands will be protected. I presumed that you understood this when I advised you by wire that odd-sections are reserved in our books for the Winnipeg Great Northern Railway."[4] Further investigation revealed that some sections in Township 18, Range 3, E. were classed as timber reserves and were thus excluded from settlement, although there was only a limited quantity of commercial timber left on them. Commissioner McCreary was determined to have these sections released for settlement, as a number of squatters had already settled in that part of the township. He therefore

[3]18. Imm./431167, Telegram, June 26, 1897: James A. Smart, Ottawa, to W. F. McCreary, Winnipeg.

[4]18. Imm., July 8, 1897: James A. Smart, Ottawa, to W. F. McCreary, Winnipeg.

wrote to the Deputy Minister, July 12, 1897, with regard to cancelling the timber reserves on which the settlers had squatted:

Referring to your letter of the 8th instant, 410595 in reference to the odd numbered sections in Townships 17 & 18 Ranges 1 to 4 East. I note what you say in regard to protecting squatters settling on these sections. Would it not be possible to have the Timber Reserve in Township 18, Ranges 1 & 2, and the Icelandic Reserve in 3 & 4 cancelled. There is no timber on any section in that reserve at present, in fact scarcely enough for settlers' buildings and as for the Icelandic Reserve they have now had it quite a number of years and have only settled a few sections along the lake shore, at least so I am informed. If all those Townships in that district were open I think quite a nice colony of Galicians and Germans from Pennsylvania and Europe might be added to the eleven families who settled there about a month ago. I may say that the six delegates whom I sent out a few days ago to look over this district returned this morning well satisfied. Two of these were Galicians from Pennsylvania who spoke good English and the others were German speaking Galicians of a superior class. I would be much obliged if you could take this matter up and let me know what can be done.[5]

McCreary met with some opposition on the part of the Dominion Lands Office, and the decision about the release of land in the Timber Reserve situated in Township 18, Ranges 1 and 2 for settlement was delayed. In the meantime, the number of settlers was rapidly growing and by the summer of 1898 well over one hundred families (about 600 souls) had made their homes in the Pleasant Home district. Reverend Paul Tymkevich, the Ukrainian Catholic priest of Edna, Alberta, related in the "News from Canada" column in *Svoboda*, November 24, 1898: "Our largest colonies in Manitoba are the Stuartburn and Dauphin colonies; they contain approximately 800 Ukrainian families. About 150 families settled in Pleasant Home, 30 in Brokenhead, 30 in St. Norbert and 30 in Gonor. . . ."[6] Settlers squatting on odd-numbered sections were reasonably certain of obtaining entries for their quarter-sections in a year and a half, as the Deputy Minister stipulated, but those who settled in the timber reserve, met with strong objections on the part of E. F. Stephenson, the Inspector of Crown Timber Agencies of the Dominion Lands Office in Winnipeg. He voiced his protest in a letter to Ottawa and in a similarly strong letter, dated September 27, 1898, that he dispatched to Commissioner McCreary in Winnipeg:

It appears a grave blunder has been made by your Galician Agent at Pleasant Home, in settling Township 18, Range 3, East, with these people.

[5]18. Imm./433089, July 12, 1897: W. F. McCreary, Winnipeg, to James A. Smart, Ottawa.

[6]Reverend Paul Tymkevich, "News from Canada," *Svoboda*, No. 47 (Mount Carmel, Pa., November 24, 1898).

When your advice first reached me, that the Galicians had been placed there, knowing that the Township was for the most part heavily timbered, I enquired of your Agent if he had been over the lands and could say that the quarter sections settled on were of the class available for homesteads. He assured me there was little or no timber upon the lands, not more than the law allowed, so the matter was allowed to rest.

Recently, numerous complaints have been received by me that in nearly every case the land taken possession of was densely timbered, and that fires had been started in the timber by some of the Galicians, as a first process towards clearing.

To satisfy myself, I detailed one of our Inspectors, Mr. Aikman, to visit the ground and investigate. I enclose you his report, which confirms the reports previously received by me, that the land was heavily timbered and that fires had been set out.

Three or four entries have been granted already to these people through your Agent, Mr. Genik, which it is thought will have to be cancelled. However, I am referring the matter to Ottawa for decision and instructions.

From what Mr. Aikman reports, I am inclined to think that even should those people be permitted to hold these lands, they will have a hard struggle for an existence. It would take years of hard labour to prepare the land for cultivation and I am afraid in most cases the result would be that little else would be done by them but traffick in wood.

The settlers living on the prairie lands to the South, who are in a large measure dependent on this Township for their supply of wood, are alarmed for the safety of this valuable timber belt, indications so far pointing to its destruction by fires set out by these people.

From the plan which I enclose it will be seen that Mr. Aikman did not cover the whole Township in his inspection.

When Ottawa is heard from, if the decision is unfavourable to allowing the Galicians to remain, I think a competent man should be sent to inspect and report upon the value and extent of timber on each quarter section.[7]

In support of his statements, Stephenson enclosed in his letter to Commissioner McCreary a copy of Aikman's report. The original of the report went to the Department of the Interior in Ottawa. It mirrored Stephenson's opinions and was definitely hostile towards the Ukrainian squatters who took up land in the timber reserve. Aikman's case against allowing the settlers on the reserve was stated at length and sounded very convincing:

Re Township 18, Range 3, East.

On Saturday Sept. 17th drove over part of Sec. 10, 4 and nine, on the timber roads and find them all heavily timbered with Spruce and Poplar, and in the afternoon over part of N.E.¼ 10, and part of 11, and find them also covered heavily with large poplar and spruce. On Monday and Tuesday went on foot over 11, 14, 15, 22 and S.E.¼ 34. All timbered with large poplar and spruce. I have not been on a quarter section in this Township on

[7]18. Imm./490976, September 27, 1898: E. F. Stephenson, Crown Timber Office, Winnipeg, to W. F. McCreary, Winnipeg.

which there is 25 acres of scrub. The timber on all is mostly large enough for saw logs and that of a size that quite surprised me. I measured numbers of trees of poplar that measured from 20 to 40 inches 3 feet above the ground and would make from 4 to 5 logs, some more. The quantity of trees suitable for firewood cannot be estimated. Turtle Mountain is but scrub in comparison. I found some 8 or 10 Galician families living in different sections and am satisfied they cannot clear and get under cultivation within the next three years sufficient land on which to make a living and unless they have means on which to live will have to be supported by the Government, as there is no work for them in the neighbourhood. On the S.E.¼ of Sec. 34, I found a house or rather shanty, occupied as I was informed by a German. Willow Creek runs through this quarter on which is a fine Mill privilege. South of the Creek there are from 15 to 20 acres of small scrub, but all North of the Creek is heavily timbered with the largest poplar I ever saw, trees measuring 24 to 30 inches and 70 to 80 feet high and along the surveyors line leading North the Westerly side of 35 is covered with the quality of timber intersperced with bluffs of spruce also large, we found spruce trees on both 34 and 35 that would measure 40 inches. A gravelly ridge runs across the South end of the S.E.¼ 34, down near and partly on the surveyed line running South between Sections 34 & 35, down to Section 10, this narrow ridge (about 150 feet) has small scrub on it all the balance of the sections on either side are well timbered. On Tuesday 21st went over Sec. 11, thoroughly. At the N.E. corner of this section where the spruce belt crosses the East & West line, I found a number of spruce trees had been lately cut and following the line to Sec. 12 & 13, found 2 Galician families living, the one on 12, and the other on S.W.¼ of 13. On N.W.¼ 12, near a Galician hut, I found 17 pieces of green spruce timber running from 12 to 22 feet in length and 8 to 10 inches square which (the boy, the only one who could speak or understand English), admitted they had cut on Sec. 11, besides a number a pieces of dead spruce, the tops of many of these trees where they had cut are large enough for saw logs, there were plenty of down trees perfectly sound, which could have been used, but harder to hew. The Galician refused to pay any dues on them. I forbid them using them, but was told on Wednesday morning that they were using them. I went from there South along the line, then West and North, at the S.W. corner of the S.E.¼ there is a piece of 20 or 25 acres on Sec. 11, of small second growth poplar, with occasional trees large enough for cordwood, this has evidently been burnt over some few years ago, then from S.W. corner of 11, went North up the old Gimli road to the spruce belt which I was over in the morning, the soil is a heavy black loam through all the sections I was over. The quality of timber suitable for saw logs is sufficient to keep a mill running or at least 3 or 4 years and the amount or quantity fit for cordwood can hardly be estimated and from what I have seen around the huts of the Galicians, I do not believe that any of it will be left another two years, as they seem very careless about fires, in fact at the Galician's hut on S.W. corner of 22, they have built fires among the spruce trees evidently with the intention of destroying, as the fires had been built in several places and *not running* from one place to another, in one place within a radius of 60 feet I counted 22 spruce trees large enough for saw logs. I measured several running from 12 to 38 inches and would cut from 4 to 6 logs of 12 feet each, here the fire had burned through under the roots of several, farther along the line I found where they had set fire to the pitch or gum on the side of the trees but did no further damage than burning off the gum.

The extension of the Stonewall branch of the C.P.R. is now graded West and North of Balmoral and is expected to reach Foxton this fall, that would bring it within 4 or 5 miles of this splendidly timbered Township, and would make the timber valuable for firewood for Winnipeg market, as it now is, the Easterly side of the Township is only 4 miles from Lake Winnipeg and I was informed by Mr. Thorsteinsson and Icelander who has resided in Tp. 18, Rge. 4, E. for 22 years, that a part of Sec. 26-18-3, E., has been bought from the Hudson's Bay Co., for cordwood, timber, &c., I may also here state that after the timber and cordwood is taken off there will remain sufficient or any quarter section for a settler's purposes.

I submit with this a rough sketch of the parts of the Township over which I have travelled. I think that it was a great mistake allowing settlers in this Tp. and I am certain that if yourself and Mr. McCreary would go up to and over this Township, you would both agree with me and I think the size and quality and quantity of timber would surprise you. Moreover, as to S.E.¼ 34, I am inclined to think that the Mill site will be valuable as soon as the Ry. is run through to Gimli.[8]

The Deputy Minister, on receiving Stephenson's letter together with Aikman's corroborative report, wrote to the Commissioner of Immigration in Winnipeg and suggested that a change of location be made for the settlers in question:

I am in receipt of a duplicate of the letter addressed to you by Mr. Stephenson on the 27th ultimo, with regard to the settling of Galicians in Township 18, Range 3, East. If the statements made in this relation are right, and I have no reason to think they are otherwise, it appears that a very grave mistake has been made in allowing these people to locate in this Township. If the matter can be adjusted in any way by having the settlers placed on other lands, I think it ought to be done. I quite agree with Mr. Stephenson's opinion as to the unsuitability of the land for settlement and it is quite clear that a change must be made even in the interests of the people themselves. I would be glad, therefore if you would consult with Mr. Stephenson and let me know what you think be done in the premises.[9]

Commissioner McCreary had a different opinion, however. He was not inclined to accept Stephenson's statements, knowing well the latter's almost obsessive zeal in guarding timber, even when there was little timber to guard. He was also aware that there existed pressure on the part of saw mill owners in this area to prevent the land from being given to settlers. He therefore replied to the Deputy Minister's letter,

[8]18. Imm./490976, September 27, 1898: T. H. Aikman, Homestead Inspector, Winnipeg, to E. F. Stephenson, Winnipeg.

[9]18. Imm., October 5, 1898: James A. Smart, Ottawa, to W. F. McCreary, Winnipeg.

informing Mr. Smart that he was having an accurate estimate made of the amount of timber in the region:

Referring to your letter of the 5th instant, Ref. 95619, in regard to the settlement of Galicians in Township 18, Range 3, East, I beg to say that I notice you qualify your remarks by saying "if the statements made in this relation are right".

Now, that is just what I have done. As you are probably aware, if Mr. Stephenson has any hobby it is that of guarding timber, and in my opinion he sometimes is over-zealous in this way. The gentleman who made the inspection for timber is a very old man, one Aikman a Homestead Inspector, seventy-five years of age, I believe. He reported on all this Township and visited it about three days. Now, I know that you could not possibly get round this Township and make any kind of an inspection in less than two weeks, and then you would have to wade through water fully a foot to two and half deep in places. Mr. Aikman did not do this; he got his information entirely from one Thomas who owns a saw mill out there and is anxious to have the privilege of cutting all the timber and selling it to the farmers. I know, as a matter of fact, that some quarter-sections on which he says there is timber there is not enough to build a hen house of timber over two inches thick, and when I questioned Mr. Stephenson on the matter very closely he is not so sure that his inspection is correct.

However, to get over the difficulty, I have sent out Roy and Harvey to go over every quarter-section and give me an estimate, in legal sub-divisions, of the timber there is in that Township. Roy has ten years' experience in the United States as a Bush Ranger and Guide besides a residence of fifteen years in this Province, so that he is in a good position to estimate exactly what is fit for cord wood and what is fit for sawn lumber.

I do not believe there will be found more than two or three quarter-sections of all that has been entered for with more than the amount allowed, that is, twenty-five acres of timber. I have asked Mr. Stephenson to give me a statement of the amount that has been paid within the last ten years for timber permits, either by the farmers or by the mill-owners, but he says that it is so small that it would not amount to anything.

Now, would it not be better that these Galicians should settle on that land and clear it up, than have the timber burnt up, as it will be eventually, by forest fires. If it is found that there is more timber than the law allows, then I would suggest that that amount be estimated by an agent of Mr. Stephenson's and charged up at 25 cents a cord against the Galician or other party who homesteads the land. However, I would prefer leaving this until Roy makes his report, when the matter will be dealt with fully.[10]

Leon Roy, following Commissioner McCreary's instructions, made an inspection of every quarter section in Townships 18 and 19, Range 3, and submitted a detailed report, dated October 26, 1898: "I beg to submit my report of inspection of land and timber in Townships 18 and

[10]Imm./492709, October 10, 1898: W. F. McCreary, Winnipeg, to James A. Smart, Ottawa.

19, Range 3, East, and to hand you herewith list with amount of timber on each quarter section. The soil of these two Townships is fairly good, being of secondary class, with some class No. 1."[11] Roy then proceeded to describe each quarter-section of land in Townships 18 and 19, Range 3, E., but did not include the names of the settlers on the sections. Some of the names were added later, probably in the Commissioner's office:

N.E.¼ Sec. 3-18-3-E. *Panko Swirski.* Good house built. Second growth poplar will cut 10 cords for cordwood to the acre in 70 acres. Balance is fire-killed timber—willow and hay marsh. Lumber Cordwood—700 cords.

N.W.¼ Sec. 3-18-3-E. *Kost Percan* resides in his good house he built. Small poplar 3 to 5 inch—quarter of the timber is rotten and 60 acres will cut 10 cords of wood to the acre—second growth poplar 3 to 5 inch. Lumber Cordwood 600 cords.

Sec. 5-18-3-E. *Onufri Bojcum,* 2 houses built. Wind-fall with undergrowth of poplar scrub. Hay marsh on S.E.¼ and about 100 spruce trees 6 to 8 inches. The best spruces are cut out.

S.W.¼ Sec. 10-18-3-E. *Kerylo Strilecki*—house built. Will cut 60,000 feet spruce timber and 60 acres will cut 12 cords of poplar cordwood to the acre. Good hay marsh. Lumber—60,000 feet; Cordwood—720 cords.

N.E.¼ Sec. 13-18-3-E. *Frank Schucki* (*Szczucki*). Fire killed timber and scrub.

S.E.¼ Sec. 13-18-3-E. *Urban Strykowski.* House built. Shanty and residing on this ¼. 10 acres covered with spruce 10–20 inch and will cut 25,000 feet lumber. 40 acres poplar 3–6 inch and will cut 10 cords of wood to the acre. Lumber—25,000 feet; Cordwood—400 cords.

S.W.¼ Sec. 24-18-3-E. *Hnat Pasieka.* House built on S.W.¼. Wind-fall with undergrowth of poplar scrub. Few spruce on the S.W.¼ and bluff poplar 3–4 inch on S.E.¼.

S.E.¼ Sec. 24-18-3-E. *Iwan Kornylo.*

N.E.¼ Sec. 34-18-3-E. *Andreas Byck.* Shanty. About 25 acres of green poplar 6 to 10 inch. Balance is dead burned or fallen timber.

N.W.¼ Sec. 35-18-3-E. *Dmytro Hobotiuk* (*Chobotiuk*) residing on his ¼. Poplar, birch 6 to 12 inch and little wind-fall—will cut 2,500 cords of wood.

From the comparison with other quarter-sections enumerated in the report, where no names of occupants were added, it would seem that these were chosen because they possessed an appreciable amount of lumber and cordwood. Here are examples of quarter-sections listed without names of occupants:

N.E.¼ Sec. 12-18-3-E. 15 acres of poplar 3–4 inch—54 spruce trees 10 to 16 inch—balance wind-fall and scrub poplar—small hay marsh. House built.

S.E.¼ Sec. 12-18-3-E. 10 to 12 acres poplar 3 to 5 inch—29 spruce trees, willows, small hay marsh and about 30 acres of swamp.

---

[11]18. Imm./495215, October 26, 1898: Leon Roy, Winnipeg, to W. F. McCreary, Winnipeg.

N.W.¼ Sec. 12-18-3-E. No timber except a few poplar trees on the W½ of the quarter-section—balance fire-killed willow & scrub.

Roy concludes his report with some observations relating to Township 19, Range 3, East, which he also inspected:

In Township 19, Range 3, East, I find Sections 3, 4 and 5 to be wind-fallen and mostly second growth poplar scrub and some swamp on Section 5. Sections 9 and 10 have a belt of spruce and tamarac running north and south parallel with the Section line, on the West of Section 10 and the East side of 9. Balance of this Section is wind-fall with second growth of poplar scrub or burnt dead timber. Homesteads on these two sections ought to be taken running East and West 80 rods by 320. By doing so settlers would have from 20 to 25 acres of timber each; and again, the land where this spruce is poor and stony. Sections 13, 14 and 15 and northern part of 16 are also dead fallen or rotten timber and scrub, except Section 15 has about 90 acres of good green poplar on the south part of the Section and a few spruce on the N.W.¼. Four good homesteads can be had by dividing this land North and South 80 rods by 320.

Sections 21, 22, 23 and 24 are dead fallen burnt poor and rotten timber poplar and Balm of Gilead. This also ought to be given as homesteads. The soil in this Section is excellent. I have marked out (blazed) a trail from this land between Sec. 21-16, 22-15, 23-14 and between 9 and 16 to a road partly cut out leading to the Village of Gimli. The Sections S½ 2-25-26-27-28-33-34-35 are timber poplar, spruce and tamarac intermixed with big swamp and muskeg. Some of the timber is big enough for saw logs and railway ties. My impression of the western part of the Township is that it is not good for settlement at this present time. Too many swamps, willow and timber.

Leon Roy's report showed clearly that Stephenson's objections were not entirely justified, although there did exist some quarter-sections which registered an excess of lumber and cordwood over the permitted quota. In forwarding Roy's report to the Deputy Minister in Ottawa on November 7, 1898, Commissioner McCreary suggested a solution which would permit the squatters on timbered sections of Township 18, Range 3, E. to retain possession of the land they occupied:

I have to-day sent a communication to Mr. Stephenson and trust that some means will be found by which these Galicians now squatted on these lands may be able to cut cordwood thereon and pay the Government so much per cord stumpage instead of being obliged to remove their houses.

I may say Mr. Roy tells me the chief objectors to these Galicians are people who have been stripping the land of wood for many years back without making returns, and I believe that the small amount which is shewn to have been received on account of timber cut in this district as compared with the large quantity taken off would bear out Mr. Roy's statement.

I will write you subsequently as to what arrangements Mr. Stephenson makes, but in the meantime you can rely upon this report as being absolutely correct.

II

The settlers in Township 18, Range 3, were not the only Ukrainians to experience obstacles in making entry for quarter-sections on which they squatted. Similar difficulties were encountered by the squatters who occupied odd-numbered sections in Township 17 (and partly in 18), Ranges 1, 2, 3, and 4. The Deputy Minister of the Interior was much concerned about the situation in these locations, and he wrote Commissioner McCreary concerning them on March 15, 1899:

By telegram dated the 26th June, 1897, which was confirmed by my letter of the 30th of the same month you were advised that the vacant and even-numbered Sections in Townships 17 and 18 in Ranges 1, 2, 3 and 4, East of the 1st Meridian, were thrown open to settlement; and on the 8th July following I advised you that you will understand that the odd-numbered sections will be in the same position as regards settlement as those of Township 30 in the Dauphin District, that is, that no entries can be given therefor for at least a year and one-half but any squatters settling on the lands will be protected. I presumed you understood this when I advised you by wire that the odd-numbered sections were reserved in our books for the Winnipeg Great Northern Railway.

In reply to your letter of the 5th August last in which you reported that some of the Galicians had squatted upon lands in Township 17, Ranges 1 and 2, East of the 1st Meridian, and asked to be advised if the odd-numbered sections therein were open to settlement, you were advised that they were not open for settlement as they were within the Winnipeg Great Northern Railway Reserve.

By letter dated the 19th January last, the Agent at Winnipeg reported that a number of squatters had gone into occupation of certain odd-numbered sections in Townships 17 and 18, in Ranges 1, 2, 3 and 4, East of the 1st Meridian, and suggested that an inspection be made in order to ascertain the rights of the squatters. From the Agent's report of such inspection it appears that a number of the squatters have made more or less valuable improvements upon the lands they had taken up.

There is no question, therefore, that if these lands were certain to afford these settlers a living they should be permitted to make entries for the lands they have respectively entered upon and improved, and I may say to you that the fact that certain quarter-sections are included in the reserve of the Winnipeg Great Northern Railway is now no obstacle to that action, as provision has been made to warrant the granting of entries in these cases.

From information I have obtained with regard to the nature of the soil of nearly all, if not all of such lands, information which I know to be reliable, I am satisfied that these settlers cannot make a living upon these lands, and that it would be in their interest and for their future welfare to remove them as soon as possible to other lands.

I will await your reply, however, before giving a formal decision.[12]

[12] 19. Imm./410595, March 15, 1899: James A. Smart, Ottawa, to W. F. McCreary, Winnipeg.

Commissioner McCreary questioned the practicability of removing settlers from the less fertile sections of Townships 17 and 18, Ranges 1 to 4, and transplanting them somewhere else. He considered it a better policy to assist the squatters in obtaining titles to the land that they had already occupied for several years than to uproot them. The release of odd-numbered sections in Townships 17 and 18, Ranges 1–4, was constantly delayed by various formalities which had to be complied with and which severely taxed the patience of the settlers. As late as February 3, 1902, the squatters on the odd-numbered sections of Township 17, Range 2, East, petitioned the Government authorities to be permitted to make entries for quarter-sections which they already occupied for a length of time:[13]

We beseech you humbly to release the odd-numbered sections in Township 17, Range 2, East, for settlement. . . . The settlers have been working the land already for some three years, they erected buildings, broke the land for cultivation, bought farm implements and cattle and acquired everything necessary for farming.

Hoping that Your Excellency will grant our request, we thank you in anticipation.

The following settlers of Township 17, Range 2, East, Post Office Pleasant Home, attach their signatures to the petition for the release of the odd-numbered sections for homestead entries.

Pleasant Home, February 3rd, 1902.

Signatures:

Wasyl Dutzek
Peter Drohomirecki
(x) Iwan Drohomirecki
(x) Pylyp Cornij
Nykola Drohomirecki
Iwan Popowicz
John Drohomirecki (Wasyliw)
(x) Mykola Szylypontiuk
(x) Oksentyj Szarhan
(x) Oksentij Szczygil
(x) Bazyli Nowak
(x) Jasko Chimczuk
(x) Jan Barczuk
(x) Ludwik Ples
Petro Hryciw
(x) Kazio Tomczak
Ignac Sochacki
Lukasz Wojtowicz
(x) Wasyl Maliczyn
(x) Fedko Kadyniuk
(x) Ilko Prokopiw
Hryhor Drohomirecki
Dmytro Genik
Michal Drohomirecki
(x) Iwan Blonarowicz
(x) Kyrylo Feduk
(x) Petro Nazaruk

The request of these settlers was apparently granted, because some twenty years later we encounter their names as occupants of their original homesteads, for instance: Peter Drohomirecki on N.E.¼ Sec. 36, Tp. 17, Rge. 2, E.; John Drohomirecki on N.E.¼ Sec. 12, Tp. 17, Rge. 2,

[13]19. Imm./189118/410595, February 3, 1902: Settlers from Pleasant Home, Manitoba, to the Minister of the Interior, Ottawa. Petition written in Ukrainian. Those who could not write signed with a cross, indicated by (x).

E.; Michael Drohomirecki on S.E.¼ Sec. 25, Tp. 17, Rge. 2, E.; Nicholas Drohomirecki on S.E.¼ Sec. 24, Tp. 17, Rge. 2, E.; Dmytro Genik on N.W.¼ Sec. 12, Tp. 17, Rge. 2, E.; Iwan Popowicz on S.E.¼ Sec. 28, Tp. 17, Rge. 2, E.[14]

Among the original settlers who took up homesteads in the Pleasant Home district in 1897 the following names are listed: Stefan Dragan (settled on N.E.¼ Sec. 32, Tp. 17, Rge. 3, E.), Wasyl Porayko (settled on N.W.¼ Sec. 28, Tp. 17, Rge. 3, E.), Anton Chreptyk, Prokop Slusarchuk, Fedor Holinski, Ilia Chreptyk (settled on S.E.¼ Sec. 20, Tp. 17, Rge. 3, E.), and Yurko Lukaszczuk. All of these settlers were naturalized on September 19, 1900.[15]

John Drohomirecki (S.E.¼ Sec. 25, Tp. 17, Rge. 2, E.) and Petro Drohomirecki (N.E.¼ Sec. 35, Tp. 17, Rge. 2, E.) belonged to the group of squatters on odd sections of Tp. 17, Range 2, who petitioned the Minister of the Interior in 1902 for permission to make entry "because they have already been working the land for some three years." These settlers were naturalized in April, 1903.[16] Michael Hawryluk (S.E.¼ Sec. 36, Tp. 17, Rge. 3, E.), Hilar Yakymiw, and Wasyl Dutczik settled in 1898 and were naturalized in March, 1902.[17] Prokop Antoniuk (S.W.¼ Sec. 32, Tp. 17, Rge. 3, E.), Jacob Jakimiszczuk, Nykola Romanczycz (S.W.¼ Sec. 18, Tp. 17, Rge. 3, E.), Nykola Szybinski (N. Sibinski) (N.E.¼ Sec. 31, Tp. 17, Rge. 3, E.), and Philip Rublowski (S.W.¼, Sec. 16, Tp. 17, Rge. 3, E.), were naturalized in September, 1902.[18]

Stefan Dragan was one of the "German speaking Galicians of superior class" mentioned by Commissioner McCreary in his report to the Deputy Minister of the Interior in Ottawa in 1897. Dragan, who was born in 1868 in the town of Zabolotiw, in the district of Sniatyn, Galicia, arrived in Canada with his family in July, 1897, and settled in Pleasant Home the same summer. He had public school education and acquired a knowledge of the German language during a three-year service in the Austrian Imperial Army. He supplemented his education while training for the rank of a non-commissioned officer. In Pleasant Home, Dragan soon became one of the leaders of the community, assisting immigration officers in locating settlers on homesteads, and acting as an interpreter and a school organizer. His wife, Anna Lukas-

[14]Cummins Rural Directory Map of Manitoba, Map No. 57, 1923.

[15]Naturalization Records, Supreme Court, Winnipeg, September 19, 1900. Nos. 2340–2346.

[16]Naturalization Records, Stonewall County Court, April 10, 1903.

[17]Naturalization Records, Pleasant Home, Nos. 165, 168, 169, March 7, 1902.

[18]Naturalization Records, Supreme Court, Winnipeg, Nos. 752, 730, 738, 772, 753.

chuk, passed away in 1929, and he himself died in 1947. They had two sons and seven daughters, and one of their sons, George E. Dragan, born at Pleasant Home in 1898, became a physician, practising in Saskatoon, Saskatchewan. In 1936 he entered politics and became the first Member of the Saskatchewan Legislature of Ukrainian origin.[19]

C. W. Speers, in his enumeration of the Ukrainian settlements in Manitoba and the Northwest Territories in January, 1901, mentions the settlement of Pleasant Home briefly, pointing to its rapid growth:

> This colony was established with 605 Galician settlers. [The first eleven Ukrainian families, according to Commissioner McCreary, were settled in Pleasant Home in June, 1897.] In 1899, 400 souls were added, in 1900, 218 souls were again added, making about 1,225 souls settled in this district. These settlers have a country possessing considerable timber and plenty of hay; the country is flat and inclined to be wet. They are clearing their land, and putting up large quantities of hay; growing excellent gardens, and a considerable quantity of grain. They are securing considerable stock and are doing well.[20]

By the end of 1902, Pleasant Home colony was spread over an area of some 260 square miles. The Ukrainian weekly *Svoboda*, of December 11, 1902, contained a brief correspondence from Pleasant Home signed by Wasyl Cichocki, a local school teacher, in which he described the development of the colony:

> About 40 miles north of Winnipeg, the capital of Manitoba, Ukrainians settled on about 260 square miles of land. . . . In Gimli, as well as in Pleasant Home, churches have been built, but they still are awaiting with longing hearts for true and devoted Ukrainian clergymen to serve them. There are four schools in this district—two of them have English teachers. In the one near Gimli a Ukrainian teacher, Wasyl Cichocki, is teaching. The fourth school, newly organized, is now advertising for a Ukrainian teacher. All four schools are public schools with English as the language of instruction and with Ukrainian as the secondary language.
>
> A spirit of mutual understanding prevails in the colony, all live in accord with one another. . . .[21]

In response to an appeal to Ukrainian farmers in Canada published in *Svoboda*, Iwan Drohomirecki, sent in a lengthy description of the Pleasant Home colony, including in it his own experiences as a pioneer settler:

> 1. Our colony is called Pleasant Home and Gimli. It lies 40 miles north of Winnipeg and 25 miles north of the smaller town of Stonewall, and it

[19]Philip Wade, "Ukrainians Built Fine Record in Canada," Saskatoon *Star-Phoenix*, Saturday, January 5, 1962.

[20]9. Rpts., January 24, 1901: C. W. Speers, General Colonization Agent, Winnipeg, to E. L. Newcombe, Deputy Minister of Justice, Ottawa.

[21]W. Cichocki, "Ruthenian Colony Gimli and Pleasant Home in the Province of Manitoba, Canada," *Svoboda*, No. 50 (Olyphant, Pa., December 11, 1902).

covers 24 square miles. It is crossed by two rivers which, in the spring, abound with fish coming up from Lake Winnipeg.

The next small town is very near, only two miles distant. It is situated on the lakeshore and is inhabited mostly by Icelandic fishermen. . . .

Following a description of the distances of Pleasant Home from the Railway lines, and a discussion of marketing procedures, Drohomirecki continues his account of the settlement:

9. Between 700 and 800 Ukrainian families have settled in this colony. . . .

16. It will be six years next spring since I settled on the farm in this locality [in 1897]. I arrived with my wife and three children, and leaving Winnipeg, we had $41 with us. At first I went with a few other new immigrants from Winnipeg to the Dauphin district and spent six weeks there looking for a suitable location to settle. After six weeks I paid $13 return fare to Winnipeg and had now only $5 left . . . but I did already buy the most necessary commodities for the house, although we did not have a house yet. Mr. Genik directed us, some eight families, to this place, and we were the first ones to settle in this colony. I built a temporary shack from poplar poles and branches, and the mosquitoes nearly killed our children before the autumn brought relief. I was unable to build a better house because I spent all my money and was obliged to go and dig ditches near Selkirk, where I earned $23. I then returned to my children whom I left with my wife in the dug-out in the bush. We built a modest house before the winter set in, and moved in, although it was only half finished, because the frosty nights made it impossible for the children to remain in the cold shanty. My wife plastered the walls inside, and I built a large stove with a flat top, which for two years served as a bed for the children during the cold weather. The next summer I again went to dig ditches and I earned $80 which enabled us to buy a cow, and thus with God's help we have been managing. Now (February, 1903), I own 10 head of cattle, 2 pigs, 25 hens, and 2 ducks. . . .[22]

Drohomirecki's story presents a typical example of the beginnings of farming in Canada by a homesteader with limited means. Initial difficulties, such as those he described, were particularly felt by those who settled on their homesteads late in the season, too late to start raising roots and vegetables to tide them over the winter and spring. Those who brought some money with them were able to buy the necessary provisions for their families. But those, like Iwan Drohomirecki, who had spent all their money even before they settled on the homestead, faced only two alternatives: either to find work before winter set in and to earn some cash to buy provisions, or to rely on an advance of flour, cornmeal, and potatoes from the immigration authorities, for which, as a rule, a lien on the homestead was demanded.

[22]Iwan Drohomirecki, "Description of Pleasant Home," *Svoboda*, No. 8 (Olyphant, Pa., February 19, 1903).

Several of the eighteen Ukrainian families who settled on homesteads in the Pleasant Home district in 1897 faced these difficulties as winter advanced. George H. Chatfield, employed at Pleasant Home, desiring to help the families in need, wrote a letter to the local Member of Parliament in Ottawa, J. A. Macdonell, informing him that some new settlers in the Pleasant Home district were in need of relief.[23] Mr. Macdonell forwarded Chatfield's letter to the Deputy Minister of the Interior who, immediately on receiving it (March 19, 1898) instructed the Commissioner of Immigration in Winnipeg to investigate the matter and to extend relief to those in need without delay: "I beg to enclose herewith a copy of a letter which has been received here through Mr. J. A. Macdonell, M.P., from Mr. George H. Chatfield, of Pleasant Home, Manitoba, with regard to the conditions of the Galicians at that place. Will you at once instruct one of your officers to proceed to the homes of those people and render what assistance is necessary. Mr. Chatfield says $100 would cover what is required now, and if you think proper you can extend relief to that amount."[24] Commissioner McCreary directed Cyril Genik to proceed to Pleasant Home and also informed George T. Zeron, a businessman at Pleasant Home who also acted as a Land Guide, that ". . . You are authorized to honor any orders for flour which may be given by Mr. Genik, at a price to be agreed on between you. . . ."[25] Genik visited Pleasant Home on March 30 and April 1, 1898, and on his return to Winnipeg he reported to the Commissioner of Immigration concerning the condition of the settlers:

> By your order I went on 29th of March as far as Stonewall and the 30th of March I went to Pleasant Home where Galician Colony is found. There are eighteen settlers which I saw all on the 31st March and 1st April. All the settlers are getting on very well and have enough food. All the houses are ready except one man's who came late in fall and he has only logs ready for the house. There are eleven cows and two horses on that colony. Three families had not enough flour so I gave them orders for eight sacks. The Engineer who now re-surveyed land gave four Galician men thirteen days of work. . . .[26]

Genik also met Mr. Chatfield, who explained that the purpose of his

23. Dest./467064, March 19, 1898: James A. Smart, Ottawa, to J. A. Macdonell, House of Commons, Ottawa. Letter referring to personal conversation with Macdonell concerning the situation in Pleasant Home.

24. Dest./467064, March 19, 1898: James A. Smart, Ottawa, to W. F. McCreary, Winnipeg.

25. Dest./56324, March 26, 1898: W. F. McCreary, Winnipeg, to George T. Zeron, Pleasant Home.

26. Dest./56324, April 2, 1898: C. Genik, Winnipeg, to W. F. McCreary, Winnipeg.

writing a letter to the Member of Parliament was not to ask for relief for Galician settlers but to request that the Government assist them in finding some occupation for the heads of families so as to enable them to earn the money necessary for the support of their families during the winter and spring. Commissioner McCreary approved this suggestion and wrote a letter to George Zeron in Pleasant Home, instructing him to arrange for some employment for these settlers:

I beg to inform you that it is desired to give employment for the Galician immigrants residing near Pleasant Home, by clearing the standing timber and underbrush from part of the road allowance by cutting a road twenty-five feet wide, between Townships 17-2, and 17-3, for four miles north; thence to be taken east between Sections 19 and 30, through Township 17-3, and west through Township 17-2, between Sections 24 and 25.

I will pay these people $120, allowing them 75 cents a day, so that, estimating the number who require work at fifteen, it would give each man about ten days' employment.

This money will be paid by supplying provisions and seed grain, some of which has already been advanced them.

An Interpreter will be sent out to supervise their work, and see that it is faithfully done, and full value given to the Government for the expenditure, and you will be allowed $5 for your services in shewing him the directions in which, as above indicated, the road should be cut.[277]

The Provincial authorities also promised to expend an equal amount of money on this project to give similar employment to the new settlers of Pleasant Home. Thus the initial difficulties that faced the settlers of Pleasant Home during their first winter and spring in Canada were overcome.

277. Dest./58028, April 15, 1898: W. F. McCreary, Winnipeg, to George T. Zeron, Pleasant Home.

Chapter Eight

STRATHCLAIR AND SHOAL LAKE

I

THE COMMISSIONER of Immigration in Winnipeg and the Superintendent of Immigration in Ottawa were very much concerned about the problem of providing homesteads for the Ukrainian settlers who were expected to arrive in the spring of 1899. Mr. Pedley entrusted C. W. Speers, the General Colonization Agent in Winnipeg, with the task of exploring regions suitable for the establishment of new colonies and of reporting his findings back to Ottawa. Groups of immigrants had arrived already in February, and they began to arrive in greater numbers in April, a fact which caused great concern to Commissioner McCreary. When one group arrived in Winnipeg in February unannounced, McCreary wired the Superintendent of Immigration in Ottawa to ask how settlers were able to come without warning: "Thirty two Galicians arrived today. No advice whatsoever. These people coming, and no place to put them. How is this?"[1]

On April 5, the High Commissioner for Canada in London cabled that the Hamburg-America steamer *Armenia* had sailed from Hamburg carrying 353 adult Ukrainian immigrants and 194 children.[2] A few days later the S.S. *Palatia* also sailed from Hamburg with 398 adults and 171 children aboard.[3] Superintendent Pedley wired Speers in Winnipeg, advising him to consult Commissioner McCreary about finding suitable

[1]5. Gal./75732, Telegram, February 27, 1899: W. F. McCreary, Commissioner of Immigration, Winnipeg, to Frank Pedley, Superintendent of Immigration, Ottawa.

[2]5. Gal., Cable, April 5, 1899: The High Commissioner for Canada, London, to the Department of the Interior, Ottawa.

[3]5. Gal./79759, Cable, April 19, 1899: The High Commissioner for Canada, London, to the Department of the Interior, Ottawa.

locations for these immigrants. Speers followed the Superintendent's instructions and then reported to Ottawa, April 4, 1899, with recommendations about new locations for the settlers who were arriving:

In complyance with your telegram to consult with Mr. McCreary, concerning the distribution of the Galician people arriving this year, I beg to say, I have talked the matter over with him to-day, he is also of the opinion that in Northern Alberta, namely the Edmonton District and at Stuartburn and Pleasant Home colonies, there are a sufficient number there at present and it would be unwise to settle these colonies with any more Galicians. The colonies that have already been established would be supplemented by 100 families in Beaver Hill district west of Yorkton, 100 families at Saltcoats, 50 families at the Sliding Hills, north of Yorkton, on the east side of Lake Dauphin. There are some new locations where colonies can be founded, these will be the districts marked out on the map submitted to you in my recent report on Lake Dauphin and can be easily reached in Shole Lake or Russel, on the north Western R. There is a very fine track of land on the west side of the north branch of the Saskatchewan River near Windgard about 15 miles from Duck Lake, on Prince Albert R. There is also several Townships of good land about 40 miles west of Yorkton directly south of the Beaver Hills. The last named districts offer excellent facilities for any class of settlers and possibly it had better be reserved for future colonizations and other european classes.

Mr. Smart intimated last fall that he thought possibly he might establish a colony of Galicians on the west side of Moose Mountain, now occupied or reserved for the Indians. I have not heard whether he has decided to do this or not. I am persuaded that the Galician people coming this year can be placed in the manner above suggested, the great difficulty, we have encountered has been the fact that those coming have relatives formally settled in different places and it is their wish to join their friends and relatives. They have been very persistent regardless of their own welfare. I think strong measures will have to be applied to place these people where it is the desire of Department that they should go irrespective of their own wishes in the matter.

I hope to look over the districts I have drawn your attention to at the earliest date. I will report to you the advantages of interest and its adaptability for settlement.[4]

After repeated consultation, McCreary and Speers came to the conclusion that the Shoal Lake and Strathclair district would be the most suitable to start a new Ukrainian colony. Speers left without delay for this district to make a personal inspection, and on April 21, 1899, he reported his findings to the Superintendent of Immigration in Ottawa:

I have the honor to submit to you a report of inspection made by me of the lands situated in Township 19, ranges 21–22, also Townships 20–21 in range 24 and Township 21 range 25.

[4]5. Gal./78874, April 4, 1899: C. W. Speers, General Colonization Agent, Winnipeg, to Frank Pedley, Ottawa.

As doubtless you will observe, these are the lands referred to in my former report and marked on a map submitted to you a short time ago. In consultation with W. F. McCreary we decided that these lands would be specially adapted for the colonization of Galician people during the present season, owing to the fact that it was your desire to have these people distributed as much as possible. Township 19 range 21, situated about 16 miles north from Strathclair station on the M. & N.W. Railway, just at the base of the Riding Mountains. (I omitted to mention that I received from the Minnedosa land office, the plan of each Township with the lands marked open for entry.) Referring to the above township—the soil is fairly good quality but inclined to be a little light in the Saskatchewan valley as that river runs through the township. On either side of the valley there are a number of small lakes and the district, generally speaking, is well watered. The country is high and rolling and possesses a good supply of hay around the ponds and lakes; these lands have been timbered, but most of it has been destroyed by fire; there is plenty dry timber for fuel and light building; the wood is principally poplar with a little spruce scattered and an occasional small tamarack swamp; this land is well adapted for Galician settlers; it is well watered; besides the Saskatchewan there are two good creeks and many lakes that abound with fish. Many places and openings have been cleared by fire and most places can be easily cleared.

Township 19-22 is very similar to 19-21 a high rolling piece of country; fires have destroyed the most of the timber; there is considerable green timber, but this is light; many good natural hay meadows; plenty of fuel, quantities of fish can be obtained in many lakes, a good stock country, most of the land with a little work will make good comfortable homes for the Galician people. Judging from the fact that some fifty Galician people have squatted on the permanent timber reservation on the north side of the Riding Mountains, in the Dauphin district, I may say that these townships will be a very similar class of land directly south on the southern slope of the Mountain and I am persuaded the Galician people would be suited with this class of land. I may say I drove north within a few miles of Lake Audy. Strathclair would be the nearest point to reach these two townships. I arranged with one Robert Foster who owns a large building within 200 ft of the Railway track, that it can be secured if required, also a small building close by that can be used for cooking in; teams can be secured for transportation at reasonable prices, about $3.00 per day and this large building 30 × 60 with the small cooking building can be secured for about $15.00 per month if we require it.

Townships 20 & 21, range 24, 21 in range 25, 22 in range 26 north of Shoal Lake—I may say that I secured a great deal of valuable information from John Menzies, Henry Roberts and others who have been operating in these townships. These lands have been timbered but, are pretty well burnt off and I might say that I noticed while driving along the base of the mountain as far west as Oakburn that the country presented a very similar appearance. It is a high rolling country and would make better grain land than range 21 and 22. It is well watered with lakes and creeks, some fish are obtained in these lakes; there is plenty of natural hay meadows for settlers; there is little spruce and this is confined to the north side of the township. This is rather a desirable Township (referring to 19-23) and pronounced by many competent judges whom I have interviewed, better than many districts already taken up, being well adapted for mixed farming.

Township 19-24 all taken up but two homesteads. Township 20-21, Townships 20-22 in the permanent timber reservation—I beg to call your attention to the fact that the south portion of the two townships last mentioned are not much value for timber reserves. The timber originally was light, fire has destroyed it and it possesses some very good country for settlement. The choice timber is confined to the northern portion of these townships; the creeks have plenty of hay and an open country near them; there are several sections of open prairie on what is called "Squaw Creek".

Township 20 range 23—there is more or less timber in this township; the southeast portion possesses some open country. This township possesses similar advantages to the others before mentioned, for settlement.

Township 20 range 24—this township has been culled of any good timber it possessed; a good deal of standing dead timber, it possesses some small tamarack in the low land; is naturally well watered having a number of good sized lakes. There are a few homesteads taken up in the southeast part. There is not valuable timber for manufacturing purposes. There is not much open Prairie in this township.

Township 20 range 25 on the Birdtail river—mostly taken up.

Township 21 range 24 and Township 21 range 25—these townships are in the Dauphin district. There is a good deal of open country along the Birdtail river, high rolling country; timber mostly burnt off; some tamarack swamps; country is well watered and possesses some good grazing land. There are many good locations in these townships; the soil is good and they are well adapted for mixed farming.

Township 21 range 22, Township 22 range 22, Township 21 range 23 and 22 range 23. Referring more particularly to Township 21 in ranges 22 and 23—these townships are mostly open and it is very desirable land for settlement; they possess many good natural hay meadows and a good stock country. This country is not high rolling and rough, but has a nice undulating surface and should be a desirable piece of country for settlement. This district can be rapidly reached from Shoal Lake, a distance of 18 or 20 miles and a good road has been built right through to these townships. The same can be said of Strathclair, which possesses a good wagon road right up to this district. I interviewed Mr. Greenshaw at Shoal Lake, who is one of the proprietors of the skating rink and he thought satisfactory arrangements could be made that we could secure that building, if it was required. The roof, although not water proof altogether, might answer the purpose and is the only building available. I may say, that I drove south to examine the police barracks at the foot of Shoal Lake. There are two or three buildings that would do and would afford shelter if they are required. The large stable has collapsed, the other three buildings could be used in the event of a number of women and children being there for a prolonged period, although this would incur a drive of five miles from the railway in the wrong direction. I may intimate that satisfactory arrangements can be made, arrangements which I have pretty well talked over, and that the charges will be reasonable for transportation etc.

In reviewing these different districts eluded to, I beg to say that I think the country is well adapted for Galician colonization. It possesses a great many natural advantages, plenty of timber, plenty of hay, well watered, fish can be obtained and has most of the natural characteristics which these people admire. I think the permanent establishment of these people can be satisfactorily looked for in this district. I will submit you a map of this report with the districts marked to which I refer.

I drove from Shoal Lake south through the municipalities of Blanchard, Saskatchewan, and Hamiota to Rapid City. I beg to intimate that while there a special meeting of the town council was held and that I addressed the council on Immigration matters, as there is a great deal of excellent land in that vicinity that could be secured at a very low price. They passed some strong resolutions, formed themselves into a Board of Trade and Immigration and thanked me for the interest the department were taking in their district. I suggested that they submit to you in Ottawa the result of their adjourned meeting, which would be to-day.[5]

After his inspection of the district, Speers returned to Winnipeg, and taking the teacher Iwan Bodrug as interpreter, departed with four delegates selected by the prospective settlers for Shoal Lake and Strathclair. On May 3, 1899, he was able to report to Superintendent Pedley in Ottawa about the establishment of a new Ukrainian colony north of Shoal Lake and Strathclair:

I beg to submit a report of the trip made through the Riding Mountain District North of Shoal Lake and Strathclair, accompanying four Galician Delegates.

The Districts inspected were the Townships referred to in my former report, being—19-22, 19-23, 20-23 and 20-24.

Referring to the Western portion of Township 19-21 and 19-22, this land is high rolling, and well covered with burnt timber. On the Eastern side of the first Township, along the Saskatchewan River, the Galicians have decided to take up the available homesteads.

They are also much impressed with Townships 19-23 and 20-23, where a large colony can be placed.

We experienced some difficulty in getting through these Townships, owing to the quantity of fallen timber and the high water in the creeks.

I herewith submit the following report taken from the delegates who accompanied me, giving their impression of the District:

Strathclair, April 29th, 1899.

To
C. W. Speers, Esq.
General Colonization Agent

Dear Sir,

We the undersigned Galicians, having accompanied you on a trip of inspection through the country north of Strathclair and Shoal Lake, at the base of the Riding Mountains, beg to submit this report of the different districts.

[5]8. Rpts./80323, April 21, 1899: C. W. Speers, Brandon, to Frank Pedley, Ottawa.

We find the East side of Township 19, Range 21, along the valley of the Saskatchewan River, a very desirable District and some fine land with nice openings, good hay, good soil, and plenty of timber. We were also shown a fine large lake. About fifteen families of our people will go in and settle there. We are much pleased with this place on both sides of the river.

Passing through the townships on the West side, we find some very good land, but it is all standing dry timber that has been killed by fire. No doubt many good farms can be found in this township pertaining to Township 19 Range 21.

The same can be said of Township 19 Range 22. There are many small lakes; the land is high rolling; we passed right through these townships and found the road very rough with heavy dead trees lying across the trail. For several miles we were obliged to chop our way through and clear the road of windfalls. It will take a good deal of work to clear these farms, although in many places this work can be done easily on account of fire. These will make good farms when cleared up.

The soil is black and sandy loam; there are a few evergreen trees scattered here and there growing.

Township 20, Range 23 and Township 19 Range 23. We find some splendid land in these townships, rolling, but not so high as the others referred to. There are some nice creeks running here and some good natural hay meadows also some very nice lakes. The soil is good, a black loam and clay sub-soil. These should make splendid farms for our people. The timber is pretty well burnt off and in many places a light scrub is growing, but this land is good, well watered and plenty of hay. Where we camped all night in Township 20 Range 23, we were well pleased with the land north of Shoal Lake. It should suit the Galician people well and we think our people would prosper here. Timber for building is destroyed by fire, but this can be got close in the other townships.

Generally speaking we are well pleased with the districts we have seen and think a large colony of our people can be placed here.

Yours respectfully

(Signed) IWAN BUKATCZUK
FEDIR BURTNYK
SYLVESTER WASYLYNIUK
WASYL KOSTYNIUK

Witness: JOHN BODRUG, Acting Interpreter.

I beg to say that this district is by no means confined to a small area, as there are several townships to the north that I think can be successfully colonized with these people and they are not far from a railroad and in a good position to secure employment being close to the Manitoba and Northwestern Railway and also close to any work that may be going on in the Riding Mountains, taking out timber during the winter months.

Observing when going through the country that time and fire had obliterated every landmark, some difficulty may be experienced in getting the proper lines started. In view of this fact I wrote Thos. McNutt of Saltcoats and we have been able to secure his services.

Returning with the delegates I accompanied them to Selkirk, where they used their influence, and have induced some forty five families to go to the new district. Those will be supplemented by about twelve additional Galician families, which would make in all about sixty families.

I have arranged for suitable buildings at Strathclair, and will accompany these people to the district and see that the work is well started and I will leave competent men to carry on the settlement.

I have been in consultation with W. F. McCreary in connection with this work and am acting in conjunction with him. I am hopeful that we will be successful and get a good colony of these people placed in there.[6]

II

About eighty families moved, in the first days of May, 1899, to Strathclair in preparation for the settlement of the selected homesteads. But a dreadful tragedy struck the families even before they reached Strathclair. This was the disease of scarlet fever, and its effects are vividly described by Speers in the report he sent Frank Pedley in Ottawa on May 11, 1899:

I am obliged to drop you a letter, owing to the fact that my work has been greatly interrupted here colonizing about 80 Galician families owing to a very malignant type of Scarlet Fever that has developed among them. I had 4 coaches from Selkirk for here and two more from Winnipeg the Disease was among the Winnipeg people. I loaded the Selkirk people myself before reaching Portage la Prairie one Child had Died, and another two hours later 2 dying in transit before reaching Minnedosa yesterday. I burried 4 in one Waggon, had a resident Clergy Man officiate and all respect shown bereaved. Today two more have died, making a total of 6 dead and 4 more are affected. I was obliged to establish an isolated building for quarantine a tent for an Hospital a small building for a morgue and have succeeded in keeping in isolation anything dangerous. Dr. Patterson of the Provincial Board of Health arrived today and says I have done all that could be done and have kept in Separate Building all that are all right. I have been obliged to go into all the details myself and have really had a dreadful time but met every emergency in practical manner and Dr. Patterson was well pleased. It is my intention to report to you very fully on the matter and some investigation I am obliged to request from yourself or Mr. Smart. I had hoped to establish a good new Colony here which I will yet do, but these people were not fit to send from Winnipeg where this disease must have developed as the fact will show with so much mortality. The men I have are all new and I have had an experience. I buried 4 in one Waggon yesterday and could scarcely restrain the Bereaved Mothers who followed the Waggons kissing the Crude Coffins and had to be turned back. I have been in communication with Mr. McCreary by wire and letter but have every detail thoroughly attended to in such a manner that the Dept. are well protected and there will be no reflection.

There is a sentiment against the Galician people and I endeavoured to dispel this but when unfortunately with their advent comes some contagion

[6]5. Gal./81369, May 3, 1899: C. W. Speers, Winnipeg, to Frank Pedley, Ottawa.

that endangers the community the situation becomes very unpleasant I am not easily intimidated and can meet and overcome anything reasonable and have done even this time in the interest of the Dept. but I feel bad to think that these people were put on me at the inception of a new colony in that condition and fully intend to submit to a very full report as soon as I get time. I have had no rest for 3 days and have had many unpleasant things to do. I started 14 Waggon Loads, the men walking to the Colony today with T. McNutt & interpreter. I will write in a few days.[7]

Commissioner McCreary wrote to Ottawa, informing Mr. Smart of the unfortunate outbreak of the epidemic and the resulting deaths of a number of children among the settlers destined for the Strathclair area:

As the matter may probably get into the newspaper by sensational despatches, I beg to advise you that we shipped about four hundred Galicians to Strathclair last Tuesday morning. From some cause or other measles seems to have broken out among them, and two children died on the way up, and two since they arrived there.

I wired Mr. Speers to at once call the services of a physician to establish a proper quarantine, which he has done.

I have to-day sent out Dr. Patterson for two days at $20 per day and expenses in order that he may assist in stamping out the disease as quickly as possible.

Dr. Corbett will likely write you on the subject, and, as far as I can learn from him, he visited the Dufferin School on Monday and found no disease there at that time, although I understand two of the children were slightly ill. Mr. Genik and Mr. Wedelbo who were looking after the shipping of these people, said they saw no illness, although they were there till eleven o'clock on Monday night. Unfortunately, although the Railway Company promised the cars to be there not later than six or seven o'clock and although the children and women were waiting upon the grass alongside the track for the cars, they did not come until well on into the night, so that the children likely contracted cold from this exposure—hence the above results.

I thought it better to advise you of this.[8]

The Deputy Minister, on reading of the tragedy, fully approved of the arrangements made by Commissioner McCreary: "I was very sorry indeed to receive your letter of the 11th instant advising me of the breaking out of measles among the party of Galicians sent to Strathclair, and I approve your action in sending out Dr. Patterson."[9] Dr. James Patterson of the Provincial Board of Health in Winnipeg visited the

[7]5. Gal./81890, May 11, 1899: C. W. Speers, Strathclair, to Frank Pedley, Ottawa.

[8]5. Gal./81959, May 11, 1899: W. F. McCreary, Winnipeg, to James A. Smart, Ottawa.

[9]5. Gal./81959, Telegram, May 15, 1899: James A. Smart, Ottawa, to W. F. McCreary, Winnipeg.

stricken colony and reported back to Commissioner McCreary about the condition of those who had been stricken:

In compliance with your request I visited Strathclair on Thursday last the 11th inst. re an outbreak of disease amongst Galician Immigrants forwarded from Dufferin School building in Winnipeg. When I reached there at 3 P.M. I found that six children had died since they left Winnipeg on the morning of Tuesday the 9th inst. Besides these there are four lying ill of an eruptive disease which I consider the Scarlet Fever, from the character of the eruption the condition of the throats. The enlarged glands about the angles of the jaws. The eruption upon the skin was modified by the exposure during cold weather, it had a natural appearance resembling Measles, except on the portions of the body warmly clothed.

The sudden and excessive mortality points to Scarlet Fever rather than Measles, of the six who died, so virulent was the poison that the majority of them died before the eruption made its appearance. This is common in Scarlet Fever, but rare in Measles. Upon my return to Winnipeg on the morning of the 12th inst. I found awaiting me an urgent call to Mr. Ed. Tumbuls boy in Fort Rouge who had taken suddenly ill that afternoon, next morning he had died at 9 A.M. This was exactly a similar case, no eruption appeared upon him, but there was no other reasonable cause of death, than toxic poisoning from some undeveloped eruptive disease, such is the opinion of myself and those who were in Consultations with me on the case, and this is the only explanation why these children were not known to be ill before leaving Winnipeg, by the parents, by the Caretaker of the building, by the Dom. Medical Attendant at the building. Nor of those in charge of these Immigrants at the beginning of their journey on the train. I am perfectly certain no charge can lie against any official of carelessness or neglect of duty. It was an unfortunate coincidence that it should happen when these people were trying to move out to their locations, I have no doubt but that the exposure unavoidable upon the trip added to the gravity of the case.

At Strathclair I found Mr. Speers in charge with Dr. Sinclair as Medical attendant both were doing everything in their power for the sick and to make all comfortable. The majority of the party had gone to their Homesteads some twenty miles North. Those remaining and well, were housed in a large warm comfortable barn with abundance of hay for bedding. I ordered Mr. Speers to forward these as soon as possible to their destinations to lessen the risk of the disease spreading amongst themselves and also perhaps to the citizens of the village.

The four sick with the other members of their families were housed in a roomy tent with a cook stove in it, in a well isolated position, and were wonderfully comfortable during such cold gloomy weather. Mr. Speers is giving them abundance of milk and a sufficiency of meat for soup and beef tea. These will have to remain until convalescent. The citizens at Strathclair were not the least reasonably alarmed, and were acting in a calm and sensible way. Every one was sorry for and sympathized with these unfortunate families. Every Official was doing his duty to the best of his ability. No amt of prescience could have foretold what happened it is simply one of those occurences which may always be looked for during such a large flow of foreign Immigration.[10]

Dr. Sinclair, the Medical Officer of the Municipality of Strathclair, was in charge of the patients and persons quarantined at Strathclair, but Commissioner McCreary thought it advisable to send an additional doctor, S. D. Cameron of Winnipeg, to assist Dr. Sinclair and report to the Commissioner on the situation. On May 26, Dr. Cameron wired his findings to the Commissioner:

Went to colony last night—inspected camp this morning—found 3 or 4 cases of undoubted scarlet fever and several cases of measles—have established an efficient quarantine. 3 deaths at colony last night and one here in Strathclair—two cases of scarlet fever here—people wanting to go to Yorkton. Have not been out to the settlement as I hurried in to make report. Mr. Reed is provisioning and attending to all their wants. We need 3 or 4 tents twelve by fourteen as we have stopped the settlement of the people. This I think necessary owing to the death and the agitation of the town and surrounding country. Please instruct as to the further movements and if possible send tents on tomorrow train. Mr. MacNutt is anxious to leave—he and Mr. Reed are invaluable assistants. You might instruct as to the desirability of his leaving for few days. Can manage with the assistance from him and interpreter. The camp is situated 26 miles north west from Strathclair but roads are exceedingly bad. Mr. Reed has warehouses for storing of necessary commodities for people's use and is selling to those able to pay. While acting on my instructions he looks after the poor. Everything much the same as commended itself to you in similar cases before. Will go back tomorrow morning and send you wire each day for a few days regarding situation. If this is satisfactory please wire further instructions.[11]

Commissioner McCreary replied the same day by wire, giving Cameron instructions and informing him of the arrangements that he had made:

Tents go up tomorrow. Establish pest tents considerable distance from suspect tents, and latter considerable distance from healthy tents. Put reliable patrol men on night and day between these tents. Municipality may nominate these men if desired, we will pay. See that sufficient food is provided for people in pest tents and table and water barrels at some distance where supplies can be left without any communication whatever. One cooking stove and some utensils had better be purchased for each tent if necessary. Also meat, milk, blankets or other supplies. Speers will likely be up tomorrow. Tell him to wire when he arrives. Tell McNutt I will want his services for three or four months, but if absolutely essential he might go home for a few days. Will not send people for Yorkton in present

10. Gal./82789, May 15, 1899: Dr. James Patterson, Provincial Board of Health, Winnipeg, to W. F. McCreary, Winnipeg.

11. Gal./83107, Telegram, May 26, 1899: Dr. S. D. Cameron, Strathclair, to W. F. McCreary, Winnipeg.

condition. If McNutt thinks he could handle a fresh crowd of people from Shoal Lake without fear of contagion will send them up next week. Cheque went to you today to Strathclair.[125]

Dr. Cameron purchased several cows for the camp, so as to have a supply of fresh milk for the sick. He also kept a strict quarantine around the isolation tents, quarantining even the teamsters in the camp until they were disinfected. Despite the strict measures taken, however, the epidemic persisted, and the mortality rate among the children continued to be exceedingly high. C. W. Speers submitted a detailed description of the situation to Frank Pedley in Ottawa on May 31, 1899. At the same time he expressed the hope that the climax had been passed, so that the original plans of establishing a large Ukrainian colony south of the Riding Mountains might at last become reality:

I have the honour to submit to you a report of a trip made to the new colony of Galicians being settled North of Shoal Lake and Strathclair. As you are aware, a contagious disease had developed among them at the time of their advent to that District, particulars of which I submitted to you in my last report. I deplore the fact that this epidemic occured from the fact that I was very hopeful that a large and progressive colony of these people would have been established there with very little trouble and in a practical economically manner. However, under circumstances, the work of colonization has been progressing, and in a district where land marks of former surveys were completely obliterated, with a heavy undergrowth of scrub in many places and deep bodies of water on Saturday last all were located except some twenty seven families out of nearly one hundred families. I may say these would have been located last Saturday had the work of colonization not been intercepted through the establishment of a quarantine at the colony, quite necessary, owing to the great percentage of mortality. Up till last Sunday night twenty children have succumbed to this fatal disease, a malignant type of scarlet fever, ranging in ages from seven years to infants of one year. These people are all at the Colony about eighteen miles North of Shoal Lake, and I may say that I am very glad that they are away from any centre of habitation or any hamlet. There has been a strong sentiment manifested against the Galician people and this feeling became more intense with the introduction of any contagion or infection with their advent. A great deal of it has been unwarranted and unjustifiable, people seemed to be affected with a sort of chronic cowardice claiming that quarantine regulations were not sufficiently rigid. However, it is a satisfaction to know that the contagion has been absolutely and solely confined to the immigrants and that we have not heard of one child belonging to any of the citizens being affected with this disease.

I beg to submit to you a letter from Dr. Sinclair:

Strathclair, May 26th, 1899.

125. Gal./83107, Telegram, May 26, 1899: W. F. McCreary, Winnipeg, to Dr. S. D. Cameron, Strathclair.

To
C. W. Speers, Esq.,
General Colonization Agent.

Sir,

In connection with the Galician Colony, and the epidemic existing among them at the various places of occupation it is a very important fact that the mortality rate the second day after their arrival was very high. That rate has been steadily diminished from that time. The fact that the children were most of them very young and had just completed a long and arduous journey had a great bearing upon the mortality; the difficulties too of keeping them nourished and warm during such a long trip contributed largely to the lack of resisting power to meet disease. The weather was the worst possible for these cases.

The quarantine was effected as efficiently as possible and in the earliest possible time, notwithstanding the fact that it was almost an impossible thing to keep the villagers out of the large barn, owing to their strong curiosity. There has not been one single case of the infection spreading to the local population.

It was extremely hard to get the mothers of children to carry out the simplest matters, their ways being much different from ours in method and cleanliness. I found in several cases that they required to be watched most closely to do what needed, and also in some cases where out of sentiment the mother tried to conceal their children from inspection. This required close scrutiny.

Thus far I may say that I have carried out the quarantine in the best manner possible, the proof of which is that the disease is confined to the immigrants, notwithstanding that the villagers had no other reason than cowardice for the extraordinary action taken by them in agitating a grievance against the officers responsible for the work.

I beg to say that every order by me under sanitary law has been carried out by yourself by promptness and despatch and I say with the greatest assurance that the best has been done under existing circumstances. I have visited the camps, and they could not be better located. There is an abundance of good dry fuel and in close proximity to a large lake of good water, the natural advantages being well adapted to quarantine regulations. The condition of things is improving, less mortality can be looked for. The weather is more propitious for treating this epidemic. The situation surely was grave enough at your advent and for a few subsequent days.

Yours etc.

(Signed) D. R. SINCLAIR, M.D.

Permit me to say that from the time of the arrival of the train at Strathclair, carrying these people Dr. Sinclair was consulted and the people put in isolation in separate buildings and that the sanitary conditions were under his control, being Health Officer of the Municipality of Strathclair and I am persuaded he carried out carefully and efficiently every function of his office as well as the conditions would permit which can be corroborated by Dr. Patterson, President of the Board of Health, Winnipeg. This is the

Dr. Sinclair who wrote the letter to the Board of Health, Winnipeg, complaining that these people arrived in bad condition; that the cars were crowded; that they were allowed to leave Winnipeg with contagious disease. To show that the cars were not crowded and that they were comfortable, good colonist cars, the four coaches contained the following number of souls namely: There was fifty in one, 56 in another, 41 in another and 50 in another, making a total of 197 souls including children in four coaches. You can readily see that we could put in many more and still not have these cars crowded.

Dr. Sinclair has given me the following letter:

C. W. Speers, Esq.
General Colonization Agent,

Sir,

The strong tendency exhibited of concealing the children from inspection has very materially changed my mind since writing the Provincial Board of Health concerning the Galician people.

In respect of the bad effects of crowding and permitting them to leave Winnipeg in the condition they were, I beg to say that suddenly are they taken down, that the child that died to-day was playing two hours before it died.

Yours, etc.

(Signed) D. R. SINCLAIR, M.D.

I found considerable excitement prevailing among the Indians in the Valley, as about fifteen Galician families have settled in the valley North of the Indian Reserve. This is largely owing to the agitation among the whites. Being pressed by the sentiments of the Strathclair people to move the Galicians from the town, I was obliged to use Campbell's barn for a short time, when I received the following letter from Mrs. Scott in charge of the premises:

Elphinstone, May 27, 1899.

C. W. Speers,
General Colonization Agent,

Sir,

I am obliged to request you to move the Galicians at present housed in the buildings on Section 24, Township 18, Range 21. I insist on their being taken away at once. They have destroyed a quantity of hay and consume a great deal of wood, besides I fear my children owing to the outbreak of disease among them.

Kindly give this matter your attention at once.

Yours, etc.

(Signed) MRS. W. SCOTT.

I beg to say that on my arrival at Elphinstone the Indians had a counsel and discussed the advisability of closing the trail on both sides of the river. I had Dr. Sinclair inspect these colonists and sent the following certificate with the interpreter or second Chief to the Council:

To Whom It May Concern,

This is to certify that I have inspected the Galicians in this neighbourhood and that I find them free from any contagious or infectious disease.

(Signed) D. R. SINCLAIR, M.D.

(Copy given to the Okenisis Indians.)

This certificate somewhat allayed the anxiety of the people and on Sunday I secured teams and moved these people out of the barn, sending them up to some old lumber camps. Proceeding from there I drove to Menzies Colony, meeting Thos McNutt in charge of the work, and after arranging matters with Dr. Cameron, I left the following instructions with Mr. McNutt:

Menzies, May 28, 1899.

Thos. McNutt, Esq.,

Sir,

Dr. Cameron has agreed to give you any number of the men to complete location, as you intimate that you have about 27 men to locate. I would request you to proceed with the location of these 27 families at once, as the Dr. has agreed to discharge them from time to time and possibly by the end of the present week we will be in a position to get some of the tents now occupied after they have been disinfected to hold the incoming people. Mr. John Menzies will accompany you to-morrow and select a suitable location for a new camp in one of the adjacent townships at a central point which you may decide will best serve your purpose to colonize those that may come. Mr. Menzies will remain with you while you may require him to assist in finishing the present locations required and to run any lines that may be of service to you that would expedite matters when the new people arrive. You had better have the physician in charge of the quarantine retain the services of Neogrege the Interpreter, and keep John [Bodrug] for your own work as he will have some knowledge of the comforts and your work by this time.

I beg again to call your attention to the fact that more or less duplicity will be practiced by the Galicians to obtain assistance. Be very positive that the case is deserving and relief necessary before giving anything. I have instructed W. H. Reed to give nothing of any kind except on your order. Be good enough to keep a check on this thing as well as you can in the interest of the department. Do not permit your work to be intercepted in the future. Of course you are quite justified pertaining to the present quarantine, as Mr. McCreary had sent up Dr. Cameron to more thoroughly establish quarantine regulations.

I am anxious for you to remain this week to close up the present work, when you can go home Saturday night to Saltcoats, returning again at once. Leave Mr. John Menzies any particulars during the day of your absence. When you have decided on location of camp and outline the prospects of settlement for incoming people from the point you have chosen. We will move these people as soon as the conditions will warrant.

I am, etc.

(Signed) C. W. SPEERS.

In conclusion I beg to state we never had a better outlook for the formation of a large colony, but this unfortunate disease developed, a thing we could in no way control. It has incurred an endless lot of worry and trouble and doubtless will incur considerable expense but we had to meet it as best we could and every dollar expenditure incurred will be necessary and judiciously laid out.

Twenty on Sunday night last had succumbed to the disease. This is a high percentage of mortality. I am hopeful that we are through the worst and a brighter phase of the situation will soon break in. I have discussed the matter with Mr. McCreary today, and we are endeavouring to adopt the most practical methods to wipe out this disease and settle these people.

I beg to draw your attention to this fact, because you might come to the conclusion that there was a great deal of expenditure in connection with these people. I was endeavouring at the onset, to locate these people very cheaply, and perhaps a little expenditure at that time would have been judicious and possibly might have curtailed the amount of mortality. I have been forced to move these people when the weather was unfavourable, sentiment of the local population has been worse to grapple with than sickness. I have observed a reticence all through that I claim was necessary, confining our operations solely to the Commissioner. The little outbreak of disease will pass away, the sentiment of the people will change and I am confident we can look to hopeful results and have a happy, progressive and industrious colony of Galician people located in that district, when all the little difficulties pertaining to their early colonization have been forgotten. Mr. McCreary has sent about fifty families. These we will commence to locate from the new camp selected by McNutt. He has also sent another large colony to Fish Creek and some other places. I will be obliged to return again to Shoal Lake for a day or two, when I hope to be able to go to Rosthern on the Saskatchewan road and other points where large numbers have been placed and submit to you a report or review of colonization work with the prospect and progress of these people.

I am, etc.

(Signed) C. W. SPEERS.[13]

A better description of the situation at Strathclair and Shoal Lake could hardly have been given. Despite all the adversities encountered, Speers proceeded with the original plan—the establishment of a new Ukrainian colony south of the Riding Mountains in a region which he thought had great possibilities and plenty of good land for expansion. His expectations proved to be correct. The colony—started with such difficulties and heartbreaking sacrifices—soon expanded over many townships and ranges and in numbers of settlers and prosperity did not lag behind the older colonies in the Stuartburn and Dauphin regions.

[13]5. Gal./83397, May 31, 1899: C. W. Speers, Winnipeg, to Frank Pedley, Ottawa.

III

With the advent of warmer weather and with expanded medical care, the scarlet fever epidemic which took so many victims seemed to be on the wane. Only two weeks after the peak Speers was able to send to Ottawa a more hopeful and cheerful report about the health of the new settlement:

I beg to submit to you a brief report of the trip from which I have just returned from the new Colony of Galicians, being placed North of Strathclair and Shoal Lake. There are about 160 families settled in this new District, and over one hundred families are at present located on the homesteads. They are already showing evidence of prosperity, many of them have from one half acre to an acre and a half cultivated, the garden seeds planted, potatoes put in and in some instances I observed barley has been sown and was well advanced for the time. They have purchased a great many cows, have built temporary shanties that are comfortable and generally speaking are manifesting a great individual interest in their own welfare. They are highly pleased with the District. Having decided to move the central camp of location about seven miles further West, we find the country there more open, more desirable and less scrub to contend with and the settlement of these people should be effected more readily. I drove from there a considerable distance North to Squaw Creek and I am persuaded that two hundred and fifty families in all of the Galicians can be placed in this District. The prospect for obtaining work in this locality should be very good, as they are close to the timber in the Riding Mountains, where for many years to come a great deal of work will be carried on in the winter months, and close to the North Western Ry. where many of these men will find employment. As you have observed by my former reports, we have had to contend with some contagious disease, the percentage of mortality has been higher than we have hitherto had in any colony ever placed in the West. It has been confined to children, and none of the residents were affected. The number of deaths to date have been about 26. Of course the conditions have been bad, the weather unusually rough, with almost incessant rains, and possibly a good deal of the above is due to exposure, which was impossible to avoid. We have had a thoroughly established quarantine at the camp, Mr. McCreary having up Dr. Cameron who is taking charge of this work and I think is succeeding well in stamping out the disease. At first he intercepted colonization work, but he agreed when I consulted him to give Thos. McNutt any number of the Galicians he might require to assist him in running lines and effecting settlement. The work has been pressed with all possible vigour without any interruption. I hope by the middle of the week that about all will be settled. I beg to say that Dr. Cameron has been very practical, discarding a good deal of professional humbug, and that under all conditions this work is being done, done cheaply and rapidly. I have looked into every detail personally, transportation, instructions for interpreters, improvements of the road, purchase of supplies and have put McNutt in charge of the work, handing over the buildings we used at Strathclair, where the sentiment of the people seemed against the Galicians, have notified Dr. Sinclair in writing no professional service will be required in future, as I considered Dr. Cameron could look after the health of the people and gave Dr. Sinclair the following letter—

. . . It will not be necessary to visit the valley nor Menzies camp in future, as Dr. Cameron will look after the quarantine.

I therefore beg to notify you that any further professional services will not be required by you for the Department of Interior at present unless advised by W. F. McCreary, Winnipeg, or your obedient servant. . . .

I beg to intimate that we had rumours of diphtheria at Strathclair, and smallpox at the colony, but there was nothing to justify this opinion developed and I think all our difficulties will end in the near future. It is possibly unwise to be too candid in confessing the conditions in health, because, happily, these things are not very serious and the public are ready to grasp every word and exaggerate every statement. Of course, owing to sicknesses the establishment of quarantine, progress of the work has been retarded to some extent, and possibly for years we have not had such heavy rain and so much surface water to deal with. I have driven my buggy through miles of water in the valley; small bridges have been carried away, transportation has been difficult, the teams have suffered through mud and heavy roads, in fact, every man in the employ of the Department has earned his money hard, and with a good deal of exposure.

I left the following letter with Thos. McNutt:—

Shoal Lake, June 7, 1899.

Thos McNutt, Esq.
Shoal Lake,

Sir,

I think it advisable to proceed at once to the new Camp, and distribute the people from there to their locations as soon as possible. The work is pretty well completed at the Old Camp, where quarantine regulations are established, and the few remaining to be located can remain for a time, pending their final discharge by the physician in charge. Yesterday I found the tents at the New Camp too close together, and the weather being extremely wet with heavy rains the people are as comfortable as I desire to see them.

Dr. Cameron has gone today to look at a few cases I observed yesterday. I will therefore advise you to take John Bodrug and your own tent and instruments and confine your operations to the new camp and get the people out as quickly as possible. I am anxious to put eighty or one hundred families in addition to those you have already in that district at as early a date as you can possibly receive them. I have arranged with John Menzies for a stove, which had better be taken over at once. Doubtless Dr. Cameron will complete satisfactory arrangements pertaining to any that may require his attention.

Be kind enough to retain all your township plans, and keep your list completed, showing the location and name of each Galician settler. This will avert difficulties we had to contend with in former colonies.

Impress the interpreter with the necessity of establishing in the minds of Galicians who have located the necessity of securing their Interim Receipt and paying the ten dollars into the land office to secure their places, provision for which will be made in the near future.

I am, etc.

(Signed) C. W. Speers

I beg to say in conclusion, that I left instructions with the interpreter [John Bodrug] as to his duty to look well after the people. Owing to this large colony being placed in a new district, owing to the development of infectious disease and the establishment of quarantine with the worst kind of weather prevailing, I think in a short time I can report the disease has been stamped out and that the people are all settled with a good prospect for their future.

According to Mr. McCreary's report yesterday, the people arriving on the last two special trains have signified their intention of going to other districts and supplementing former colonies. Of course, some of these we may be able to secure.

My time has been pretty well confined with this Colony owing to the above mentioned fact, keeping down expense and colonization work going ahead. I will visit Fish Creek very soon, where Leon Roy is placing a number of Galician people near the old Colony established there last year.[14]

The progress of the new colonies was carefully watched by the Commissioner of Immigration in Winnipeg, by the General Colonization Agent—who constantly moved about and produced detailed reports to the Superintendent of Immigration in Ottawa—as well as by the various homestead inspectors, interpreters, and minor officials whom the Commissioner of Immigration or the Colonization Agent detailed to visit individual homesteads to report on the condition of the settlers, their progress, and any need to render assistance. As the immigration budget of the Department of the Interior was very limited, the officers were advised to use discretion in spending money. Nevertheless, where distress was found it was alleviated, even to the extent of purchasing cows to supply milk for destitute families. Speers visited the new Strathclair and Shoal Lake colony every few months from the date of its establishment in May, 1899, because the Department of the Interior was particularly anxious to keep informed about the condition of the settlers who had suffered such severe losses due to the scarlet fever epidemic. Returning from one of these routine visits during the

[14]5. Gal./83911, June 10, 1899: C. W. Speers, Winnipeg, to Frank Pedley, Ottawa.

first week of August, 1899, Speers provided this progress report for Ottawa:

I beg to submit a short report of a trip made to the Galician colony at Strathclair and Shoal Lake, from which place I have just returned and closed up for the time the work of colonization.

There will be about 200 Galician families settled in this district. The townships they occupy have been frequently referred to in my former reports. I do not consider there will be any more land available for homesteads in this district without encroaching on the permanent timber reservation. I have drawn the attention of the Deputy Minister to some lands within the limits of that reserve that is not valuable for timber but evidently it is not the wish of the Department to open any of these lands, as I am in receipt of a letter to that effect. This new colony is very well established; plenty of work is obtainable, most of the men are doing work at present; plenty of fish about in the lakes and the women are making money picking wild fruit. As a colony, they have already purchased 125 cows and 18 head of horses. There are a few families yet to locate, but the men have gone out to work, preferring to defer their selection of land for a short time. I think these people will do well in this district and that this will be a very prosperous colony. The country is very suitable for them.[15]

The Superintendent of Immigration in Ottawa, in acknowledging Speers' report, stated that he was glad to learn that the colonists were doing well. When Speers visited the new colony again eight months after its establishment, in January, 1900, he provided an even more optimistic report for Mr. Pedley:[16]

I find these people are all in very good shape, have good comfortable houses, have made ample provisions for their stock, of which they have purchased a great many, and are taking hold with will to get themselves permanently established. They are all healthy—I did not observe one case of sickness in the town. They have made provisions for their own support and I did not see one individual case requiring assistance. As there are about 1,000 souls in these colonies and they had encountered a great deal of sickness this speaks for them.

Living close to the Manitoba and North Western railway they have been able to secure all the work they wanted through the fall and late in the winter at good wages and evidently made good use of their time. As they have improved their surroundings very much since they were settled there last June they have given perfect satisfaction to their employers. I submit to you the following letter from Roadmaster Waters:

Portage la Prairie Jan. 19/1900.

[15]8. Rpts./87890, August 3, 1899: C. W. Speers, Winnipeg, to Frank Pedley, Ottawa.

[16]8. Rpts./103918, January 24, 1900: C. W. Speers, Brandon, to Frank Pedley, Ottawa.

C. W. Speers Esq.

Sir,

During the year just closed, 1899, I have had under me and my foreman on the M. & N.W. railway about 500 Galicians and Doukhobor laborers employed doing repair and construction work. About 60% of the above were Galicians, the balance Doukhobors. The men have all been very satisfactory. The Galicians are first class men and have given perfect satisfaction. I retained them until my work closed on the 23rd day of December 1899. I have paid them from $1.40 to $1.75 per day—many of them have earned $30 per month for several months clear of their expenses.

We have paid 20% higher wages during 1899 than we ever did for the same class of work and could not get men enough and took all we could get. Some of these Galicians have been with me for the last three summers. They are improving all the time. I would not want better men.

I was obliged to hire 96 men through an employment agency in Winnipeg a few years ago—I put them to work and they were anything but satisfactory. Since getting the Galicians I have had no trouble.

(Signed) Robert Waters—Roadmaster.

You will observe by the foregoing letter that the Galician laborers are giving perfect satisfaction to their employers and that instead of congesting the labor market there has been ample work.

Speers also described various enterprises which gave employment to the Ukrainian settlers who were in need of money to start homesteading. He pointed to changes in the general attitude towards the new arrivals. Only a few months previously, when some fifteen Ukrainian families took up homesteads in the vicinity of the Okenisis Indian Reserve, there were signs of open hostility against the settlers, but gradually more friendly relations were established: "I also interviewed the chief of the Okenisis Indians and he says the Galician settlers are very industrious settlers and have done remarkably well and are acceptable neighbors. They are very guarded about putting out fire and are cleaning up the old dried timber that had fallen. This will lessen the possibility of fires doing any damage. He says that the Indians are friendly with them and are pleased that they came." Speers was informed about some cases where wages earned by these settlers were withheld by the employers: "There was also a number of cases where Galicians were employed and had not received their money in full. These cases I am looking into and expect to have adjusted." But in general, he was satisfied with the progress made by the settlers in the eight months: "In conclusion I beg to say that this large new colony is in a very progressive state and requires no assistance at present. They have done well and promise to be a very satisfactory colony."

The next visit that Speers undertook was in June, 1900, one year after the first families were located on homesteads to start the colony. Speers' report to Pedley indicated that the colony was prospering:

. . . [I was] accompanying about fifty families of Galicians who intended settling in that district, they being very anxious to go to the Shoal Lake district and join friends who had formerly settled there irrespective of the fact that every influence was used to induce them to settle in other districts. Previous to the advent of this late number I have placed about eight hundred people, Galicians, in that district. They settled along the base of the Riding Mountains from Township 19, Range 21 as far West as Township 21, Range 26 the settlement running in a North-Westerly direction and hugging the permanent reservation of timber lands stretching about twenty five miles.

This district is well adapted for these people, well supplied with wood, water and hay and an excellent soil. The country is high rolling. It is not far from a railway and work has been readily obtained and the requirements of these people during the past winter have been very little. I also think generally speaking that they are satisfactory settlers in the minds of people of other nationality in that district.

Doubtless you are aware that we are confined to a small area owing to the enormous amount of land contained in this timber reserve and the last camp I located was on section 16, Township 21, Range 25 and when locations are found for those already there I may say every available homestead will be occupied. I have called the attention of Mr. E. S. Stephenson, Crown Timber agent, to two townships on the extreme West of the Reservation being 24 and 25 in Range 27. Mr. Stephenson promised to go into the matter when in Ottawa. I wrote Mr. Smart [Deputy Minister of the Interior] from Shoal Lake about these two townships and hope to have his reply at an early date.

It was my privilege while there to meet Mr. J. W. Thompson, Homestead and Timber Inspector, and as he was on a trip to Russell I requested him to report on these two townships of land if it would not interfere with his duties too much, which report I hope to be able to send you at an early date.

I would be glad to hear from you with reference to this portion of the reservation and to know that all sections odd and even could be utilized for the settlement of Galicians. I think they are going to be a very satisfactory community and some of them have considerable means and may be able to purchase. I had a very large list of cheap lands prepared by Mr. Webster of the M. & N.W. Railway Lands were about three dollars per acre, terms ten years, annual instalments at six per cent. I left this list and would have the attention of those able to buy directed to it, as quite a number seem to have considerable money.

There were also some who had no means and a few aged and infirm. It would be a good thing if some discrimination would be made at the port of embarkation against this class but I presume it is a hard matter to get a large number of people without receiving a percentage of the above named and doubtless this matter has been fully gone into by yourself and the deputy-minister. I remember when accompanying Mr. Shultz [Eduard Schultze, Austro-Hungarian Consul General] through the West he intimated that a discrimination had been made and that a certain amount of capital would be required before the Austrian people would be accepted. This did not seem to meet his views and I think he told me the order was revoked however I presume the best is being done under all the circumstances and not being aware of the difficulties that present themselves I make the above suggestion which would be very desirable if it could be carried out which fact I implied in my letter to Mr. Smart. I have also been in communication with Mr. McCreary on account of a report by wire that dyphtheria had broken out among the Galicians at Rossburn. The message was sent by the Health officer of the municipality, Dr. Wickware, at the instigation of the Reeve, R. R. Ross.

I arranged a meeting with the two above named gentlemen at Rossburn on Thursday last the results of which will be that I think an understanding will be reached. I had received a good deal of information from Dr. Brothers of Shoal Lake and health officer of the Shoal Lake municipality. He says "Dyphtheria has existed in Rossburn for eight or ten years. It broke out in January 1898 and again last summer 1899. It will likely break out again and the people you bring in may contract it from the old settlers in the municipality. Proper dissinfecting has not been used and the germs linger in any event this has been the history of the disease." I pointed out the above facts to Mr. Ross, the Reeve, showing him that if the new settlers were affected that in all probability they had been contaminated with the old settlers and that it was the duty of the municipality to protect themselves and assume the responsibility. Mr. Ross quite agreed with me as well as did Dr. Wickware. They were both very gentlemanly. There was no unkindly reflection against the Galician people with the slightest political significance or otherwise. Mr. Ross requested me to write a letter that he would lay before his council and thought everything would be very satisfactory.

I had Dr. Wickware examine the suspects and they were all in healthy condition except one or two trifling cases so that the rumor was entirely unfounded. Reeve Ross says a Galician came to a settler called McBride and also to Harry Slay and said his child had died and a number of others were sick and that dyphtheria had broken out. Slay went immediately on horseback to the Reeve who notified the health officer to ask the department to take action. This report was entirely unfounded and gave us considerable trouble.[17]

Speers requested Dr. J. W. Wickware, Health Officer of Rossburn Municipality, to write a statement on the results of the inspection of Ukrainian settlers which he undertook together with Speers. Dr. Wickware's report, enclosed in Speers' letter to Mr. Pedley, read: "This is to certify that I have this day [May 31, 1900] inspected a number of Galicians in this municipality for the Immigration Department of the Dominion Government who were reported by the Reeve, R. R. Ross, to be affected with dyphtheria. The cases were on section 10 and section 2 in 21, 25. I found these people all in comparatively good

178. Rpts./117263, June 4, 1900: C. W. Speers, Brandon, to Frank Pedley, Ottawa.

health and no sign of any infectious disease among them. . . ." The reeve of the municipality was duly informed about the findings of his health officer, and Speers concluded his report with a note on the precaution that he had taken with regard to a possible epidemic of diphtheria: "Considering the fact that this disease is epidemic and may break out at any time in that municipality I considered it wisdom to have some understanding with the council as to who should take the responsibility."

IV

When the winter of 1900 approached, rumours of destitution among the more recent arrivals in the Strathclair and Shoal Lake district reached Ottawa. The Deputy Minister of the Interior was anxious to learn the true facts. Mr. Speers therefore visited the colony in December, 1900, and reported his findings concerning destitution in the colony to the Superintendent of Immigration:

> In compliance with instructions from the Deputy Minister pertaining to destitution I may say that this colony is in a very satisfactory condition. These people have had good gardens; they have also improved their dwellings; they have purchased a great number of cattle. I find the original twelve settlers in the Saskatchewan Valley own 63 head of cattle, and this might be accepted as an estimate for the cattle owned by these colonists, as something over 200 families are settled in that district. They stretch over about thirty miles of country, commencing at Township nineteen, Range twenty-one, north and westward to Township twenty-one, twenty-six, settled at the base of the Mountain outside the Permanent Timber Reserve. I consider this colony has made rapid progress since its establishment, wages have been good during the past summer, they have earned a lot of money, from the farmers of Manitoba and also from Railway Corporations. They have carried their money home and the merchants recognize the fact that they are good customers paying cash for everything and that they consume large amounts of our manufactured products. Robert Scott, Merchant of Shoal Lake, informs me that in the last twenty days he has sold the Galician people 1200 sacks of flour and 400 sacks of cornmeal. They pay cash for everything. They also purchase large quantities of clothing and other commodities. Other merchants speak highly of these people, and I beg to say that there is an air of thrift and progress all through their colony.
>
> Pertaining the cases that required attention, I may say that I only found four—three in the vicinity of Rossburn and one a little further east in the colony. The one case is an infirm old couple who have been in the Hospital here for some months. They are feeble and unable to work, and as their demands are modest there is no alternative than to provide for them, or send them back to Austria. The other cases are a man with a broken leg, a man who was defrauded out of his earnings and another case of sickness. Now, these are the only four cases requiring attention or assistance. I beg to say that I purchased a load of flour and cornmeal, had it sent to Rossburn

and put in charge of one Wakefield who will look after these four destitute cases, carefully guarding the goods of the Department, and only relieving deserving cases that cannot be avoided.

All other portions of the country where these settlers are placed they seem to be getting along very nicely, they are all healthy, contented and are doing well. I consider that in a new colony of eleven or twelve hundred people three or four cases are a very small percentage that require a little attention, and I am convinced that a larger percentage of needy people can be found among other nationalities, and even in our cities. I am convinced there will be a few of these cases from time to time among all our colonists. However, I find there is a lingering sentiment against these people and against their advent into the country, and although this is not general, from time to time it presents itself. I might intimate, by way of example, that I attended a Church festival in that district, and at the request of the resident Clergyman made a few remarks, confining myself absolutely to the lines of christianity and high moral attainment. I was followed by an Episcopalian Clergyman who said he was very much pleased with my remarks although he was opposed to the bringing in of the Galician people and policy of administration. I merely give this statement to shew that in some places there is a most unwarranted and unjustifiable sentiment, but I am thankful to say it is only confined to a few.

I consider the Galician Colony referred to in this report is in first class condition. Minor matters of unpaid wages, reported irregularities in homestead entries, adjusting locations and other matters of detail were gone into when I was in that district as I remained several days endeavouring to go carefully into any matters of importance.[18]

Although Speers considered the colony to be "in first class condition," a certain degree of destitution did exist among the later arrivals. This was not, however, in the degree depicted in sensational reports published abroad about "destitution in the colony of Polish Jews from Galicia settled in the Canadian North West." The High Commissioner for Canada in London cabled the Department of the Interior in Ottawa on March 30, 1901, requesting information pertaining to the terrible conditions reported in British newspapers:

Liverpool papers publish following despatch from Winnipeg state widespread destitution and suffering prevails colony Polish Jews from Galicia settled North West—Manitoba Government sending supplies food and warm clothing following telegram via New-York published London papers last evening shocking accounts received Winnipeg destitution colony Galician emigrants recently settled since winter commenced have been dying hunger through failure supplies have been neglected by Government which duly warned starvation had beset colony—cable full particulars.[19]

[18]8. Rpts./134541, December 18, 1900: C. W. Speers, Winnipeg, to Frank Pedley, Ottawa.

[19]7. Dest./149975, Cable, March 30, 1901: The High Commissioner for Canada, London, to the Department of the Interior, Ottawa.

In reply to an urgent telegram dispatched to the Commissioner of Immigration in Winnipeg about the contents of the cable from London, Commissioner Smith wired Ottawa as follows:

> Telegram re alleged destitution received. Have communications frequently from agents Rosthern, Edmonton, Yorkton, Swan River, Sifton, Dauphin, Shoal Lake, Teulon, Stuartburn and Gruenthal and there is not here a single report of destitution or suffering in any locality. We know nothing here of Manitoba Govt. or officials or any organization or individual sending feed supplies and clothing to these people. Absolutely no case reported to government, or any agent had been refused adequate and immediate relief. We have no knowledge of any such cases and these reports false. Our agents report Galicians are in better conditions financially and otherwise than at any time since they have been in the country and claim they are prospering in some localities better than English speaking settlers contiguous. I have recently laid out nine public school districts in purely Galician settlements. No Winnipeg, Manitoba or Northwest Territories journal has published any statement of destitution or death among these people and they surely would if there were any.[20]

The High Commissioner for Canada in London received these particulars on the same day that he cabled Ottawa. The Deputy Minister, although reassured by the Commissioner of Immigration as to the prevalence of satisfactory conditions in Ukrainian colonies, cautioned Mr. Smith to attend to any case of destitution that might occur: "I would again urge the importance of Mr. Speers being in closest touch with these settlers in order that he may detect anything approaching distress among them. It is always more satisfactory, I think, to provide ahead than to wait until reports in such cases are received in the Department."[21]

Speers remained in close touch with the colonies and with that of Strathclair and Shoal Lake in particular. His reports arrived with clock-like regularity every few months, describing the conditions, growth, and progress of the now quite large settlement of the Riding Mountains. The settlement bordered on a timber reserve, and with the influx of hundreds of new settlers, there occurred cases of squatting in the reserve, which necessitated investigations prior to obtaining permission to enter those quarter-sections as homesteads. A number of squatters settled in Township 20, Range 22, and the Inspector of Timber Agencies in Winnipeg instructed the Land Agent in Shoal Lake to investigate the matter and to report to Winnipeg. The agent sent back a detailed report, dated

20. Dest., Telegram, March 30, 1901: J. Obed. Smith, Commissioner of Immigration, Winnipeg, to James A. Smart, Ottawa.

21. Dest./155521, May 8, 1901: James A. Smart, Ottawa, to J. Obed. Smith, Winnipeg.

October 28, 1901,[22] setting forth the locations of the various settlers. As a comparison with Cummins Rural Directory Map No. 69, Manitoba, 1923, shows, most of the squatters of 1901 received their entries, and they or their children were in possession of their homesteads by 1923.

I have the honour to inform you that acting under instructions from H.Q. I made an inspection of S½ Tp. 20, R. 22, W. and found that nearly all the even numbered sections were occupied by Galician settlers who had squatted upon these lands.

The following are the names and locations of these squatters together with their improvements.

Sec. 2-20-22 W. was settled upon last spring by *Fedko Karasiewich* and three other Gallicians, whose names I could not learn. They have each small comfortable log houses and stables and garden patch cultivated and have among them 15 head of cattle. Their families have been in constant residence to date. No timber of any consequence on this land.

Cummins Rural Directory Map registers the following occupants of Section 2 in 1923: P. Karasiewicz N.W.¼, S. Karasiewicz S.E.¼, M. Michailyshyn N.E.¼, and W. Dunec S.W.¼. The Land Agent's report continued:

Sec. 4-20-22 W. is occupied by *Klymko Kaskiw*, *M. Kaskiw* and *Jno Stadnyk* who went into residence last Spring and have been in continuous residence since. They have each small comfortable house, stable and small patch of cultivation and have among them 10 head of cattle. Very little timber.

On the Cummins Directory Map, J. Stadnyk is registered on S.E.¼ Sec. 4-20-22 W. Klymko Kaskiw is not registered on that section, but a certain A. Kaskiw is listed on N.W.¼ Sec. 17-20-22 W. M. Kaskiw is not registered. The agent reported further:

Sec. 6-20-22 W. is occupied by *Roman Oleniuk*, *H. Oleniuk*, *Antoni Krynicki* and *Andrew Procak*. These have been in constant residence since Spring of 1899 and have comfortable log houses, stables etc. and have each about 2 acres under cultivation and 2 to 3 cows each. Very little wood on this section.

Roman and H. Oleniuk are not registered on the Cummins Map. A. Krynicki is listed on N.W.¼, and Wm. Procak on S.W.¼ of Section 6.

Sec. 10-20-22-W. *Fedko Barabash*, *Wasyl Kitch* and *Stefan Darkach* have been in constant residence on this land from Spring of 1900 and have each small comfortable houses stables etc. Have about 1 to 2 acres cultivation and 1 or 2 head of cattle each. No timber of value.

[22]19. Imm./163877, October 28, 1901: Land Agent, Shoal Lake, to E. F Stephenson, Inspector of Timber Agencies, Winnipeg.

On the 1923 Cummins Map, the following are listed on Section 10: M. Barabash N.E.¼, J. Kutch S.W.¼, S. Dyrkach S.E.¼.

Sec. 12-20-22 W. *Jos. and Wasyl Dunec* are in residence on this land. They both occupy the same house and have small stable and garden patch. Keep one cow. Went into residence Spring 1901. Gillead timber.

Cummins Map lists J. Dunec on N.E.¼ and F. Dunec on S.E.¼ of Section 12.

Sec. 14-20-22-W. *P. Twerdun, P. Macyoski, Simko Macyoski* and *Stefan Hnatiw* went into residence on this land Spring of 1900 and have been in constant residence to date. Have each about 2 acres breaking, comfortable house and stables and keep from 3 to 10 head of cattle and 1 to 3 horses. No timber of value.

On Cummins Rural Directory Map, the following are listed on Section 14: S. Macijowski N.E.¼, N. & J. Macijowski S.W.¼, A. Macijowski S.E.¼, and S. Hnatiw N.W.¼.

Sec. 16-20-22 W. *Gresko Skawinski, M. Danyluk, Jno Bodnarciw* and *Mathew Danyluk* went into residence on this land in Spring of 1901 and have each small comfortable log house and stables. A small patch broken and 1 or 2 head of cattle each. No timber of any value on this land.

Cummins lists these persons on Section 16 in 1923: M. Matieshyn N.W.¼, S. Bomak N.E.¼, O. Nowosad S.W.1, and J. Stadnyk S.E.¼.

On December 18, 1901, Speers sent another report to Ottawa, when he had returned from an inspection of the Ukrainian settlement North of Shoal Lake and Strathclair, and pointed out that there were no longer any destitute cases in the colony:

I beg to submit a brief report of the Galician colonies North of Shoal Lake and Strathclair at the foot of the Riding Mountains. A number of the Galicians have settled North of Newdale, Township 18, Range 20 and extend North-west to township 21, Range 26. These settlers are in a very prosperous condition and a number of them have purchased C.P.R. lands. They have had a very good crop of grain and an excellent root and vegetable crop this year. They have improved their homes, houses—many of them have good shingled roofs. This settlement of Galician people comprise two thousand souls. It would be safe to estimate that they have an average of four or five cattle per family and one horse. They have purchased a good deal of machinery such as mowers, rakes and waggons. This colony is in a very satisfactory condition. There is not one case of existing destitution in the entire colony. A few families who arrived last spring required a little assistance but less than Fifty Dollars has been advanced to this entire colony during the year. There is not a very great acreage under cultivation among these settlers—in many places the land had to be cleared of scrub and as they are all new settlers starting without means the men were obliged to go out and earn money before they could devote their attention to the land. There is enough of these settlers in this particular district as all the available land is pretty well occupied and there are a great many young people among them who will soon want homesteads in addition to the fact that they are multiplying fast and the natural increase of these people will be very great. They are settled adjacent to the large timber reservation in the Riding Mountains and we are constantly warning them that they must not intrude upon this reservation. I have requested John Menzies to check up a number of these settlers to show what they had when they started and what they now possess. I would like to get information in detail concerning a number of our colonies which I will endeavour to submit to you at a later date.[23]

Towards the end of 1903 the Shoal Lake and Strathclair colony, established with great sacrifice in May, 1899, was a thriving community of over three thousand settlers. On November 20, 1903, Speers sent this brief report to the Superintendent of Immigration in Ottawa, reporting on the general progress of the colony since its establishment:

I beg to submit a brief report on the Galician settlers in the Riding Mountain District, after an investigation into their progress.

This colony was established in 1899, when I placed about 900 souls north of Shoal Lake and Strathclair. The subsequent year an additional 900 was placed there. This has been supplemented from time to time, each succeeding year, contributing its regular quota, until about 3,000 souls are resident in that district. They have occupied the territories south of Riding Mountain, following the base of the permanent timber reservation, reaching from Newdale to Russell, a distance of fifty miles. A few of these settlers have encroached upon the timber reservation as squatters, contrary to the advice given them by the Officials of the Department. The district is well filled with these homesteaders, and they have made great progress. It would be a conservative estimate to place their horned stock at 4,000 head, and their horses at 1,000 head. They are well supplied with swine and poultry. They have improved their houses and outbuildings, and have adopted Canadian customs in methods of living and dress. They have bought a great deal of Canadian Pacific and other lands. They are very progressive; and, although they commenced life a few years ago poor, they are now very comfortable, and soon will be well fixed. This is seemingly characteristic of the Galician settlers, who are among our very most progressive.[24]

In the first years of the twentieth century, the district described by Speers was being shaped into rural communities, including post offices, schools, churches, and community halls. The names chosen by the immigrants for their institutions are interesting and revealing. The

[23]9. Rpts./182470, December 18, 1901: C. W. Speers, Brandon, to Frank Pedley, Ottawa.

[24]9. Rpts./283988, November 20, 1903: C. W. Speers, Winnipeg, to W. D. Scott, Superintendent of Immigration, Ottawa.

settlements bore names such as "Horod," with a post office and school district of the same name in Township 19, Range 21, and "Seech," a settlement, post office, and school district in Township 20, Range 22. Another school in the latter Township bore the name "Zaporozhe." "Olha" settlement, post office, and school district (N.W.¼ Sec. 34) was established in Township 19, Range 23; another school in the same township bore the name of King George. The settlement "Marco" was established in Township 20, Range 23, and the school district in this township bore the name "Rawa Ruska." In Township 21, Range 24, two schools were established, "Mohyla" School and "Chmelnycky" School. In Township 21, Range 25, the settlement were called "Ruthenia," and the school districts had the names "Ruthenia" School and "Valley" School. This large Ukrainian community was in time to produce from its institutions a number of prominent citizens, among them doctors, educationists, lawyers, and businessmen—all of them the sons of hardy Galician immigrants.

Chapter Nine

YORKTON AND ROSTHERN REGIONS

I

ON JANUARY 17, 1898, C. W. Speers, in his yearly report addressed to Clifford Sifton, Minister of the Interior, wrote this brief description of the establishment of a new colony at Yorkton: "In June (1897) I took the first Galician colony to Yorkton, some fifty one families, and settled them at Beaver Hills, which is on the surveyed line of the Manitoba and North-Western Railway, about thirty-five miles north west from Yorkton. This is a beautiful country, with plenty of timber and well watered. Subsequently I took 457 souls, about 110 families, and settled a large colony at Crooked Lakes, twenty-five miles north of Yorkton, and a colony of thirty-one families settled about twenty-five miles north-east of Saltcoats. . . ."[1] This concise, matter-of-fact account gives no indication of the great struggle, fraught with hard work and intense suffering, that the settlers of the Yorkton region underwent as they began their new life in Canada.

In 1897, the Assiniboia and Saskatchewan districts in the Northwest Territories were just emerging from a prolonged period of depression after persistent droughts which had lasted many seasons, and which had resulted in disastrous crop failures and financial ruin for the early settlers, who depended almost entirely on their wheat crops. In many cases the Government had to come to the assistance of the stricken settlers. Hundreds left their homesteads. Those who came from the United States headed south, and those who came from the United

[1]Canada, Department of the Interior, *Annual Report*, 1898, No. 4, 191, C. W. Speers, Travelling Agent, Winnipeg, to Clifford Sifton, Minister of the Interior, Ottawa, January 17, 1898.

Kingdom moved to towns or sought farms situated nearer to centres of settlement and communications that were less affected by drought.

The settlers who came to the Assiniboia and Saskatchewan districts during the early 1880's originated mostly in the United States and Great Britain. The American settlers were attracted by the prospects of abundant cheap land which was becoming scarce south of the border, and the British settlers were encouraged to emigrate to Western Canada by the agents of the Canadian Government, as well as by various societies and settlement companies. Comparatively few of the British immigrants were prepared for the rigours of pioneer life in the Canadian Northwest Territories. In most cases the companies or societies sponsoring the settlers offered them financial assistance in the form of loans, as well as other types of aid. Those who persevered and endured initial difficulties, who were prudent in their use of the money loaned them, succeeded in the long run, but the less experienced and less careful left their homesteads after the first crop failure. Superintendent Perry of the North West Mounted Police reported in 1895 that "some districts which were once well settled are now deserted and others have only two or three settlers left."[2]

Saltcoats was one district which the original British settlers abandoned after years of successive failures. It was originally settled in 1889 by crofters from the United Kingdom. Their progress was slow, mainly because of inexperience and lack of knowledge about farming methods. Many settlers also spent most of the money loaned to them extravagantly. They were, of course,

> . . . encouraged in their improvidence by the fact that the promoters of the movement advanced to them loans of $500 to $600. Many of the first settlers became discouraged and abandoned their homesteads, but those who tenaciously stayed on the land have prospered in the end.
>
> Financial aid was also extended to old country immigrants to the East London Artisans' Colony, south of Moosomin, prospected by Major-General Sir Francis DeWinton and other prominent citizens of London.[3]

W. T. R. Preston, Inspector of Agencies in Europe, in his yearly report to the High Commissioner for Canada in London, suggested that British immigrants should preferably be directed to old established farming regions in the East, as they would not be able to surmount the difficulties of pioneering life in the Northwest:

> A great deal has been said and written in Canada about the desirability of securing a movement on the part of the so-called tenant farmers towards

[2]Norman Fergus Black, *A History of Saskatchewan and the Old North West* (Regina: North West Historical Company, 1913), 433. [3]*Ibid.*, 502.

the North-west Territories. Upon one occasion, at least, representatives of this class of English agriculturists visited Canada for the purpose of personally inquiring into its sources, and the most optimistic calculations were indulged in as to the result of the visit in question. But one has only to be thrown into contact with these people here to be assured that they are not likely to leave their positions of ease and comfort upon English farms, and assume cheerfully the alleged responsibilities attached to pioneer life in a new country. I am not prepared to say that a time is not coming when an organization having for its object the presentation of a scheme to induce this class to consider, with some degree of favour, settlement upon cultivated and comfortable homesteads in the older provinces, might not be more successful. But the project to induce them to emigrate to Manitoba and the North-west might, in my humble opinion, be abandoned.[4]

The settlers best suited for the Northwest Territories were those who had the ability to make a living under the most severe conditions, who were used to hard work and a frugal life, who had a thorough knowledge of farming, who could take good care of their animals, and who were to a marked degree self-sufficient, since most of the homesteads were many miles distant from towns and railways. The Ukrainian peasant settlers seemed to meet these requirements, and therefore they were encouraged to come to Canada and to settle on homesteads in the West.

Dr. Oleskow's emigration activities in 1897 produced even greater results than originally anticipated. When the spring arrived, the Winnipeg Immigration Hall was filled to capacity, and still more immigrants were arriving with each successive boat. On May 5, 1897, the Commissioner of Immigration in Winnipeg, commenting on one such arrival, informed the Deputy Minister in Ottawa that: "The whole party of 1100 came in within six hours of each other, and you may depend upon it it was no easy task to manage them."[5] A few days later, May 12, a cable from the High Commissioner in London announced that "539 souls, 258 adults mostly Galicians sailed from Hamburg by Arabia 8th instant."[6] Two days later, another cable informed the Department of the Interior that "672 Galicians, 320 adults sailed from Hamburg. . ."[7] A letter from Dr. Oleskow to the Commissioner of Immigration advised that still more settlers would be on their way before the summer season closed. All of these immigrants were bound for the West, and their first stop was Immigration Hall in Winnipeg. To be able to cope with this

[4]Canada, Parliament, *Sessional Papers*, X, No. 23, 1900, Paper No. 13, Report No. 2: W. T. R. Preston, Inspector of Agencies in Europe, to Lord Strathcona, November 28, 1899, 12–19.

[5]3. Gal., May 6, 1897: W. F. McCreary, Winnipeg, to James A. Smart, Ottawa.

[6]3. Gal., May 12, 1897: Cable, Sir Donald A. Smith, London, to Clifford Sifton, Ottawa.

[7]3. Gal./37498, May 15, 1897: Cable, Sir Donald A. Smith, London, to Clifford Sifton, Ottawa.

difficult situation, Commissioner McCreary tried to sort the settlers out on arrival in Winnipeg, so that those travelling to Edmonton, Dauphin, or Stuartburn were put in separate coaches and dispatched to their destinations without stopping over longer than necessary in the overcrowded Immigration Hall. This distribution helped considerably to relieve the pressure, otherwise the situation would likely have gotten out of hand.

Not all the Ukrainian immigrants who arrived in Winnipeg that season were sent by Dr. Oleskow. A considerable number of them were picked up without selection by steamship agents in the neighbouring province of Bukowina. As long as they could afford to pay their passage they were dispatched to Hamburg, and from there to Halifax or Quebec. These immigrants were given fantastic promises by the agents, and when on arrival in Winnipeg the promises failed to materialize, they protested vigorously, refusing to be moved from the Immigration Hall until the promises would be fulfilled. To make matters worse, few of them had any means at all. The Commissioner of Immigration was in a quandry as to what should be done. He wrote the Deputy Minister for his suggestions on the problem:

> . . . Now, I cannot see what these people will do without a single dollar if they should be placed on land; it would be a case of assistance from the Government for some time, and the expense would run up very high.
>
> I secured a contract of 1,000 cords of wood to be cut about fifteen miles from the City, at 45 cents per cord, and they to board themselves. I thought when I had secured this contract that I should be able to get them to go at once, and thus enable them to earn a little money at least during this month (May, 1897) and after that I would probably be able to engage them with farmers during haying and harvest, for, as you know, for the next month farmers will not require any help. They are raising a row over the matter however with Genik, the Interpreter, and he seems entirely in a quandry as to what to do with them. They are an obstinate class, and complain that misrepresentations were made to induce them to come out here. They were told that the Crown Princess of Austria was in Montreal, and that she would see that they got free lands with houses on them, cattle and so forth, and that all they required to do was to telegraph to her in Montreal in case their requests were not granted. These and other similar stories have been so impressed on their minds that they now seem very unsettled, and talk about going back to Austria. . . .
>
> I do not quite despair of being able to satisfactorily locate these people, but when you consider that 539 more will be here at the latter part of this month, and as I would infer from Oleskow's letter that still more are to follow, then I would anticipate some trouble, as I tell you plainly that it is simply impossible to get even one of these people out to work without all the persuasive powers I can use. . . .[8]

[8]3. Gal./37582, May 15, 1897: W. F. McCreary, Winnipeg, to James A. Smart, Ottawa.

The trouble that the Commissioner anticipated arrived sooner than expected. The imminent arrival of hundreds more new immigrants from Halifax and Quebec necessitated the removal from the Immigration Hall of those who had overstayed their time and who should either have taken up homesteads or accepted employment to secure the means to start farming. The Commissioner was able to offer two alternatives to the settlers. The first of these was to take up residence in the district around Yorkton, which possessed good farming land, suitable for cattle-raising as well as grain-growing, and which was well-timbered, with an abundant supply of water. The second alternative that the Commissioner could offer was simply that the settlers vacate the hall and proceed on their own. The Bukowinians refused to accept either alternative, and thereby created a crisis.

On Wednesday, May 26, 1897, with the new immigrants scheduled to arrive at any time, the Commissioner was compelled to take drastic action. He ordered the evacuation of the Immigration Hall but was met with determined resistance on the part of the occupants. The police were then called in, and the local press afterwards gave sensational descriptions of the ensuing "revolt" of the obstinate Bukowinians. The *Winnipeg Tribune* of Thursday, May 27, 1897, reported the colourful event as follows:

MAYOR'S ESCAPE

An Old Galician Woman Threw Her Big Boot at His Head—Galicians Excited

The stubborn Bukowinian immigrants referred to in yesterday's Tribune had to be turned out of the immigration hall yesterday by main force. Some of them threw themselves on the floor and had to be carried out. An old woman who had been very outspoken in her foreign way, finally pulled off her long boot and threw it at the commissioner's, Mayor McCreary's head, fortunately missing her aim. The men also became so excited that four policemen had to be called in clearing the place.

The immigrants had been in the hall over a fortnight and longer than the time allowed and it was necessary to get rid of them to make room for the new arrivals. Many of their number refused work.[9]

The press gave the "revolt" the type of coverage which McCreary was afraid might cause some concern in Ottawa, and therefore he prepared a detailed report about the events. He informed the Deputy Minister that the incident was closed and that the reluctant immigrants had proceeded to Yorkton to be settled on homesteads in the vicinity of Saltcoats, south of Yorkton:

I have not been able to find time to write you for three or four days, as I have been continuously at work from 6 in the morning till 11 o'clock at

[9] *Winnipeg Tribune*, Thursday, May 27, 1897.

night, and never even get home for my meals, so that I am now pretty well tired out. However, I have just despatched another party to Yorkton, and as the new Special containing the Arabians [passengers from the S.S. *Arabia*] will not arrive here till about 2 o'clock this afternoon, I thought it better to advise you roughly how matters are getting on, as, owing to certain criticisms of the press which may possibly reach the eyes of the Minister, a mis-contruction might be placed on some of the actions of this office. I send you the clippings referred to, but as none of them are absolutely correct, I deem it better to give you a true version of the entire matter.

I have already written you at considerable length about the Bukowinians. A number of them were not only poor but they all were a most obstinate class. I had tried every peaceable means to induce them to settle; first, as you know, at considerable expense taking a large delegation of them, forty-six in all, to Stuartburn, and driving them over that country for three or four days with no less than three Livery teams. The result of that was that I placed probably twenty families; about two hundred continued to remain here despite all my efforts, some of them having money, some none. I finally made arrangements with Mr. Baker of the North-Western Road, that he would take them up to Yorkton at a very low rate, and give those who had no money work on the Road for fifty days, and see that the others were protected in his Sheds there till they were located.

I submitted this proposition to them, and they talked about consenting at first. However City parties got among them, and by pouring into their ears all sorts of stories, induced them not to go. As the large party of six hundred and seventy-five were billed to arrive here at 4 o'clock on Thursday morning, and as we would require all the Shed accommodation for these people, I came to the conclusion that the climax which had been approaching for the last two weeks might as well be now reached, so I told those people in the Sheds that I wanted them to get on the cars on Wednesday night ready for transportation early Thursday morning to Yorkton. They sullenly refused, and said they wanted free land at Cook's Creek with houses thereon, two cows for each settler, and keep for a year—or to go back to Austria. This, of course, was impossible, so I then told them that 4 o'clock if they did not get on to the train of cars which I had placed on the siding, I would use force. A number of them laid down in the Building and commenced to play sick and made all sorts of excuses. However, I called in a requisition, Sergeant Munroe and five officers of the City Police, and we had their baggage carried downstairs and put into the yard and forced them that far, not, of course, without great deal of yelling, crying and shrieking on the part of the women and considerable hard feeling; the job being not at all pleasant one, I might say. However, no injury was done; none of the sick were ejected, nor was any force used; merely the baggage carried out and one or two of the boisterous ones given a slight shake.

Getting them into the yard was one thing, but putting them on to the train was another. They would not go on the train, but as soon as we had got their baggage on to the trucks they would upset the trucks, take the baggage on their backs and marching north, squatted along the street at different points around the Vulcan Iron Works, and many of them took possession of one or two vacant houses north of the track. The parties who had been doing most damage all lived in the district to which they went, their names being one Pole McCorski, one Pole Saborski, one German Edinger and some others.

Only two or three families actually got on the cars that night, and when I found the others would not get on I adopted the other alternative and told them through the Interpreters that as these parties had been advising them, they had better go there now and board with them. Apparently Mr. Saborski and McCorski did not like so many boarders of this class, and as the train of cars was left on the siding all night we found by the next morning that about twenty-one families had come back during the night and got into the cars for protection, and were willing to go to Yorkton. I might say that the rain fell in the night, and this also had a cooling effect upon those who were sleeping out.

Of the new arrivals there were some nine families from Bukowina, and we at once sent those forward with this same special train. I put Mr. Speers in charge and sent him out two Interpreters from here, and from reports from Mr. Speers the party landed safely at Yorkton; all were satisfied, and he is now busy locating them.

I have told Speers to stay out there till the 7th of June in order that these parties may all be placed on farms, and I have also advised him to plough an acre or two on the land of each, and give each one two sacks of flour and two bushels of potatoes, that is, all those who have no money. I, of course, also gave them some flour when they left here. I think with this assistance and the work they get on the line of railway they will be able to get along. I kept close track of those who were scattered round the City, as I expected they would capitulate in time, and yesterday morning the entire number in one deputation came into this office with the flag of truce, saying that they were now willing to go to Yorkton. Seven of these families I found had among them $701, and the others were without means. I have shipped all those on the 9.55 train this morning, and they all seem contented and happy. They admit they were ill-advised, and it was certainly a source of gratification to this office that the policy we adopted of firmness towards them was successful, as I am now convinced that had I not taken this course, we would have had those people on our hands for most of the summer.

All the party of Galicians who came in yesterday we have had no trouble whatever. All of them have been despatched to their respective destinations except a very few families whom we are endeavouring to get out to work; but as this is a different matter, and is not immediately pressing, I will write you later.

In the meantime, I enclose you copy of the list of all the Galicians who are now in the Building. Of course, we have a few in Brandon not yet placed, and also a few at Calgary, but I shall easily be able to handle this small number.

I think, under all the circumstances, we have done remarkably well, as you cannot conceive all the difficulties of handling such a large number of foreigners in so short a time.

As soon as the train arrives this afternoon, it is my intention to divide them into three parties; those going to Stuartburn I will put in one portion and get all their baggage separated from the others and transportation arranged as their train goes on Monday morning at 8 o'clock. I expect only

> about fifteen families will go there—in fact, that is as many as we can afford to forward to that point, as there cannot be much more room there, and as Burrows is pretty well crowded with the four hundred and thirty-three we sent to Dauphin a few days ago, I will try and get thirty or forty of the families of this last party to go to Yorkton, and the balance I will try to induce to go to Edmonton—but of course I cannot say until they arrive.[10]

Some eleven days later, McCreary was able to inform the Deputy Minister in Ottawa that "the parties sent to Yorkton, I may say, have nearly all settled and seem well satisfied and the Management of that road have written Professor Oleskow, in Russia [Austria is meant] that they would take 1000 to 1200 more families, provided he can send them straight through to Yorkton; in fact, this is the way in which all this immigration will have to be handled hereafter. . . ."[11]

II

The Ukrainian colony in the Saltcoats district, established with such difficulty at the end of May, 1897, steadily grew in numbers. New settlers arrived almost every week. Commissioner McCreary sent C. W. Speers to the Yorkton district to supervise the distribution of settlers and their location on homesteads. The Land Guide, Thomas MacNutt of Saltcoats, described the process of settling the new arrivals in a note to Speers:

> In reply to your note asking for a synopsis of proceeding in connection with settlement of Saltcoats Galicians and Bukowinians, I think I cannot do better than give extracts from my Diary.
>
> Monday [June 28] being wet, was spent in housing and making them comfortable at Saltcoats.
>
> Tuesday was a Greek holiday, and was taken advantage by the citizens to give them all a welcome and feed all round.
>
> Wednesday I started out with Mr. Steinhard and two delegates to examine the country. I arranged for a change of teams so as to cover ground. I first took them to see a number of Russo-Germans who were doing well and could converse with them. This made a good impression, and afterwards drove through a part of the locality that it was proposed to settle them in. The delegates seemed well satisfied with all they saw and heard, and reported favourably to their compatriots.
>
> Thursday being 1st July, they took in the sports, special races and sports were gotten up for the foreigners and they enjoyed themselves immensely.

[10]3. Gal./38150, May 29, 1897: W. F. McCreary, Winnipeg, to James A. Smart, Ottawa.

[11]3. Gal./38814, June 9, 1897: W. F. McCreary, Winnipeg, to James A. Smart, Ottawa.

At the Dramatic entertainment in evening some twenty of them gave their national songs and dances on the stage and was a feature of the evening. The object of all this was to make them feel at home and give them a good impression.

Friday I was with two teams early to take a number out to make a start, but on account of rain did not get off till 7.30 in evening—drove 18 miles to an Icelanders and camped in his stables.

Saturday, went on ground and started running lines. On account of frequent fires nearly all survey marks were obliterated and I will have to make a re-survey. The country being scrubby and bluffy, renders the start slow, but I hope to get on well now, as a good start has been made. In order to get my first point I have to start three miles south of where the first locations will be and cut through some timber and scrub. I intend to run a main line straight north and turn an angle every ½ mile, which I will run with pickets east and west. In a couple of days I hope to have made some progress, but have been handicapped by wet weather; the fact that all baggage and tools had gone on to Yorkton and principally the destruction give necessity for renewal of survey marks. . . .

I may say that so far my opinion is that these people will eventually make successful settlers although the start will be hard.

I can get employment for a number of them, as soon as they have selected their homesteads.

I may add that I feel a good deal of interest in them and will do my best to establish them. . . .[12]

Speers returned from Yorkton to Winnipeg on Monday, July 5, and submitted his report on the progress of settlement in the Yorkton and Saltcoats districts. McCreary forwarded it to the Deputy Minister in Ottawa and added his own observations on the fine treatment of the new settlers by the other inhabitants of the area:

I do not know that I can enlarge upon this report except to say that I have telegrams up to yesterday to the effect that they are being settled rapidly. I think most of those at Saltcoats will be located to-night, and of the larger number at Yorkton, the land guide there will likely finish his work some time next week. . . .

The colony is getting along very well in both places, and the people, I am glad to say, are receiving these foreigners in a better spirit than has been manifested by English settlers in other localities. The Board of Trade, both at Yorkton and Saltcoats, have held meetings and have assisted in every way to make the people feel at home, and have also wired me to the effect that others will be received there and well used.

In a report of Mr. MacNutt's, which I also enclose you will notice they went so far as to get up games on the first of July for the special edification of the Galicians, both at Yorkton and Saltcoats, at which, I understand, the

123. Gal./40035, July 4, 1897: Thomas MacNutt, Land Guide, Saltcoats, N.W.T., to C. W. Speers, Yorkton, N.W.T.

foreigners enjoyed themselves immensely, and contributed to the festivities by their own national songs and dances.

In view of the criticism and prejudice against these people from many quarters, it affords me considerable gratification to know that they are being treated so well in those localities. A large number who went to Yorkton, and some of those to Saltcoats have already bought waggons and horses; I believe some twenty teams of horses and twenty waggons have been purchased, and I think that they are in a fair way to succeed. . . .

I have to-day written the Interpreters at Yorkton and Saltcoats to see that each family has a house of logs put up, with good thatched roofs, at least 12 × 16, or larger if the family is large, and when this has been done, to instruct their wives to cut some hay for a cow, and also have those with sufficient funds buy not only a cow, but a pig and some hens. For those who have no money, I have instructed them to give them sufficient flour and cornmeal, keeping close track of it, until such time as they are able to get their families into the houses, and procure work.

It is desirable that these people should be employed with farmers, if possible, as, not only will then learn farming, but they will learn English more rapidly than if sent on to do railway work. However, if none of them can get work with farmers, I have arrangements made to get them on the railway, having closed negotiations with Mr. Haney to that effect.

The children I have instructed to pick snake root and fruit in season, so that these colonies are now in good working order, and it is my intention to try and have the 191 now en route shipped straight to that district.[13]

Speers' report of July 9, 1897, enclosed by McCreary in his letter to the Deputy Minister, gave a more detailed and vivid description of the establishment of the Ukrainian colonies around Saltcoats and north of Yorkton. His report testified to his humane qualities as well as his extraordinary abilities of organization:

I beg to submit report of the large arrival of Galicians at Fort William on the 26th day of June, having in charge Mr. Akerlindh, of Ottawa.

I was informed by the Government Agent that they had been checked and their destinations telegraphed to you at Winnipeg, and that they were mostly for Edmonton, N.W.T. I left for Fort William on the first special, having with me Mr. Steinhard as Interpreter from the Winnipeg Office. I asked Mr. Steinhard if these people had decided to go to Edmonton, and he said "No." I told him as soon as daylight would permit, we would go through the train and consign all we possibly could to Yorkton, checking up the train again, and getting the numbers of their baggage checks. Early in the morning before daylight, W. F. McCreary, to whom I respectfully submit this report, with two doctors, boarded the train, to whom I submitted my suggestions and intentions, and who gave assent, requesting me to carry the matter out. The train was under your direction and your wishes carried out until we arrived at Winnipeg.

13. Gal./40035, July 10, 1897: W. F. McCreary, Winnipeg, to James A. Smart, Ottawa.

After a few hours' delay the second section arrived, and I started to Yorkton with thirteen coaches of Galicians, in all 587 souls. At Rosser a number got off when the train stopped, and with all the assistance I could summon and a struggle, we forced them back into the cars, after a short delay.

Before reaching Portage la Prairie a child was born, and I had the Interpreter do everything possible to make mother and child comfortable. As you had given me a generous supply of milk and bread, I made the men use it freely, and soon the mal-contents were in a better mood, and no difficulty was experienced.

I arrived at Saltcoats about 10 o'clock on Monday morning and left five coaches containing 31 families and two single men, in all 142 souls, having telegraphed Thomas MacNutt he met me, also leaving Mr. Steinhard the Interpreter in charge of the people at Saltcoats, and instructed Mr. MacNutt to proceed at once to get the people settled, I proceeded to Yorkton with 96 families, in all 440 souls, contained in eight coaches.

Not having accommodation in the Sheds, I sent for R. Mitchell, the owner of a warehouse, and rented it for $20 for one month. You will find agreement made with him for the Department.

I had Dr. Patrick inspect the train, and fumigate the Sheds, and as a result was obliged to put two families in isolation, securing a team and moving them from the train first, causing some delay. I had the trainmen pull the cars as near the warehouse as possible; the rain was falling fast; then we commenced getting the people out. They clung to the cars, and I was obliged to secure some assistance, and lock each car as we got it empty. We filled the warehouse, which has two floors, upstairs and down, and then backed the train a short distance to the Immigration Sheds and got all the cars empty. After the Immigration Sheds were filled, we put up the Government tent, and had the entire lot under cover. I purchased some twenty sacks of flour to give to the poor. This was divided, each family getting 25 pounds, or a sack to four families. I bought 25 bushels of potatoes, and gave each about 15 lb. or a small shovel full.

I wired Steinhard at Saltcoats to give proper attention to the mother and child, and procure medical aid if necessary. I wired Dr. Mason, at Saltcoats, to inspect colony and report to me by wire their condition, and if there were any cases requiring quarantine.

Herewith find Dr. Mason's answer by telegraph—

C. W. Speers, Yorkton—

Having inspected thirty-one Galician families here on Railway premises found them all in fair state of health. There is one case of vaccinia, three cases of dermati(tis) slightly infectious, one case maternity confined on train.

—(Signed) Dr. R. M. Mason.

After arrival I was invited to attend a meeting of the Board of Trade and Immigration, which I did, and was highly pleased to see the great interest manifested by all in this colony of people at Yorkton. The Board passed a Resolution recommending a district north-east of Yorkton in the vicinity of Crooked Lakes, and requested the President, Mr. J. S. Crerar, to accompany me to look over the country. A copy of the Resolution passed I have the honour to submit to you with this report. I addressed the meeting, and thanked them in the name of the Department for their interest and consideration, and agreed to go in the morning and visit the district.

I called all the Galician men to an open meeting, and through the Interpreter requested them to select four or six from among themselves to accompany me with Mr. Crerar, Mr. Hill and an Interpreter. They were quite pleased, and after a little trouble which arose, the Galicians, not wishing to go with the Bukowinians—verily the Jews not wishing to deal with the Samaritans—I assured them they were all Canadians now under free institutions, and they were all satisfied as we agreed to colonize them in different parts of the Townships. They balloted and chose their men; I proceeded to the Land Office and secured the lands vacant in Townships 28, 29, and 30, in Ranges 2 and 3, W.2.M., and getting two teams we started off.

After arriving at this district about twenty-five miles from Yorkton, it is a beautiful country, well timbered, high rolling land, warm and sharp, free from stones and affording every facility for poor settlers, plenty of hay and water. The Galicians said they would rather go to the Beaver Hills, where the former colony had gone. All discussion seemed of no avail, and we camped awhile, and then I promised them to shew them the Beaver Hills.

The country passed through was not so good as the Crooked Lakes district and they cast their eyes back frequently. In close proximity of the Beaver Hills, on a summit, I stopped. I took out the maps and shewed them the advantage of settling in the Crooked Lakes country, reviewing the country over which we had travelled, and pointing out the fact that they would have to go north of the White Sand River, which would be some distance from the Beaver Hills. They agreed to go back and take up the Crooked Lakes country and report favourably to the people at Yorkton, as I shewed them their responsibility, and that having a knowledge of the country myself their poor countrymen would do better to select the Crooked Lakes district.

We returned to Yorkton, and where we camped to feed, a large, beautiful deer came within fifteen yards from the camp, and the Galicians were delighted at the sight of such Canadian game.

After arriving at Yorkton, they held councils for an hour or two, then I convened all the men, putting the delegates in the front of me, and through Interpreter Harvey gave them an address, reviewing our trip and pointing out their duty to this their new country. They all seemed highly pleased, and I told them the next day being a holiday, Federation Day, if they wished to see the sports, etc., they could remain and make preparations and that we would all start on Friday morning the 2nd instant for the colony, and all who had money could get assistance for themselves.

Friday morning broke wet and cold, rain at intervals all day, we were obliged to put off until Saturday morning the trip.

On report from Dr. Patrick, I forwarded 20 sacks of flour to the colony at Beaver Hills, sent out Mr. William Laurie with the following instructions hereto attached, which I requested Dr. Patrick to give. You will also find a report from Dr. Patrick attached to this my report, which I requested concerning the health of the Beaver Hills colony, and the large colony I had with me. The following message came from Interpreter Steinhard, Saltcoats—

C. W. Speers, Yorkton—

I have here a few families without a cent. Shall I give them Food? Please answer quick.

—(Signed) I. S. STEINHARD.

I answered to get some flour and potatoes and milk for the poor children and feed them. The car with flour had arrived, and I sent a team drawing thirty-five hundred to Saltcoats, with instructions to Steinhard to use it judicially and have it put in safe, dry place. I also wired Thomas MacNutt full instructions to proceed with colonization as rapidly as possible, get what he required to efficiently carry out his work, and use judicious, but make every effort to get people settled. I received the following answer by telegraph:

C. W. Speers, Yorkton—

Baggage with axes, shovels, etc. having gone on causing some delay, I must first establish points and lines of survey markers completely obliterated. I am taking Interpreter, few men, and couple of women to-morrow to run lines and plant stakes. Have rented a surveyor's instrument have tents and supplies after this is done no trouble to locate and start building, but this is the first move, otherwise might locate on wrong place—hope to have all settled next week, having hired two teams for present—am arranging for good oxen and second-hand wagon for those who can buy them. If inconvenient do not come down for a few days, as I can manage, your telegram being clear. Can accommodate 25 or 30 more families, some will settle alongside of Old Russo-German settlers who are prosperous and gladly welcome the Galicians. Expect to be back late Saturday night and return Sunday.

—(Signed) THOS. MACNUTT.

Also the following message from Steinhard—

C. W. Speers, Yorkton—

Our Galicians are very satisfied with the land. If you have too many send some families here.

(Signed) I. S. STEINHARD.

You will also find a number of messages hereto attached pertaining to supplies, etc., as well as from others.

I wired Mr. W. R. Baker, General Manager of the Manitoba and North Western Railway Company the district I had selected, the contentment of the people, and particulars.—Mr. Webster also the Land Commissioner. Mr. Baker kindly placed the use of the telegraph lines on his system at my service free of charge, and exhibited a great interest in doing all in his power to assist in every way to make this large and important colony a success; as also did Mr. Webster, gladly giving useful and generous assistance; in fact, the courtesy of all the Manitoba and North Western Railway officials and others in connection with the Road makes it a pleasure to place people along their line; and as it is really a wonderful country with great natural facilities, important colonies of immigrants should be directed along that line. There is room for thousands, and with industry they are bound to succeed.

After seeing that every detail of the work had been carefully gone into, in fact, going into it myself, pertaining both to the Saltcoats colony as well as that at Yorkton, I hired on Saturday morning early 16 teams and waggons, giving to Interpreter a complete list of those who had no money, and told him to get them ready—the sixteen teams also including a team and buggy for myself, loaded 55 families and their boxes, baggage, etc., my men loaded every waggon heavily. The men mostly walked, and with tents also one load of flour, provisions, six axes, six spades, lanterns, coal oil and a few other necessaries, we left Yorkton for the colony.

We arrived at a point about 25 miles north-east of Yorkton, I should think between Townships 28 and 29, in Range 2, on Crooked Lakes. These Lakes are dry and constitute a deep ravine running in the serpentine course with high banks of fertile land and the Valley covered with long grass with an occasional body of water. The country is well timbered, and the Galicians were exceedingly joyful. We commenced to put up tents, having two large ones and 2 small tents. I purchased 500 feet of inch lumber which we used for the tent, getting timber for a ridge pole, and at dark all were under cover, but crowded in like sheep. The rain fell fast nearly all night, but no murmuring was heard as the body of the people, including the women, were working and pleased with the prospect of the country.

I secured the services of J. S. Crerar, a very competent man, also had George H. Hill, two teams, another Interpreter and through the night carefully gave written instructions to each. I selected a beautiful opening, surrounded by heavy good building timber, and instructed Mr. Crerar to build a large Reception Hall with the Galician men while Hill was getting the lines run and locating a few homesteads. This Hall can be protected and used for future consignments, as thousands can be put in this country.

I herewith submit instructions given by me to each man in writing—

To J. S. Crerar, re Galician Colonization—

1st. Build large camp at spot selected by me out of logs, sod roof, build it spacious as material is plentiful and close. Use Galician men to assist. Leave room in one end for supplies.

2nd. When you have sufficient room at camp for all, notify Interpreter Harvey at Yorkton all can be moved out as well as supplies which Harvey will take charge of as well as assist in doing other work by interpreting.

3rd. As soon as Mr. Hill notifies you that locations are ready, commence building houses on quarter-sections. Build them small but permanent out of logs, and have the Galicians plaster them with mud while in course of construction. See that they are dry before families go into possession if they have small children.

4th. Settle families without money first, and permit those who have money to assist themselves.

5th. Get what you want to efficiently carry out the work and do not keep any idle or indolent men or teams nor any men longer than they are required to do the work.

6th. Get the Galicians to assist. Mr. Hill will take from time to time what he requires to assist him to run the lines.

7th. Press the work as vigorously as possible to get these houses built and move each family into location.

8th. Keep record of dimensions of each house built.

9th. If any difficulty arises in connection with your work, wire to the Commissioner W. F. McCreary, Winnipeg, and await his instructions.

10th. Avoid useless or needless expenditures and get what you want to efficiently carry out the work.

11th. In building the Reception House for immigrants and to hold the present large colony, try and select odd numbered Section and report the same to Mr. Webster at once. He will hold it for the use of the Government to hold future consignements until they are located on these lands. Assist Hill to get a stake to start his work, and keep the Galician men as well employed as possible to put up proper buildings as the timber is good. Harvey will go out when you give him notice.

(Signed) C. W. Speers, For Commissioner of Immigration.

To efficiently carry out the work, I engaged Mr. J. S. Crerar, for the Immigration Department of the Dominion Government, for the sum of $3.00 per day, as director of work. I engaged another man to assist at $1 per day, two men and two teams at $3 each per day, under Mr. Crerar.

Instructions given to Geo. A. Hill, re Galician Colonization—

1st. Proceed at once to run lines with as much despatch as possible.

2nd. Keep record of each man's location, number of quarter-section and name.

3rd. Let Mr. J. S. Crerar know when you are ready so that he can proceed with construction of houses, as directed.

4th. Take any or all men you require to carry out your work, via running lines.

5th. If assistant comes on, direct him where to work in the south or north of Township, so as not to conflict with your work.

6th. Do all you can to settle these people as quickly as possible.

7th. Keep record so that you can report your work to Commissioner or myself in the future.

8th. If anything difficult presents itself, send a messanger to Yorkton and wire difficulty to W. F. McCreary, Commissioner, and await his instructions.

9th. Proceed as vigorously as possible with the work and assist Mr. Crerar all you can without any conflict or discord, and try to press the work. Mr. Crerar will assist you all in his power to make a success of this work.

(Signed) C. W. Speers, For Commissioner of Immigration.

Written instructions to Interpreter Harvey.

1st. Get the names of men, women and children, making the entire Yorkton Colony, with any particulars.

2nd. See that the baggage is all right and take note with particulars of any missing.

3rd. Keep as much reserve of flour as you can until people are settled as some of the poor families will require some in their homes.
4th. As all the poor people are moved out, let the rest go themselves and in case a few families, move them to colony when the Reception House is ready. Mr. Crerar will notify you when he is ready with building.
5th. Assist in any way you can to get these people on their lands. Settle the poor with large families first.
6th. Take the cow up I bought and distribute milk among the poor in small quantities.
7th. I would leave the flour in Yorkton unless what you want for use until the settlement is pretty well effected. Wire Mr. McCreary, Commissioner, for any instructions in case of difficulty.

(Signed) C. W. SPEERS.

SALTCOATS COLONY.

Instructions to Steinhard.

1st. Have your flour and supplies kept in a safe place under lock and sell to those who can pay for it at 80 cents per sack.
2nd. When Mr. MacNutt is ready and has some lines run and you can safely move the people, go out with them and assist in getting them on their lands.
3rd. See that the houses are dry before small children go into them.
4th. Secure teams for transportation of poor to colony with their baggage and see them located first—give them each a sack of flour at present.
5th. Do all you can to secure the early settlement of these people, and assist Mr. MacNutt with colony.
6th. When baggage is claimed that belongs to your people at present in Saltcoats, send or have forwarded to Winnipeg what is left.
7th. Do not incur any needless expenditure only get what is really required to carry out the work in supplying the wants of these people that are without money.
8th. Wire if you are in any trouble about anything to Commissioner W. F. McCreary, and await his instructions.

(Signed) C. W. SPEERS.

You will find hereto attached a synopsis of report from Thomas MacNutt pertaining to the work as far as the present which I requested him to submit to me. Pertaining to the dispute in the Beaver Hills of certain settlers on the same land, I have instructed Mr. Hill, when time will permit, to adjust the difficulty, which has occurred only in two cases.

I purchased a very fine cow for $30, instructing Harvey to take her to the Yorkton Colony and deliver milk in small quantities to poor families. The cow is in excellent condition, and as I did not want the calf, which was two weeks old, the man kept it at $5. You will find attached to this report agreement made with Robert Mitchell for rent of Warehouse for one month; also physician's report at Saltcoats and Yorkton all bills pertaining to transportation of all telegrams of importance, agreements made with men employed by me for the Department.

In the Yorkton colony there are several Townships of land available, all seemingly of good quality. The Galicians while in Yorkton purchased thirteen new waggons, several teams of horses, $275 worth of new harness, $250 worth of timber and hardware, and gave a great impetus to the commerce of the village. It was pleasingly significant that both dealers and merchants tried to place their implements and wares at a very low price, and did what they could to place a cheap equipment in the hands of their new settlers.

As this work has been gone into very fully, and every detail of it taken up, I would suggest that no additional expenditure pertaining to survey or inspection take place until about the 19th instant. Having efficient men, I believe, conducting its different departments, the colonization and settlement of these people should be effected on a low per capita allowance. I endeavoured to carefully go into every detail of the work, that no subsequent hitch nor excuse could be made, and permit me to say, Sir, that had I your counsel and mature judgement at times, it would have been very acceptable but in your absence did the very best to reflect credit on the Department and colonize these people in a satisfactory manner, looking well to the future.[14]

The Yorkton colony, so vividly described in its initial stages by Speers, was eventually to become the largest in Ukrainian settlement in Saskatchewan.[15]

Shortly after Speers' visit, in the last week of August, 1897, Father Dmytriw, attached to the immigration office in Winnipeg, visited the new colony at Crooked Lakes to attend to the spiritual needs of the settlers. His companion, whose name is not given, sent a description of their visit to *Svoboda*. Here are some interesting excerpts from the article:

I left for Yorkton in the company of the Reverend N. Dmytriw intending to visit our largest colony in the Assiniboia district. There exists an older colony in that district, called Pleasant Forks, but only a few (Ukrainian) families settled there. . . .

We arrived at Yorkton rather late, about 2 A.M., and in the morning we visited the immigration hall where we found some of our people waiting to be taken to Arden, Man., to start working on the rail road.

Yorkton is a small town, two mills, two hotels, a few stores and that's all. Our colony, named New Yaroslau, is situated some 52 miles north of Yorkton. . . . About 110 families settled in that colony, some coming from Galicia and some from Bukowina. They arrived there in July of this year. . . . As I already mentioned, the soil here is good with plenty of bush and excellent hay meadows. You can cut as much hay as you desire, if only you had the cattle to feed it to. But there are two main drawbacks here: scarcity of water and ground frosts which occur in May and towards the end of August. Some farms have abundant water and on some you cannot reach

[14]3. Gal./40035, July 9, 1897: C. W. Speers, Winnipeg, to W. F. McCreary, Winnipeg.

[15]Census of Canada, 1951, II, Table 34. Census Division No. 9, Yorkton, showed the following percentage division of the population: Ukrainian origin, 44.6%; British origin, 18.8%; German origin, 10.1%.

water no matter how deep you may dig. Ground frost in moist seasons is harmful, but in dry years it does not cause any damage at all. For instance, this year it caused no harm.

The settlers of this region predominantly raise stock, and the best cattle comes from Assiniboia. Our good people, those who brought some money with them have already started farming, but those who ventured out pennyless will have a hard time, although, the enterprising and the willing to work among them will get their bread, only the dumb and the lazy are bound to suffer.....

We visited several sections and on the third day of our stay we called on our good friends from Mt. Carmel, Pennsylvania. Alex Warcholyk, Iwan Khokholak and Roman Slezin settled on Sec. 34-Tp. 29-Rge. 3. They arrived here in the first days of August and in one month they managed to store a good supply of hay, dig a well and cut lumber for the erection of farm buildings. They live temporarily in a hut made out of hay, cook their own meals and are about to put up houses in order to be able to bring over their families. We spent three nights with them, sleeping on fragrant hay.

On the day of the Feast of Assumption [August 28] as well as on the following Sunday, August 29th, Father Dmytriw celebrated Mass in the new house of the well-to-do-settler Wasyl Krypiakevich. We returned to Yorkton on Sunday evening.

There are other colonies in the vicinity, at Beaver Creek and Saltcoats but we were unable to visit them....[16]

In September of the same year, the Ukrainian colonies of Yorkton and Saltcoats were visited by the Austrian-Hungarian Consul Eduard Schultze, accompanied by C. W. Speers, and after the visit Schultze dispatched the following telegram to the Commissioner of Immigration in Winnipeg:

Yorkton, N.W.T., September 9, '97.

W. F. McCreary, Winnipeg—

Have inspected colonies at Saltcoats and Yorkton accompanied by officer Speers from Whitewood. Am delighted for what I have seen. Beautiful country, specially adapted for settlement; far exceeds my expectations, good houses, spendid farms; am very thankful for your wise policy in placing these people. Mr. Speers has taken great pains to show every advantage of the people, the work done reflects great credit, is really wonderful. I extend to you the congratulations of my government for what I have seen. Hungarian colony at Whitewood very prosperous.

ED. SCHULTZE—Austrian-Hungarian Consul.[17]

III

For the settlers of Saltcoats, Crooked Lakes, and Beaver Hills—as for all homesteaders—the first year was the hardest. There was no abun-

[16]*Svoboda*, Mount Carmel, Pa., No. 38, September 16, 1897.

[17]3. Gal./43592, printed in *The Argus*, Stonewall, Manitoba, Thursday, September 16, 1897.

dance, but the danger of starvation for some of the destitute was staved off by Government assistance, modest as it was. During the second winter, 1898–1899, very few families required relief. Speers informed J. S. Crerar, the Dominion Immigration Agent in Yorkton, on January, 1899, of the fine progress made by the settlers:

In looking over the various Galician Colonies settled in the vicinity of Yorkton, I have found them, generally speaking in a satisfactory condition and making excellent progress. But there are a few, probably five or six families in the Saltcoats Colony, whose names I have submitted to you, and possibly two or three families in the large colony at Crooked Lakes, and the two families I have been referred to in the Beaver Hills that may require a little assistance. Considering there are 275 families in these three colonies, this is not a great number to be dependent. . . . I have drawn your attention to two or three cases, giving you particulars where Galicians have been defrauded out of their earnings. Kindly look into these matters and report to the Commissioner of Immigration in Winnipeg. . . .[18]

Speers sent the Superintendent of Immigration in Ottawa a report of inspection of the Colonies of different nationalities around Yorkton, which included a detailed description of the Ukrainian colonies in that region, particularly of "the Crooked Lake Colony of Galicians, established in June 1897, situated in Townships 28, 29, and 30, Ranges 2 and 3, W.2.M., thirty miles north-east of Yorkton."

This colony comprises 180 families, and they occupy a very desirable tract of country; a country rolling, rich and fertile, well timbered and well watered. They have sufficient building timber and fuel, possibly for light construction for many years to come, and their country is free from scrub and there are plenty of beautiful openings on each holding where every man can cultivate all the land he requires without loss of time being incured in clearing. This location is about ten or twelve miles from the selected site upon which the Doukhobors will be colonized, and the country in and around the vicinity of Pelly is considered very desirable.

Speers took understandable pride in the new colony, and indeed he was in great measure responsible for the settlement and the high level of progress attained by the immigrants. His report continued:

Accompanied by Mr. Crerar on Sunday morning, when we reached the summit of Sliding Hills, I could not help but notice the fact that where eighteen months previous to that date it has been my privilege to raise a number of tents and where there was no sign of improvement nor habitation, I could see with the naked eye the smoke ascending from no less than thirty or forty well erected houses, large hay stacks, a good deal of the land fenced and every evidence of thrift, progress and development. The

[18]8. Rpts./72482, January 12, 1899: C. W. Speers, Winnipeg, to J. S. Crerar, Dominion Immigration Agent, Yorkton, N.W.T. Copy of this letter forwarded to Frank Pedley, Ottawa.

contrast within the short space of time I have referred to was very striking, and evoked the remark that this truly was developing, to some extent, the agricultural resources of our country, as there is considerable cultivation in this colony.

I find this colony of Galicians have earned in cash this year from the Manitoba and North-Western Railway some $9,926, and as wealth is the product of labour, these people by their industry, are bound to succeed.

I also find that they are the owners of four hundred cows in that settlement, from information I have obtained from Mr. J. S. Crerar.

The women have made good use of their time while the men were employed in the Railways—have succeeded in putting up large quantities of hay and their stock is in excellent condition. They are a progressive colony, industrious, frugal and good settlers, and are giving the best satisfaction.

I will submit to you a few names to give you an idea of how they are getting along. [The information in parentheses is from C. W. Speers' Survey of August 8–13, No. 8, No. 65307, and from "Patents for Homesteads Records" in the Saskatchewan Archives.]:

Stefan Graber—Sec. 6-29-2 W.2.M. (Stefan Graba—SW¼-6-29-3) Good house and stable—$100. 21 tons of hay—$63. 2 acres ploughed—$6. One cow—$35. Has earned in cash at work on Railway this year $110. Came in June, 1897, with 25 cents capital.

Wasil Stefaniuk—6-29-2. (Wasyl Stefanuk—NE¼-6-29-3) House and stable—$125. Two horses—$100; Two cows—$60. Two calves—$20. 40 tons of hay—$120. 3 acres ploughed—$9. Came in June 1897 with capital of $110. Has earned considerable money with team.

Petro Jaholnizki—4-29-2. (Petro Jaholnitski—NW¼-36-28-3) Buildings—$100. 20 tons of hay—$75. 10 acres broken—$30. 2 horses—$100. 3 cows—$90. 4 calves—$40. Plough, waggon, mower and rake—$125. Has earned money cutting hay. Had $250 capital when he started.

Wasil Kreipokowicz—4-29-2. (Wasyl Krypiakevich) Good houses and stables—$250. 2 horses—$150. 6 cows—$180. 6 calves—$60. One bull—$40. Waggon, mower, rake and plough—$150. 4 acres broken—$120. 75 tons of hay—$200. Started with considerable capital.

Wasil Oystruk—6-29-2. (Wasyl Oystryck—NE¼-32-28-2) 2 oxen—$100. 3 cows—$90. 3 calves—$30. 40 tons of hay—$120. Good house and stable—$100. Started with capital of $100.

Simeon Jurko—16-29-2. (Hawrylo Jurkow—NE¼-16-29-2) Good house and stable—$70. 2 horses—$100. One cow—$30. One calf—$10. Waggon—$40. 40 tons of hay—$100. Came in spring of 1898 with $120 capital.

Simeon Kushner—4-29-2 (Semko Kushnir—SW¼-4-29-2) Good house and stable—$100. 2 oxen—$75. 3 calves—$30. 3 cows—$90. 30 tons of hay—$90. Waggon—$50. Came to the country in 1898 with about $200.

Joseph Korchinski—36-28-3. (Josef Gorczynski—SW¼-36-28-3) House and stable—$75. 2 horses—$100. 3 cows—$90. 3 calves—$30. 10 acres broken—$30. 40 tons of hay—$100. Waggon—$35. Came in June 1897 with $200 capital.

Franko Bandura—12-29-3. (Francis Bondura—SE¼-12-29-3) House and stable—$100. 3 acres ploughed—$9. One horse— $50. One cow—$30. One calf—$10. 40 tons of hay—$120. Came in June with capital of $75.

Anton Burchinski (Anton Brezinski—SW¼-12-29-3) House and stable—$150. Horse—$50. Cow—$30. Calf—$10. 30 tons of hay—$90. 5 acres ploughed—$15. Came in June 1897, with capital of $100.

Anton Auchamachuk—16-28-2. (Anton Achtymijczuk—NW¼-18-28-2) House and stable—$150. 2 cows—$60. 2 calves—$20. 5 acres ploughed—$15. 15 tons of hay—$45. Earned this year on the Railway $150. Came in June 1897, with no capital.

Wasil Nadurak—32-29-3. (Wasyl Nadureck—NW¼-32-29-3) House and stable—$150. 2 horses—$100. 2 colts—$40. 2 cows—$60. One heifer—$15. 2 calves—$20. 50 tons of hay—$150. 15 acres of land ploughed—$45. Waggon and plough—$80. Came in June 1897 with a capital of $220.

Tanis Harris—36-29-4. House and stable—$150. 2 horses $100. 3 cows—$90. 2 calves—$20. Waggon—$40. 45 tons of hay—$135. 15 acres ploughed—$45. Came in June, 1897, with a capital of $250.

Wasil Churney—24-28-3. (Wasyl Chornyj—NE¼-24-28-3) House and stable—$125. 2 cows—$60. Yearling—$15. 2 calves—$20. 40 tons of hay—$120. 10 acres of ploughing—$30. Came in June, 1897, with a capital of $100.

Iwan Tamaruk—6-29-2. (Iwan Temeruk—NW¼-6-29-3) House and stable—$75. 5 tons of hay—$15. 2 acres ploughed—$6. One cow—$30. Earned $100 this year on Railway. Came in June 1897 without any capital.

Rusko Olinski—House and stable—$100. 2 cows—$60. 20 tons of hay—$60. Had no capital when he came in June 1898.

In submitting to you the above number of Galicians, this can be generally accepted to govern the entire colony. There has been no disposition to single out or set apart a few of the more thrifty and frugal to put you in possession of other than actual facts that I have tried to elicit. But generally speaking, the colony is in good condition.

The want of an English-speaking school is felt, and, as I have hitherto reported on other Galician colonies, would be a rapid way to Canadianize these people and teach them our language. There are about 350 children of school age in this colony. A few are attending an English-speaking School which has been established near Jacob Wurtz' residence, and the teacher speaks very well of them as being bright and attentive.

There is no Church, but they contemplate building soon. This colony are mostly of the Greek Catholic faith.

I would next direct your attention to that colony of Galicians settled north-east of Saltcoats, in Townships 25, Ranges 31 and 32—consisting of about 45 Galician families—31 families settling there in June 1897 and the others coming in during the season of 1898. These Galicians possess a very good country, similar in many respects to that of the other colony, plenty of wood, ensuring a supply of fuel for many years; great quantities of hay, the country well watered and a rich loam, black soil. There is every evidence of thrift and prosperity among this Galician colony, and a great many are wintering cattle for the Firm of Messrs Gordon and Ironsides, Livestock Exporters, for which they receive from $6 to $7 per head.

There is no public school of any kind in this colony, although we concede there are about 125 children of school age. Therefore, the necessity of the establishment of English-speaking schools must be apparent, as this seems to be the universal wish of the Galician Colonies that have been established; they want national schools which will be English-speaking, and thinking that you might wish to direct the attention of the proper authorities, be they the Provincial Legislative Assembly or the North-West Government, to this fact, I have submitted it for your consideration, and you will find it pertains to the inspection of almost every large colony recently established. These people have expressed themselves that they do not want parochial or religious schools. They are mostly of the Greek faith. There is no Church or religious service held in this colony, but they are all anxious to have a Church of their own for public worship, and are making application to the Manitoba and North-Western Railway Company for a piece of land that will be used for a burial plot and a subsequent date they can erect a Church thereon.

Mr. Thomas MacNutt, who accompanied me, has consented to do all the correspondence for these people that will be necessary to the Railway Company.

I find in this colony a number of poor people who had made application to the Commissioner of Immigration for some relief, consisting of seven or eight families. You will find in a former letter of mine to you this matter was dealt with, and a copy of letter of instruction left by me handed to Agent Crerar in Yorkton. The causes, as nearly as I could ascertain, of these people being in want, are the following—Some through sickness. Some late arrival in 1898 that could not grow a crop. Some purchased cows and had no money left and could not get work. You will notice that I advised Mr. Crerar to permit these people to sell stock and assist themselves, where it would not militate against their future prosperity. But I considered it a mistake to have a settler sell his only cow to buy flour when perhaps a few bags of cheap flour would put him through the winter and the Department could be secured by regular form of lien, arrangements for which have been completed by the Commissioner of Immigration.

Again, it seems that this Saltcoats Colony, from the report that I took on the ground, have not been in receipt of all the information pertaining to work that could be obtained by the Railway Companies, and they say they did not know that they could get work. The same thing presented itself, permit me to say, at Edmonton, in the large Edna Colony. . . .

I am now convinced of [the settlers'] permanent establishment, and glad to know that they have been so satisfactory as labourers to the men who have given them employment, and I think we can rest assured that they will require little, or no attention after the present winter.[19]

Five years after the establishment of the Saltcoats colony, on July 10, 1902, Speers was able to report to Ottawa that in all respects the settlers were flourishing: "I beg to report that the condition of the Galician Colony at Saltcoats, comprising about 1000 souls, or 200 families, is in a most prosperous condition. Some of the Galician settlers have 50 acres of wheat. They will produce large quantities of grain to market this

19. Rpts./73855, January 31, 1899: C. W. Speers, Winnipeg, to Frank Pedley, Superintendent of Immigration, Ottawa.

fall, and their crop all looks very promising. They are getting machinery and comfortable homes, and I can estimate fairly that this one settlement possesses 800 head of cattle. The Galician settlers, whenever I have been in a position to come in contact with the Colonies, either in Saskatchewan or other districts in Manitoba or the Territories, are very prosperous, and among our best settlers."[20]

IV

Another Ukrainian colony, that of Fish Creek, on the South Saskatchewan River in the District of Saskatchewan, was established in June 1898, one year after the founding of the colonies at Saltcoats, Crooked Lakes, and Beaver Hills. It was born with greater pains and more stubborn resistance on the part of the pioneers of the colony than even its sister colonies in the Yorkton region. The location of the settlers who arrived in Winnipeg in a seemingly endless stream during the spring of 1898 put a great strain on Commissioner McCreary and his staff. The new arrivals, reluctant to take up homesteads offered to them in new locations, away from their fellow-nationals, created disturbances in the Immigration Hall. McCreary complained to Ottawa about the problem of handling the new settlers and the Superintendent of Immigration answered McCreary's letters, explaining to him that difficulties had to be expected and that patience had to be exercised with new immigrants:

> With reference to your letters, addressed to the Deputy Minister and myself, regarding the difficulties under which you are labouring in handling Galician immigrants, Mr. Smart and I have talked this matter over and realize that in the beginning there would necessarily be considerable trouble in dealing with them. We are satisfied, however, that once they are properly settled any trouble or money, within reasonable bounds, expended on them will be amply repaid in the near future. Coming as they do from a foreign land, unused to Canadian habits and customs, a policy to give and take must be exercised at first. The full effect of the work which is now being done by yourself and staff in connection with these people may not be seen for a few years but there is every evidence that this work is of a substantial character and that the younger members of these immigrants will prove first-class citizens even though as much may not be said of the older members.[21]

But the situation in the West was more complicated than the Deputy Minister and the Superintendent of Immigration believed it to be. News

[20]9. Rpts./215279, July 10, 1902: C. W. Speers, Winnipeg, to W. D. Scott, Superintendent of Immigration, Ottawa.

[21]4. Gal./34214, April 28, 1898: Frank Pedley, Ottawa, to W. F. McCreary, Winnipeg.

of unrest among the new immigrants appeared even in the pages of the eastern papers. The Toronto *Globe* of May 21, 1898, contained the following article on the problem:

GALICIAN IMMIGRANTS REVOLT AND MOUNTED POLICE ARE CALLED ON

(Special Despatch for The *Globe*)

C. W. Speers, western immigration agent, who accompanied the party of Galicians west on Tuesday [May 17] wires to the Commissioner from Saskatoon that the members of his party are in open revolt, and have got beyond his control. Mounted Police have been called in to assist the agents in quelling the disturbance. The trouble was caused partly by some of the Galicians being sent to a different part of the country than that to which they wished to go, and partly through a disposition of several of the leaders to be quarrelsome.[22]

It appears that the party of immigrants which Speers took from Winnipeg to settle in the Fish Creek region were not informed about their destination. When they arrived in Saskatoon and found out that they were going to Fish Creek rather than Edmonton, they refused to proceed and demanded to be taken to Edmonton, where they claimed to have relatives and friends. When their demand was refused, a number of them started to walk back to Regina. Speers wired Winnipeg for advice:

Almost distracted with these people, rebellious, act fiendish, will not leave cars, about seventy-five struck off walking Regina, perfectly uncontrollable. Nothing but pandemonium since leaving Regina. Have exhausted all legitimate tactics with no avail. Policeman here assisting situation—eclipses anything hitherto known. Edmonton, Edmonton or die. Will not even go inspect country, have offered liberal inducements, threatened to kill interpreter. Under existing circumstances strongly recommend their return Edmonton and few Dauphin and get another consignment people special train leaving here this afternoon. Could take them Regina. Answer immediately am simply baffled and defeated—quietest and only method will be their return. Waiting reply. Mostly have money and will pay fare. They are wicked.[23]

North West Mounted Police Commissioner Herchmer also wired McCreary in Winnipeg:

The following from Police Saskatoon—Galician emigrants under impression on road to Edmonton refuse to locate Fish Creek.[24]

[22]4. Gal./59571, The *Globe*, Toronto, Saturday, May 21, 1898.

[23]4. Gal./59672, Telegram, May 19, 1898: C. W. Speers, Saskatoon, to W. F. McCreary, Winnipeg.

[24]4. Gal./59672, Telegram, May 19, 1898: L. W. Herchmer, Commissioner, N.W.M.P., Regina, to W. F. McCreary, Winnipeg.

The situation was becoming serious, and McCreary answered Speers' telegram with instructions on how to deal with the settlers.

> Am trying to see Fred Jones about these people. Tell them we have letters from Edmonton, Dauphin today that Homesteads those places all taken up. Leave them bread; have interpreter tell them where they can buy more milk, and you and he leave them for a while to think over. Tell them teams are ready to take them out free, with three sacks flour and five bushels potatoes for each family. Will wire you later when I see Jones. Answer. Will it avail anything to send Genik and Harvey up Saturday?[25]

At the same time, McCreary sent a wire to the Commissioner of the Mounted Police in Regina, asking that police be sent to assist Speers:

> Please instruct your detachments Saskatoon and Fish Creek or nearest points assist C. W. Speers maintaining order and locating Galicians and advise him. Immigrants reported very unruly.[26]

Herchmer complied immediately with this request:

> Have ordered experienced sergeant and two men to Fish Creek to assist Speers in maintaining order and locating Galicians.[27]

On the same day, May 19, a second wire arrived from Speers to McCreary, emphasizing the seriousness of the situation:

> Seventy-five souls walking Regina intercepted them with police thirteen miles away, sending bread could not turn them. They have few guns and are determined—will take several policemen return them—have submitted every liberal proposition fully appreciating your anxiety. Send Genik and Harvey Saturday.[28]

McCreary informed the Deputy Minister in Ottawa about the happenings in Fish Creek and Saskatoon and also mentioned that in order to persuade the immigrants to proceed to Fish Creek, they had been told that their train was bound for Edmonton and Dauphin:

> Referring to previous correspondence with yourself and the Minister, and to your letter of the 17th instant, expressing your anxiety that a number of settlers should be placed in the Saskatoon district, about Fish Creek, as I have already written you, I despatched Mr. Speers there some time ago, located a suitable place for a colony and forwarded a number of Galicians about 200 a few days ago.

[25]4. Gal./59672, Telegram, May 19, 1898: W. F. McCreary, Winnipeg, to C. W. Speers, Saskatoon.

[26]4. Gal./59672, Telegram, May 19, 1898: W. F. McCreary, Winnipeg, to the Commissioner, N.W.M.P., Regina.

[27]4. Gal./59672, Telegram, May 19, 1898: L. W. Herchmer, Regina, to W. F. McCreary, Winnipeg.

[28]4. Gal., Telegram, May 19, 1898: C. W. Speers, Saskatoon, to W. F. McCreary, Winnipeg.

> They did not want to go, but we represented that the train was going to Edmonton and Dauphin, and by this means they were induced to go up.[29]

McCreary should, of course, have anticipated that when the settlers found out that they had been deceived, they would protest. In the same communication, he notified the Deputy Minister of his next step:

> I intend going up tonight (May 20th) myself, although I have been ill for two days, and taking two Interpreters, Harvey and Genik my regular interpreter who is down the line to-day meeting the 132 who came from Genoa by the "Spartan Prince". We will all go up and try to assist Speers; but if we fail, we shall just have to move them away on Monday to Edmonton and Dauphin. . . .

Commissioner McCreary arrived in Saskatoon on May 21, 1898, accompanied by the two interpreters, Cyril Genik and Philip Harvey. They all went to Rosthern, visited Fish Creek, and learned that Speers had already established a nucleus of the colony with the settlers who did not join the trek to Regina, but who, after an inspection of the region, found it satisfactory and decided to stay. McCreary returned to Winnipeg and sent a detailed report on the situation to Ottawa, pointing out that changes had to be made in the selection of destinations for settlers:

> Referring to my letter of a few days ago in reference to the turbulent Galicians at Saskatoon, I beg to say that I returned from Saskatoon this morning [May 25] and brought with me quite a large number of the people who had been taken up there. However, we succeeded in our purpose to a certain extent, that is, we formed the nucleus of a new colony in Township 41, Range 1, some twelve families remained there and forty-seven returned, thirty of whom are destined for Edmonton and seventeen for Sifton.
>
> You cannot imagine the difficulty there is to get these people to go to a new place; it either has to be done by force or deception.
>
> Now, there is no doubt some change has got to be made in the way of handling these people. They cannot be allowed to come here and select for themselves where they are going; there must be some means of compelling them to go where the Government Agents select. . . .[30]

McCreary thought that some feasible plan could be evolved to prevent the repetition of confusion they experienced first in Yorkton, and now in the Fish Creek region, and he put forth his own suggestion:

> My own idea would be to try on the party now at Halifax a new experience, that is, that I should go to Halifax with Mr. Genik, decide at that point

[29]4. Gal./59672, May 20, 1898: W. F. McCreary, Winnipeg, to James A. Smart, Ottawa.

[30]4. Gal./55942, May 25, 1898: W. F. McCreary, Winnipeg, to James A. Smart, Ottawa.

where the people should be sent, that is, those having close relatives, such as brothers, fathers, sisters and mothers in any one of the present colonies, send them there; those having no relatives, or distant relatives in any of the colonies, send them to Fish Creek or some new settlement. If a train load could be secured for Fish Creek have that train run through to that point without change, running through Winnipeg and Regina in the night. Those for Yorkton would be ticketed through to Yorkton and stop them only at Portage la Prairie to change cars. Those for Edmonton would go straight through to Calgary, or, if sufficient in number, by a special train to their destination. If a lot of them refused to decide where they were going, or refused to go where they were told to go, then they should be instructed there and then to return to Austria unless they would follow the advice of the officials. . . .

His letter also contained the lists of those who were sent on to Edmonton and to Dauphin because they refused to settle at Fish Creek:[31]

List of Galicians who went to Saskatoon and returned to Edmonton—

<table>
<tr><th></th><th></th><th>Capital</th></tr>
<tr><td>1.</td><td>Iwan Melnyk, wife and 7 children</td><td>$1000</td></tr>
<tr><td>2.</td><td>Franz Witwicki, wife and 6 children</td><td>50</td></tr>
<tr><td>3.</td><td>Pawel Fedorkiw, wife and 4 children</td><td>100</td></tr>
<tr><td>4.</td><td>Harasym Juzda</td><td>—</td></tr>
<tr><td>5.</td><td>Ilko Jakimishyn, wife and 4 children</td><td>80</td></tr>
<tr><td>6.</td><td>Todor Nykyforuk, wife and 3 children</td><td>115</td></tr>
<tr><td>7.</td><td>Jakym Chmelyk, wife and 1 child</td><td rowspan="2">500</td></tr>
<tr><td>8.</td><td>Kindrat Chmelyk and wife</td></tr>
<tr><td>9.</td><td>Fed. Bojko, wife and 6 children</td><td>500</td></tr>
<tr><td>10.</td><td>Hnat Lisowyj, wife and 2 children</td><td>100</td></tr>
<tr><td>11.</td><td>Andran Hasij, wife and 2 children</td><td>150</td></tr>
<tr><td>12.</td><td>Semon Widoniak, wife and 1 child</td><td>50</td></tr>
<tr><td>13.</td><td>Oleksa Podruski, wife and 1 child</td><td rowspan="2">600</td></tr>
<tr><td>14.</td><td>Michal Podruski, wife and 3 children</td></tr>
<tr><td>15.</td><td>Gawrylo Odynski, wife and 3 children</td><td>164</td></tr>
<tr><td>16.</td><td>Leop. Wincentowicz, wife and 1 child</td><td>180</td></tr>
<tr><td>17.</td><td>Safat Perun, wife and 1 child</td><td>—</td></tr>
<tr><td>18.</td><td>Wasyl Herman, 2 children</td><td rowspan="2">60</td></tr>
<tr><td>19.</td><td>Anna Herman, 1 child</td></tr>
<tr><td>20.</td><td>Fedor Jabowica, wife and 2 children</td><td>100</td></tr>
<tr><td>21.</td><td>Dmytro Gregorashchuk, 2 children</td><td>54</td></tr>
<tr><td>22.</td><td>Georg Puchalski, wife and 2 children</td><td>200</td></tr>
<tr><td>23.</td><td>Georg Lupul, wife and 1 child</td><td>150</td></tr>
<tr><td>24.</td><td>Wasyl Lupul, wife and 5 children</td><td>400</td></tr>
<tr><td>25.</td><td>Jakym Krys, wife and 2 children</td><td>100</td></tr>
<tr><td>26.</td><td>Georg Bidniak, wife and 2 children</td><td>380</td></tr>
<tr><td>27.</td><td>Georg Melaychuk and wife</td><td>400</td></tr>
<tr><td>28.</td><td>Dmytro Danyluk and wife</td><td>17</td></tr>
<tr><td>29.</td><td>Dmytro Klymochko, wife and 3 children</td><td>200</td></tr>
<tr><td>30.</td><td>Michael Ferlecki</td><td>—</td></tr>
</table>

314. Gal./59943 and 59944, May 25, 1898: W. F. McCreary, Winnipeg, to James A. Smart, Ottawa.

List of Galicians who went to Saskatoon and then to Sifton:

1.	Pantelej Krupa, wife and 1 child	$ 100
2.	Pawel Sopel, wife and 2 children	80
3.	Kath. Perzylo	—
4.	Wojciech Skulmowski, wife and 4 children	100
5.	Janko Kicherawy, wife and 3 children	70
6.	Jakiw Kindrat, wife and 3 children	100
7.	Hnat Kuzyk, wife and 4 children	80
8.	Michas Kuzyk, wife and 3 children	100
9.	Andrij Kendzierski, wife and 2 children	70
10.	Iwan Kindzierski and wife	100 (10–11)
11.	Elena Kindzierska	
12.	Iwan Lukijanchuk, wife and 4 children	100 (12–13)
13.	Jurko Hrushka	
14.	Iwan Marcyniuk, wife and 4 children	50
15.	Michael Atamanchuk, wife and 2 children	40
16.	Stefan Atamanchuk and wife	33
17.	Iwan Saranchuk, wife and 3 children	70

Some ten days after the disturbing events of the revolt, C. W. Speers returned to Winnipeg and presented his report to the Commissioner:

I beg to submit a report of the arrival of Galicians at Fort William on the 15th instant.

Assisted by Interpreter Genik and Wendelbo we endeavoured to persuade a large number of these to go to Saskatoon and colonize in the Fish Creek district, in that good country, which I had inspected the previous week. Without much consultation with the people we had decided to move about fifty families to that place, knowing its special adaptability for Galician colonization, and keeping before our minds the fact that you were anxious to place a colony there, knowing that as many for the present had been placed at Edmonton and Dauphin as it was your desire to send.

Having experienced difficulty in the past in founding a new colony of these people at Yorkton and other places, I may say that the same difficulty presented itself at Saskatoon, but the Galicians were more persistently obstinate in this case than in any other hitherto. As you are aware from the messages and correspondence passing between yourself and me, and finally necessitating your trip to Saskatoon, matters were in an unsettled condition.

I may say that I could not induce a large number of these people to listen to reason. I held out very liberal inducements to them; treated them with every consideration, but they were so self-willed and determined that there was no alternative other than the one resorted to. The only plea made by these people was the one that they had some relatives, either near or distant, living at some other point. . . .

The Fish Creek district possesses every natural advantage for these people, and I may say now that the nucleus of a colony has been established there, you can send five or six hundred souls in at any time, and they can be located at a very low expense.

Although somewhat disappointed in not placing all the people, when we consider the success of permanently locating a number of families that are so contented and so happy, little difficulty will be experienced in the future. . . .

Speers relates how some families expressed their joy over selecting their new homesteads. The families of Macko Michalkow, Nykola Lucyshyn, Franko Rozdolka, Jasko Waliduda, Jasko Matuszewski, Jignac Ganczar, Wasyl Toms, Jasko Michalkow, Antoni Michalkow, and Stefan Wawryk ". . . were all so happy on the night of the 24th instant, that around a large camp fire on the prairie they sang their national songs; they were delighted with the surroundings, and gave every tangible evidence that they were more than pleased with their location. I selected for the camp a spot looking down upon a beautiful lake, well wooded, and the prairie all that could be desired. . . ."[32] Despite Speers' optimism, however, his difficulties were far from over. On June 6, an additional transport of 738 Galician immigrants arrived in Halifax on the S.S. *Italia.* These people headed west and were met by Speers. He selected twenty-one families from this group and conducted them to Fish Creek. Having put them up satisfactorily in the camp, he returned to Winnipeg, only to receive an urgent telegram from R. S. Cook, the Homestead Inspector at Duck Lake, who informed him that 35 men of the newly-settled group had come back to Duck Lake seeking to hire teams to bring their families and baggage from Fish Creek to the rail point, as they wished to be taken to Edmonton. When Commissioner McCreary learned this news, he wired Ottawa for advice. The Deputy Minister sent back his instructions: "Think you should send Father Dmytrow to urge Galicians to settle Fish Creek. He must remain now until these people are settled. Think it a great mistake in their own interest to go to Edmonton and advise instance on their location."[33]

Mr. Cook outlined in a letter to McCreary a possible reason for the sudden decision of the newly-settled families to quit Fish Creek:

So far we have not been able to do anything with the last batch of Galicians. The heavy frost of Sunday and Monday night spoiled everything and could reason with them no longer. 34 of the men started for Duck Lake yesterday leaving their families behind, they are now waiting for the down train and seem determined to go. They tried to get teams to go for their families but so far we have been able to stop them. Measles have broken out in the camp and I came in to consult a doctor. We have rigged up a small tent and put a stove in it and will do all we can for the sick children.

[32]4. Gal./60179, May 30, 1898: C. W. Speers, Winnipeg, to W. F. McCreary, Winnipeg.

[33]4. Gal., Telegram, June 17, 1898: James A. Smart, Ottawa, to W. F. McCreary, Winnipeg.

There are only three cases as yet; the weather has now turned warm and I am in hopes we may yet be able to settle them.[34]

In view of the mounting unrest, Speers left Winnipeg for Duck Lake and Fish Creek to tend to the matter personally, accompanied by Father Nestor Dmytriw, as the Deputy Minister suggested. On June 19, Speers reported to the Commissioner in Winnipeg, indicating his determination to settle the immigrants satisfactorily if at all possible:

To-day has been a busy day, all the people have been here except five families that Roy Cook located at Fish Creek. The heavy frost drove them out.

I got them all to attend the Catholic Church here to-day and Father Dmytriw gave them the right sort of a lecture, and after Church again we talked off the Station platform and have kept constantly after them. It is needless to tell you how they worry one. Tomorrow I will try another location taking out some of the men first. I am determined that these people must settle here, if such a thing is possible and am hopeful that it can to a great extent be accomplished. You need not fear, I am not weak about the matter, but fully decided to try everything, and knowing that you have plenty of trouble there will endeavour to work this out alone. These are a self willed lot and stubborn with a few very bad ones that help keep the matter inflamed with the others.

They are sleeping everywhere, baggage and people.

I will endeavour to get location to suit them and will telegraph you. I enclose Dr. Stewart's certificate these are all healthy enough.

If John [Steinhard] gets in I will send him down as Schultz will do here and T. O. Davies is very anxious that Ens should try his hand for a day or two. Father Dmytriw feels bad the people said he sold them to the Government. I am almost too tired to write as I have been on the go since early morn.[35]

Commissioner McCreary informed Deputy Minister Smart about the dissatisfaction of the settlers:

I have your letter of the 18th instant and in reply beg to say that prior to receipt of same I had already arranged that Father Dmytrow should go up to Fish Creek, accompanied by Mr. Speers, and endeavour to conciliate these people. Father Dmytrow was inclined to think that they should be allowed to go where they wished, but after considerable discussion he and I agreed that if at all possible they should be forced to remain there.

I learn from an Interpreter who I had up there, and who returned this morning, that there was a heavy frost about the morning they moved out to the Colony from Duck Lake. It cut down the potato vines and garden stuff, and discouraged the people.

[34]4. Gal., June 13, 1898: R. S. Cook, Homestead Inspector, Duck Lake, N.W.T., to W. F. McCreary, Winnipeg.

[35]4. Gal./61631, June 19, 1898: C. W. Speers, Duck Lake, to W. F. McCreary, Winnipeg.

In addition to this, of course, there was the hardship of their children sleeping on the ground without very much covering. In fact, he said the white frost was so thick you could gather it up in your hand like snow; so it is not much wonder the people became somewhat dissatisfied.

As soon as Father Dmytrow returns I will let you know the result at this colony.[36]

Gradually the immigrants quieted down and some of them came to the conclusion that it would do no harm, before making their final decision, to have a better look at the surrounding country which, from a farmer's point of view, did not perhaps look so bad after all. C. W. Speers reported to the Commissioner on June 22 that some progress was being made despite the obstinacy of many of the settlers:

I have just returned from East of Rosthern, in Tp. 42 Range 3, where about ten or twelve families of the Galicians will settle, the rest have had every conceivable inducement; held out.

I sent them North West to Windguard [Wingard] five delegates accompanied by Father Dmytrow and good guide. To-day I accompanied them South, in fact, they have had every chance, and many of them remain sulky, indifferent and obstinate.

They have not received one pound of flour nor anything else and they may come to [in] time.

Father Dmytrow leaves to-morrow morning as I left him at Rosthern to-night and have just got here. He is anxious to get back and has done all he could with these people. The families near Rosthern will be settled in a few days by Friday night.

If nothing can be done to-morrow in the morning early as I will try to get some more out, but if I fail I will send Cook home, store the Government tents, put supplies away, put everything in order, show the Galicians the Land Office and tell them when they make up their minds they can enter. I have tried everything and the paupers are the worst. I am trying to get them settled on vacant land anywhere, and do not consider any such idea as to let them go back. Write me here, as I will suspend operations leaving [Schultz] until these people become reasonable. I will, I hope, get away next Monday before which time something may be done.[37]

At last the immigrants found a place of settlement that suited them. Speers wired the good news to Winnipeg on June 27: "Galicians contented; successfully and permanently located east of Rosthern near Fish Creek. Most of them have taken land—Everything well."[38]

[36]4. Gal./61663, June 21, 1898: W. F. McCreary, Winnipeg, to James A. Smart, Ottawa.

[37]4. Gal./61865, June 22, 1898: C. W. Speers, Duck Lake, N.W.T., to W. F. McCreary, Winnipeg.

[38]4. Gal./61935, June 29, 1898: W. F. McCreary, Winnipeg, quoting C. W. Speers' telegram of June 27 to the Superintendent of Immigration in Ottawa.

V

The settlement of Fish Creek colony was thus accomplished in June of 1898. On his return to Winnipeg, Mr. Speers submitted his report, summarizing the details of the arduous task that was now completed:

I beg to submit my report of the final settlement of the Galician Colony at Fish Creek and Rosthern—leaving Winnipeg on Thursday, the 16th instant [June] accompanied by Father Dmytrow. Getting off at Brandon with J. H. Pettifer, representing the United Empire Trades League, and engaged as a Lecturer in England, I shewed him the Experimental Farm and drove him through a portion of the best country for about twenty-five miles by Alexander, the Assiniboine River, taking the train with him at Griswold and proceeding to Fish Creek.

On arriving at Duck Lake, I found the Galicians all camped around the Station, and determined to return. A very heavy frost which occured on Monday night [June 13], also on Sunday night previous had so frightened them, that they had decided to leave the district. I may say the frost was unprecedented, even old settlers told me that in twenty years they had never seen its equal. Ice was formed three quarters of an inch thick; many of the small trees were blighted, the foliage entirely black.

I arranged with Father Poquette to permit Father Dmytrow to address the people in the Church at Duck Lake, believing that he could wield more influence in this way. We got most of them out to the Church, and Father Dmytrow addressed them at some length. This may have had some effect, but I am under impression they are not very susceptible to clerical influence, remaining obstinate, sulky, indefinite in purpose and difficult to manage.

On Monday morning I sent one deputation to Wingard, accompanied by the Priest, and being specially requested by T. O. Davis, Member for Saskatchewan, had Mr. Ens and Mr. Roy take four or five more to Rosthern. All delegates returned seemingly well pleased, and after considerable delay I loaded eight families in wagons with their baggage, sending them to the Rosthern Colony. Twenty-two paid their fare as far as Rosthern on the first train, determined to leave. I sent Mounted Police on the train, but they were put off without any difficulty. Twenty-five or thirty more walked from Duck Lake to Rosthern. I followed them there, and after considerable persuasion induced them to go down and settle. It was Saturday morning when I got the last nine families loaded at Duck Lake and all sent to the one colony. We had incessant rain Thursday, Friday and Saturday, but I may say that after the continued fight, the contention, the trouble and worrying, they were all in the Government tents seemingly very contented and happy, and on Sunday morning at 12 o'clock twenty-eight of them had been located on their land.

The more dependent portion of these people have been the most troublesome. I did not give them one morsel of anything until they had decided where to go, but they would gather toadstools and fungus in the woods, and with the little assistance they secured from the citizens, were enabled to continue their fight. I expect by Monday or Tuesday this colony will be finally settled.

I built one house; built it very substantially, putting a heavy ridge pole and heavy poles leaning from the ground, being A shaped. I instructed Mr. Roy to build about fifteen such houses; this can be done in two or three days; put two or three sacks of flour, according to the number in family; a sack or two of potatoes in the houses of the people who are dependent, and get them in a position that the men can go to work forthwith.

We have been, I can safely say, very judicious with supplies, but we have been necessitated to give the dependant families and possibly even some with a little means, an occasional sack of flour and some potatoes. The expense incurred will be very considerable, as some of the supplies have been freighted from Saskatoon to the Fish Creek Colony, and from Fish Creek to Duck Lake to the new colony, incurring a haul of about eighty-five miles.

These people have been well supplied with boxes and bags and heavy baggage; the roads have been very muddy, and although the teamsters have worked at starvation prices, only $2.50 per day for man and team and they boarding themselves, still even at these low prices securing the peaceful and successful settlement of these malcontents has incurred a good deal of hauling. There are about fifteen families in Township 41, Range 1—the others will be in Township 42, Range 1, and Township 42, Range 2. They will only be divided by the Saskatchewan River, and as the North-West Government are putting a ferry on, these people will be mostly together.

I let a contract to Tremblay to put in an additional 2½ acres of potatoes, and owing to the recent rains, they should be a very good crop. This will make eight or nine acres of potatoes the Government have planted in close proximity to these people, and in the Fall they should largely assist in any maintenance that may be required in that district.

I telegraphed Mr. Milestone, Superintendent, and secured employment for fifteen men on Section work between Moose Jaw and Estevan. I requested Mr. Roy and Mr. Ens to make all haste to get these men to work. Others are obtaining work from the Mennonites in the vicinity of Rosthern; a number of young girls are at service and giving good satisfaction. These people have been well received by the settlers; they have a very fine piece of country, and should in future give very little trouble. With a little encouragement and assistance to get work, even the poor families should be in a position to make the situation self-sustaining. They are all happy and contented, and I look for no future trouble. As the first work in establishing a new colony has hitherto been troublesome and somewhat expensive, this class has been only similar to the others—the work has been done economically and in a practical manner, simply satisfying the people; those who were dependant put in a position to live, and employment being found.[39]

Five months later, in November, 1898, Speers made an inspection of the already well-established colony and sent his report to the Superin-

394. Gal./62333, June 29, 1898: C. W. Speers, Winnipeg, to W. F. McCreary, Winnipeg.

tendent of Immigration in Ottawa. He made special mention of the exceptional rate of progress of the Fish Creek colony:

I beg to submit a report of inspection of the Colony of Galicians at Fish Creek, from which place I have just returned. This is the last Colony of Galicians established in the North West, the first being placed there in June 1898, and subsequently supplemented in July and August. The ensuing report will show the progress made by these settlers in the short period of time since their advent to the country.

I have carefully gone into the matter and visited every settler and consider these people have done remarkably well, and are very permanently settled in good substantial houses, many of which are a credit to these people. They have made as great progress for the time and their improvements are more permanent than any other colony of their nationality hitherto established by the Department. The evidence of the people in the district goes to prove that they are desirable settlers, almost unanimously. They are industrious, thrifty people and where they have been employed on the Railway as laborers either doing section work or in Gravel Pits have given excellent satisfaction. . . .

I might intimate that the Galician Colony at Fish Creek is divided by the Saskatchewan River, and that a portion of the colony are on the east side of the South Branch in the vicinity of Fish Creek, and the remainder are on the west side of the River in the vicinity of Rosthern. The Northwest Government has placed a ferry which connects the colony and makes the means of egress and ingress to and from Fish Creek to the market at Rosthern very desirable. There has been a disposition on the part of the Executive of the North West Assembly to do all they can to meet our wishes in every respect to make the colonization of these people a success, they having agreed to put down some wells with their boring machine and placing a ferry on the river.

You will find the settlers on the south side in the Fish Creek vicinity in Township 41, Range 1, and Township 42, Range 1, are as follow, with their respective improvements, which demonstrates the fact that progress has been made—[40]

Iwan Yurasyk (NR: Yurasick, Iwan; Residence: Alvena, Sask.; Occupation: Farmer; Former Residence: Kolomea, Austria; Nationality: Austrian; Date when granted: May 16, 1902; Name of Court: Supr. Court, Prince Albert; No. of return: 34.) 7 souls—River Lot 9. House 14 × 24—$50; Log stable—$25; 2 cows—$50; 7 chickens; 5 acres fenced; 1 acre ploughed; 3 sacks of flour; 10 bushels of potatoes. Has earned $30 in cash on railway at $1.25 per day. Good well; 5 tons of hay—has $18 cash.

Ilko Bukurak (NR: Bukuryk, Ilko) 2 souls—River Lot 10. House—$25; Log stable—$25; Cow and heifer—$40; 4 tons of hay—$8; Cash—$18. 30 days at $1.25 per day.

---

[40]In order to verify the proper spelling of the names of the settlers, Naturalization Records in the Saskatchewan Archives, as well as the Cummins Rural Directory Map, 1922, have been consulted. The information from these two sources appears in parenthesis, preceded by the abbreviation NR or CM.

Onofry Romancyz (NR: Romanczycz, Onufry) River Lot 12. House 18 × 20; Supply of potatoes; has worked 1½ months at $1.25 per day. Cash $40. Good well.

Frank Hulick (NR: Hulyk, Fedor) House—$40; Stable—$20; Cow—$25; Cash—$20; 20 sacks of flour in house. Not properly located on land.

Joseph Hryzak (NR: Hrycak, Joseph) 7 souls—Section 6-41-1. Good house 18 × 24—$80; Good stable—$75; Cow and heifer—$40; Good well; 20 tons of hay—$40; Chickens; 800 lbs of flour in house. 3 boys—worked all summer on Railway.

Michalo Michalko (NR: Michalkow, Maciej; CM: M. Michalkiw) SW¼-4-41-1; SE¼-3-41-1. Good log house 20 × 26—$100; 2 horses—$95; 2 colts—$40; Good stable—$50; One cow and calf—$35; New wagon—$70; Harness—$15; Plough—$25; 25 tons of hay—$50; Cash on hand—$100; One acre garden; 8 sacks of flour in house; Quantity of potatoes—a splendid settler.

Jasko Matuschowski (NR: Matuszewski, Jan) 4 souls—Section 4-41-1. Good log house 18 × 24—$100; 5 acres ploughed; 2 horses—$70; One colt—$20; Good log stable 18 × 30—$50; One cow and calf—$40; 20 tons of hay—$60; New Wagon—$70; Plough—$25; Harness—$15.

Wasyl Doms (In another Speers' report: Wasyl Toms) 7 souls—Section 4-41-1. House 18 × 30—$30; Stable 14 × 18—$25; 20 tons of hay—$40; 10 acres ploughed—$30; One wagon—$25; 2 horses—$50; One cow and heifer—$35; One plough—$10; 7 sacks of flour in house—working 3 months at $1.25 per day. This family suffered a small loss by fire but are well provided for the winter.

Jaska Waleduda (NR: Waleduda, Jan; CM: M. & D. Waliduda; NW¼-41-1) Good log house 18 × 24—$100; Stable 18 × 20—$50; One horse—$34; 2 cows—$46; 3 calves—$26; One wagon—$25; One plough—$5; 3 acres ploughed—$9; 8 tons of hay—$16; Cash—$10; 2 sacks of flour. Everything in good shape; but no water on this section. This is one of the sites on which the Government will bore.

Michalo Luczichen (NR: Lucyszyn, Mikolaj) 5 souls—Section 10-41-1—Good log house 18 × 24—$100; Good stable 18 × 20—$50; One horse—$23; One cow—$20; 2 calves—$15; 9 tons of hay—$18; Wagon—$20; Plough—$5; Cash—$3.

Franko Rasdoljko (NR: Rozdolka, Franko; CM: F. Rozkolka; NW¼-3-41-1) Section 10-41-1. Good log house 18 × 24—$100; Good stable—$50; One horse—$30; One cow—$22; 2 heifers—$15; 9 tons of hay—$18; one acre broken. Working on railway at $1.25 per day.

Stefan Wawrik (NR: Wawryk, Marcin; CM: S. Wawryk—NE¼-3-41-1; NW¼-2-41-1) Section 10-41-1. 5 souls. Good log house 20 × 24—$125; Good stable 20 × 20—$50; 2 horses—$60; 2 cows—$50; 2 calves—$15; Wagon—$50; Plough—$25; Harness—$10; 2 acres ploughed—$6; 10 tons of hay—30; Cash—$50; 3 sacks flour in house—Very good settler.

Barchenski, John—5 souls—Section 16-41-1. House 16 × 18—$50; Log stable—$20; One horse—$20; One cow—$20; One calf—$10; 6 tons of hay—$12; Cash $4. Good well—2 acres ploughed.

Alexander Chrick (CM: A. Chryk SW¼-16-41-1—Section 16-41-1) House 16 × 18—$40; Stable 20 × 30—$60; 10 tons of hay—$20; No money—wife in Austria.

Jacob Matkowski—6 souls—Section 16-41-1 (NR: Matkowski, Jakub; CM: J. Matkowski NE¼-16-41-1) House 16 × 18—$50; Stable 14 × 18—$25; One horse—$20; One cow—$25; One calf—$10; 5 tons of hay—$15. No money.

Wasel Romanchuk—Section 6-41-1. House—$50; One cow—$30; Two horses—$70; One wagon—$30. Is settled on Rosthern side; selling out to another Galician for $100—has earned considerable money with team.

Michal Turton—Section 20-41-1 (NR: Turta Michal; CM: N. & A. Turta; SE¼-20-41-1). Has taken up the entire Section on three sons, Ivan, Andre and Anton—Log house 18 × 30—$100; Stable 16 × 20—$30; Two horses—$70; One cow—$39; One calf—$15; Wagon—$60; Harness—$20; 25 tons of hay—$50. Cash $30. Two sacks of Flour. Three sons working out—well-to-do for winter. Has dug wells but no water. This is another point selected for Government well-borer. They having decided and agreed to put down two in that colony.

Kachimir Biletzky—4 souls—Section 22-41-1 (NR: Bilecki, Kazio) House 16 × 20—$30; Stable 12 × 14—$30; One horse—$60; Cow and calf—$40; wagon and harness—$40; 10 tons of hay—$20; Three acres ploughed. No flour—no money.

Constantine Schumakah—4 souls—Section 22-41-1 (NR: Szumelak, Kost; CM: Schumelak, K. NE¼ 22-41-1) House 16 × 18—$30; Stable 14 × 18—$10; 10 tons of hay—$20; Four acres ploughed—$12; One horse—$36; One cow and calf—$40; Cash—$20; 650 lbs. of flour.

Andre Hawraschuk—2 souls—Section 22-41-1 (CM: A. Hawryshchuk NW¼ 22-41-1) House 16 × 18—$30; Stable 14 × 20—$30; One horse—$23; One cow and calf—$40; 6 tons of hay—$12.

Nicholi Viciniski—4 souls—Section 22-41-1 (CM: N. Wyzinski SE¼ 22-41-1) House 14 × 16—$25; Stable 12 × 12—$15; Cow—$30; 4 tons of hay—$8; 4 acres ploughed—$12; Cash—$17.

Joseph Bilenski—8 souls—Section 28-41-1 (NR: Bilinski, Joseph) One horse—$28; One cow—$26; One plough—$12; 12 tons of hay—$24; 2 sacks of flour. No buildings; came late; living on same Section with another Galician. (CM: Bilinski, J. NE¼ 28-41-1.)

Anton Walkoo (Anton Michalkow?)—3 souls—Section 28-41-1. House 18 × 24—$60; Stable 14 × 16—$30; Small building 12 × 14—$15; Horse—$20; Cow—$26; Calf—$10; Wagon—$27; 6 acres ploughed—$18; 4 tons of hay—$8; Cash—$2.

Thomas Kosack—6 souls—Section 28-41-1 (CM: T. Kozak SW¼ 28-41-1) cow and calf—$30; 4 tons of hay—$8; Cash—$14.

Marzin Oleskow—4 souls—Section 28-41-1 (NR: Oleskow, Marcin; CM: M. Oleskiw SE¼ 28-41-1) House 18 × 24—$75; Stable 14 × 20—$50; 12 tons of hay—$24; One horse—$20; Cow and calf—$40; Wagon—$27; One sack of flour—No money.

Simon Bunjka—7 souls—Section 34-41-1 (NR: Bunka, Semen; CM: S. Bunka SW¼ 12-42-1) House 16 × 20—$50; Stable 16 × 18—$25; One horse—$34; One cow—$30; Heifer—$10; Ten tons of hay—$20; Good well—6 sacks of flour—Some money.

K. Scherbiniuk—3 souls—Section 34-41-1 (NR: Szczerbaniuk, Kyr.) House 16 × 20—$40; Stable 18 × 20—$40; Cash—$42; Six sacks of flour.

Janko Zajenczkowsky—3 souls—Section 34-41-1 (NR: Zajackowski, Yan, or Zajaczkowski) Horse—$35; Cow—$28; Calf—$10; 7 tons of hay—$14; 600 lbs. of flour. No buildings.

Michalo Czlischuk—Section 34-41-1 (CM: M. Zaleschuk) Young man, working out for wages at Rosthern.

Nicholi Czichik—6 souls—Section 32-41-1 (CM: Czyzyk, M. SW¼ 30-41-1) House 20 × 20—$100; Stable attached—$40; One horse—$40; One cow—$35; 2 calves—$18; 6 tons of hay—$12; Wagon—$65; Cash—$40; Six sacks of flour and six sacks of potatoes. Good settler.

Yakem Trach (NR: Tracz, Yakiem)—Living with former settler—will enter for quarter of Section 34-41-1 in Spring. Has been working three months at $1.25 per day.

ROSTHERN SIDE

Petro Reherchuk—4 souls—Section 28-41-1 [Should read "28-41-2"] (NR: Rehorczuk, Peter; CM: P. Rehorczuk—SW¼-33-41-2) House 18 × 24—$75; Stable 14 × 18—$25; One cow—$30; One horse—$25; 5 tons of hay—$10; No flour. No money.

Nichola Zilkowski—4 souls—Section 28-41-1 [2] (NR: Zilkowski, Nikola, Hague) Wagon—$35; No money. No flour.

Iwan Twomisky—one soul—Section 28-41-1 [2] (CM: J. Twarinsky—SW¼-28-41-2) House—$50; Stable—$25; Cow—$30; Ten tons of hay—$20; Wagon—$25. Some wheat and flour.

Fecko Sraigko—5 souls—Section 32-41-2. House 16 × 20—$40; 10 Tons of hay—$20; 10 acres ploughed—$30. No money—no flour. Lost one horse, which died.

Lech Howrick—5 souls—Section 32-42-2 (NR: Hawrysz, Leo) House and stable combined—$40; 10 tons of hay—$20; Cow—$30; 15 acres ploughed—$35; Wagon—$15; Colt—$10; 2 sacks of flour.

Petro Belek—7 souls—Section 32-41-1 [2] (NR: Bilek, Petro, Hague) House and stable combined—$25; Cow—$25; 3 acres ploughed; Working and got hurt on Railway—Not serious.

Safat Kaminski—5 souls—Section 6-42-2 (NR: Kaminski, Safat, Rosthern; CM: S. Kaminski NE¼-6-42-2) House 16 × 22—$40; Stable 18 × 30—$40; 20 tons of hay—$40; 5 acres ploughed—$15; One horse—$23; One cow—$23. Good well—Earned $30 threshing.

Jacob Hutchkowski—10 souls—Section 6-42-2 (NR: Huczkowski, Jacob, Rosthern) House—$40; Stable—$25; 5 acres ploughed—$15. Himself and son have worked all summer on the railway—Has $100 in cash—In good shape—Good well.

Jacob Manik—4 souls—Section 6-42-2 (NR: Manick, Jacob, Rosthern; CM: J. Manika—SE¼-6-42-2) One heifer—$20; 4 acres ploughed—$12; 2 tons of hay—$4. Working at Hague with farmer—All right for winter.

Hrenko Wesnuk—4 souls—Section 6-42-2 (NR: Wizniuk, Hrynko) House—$50; Stable—$20; Cow—$20; 4 acres ploughed—$12; 10 tons of hay; Working out for farmer—All right for winter.

Alexander Ripchinski—9 souls—Section 36-41-2 (NR: Aleksander Rybzenski) House 18 × 30—$100; Stable 20 × 20—$75; 30 tons of hay—$60; 2 oxen—

$110; One cow and heifer—$40; Wagon—$70; Plough—$18; New mower and rake—$80; 20 acres ploughed—$60. Has purchased quarter-section of Railway land adjoining homestead and $1500 cash left. 16 sacks of flour in house. Intends to select three farms for his brothers in Austria, who are all well-to-do. This is an excellent settler and is making marked progress.

Anton Thewczewski—5 souls—Section 36-41-2. House—$25; 5 acres ploughed —$15; Been working among farmers.

Kerilo Klepack—2 souls—Section 36-41-2 (NR: Klepak, Kierylo) House—$40; Stable—$15; Cow—$25; Wagon—$25; Working at Rosthern.

Stefan Rogusenski—6 souls—Section 36-41-2 (NR: Rogozinski, Stefan) House 18 × 20—$50; Stable 14 × 16—$25; One horse—$23; 2 oxen (young)—$60; 10 tons of hay—$20; Wagon—$14; Plough—$5; 12 acres ploughed—$36; Cash —$24.

Nichol Tmowsky—4 souls—Section 18-42-2 (CM: N. Ternowski—NE¼-18-42-2) One cow—$25; Working for farmer called Rempel—Himself and family living there for winter.

Wasyl Mukanik—7 souls—Section 18-42-2 (NR: Mukanik, Wasyl, Rosthern) House—$40; Stable—$20; 10 acres ploughed—$30; One cow—$33. No money—Good settler.

Michalo Czerepacha—4 souls—Section 12-42-2. Cow—$30; 4 tons of hay—$8. Came late—living with Alex. Tanaska. No money; 14 bushels of wheat—going to Grist Mill at Rosthern.

Stefan Czany—6 souls—Section 12-43-2 (NR: Czarny, Stefan) House—$40; Cow—$30; 4 tons of hay—$8; Taking load of wheat to mill to grind; $5 in cash—no buildings.

Wasyl Czapenda—4 souls—Section 2-43-2. 2 oxen—$60; One cow—$25; 5 acres ploughed—$15; Plough—$13; Cash—$10. Quantity of wheat—No buildings —Few families living together for winter. All right.

Iwan Ruczewsky—6 souls—Section 2-43a-2—Living alone—family in Austria —coming in Spring. Has earned $50 cash; has sent his wife money to come—has $40 cash left.

Tomko Prokopy—5 souls—Section 36-42-2 (NR: Prokopiw, Semko, Rosthern) House 16 × 18—$50; Stable—$15; 10 tons of hay—$20; Cow—$20; 2 acres ploughed. No money—no flour. (Comes from distr. Borshchiw, Galicia).

John Churawinski—3 souls—Section 36-42-2 (CM: T. Zurawinsky—SW¼-36-42-2) One cow—$25; Has earned in three months $30 wages. Living with brother-in-law for winter.

Nichola Pusty—7 souls—Section 36-42-2 (CM: N. Pustai—NE¼-36-42-2) House 16 × 20—$75; Stable—$40; One horse—$20; One cow—$20; Sleigh—$10; 6 tons of hay—$12; One acre ploughed—$3; Cash—$5. One sack of flour.

Alexander Tanaska—2 souls—Section 36-42-2 House 16 × 20—$40; Stable 16 × 16—$35; 5 tons of hay—$10; 4 acres ploughed—$12; One cow—$26; One horse—$20; One plough—$11; No money—No flour.

Cachary Vosnak—6 souls—Section 26-42-2 (CM: C. Woznack NE¼ 26-42-2) House 18 × 22—$80; Stable—$50; One horse—$25; One cow—$25; 10 tons of hay—$20; Good well; Sleigh—$10; Cash—$13; One acre ploughed—$3; 2 sacks of flour.

Iwan Hladie—6 souls—Section 24-42-2 (CM: I. Hlady, NW¼-24-42-2; NE¼-23-42-2) House 16 × 24—$30; Stable 14 × 14—$45; One cow—$25; 5 tons of hay—$10; Cash on hand—$10. 2 sacks of flour.

Iwan Rawlick—3 souls—Section 24-42-2 (CM: I. Rawlick—NE¼-24-42-2; NR: Rawlyk, Onufrij, Residence: Rosthern, Sask. Former residence: Horodenka, Austria) House 16 × 20—$40. Working all summer. Cash—$100.

Iwan Lazarowitch—6 souls—Section 14-42-2 (NR: Lazarowicz, Iwan, 52 years, 5′ 10″, Rosthern, Sask.; CM: NE¼-14-42-2) House 18 × 24—$60; 8 tons of hay—$16; 10 acres ploughed—$25; One cow—$25; Calf—$10; Cash $4.

Dmytro Byckalo—5 souls—Section 10-42-2 (CM: Mrs. W. Betzkalo—NW¼-10-42-2) House and stable combined—$50; One cow—$15; 10 tons of hay—$20; 15 bushels of wheat; 1½ sacks flour; Good well; 2 acres ploughed.

Iwan Huzan—4 souls—Section 4-42-2. House 16 × 20—$40; Good stable—$40; 2 horses—$71; 2 cows—$55; Wagon—$20; Harness—$15; 5 tons of hay. No flour—no money.

Howril Orizskij—4 souls—Section 4-42-2 (CM: H. Oriltzky—NE¼ 4-42-2) One horse—$35; Cow—$30; Wagon—$20; Cash—$2. No money—No flour.

Michalo Michajena—6 souls—Section 12-43a-3. (NR: Michalkiw, Michailo—SE¼-4-41-1) House and stable—$50; Cow—$25; Good location west of Rosthern.

The foregoing report shows every settler upon his land in the Colony. It will be observed that in some cases two or three families are living together, some of the settlers having come very late, but the houses are good, substantial permanent and warm and many of them are a very great credit to the people. Perhaps thirty per cent are built on the style of an excavation with strong posts leaning to a ridge-pole incline heavily mudded, but others are built above ground, neatly plastered inside with smooth finish and in several cases good cooking stoves, with proper utensils, are being used. All the houses are very warm and only in one or two cases could I notice where better ventilation would have been desirable. I have in some cases given an order for one sack of flour to meet the present emergency, but have impressed the settlers with the necessity through the Interpreter, in all cases of drawing wood out to Rosthern as a good deal of fallen timber, that is dry, can be obtained where the Grist Mill and other people will purchase it at $1.50 per cord. This will enable them to make the situation self-sustaining during the winter. I have also impressed them with the necessity of putting in a supply of flour sufficient for the coming inclement weather and keeping, in many cases, a greater stock on hand than I observed.

All considered, the colony is in first class shape. There is no perceptable sickness among any of the people, and, with the exception of one case of toothache, every man, woman and child in the colony seems to be in perfect health, except one case of confinement, which I noticed. There has been little or no mortality. One young woman on Section (SE¼) 4-41-1, daughter of Michal Mikaldo [Michalkiw] died a few weeks ago at the age of twenty years. I could not ascertain the nature of the sickness, but the parents both seemed quite satisfied that it was from natural causes and are quite reconciled.

> There may be a small quantity of seed grain required in the Spring by some of these settlers, and they will require some little attention during the coming winter. But, all considered, they are in a very satisfactory condition. A significant fact is that they are most acceptable to the other nationalities settled in the district, and it is generally conceded that they will make useful settlers.[41]

In August, 1901, Speers made another of his routine inspections of various colonies in the Northwest. In the report he made to Frank Pedley, the Superintendent of Immigration in Ottawa, he mentioned his impressions of a visit to the Ukrainian colonies at Rosthern and Fish Creek in that year, noting the improvements that had taken place in the living conditions of the settlers:

> . . . I beg to submit a brief report on the colonies in the Saskatchewan district in the vicinity of Rosthern, which I visited last week. The Galician settlers are in a very prosperous condition. They were busy cutting a very good crop and they have made ample provision for their stock for the winter. They have excellent gardens and in a drive of about sixty miles I was very much impressed with the progress they are making. Their buildings are very much improved, their families much more comfortable. They are very industrious and I think all the early difficulties of settlement have been fully overcome. These people are good settlers and will do their share in developing the country.
>
> I wish to recommend at an early date that there be a subdivision of a few townships of lands adjoining this settlement Townships 39 and 40 ranges 26 and 27. There are a number of these settlers beginning to squat on this land and as there are a number of locations that require adjusting in this district, even on the lands that have been surveyed which will have to be done in the near future a further survey or subdivision of additional territory is very desirable.[42]

That the growth of the settlements was indeed rapid can be seen from a statement that the Commissioner of Immigration in Winnipeg prepared in February, 1901, listing the approximate number of persons in the various colonies of Manitoba and the Northwest Territories. According to this report, the Galician colonies of Rosthern and Fish Creek, established in 1898, had grown to an approximate population of 1,000, and Yorkton and Saltcoats, established in 1897, counted approximately 4,500 persons.[43]

[41]8. Rpts./69304, November 23, 1898: C. W. Speers, Winnipeg, to Frank Pedley, Ottawa.

[42]9. Rpts., August 28, 1901: C. W. Speers, Brandon, to Frank Pedley, Ottawa.

[43]9. Rpts./140941, "Settlements In Manitoba And North West Territories of Different Nationalities."

Chapter Ten

EDNA–STAR

I

THE OLDEST Ukrainian settlement in Canada was established in 1892–94 in Edna, or as it was later called, Star, in the district of Alberta, Northwest Territories. Dr. Oleskow visited the settlers in August, 1895, and afterwards described the settlement, and especially the houses of the immigrants, in his booklet *O emigratsii*:

The country behind Fort Saskatchewan is flat and resembles a steppe. This region is also settled by prosperous Galician Germans. Among them lives one Ruthenian settler, who moved there four years ago, Anton Paish from Nebyliw.[1]

The life of farmers in this district is as follows: there is plenty of grain—all kinds of grain—but there is a shortage of ready cash. Helwich, a Pole from Lviw, settled near Paish this spring; he was a locksmith in his home town but went into farming in Canada. . . . Several families from the village of Nebyliw settled a few miles further, in Beaver Hills, Edna post office, on the edge of the civilized world, since there are no other settlements beyond that place. They arrived this spring, took a long time to examine the land available for settlement, to make the choice to finally settle here. The soil is black but rather light in this region.

Those who settled here are: Andrij Paish, Stefan Chichak, Mykhailo, Mykola and Fedir Melnyk, Wasyl Fenniak, Iwan Pylypiw, Mykhailo Pulishiy, Mykola Tychkowsky, Petro and Matey Melnyk from Perehinsko, Mykhailo from the vicinity of Sambir, and Iwan Dubrowski from the district of Zolochiw. . . .

We were particularly interested to find out how our people, who arrived in Canada practically without any means, are getting along. The first thing that attracted our attention was the houses of these settlers. Our people

[1]Hugo Carstens, the Immigration Officer who accompanied Dr. Oleskow, mentions in his report that Anton Paish came to Beaver Hills "two years ago," that is, in 1893.

generally build nicer houses than the German or English farmers do in Canada. One of the Melnyks even covered his house with ornaments, which he made himself. The house looks very nice from a distance, but it is senseless to waste valuable effort like that at this early stage. The first house of a settler is usually very simple. It is a box made of poplar logs without a ceiling, and with a roof made of tree trunks. The roof is sometimes plastered with clay from the inside, and the house is then ready for occupancy. A house with a roof like that is possible only in Canada, where there are no rainy seasons. As a rule, but not invariably, the house has a lean-to, where an iron cooking stove is placed. An immigrant farmer lives in such a house for several years and later builds for himself a dwelling of seasoned lumber according to American methods, when he has saved enough money to do so.

Everything indicates that in a few years our farmers will achieve prosperity, but engrossed at present in the struggle to establish themselves, they let themselves go to such an extent that they hardly resemble the image of God's creatures. . . .[2]

These pioneer families whom Dr. Oleskow visited in 1895, came, with few exceptions, from the village of Nebyliw in the district of Kalush. They settled in what was soon to become the largest Ukrainian colony in Alberta, extending over several townships and ranges.

One and a half years later, in April of 1897, the colony was visited for the first time by a Ukrainian Catholic priest, Father Nestor Dmytriw from the United States. Father Dmytriw spent several days in the colony, solemnizing the Easter services, baptizing children, and performing other religious functions. He arrived at Fort Saskatchewan during Easter week and proceeded to Edna:

At the post office at Edna, I met several Ruthenian settlers who came to collect their mail. They were overjoyed to learn that they will eat blessed Easter bread (*paska*) this year, and they accompanied me on the one-mile walk to the home of Michael Melnyk, from Nebyliw, where I was to stop (during the visit to Edna). He settled here three years ago and has a presentable house with plank flooring and a roof covered with shingles. He has a granary filled with all kinds of grain and white flour. He built a stable and has a pair of beautiful young horses worth 400 florins, also three cows, one pair of magnificent oxen, a heifer, and several pigs. Two of his brothers, Fedor and Nikola, are also well off, and so are all other farmers who have been farming here three years. They are working about 35 acres on the average, and some even more.

The same day, I visited the farms of all the old established farmers and also went to the school-building under construction to make the necessary preparations for Holy Mass to be held there (on the next day, Easter Sunday).[3]

[2]Dr. Josef Oleskow, *O emigratsii*/"About Emigration" (Lviw: Publication of the Michael Kachkowsky Society, No. 241, December, 1895), 63.

[3]Reverend Nestor Dmytriw, *Kanadiyska Rus: Podorozhni spomyny*/"Canadian Ruthenia: Travel Reminiscences" (Mount Carmel, Pa., *Svoboda* Publishers, 1897), No. 4, 34–41.

There follows the description of the Easter festivities, the blessing of the *paska*, and other events. Then Father Dmytriw provides a great deal of detail about the settlers and their establishment, especially concerning the crops that they planted:

This Ruthenian colony is undoubtedly the most northerly settlement of Ruthenians in the whole world. The settlers, 75 families of them at the time of my visit [April, 1897], were distributed over the following townships: 55-x-18, 56-x-18, 56-x-19, 56-x-20, 57-x-18, 57-x-19, and 57-x-20. The distance between the East end and the West end, that is, from Kost Nemirsky to Iwan Dombrowsky, who came from the village of Krasne, in the district of Zolochiw, is 12 miles.

I shall divide the settlers into four groups, according to the time of their arrival.

(1) The oldest settlers came from the village of Nebyliw, in the district of Stryj. [Dmytriw erred—Nebyliw is in the district of Kalush.] One of them, Nykola Tyshkowsky (Tychkowsky, according to Dr. Oleskow) settled here five years ago (i.e., in 1892, and according to Dr. Oleskow he settled early in the spring of 1895), and the other nine came 3 years ago, almost all of them from Nebyliw. (2) To the second group belong Iwan Dombrowsky (Dubrowsky, according to Dr. Oleskow) from Krasne (district of Zolochiw), Ilko Senetowich, and his son-in-law Tymiak from Hlyniany, Fedko and Peter Kinash from Poluchiw, and others. (3) The group of the more recent arrivals [May 1896] who came under the leadership of Wladimir Oleskow [Dr. Oleskow's brother], originated mostly in the district of Borshchiw. (4) The last group is composed of those who came last winter, or even last month.

It is difficult to describe the condition of each farmer individually. I shall therefore take an average farmer and shall demonstrate, using actual figures, how a Ruthenian settler has progressed in about three years time since his settlement in the district of Edna.

Wasyl Fenyk (Fenniak, according to Dr. Oleskow) from Nebyliw, had $450 in cash on arrival in Winnipeg. Immediately on arrival, he bought 3 horses (1 died shortly afterwards), 2 cows, 3 calves, a wagon, a plough, harrows, a stove, some flour, etc., and when he arrived on the place of settlement, he had $27 left. He arrived late in the spring and therefore he was unable to put in any seed. The next spring he ploughed 8 acres, sowed 8 bushels of wheat and harvested 88 bs.; sowed 5 bushels of oats and harvested 44 bs.; planted 12 bushels of potatoes and harvested 120 bs. He also planted some cabbages, tobacco, and vegetables. He had enough wheat to last him until the next spring, and he even sold some.

The third spring he ploughed 20 acres, put in 24 bushels of wheat, and harvested 365 bs. He sold 300 bushels at 60¢, 55¢, and 57¢ per bushel. He also put in one gallon of rye and harvested 8 bushels. He sowed 21 bushels of oats on 5 acres and harvested 220 bs. He sold 50 bushels at 22¢ per bs. He sowed 1 bushel of barley and harvested 15 bs.; from 20 bushels of potatoes which he planted, he gathered 220 bushels. Peas—planted 3 pints, gathered 3 bushels. He sold some cabbages and received $3.00. In his stable he has 4 cows, 4 calves, 3 horses, and some pigs. He already sold a pair of young oxen for $44. He built a house, a stable, and a barn, and fenced his farm in. It must be pointed out that this settler was ill during the whole of the last summer and had to keep a hired man. One horse escaped in the middle of ploughing season, and he had difficulty to complete the ploughing of his field. This is a typical example of an older settler.

Let us now take a settler who came two years ago from the village of Krasne, district of Zolochiw. As it happens, I know the conditions in that village very well. I know the quality of the soil, etc., and therefore it will be easy for me to evaluate whether Iwan Dombrowsky would have done better in two years of farming in Krasne than in Canada.

Iwan Dombrowsky arrived in Winnipeg with $400 in cash. During the first spring, he ploughed 4 acres of land and sowed 8 bushels of wheat, harvesting 106 bs.; on the other 4 acres he sowed barley, oats, rye, etc. The second spring he ploughed 15 acres of land and put in 14 bushels of wheat, 10 bs. of oats, 6 bs. of barley, and also planted 12 bs. of potatoes. He added another horse recently to his outfit and now has 4 horses, 2 cows, and a pair of pigs. He has a house, a modest house, but clean and well kept. You can see he is a "wheat-bread country man," as people from Krasne are called. This man, through his intelligence and perseverance, would have been much better off than any of his neighbours if he had not been hit by a misfortune—his wife died and he was left with 5 small children. His two elder daughters (the oldest 10 years of age) help him to run the household. This is his third farm. In Krasne, Iwan probably would have owned a pair of horses and a cow, which he would have had to pasture along the road, leading it on a string.

And now let us take an average settler from Oleskow's group [arrived in May, 1896]. Iwan Lakusta, from the district of Sniatyn, brought $400 with him. He bought (a pair of) oxen, 2 cows, 2 calves, and 7 sheep. He owns, jointly with another settler, one plough and one wagon. He broke 8 acres of land and put in wheat, oats, rye, etc. Lakusta built a house and a stable. He was short of wheat and oats for seed. He took one of his cows and exchanged her at one of the older settler's for 14 bushels of oats, 16 bushels of wheat, $10 in cash, and a tanned hide of ½ an ox. This is how they trade here—on the spot.

About those destitute immigrants who arrived after Oleskow's settlers, and who are still arriving, it is difficult to say anything, as they have not had enough time to even make a start. Generally speaking, the settlers who came with the Oleskow group are the best off in every respect.

For the sake of curiosity, and perhaps for the sake of study as well, let us take two more examples—the oldest settler and his achievements during 5 years of farming, and the most successful recent settler from Dr. Oleskow's group, who arrived on May 22, 1896, and took a homestead. The oldest farmer, Nikola Tyshkowsky, came from Nebyliw and brought $400 in cash with him. It should be born in mind that he is an elderly man and illiterate. He broke 35 acres of land, has a pair of horses, a pair of working oxen, 4 young oxen, 4 cows, and 6 heifers. He has a modest house, a barn, a stable, and some implements.

Kost Nemirsky from Bilche Zolote, in the district of Borshchiw, arrived on May 22, 1896. A middle-aged man, who can read and write, he was in Russia and in Bessarabia as seasonal worker. In Galicia he owned a village store. He brought $500 in cash with him. During the first year it was too late in the season to put in any seed, but during this spring he has already ploughed 4 acres and sowed some wheat, one acre of rye, and in one acre he put in potatoes, planted cabbages, tobacco and other vegetables. He bought a pair of oxen for $55 (big-sized beasts), 2 cows for $56; a wagon for $75, a plough for $26, a stove for $16, a tent for the summer for $10, kitchen utensils for $60, and some implements for $35. He also bought two rifles for $20 and is living now on the money which was left. He has already built a big house and is now building a big barn, which in Galicia would have been worth at least 800 florins. During the winter he brought in a great amount of lumber. I saw a fir tree log in his yard 4½ yards in circumference, and this does not cost him a penny, except for the labour he has to expend. The farm of this settler is almost all covered with bush. It will require considerable effort to have it cleared. On that farm I saw a beautiful grove of fir trees and a pond where he killed a great number of wild ducks. Generally speaking, this man represents a valuable asset for Canada. Moreover, he speaks German as well and won't be cheated.

The colony possesses three jointly-owned mowers and 4 harvesters.

Father Dmytriw's description of this colony is a fairly accurate one, although it contains a certain partiality for Dr. Oleskow's group of settlers, and perhaps justifiably so, since it was a carefully selected group conducted by Oleskow's own brother.

II

During the spring and early summer of 1897, several hundred families of Ukrainian settlers arrived in Edna, a great number of them almost completely destitute. Dr. Oleskow advised prospective settlers to emigrate only when they had enough money to pay the passage and to live in Canada for several months until the first harvest could be reaped. The steamship agents, on the other hand, were principally concerned with commissions, bonuses, and whatever other legitimate and sometimes less-legitimate benefits they could reap from a prospective immigrant. This fact was well known to Canadian immigration officers:

Certain Galicians in the party who arrived yesterday [May 27, 1897] ex S.S. *Prussia* à Hamburg have, upon examination, corroborated my previous suspicion that they were induced to emigrate although in a destitute condition by promises of Shipping Agent Mr. Michael Morawec of Hamburg, who distinctly promised them not only free land but that the Canadian Government would further assist them by grants for subsistence, and by gifts of cattle and tools.

Were such shamefully dishonest practices exposed in the proper manner by proper officials in Hamburg and elsewhere, the result would be very beneficial.[4]

[4]3. Gal./38073, May 28, 1897: W. F. McCreary, Commissioner of Immigration, Winnipeg, to James A. Smart, Deputy Minister, Department of the Interior, Ottawa.

The S.S. *Prussia*, to which Commissioner McCreary referred, was only one of many ships which brought several thousands of Ukrainian settlers to Canada that spring. Steamship agents were particularly active in the province of Bukowina, from which great numbers of people emigrated during 1897 and 1898. These were mostly of the poorer peasant class, who arrived in Canada without any means at all, misled by the promises given by steamship agents that the Canadian Government would support them in various ways.

The Canadian immigration authorities were greatly annoyed at the activities of these steamship agents, and stern letters were dispatched to the steamship companies who carried such passengers, warning them that if they persisted in this action, destitute immigrants would be refused permission to land, and the companies would be forced to take them back to Europe. But in the meantime, those who were already in immigration sheds in Winnipeg, Edmonton, and Dauphin had to be placed on homesteads or helped in obtaining work to be able to feed their families. Hundreds of these families also arrived in Edmonton during 1897, and most of them went into the Edna district, where some had friends and hoped they would be able to survive the difficult first year. These settlers did remarkably well under dire circumstances; they built temporary shelters for the winter, and those who came in May and the beginning of June even succeeded putting in some vegetables in hastily-dug garden patches. But their meagre means were soon exhausted, and the situation became alarming towards the end of the year. Not only the immigration authorities, but everybody who came into contact with these settlers grew concerned about their well being. On September 7, 1897, the Commissioner of the North West Mounted Police in Regina wrote the Comptroller of the Mounted Police in Ottawa, warning of impending destitution among the settlers:

> I have the honour to inform you that there is certain to be great destitution among the Galicians, and other foreigners, who have grown nothing of any account this year, and are now living in a most miserable manner and many of them sick, caused, it is said by want of nourishment. Cprl. Butler on duty in their District is now investigating the conditions of each family, but it will be necessary to give temporary relief I fear before this investigation is finished. Please obtain authority required.[5]

The Comptroller transmitted the communication received from Regina to the Department of the Interior, and was informed, that: "Copies of your letter and of its enclosures are being forwarded to the Com-

[5]7. Dest., September 7, 1897: L. W. Herchmer, Commissioner, N.W.M.P., Regina, to Fred White, Comptroller, N.W.M.P., Ottawa.

missioner of Immigration in Winnipeg, who will at once deal with the matter."[67]

Corporal G. D. Butler, stationed at Edna in the heart of the new Ukrainian colony, sent a report to his commanding officer at Fort Saskatchewan in which he described the conditions in the district. The report revealed that despite their late arrival and lack of means, most of the new immigrants had erected shelters for their families and had even tried to begin farming operations on their homesteads. They had been settled only a few months when Butler's report was made. Corporal Butler enumerated thirty-five families who in his opinion required immediate relief. His description of these families follows:

I have the honour to forward the following report re settlers that came in this Spring, who I visited with the Interpreter:—

Wasel Mariajan (Wasyl Marian, S. 22, Tp. 56, Rge. 17, W4). Has no horses, 1 cow. Said he had about $150.00 stolen from him on board the ship. This man is very good to work, having built a house and fixed it for the winter. Has 3 small children.

Danytra Balan (Dmytro Balan, S. 16, Tp. 56, Rge. 17, W4). Has nothing. This man has also built a house and is working out when he can get any work. Has 4 small children.

Giorgi Klapacyuk (George Klapatiuk, NE¼ 16, Tp. 56, Rge. 17, W4.) Has nothing. Three children. He owed Iwan Scraba $200.00 for passage money to this country.

Wasel Hunka (Wasyl Hunka, SW¼ 32-56-17-W4). Has two cows, but nothing else of any account. Has 6 children.

Gregori Waselncyuk (Gregory Wasylynchuk, SW¼ 28-56-17-W4). One team of ponies, 1 cow & calf, 4 children. Has nothing else.

Tanaska Skintej (S. 28-56-17 4W). Has nothing at all, living on what they can make from day to day.

Michal Hyhercyuk (Michael Hryhorchuk). Has one horse. Has left his wife at home and gone to find work round Edmonton. His father and mother are living on the farm with him.

Gavril Andrite (Gabriel Andriets, NW¼ 20-56-17-W4). Working out at Deep Creek. Has 3 children. Has not got anything at all. His wife is staying with Giorgi Melnyk, looking after the sick woman.

Giorgi Melnyk (SW¼-20-56-17-W4). Has one horse, 1 cow, and 4 children. His wife had twins about two months ago and caught cold from laying on the ground. He started to take her to Edmonton once, but had not gone any more than a quarter of a mile before she started to groan and say she could not stand being taken that distance. She has not been any better since.

Danelo Kutzengavitz (Daniel Kuzengewitz, S.20-56-17-W4). Has one horse, 4 children and nothing else.

---

67. Des./32246, September 15, 1897: Frank Pedley, Superintendent of Immigration, Ottawa, to Fred White, Comptroller, N.W.M.P., Ottawa.

Wasel Statskow (Wasyl Stecko, NE¼ 36-56-18-W4). Has nothing. Sends wife amongst the neighbours to work. Has 3 children.

Nycola Tapylnitzki (Nykola Topolnitsky, NW¼ 28-56-17-W4). Has nothing at all. This man has been sick for about 5 weeks and is just getting round again. Symptoms like grippe. (Three in the family.)

There are 5 families who had had the misfortune to lose their boxes with all their clothes. The only clothes they have now is what they stand in. The last they saw of the boxes was in Galicia. When they got to Hamburg the Shipping Agent, Spiro & Co., got the checks from them and promised to send them on the next steamer; that was on the 1st May. The Land Agent on the Sth. Side has a receipt for the check which he got from one of them; 3 of them are mentioned in the report. Their names are Danytra Balan, Tanaska Skintej, Gregory Waselncyuk and Teodor Lupul.

Most of these people when asked how they are going to get through the winter, and what they are going to live on, say they do not know, they will have to get through somehow. They all want to know if they cannot get work somewhere from the Government, the Government to give them flour and meat in exchange.

There are only 3 of the whole lot who came in last Spring who have any money at all, I have not mentioned them in the report at all, and there are quite a few more who will need looking up, but I have not time before sending in this report.[7]

A few days later, on September 9, Corporal Butler forwarded "a more complete list of Russians [*sic*] who will want relief." The additional names were:[8]

Nicola Hyhyrcyuk (Nykola Hryhorchuk)—3 children, 1 horse. Nothing else.

Hyhory Hyhyrcyuk (Hryhorij Hryhorchuk)—4 children. Nothing at all.

Aterni Rehyrcyuk (Achtemij Hryhorchuk, SW¼-20-56-17-W4)—1 horse, 1 cow & calf, 3 children. Nothing.

Philip Wetaz (Philip Woytas)—1 child, 1 cow in partnership with Ivan Makovilyski (Iwan Makowicki, NE¼ 36-56-20-W4).

Ivan Makovilyski (Iwan Makowicki)—3 children. Nothing else.

Antonian Coubar (Antony Gurba, NW¼-30-56-19-W4)—2 children, 1 cow. Nothing else.

Pawlo Gudza (Paulo Gudzan, SE¼-36-56-20-W4)—2 children, 1 cow. Nothing else.

Ivan Farjon (Iwan Farion)—3 children. Nothing else.

Rammon Kitchitski (Roman Kulchytski ?)—3 children. Nothing else.

Ivan Borasa (Ivan Bucza, NW¼-22-56-20-W4)—3 children. Nothing.

---

7. Dest./43727, August 28, 1897: Corporal G. D. Butler, N.W.M.P., Edna, Alberta, to the Commanding Officer, "G" Division, N.W.M.P., Fort Saskatchewan. The names in parentheses are those found in the Naturalization Records.

8. Dest./43727, September 9, 1897: Corporal G. D. Butler, Edna, to the Commanding Officer, "G" Division, N.W.M.P., Fort Saskatchewan.

Jashko Kolenczuk (Ilko Kalanczuk, NW¼-36-56-18-W4)—2 children, 1 horse. Nothing else.

Jasko Malinka (Jasko Melenka, SE¼-22-56-20-W4)—1 child. Nothing else.

Iwan Selowka (Iwan Slywka, SW¼-36-56-18-W4)—3 children, 1 cow. Nothing else.

Wasel Glucki (Wasyl Gluchie, SW¼-30-56-17-W4)—1 child. Nothing else.

Michael Babiak—2 children. Nothing else.

Wasel Saharji (Wasyl Zachary, SE¼-30-56-17-W4)—4 children. Nothing else.

Petro Palanak—Nothing, is too old to work.

Wasel Hrynkuw (Wasyl Hrynkiw)—3 children, 1 team of ponies. Nothing else.

Ivan Kuryski—5 children. Nothing else.

Wasel Strazok—3 children, 2 cows. Nothing else.

Fedor Sochacki—1 child. Nothing else.

Michael Kachupski—1 child. Nothing else.

Corporal Butler's report was sent to the Comptroller of the North West Mounted Police in Ottawa, and the latter enclosed it with his own letter to the Deputy Minister of the Interior, adding: "Will you be good enough to advise me whether the Hon. The Minister of the Interior desires relief to be furnished to these people, through the medium of the Mounted Police, during the coming winter."[9]

The Commissioner of Immigration was visibly annoyed that officers of the Mounted Police were interfering with the work of his division. He sent a strongly-worded letter to the Immigration and Land Office in Edmonton, demanding an explanation of why cases of destitution, if they in fact existed, were not reported and attended to within the Department. From the correspondence which followed, it becomes apparent that there was an acute rivalry, bordering on open hostility, between the immigration officers and members of the North West Mounted Police. On the upper level there was a polite, formal exchange of letters—but on the lower levels sharp blows were exchanged with definite intent to discredit one's opponent. In reply to the Commissioner's letter, which contained a sharp reprimand, C. W. Sutter, the Agent of the Dominion Lands Office in Edmonton, wrote this account of his investigation:

I left Edmonton on the morning of the 22nd inst. [September, 1897] with Mr. P. Wagner (as interpreter) for the Galician Settlement to investigate the alleged destitution and sickness which was supposed to prevail among foreign settlers north of Fort Saskatchewan.

97. Dest., September 29, 1897: Fred White, Comptroller, N.W.M.P., Ottawa, to James A. Smart, Ottawa.

We first visited several of the Galicians who are settled on Township 55, Range 21. They are some of the ones who settled first in this part of the country and have considerable land under cultivation and their crops are all good. They had not been troubled with any sickness but were all happy and contended.

We next went to Township 56, Range 18. This Township is partly settled with those who have been in the country for two years and over, also some Canadians and Norwegians. After making full enquiries here we were informed that they had not been in want neither had they been troubled with any sickness.

We then drove to Township 55, Range 17, where the last arrivals of Galicians are settled. We drove to H. Belcher's to stay for the night. Here I met Mr. Bennett who is also investigating and had just arrived ahead of me. G. Butler of the North West Mounted Police is stationed here with Mr. John Creps [John Krebs] as interpreter; for what purpose I know not.

At 6 o'clock the next morning we started to visit the settlers here who were supposed to be living in miserable and destitute circumstances. To my surprise I found it quite the reverse. We went into every house and mudded hut. Those who have their homes finished have made them comfortable and warm; and inside looked clean. The children were also well kept. In no place did we see any want or suffering. The least flour we saw in any one place was 2½ sacks and in this case the man had his house finished and he and his son are working out with farmers and earning money. Most of them have from five to seven sacks of flour and one man had ten. Every one has one or two cows and a team of horses. Nearly all have land broken for a crop next summer. They informed me that they enjoyed good health ever since they came out and had not been troubled with any sickness except one woman who had given birth to twins; she was sick for some time but is better. We called at the house and found the woman at work baking bread; the children neat and clean; five and a half sacks of flour in the house. I enquired of the man if he had asked the police for any assistance. He said, NO, but that the Police asked him if he wanted anything and he told him that he would take some flour and the Police told him that he would write to the Government and see what he could do.

Several of them said that they would like if the Government would advance them some seed grain and flour in the spring and they would pay it back in the fall with interest. I gave them to understand that they must not expect any help from the Government and that they must go out and work among the farmers and earn their grain and flour and that there was plenty of work all over the country this year. Several have promised to come to Edmonton and to go to work in the coal mines.

I think it would be well if I would go out there occasionally and see that they do go to work. Some of them think that the Government have sent the Police out among them to see that they are not in want and should they be, the Police would at once send them flour.

On my way back to Edmonton I met Mr. Porte, President of the Fort Saskatchewan Agricultural Society. He had been to every house to ascertain in how much crop per acre each farmer would have and he informed me that he had never seen a more contended and happy lot of farmers than the

Galicians. They are all doing well and had considerable crop and land cultivated for next spring.[10]

On receipt of this optimistic report from Sutter, Commissioner McCreary wrote the Superintendent of Immigration in Ottawa, and in his letter he alluded to the rivalry between the Department and the Police: "I felt that it was a certain reflection upon the officials of my Department at that point, if the condition of affairs alleged in Commissioner Herchmer's communications were true, and at once upon receipt of the communication I wrote rather sharply to Messrs. C. W. Sutter and Thomas Bennett, of Edmonton, telling them that it was strange news of this kind had to reach the Department through channels of the Mounted Police when those men were supposed to be on the ground and know all about such matters. . . .[11] The conflict between the immigration division and the Mounted Police benefited the settlers concerned, because attention was drawn to their needs and, as a result of it, they received additional assistance. The reports of both parties contain information on how the immigrants arrived without means, how they gradually overcame seemingly insurmountable difficulties, the privation they had to endure, and the great sacrifices they had to make.

On September 21, 1897, Thomas Bennett, the Immigration Agent in Edmonton, presented his report to the Commissioner of Immigration in Winnipeg concerning the rumours of destitution among the settlers:

. . . Regarding distress in the Galician Colony East of Fort Saskatchewan I beg in reply to say that no word of such nature has reached me from that or any other colony in the district. I had four of them yesterday, and two on Saturday looking for their lost baggage. One of them gave me $21.00 to pay charges on part of their baggage which had arrived. Some it have not yet come. They had no complaints, nor word of any hardship or suffering among the people of the Colony. But if there are any individual cases of distress, I quite agree with you that it should not be learned for the first time from an outside source, but through the Agent of Immigration for the district in which it occurred. It should be his duty to know every settler in his district and as far as possible his circumstances. He should also be able through visiting the colonies and settlements to ascertain if those who had made entry for homesteads were making the improvements required, or if some of these neglected homesteads were not liable for cancellation, and direct new-comers to such places which if suitable they might cancel. But to enable the Agent to do this he should have permission with such

[10]7. Dest., September 27, 1897: C. W. Sutter, Agent, Dominion Lands Office, Edmonton, to W. F. McCreary, Winnipeg.

[11]7. Dest./43991, October 1, 1897: W. F. McCreary, Winnipeg, to the Superintendent of Immigration, Ottawa.

instructions as the Department thought necessary to visit every settlement in his district and report thereon twice a year. It would be beneficial to the Agent, encouraging to the settler and as far as possible a perfect source of information to the Department, and should not be dependant on a branch of the service whose duties are as foreign to immigration work as would the inspection of Public Works. I have only to add that I have asked permission of the Agent here before your taking charge, to visit the different setlements in the district but lack of funds would not permit my getting permission and I would respectfully refer to my letter dated April 5th and May 6th—asking permission to visit these colonies, but did not until last night receive the permission asked for. Moreover I will start at once and follow wour instructions, and wait taking my holidays until I return. I will be very much pleased to see you here, you will then see the situation as it is.[12]

Immigration Officer Sutter also wrote a "strong" letter to Commissioner McCreary—afterwards sent on to the Comptroller of the North West Mounted Police in Ottawa for his information—in which he criticized the officers of the Police for interfering in what he considered was not their business:

I have been informed by Major Griesbach who is in command of the Mounted Police at Fort Saskatchewan, that some of the Galicians at Edna have applied for provisions through Corpl. Butler who is still stationed there, and that he had sent word back from them to get up a petition and send it to the Government as he could do nothing himself. I said it would have been better for them to work but they have got the idea into their head that the Government will provide for them, because a Police officer and an interpreter is stationed among them which I think is a great mistake. Because they would then more fully realize the responsibility of looking after themselves but as long as some one is among them representing the Government they will never cease begging.

The idea of instructing them to get up a petition to the Government when they ask for provisions, should be stopped, for we well know that every one whether he has plenty or little will sign the petition in hopes of receiving more, and would send one to the Government every month.

It is my intention to go to Limestone Lake and Edna in a few days and have another interview. At present I am looking after four Galicians from Edna who had been working on the C.P.R. Section at Calgary two months ago and who have not yet received their wages and are in need of provisions. I have wired the road master at Calgary asking him why the money had not been sent to these men. I wanted these men to go to work in a coal mine but they refused. They are going to wait in the Immigrant Shed until the money comes.[13]

[12]7. Dest./44133, September 21, 1897: Thomas Bennett, Immigration Agent, South Edmonton, to W. F. McCreary, Winnipeg.

[13]7. Dest./48986, November 22, 1897: C. W. Sutter, Edmonton, to W. F. McCreary, Winnipeg.

The accusations voiced by Sutter were denied by Police Interpreter Krebs and Corporal Butler in the most energetic way—both men signed affidavits witnessed by a Justice of Peace. The text of their sworn statements follows:

I, John Krebs, Police Interpreter at Mole Lake, Sec. 14, Tp. 56, R. 18 W. of the 4th, declare that I never asked the Galicians if they wanted anything, neither did I tell them they could get flour from the Government if they asked for it. When any of them have asked me if the Government would give them flour I have said the Government would not. And I make this solemn declaration conscientiously believing the same to be true, knowing it is of the same force and effect as if made under and by virtue of the Canada Evidence Act of 1893.

(Signed) JOHN KREBS.

Declared before me at Mole Lake on the 5th day of January, 1898.
(Signed) P. C. H. PRIMROSE, J.P.[14]

I, George Butler, Corporal N.W.M.P. stationed at Mole Lake, Sec. 14. Tp. 56. R. 18 W of the 4th. do solemnly declare that I am in charge of the North West Mounted Police at this point. That I visit the different settlers in my section and, as is my duty, ask if anything is wrong and if there are any complaints. I never asked the Galicians in this section if they wanted anything, neither did I tell them they could get some flour from the Government. And I make this solemn declaration conscientiously believing the same to be true and knowing that it is of the same force and effect as if made under and by virtue of the Canada Evidence Act, 1893.

(Signed) G. D. BUTLER

Declared before me at Mole Lake on the 5th day of January, 1898.
(Signed) P. C. H. PRIMROSE, J.P.[15]

Inspector P. C. H. Primrose of the North West Mounted Police was instructed by Major Griesbach, the officer in command at Fort Saskatchewan, to proceed to the new colony and to verify the statements made by Corporal Butler and Mr. Sutter. Primrose's report, submitted January 7, 1898, is precise and very clear. It offers a description of the conditions of the settlers who arrived in Edna in May, 1897, as they appeared to him some seven months after their arrival:

Re Police asking Galician settlers if they want anything, etc.

I have the honour to report that in accordance with your instructions on Monday 3rd Instant [January, 1898] I proceeded to H. Belcher's Sec. 14. Tp. 56 R 18 W of the 4th M., to enquire into the above matter.

147. Dest./49694, January 21, 1898: Affidavit signed by John Krebs and witnessed by P. C. H. Primrose.
157. Dest./49694, January 21, 1898: Affidavit signed by G. D. Butler and witnessed by P. C. H. Primrose.

I spent all Tuesday and Wednesday the 4th and 5th inst going round amongst these people, and I attach a schedule of the 35 heads of families interviewed by me on this subject, returning to Fort Saskatchewan on Thursday the 6th Instant.

Before proceeding further I would point out that I discovered on arrival at Belcher's that the Russian [*sic*] Christmas Festival (which this year lasts for 4 days) was to start at sundown Wednesday evening, and in nearly every house which I visited on Tuesday and Wednesday I found active preparations going forward towards this celebration; further I am given to understand that all, according to their means, strive to make it a point to have some little better and additional food at this season for the year if possible, and borrowing from their richer neighbours is not infrequent if the wherewithall cannot be procured in other ways.

I just mention this as for this reason I consider that I have seen these people under more favourable circumstances than I otherwise would have done.

Explaining further I might mention that the conditions of a number of these people have changed since September, and that my visits were only to some of those families who were reported as being in good circumstances.

Taking up the various statements made by Mr. Sutter in his report of the 27th Sept. I would say:

1st He must surely be aware that Det's of Police are stationed at various points throughout the Territories for the purpose of maintaining Law and Order, and that where the bulk of the settlement near a Det. do not speak the English language, the services of an Interpreter become necessary in order to carry on the work.

2nd That I should hesitate before I would state that some of these people were living in a state quite the reverse of miserable and destitute.

3rd A number of these people informed me that Mr. Sutter was not in their houses at all, which if correct would make his inspection cursory instead of going into every house and mudded hut.

4th The houses I found with few exceptions very hot, there being not much ventilation. All these houses with the exception I think of 2 had mud floors, and I would not consider any clean and in great many they keep their hens in with them, and in some the hens were nesting on the beds. The insides of some of these houses struck me as filthy with mildewed walls as soft as putty. . . .[16]

Inspector Primrose then goes on to describe the extreme poverty of the settlers. The children he saw had hardly any clothes or shoes and had to stay indoors all the time. The settlers, he related, had no money to buy any blankets for their beds, and were compelled to sleep with their clothes on. He continued his report thus:

5th The most flour I saw in any house was 3 bags.

6th The statement "Every one has one or two cows and a team of

[16]7. Dest./49694, January 7, 1898: P. C. H. Primrose, Inspector, N.W.M.P., Fort Saskatchewan, to the Commanding Officer, N.W.M.P, Fort Saskatchewan.

horses" is incorrect as you will see from the attached schedule about 20 have no stock.

7th The following cases of sickness were reported viz:—Wasyl Myryan [Marian] sick for about 4 weeks during the summer. Giorgi Klapaczuk at present suffering from bad teeth and sore throat. Danelo Kucenzack laid up about 4 weeks having run something into his foot or leg (I saw his wife). One of his children has died and one now has a much distended stomach, due I am told to eating bread made from shorts. Giorgi Maylnk's [Melnyk's] wife who is reported by Mr. Sutter as having twins but being better, *died not long after he was there*, and Corpl. Butler informed me he had to come to Fort Sask'n for 4 boards to make a coffin, as they had nothing. *The twins are also dead.* Grovella Andros [Gabriel Andrietz] reported a child sick, does not know what is wrong, but thinks it is caused by bread made from the shorts. Iwan Scrabba is hobbling around having broken his leg about a month ago whils't on the trail, to Fort Saskatchewan. Demetrius Siliaco [Dmytro Chilko] was in Calgary Hospital, and has been sick since. Michael Kachupski's wife has been ailing for about 3 months, some chest trouble. He has been sick also for some days. Iwan Macyloytski [Ivan Makowicki] cut himself on the foot 3 months ago and has been unable to work, now recovering. Maxim Zacharcho's wife is sick—cough. Wasyl Kryz has something wrong with a child, does not know what it is. Panko Omisyko [Panko Onysko] has had two children die and one now in Hospital in Edmonton. Ivan Tameyack has a frozen foot: his wife has left him and is reported to be living at Knowltons. Nastya Zacharko has two children sick. Krebs who accompanied me says it is measles. I notice that Corpl. Butler reports a number of cases but I only mention those brought to my notice.

8th Mr. Sutter says "I enquired of the man if he had asked the Police for any assistance. He said no, but that the Police asked him if he wanted anything and he told him that he would take some flour and the Police told him that he would write to the Gov't and see what he could (do)." The husband of the woman who had twins is Giorgi Malnyk and he informed me in answer to my questions "that the Police did not tell him to ask for grub; they did not tell him that the Govt. would give him flour if he asked for it: He went and asked himself and Corpl. Butler said he would write about it."

At every house to which I went I asked them if the Police had told them to ask for flour or if the Police had told them they would get grub from the Govt., if they asked for it and the invariable answer was that the Police had not told them to ask or that they would receive if they asked, but that they went themselves and that Corpl. Butler told them (so a number told me) that he would write and see about it, I attach declarations from Corp. Butler and Interp. Krebs to this effect. Wasyl Myryan [Marian] informed me that the old timers (Galicians) told him if he could not pull through to go to the Police. Filip Wojtas says some of the old settlers told him to go and ask the Govt. for help as they had given grub to them and from what these two men say I think I see how this business came about and that a number if they saw a chance to get flour from the Govt. would not be slow to avail themselves of it, if they thought that they could get away with it.

9th Mr. Sutter's idea that they who are in poor circumstances should go to work, I think an excellent one, but some of them are prevented from doing so through having no wives, and children to look after: through having to get out the logs for their houses: through sickness: through not having the proper clothing in which to go and look for work etc. Whilst on this subject of work I may say some are reluctant to go to work as they say they do not get their pay. I have asked about some of these cases and some are due to the people who owe them not having had their threshing done and quite a number are being paid in wheat etc. I have instructed Corpl. Butler to enquire into a couple of cases (not due to want of threshing) and that if the people did not pay them to instruct the Galicians to lay informations before the nearest magistrate for non-payment of wages. There is another point I would bring to your notice namely that the fruits of the work of a number will not do them much good for some time as they owe money which they had to borrow to bring them to this Country, for instance Nycoli Topolitski [Nycola Topolnitsky] and his son each owe $90.00 which is going to take them sometime to repay: this is the largest amount I heard about but others owe various smaller sums.

If either Messrs Sutter & Bennett were to take up their residence in the settlement for a month or two and see that those who were able went to work also prosecute those people who employed but did not pay them: assist those who are not yet located on land (of which there are 5 or 6) to obtain their homesteads and be in a position to thoroughly look into any cases where relief (strictly as a loan) was asked for, it would be a good idea, and in this connection I might say that I think no relief should be given until a couple of visits at least at uncertain times, have been made to the homes of these applying for the same, and also careful enquiries to be made amongst their neighbours as to their circumstances, etc.

With regard to their circumstances as shown by the attached schedule I may say that their houses are small and that I looked about to see if anything more than was shown was concealed, but I could find nothing and I was struck by the absence of blankets or other clothes. I failed to obtain the location of a few and the reason I put in No. 31 who has been in the Country for several years was because his crop had been destroyed.

I visited a few whom I declined to take notes of, as they had 3 or 4 head of stock and if in want could sell an animal if they could or would not work out for wages.

Nearly all of these people have log houses with thatch or mud roofs, but four or five which I visited had mudded huts i.e. poles placed together as an ∩ and heavily covered with sods.

Inspector Primrose also enclosed a tabular statement on the thirty-five settlers he visited. They were:

1. Wasyl Myryan (Marian): 22-56-17-W4. Total Family—5; Acres broken about 3; Arrived May 1897. 1 bag Flour, 1 bag Bran; 3 bags of Wheat, about 15 bs. potatoes.

---

3. Dymtria Balan (Dmytro Balan): 16–56–17–W4. Total family—6; Acres broken—about 4; Arrived May 1897; ½ bag flour ½ bag wheat.

2. Hot. Babitch (Babych): 22-56-17-W4. Total Family—6. No acres broken. Arrived May 1897; about 10 head of cabbage and about 2 bus. potatoes.

3. Dymtria Balan (Dmytro Balan): 16-56-17-W4. Total family—6. Acres broken—about 4; Arrived May 1897; ½ bag flour, ½ bag wheat.

4. Giorgi Klapaczuk: 16-56-17-W4. Total family—6; Acres broken about 2; Arrived May 1897. 3 bags Flour.

5. Danelo Kucenzack: 20-56-17-W4—Total family—6. Acres broken about 4. Arrived May 1897. ⅛ bag flour, 3 bags Bran, 4 bags Potatoes.

6. Giorgi Malnyk (Giorgi Melnyk): 20-56-17-W4. Stock—1 horse, 1 cow, 1 calf. Total family—5; Arrived May 1897; ¼ bag Flour, 3 bags Bran, 4 bags Potatoes.

7. Govrella Andrews (Havrylo Andrietz): Total family—5. Acres broken—about 2; Arrived May 1897. ¼ bag Shorts. Living in the same house as 6.

8. Ivan Scrabba: 32–56–17–W4. Total family—7. 2 horses, 1 colt, 1 cow, 1 calf. Acres broken—about 5. Arrived May 1897. Piece of pork, ½ bag of Flour.

9. Wasyl Hounka (Wasyl Hunka): 32-56-17-W4. Total family 8. Has 2 cows and 2 calves. Arrived May 1897. I bag Flour, 1 bag Shorts, 3½ bags Wheat.

10. Nycoli Topolnitski: 28-56-17-W4. Total family 3. Acres broken about 2. Arrived May 1897. About 25 lb. Shorts, about 15 bs. Potatoes.

11. Nycoli Topolnitski Jr.: Total family—3. Arrived May 1897. Living in same shack with his father.

12. Gregori Wasylnczuk (Gregori Wasylynczuk): 28-56-17-W4. Total family 6. Stock—2 horses, 1 cow, 1 calf. Arrived May 1897. Acres broken—about 2. 2 bags flour, 4 bags Shorts, about 15 bs. Potatoes.

13. Tanaska Skintij: 28-56-17-W4. Total family 6. Acres broken about 6. Arrived May 1897. 1¼ bags flour, 1 bag Shorts, 4 bs. Potaoes.

14. Nycoli Verenka: 28-56-17-W4. Total family—8. Stock—1 horse. Acres broken—about 4. Arrived May 1897. ½ bag Flour, 1 bag Shorts, 16 bs. potatoes.

15. Gregori Rhyrczuk (Gregory Hryhorczuk): Arrived May 1897. Everything included with his son-in-law; No. 14.

16. Demetrius Siliaco (Demetrius Chilko): 14-56-18-W4. Total family—3. Acres broken—about 6. Arrived October 1896. 1 bag Flour, 1 bag Wheat, 15 bs. Potatoes.

17. Eliuck Solunuck (Elia Soloniuk): 18-56-17-W4. Total family—6. Stock 1 horse, 1 cow. Arrived May 1897. Acres broken about 3. 1 bag Flour, 3 bags Shorts, 1 bag Wheat.

18. Andro Polinski: 10-56-18-W4. Total family—3. Acres broken—about 2. Arrived May 1897. 1 bag Flour, 2 pails potatoes.

19. Iwan Macyloytski (Iwan Makowicki): 36-56-20-W4. Total family—5. Stock 1 cow. Acres broken—about 5. Arrived May 1897. ½ bag Flour, ¼ bag shorts, about 15 bs. Potatoes.

20. Filip Wojtas: 36-56-20-W4. Total family 2. Stock—1 cow. Acres broken—about 3½. Arrived May 1897. 1 bag Flour (Living with 19).

21. Maxim Zaharcho (Maxym Zacharko): 36-56-20-W4. Total family—3. Arrived November 1897. 1 bag Flour (also living in same House with 19 & 20).

22. Paulo Gudza (Paulo Gudzan): 36-56-20-W4. Total family 5. Stock—2 colts, 1 cow, 1 calf. Acres broken about 5½. Arrived May 1897. 1 bag Flour, ½ bag Shorts, 10 bs. Potatoes.

23. Michel Kachupski: 56-18-W4. Total family 3. Acres broken about 2½. 1 bag Flour.

24. Vavro Mrycyak (Vavro Mrycak, arrived Feb. 1897): Total family—6. Acres broken about 3. 1 bag of Flour.

25. Fedor Lacousta (Fedir Lakusta): Total family 4. Stock—1 cow. No acres br. About 10 bus. Potatoes (living with 24).

26. Wasyl Kryz: 2-57-20-W4. Total family—6. Stock—2 horses, 1 cow, 1 calf. Acres broken, about 6. Arrived May 1897. About 4 bush. Potatoes.

27. Panko Onusyko (Panko Onuczko): Total family—4. Arrived November 1897. 1 bag Flour, 1 bag Bran (lives with 26).

28. Iwan Tansovini (Iwan Tancowny): Total family—2. Arrived December 1897. 1 bag Flour, 1 bus. Potatoes, is father of 2, both living with 22. and food is between them.

29. Antoni Tancovini (Anton Tancowny): Family of 3.

30. Antonie Gourba (Gurba): 30-57-19-W4. Total family 6. Stock—1 cow, 1 calf. Arrived May 1897. 20 bs. Potatoes, 15 lb. flour 2 bags Bran 1 bag Wheat.

31. Ivan Tameyuck: 1 person. Stock—1 cow. Acres broken—5½. Arrived 1895. about 15 bus. Potatoes, 20 lb. Flour.

32. Nastya Zaharco (Nastia Zacharko): family of 6. Arrived December 1897. Living with 31 in same house.

33. Ivan Matcheo (Iwan Macko): SE¼-4-57-20-W.4.M—Total family—2. ½ bag Flour, 1 big bag Potatoes, also living in the same house with 31.

34. Yurko Couzhek (Yurko Kuszek): Total family 7. Stock—cow, 1 calf. Acres broken, about 10. Arrived May 1897. ½ bag Flour, 4 or 5 bs. Potatoes.

35. Mrs. Linechuck: Total family 2. Arrived May 1897. Living in House with 34.

Inspector Primrose's report and tabular statement were passed on to Commissioner Herchmer in Regina, and he sent it on to Comptroller White in Ottawa, adding an observation of his own about the comparison of Primrose's report with Sutter's:

I have the honour to return file of correspondence regarding the alleged cases of destitution among Galician settlers near Edna, N.W.T., together with a report from Inspector Primrose on a special visit he made to thirty-five Galician families, and a tabular statement showing the number of souls in each family, their horses, cattle, acres broken, date of arrival, and the amount of food in possession of each. From this I think it is apparent that my statements, and those of Corporal Butler, are not rash ones, as Mr. Commissioner McCreary is pleased to characterize them.

I will observe that out of the 35 settlers visited, only 3 have teams at all, and only 3 have a horse, only 13 have any horned animals, and only one has more than a cow and a calf; 15 families have no land broken at all. Only one has 10 acres, and the others 6 and under. You will also notice that but one family had meat of any sort of description in the house. Several had nothing but a few potatoes, and many are deriving most of their sustenance from bread made of shorts, which diet is hardly suitable for human beings in mid-winter, and as the visit was made the preparations were in progress for the celebration of their New Year's Festival, it is to be presumed that they were as well provisioned as they could be.

I would draw your attention to that part of Mr. Sutter's report which says "The children were also well kept. In no place did we see any want or suffering." Inspector Primrose's description of the clothing worn by women and children does not quite agree with Mr. Sutter's account.[17]

Comptroller White then forwarded all of the correspondence to the Department of the Interior with a notification that no further visits would be made by the Police to the settlers unless they were requested: "Under the circumstances I have asked the Commissioner of Police to instruct members of the Force not to visit these settlers again until requested to do so through your Department, and that in the event of any of them applying to the Police for assistance they must be referred to the Agents of the Dept. of the Interior."[18] The Superintendent of Immigration sent the copies of the correspondence enclosed by White to Commissioner McCreary in Winnipeg, with a request that the matter be looked into fully: "Please make a thorough investigation into this matter and if necessary provide the needed relief."[19]

Commissioner McCreary, although recognizing that Sutter's report had its flaws, was determined to find out the truth with regard to the whole matter. He therefore sent the copies of all related correspondence to Sutter, who was away on duty in Chicago at the time. McCreary then informed the Department of the Interior of his action:

. . . I have forwarded the copy (of the correspondence) to Mr. Sutter, but as he is now doing immigration work in the States, he will not likely be able to make a reply until his return. I have sent another copy, however, to Mr. Bennett, the Immigration Agent in Edmonton, with instructions to take an interpreter and spend a week among those people, in order that we may get at the real truth in regard to them.

I cannot personally visit all these colonies, and of course, have to base my reports entirely upon information the officials in the different districts send in to me. From the letter of Inspector Primrose, I would say, however, that his ideal is a little too high for European immigrants. I do not believe the condition of this colony is any worse than that of many others who have come here in years past; in fact, I think the condition of the Mennonites for a few years after their arrival as well as the Hungarians, Germans and others, was worse than that of the Galicians.

17. Dest./49694, January 15, 1898: L. W. Herchmer, Commissioner, N.W.M.P., Regina, to Fred White, Comptroller, N.W.M.P., Ottawa.

18. Dest./49694, January 21, 1898: Fred White, Comptroller, N.W.M.P., Ottawa, to the Secretary, Department of the Interior, Ottawa.

19. Dest./49694, January 26, 1898: Assistant Secretary, Department of the Interior, Ottawa, to W. F. McCreary, Winnipeg.

To insure success, I believe it will be necessary, should this class of immigration continue, to have a man established in the colony, and do nothing else but drive round among them advising them as to building their houses, ventilation of same, getting fire wood, modes of farming, securing employment, and so forth. While it might cost perhaps $1200 to keep such a man and to provide him with a horse, in my opinion, it would be money well spent.[20]

Although Sutter was away in the United States, he nevertheless sent in his reply to Commissioner McCreary's letter, informing him: "I am writing to Mr. Bennett and will give him some instructions to follow before he makes out his report."[21] Sutter also answered some of the accusations voiced by Inspector Primrose in his report. From his letter, Sutter appeared to have a personal grudge against John Krebs, and would have liked to see him removed:

. . . I might also state that Mr. Creps did all he could against me during the election to hurt Mr. Oliver and is still continuing his warfare against me and as long as he is employed as interpreter there, trouble will never cease.

Now in Rabbit Hills District there are also a number of Galicians who just came in last summer and are no better off than those settled around Edna and we have not heard any complaints from that quarter.

In the meantime, Thomas Bennett was busy at Edna. He visited some sixty settlers and found that even more persons than those enumerated by Corporal Butler and Inspector Primrose were in need of assistance. Following instructions given to him by Commissioner McCreary, he rendered relief to forty-five heads of families and prepared a detailed report on the condition of each family. To repair in some small way his tarnished reputation, Bennett also secured affidavits signed by two settlers, Jan Stroczynski and Leon Proczynski, who solemnly swore (through the interpreter, as they could not speak English) to statements quite the opposite of those Corporal Butler and Inspector Primrose had made. Iwan Stroczynski made this statement:

I Iwan Stroczynski of S.E.¼ 30-55-17-W of the 4th M. in the County of Alberta do solemnly declare that John Krebs the Police Interpreter told me in presence of Corporal Butler & several others of the settlers who were present that the Government would supply us with provisions, and told me I could have 4 or 5 sacks of flour. Krebs knew I had 2 horses 2 cows and 2 calves. Waggon, plough, harrow. I arrived in June 1897, and was then possessed of about $500.00. This promise of relief by Krebs was made generally throughout the colony. This statement was made in Harry Belcher's

[20]7. Dest./51500, February 3, 1898: W. F. McCreary, Winnipeg, to the Secretary, Department of the Interior, Ottawa.

[21]7. Dest./52998, February 7, 1898: C. W. Sutter, c/o Canadian Government Agency, 1223 Monadnock Block, Chicago, Illinois, to W. F. McCreary, Winnipeg.

house. And I make this solemn declaration conscientiously believing the same to be true, and by virtue of Chapter 141 Revised Statutes of Canada, intituled "An Act respecting Voluntary and extra-Judicial Oaths".
Declared before me at South Edmonton
in the County of Alberta, this 24th day of
February, A.D. 1898

(Signed) JAN STROCZYNSKI.

(Signed) THOS. BENNETT, A Commissioner, etc.[22]

An identical "solemn declaration" was signed by Leon Proczynski, of SW¼ 34-55-18-W 4th M., who, since he did not know how to write, put his cross under the document. The Commissioner who took the oath was Thomas Bennett himself.

Bennett's description of the settlers who arrived in Edna in the spring of 1897 and settled mostly in Townships 55, 56, and 57, Ranges 17 and 18, contains more detailed information than the report submitted a few months earlier by C. W. Sutter. Bennett makes observations on the modes and habits of the settlers, and describes the conditions prevailing in the new settlement:

Acting on your instructions I proceeded to the colony with my interpreter J. A. Lipinski on Wednesday the 9th inst. (February, 1898).

Previous to receiving your letters several Galicians came into town asking for assistance stating at the same time that they had been sent by the police. Some of them I knew to be in need of assistance, and followed your instructions by giving them relief, taking a lien on their homesteads. I also met several on the way coming in with teams. Some of these I knew to be in good circumstances whom I directed to wait in South Edmonton until my return.

On arriving in Edna I proceeded to the S.W. part of the Colony in Township 56, Range 20, working my way N & E returning S & W again to Edna, having visited over 60 families regarding whose condition I make the following report—

1. Paulo Guzan (Paulo Gudzan) S.E.¼ 36-56-20. Wife and 3 children, arrived in May 1897. Has 1 cow and calf, good house and cook stove but was short of provisions, sufficient to carry him through until he could get crop in. I explained that any assistance the Government might give must be secured by a lien on his homestead, to which he willingly assented. I therefore gave him relief to the amount of $10.00.

2. Philip Waytas (Philip Woitas) S.W.¼-36-56-20. Wife and child. Arrived in May 1897. Has 5 acres broken—1 cow, but no team of any kind. Log house and cook stove. I allowed relief to the amount of $5.00.

3. Iwan Mackowicki, N.E.¼-36-56-20—Wife and 3 children. Arrived in May 1897. Has 5 acres broken—1 cow. He expects 400 guilden from Austria but had only ½ sack of flour (shorts) in the house. Gave him relief to the amount of $10.00 which he will pay as soon as he receives his money from the old country.

---

22. Dest./55512, February 24, 1898: Solemn Declaration by Jan Stroczynski of SE¼ 30-55-17-W4.

4. Iwan Bucza—N.W.¼-22-56-20—Wife and 3 children. Arrived in May 1897. Only took up land in November so has nothing broken. Was very poor when he came and worked out all summer for provisions and clothing. Granted relief to the extent of $10.00.

5. John Polowy—S.W.¼-32-55-20. Has a mother depending on him. Arrived in May 1897 and has been working for farmers for board of self and mother. He has 2 acres broken and some timber cut to build a house in spring. Has not been able to make entry. He is at present living with a neighbor. Allowed him relief to the amount of $5.00.

6. Wasyl Kryz. N.E.¼-2-57-20. Wife and 4 children. Arrived in May 1897. Has 6 acres broken—good house, cook stove, 2 horses and 1 cow and calf. Spent all his money and had not provisions to last his family through winter. Gave him relief to the amount of $10.00.

7. Franko Wozniak—N.W.¼-14-57-20. Wife and 1 child. Arrived in May 1897. Has 3 acres broken. Small house and Russian stove very poor—was unable to make entry. Granted relief to the amount of $10.00.

8. Panko Onuczko—N.E.¼-4-57-20. Wife and 1 child. 2 children having died since his arrival in December 1897. No land broken but timber cut and hauled to build a house. At present living with a neighbor. Granted relief to the amount of $10.00.

9. Anton Gurba—N.W.¼-30-56-19. Wife and 4 children. Arrived in May 1897. Has 5 acres broken. Log house, cook stove 1 cow and calf. Would be short of provisions before he could do anything. Granted relief to the amount of $10.00.

10. Wasyl Stecko—N.E.¼-36-56-18. Wife and 1 child. Arrived in May 1897. 2 acres broken but has not been able to make entry. Has small house and Russian stove. Very poor no food except potatoes. Gave relief to the amount of $10.00.

11. Elko Kalanczuk—N.W.¼-36-56-18. Wife and 3 children. Arrived in May 1897.—1 Acre broken but has not been able to make entry. Small house and Russian stove.

12. Joseph Wispinski—S.E.¼-36-56-18. Wife and 1 child. Arrived in May 1897. No house or food. Living with a neighbor. Has not made entry. Granted relief to the amount of $10.00.

13. John Sliwka—S.W.¼-36-56-18. Wife and three children arrived in May 1897. 2 acres broken. Home Russian stove. Has not made entry. Gave relief to the amount of $10.00. This man owes $7.00 for baggage but has given order on C.P.R. for that amount as he has been working for that company and has not yet been paid.

14. Mikal Zatzbski (Jastrembski?) S.E.¼-14-56-18. Wife and 1 child. Arrived in November 1896, 2½ acres broken. His house was burned last spring but has built another. Very poor. Worked on the Railway and earned a little. Granted relief to the amount of $5.00.

15. Andro Topolinski (Andrew Topolniski) N.W.¼-10-56-18. Wife and 1 child in Calgary arrived in March 1897. 3 acres broken. Poor house, Russian stove. Baggage has been in Edmonton Station all winter with charges of $10.50, which I released and gave him $5.50 in provisions. Total amount of relief given $16.00.

16. Dmytro Zahazko (Dmytro Zacharko) S.W.¼-14-56-18. Wife and 1 child, arrived March 1897. 5 acres broken. No cattle or house. Very poor house with Russian stove. Was injured last summer working on Railway by being thrown from hand car. Granted relief to the amount of $16.00.

17. Feodor Lakusta—S.E.¼-14-56-18. Wife. Arrived in March 1897. Has 3 acres broken 1 cow and calf. Log house, Russian stove. Has very little provisions. Granted relief to the amount of $10.00.

18. Iwan Lupul—N.W.¼-16-56-17. Wife and three children. Arrived in May 1897. 5 acres broken. Pair oxen, cow and calf, waggon, plough, harrow and sleigh. Good house, Russian stove. Spent all his money in buying cattle and implements. Had no provisions to carry him through. Granted relief to the amount of $10.00.

19. Iwan Tkaczuk—S.W.¼-18-56-17. Widower, 2 children. Arrived in March 1897. 6 acres broken. Horse, cow and calf, plough and harrow. Small house, Russian stove. Has logs cut to build a good house. Spent all his money in improvements. Granted relief to the amount of $16.00.

20. Iwan Scraba—N.E.¼-32-56-17. Wife and 5 children. Arrived March 1897. 6 acres broken, 2 horses, cow and calf, waggon, plough, harrow and sleigh. Shanty only poles covered with sods in the shape of a roof. Is hauling logs to build a new house. Spent his money on cattle and implements. Had no provisions. Granted relief to the amount of $16.00.

21. Wasyl Zachary—S.E.¼-30-56-17. Wife and 3 children and father-in-law. Arrived May 1897. 4 acres broken. Horse, cow and 2 calves. A very poor house. Russian stove. No provisions. Gave relief to the amount of $16.00.

22. Wasyl Hunki (Wasyl Hunka)—S.W.¼-32-56-17. Wife and 6 children. Arrived May 1897. 5 acres broken, 2 cows and 2 calves. Log house. Russian stove. Earned $30.00 on railway which was all used up in buying provisions in the early winter. Gave relief to the amount of $16.00.

23. Nikolas Warenko (Nicholas Verenka) N.E.¼-20-56-17. Wife and 4 children also father and mother. Arrived in May 1897. Has 4 acres broken. 1 horse, plough, harrow and sleigh. A poor house. Russian stove. Earned $30.00 on railway which was spent the same way as Hunki. Granted relief amounting to $16.00.

24. Dmytro Balan—N.E.¼-16-56-17. Wife and 4 children. Arrived in May 1897. 4 acres broken. Fairly good house, Russian stove. Very poor—no provisions. Granted relief to the amount of $16.00.

25. Gregory Waszelinczuk (Gregory Wasylynchuk)—S.W.¼-28-56-17. Wife and 4 children. Arrived May 1897. 5 acres broken, 2 horses, cow and calf, waggon, sleigh and harrow. Poor house, Russian stove, Hauling logs to build new house. No provisions. Gave relief to the amount of $16.00.

26. Danielo Kacinadak (Danylo Kucenczuk) N.E.¼-18-56-17. Wife and 4 children. Arrived in May 1897. 5 acres broken, 1 horse, poor house, Russian stove. Relief granted $10.00.

27. Gavrelo Andrezasz (Havrylo Andreyasz)—N.W.¼-20-56-17. Wife and 3 children. Arrived May 1897. 3 acres broken. Shanty made of poles covered with sods. Russian stove. Gave relief amounting to $10.00.

28. George Klapaczuk—N.E.¼-16-56-17. Wife and 4 children. Arrived in May 1897. Has only a hovel, children almost naked. Very poor. Has not made entry. Gave relief to the amount of $10.00.

29. Wasyl Maryan—N.E.¼-22-56-17. Wife and 3 children. Arrived in May 1897. 4 acres broken. Cow and calf. Snug house clean and tidy. Very little provisions. Gave relief amounting to $10.00.

30. George Melnik—S.W.¼-20-56-17. Widower, 4 children, arrived May 1897. 4 acres broken. Very poor. Shanty made of poles—sod roof. Has 1 cow. Granted relief amounting to $10.00.

31. Iwan Topolinski (Iwan Topolniski)—N.E.¼-28-56-17. Widower and 3 children. Arrived May 1897. 2 acres broken. Poor—has not made entry. Very poor house, Russian stove. Granted relief to the amount of $10.00.

32. Nicolas Topolinski (Nicola Topolniski)—N.W.¼-28-56-17. Wife and 1 child. Arrived May 1897. No improvements. Poor. Has not made entry. Very poor house, Russian stove. Gave relief to the amount of $10.00.

33. Tleo Salonak (Elie Soloniuk)—S.W.¼-18-56-17. Wife and 4 children. Arrived May 1897. 3 acres broken, 1 cow. Wretched poor house and entirely destitute. Has not made entry. Granted relief to the amount of $10.00.

34. Achtemi Herchorczuk (Achtemy Hrehorczuk) S.E.¼-20-56-17. Wife and 3 children. Arrived May 1897. 6 acres broken. 1 horse, 1 cow. Poor house, Russian stove. Granted relief to the amount of $10.00.

35. Tanasko Skinti (Tanasko Skintij)—S.E.¼-28-56-17. Wife and 3 children, also mother-in-law. Arrived May 1897. Has 3 acres broken. Wretchedly poor. Granted relief to the amount of $16.00.

36. John Yorkow (John Yurkiw)—S.E.¼-36-55-18. Wife and 5 children. Arrived Nov. 1896, 3 acres broken. Only 1 pig. Raised 18 bushels potatoes and 12 bushels of poor barley and has been living on that. Poor house, Russian stove. Granted relief to the amount of $10.00.

37. Franc Mack—S.E.¼-14-50-23 (Tp. 56?). Wife. Arrived January 1898 from Regina. Is building house on his homestead. Gave him relief to the amount of $10.00.

38. John Talbash—S.W.¼-14-50-23. Wife and 2 children. Arrived January 1898, from British Columbia. Has gone out with Mack and is also building a house. Granted relief to the amount of $8.00.

39. Rozalia Sawkowa—N.W.¼-22-56-18. Widow and 4 children. Arrived May 1896. Husband Anton Sawkowa (Sawka) died in December 1897. Good house and cook stove, 8 acres broken. 2 horses, 2 cows and 2 calves. Raised 14 bushels of wheat but such poor quality that they would not grind it for her at the mill. She has no provisions. Gave her relief to the amount of $10.00.

40. Wasyl Gluchi (Wasyl Gluchie)—S.W.¼-30-56-17. Wife and 2 children. Arrived May 1897. Has 2 acres broken. House, Russian stove. 1 cow. Poor. No provisions. Granted relief to the amount of $10.00.

41. Bartko Prus—N.E.¼-16-56-18. Wife and 4 children. Arrived March 1897. House and Russian stove. Has 3 acres broken. 1 cow and 1 calf. Clean generally but poor. Granted relief to the amount of $10.00.

42. Sobko Andruchiw—S.W.¼-4-56-18. Wife and 6 children. Arrived May 1897. 5 acres broken. House, Russian stove, cow and calf. Poor, no provisions. Gave relief to the amount of $10.00.

43. Iwan Kuczy (Kucy)—S.W.¼-16-56-18. Wife and 3 children. Arrived May 1897. 5 acres broken. Good house and Russian stove. Very clean. No cattle, poor. Gave relief to the amount of $10.00.

44. Iwan Karszoryszyn (Kaszczyszyn?) N.W.¼-16-56-18. Wife and 5 children. Arrived May 1897. 4 acres broken. House and Russian stove. Clean but poor. Gave relief amounting to $10.00.

45. Nicholai Szparzuski—S.W.¼-36-56-18. Wife and 1 child. Arrived May 1897. Has 2 acres broken. 2 calves. Good house and Russian stove. Very poor. Gave relief amounting to $10.00.

There are upward of 90 families in the Colony of which about 30 came in 1896 and about 20 in 1897, who are well off and require no assistance. In many cases amongst the best off of these when I demanded giving any assistance they informed me that the police interpreter told them they could get what they wanted by asking the Government for it. This information was given voluntarily and without any solicitation on my part. Amongst the number who made this statement (are)

Dmytro Melinka —S.E. 22.56. 17.
Philip Ojats —S.W. 36.56. 20.
Jurko Koziak —S.E. 32.56. 19.
Anton Sloboda —S.W. 30.55. 17.
Iwan Stroczynski—S.W. 30.55. 17.
Leon Proczinski —N.E. 34.55. 18.

From the latter two I enclose declarations made before me in the office here substantiating the above statement. I may say that these promises have given me endless trouble in combatting the requests for provisions made by many who could have pulled through without assistance.

You will see I have granted relief to some who possess cattle etc. I weighed the question of relief well and came to the conclusion that it would be better to give them relief than to allow them to sell any of their stock. All were willing to give security on their homesteads and I consider them quite safe, as every one I believe is good for the debt and will pay when it becomes due. I have explained to them that now as the Government has been so good to them they must go to work and get out fence rails and building logs for stabling etc., and show that they appreciate what has been done for them, which they all promised to do.

The report of Inspector Primrose in many points is true but his ideas of the requirements of these people are not in accordance with their habits even when they are well off—as for instance he speaks of the women and children having no clothing except a linen shirt. I may say that in the whole colony it would be impossible to find a woollen under garment and I have never seen any of them yet wear stockings. This is their mode of dressing and I would consider it impossible to attempt to change their habits in this respect. In the houses the women and children all go bare footed. In one case where I called the man being one of the best off in the colony was building a hand loom and had about a dozen head of cattle. Upon my making a remark about his stock looking well he seemed pleased and said he would show them to me. He went with me out to the stable about 6 rods distant and on the way I noticed he was bare footed and on my drawing his attention to it he said it was all right and went on through the yard and stables without appearing to suffer any discomfort. His name is Iwan Lakusta and lives on S.W.¼ of 22. 56. 18.

The houses upon the whole are warm the majority being heated with the Russian stove. Very few have cook stoves. In this respect I don't consider they suffer. As you have doubtless seen in the Dauphin district part of the back of these stoves are made specially for the children to sleep on.

It is also true that some of the houses which were built late in the fall and plastered with clay are not yet dry, but I only saw one where the walls appeared mildewed.

I did not find a case of sickness in the whole colony which required medical treatment. One woman suffered from toothache and one man had a frozen toe and two children appeared to have distended stomachs caused I believe by living on bread made from shorts. In one house I found bread made from bran only, they had a few bushels of potatoes, but were very destitute. With these few exceptions they appeared to be in a healthy condition.

With regard to their beds and bedding, Inspector Primrose's report is also correct. The beds are broad and generally reach from the side of their Russian stove to the end of the room and are generally large enough for the whole family to sleep upon—the smaller children sleeping over the oven. The bed consists of straw or hay with a coarse linen cover, but no blankets or eider down quilts were visible in the colony, so that while Inspector Primrose's kind heart was touched by their apparent discomfort it is evident they are quite content to sleep in their sheep skins coats as their fathers have done before them, and would consider our requirements an extravagant luxury.

I have only to add that the amount of relief has exceeded very much what I considered would be necessary before visiting the colony—but owing to the encouragement they had already received to obtain relief, and what they have secured to the Government the amount of their indebtedness by lien on their homesteads, I have taken the responsibility of giving so many assistance believing it to be for the best.[23]

Some of the observations made by Bennett point to his lack of knowledge about the background of the Ukrainians. A shelter erected with mud floors, sod-covered roof, mildewed walls "Soft as putty," with primitive beds and hens nesting on them, were not typical of the settlers' abodes in the country of their origin. W. T. R. Preston, the Inspector of Agencies in Europe, who visited the province of Galicia in 1899, described a Ukrainian village in these words:

. . . To see one such peasant community is practically to understand the mode of living in all. . . . One cannot avoid admiring the care and labor expended in that direction to make their habitations attractive. In very few cases did I observe a failure to whiten the outside of the cottages, and in not a single instance did I find cattle or fowl sheds annexed to the living apartments. What might be termed the barnyards were very limited, and the people of the village were, as might be termed, living closely together. Yet there was evidence of order and cleanliness that could not escape observation.[24]

[23]7. Dest./55622, February 21, 1898: Thomas Bennett, Immigration Agent, South Edmonton, Alberta, N.W.T., to W. F. McCreary, Winnipeg. The names in parentheses are those found in the Naturalization Records.

[24]Canada, Parliament, *Sessional Papers*, 1900, XXXIV, No. 10, Paper No. 13: Report of W. T. R. Preston, Inspector of Agencies in Europe, London, December 23, 1899, 12–19.

The much-derided dress in which the Ukrainian peasant-immigrants arrived in Canada—and which the immigrants themselves (the women in particular) tried to exchange as soon as possible for "Canadian" dress, mostly made of cheaper cotton—was unjustly condemned. The women's long shirts, which served at the same time as under-skirts, were made from home-grown, home-spun flax or linen. These linen shirts could be of exquisite workmanship, decorated with hand-embroidery, and still more important, they could be of almost indestructable durability. Peasant girls often received as a dowry homespun skirts and shirts inherited from their grandmothers, which would sometimes wear for another two or three generations.

During the summer, shoes were seldom worn around the house. The lowland girls and women wore high leather boots when visiting on Sundays in the cold weather. For festive occasions soft yellow or red morocco leather boots were usually worn. The Highlanders (*Hutsuls*), men and women, wore sandals (*postoly*) made of strong tanned cowhide and laced with leather thongs which encircled the lower part of the calf. Their legs were wrapped in home-woven wool leggings, often of artistic workmanship, which reached below the knee. During the summer, the Hutsuls wrapped their feet in linen squares (*onuchi*), and during the winter the men and women wore heavy woollen home-made socks (*kapchooree*). Highland women wore woollen undergarments (*kholoshni*) in the winter, as they all, including the grandmothers, rode their ponies, the main means of transportation. An industry carried on in most of the Hutsul homes was the weaving of blankets of home-grown wool, artistically designed in colors derived from vegetable dyes. These thick, furry blankets, called *lizhnyky*, were used as bed covers, as saddle blankets, and for trade. *Lizhnyky*, a collector's rarity in Canada, can now be seen at Ukrainian folk-craft exhibitions or in private homes.

The Ukrainian peasant-settlers who arrived in Canada in the late 1890's, often with very limited or no means at all, were forced to fight for survival, and consequently shoes for the children, or a piece of cotton fabric for a skirt for one's wife and daughter, were luxuries to be acquired only after flour and potatoes for the family had been secured. The memoirs of the pioneers yield touching descriptions of such important events in the lives of the settlers. Maria Adamowska, who came to Canada as a nine-year-old girl in 1897, and settled with her parents on a homestead in Saskatchewan, provides this amusing description of her first pair of Canadian shoes:

> That autumn (the second in Canada) father earned a little more money. We bought an additional cow and a young ox. And finally they bought

shoes for me and some fabric for a skirt. The shoes were something to behold. If you want to know what they looked like, read Iwan Franko's fable "Abu Kazim's Sandals." His description fitted my shackles well. In size they resembled medium-sized sleds. They were made of iron-hard leather and had two rows of six cow's-eye-sized holes to put the shoe string through. You couldn't miss them in the darkest night. They pinched and burned so hard that tears came into my eyes when I wore them. And as for durability, there was no complaint—for each one of us girls wore them. As soon as the elder one was to be married, she bequeathed the pair to her next eldest sister, and thus four of us have worn the shoes in succession. . . .[25]

Commissioner McCreary shared Bennett's ideas on the "standard of comfort" to which the Ukrainian settlers were accustomed. He wrote the following opinion to Superintendent Pedley when he sent on Bennett's report:

Undoubtedly a fair proportion of these people have come out altogether too poorly provided with means to make a satisfactory start on their land, but I do not think that the general condition of the Colony warrants the belief which appears to be held by the Police authorities, that actual suffering exists, except in a few isolated cases.

I quite agree with the remarks made by Mr. Bennett as to judging of these people's surroundings by the standard of comfort which is expected by English or Canadian immigrants. As it appears from the Comptroller's letter of the 21st January that the supervision of these Galicians will thereafter be left to our officials, I have instructed Mr. Bennett that he will this year be held entirely responsible for looking after and caring for the interests of these people.

I am writing separately with regard to the remarks made in his report as to the action of the Police Interpreter.

You will find enclosed the liens which have been taken for relief supplied to these colonists, amounting in all to $493; one form of each lien has been filed with the Dominion Lands Agent at Edmonton.[26]

Every cent of the $493 loaned to the settlers of Edna was repaid, the reports of the Dominion Lands Office reveal. This conscientious discharge of the settlers' obligations was commented on in the House of Commons, April 26, 1901, when T. O. Davis, the Member of Parliament for Saskatchewan, observed: "The Galicians may not have much capital when they come in, but when they settle on the soil they are there for good. And, if the government advances them any money or loans them seed-grain or gives them any other assistance, the govern-

[25]Maria Adamowska, "Pochatky v Kanadi"/"Beginnings in Canada," "*Ukrainian Voice*" *Almanac* (Winnipeg, 1937), 93–102.

[26]7. Dest./55622, March 14, 1898: W. F. McCreary, Winnipeg, to Frank Pedley, Ottawa.

ment may be certain that it will get back that money, every dollar of it, with interest. . . ."[27]

III

The Edna colony settled down to a quiet life. The Edmonton Immigration Office and the Dominion Lands Office kept a watchful eye on the progress of the settlers. After they had overcome the difficulties which every new immigrant experienced who arrived without sufficient means to carry him over the first difficult months, the settlers gradually began to breathe more freely. The spring and the summer of 1898 helped those who arrived in 1897 to greatly improve their material condition. With the approach of the winter of 1898, after the harvest had been garnered, the Commissioner of Immigration sent C. W. Speers to the Edmonton area to view the situation around Edna and to report on it to Superintendent Pedley in Ottawa. On December 13, 1898, Speers presented his report, including an excellent description of the type of country in which the immigrants settled and news about their rapidly improving social conditions:

. . . I found at Edmonton eleven Bukowinians in the Immigration Hall asking relief, and after eliciting all the facts, ascertained they had mostly arrived in August (1898), having been detained in Quarantine at Halifax and Winnipeg. I instructed Mr. T. Bennett, the Agent there, to give them a small quantity of flour, fixing the amount from one to three sacks, according to number in family, and to take the necessary lien in each case, provision for which has been made by the Commissioner of Immigration.

After completing arrangements for any subsequent emergency, of that nature, I proceeded to inspect the large colony of Galicians at Edna, and other small colonies in that district. . . .

I may here say that this is a very fine tract of fertile land, commencing at Edmonton south through the celebrated Clover Bar and Agricola districts on to Fort Saskatchewan, and still on to Victoria, a distance of a hundred miles. The country is perceptably rolling, almost level, well watered, with occasional streams that have good, deep beds—also well wooded, although prairie fires have left a great deal of standing dry timber. The timber is principally poplar, with an occasional bluff of spruce. In most places a growth of light scrub covers the surface, but this is no drawback, as it is light, mostly dead and will plough down. The soil is unequalled, and a striking fact is the sameness of the country. Every few miles passing along, one thinks the country improving, if anything, with every acre rich, fertile and desirable; no bad sections, but a grand tract of beautiful land of excellent quality—such is the kind of country possessed by the Galicians at Edna, and there still remains a number of Townships open for colonization.

[27]Canada, Parliament, House of Commons, *Official Report of Debates*, 1901, I, April 12, 2956: T. O. Davis, Saskatchewan.

There is every evidence of prosperity among them; they are in good, comfortable houses and are doing remarkably well, as I will endeavour by this report to show.

Their social conditions are rapidly improving; they are fast adapting themselves to our customs; their homes are comfortable; many have good cooking stoves and proper cooking utensils and are very cleanly and are setting their tables for regular meals as Canadians do, and fast conforming to our usages, both in dress and custom. They have built two large churches in this colony—one a Union Church of Greek and Orthodox Catholic, and the other the Greek Church. These churches are in the course of construction and nearly completed, and are well built, substantial and good size. Two burial plots are laid out where a few of their number are laid at rest, evidently with respect, as the places are marked with a neat cross and evergreen wreath. The Church of the Russian Orthodox faith is 35 × 75, and will cost $1200. The Union Church will be 35 × 54 and cost $1000. They are situated on Section 23, Township 55, Range 18, and on Section 27, Township 56, Range 19, respectively, both West of the Fourth Principal Meridian.

There are two schools already established on the Colony, one at Limestone Lake, and the other at Beaver Creek, which are open eight months in the year. These colonists are very anxious to learn our language, and are keeping their children at school where they have had an opportunity and in all cases the teachers speak highly of the progress of the pupils—they are quick, bright and attentive.

In going over Nemerski's book, who acts as guide in locating this large colony, I find he has settled 281 families in this colony, and we place the colony at 360 families. Conceding that there are 800 children of school age in this settlement, the necessity of an early establishment of more schools must be apparent. This will be the most perfect way to Canadianize these people and make them more useful at an early date. The action of the Deputy Minister when at Dauphin establishing a school there, is wisely meeting the requirements. In conversation with a Mr. McDonald, a Barrister at Edmonton, he informs me he has been giving special instructions to two Galicians named Kota [Gowda] and Mans, and claims they are both bright young men. This is the Mr. McDonald who accompanied Mr. F. Oliver, M.P., and Agent Sutter through the colony, and subsequently defended these people through the "Toronto Globe" by an article which has evidently come to your notice. He says—"I was very much opposed to these people at first, but after seeing for myself the progress they are making I changed my mind. They are good settlers."

Permit me to suggest that just such young men as I have referred to could be speedily qualified, even without holding certificates, to do the first good work as teachers among these people, at even low salaries. I may say that some of these people have been communicating with the Right Reverend Bishop Nicholls, 1715 Powell Street, San Francisco, California, concerning the establishment of schools in this colony. I have no particulars as to the result of the correspondence, but thinking the Department might wish to take the initiative along national lines, I merely submit to you the fact for your consideration and action.

I had a conversation with D. J. Goggin, Superintendent of Education for the North-West Government, and felt impressed that your wishes would be carried out when submitted.

The Ruthenian people have large families—and the sanitary conditions of the colony, generally speaking, are very good.

In addition to a Grist Mill at Fort Saskatchewan owned by R. A. Bell, who informs me that he has ground into flour for Galicians this Fall two thousand bushels of wheat and purchased about five thousand bushels at 45 cents. They have in two places small mills in the colony made by themselves—one operated by two horses on a stationary power, with rope belting turning two large stones that have been chiselled and fitted to grind with small agitating hopper suspended above. This does fair work and is keeping things going in the vicinity. At another place I saw a small mill in a house that would grind two bushels of wheat per day; a woman working it by hand—verily "a woman grinding at the mill." Thus they are enabled, by their industry and ingenuity to save a long haul of thirty miles to the Grist Mill. But these Oriental habits will soon pass away, and as they are possessing a great producing district, we can look for good results in the future, owing to their frugality and industry.

Some have been engaged in placer mining on the Saskatchewan River, when not otherwise engaged on their farms. This is quite an advantage, as their time can be profitably employed at home. I will submit a few names—

Theodor Kenis [Kinash] Section 6-57-19—took $160 in gold out of the Saskatchewan River in four months besides putting up hay for his stock during interval.

William Piche [Paish] in eighteen days took $25.

Sefat Leperchinski [Lopushinsky] $50—Olag Ogli $25—making in short days from $1.50 to $2 clear—almost at their door in the River. The gold was sold to the Imperial Bank of Canada in Edmonton. This many will take advantage of next year when not busy on the farm, and it should prove quite an assistance to them.

These people have quite a lot of stock, and have made ample provision for them, as large quantities of hay have been put up, and they are good caretakers and feeders. But in many cases, late arrivals have purchased small ponies that are practically useless and are retarding their progress. These ponies run off when allowed their freedom, and when the Bukowinian is not looking on the prairies to find them he is running round with them. This is a mistake that a few of them are making, and I have pointed out and invariably impress our Agents to ward off the Broncho dealer and advise these people in their interests. But in many cases some have preferred to use their own judgement against the best advice that could be given. This more directly applies to the late arrivals of the Bukowinian class.

The production of this country in grain and stock will soon warrant railway construction, not only as a colonization road but as a commercial highway, whereby the products of the country can be carried to the market. The road, when built, would reap large revenues from the day the iron is laid as a common carrier of grain and stock by export and necessaries and commodities essential in great agricultural development by way of import. I am so impressed with that great belt of land running from Dauphin or Yorkton by way of Stony Creek or Carrot River to Prince Albert, thence to Battleford along Battle River, and through to Edmonton, and having been priviledged to report to the Department on many portions of it, that if such a road is completed right through to the Yellow Head Pass all along its entire permanent way, will be one grand fertile productive country that no man can accurately forestall its possibilities.

I am anxious, if permitted, to drive from Edmonton to Battleford—thence to Prince Albert by way of the Carrot River district to Yorkton at any time that would be in the interests of the Department and at the propitious season to see the country to advantage.

Returning again to Edmonton, I visited the Galician Colony at Rabbit Hills, comprising about thirty families, laying south-west of South Edmonton, at a distance of eighteen miles. The first of these Galicians came here about three years ago and are settled among some Russian Germans. This colony is making remarkable progress and are very permanently established. The country is a good one, lying adjacent to the White Mud River and just beyond the Rabbit Hills. The district is rather thickly covered with timber, principally poplar, and Balm of Gilead—in fact, for a few miles it could be called solid bush—the timber of fair dimensions. Just passing through this we come to the settlement with nice openings here and there and everything in a prosperous condition. About 60,000 bushels of grain will be grown in this settlement this year by the Russian Germans and Galicians. This information I got from the thresher in the colony. They have plenty of horses, cattle and hogs; everything is looking well and the Galician people are going into mixed farming. These Galicians are a very superior lot, and all come from the same place in Austria, namely, the Municipality of Jaroslaw—which may account for their advancement, they having had considerable means. There are no Bukowinians in this colony. They intend to build a church next year. They are all Greek Catholics. There are three public schools in the district, namely, White Mud, Rabbit Hills and Spruce Grove. Two of these schools have an attendance of 45 and 20 Galician children all learning English and making marked progress. They are anxious to have the school open the entire year. This colony is in a very satisfactory state—good houses and stables, plenty of roots, vegetables and grain, some threshing as much as 1500 bushels.—Stock in good condition, and with good prospects for the future.

There are other small colonies that have been founded, and where I have received very encouraging reports. The Austrian Germans at Stony Plain are doing very well and making marked progress. [These were German settlers from Galicia mentioned in Dr. Oleskow's booklet of 1895.] They first settled at Dunmore and moved from there to their present location in 1890 or 1891, which is twelve miles west of Edmonton. There are about eight families of Swedes among these—in all, possibly, fifty families. The Josephsburg Colony of Austrian-Germans have done well and many have this year—fourteen farmers threshed 26,780 bushels of wheat. . . .

In reviewing the condition of the different colonies that have been established by the Department, as well as those that have been supplemented within the past two years, I think, generally speaking, they are in a very satisfactory condition, and there is every evidence of prosperity and their prospects for the future are very good. The building of churches, the large attendance at the public schools, the desire of these people to acquire the English language, the very significant manner with which they wish to become identified with our citizenship, as well as the great amount of grain and stock being produced by these people, must be a source of gratification to the Department. With the exception of a few in the Edna Colony, there will be no demands upon the Department for assistance, and this should be very limited and will be effected in practical manner, several of the Bukowinians who were detained in quarantine at Halifax and Winnipeg will require a little assistance, but many Galicians in that settlement have as much as from a thousand to twelve hundred bushels of wheat in their granaries, and from two to three hundred bushels of potatoes in their cellars.

Speers further quotes the instructions which he gave in writing Bennett with regard to assistance to be extended to some Bukowinian families who were detained in quarantine at Halifax and Winnipeg:

It has been a satisfaction to notice that much of the ill feeling in the district of Edmonton held by certain people with reference to the advent of the Galicians into that district is becoming slowly, but surely, dissipated, and that the evidence of prosperity, with the other redeeming qualities of the people, is largely changing the sentiment in that locality. And I am persuaded the day is not far distant when all will concede that these people are desirable settlers. They are all producers and in looking over the short time they have settled, have made as much progress to do them justice as any other nationality could be expected to do.

I will submit to you a number of names, not going into the entire colony, showing capital they had at the time they arrived at their destination, and what progress they have made since that time.
Among the earlier settlers we have—

Ivan Pylypi (Pylypiw)—came three and a half years ago—Family comprising eight souls. He has built a comfortable house worth $100; stables and outbuildings $150; a good granary worth $75; 75 tons of hay $150; 6 horses $300; 14 cattle $400; 80 acres under cultivation $240; 1300 bushels of wheat in the granary. He has a new binder $150; mower and rake $80; wagon $50; disc harrows and ploughs; two good wells $100. 12 hogs worth $60 and two sheep. He came in 1894 with capital of $200. He has a clear deed of his farm unencumbered, and a very complete equipment.

Michal Polishi (Pullichie)—Section 22-56-19 W.4.M.—came four years ago. Has a good large frame house worth $400; good stable worth $150; 5 horses $250; 17 head of cattle $375; 8 hogs $60; binder, mower and rake $200; 70 acres under cultivation; has 1560 bushels of grain this year; 300 bushels of potatoes. Has all necessary equipment for farming. Farm is fenced. Came in 1894 with $350 capital and has a deed to his farm unencumbered.

Michalo Manick (Michael Melnyk)—Section 2-56-19—House worth $200; stable $100; granary $75; machine-house $40; 4 horses $200; 10 head of cattle $250; wagon and plough $100; Binder $120; mower and rake $80; 900 bushels of grain in his granary; 400 bushels of potatoes; 50 tons of hay; 6 pigs. Has everything paid for. Came four years ago with $350.

Feodor Melnak (Fedor Melnyk)—House worth $400; stables worth $200; granary $75; 4 horses $200; 10 cows $300; 50 tons of hay $100; 1100 bushels of wheat; 300 bushels of potatoes on hand. Has binder, mower, rake, wagon, harrows and a full agricultural equipment. Has purchased some railway land. 25 hogs $75. A little cash on hand. Farm all fenced—Does not owe one dollar. Came four years ago with a capital of $500.

Nicholi Manick (Nykola Melnyk)—Good house $200; stables and granary $200; 2 horses $120; 5 cattle $125; has 600 bushels of grain on hand; 300 bushels of potatoes; 25 tons of hay; 35 acres under cultivation; has a deed on his farm; a good agricultural equipment; is out of debt. Started there four years ago with a capital of $85 on leaving Winnipeg.

Elias Finitosh (Ilko Senetowich)—House $150; stables and out-buildings $150; 2 oxen $100; 8 cattle $200; mower, rake and wagon $150; 60 tons of hay $120; 400 bushels of grain; 200 bushels of potatoes; 8 sheep; a number of pigs $75. Started three years ago with $400 capital.

Michalo Spiche (Paish?)—House $200; outbuildings $150; 2 horses $60; 9 cows $200; 400 bushels of grain; 200 bushels potatoes; wagon, sleigh and plough, $100; two good wells $60. Settled three years ago with $175 capital.

Petro Melnak (Petro Melnyk)—Section 28-56-19. Came four years ago in July; has 40 acres broken $120; 3 horses $150; 6 cattle $125; wagon $40; plough, mower and rake $70; 50 tons of hay $100; house $100; stables, granary and outbuildings $200; 6 pigs; building material ready for new house; 645 bushels of grain and 150 bushels of potatoes. Has the deed to his farm; speaks a little English and is highly pleased with the country. Arrived with only $6 capital in July 1894 and had nothing else.

Nikoli Tryskovsky (Nykola Tychkowsky)—The first Galician settler, has 320 acres of land; house $150; stables, granary and outbuildings $250; 4 horses $200; 11 head of cattle $240; wagon, mower, rake and binder $300; Has 1100 bushels of grain; 200 bushels of potatoes; 13 pigs worth $60. Left Winnipeg with $150; had no other capital; settled on Section 28-56-19 W.4.M.

Andrew Spiche (Paish)—Section 34-56-19—House $200; stable and outbuildings $100; 2 horses $150; 7 cattle $175; 500 bushels of grain; 50 tons of hay; 150 bushels of potatoes; plough, mower and rake $100. Came with $200 capital three years ago.

I have submitted the above ten names who are ten of the earlier settlers settled in the Edna district. I have invariably found that these people after a few years have accumulated a very considerable property. I have checked up about 200 families, and consider the progress made by these people has been very great.

I submit a few names of the others who arrived at a more recent date, all of which are permanently established, and making very good progress—

George Klapatchuk—Section 16-56-17—House $75; stable $50; one horse $50; 80 bushels of grain; 25 bushels potatoes; 30 tons of hay; 8 acres broken. Came in 1897. $40 in debt when he arrived.

Metro Balan—Section 16-56-17. House $80; stable $40; 2 horses $60; 12 tons of hay $24; 8 acres ploughed. Came in 1897 with $20.

Wasyl Stratijchuk—Section 36-55-18—House $80; stable $60; 3 horses $120; 6 cattle $150; wagon, plough, $80; sleighs and harrow $40; mower, and rake $80; 35 tons of hay $70; 20 acres ploughed $60; has 400 bushels of grain; 150 bushels of potatoes. Came in 1897 with a capital of $500.

Ivan Jurkow—Section 36-55-18—House $80; stable $60; 2 horses $80; 2 cattle $50; 15 tons of hay $30; 14 acres ploughed $42; plough and harrow $40; 200 bushels of grain; 60 bushels potatoes. Came in 1896 without any capital.

Peter Nimchuk—Section 34-55-18—House $80; stable $50; 4 cattle $100; 15 tons of hay $30; 14 acres ploughed $42; 200 bushels grain; 100 bushels potatoes. Came in 1897 with $40 capital.

Michael Wichinski—Section 28-55-18—House $70; stable $50; 2 horses $60; wagon, plough and harrow $100; 2 cattle $50; 15 tons of hay $30; 7 acres ploughed $24. Came in 1897 with $20 capital.

Metro Zacho (Dmytro Zacharko)—Section 14-56-18—House $70; stable $50; cow and calf $40; 80 bushels of grain; 40 bushels potatoes; 8 tons of hay $16; 8 acres ploughed $24. Came in 1897 with $20 capital.

Michalo Zakopsky (Kasubski)—Section 14-56-18—House $80; stable $40; 2 cattle $45; 30 bushels of grain; 20 bushels of potatoes; 8 tons of hay $16; 6 acres ploughed $18; Came in 1897; was in debt $90.

Stefan Petnitz (Stefan Panych)—Section 12-56-18—House $70; stable $50; 2 horses $75; wagon and plough $80; 4 cattle $100; 20 tons of hay $40. Has 180 bushels of grain; 35 bushels potatoes; 8 acres broken $24. Came in 1897 with a capital of $120.

Ivan Wilaschuk (Ivan Weleschuk)—Section 12-56-18—House $60; stable $50; Blacksmith shop $30; 2 horses $85; 6 cattle $140; 20 tons of hay $60; 250 bushels of grain and 80 bushels of potatoes; 20 acres ploughed $60; came in 1897 with capital of $400.

I will herewith submit three or four names from the Rabbit Hills Colony of Galicians to shew you that the progress made in that district has been very great and the condition of things is very satisfactory.

Theodor Fuhr—Section 4-51-25 W.4.M.—Has been there three years; has 700 bushels of grain in granary; 7 cattle $175; 3 horses $150; 15 pigs $40; house, stable and granary $400; all good; wagon, binder, plough, sleigh and harrows $300; 40 acres under cultivation; 30 tons of hay; 100 bushels of potatoes. Came in April 1896 with $500 capital.

Iwan Hunis (Halkow ?)—Has 800 bushels of grain; 300 bushels of potatoes; 2 horses $100; 6 cattle $150; wagon and plough $100; 40 acres ploughed $120; 17 pigs $70; house, stable and granary $350; has 320 acres of land. Started in 1896 with a capital of $700.

Gregory Tamara (Hryc Czymera)—House and stable $150; 400 bushels of grain and 100 bushels of potatoes; 2 horses $80; 2 cows $50; mower, rake and plough $100; Came a little over a year ago with no capital.

Timko Perch (Pyrch)—House and stable $300; 2 horses $100; 4 cattle $100; 25 acres ploughed $75; 7 pigs $35; 400 bushels of grain; 100 bushels of potatoes; wagon, plough, mower and rake $150. Came over a year ago with $700 capital.

In speaking with A. McLeod, who has settled in this Rabbit Hills district, he says the thirty Galician families there are as good settlers as could be desired in any country, and had it not been for them it would have been impossible to keep the school open during the late year.

As I have submitted to you the above four settlers, I wish to intimate that there is evidence of universal prosperity in this district. I have checked up about 200 or more of these families; have visited a great many of their homes; have looked over the features of interest in the different colonies, but will only submit to you a portion or a few of the above arriving at different periods to shew you that the greatest possible progress is attending their efforts. I am in receipt of a good deal of information that can be used for future reference, but which would be very cumbersome and uninteresting to you, and you can accept the above as a criterion to govern the progress and advancement of the late arrivals in our country.

It was my intention to visit the Mormon Colony south of McLeod, but I thought it better to return and submit some reports that I have on hand, and look over some of the German Colonies between the main line and the North-Western, and possibly run in to the Beaver Hills Colony of Galicians, the Yorkton and Saltcoats Colonies before the close of the year. These Colonies were inspected and a tabulated report made by Mr. E. H. Taylor, late of this office, so that possibly a general review of their prosperity and progress will be sufficient to submit. I will endeavour to accomplish this at an early date.[28]

IV

The report of an inspection of the same district made by Speers two years later, in 1900, contains his observations relating to the further development of Ukrainian colonies in the Edmonton area. He enumerates a number of settlers that he mentioned in previous reports and describes their economic condition, which enables us to make comparisons. There are certain discrepancies in the statements about the amount of money each settler had on his arrival in Canada, ones similar to those that we noticed in reports on other colonies. Speers had to rely on information supplied by the settlers themselves, probably made from memory and not substantiated by documentary proof. All other information Speers was able to verify, and it therefore can be assumed to be correct. The report dated 1900 was submitted to the Superintendent of Immigration in Ottawa at the beginning of February. It was written on the day of Speers' return from his inspection trip:

I have the honour to submit to you a report of a trip of inspection of the various colonies settled in the Edmonton District having returned from there this morning (February 9, 1900). I drove to the large Galician colony 50 miles East of Edmonton accompanied by Agent Sutter of the Department. I find these people are steadily making progress and are doing very well. Their continued success fully warrants everything implied in my former report.

To ascertain how acceptable they were as settlers and to find out the feeling of merchants and others in that district I made considerable enquiry and I found upon the best information that I could gather from all sources that these people were all right and were proving quite an acquisition to the commerce of Edmonton and vicinity as well as displaying a progressive

[28]8. Rpts./70396, December 13, 1898: C. W. Speers, Winnipeg, to Frank Pedley, Ottawa.

interest in promoting the industries of the country. They have already become a potent factor in consuming the production of the East as well as being large producers where they live.

Mr. N. B. Peck, Manager of the Massey-Harris Co., says:

I find the Galicians good men and honest, meeting their notes before they mature. Our sales during 1899 made to them for machinery would be $14,000 or $15,000. They are good settlers and making progress. I sold them a steam thresher for over $2,000. It went to the large colony 50 miles East of here. They have met their payment before it was due.

(Signed) N. B. Peck, Agent Massey-Harris.

Nor have their purchases been confined to this one company. In addition they have purchased largely from McCormick Man'g Co., Deering, Frost & Wood. I find that their total purchase in agricultural implements would be over $40,000 last year in Edmonton alone. Frost & Wood's agent at Edmonton claimed that they will purchase 100 binders next year. As an evidence that their trade is valuable some of these firms have Galicians employed as interpreters who have acquired the language.

The merchants speak highly of them stating that they are honest and men who were against them and their advent are now catering for their trade. Thus it will be observed that they are honest and industrious and are not only producers but are being felt as great consumers of our manufactured products. About 350 of these people have been employed on the railway they have earned a great deal of money. They have all been self sustaining. None wanting any support no destitution and the majority of them very comfortably off. They possess a beautiful country, rich and fertile and all they want is a railway.

Conceiving the idea that it would be well to take the first Galician settlers that settled in that district, comprising nine families who settled there in 1894, take a statement of what they had individually when they went in there and take also an inventory of what they now possess to establish the fact that they succeeded financially and are good settlers, I went to this trouble, and I beg to say that no nine men of any nationality ever made greater progress in Western Canada than these and if the record of the past is any criterion to govern the future the Galician people will be all right.

I beg to submit the following:

Name of Settler	1894
Michael Pullishy (Pullichiy)	$ 18.00
Peter Melyneck (Melnyk)	6.00
Andre Biche (Andrij Paish)	150.00
Michael Melyneck (Melnyk)	350.00
Antoine Biche (Antin Paish)	100.00
Fedor Melyneck (Melnyk)	250.00
John Pilipoo (Ivan Pylypiw)	100.00
William Finuck (Wasyl Fenniak)	200.00
Nicoli Melyneck (Melnyk)	120.00
Total Capital	$1294.00

This is all these men had when they came and settled in 1894. Herewith I beg to submit the present valuation of these men's holdings:—

	Valuation	
Michale Pullishy (Pullichiy)		
Horses 6 head	$ 450.00	
Cattle 22 head	550.00	
480 acres of land	2400.00	
1 binder	120.00	
Mower and Rake	80.00	
Seed drill, harrows and Plows	100.00	
Share in Steam Thresher	500.00	
Wagon and Sleigh	113.00	
Share in Flour Mill	60.00	
	$4373.00	$4373.00
This land is fenced and the buildings are worth $1,000.00		
Michael Melyneck (Melnyk)		
160 acres of land	$1000.00	
Horses 5 head	375.00	
Cattle 20 head	500.00	
Binder, Mower and Rake	200.00	
Seed Drill, Harrows and Plows	100.00	
Wagon and Sleigh	115.00	
Share in Steamer Thresher	500.00	
Share in Flour Mill	60.00	
	$2850.00	$2850.00
Nicolo Melyneck (Nykola Melnyk)		
¼ section of land	$1000.00	
3 head of horses	250.00	
8 head of cattle	200.00	
Wagon and Plow and Harrows	100.00	
	$1550.00	$1550.00
Fedor Melyneck (Fedir Melnyk)		
320 acres of land	$2000.00	
Horses 4 head	300.00	
Cattle 20 head	500.00	
Binder, Mower and Rake	200.00	
Harrow, Disc Harrow	60.00	
Plow and Wagon	100.00	
12 Hogs	60.00	
Share in Steam Thresher	500.00	
Share in Flour Mill	60.00	
	$3780.00	$3780.00
Buildings worth $1000 Farm all fenced.		
Petro Melyneck (Melnyk)		
160 acres of land	$1000.00	
4 Horses	300.00	
8 Cattle	200.00	
13 Hogs	75.00	
Binder, Mower and Rake	150.00	
Harrows and Plows	50.00	
Wagon and Sleigh	115.00	
	$1890.00	$1890.00
House worth $600. Farm all fenced.		

Antoine Biche (Antin Paish)		
160 acres of land	$1000.00	
3 horses	225.00	
15 cattle	375.00	
10 hogs	75.00	
Mower and Rake and Wagon	130.00	
Plows and Harrows	45.00	
Seed Drill	40.00	
	$1890.00	$1890.00
Farm all fenced. Comfortable Buildings.		
Andre Biche (Andrij Paish)		
160 acres of land	$1000.00	
2 oxen	125.00	
6 cattle	175.00	
Binder, Mower and Rake	100.00	
Wagon and Sleigh	80.00	
Plows and Harrows	50.00	
4 hogs	25.00	
	$1555.00	$1555.00
Farm all fenced. Comfortable Buildings.		
William Finuck (Wasyl Fenniak)		
320 acres land	$1600.00	
4 horses	300.00	
12 cattle	300.00	
8 hogs	75.00	
Binder, Mower and Rake	200.00	
Wagon and Sleigh	115.00	
Harrows and Plows	50.00	
	$2640.00	$2640.00
Buildings worth $1000 Farm all fenced.		
John Pillipoo (Ivan Pylypiw)		
320 acres land	$1600.00	
7 horses	450.00	
16 cattle	480.00	
16 hogs	100.00	
Binder, Mower and Rake	200.00	
Seed Drill, Plows	80.00	
Disc Harrow and Harrow	80.00	
Wagon and Sleigh	100.00	
Share in Steam Thresher	500.00	
Share in Flour Mill	60.00	
	$3650.00	$3650.00
Buildings worth $1000 Farm all fenced.		
		$24,278.00

In addition to the above I find these farms all well fenced, with good buildings. These improvements might be valued at . . . $7000.00.

Thus it will be seen that these nine Galician settlers the first coming to Western Canada have done remarkably well. I also wish to remark that a farmers grist mill is being built at Fort Saskatchewan and that these Galicians have taken $1500 in stock in the joint stock company. The secretary of the company informs me that they are the first men ready with their money on any and every demand of the company.

These Galicians have already built two fine churches and have established schools.[29]

To round out the description of the Ukrainian settlements in Alberta, here is Cyril Genik's report on his visit to the "Ruthenian (Little Russian) Colony" in the Edmonton area, presented in December, 1903. Genik, the Ruthenian Interpreter from the Winnipeg immigration office, spent twenty days in the Edmonton area, but his report is brief in comparison to others and lacks the detail given as a rule by Speers and by the local immigration agents in their reports:

By your order I went to Alberta in the neighbourhood of Edmonton to visit the Ruthenian (Little Russian) Colony, and where I stayed from the 9th of August to the 29th, 1903. The Ruthenians from Galicia and Bukowina provinces of Austria, settled near Edmonton in two places. The first place can be found 50 miles East from Edmonton, where they are scattered over 50 townships. The first settlers came were nine families who settled east of Edmonton 56 miles, near Post Office Star, and came from Galicia. In 1897 15 families arrived from Galicia and Bukowina, and settled near the first settlers further east. From the year 1898 until this day, there came such large number of settlers to this place, that now they take up 50 townships. The colony consists of about 2500 families of which about 2000 settled on homesteads, and about 500 families are scattered on homesteads. On both these colonies there are about 16,000 Ruthenians. The economical position of the whole colony is most satisfactory, each of the settlers having from 5 to 100 acres of land under cultivation, from 5 to 20 head of cattle, besides having a team or two of horses. Every settler raises a big lot of poultry. I met a lot of these people who a few years ago had no means at all, and to-day they are in very good shape. Nearly every settler has the necessary farm implements, and the whole colony has five threshing machines, the engines of which are used in the milling process afterwards. They are settled on the East side of Edmonton in the following townships:

Township	Range
46,	17
47	15, 16
48	16
50	16
51	15, 16, 17
52	16, 17
53	13, 15, 16, 17, 18
54	13, 15, 16, 17, 18, 19
55	13, 14, 16, 17, 18, 19, 21
56	13, 14, 15, 16, 17, 18, 19, 20, 21
57	14, 15, 16, 17, 18, 19, 20, 21
58	15, 16, 17, 18, 23, 24
59	15, 17.

29. Rpts./109279, February 9, 1900: C. W. Speers, Brandon, to Frank Pedley, Ottawa.

On the West side of Edmonton in Township 26, ranges 48, 49 and Township 27, ranges 48 and 49.[30]

Every settler is satisfied that he settled on this colony, and the growing welfare encourages the people more and more. I also have to add that in this colony the people have purchased a big lot of C.P.R. land, at the time when the lands sold at $3.00 per acre, and the settlers bought over 500 quarter sections. In this neighbourhood among the Ruthenians there is no more free land, as the newly arrived settlers finds, and they are moving farther and farther east, where more free land can be found. Up to this time there have only been organized a very few schools on these colonies, and also a few churches. On the East Colony are the following Post Offices: Star, Wostok, Whiteford, Vegreville and Beaver Lake. The settlers on the West side of Edmonton going to Edmonton and LeDuc Post Offices. I visited also Edmonton town, and found here about 100 families, who have bought property and settled in the town, and have made very good progress.[31]

V

It did not take long before the children of those pioneer settlers about whom Corporal Butler of the North West Mounted Police reported to his superiors as suffering hunger and privation began to participate in the public life of the province and of the nation in general. Andrew S. Shandro, the son of a Bukowinian settler who came to Canada in 1899, became a pioneer in the political field. As early as 1913 he was elected to the Alberta Legislative Assembly, representing Whitford constituency. Although his election was contested and annulled, he was re-elected in 1915 and again in 1917.

Institutions of higher learning, almost inaccessible to peasant sons in their country of origin, were not beyond their reach in Canada, and these Ukrainian Canadians took advantage of the opportunities offered them. An outstanding example of this fact was recorded in the *Edmonton Journal* of May 21, 1948:

BELIEVED RECORD

10TH DEGREE IN FAMILY AWARDED VEGREVILLE MAN

Ladimer L. Kostash, youngest of a large Vegreville family, was awarded the degree of Bachelor of Education at the University of Alberta convocation Wednesday. It was the 10th university degree won by immediate members of his family since 1921.

It is believed to be a record number of degrees for members of one family.

[30]After each set of range numbers in the above list, Speers included the phrase "West of the 4th Meridian."

[31]9. Rpts./287573, December 16, 1903: C. Genik, Winnipeg, to J. Obed. Smith, Winnipeg.

Ladimer Kostash, now 36, won his Bachelor of Arts degree from the University in 1934 and has been teaching in Alberta schools since that date. Formerly principal of a Willingdon school, he has been teaching at McKay Avenue School in Edmonton for the past two years.

He is one of six sons of Mrs. Anna Kostash and the late Frederick Kostash of Vegreville. All six won degrees from the university.

Harry, 49, the eldest son, received his B.A. in 1921 and subsequently his B.Ed. degree. He is inspector of schools for the Smoky Lake division.

Elias, B.Sc. graduate in electrical engineering, was forced to give up his profession some years ago, because of a knee injury. He now is directing the operation of the family farm 10 miles out of Vegreville.

John, holder of B.Sc. and M.Sc. degrees in mining engineering, died in 1943 in Ottawa. He was working with the Canadian bureau of mines at the time.

William, holding degrees in commerce and in education, is a member of the staff of the correspondence branch of the Alberta department of education.

Marshall, graduate in honors chemistry, is assistant superintendent of the International Nickel's operations at Sudbury, Ont.

In addition, a sister, Mrs. D. Fodchuk of Vegreville, has two daughters who are university graduates. Mrs. D. Lutsak of Hairy Hill graduated with a B.Sc. in arts. Eugenia Fodchuk, graduate in nursing, is on the staff of a Vegreville clinic.

Boris Fodchuk, a younger brother of Mrs. Lutsak and Eugenia is carrying on the family tradition. Last year he won the lieutenant-governor's medal for grade nine proficiency in the Vegreville School Division.

But it was in the field of agriculture that the Alberta Ukrainians excelled, true to their inherited tradition, as P. J. Lazarovich, Q.C., himself the son of a pioneer, pointed out in an address delivered before the Alberta Historical Society in Edmonton in 1957:

Basically, the Ukrainians have remained an agricultural people to this day. Consequently, it is in agriculture that they have achieved the greatest measure of success and made the greatest contribution to the wealth and prosperity of this country. And in this industry the Ukrainians in Alberta lead the other two provinces. To illustrate, let me enumerate some of the more important provincial, national, and international awards and honours which the Ukrainian farmers in Alberta won over the past several years.

In 1940 at the District Seed Fair held in Edmonton, the Ukrainian boys won 50 different awards. Between 1930 and 1955 the Ukrainians won 12 provincial championships in livestock-raising, 2 in dairying, and 3 in grain-growing. They won 3 national grain-growing championships at the Toronto Winter Fair. But at the various international or world Grain Shows in Chicago, the Ukrainians won 18 major awards in grain-growing. Among these awards there were 9 Grand awards for oats and 3 Grand awards for barley, each of which entitled the winner to the title of "World Oat King or Queen" or "World Barley King or Queen." William Skladan of Andrew, Alberta, won the world oat crown twice—first in 1939 and again in 1941.

Then the Pawlowski family of Vilna established a record which can scarcely be equalled anywhere. Paul won the world oat crown in 1940 and the barley crown in 1941. Sidney won the oat crown in 1949. Two Kings in one family! In addition to that, they won several provincial awards.

John T. Eliuk of Hairy Hill won his first oat crown in 1948 at Chicago and Canada's championship for oats and barley in Toronto in 1949. In 1950 he won the oat championship in Toronto and world barley crown in Chicago. In 1953, he again won the oat crown in Chicago. Three times, a King! That would gratify the vanity of any wife.

But it was in 1941 at Chicago that the Ukrainian boys or junior farmers from Alberta covered themselves with glory. Out of the first 12 highest prizes including the crown, they won 9 of them. They won the first six top prizes in a row and missed only the 7th, 10th and the 11th. . . . Two Ukrainian farmers have won the Master Farmer awards in Alberta—John Melenka of Warwick and John Skripitsky of Mundare.

In addition to grain-growing and stock-raising many Ukrainians have achieved more than local fame in other branches related to agriculture. Many pioneered in introducing fruit-growing in Alberta, four names are well known to fruit-growers—the late, William Salamandick of Vegreville, William Fedun of Krakow, William Zazula of Lamont and Peter Svarich of Vegreville.

Chapter Eleven

ON THE THRESHOLD OF THE NEW CENTURY

THE CURRENT of Ukrainian immigration which began to flow in 1896 continued unabated into the twentieth century. For a full decade the Ukrainians formed one of the major immigrant groups arriving in Canada. The flow was directed almost exclusively to Manitoba and the Northwest Territories (the Districts of Assiniboia, Saskatchewan, and Alberta), contributing substantially to the growth of the population in these regions. A comparison of immigration statistics illustrates the tempo of the increase in volume of the Ukrainian immigration:

YEAR	NUMBER OF PERSONS OF GALICIAN ORIGIN WHO ARRIVED[1]	TOTAL IMMIGRATION FIGURES FOR CANADA[2]
1893	254	29,633
1894	616	20,829
1895	489	18,790
1896	1,275	16,835
1897	4,999	21,717
1898	5,509	31,900
1899	7,276	44,543
1900	6,618	41,681
Totals	27,036	225,928

The "Galician immigration" between the years 1891 and 1895 consisted predominantly of persons of German origin who began to emigrate from Galicia during the late 1880's. The number of persons of German ethnic origin in the province of Galicia amounted to slightly over 2 per

[1]6. Gal./139859, February 1, 1901: J. Obed. Smith, Commissioner of Immigration, Winnipeg, to the Secretary, Department of the Interior, Ottawa.

[2]The census figure for 1899 is higher than the preceding figures, due to the arrival in that year of 7,350 Doukhobors: *Sessional Papers*, XXXIV, No. 10, Paper No. 13, 1900, 5.

cent of the total population. After 1895, according to immigration reports, 90 per cent of the Galician immigration consisted of persons of Ukrainian ethnic origin and about 10 per cent was made up of persons of Polish origin. The official figures for 1902 were given as follows:[3]

GALICIAN SETTLEMENTS IN MANITOBA		
1. Ruthenians from Galicia	11,378	
2. Ruthenians from Bukowina	5,690	
3. Polish people from Galicia	1,896	
		18,954
NORTH WEST TERRITORIES		
1. Ruthenians from Galicia	8,762	
2. Ruthenians from Bukowina	8,762	
3. Polish People from Galicia	1,947	
		19,471
Total number of Galician (and Bukowinian) settlers from Austria up to 31st July '02		38,435

(Signed) C. GENIK, Ruthenian Interpreter.

The immigration movement of Ukrainians to Canada before 1895 was sporadic, consisting only of single persons and a small number of families, almost all of them originating in the district of Kalush, with the village of Nebyliw contributing the bulk. The organized flow of Ukrainian peasant-settlers to Canada began in the spring of 1896. It was initiated and directed by Dr. Oleskow and supported by the popular educational associations of Galicia and the Emigrants' Aid Committee, of which Oleskow was the *machina movens*. By the year 1900, the number of Ukrainian settlers in Canada passed the twenty-thousand mark. The incentive to emigrate was now stimulated less by the activities and writings of Dr. Oleskow and the committee supporting him, or by the efforts of steamship agents, than by the letters the settlers themselves wrote to their friends and relatives in Europe. "I was sixteen when the emigration movement from our village to Canada started," wrote one

36. Gal./227379, October 25, 1902: Memorandum submitted to the Commissioner of Immigration in Ottawa by Cyril Genik, Ruthenian Interpreter, Office of the Commissioner of Immigration, Winnipeg. The number of "Ruthenians from Bukowina" on Genik's list is identical with the number of "Ruthenians from Galicia" (for the Northwest Territories). This is not probable. The population of Bukowina in 1890 amounted to 640,000 persons, whereas that of Eastern Galicia exceeded three million. This division was also reflected in the proportion of persons who emigrated from the two provinces. It may also be noted that the "Polish people from Galicia" group is calculated at exactly 10 per cent of the total number. This suggests that Genik used correct total figures of immigrants, but that the division into separate groups was made arbitrarily.

of the pioneer settlers in his memoirs, "It began when letters started to arrive from the families who left for Canada a few years earlier."[4] The writing of letters back to Galicia was based on psychological as well as familial reasons. The immigrants were going through a difficult process of adjustment, often accompanied by deep frustration and a general feeling of insecurity. In order to overcome these hardships and to maintain their psychological balance, the immigrants tried to reconstruct an environment which was familiar to them, one similar to that which they had left behind in Europe. They named their Canadian settlements after their native villages, built houses on the old country pattern, and settled in village groups. Relatives and former neighbours in their original homeland were induced to come over and join the settlers in Canada because they fitted into the pattern that the immigrants were anxious to follow in the new land.

As we have seen, letters written to relatives and friends sometimes exaggerated the extent of success attained in Canada. On the other hand, the settlers' friends in Europe tended to imagine that their Canadian relatives were living in opulence like the landlords in Galicia, because they heard that in Canada their friends owned 160 acres of land. This misconception sometimes led to painful disappointments, as the memoirs of pioneers testify. Anna Farion wrote:

> I arrived in Canada from the village of Zawale, district of Terebowla, Galicia, in 1897. Several other families arrived together with us. I was 17 at that time. The son of my father's sister, Wasyl Ksionzyk, and another relative of ours from Terebowla, emigrated to Canada one year earlier. They wrote to my father that they were doing fine in Canada, that they had plenty of land with woods and meadows. They never lacked meat—rabbits came to their very door, and herds of deer and moose roamed about in the bush. (That they often lacked bread and salt, they did not tell us; we found that out when we came to Canada). . . .[5]

The initial disillusionment on the part of those who came at the suggestion of established settlers did not last long. The joy of reunion and the hope for a better future quickly absorbed all their attention.

The more cautious individuals among the immigrants did not immediately dispose of their land and property in the old country and took along only enough money to pay their passage and rail transportation to their destination in Western Canada. After some time, finding the conditions in Canada satisfactory, these settlers obtained home-

[4]M. Dalyk, "Spomyny pionira"/"Memoirs of a Pioneer," *Kalendar "Ukrainskoho Holosu"* (Winnipeg, 1942), 99–104.

[5]Anna Farion, "Moi spomyny"/My Memoirs," *Kalendar "Ukrainskoho Holosu"* (Winnipeg, 1942), 87.

steads, built temporary shelters, and sent their power of attorney to their families to dispose of their property and join them in Canada. It became a common practice for the settlers who had lived in Canada several years, and who had established themselves and sold their first crop of wheat or barley, to pay the passage for their relatives or to advance money to friends who wished to join them. Deputy Minister Smart noted this fact in a letter addressed to W. T. R. Preston, the Inspector of European Agencies in London, "I understand a great many Galicians have and are continuing to send money to bring out friends from Austria. . . . I have also been told that many Galicians left Austria with only sufficient money to reach Canada and before coming did not dispose of their lands. Since arrival they are so satisfied with their new homes that they have sent back powers of attorney to agents to dispose of their properties and send the money here to them. . . ."[6]

Once settlements were founded, they grew with astonishing rapidity into extensive colonies. The Ukrainian colony at Rosthern (Fish Creek, Duck Lake, etc.) on the South Saskatchewan River, for instance, which was reluctantly established in 1898 with a few families, counted five thousand settlers, spread over several townships, only five years later. Speers reported, in July, 1903, on the astonishing progress made in this colony:

> The Galicians are established in the Saskatchewan River. . . . In June 1898, I placed the first twenty families in Townships 41 and 42, Ranges 1 and 2, West 3.M. This colony has been supplemented annually and at present we have 5,000 souls occupying the territory between Townships 38 to 43 inclusive, from Ranges 25 to 3.W.3.M. These settlers have made marked progress and are comfortably off at the present time, and have been in a position for the past few years to receive their fellow-countrymen and put them in a position to become established without incurring much trouble to the Department. They have proved excellent workers and have in the past, as they are at present doing most of the railway construction work in their own and many other districts on the line of railway. . . . I beg to state that I was astonished at the progress of these people; their agricultural equipment; their horses and their cattle; and they have built good comfortable homes. Their adaptability to our customs, both in manner and dress, their anxiety to acquire the English language with many other qualities possessed by these people, make them most desirable settlers.[7]

Besides those who had relatives or friends in Canada, the emigration

[6]6. Gal./105479, February 9, 1900: James A. Smart, Deputy Minister, Department of the Interior, Ottawa, to W. T. R. Preston, Inspector of European Agencies, London.

[7]6. Gal., July 24, 1903: C. W. Speers, General Colonization Agent, to W. D. Scott, Superintendent of Immigration, Ottawa.

movement also embraced those who had no direct connections in the new land. The more enterprising of these persons wrote directly to the Canadian Government in Ottawa, requesting information about Canada. These requests were often disarmingly frank and simple:

> I like to emigrate to Canada and I will be very much obliged if you will send me all information about the country. I like to get some pamphlets and maps.
>
> Yours Truly,
>
> (Signed) MATWIJ CZORNIJ,
>
> Kozaczyzna, P.O. Jezierzany by Czortkow, Galicia, Austria.[8]

Czornij's request was promptly granted. The Commissioner of Immigration in Winnipeg mailed him pamphlets and maps, and Cyril Genik translated the Commissioner's letter. Another writer from the same village, Teodor Skalczuk, went a little further in his request. He wrote: "The people of the whole world are thankful for giving them free land. There are many people who wish to come to your country but they are poor and have no money for journeys from Europe to Canada. We are 11 persons who want to come to Canada but we are poor, 5 adults and 6 children but we have not enough money. If the Canadian Government would back us for our own expenses we promise to pay back."[9] Unfortunately for Skalczuk, the Canadian Government did not have a fund for such a purpose, and the answer he received was in the negative. Had such a fund for prepaid passages existed, the borrowers would doubtless have honoured the obligations incurred, just as those who received advances on seed grain or rail passages did. Sir William Van Horne, the President of the C.P.R. Company commented on the honesty of the Ukrainians in an interview with the *Montreal Star*:

> When the Galicians were taken out there [to the West] the railway company had got pay for their transport only as far as Winnipeg, and had carried them the rest of the journey west on credit.
>
> "We had little hope of ever getting what they owed us," said Sir William, "but they have paid up every cent. Don't you think people whose sense of honesty is so keen that they will pay a railroad corporation a debt that they could easily have got out of are a good class of colonists to get hold of?"
>
> "When they are completely 'assimilated' they may get over that," suggested the reporter.

[8]6. Gal./110394, March 1900: Matwij Czonij, Kozaczyzna, P.O. Jezierzany, Galicia, Austria. Translation from the Ukrainian by Genik.

[9]6. Gal./110394, March, 1900: Teodor Skalczuk, Kozaczyzna, P.O. Jezierzany, Galicia, Austria, to the Canadian Government. Letter translated from the Ukrainian by Genik.

"I am afraid they will," admitted Sir William with a smile. "We can hardly hope to keep them up to the present standard long, I suppose. . . ."[10]

Sessional papers for the years 1901 and later, in the Dominion Lands Revenue section, record long lists of the names of these Ukrainian settlers who refunded "Relief Advances" received two and three years before.

After the first back-breaking years of homesteading, changes gradually became apparent in the Ukrainian settlements and in their relationship with other Canadians. Neat houses dotted the countryside, and people who were critical of or even hostile towards the immigrants began to alter their original opinions. One of these persons was Dr. R. H. Mason of Saltcoats. W. F. McCreary commented on Dr. Mason's change in attitude towards the Galicians: "Enclosed I beg to hand you extract from a letter I received a few days ago from Dr. Mason, who is attending the Galicians at Saltcoats where they were quarantined for scarlet fever and measles. The doctor was a very bitter opponent of the Galicians last year, but as you can see that his opposition came entirely from the fact that he was not acquainted. This shews that after going into the colony and attending their patients, he is highly pleased with the success they are making."[11] This is what Dr. Mason wrote to the Commissioner of Immigration:

> In accordance with instructions from Mr. Thos. MacNutt [Land Guide, Saltcoats, Man.], I proceeded to this colony on the 6th (June, 1899), reached Logberg about noon and was storm-bound the balance of the day—also experiencing some difficulty in persuading the interpreter to accompany me until the following day. I was agreeably surprised to find the amount of breaking, cultivation and building done by the Galicians, fencing and even tree planting, and the houses as a rule compare favourably with the German and other settlers—a great many have dogs to each house. It was all a revelation to me. I never expected anything—a demonstration that proves these people to be worthy, industrious, sober and ambitious to make homes for themselves—good settlers. I found several clever carpenters, waggon-makers, gardeners. As a result of their abilities in these lines I noticed two waggons complete—nothing but the poplar wood—also some furniture planed and carved equal to a great deal offered for sale. I also found a grist mill, which seemed to turn out good chop, and feed made entirely with poplar strongly constructed—a large flat or nearly flat rock turned by a shaft swung from the roof.
>
> I found a musician who constructed a very good violin and played

[10]6. Gal./Original in File 76054/100670, Extract from the *Montreal Star*, Monday, May 22, 1899: Interview with Sir William Van Horne.

[11]6. Gal./85345, June 24, 1899: W. F. McCreary, Winnipeg, to James A. Smart, Ottawa.

selections from Mozart, and others also made a good flute, out of a piece of poplar wood. An expert shoemaker also is to be found in the colony.[12]

No less surprised at the progress that the settlers had made was the Dominion Immigration Agent from Halifax, F. W. Annand, who was sent to Western Canada in September, 1900, by the Department of the Interior to inspect the Ukrainian colonies in Alberta:

I left Winnipeg on the morning of the 26th (August, 1900), on my way to Edmonton, and on my journey I passed through a fertile belt of Manitoba. . . . On my arrival at Edmonton, I met Mr. Wagner, the interpreter, the Agent Mr. Sutter being absent, and I informed him of my mission to visit the Galicians. We at once arranged for a team, and started across the prairie to Edna. I must say that although I had read a good deal about the agricultural resources of the North West Territories, I found the vastness of the Country was far beyond anything that I had previously conceived, as I travelled for miles and miles through what seemed to be an illimitable ocean of the finest agricultural lands, in a natural state, inviting the hand of the husbandman.

We found very comfortable quarters at Edna with an Ontario farmer, whose housekeeper was a Galician woman, and who for the neatness of her appearance, the condition in which she kept the house, and the way she prepared the meals would put many of our Canadian women to shame. I requested the interpreter to ask her how long she had been in this Country. He said it was not necessary to employ his services as she spoke English fluently, and to my surprise when I entered into conversation with her, I found that she spoke good English, and without the slightest foreign accent. I found on enquiry that this is a characteristic of the Galicians that they pick up our language with surprising facility, and speak it as though it were their native tongue. I would not have suspected from her appearance, manner or speech, that she was not a Canadian, and of a rather superior type at that, in the position she held.

Early next morning we started for Beaver Creek, to visit the Galician homesteads, passing many thrifty Canadian and German farms on our way. These showed all the signs of prosperity, comfortable looking houses, small but neat, fields well fenced, containing large crops of wheat, oats and rye; and vegetables of every variety. The horses were large and the cattle rolling in fat; everything indicating that these settlers should become in a short time free from the financial cares of the world.

We at last arrived at Beaver Creek, the home of the Galicians, and after paying our respects to the Greek Catholic priest, we started out to inspect their homes and surroundings.

We found the old people about the same, at least so far as their dress went, as when they arrived in Canada, but a wonderful transformation has been going on with the younger people. In a great many instances they

[12]6. Gal./85345, June 12, 1899: Extract from Dr. R. H. Mason's letter from Saltcoats, to W. F. McCreary, Winnipeg.

speak English fluently and have discarded the sheepskins, falling in with the customs of the country with regard to wearing apparel. I was informed that they were anxious to have legislation passed, so that they could substitute their unpronouncable Russian names, for English [substitute English for the Ukrainian], as they recognize the difficulty Canadians have in doing business with them, under present circumstances. The community is thrifty and prosperous, the people adapting themselves to their new conditions with amazing facility, their farms are well cultivated, and have yielded such large crops, that they are already agitating for a grain elevator. They purchased last year, and paid for, over $50,000, worth of agricultural machinery of up to date kinds. Several Galicians have shares in the Fort Saskatchewan Milling Company. Most of the merchants of Edmonton speak in high terms of the quality of these people. I understand that it is only six years since the first lot of Galicians settled in this district, and the progress they have made is the best evidence of the intelligence, thrift and industry they possess. In their schools, by their own choice, the English language is taught, and their children are bright and intelligent. From a careful examination of the condition of these people after their short existence in this Country, and from enquiries conducted in quarters well fitted to give reliable information, I have no hesitation in submitting my humble opinion that, notwithstanding all that has been said in objection to them, they are a desirable class of immigrants to people our fruitful North West lands with. Every evidence goes to show that in an exceedingly short space of time they will drop into the customs and manners of the Country and in all respects discharge the duties of good citizenship, in the spirit of our institutions.[13]

Annand's report may seem too optimistic, but it should be born in mind that he visited the oldest Ukrainian colony in Canada, established four to six years before his visit. The settlers of the colony had already obtained titles to their farms and were reasonably well off, as C. W. Speers' survey of the same settlement, made in 1902, testifies. These are some settlers of Edna (later Star) whom he visited:[14]

Ivan Havrelenko, Star, P.O.; Number in family—6; Arrived—1896; Capital on arrival—$100; Land now owned—160 acres; Acres under cultivation—60; Present value of land—$2,000; Horses—4; Cattle—10; Swine—10; Value of implements—$500; Total worth of Settler—*$3,000*.

Michael Pulliczie, Star, P.O.; Number in family—5; Arrived—1894; Capital on arrival $360; Land now owned—400 acres; Acres under cultivation—140; Present value of land—$3,000; Horses—6; Cattle—32; sheep—5; Swine—28; Value of implements—$933; Total worth of Settler—*$5,000*.

Wm. Pulliczie, Star, P.O.; Number in family—single; Capital on arrival—nil; Arrival—1894; Land owned—160 acres; Acres under cultivation—40; Recent value of land—$1,200; Horses—2; Cattle—8; Value of implements—$200; Total worth of Settler—*$1,800*.

[13]PAC File 99,993, and 6. Gal./125572, September 19, 1900: F. W. Annand, Dominion Government Agent, Halifax, N.S., to James A. Smart, Ottawa.

[14]17. Rpts./198139, April 9, 1902: C. W. Speers, Winnipeg, "Progress of Galicians at Edmonton."

Peter Melnyk, Star, P.O.; Number in family—9; Arrived—1895; Capital on arrival—$600; Land owned—320 acres; Acres under cultivation—50; Recent value of land—$1,600; Horses—7; Cattle—10; Swine—30; Value of implements—$50; Total worth of Settler—*$3,000.*

Joseph Deziwanka (Dziwenka), Star, P.O.; Number in family—6; Arrived—1896; Capital on arrival—$18; Land owned—160 acres; Acres under cultivation—30; Recent value of land—$1,000; Horses—3; Cattle—7; Swine—9; Value of machinery—$200 Total worth of Settler—*$1,500.*

Controversial and even contradictory opinions concerning the Ukrainian settlers were quite frequent and sometimes bordered on the sensational, a fact that caused confusion in the minds of the public. The question of the destitution of settlers was one of the topics frequently discussed, as we have already noted. Immigration authorities scrupulously investigated every rumor that came to their attention, so as to safeguard their reputations. Whenever complaints of destitution revealed cases of need, relief was rendered. Usually such relief consisted in sacks of XXXX flour (the cheapest brand of wheat flour), cornmeal, and potatoes. In some cases, even cows were given to destitute families which had small children, with the stipulation at the same time that the cows were government property on loan. An interesting example of a controversial report about destitution among the settlers is seen in a complaint lodged by Dr. W. H. Brothers of Shoal Lake to the Commissioner of Immigration in Winnipeg against the Ukrainian settlers north of Shoal Lake. Dr. Brothers forcefully called to the Department's attention the unfortunate diets of many Galicians:

. . . The majority of these (Galician) patients suffer from diseases due chiefly to improper and insufficient food. . . . In the past 3½ months most of the illnesses from which they want treatment, are illnesses due to dietetic causes, scurvy, partial starvation and worst of all poisoning caused by a fungus which the poorer families cook and use as a food. The fungus is, I think, the punk found growing on standing dead trees. There are many varieties of punk and all of them more or less poisonous even if eaten only once, but almost impossible as a food. Punk-poisoning is a new thing to me, especially chronic punk-poisoning. No doubt you will grant that it may happen in isolated cases but I hardly expect you to believe that Galician families use this poisonous fungus as a food. I could not believe it until I had seen three cases of poisoning and had heard three or four Galicians, besides the patients, state that they were living on punk.

I have attended 3 cases of scurvey from the Galician colony north of this place, 3 cases of punk-poisoning two of which had signs of scurvy and starvation, and one case an infant one year old which was apparently in the last stage of starvation owing to the mother's not being in fit health to nurse it, and cow's milk could not be obtained. This woman would not stay in the Shoal Lake Hospital nor leave her child there.

The condition of some of these Galician families is simply barbarous. Even if some of them have plenty of bread and meat this does not prevent them from having scurvy. But when they have not even enough bread and meat and have to fill up with punk, it seems to be almost too late for help. Such conditions would not be allowed to exist in any city in Canada, and if the Department of Immigration cannot do something very soon, then the public should know and should assist those who need it.

Please do not take me for an alarmist nor for a writer to the newspapers. There are kickers enough here who would pay for material such as this letter contains, in order to make use of it in an article on the Galicians and so forth.[157]

The accusation voiced by Dr. Brothers was very serious indeed, and the Commissioner of Immigration in Winnipeg immediately informed the Deputy Minister in Ottawa about the contents of his letter. Commissioner McCreary also dispatched officer Philip Harvey to Shoal Lake Colony to investigate the situation and to report on it. On his return from Shoal Lake, Harvey turned in a report that was quite different from that of Dr. Brothers:

According to your directions I visited the Colony of Galicians north of Shoal Lake in company with Mr. John Menzies, for the purpose of investigating the complaint made by Dr. Brothers, of Shoal Lake, to the Department, that a number of the Galicians were insufficiently supplied with food, and had been eating punk.

On my arrival in Shoal Lake, Mr. Menzies and myself waited upon Dr. Brothers for the purpose of receiving all information at his disposal, and we assured him that we proposed to make the fullest investigation into the circumstances, and on the 19th instant (April, 1901) Mr. Menzies and myself left by team for the purpose of visiting, in the first place, the three Galician women whom Dr. Brothers had attended for alleged scurvy and blood-poisoning. We found the women apparently well, and very much surprised to know that Dr. Brothers had reported that they had been eating punk, and they were emphatic in their statement that they knew what was good to eat as well as Dr. Brothers, and had not been eating punk, but they had during the summer dried a supply of mushrooms and capstools which Dr. Patterson and many others admit is first-class food, and one frequently used in the same manner as dried apples.

The names of the three women in question are Magda Tuwbyk, Kaska Dzievir and Mrs. Mikola Lezarsky. All the women in question had a supply of provisions in their houses, and were surprised to find that reports of their destitution had been made to the Department.

Mr. Menzies and myself continued our journey and visited Townships 19, 20 and 21, in Ranges 22, 23, 24 and 25, W.P.M., calling upon as many Galicians as we could, and also calling upon Mr. A. G. Wakefield, of Ranchvale, and we found, on the whole, that the colony was progressing as

157. Dest./154991, April 15, 1901: Dr. W. H. Brothers, Shoal Lake, to J. Obed. Smith, Winnipeg.

well as could be expected. There was no destitution, but on account of the men of one or two families being absent, I advanced 18 sacks of flour and six sacks of cornmeal to divide among six families, and took a lien upon the land for $5.50 from each family. During our tour through the colony we were impressed with the fact that a large number of men had already left home and gone to work, but with the exception above mentioned, there were apparently, ample provisions with the families to maintain them from time to time.

We also made enquiries as to the prevalence of small-pox in that vicinity, and found that the epidemic was confined to the Indian Reserve in the first place had entirely subsided, and the patients were out of quarantine. We found the health of the colony good, and on our return to Minnedosa Mr. Menzies and myself waited upon Dr. Brothers and mentioned to him the result of our trip. The Doctor then told us that a man named Barres, and a Jewish Interpreter living in Shoal Lake, had told him that the Galicians were destitute and living on punk taken from standing dead trees; he did not know of it himself, but on the strength of this statement he had been treating the women for punk-poisoning, and when it was proved that this was not the case, the Doctor suggested they must have been eating too much bread and meat. I need not comment upon the last remark, as the destitution he reported could hardly go hand in hand with the statement made that they had been eating too much bread and meat. However, Dr. Brothers was satisfied with our report, and pleased to know that the statements made to him were inaccurate.[16]

No doubt a certain degree of destitution did exist in the colonies, particularly among the newly arrived settlers who came too late to plant potatoes and other vegetables and to cut hay for the cow for the winter. Having little or no cash at all to start with, they were compelled to live on rabbits, mushrooms, and bread made of the low-grade XXXX flour supplied for them by the immigration authorities.[17] Conditions improved after the first season. Even the first modest crop of cereals and vegetables produced by the settlers was usually sufficient to face the second winter in Canada. This crop was almost invariably supplemented by the first few months' earnings of the older members of the family, mainly the husband. His wife usually remained on the homestead to tend the garden, make improvements in and on the house, take care of the children, and perform other such tasks.

The colonies that were established in or around 1896 in Manitoba

[16]7. Dest./154991, April 25, 1901: Philip Harvey, German Interpreter, to the Commissioner of Immigration, Winnipeg.

[17]Reverend A. Page, O.M.I., who visited the Galician colony in Beaver Hills on September 24, 1897, had this to say about XXXX flour: ". . . One family had only about ten lbs. of flour, the bread made from this flour was unfit to eat. . . . I tried to eat the bread made from this flour but could not, I never saw such bad bread in my life. . . . " 7. Dest./44027, September 24, 1897: Reverend A. Page, Yorkton, to Constable Ashe, N.W.M.P, Yorkton.

and the Northwest Territories grew into populous communities by 1900. The original settlements formed nuclei around which new colonies developed. The report submitted by the Commissioner of Immigration in Winnipeg to Ottawa, February 1, 1901, enumerated the following Ukrainian settlements:[18]

Manitoba Settlement		
Dauphin, including Sifton and Ethelbert	5,000	
Shoal Lake	1,200	
Pleasant Home-Gimli	1,400	
Stuartburn	3,000	
St. Norbert	100	
Gonor	300	
Whitemouth	200	
Cook's Creek	200	
Poplar Park	36	
Brokenhead	600	
Total for Manitoba		12,536
Northwest Territory Settlement		
Edmonton District	9,000	
Rosthern District	1,000	
Yorkton & Saltcoats	4,500	
Total for N.W.T.		14,500
Grand Total		27,036

Two years later, in 1903, W. D. Scott, the Superintendent of Immigration in Ottawa submitted a report on the Galician colonies to the Deputy Minister in which he listed the following settlements:[19]

Manitoba:
Dauphin, Sifton, Shoal Lake, Pleasant Home, Gimli, Stuartburn, Whitemouth, Brokenhead, Poplar Park, East Selkirk, Gonor, Cook's Creek, St. Norbert and Steinbach.

Northwest Territories
Assiniboia: Yorkton, Saltcoats, Langenburg, Pheasant Forks, Weyburn and Regina; *Saskatchewan*: Rosthern, Duck Lake; *Alberta*: Edmonton, Leduc. Total number of Galician settlers in 1903: *38,435*.

The colonies also showed signs of growing prosperity. With the adjustment to Canadian life the factor of strangeness gradually wore off, and the antagonism which was dominant when large numbers of strange settlers made their appearance in the Canadian West diminished

[18]6. Gal./139859, February 1, 1901: J. Obed. Smith, Commissioner of Immigration, Winnipeg, to the Secretary, Department of the Interior, Ottawa.

[19]6. Gal./227379, October 25, 1902, and /259502/ June 6, 1903: Memoranda, Galician and Bukowinian Immigrants from Austria.

considerably. The Ukrainians were even held up among other inhabitants as an example of honesty and frugality. Fred Villeneuve, a practicing lawyer in Edmonton and Member of the North West Assembly in Regina, gave an interview to the *Montreal Gazette* in 1901 in which he summed up the new viewpoint about the Ukrainian settlers in the district of Alberta:

> They are certainly fine settlers, and in a comparatively short time will develop into good and patriotic Canadians. When they first take up their 160 acres of land, each occupant proceeds at once to build a fence around his possessions, this immediate fence building being the distinctive trait in the character of the Galician people. They are industrious, honest and exceedingly frugal in their habits. If they need anything and have the money on hand, they make the purchase, but if they do not have the cash they will wait rather than go in debt.
>
> Mr. Villeneuve also remarked that a good many people born in this country might take valuable lessons in frugality from the Galician settlers of the Northwest. . . .[20]

A similar sentiment of admiration and approval appeared in an article in the Toronto *Globe*, written by a journalist, traveller, and lecturer, Frank Yeigh, who visited the Ukrainian settlement of Gonor on the Red River in 1902. His lengthy article was entitled "A Day in a Galician Village." In it, Yeigh described a visit to the home of a Ukrainian gardener who had been in Canada for five years:

> . . . Farther along the winding highway—and a Manitoba road is as capricious in its course as a Manitoba river—stood the home of a Galician settler of five years' residence, now a prosperous market gardner, raising potatoes and hens, onions and garlic, cabbages and beets for the Winnipeg market, to which he drives his ox team once a week. If the weather be too hot for his sleek beasts of burden, he will mercifully make the tedious journey by night, even though his own rest is sacrificed. The cattle in the grove nearby are his, too, and the milk and butter therefrom further add to the savings, for the Galician can give pointers to a Scotchman in economy. "I sell 400 bushels potato; this year I sell 200 more," boastfully remarked this proud land-owner in his pulverized English. His house showed corresponding prosperity. The logs were plastered over, and he made the plaster. The clay floor had been planked, the one original room had been expanded into two and a lean-to, and a porch added dignity to the front door.
>
> Hardworking are these simple-minded peasants, rising before sunrise and laboring till darkness, the women doing a man's part in the field. Only the babies are immune from work, and there were enough of them to give promise of thickly populating the colony in the near future. Besides those which swarmed around my feet, I found others stowed away in the nooks and corners of the interiors.

[20]Extract from the *Montreal Gazette*, Friday, June 21, 1901. Interview with Fred Villeneuve. 6. Gal./162304, July 15, 1901.

The groups in the fields, the bright-colored headgear outlined against the cloud-flecked sky, transplanted many a Millet canvas from Brittany to Manitoba.

Everywhere cordial was their greeting to the stranger. "We are pleased to have you," greeted one at the threshold, and the language of gesture was no less eloquent than that of words. The proferred right hand was often grasped in both hands of a host, followed by a deep obeisance. The universal language of a smile is understood and answered by a smile, and a welcome unmarred by sham characterizes these children of Europe who, passing by scores of countries and crossing the, to them, unknown seas, have planted their stakes on Canadian soil. God grant them peace and prosperity in their new home![21]

As economic conditions grew better, attention was turned to social and cultural spheres, and the Ukrainian communities made rapid strides forward on the road to integration. Municipal and school districts were organized, churches were built, and in 1903 the first Ukrainian-language newspaper to be published in Canada made its appearance. The settlers were so deeply preoccupied with organizing life in the new land that the death of Dr. Oleskow, which occurred on October 18, 1903, passed almost unnoticed in Canada. The original settlers who had come to Canada under Oleskow's direct auspices in the years 1896–97 were now a vanishing band in the vast sea of immigrants who came after them, without his direct solicitation and assistance. At the time of Oleskow's death, the younger generation—the children of the settlers—were already entering intermediate educational institutions.

The organization of rural schools was often done by the pioneer settlers themselves, as in the Stuartburn district by Theodosy Wachna, or a few years later in the Vegreville district of Alberta by Peter Svarich:

. . . He set out organizing school districts in the Vegreville area for the benefit of pioneer settlers' children. The first school district which he helped to organize, Kolomya S.D. 1507, was named after his home town. During the same year (1905) there were organized additional school districts: Sich, Brody, and Spring Creek. In 1908 he organized school districts called Stanislaw, Oleskow, and Volodymyr; in 1909 followed the districts Myroslaw, Kiev, Wolia, Krasne, and Zaporoze; and in 1910 the districts Franko and Pobida. Not only did he organize school districts, he also erected five school buildings and acted as Secretary Treasurer of the districts. . . .[22]

[21]Toronto *Globe,* LVIII, No. 16, 472, November 29, 1902.

[22]Information taken from "Uryvky zi spomyniw P. Zvarycha z Vegreville, Alta."/"Excerpts of the Memoirs of P. Svarich, Vegreville, Alta.," *Propamiatna Knyha Ukrainskoho Narodnoho Domu v Winnipegu*/"Memorial Book of the Ukrainian National Home Association in Winnipeg," (Winnipeg, 1949), 641–660. Peter Svarich was born on March 24, 1877, in the District of Kolomyja, Western Ukraine, and emigrated to Canada with his parents in March, 1900. In 1964 he was residing in Vegreville.

A great obstacle in utilizing urban educational facilities was the weak economic position of the parents, who needed every cent derived from the sale of their farm produce to buy machinery and stock, and to make other improvements. Nevertheless, the parents bore the great sacrifice of letting their children leave the farms to go to schools in towns, even though they were often badly needed on the farm. In most cases the children had to manage on a very meagre allowance—usually in the shape of farm produce—for their upkeep, but they were encouraged to surge ahead with their own initiative, and a great majority of them did precisely that. The son of one of the first Ukrainian settlers and the second child born to Ukrainian pioneer parents in Canada (his elder brother is considered the first), who later became a distinguished Ontario lawyer, a Queen's Counsel, a university lecturer in criminal law, and the recipient of the degree of Doctor of Laws, summed up the spirit of sacrifice and resourcefulness that characterized the first settlers when he said in an interview: "When I left our farm to go to high school in Winnipeg, my father gave me seven dollars and fifty cents, all the cash he had on hand, and advised me to show the Canadians that we can do just as well as they in schools."[23]

Fifty-three years after the death of Dr. Oleskow, the *Toronto Daily Star*—on the occasion of the election of Steven Juba, a son of Ukrainian immigrants, as mayor of Winnipeg—paid a fine tribute to the Ukrainian ethnic population of Canada:

> Steven Juba, a man of Ukrainian ancenstry, has been elected mayor of Winnipeg. Which should be no occasion for surprise, for this energetic and able ethnic group has been forging to a position of leadership in almost every field of Canadian endeavour. They are to be found in the top ranks of every profession, in commerce, the arts, and politics, while it was recently stated that at least 150 of our leading scientists are either Ukrainian-born or of Ukrainian ancestry.
>
> Hon. Walter Harris once lauded Ukrainians as a splendid example of an ethnic group that has become wholly Canadian in outlook and loyalties while retaining the best of its old world culture and traditions. Like the Scots, the Ukrainians are proud of such features of their national culture as their dancing, their folk songs and their national dress, without prejudicing in the least their very real Canadianism. . . .[24]

One year later, in 1957, another son of Ukrainian immigrants stepped into the limelight as the former mayor of Oshawa and a Member of the House of Commons for the Ontario riding, Michael Starr, entered the Federal Cabinet as Minister of Labour. The Provincial Cabinets of

[23]Personal interview with Dr. John Yatchew, held in 1951 at Windsor, Ontario.
[24]*Toronto Daily Star*, October 30, 1956.

Ontario, Saskatchewan, and Manitoba have all included ministers of Ukrainian descent at one time or another. Three representatives of this ethnic group have been called to the Senate, and from the time of the entry of the Ukrainian settlers and their descendants into the political field in 1913 until 1962, some sixty-four persons of their ethnic origin have served in Provincial or Federal Parliaments. A news item which, at the time of Dr. Oleskow's visit in 1895, would have seemed fantastic, surprised no one sixty-five years later:

> Labour Minister Michael Starr, accompanied by Mrs. Starr, Deputy Minister George V. Haythorne and executive assistant Thomas Van Dusen, will visit Washington April 26–27. Mr. Starr is to meet President Kennedy and Secretary of Labor Arthur Goldberg and to attend a formal luncheon and official reception.[25]

Dr. Oleskow never doubted that the Ukrainian settlers and their children would "become very soon truly Canadians," as he wrote in one of his letters to the Minister of the Interior in 1896.[26] Oleskow's unstinting efforts on behalf of his people and his tireless striving to improve their lot through emmigration to Canada have indeed been well rewarded—his vision has come true.

[25]*Ottawa Journal*, Thursday, April 20, 1961.

[26]I. Oles./29051, April 18, 1896: Dr. J. Oleskow, Lemberg, Austria, to T. Mayne Daly, Minister of the Interior, Ottawa.

Biographies

BADENI, CASIMIR, COUNT (1846–1909)

Count Badeni was the Prime Minister of the Austro-Hungarian Empire from 1895 to 1897. He was born at Suchorów, in Galicia, and on completion of his university studies entered the Austrian civil service. He resigned from the civil service in 1886, but two years later he was appointed Governor (*Statthalter*) of Galicia. In September, 1895, Badeni became Austrian Prime Minister, and remained in office until November 28, 1897. Count Badeni, when asked by the Marquess of Salisbury to supply information concerning Dr. Oleskow and his activities, turned in a very favourable report.

SOURCES

Public Archives. Department of the Interior. Immigration files, 1895–1897.
Encyclopaedia Britannica, 1952, 915–16.

BAKER, WALTER REGINALD (1852–1929)

W. R. Baker entered the railway service in 1873. He was General Superintendent of the Manitoba and North West Railway from 1882 until 1892, and General Manager of that Railway during 1892–1900, when the immigrants sponsored by Dr. Oleskow began to arrive in Western Canada. From 1878–1881, Baker was the private secretary to the Earl of Dufferin, the Governor General of Canada.

SOURCES

Canadian Annual Review, 1928–29, 628.
Canadian Men and Women of the Time, 54.
Public Archives of Canada. Department of the Interior. Immigration files, 1896–1900.

BUDZYNOWSKYI, VIACHESLAW (1868–1935)

Born in Galicia, Budzynowskyi was an economist, a writer, and a politician. He was also one of the founders of the Ukrainian Radical Party and the editor of its organ *Hromadskyi Holos*/"The Voice of the People." Budzynowskyi was a member of the Emigrants' Aid Committee that supported Dr. Oleskow. In 1907, he was elected to the Austrian Parliament in Vienna.

SOURCES

Encyclopedia of Ukraine. "Biographies," II, 1, 180.
Makukh, Iwan. *Na narodniy sluzhbi*/"In the Service of the People," 555.

BURROWS, THEODORE ARTHUR (1857–1929)

Burrows was born in Ottawa, the son of Henry J. Burrows and Sarah Sparks, Ottawa pioneers. In 1875, he emigrated to the West and became a lumber manufacturer, eventually operating the largest mills in Manitoba. Burrows married Georgina K. Creasor, of Owen Sound, Ontario, the daughter of a lumber manufacturer with mills at Dauphin, Manitoba. A Liberal in politics, Burrows represented Dauphin in the Manitoba Legislature, 1892–1903, and in the House of Commons, 1904–1908. He succeeded Sir J. A. M. Aikins as Lieutenant-Governor of Manitoba, but he died before the end of his term. Burrows was Land Commissioner for the Lake Manitoba and Canal Company in Winnipeg, and he is frequently mentioned in correspondence with the Department of the Interior during 1897 and 1898.

SOURCES

Encyclopedia Canadiana, II, 144.
Canadian Men and Women of the Time, 178.
Public Archives of Canada. Department of the Interior. Immigration files, 1897–1898.

CARSTENS, HUGO E. (1866–1941)

Hugo Carstens was born at Jever, Oldenburg, Germany. Carstens was educated at Oldenburg, where he studied law. In 1884, he emigrated to Canada and settled on a homestead in the Yorkton district, Assiniboia. After some time he abandoned farming and became an accountant with a Gretna bank. After leaving Gretna, Carstens taught school at Ebenezer, Saskatchewan. He then joined the Manitoba and Northwestern Railroad, a line running from Portage la Prairie to Birtle, and became its colonization agent. At the same time, he was also manager of the Canada Settlers' Loan and Trust Company, a British institution which lent money to homesteaders. When the Manitoba and Northwestern railway was taken over by the Canadian Pacific Company, Carstens, who had been actively engaged in colonization work in the Northwest, entered the service of the Department of the Interior as an immigration agent and interpreter with the office of the Commissioner of Dominion Lands in Winnipeg. He remained in that position until the beginning of 1897.

While serving as an interpreter with the office of the Commissioner of Dominion Lands, he was detailed, in the summer of 1895, to accompany Dr. Oleskow on his trip across Western Canada, and acted as interpreter during Oleskow's conference with the Minister of the Interior in Edmonton in September, 1895.

After leaving the Dominion Lands Office, Carstens became manager of the German-language newspaper *Der Nordwesten*, published in Winnipeg, and in 1903 he became its sole owner. In 1911 he sold the newspaper and its modern printing establishment to a company of shareholders and devoted his time to consular duties, having been appointed Imperial German

Consul for Manitoba in 1907. He held this office until the outbreak of the First World War in 1914.

Hugo Carstens married Kaethe Kort, of Wittenberg, in 1900, and had three sons: Hugo, of St. Paul, Minnesota, Hans, of Vancouver, B.C., and Rolf, of Winnipeg. He also had three daughters: Mrs. E. C. White of Thornhill, Man., Mrs. William Foster of Rumford, England, and Mrs. W. G. Neill of Winnipeg. Carstens is buried in Winnipeg.

SOURCES

Canada. Parliament. *Sessional Papers*, XXXI, No. 10, Department of the Interior, Immigration, 1897. 118.

Public Archives of Canada. Sifton Papers. Letter from W. T. R. Preston to Clifford Sifton (no date, presumably 1900).

Who's Who in Western Canada, 1911, I, 133.

Winnipeg Tribune, Obituary, October 7, 1941.

COLMER, JOSEPH GROSE (1856–?)

J. G. Colmer was born and educated in London, England. In 1886 he married Margaret Black. Colmer gained his business experience in the Merchants' Bank of Canada, as secretary to the General Manager. He served as secretary to the High Commissioner for Canada from 1880 to 1903, except during 1891–1892 when he was secretary to Sir John Abbott, the Prime Minister of Canada. During his term as secretary to the High Commissioner for Canada, and particularly during the years 1895–1900, he was in direct correspondence with Dr. Oleskow and met him personally during the professor's visit to London.

SOURCES

Canadian Men and Women of the Time, 251.

Public Archives of Canada. Department of the Interior. Immigration files, 1895–1900.

DALY, THOMAS MAYNE (1852–1911)

Daly was born at Stratford, Ontario, the second son of Thomas Mayne Daly and Helen McLaren. He was educated at Upper Canada College, Toronto and was called to the Ontario bar in 1876. In 1881, Daly went to Manitoba and in 1882 became the first mayor of Brandon. From 1887 until 1896 he represented the Selkirk constituency in the House of Commons in Ottawa, and from 1892 until 1896 he was Minister of the Interior in the administration of Sir John Thompson and Sir Mackenzie Bowell. Daly was not included in the cabinet formed in 1896 by Sir Charles Tupper, and he declined to stand for re-election at the polls. From 1901 until 1908 he was a police magistrate in Winnipeg, and from 1909 until his death, he was a judge in the Juvenile Court.

T. M. Daly was Minister of the Interior in the Conservative cabinet of Sir Mackenzie Bowell in 1895, when Dr. Oleskow visited Canada. He met Oleskow personally and had two conferences with him, one in Edmonton and the other in Ottawa on the eve of the professor's departure for Europe. A few months after the second meeting, Daly relinquished his post of Minister of the Interior.

SOURCES
Encyclopedia Canadiana, III, 198.
Dictionary of Canadian Biography, I, 148.
Parliamentary Guide, 1888–1896.
Public Archives of Canada. Department of the Interior. Immigration files, 1895–1896.

DMYTRIW, REVEREND NESTOR (1863–1925)

Father Dmytriw, a Ukrainian Catholic priest, was born in Galicia, Austria. He attended the Theological Academy at Lviw and acted as a curate in various parishes in Galicia. In March, 1895, Father Dmytriw obtained permission from the church authorities to leave for the United States. On his arrival, he was appointed parish priest at Mount Carmel, Pennsylvania. An able writer, he became assistant and later associate editor of *Svoboda*, the only Ukrainian-language newspaper published on the North American continent.

Dr. Oleskow visited Father Dmytriw at Mount Carmel in September, 1895. On Oleskow's recommendation the Canadian Department of the Interior appointed Father Dmytriw an immigration agent in 1897 enabling him to travel across Canada and administer to the spiritual needs of the newly arrived Ukrainian settlers. He obtained permission from his superiors to spend two months in Canada, and on April 1, 1897, he came to Winnipeg. The arrival of thousands of Ukrainian peasant-settlers during the spring and summer of 1897 called for the engagement of additional interpreters and immigration officers, and Father Dmytriw was invited to act in both capacities. On June 2, 1897, he returned for a few days to the United States and arranged for permanent transfer to Canada. On his return to Winnipeg, he assisted the Commissioner of Immigration. Father Dmytriw accompanied trains that took the Ukrainian immigrants from the various sea ports to Winnipeg, helped locate them on homesteads, and at the same time performed his duties of a priest for the settlers. At the time he was the first and only priest of the Ukrainian Catholic rite in Canada.

The combination of all these duties proved, however, beyond his strength. In the summer of 1898 Father Dmytriw fell ill, and in August of 1898, he returned once more to the United States, where he died in 1925. His numerous articles describing his experiences in Canada appeared regularly in *Svoboda*, and parts of them were published in a separate booklet in 1897.

SOURCES
Dmytriw, Reverend Nestor. *Kanadiyska Rus: Podorozhni spomyny*/"Canadian Ruthenia: Travel Reminiscences."
Public Archives of Canada. Department of the Interior. Immigration files, 1897–98.
Svoboda, 1897–1898.

DUMKA, PAVLO (1854–1918)

Pavlo Dumka was born in Kupchyntsi, Galicia. Dumka attended the conference on emigration arranged by Dr. Oleskow on November 14, 1895, as the representative of the peasants of his district. He was active in politics, and was one of the founding members of the Ukrainian Radical Party. In 1908, Dumka was elected a Member of the Provincial Diet of Galicia.

SOURCES
Encyclopedia of Ukraine, II, 605.
Makukh, Iwan. *Na Narodniy Sluzhbi*, 558.
Svoboda. 1895.

GENIK, CYRIL (CHARLES) (1857–1925)

Cyril Genik-Berezowskyi was born at Bereziw Nyzhnyi, district of Pechenizhyn (later Kolomyja), Galicia. He was the youngest son of Wasyl and Ann (Pertsovytch) Genik-Berezowskyi, and had two older brothers, Stephan and Anton. Genik attended the Teachers' Seminary at Stanislaviw, and after graduating attended the academic *Gymnasium* at Lviw, where he obtained his baccalaureate. He taught public school at Bereziw Nyzhnyi, in a school established through his efforts in 1880. Genik passed the civil service examination for the position of postal clerk, but was refused appointment due to his political affiliations. He was closely connected with the leaders of the Ukrainian Radical Party, particularly with the poet and writer Dr. Iwan Franko, who was arrested by the Austrian authorities for his socialist leanings and writings. After he left the teaching profession, Genik established a general store in the neighbouring town of Yabloniw. Actively interested in emigration matters, he collaborated with Dr. Oleskow in advocating Canada as the country for the settlement of Ukrainian emigrants, and attended the conference on emigration convened by Dr. Oleskow at Lviw on November 14, 1895.

Genik married the daughter of Reverend Tsurkowskyi, the parish priest of the neighbouring village of Liutcha. On Dr. Oleskow's advice, he emigrated with his family to Canada as the leader of the second group of emigrants assembled by Dr. Oleskow in June, 1896. At that time the Genik family consisted of Cyril, 39, his wife Pauline, 33, and his children, Eugenia, 11, Constantine, 9, Sophia, 6, and Olena, 3. They sailed from Hamburg on the S.S. *Sicilia*, and arrived in Quebec on July 22. On July 25, 1896, they reached Winnipeg.

The Geniks remained in the Immigration Hall in Winnipeg for about two weeks before settling on a homestead in Stuartburn in August, 1896. Cyril Genik registered on NW ¼ Sec. 16, Tp. 2, Rge. 6 East, in the vicinity where other members of the group also registered their homesteads. With a good command of German, Ukrainian, and Polish, as well as a working knowledge of English that he acquired, Genik was of great assistance to immigration officers. In October, 1896, the Genik family moved to Winnipeg in order to be able to send their children to school and made their home at 11 Lusted Street. Dr. Oleskow recommended Genik to the Minister of the Interior for employment as an immigration officer, and the Commissioner of Dominion Lands in Winnipeg received consent from Ottawa to hire him on a temporary basis. In due time this temporary status was changed to permanent, and Genik remained in the civil service until his resignation in March, 1911. He was naturalized on October 24, 1900.

While in Canada, Genik remained in close contact with Dr. Oleskow in Lviw. Genik became known to thousands of Ukrainian settlers in Canada, since he acted not only as their official interpreter but as their adviser and guide as well. He was one of the first Ukrainian intellectuals to emigrate to Canada, and the first Ukrainian to enter Government service. In his later years Genik moved to the United States with two of his children, his eldest daughter Eugenia, and a Canadian-born son John. He died in Winnipeg on February 12, 1925.

The Genik-Berezowskyi family belonged to a large and ancient clan of Ukrainian gentry, the Berezowskyis of Bereziw, who, after the occupation of Galicia by Poland in the fourteenth century, gradually became impoverished. This group multiplied profusely and formed a large settlement of free yeomanry who jealously guarded their patents of nobility as a safeguard against falling into servitude. During the early period of Ukrainian settlement in Canada, almost one hundred families of various branches of this clan emigrated to Canada. Some twenty different Geniks are listed in the Naturalization Registers of the Citizenship Registration Branch.

SOURCES

Memoirs of contemporary pioneers and data supplied by close relatives of Cyril Genik.

Naturalization Records.

Public Archives of Canada. Department of the Interior. Immigration files, 1895–1900.

Sailing Records.

Svoboda, 1896–1900.

HARVEY (HERVEY), PHILIP

The dates of Harvey's birth, arrival in Canada, and death, are not available. It appears, however, that Harvey emigrated to Canada from Galicia in the late 1880's, when he was about 20 years of age. He was the son of German colonists from the German village of Landestreu, in the district of Kalush, Galicia. Harvey spoke fluent Ukrainian and became an interpreter with the office of the Commissioner of Dominion Lands in Winnipeg when the Ukrainian immigrants sent by Dr. Oleskow began to arrive in larger numbers. He was engaged as an interpreter on a temporary basis by the Commissioner of Immigration in Winnipeg in May, 1897. From that date on his name is frequently mentioned in reports written to Ottawa by the Commissioner of Immigration.

SOURCES

Boberskyi, Iwan. "How the First Two Ukrainians Came to Canada," *Canadian Farmer Almanac for the Year 1937*, Winnipeg. In Ukrainian.

Lehman, Heinz, *Das Deutschtum in West Kanada.*

Naturalization Registry. Naturalization Certificate dated December 4, 1899.

Public Archives of Canada. Department of the Interior. Immigration files, 1897–1900.

Yatsiw, Wasyl. "38 lit v Kanadi"/"Thirty-eight Years in Canada," *"Providnyk"/"The Leader" Illustrated Calendar for Canadian Ukrainians*, 1931.

KREBS, JOHN (1860–1929)

John Krebs was born in Kryvula, near Bilche Zolote, Galicia. He married Katherine Berg, and they had five sons and five daughters. Krebs acted as an interpreter for the Department of Immigration and for the North West Mounted Police at Fort Saskatchewan, and his name is frequently mentioned in reports of N.W.M.P. officers during 1897. The Naturalization Records reveal the following information about Krebs: *Residence*: Deep Creek, Alta.; *Former Residence*: Austria; *Nationality*: Austrian; *Date granted*: October 24, 1894; *Where granted*: Calgary Supreme Court; *No. of return*: 17. The Naturalization Records also list a Daniel Krebs, of Deep Creek, Alberta (Naturalization granted June 13, 1896, Edmonton, Supreme Court; No. of return: 117), and a Philip Krebs, of Deep Creek (Naturalization granted the same day as to John Krebs). John Krebs died at Fort Saskatchewan, Alberta.

SOURCES

Information received from Mr. A. Krebs of Fort Saskatchewan, Alberta, in 1962.
Naturalization Records.
Public Archives of Canada. Department of the Interior. Immigration files, 1896–97.

LEWYTSKYI, DR. KOST (1859–1941)

Born in Tysmenytsia, district of Towmatch, Galicia, Dr. Lewytskyi became a barrister. He was active in the political and social life of Ukrainians in Austria, and was elected a Member of the Provincial Diet of Galicia and a Member of the Austrian Parliament in Vienna. Lewytskyi became the Prime Minister of the West Ukrainian Republic, 1918–1919. He was also a member of the Emigrants' Aid Committee that supported Dr. Oleskow's emigration activities, and the director of the Centro-Bank at Lviw. The Soviet police arrested him in 1940, and he died soon after his return to Galicia in November, 1941.

SOURCES

Information obtained after the War from Vice-Speaker of the Polish Parliament.
Makukh, Iwan. *Na narodniy sluzhbi*, 559.
Svoboda, Shamokin, Pa., No. 18. April 30, 1896.

MCCREARY, WILLIAM FORSYTHE (1855–1904).

McCreary was born at Pakenham, Lanark County, Ontario. He was the son of James McCreary of County Armagh, Ireland, and Elizabeth Wallace, of Glasgow, Scotland. McCreary gained his education at Arnprior, Ontario. In 1882 he married Anne Ellis Greene. He was an alderman in Winnipeg during the years 1883–84 and 1895–96, and in 1897 he served as mayor of the city. McCreary was appointed Commissioner of Immigration by Clifford Sifton in 1897, and remained in office until 1900, when he was elected to the House of Commons, representing the Selkirk constituency.

SOURCES

Canadian Annual Review of Public Life, 1904, 603.
Parliamentary Guide, 1903, 111.
Public Archives of Canada, Department of the Interior. Immigration files, 1897–1900.

MAVOR, PROFESSOR JAMES (1854–1925)

Mavor was born at Stranraer, Scotland, the son of the Reverend James Mavor and Mary Ann Bridie. On graduation from the University of Glasgow, he taught in Glasgow and edited the *Scottish Art Review*, later becoming professor of political economy at St. Mungo's College. Mavor occupied the chair of political economy at the University of Toronto from 1895 until his retirement in 1923. Professor Mavor was connected with the Department of the Interior, and was interested in immigration. He visited Russia and was the chief agent promoting the emigration of the Doukhobors to Canada. He was the author of numerous reports and books, for example, *Economic Survey of Canada* (1914), *An Economic Survey of Russia* (1914), *My Windows on the Street of the World* (1923), and *The Russian Revolution* (1926). In 1882 he married Christine Watt of Glasgow; they had a family of three sons and one daughter. In 1899, Mavor visited Galicia in the company of W. T. R. Preston and met Dr. Oleskow.

SOURCES

Canadian Men and Women of the Time.
Dictionary of Canadian Biography, II, 447.
Encyclopedia Canadiana, VI, 413.
Proceedings of the Royal Society of Canada, 1926.
Public Archives of Canada. Department of the Interior. Immigration files, 1899.

NAHIRNYI, WASYL (1847–1921)

Wasyl Nahirnyi was the founder and director of the largest consumers' co-operative organization "Narodna Torhovla" at Lviw. An architect and economist, he was active in the social and economic life of the Ukrainians under Austrian rule. Nahirnyi was the founder of the *Sokol*/"Falcon" gymnastic society, a group organized on the Czech pattern, which played a prominent part in the political emancipation of the Ukrainians in Galicia. He was elected chairman of the Emigrants' Aid Committee which supported Dr. Oleskow's emigration activities.

SOURCES

Makukh, Iwan. *Na narodniy sluzhbi*, 560.
Svoboda, April 30, 1896.

NEMIRSKY, THEODORE (1869–1946)

Born in Bilche Zolote, district Borshchiw of Galicia, Austria, now Western Ukraine, Theodore Nemirsky came to Canada in 1896, on the S.S. *Christiania*, with the first group of Ukrainian settlers sent over by Dr. Oleskow under the leadership of his brother, Vladimir. He married in 1898 and, with his wife Katherina, settled on a homestead in the Edna–Star district of Alberta, in what later became the Wostok community. In 1899, he became the first postmaster of the newly established Wostok post office, and for a number of years acted as Land Guide for the Dominion Land Office in Edmonton. He was the father of eight children and died at Wostok in 1946.

SOURCES

Private information.
Public Archives of Canada. Department of the Interior. Immigration files, 1896.

OLESKOW, DR. JOSEF (1860–1903)

Dr. Oleskow was born in Skvariava Nova, district of Zhovkva, Galicia, the son of a Ukrainian Catholic clergyman. On the completion of his public school education he attended the *Gymnasium* at Lviw, and after eight years of study obtained his baccalaureate in 1878. He studied in the Faculty of Arts at the University of Lviw, majoring in botany, chemistry, and geology. Oleskow then continued on with post-graduate studies, which culminated in the Ph.D. degree. He married the adopted daughter of Reverend Budzynowskyi and left for Erfurt, Germany, to take up specialized studies in botany, agriculture, and political economy. At Erfurt he wrote several papers on fruit-growing and dairying which were subsequently published. On his return from abroad, Dr. Oleskow became a lecturer at the Agricultural College at Dublany, near Lviw, and on passing the prescribed examinations, he was appointed Professor of Agriculture of the Teachers' Seminary at Lviw.

Dr. Oleskow had four children—two daughters and two sons. The eldest daughter, Sophie, born in 1886 (her married name was Fedorchak), later became the principal of the girls' school of the Ukrainian Pedagogical Society at Lviw. She died in 1943. Oleskow's younger daughter, Maria, became a pianist, and his sons studied engineering. On the death of his first wife in 1899 Oleskow remarried. After his appointment as director of the Teachers' Seminary at Sokal, he moved to that town in 1900. Not long afterwards, he became ill and died on October 18, 1903, at the age of forty-three. He was buried in the Lychakiw cemetery at Lviw.

Dr. Oleskow belonged to the younger generation of his era, which was brought up on Western, progressive ideas, with the stress on democratic principles, as opposed to the conservative tendencies of the older generation. Together with others who believed in these ideas, he set about working for the betterment of the status of the Ukrainian peasantry. Driven to despair by the lack of land—a situation caused mainly by the constant dwindling of land-holdings due to partitioning through inheritance—the peasants of Galicia looked to emigration as their salvation. This state of affairs was taken advantage of by unscrupulous steamship agents, who were encouraged by plantation owners in Brazil to present emigration to that country as an ideal solution to the peasants' dilemma. Well aware of the dangers of emigration to Brazil, Dr. Oleskow and a group of young Ukrainian intellectuals (the popular educational "Prosvita" Society and the M. Kachkowskyi Society) banded together to counteract the agitation for emigration to South America—a movement that begun to have disastrous consequences. They decided to direct the stream of emigration to some country better suited for settlement than Brazil, and Canada was their choice.

Dr. Oleskow made a very thorough study of conditions in Canada, and as a result wrote a popular booklet entitled *Pro vilni zemli*/"About Free Lands," warning peasants against emigrating to Brazil and pointing to Canada as a much more suitable country for settlement by agriculturists. The booklet was published by the "Prosvita" Society in the spring of 1895 and was distributed to its 351 village reading halls across the province of Galicia. In this booklet Oleskow announced that he intended to visit Canada personally in order to investigate conditions there and to discuss with Canadian authorities the possibility of settling several thousand Ukrainian peasant families in that country. He advised those intending to emigrate to Brazil to postpone their departure until his return from Canada and to hear his report.

In the summer of 1895, Dr. Oleskow, accompanied by a peasant-delegate from the district of Kolomyja, set out for Canada. He made an extensive tour of the country "from coast to coast," discussed immigration possibilities with representatives of the Canadian Government, and returned determined to direct the flow of emigration to Canada. In December of the same year he published his second popular booklet, entitled *O emigratsii*/"About Emigration," describing what he had seen in Canada, and what Canada had to offer its settlers. The booklet was read eagerly by peasants across the country, and Canada became the topic of daily conversation. Dr. Oleskow's visit to Canada was also welcomed by Ukrainians in the United States. The weekly *Svoboda*/"Liberty," published at Shamokin, Pa., wrote on August 1, 1895: ". . . Among our many patriots in Galicia, one really great and wise patriot has been found: Dr. Oleskow, professor of agriculture at the Teachers' Seminary at Lviw, a truly learned person, who decided to visit Canada at his own expense in order to explore in detail the possibilities of our people emigrating to Canada instead of Brazil. . . . We repeat with emphasis once more, Dr. Oleskow is undertaking this long and important journey at his own expense. . . ." (*Svoboda*, 1895, No. 21, 1.)

Hundreds of enquiries began to pour in, and delegations from the villages arrived at Lviw to consult with Dr. Oleskow on how to proceed to Canada. In order to be able to cope with the demand, it was decided to form a special committee which would deal with emigration matters. A conference of representatives from the province was called to Lviw for November 14, 1895, during which Oleskow reported on the results of his trip to Canada. Dr. Oleskow was entrusted with conducting the emigration activities, the committee, and the educational societies supporting him.

It was Oleskow's firm belief that the emigration movement had to be planned and properly organized to be successful. Among his proposals concerning the emigration was that (*a*) prospective emigrants should be able to sell their land at fair prices to their fellow villagers, who would be given credit from co-operative loan societies to enable them to pay cash for the land without falling victims of usurers and land sharks; (*b*) emigrants should be carefully chosen, and only those with sufficient means should be allowed to emigrate; (*c*) steamship tickets should be bought directly from steamship companies and not through sub-agents who often charged arbitrary prices for steamship tickets; and (*d*) groups of settlers should be conducted by experienced guides to protect them from exploitation on their long journey. Dr. Oleskow also worked out a plan to make the emigrants self-supporting on arrival in Canada and to assist them to become "truly Canadian."

In order to retain control over the emigration movement the committee hoped to obtain approval of a concession for Dr. Oleskow to establish and conduct an emigration agency that would protect the peasant-emigrants from exploitation and save them money for the start in Canada. Provincial authorities were favourably inclined towards the proposition, but when the matter was referred to Vienna, pressure was raised by the Polish group in Parliament to refuse the granting of such a concession, as it would encourage emigration. The Prime Minister of Austro-Hungary, Count Casimir Badeni, who knew Dr. Oleskow personally and had a high opinion of his integrity, was forced to resign his position in 1897 before the matter came up for discussion, and Oleskow's hopes to obtain the concession faded away. For two years, 1898–1899, Dr. Oleskow and the committee were able to conduct emigration activities with the financial assistance granted to Dr. Oleskow by the Canadian Government, but as they were unable to control the emigration movement, their work was taken advantage of by steamship agents.

Following his transfer to the provincial town of Sokal, Dr. Oleskow retired from emigration activities. He died shortly afterwards in 1903 at the age of forty-three. The wish for a long and prosperous life expressed for Dr. Oleskow in the following tribute by an Alberta farmer thus remained unfulfilled: "May God grant health and a hundred years of life to that good man whose name is Oleskow, who guided us here, as Moses guided the Jews from the Egyptian bondage, thus did he lead us here from Galicia. Once more—may God grant him health." (*Svoboda*, August 12, 1897, No. 33.)

ITINERARY OF DR. OLESKOW'S VISIT TO CANADA (JULY 25–OCTOBER 15, 1895)

Thursday, July 25: Dr. Oleskow and Iwan Dorundiak left Lviw for Hamburg, Germany.

Friday, July 26: On the train. In Berlin, changed train stations (to Lehrter Bahnhof).

Saturday, July 27: Arrived in Hamburg and after a brief stop boarded a steamer for England.

Monday, July 29: Arrived in London and remained there three days.

Thursday, August 1: Arrived in Liverpool and boarded S.S. *Sardinian* of the Allen Line bound for Montreal.

Monday, August 12: Landed in Montreal and remained there one day.

Tuesday, August 13: Oleskow arrived in Ottawa and stopped at the Windsor Hotel, Metcalfe and Queen Streets.

Thursday, August 15: Oleskow left Ottawa for Winnipeg.

Saturday, August 17: After two days on the train, Oleskow arrived in Winnipeg and was met by Hugo Carstens who, on orders from the Department of the Interior in Ottawa, was to accompany Oleskow and Dorundiak on their Western trip.

Sunday, August 18: Oleskow and Dorundiak, accompanied by Carstens, visited several Ukrainian families.

Monday, August 19: Oleskow called on the Commissioner of Dominion Lands, H. H. Smith. In the evening of the same day, Oleskow, Dorundiak, and Carstens left by train (C.P.R.) for Calgary.

Wednesday, August 21: The party arrived in Calgary and was received by Mr. Rowe, the Agent for the Dominion Lands Office, and by Mr. W. Pearce, Superintendent of Mines. They visited farms.

Thursday, August 22: The party left Calgary by train and arrived in Edmonton in the evening.

Friday, August 23: Called on R. A. Ruttan, the Agent for Dominion Lands, who mapped out for them the whole plan for inspection of the lands in the Edmonton district. The party stopped overnight on the farm of Frederick Goebel, who came to Canada from a village near Stryi, Galicia.

Saturday, August 24: The party inspected the land around Stoney Plains. They called on several German homesteaders and stopped for the night on the farm of Philip Mueller, originally from the Galician village of Zavadiw.

Sunday, August 25: Having spent the night at Mueller's farm, the party set out on Sunday morning to view more lands suitable for settlement. Towards evening they returned to Mueller's farm and stayed for the night.

Monday, August 26: Early in the morning they started on their way back to Edmonton and arrived there in the evening. Oleskow had barely enough time to wash and change before proceeding to the Hotel Edmonton where the Minister of the Interior, T. Mayne Daly, was expecting him. They had a two-hour conference.

Tuesday, August 27: A new team of horses was hired, and the party started early in the afternoon for Fort Saskatchewan, reaching there by evening. They stayed in town overnight and bought provisions for the journey to be undertaken on the following day.

Wednesday, August 28: They left for the Beaverhill settlement. From Beaverhill the party took to the Victoria Trail until Beaver Creek. On their way to Beaver Creek they passed through a Moravian settlement. From Beaver Creek they again turned north towards Limestone Lake. In Township 56, Range 19, West of the 4th M., they found 16 Ukrainian families from the village of Nebyliw, who had settled there a short while before. After a visit with the Ukrainian settlers in Township 56, Range 19, Oleskow returned to the Victoria Trail and stopped overnight at Edna.

Thursday, August 29: They followed the same trail until they arrived at Long Lake, on the east side of Township 56, Range 18. Oleskow observed that the country between Egg (or Whitford) Lake and Township 56, Range 18, became more bluffy with lighter soil, well-suited for agricultural purposes.

Friday, August 30: They visited the country around Stoney Creek, an arm of the Battle River, and camped for the night on NW¼ 14-Tp. 46-Rge. 20.

Saturday, August 31: They reached Driedmeat Hill, proceeded west along the Battle River and arrived in the evening at Wetaskiwin, where they stayed overnight.

Sunday, September 1: After six days on the move without change of horses they returned to Edmonton. Oleskow made an excellent survey of the whole country, centring around Fort Saskatchewan. He considered this district the best suited for the settlement of Ukrainian agriculturists.

Monday, September 2: Visited an Indian Reserve south of Edmonton, returning to town the same evening.

Tuesday, September 3: The party left Edmonton for Calgary, arriving there in the evening of the same day. Oleskow and Carstens boarded the train for the Pacific Coast. Dorundiak, having received letters of introduction to settlers in Balgonie and Grenfell districts, left for the east.

Thursday, September 5: Oleskow arrived in Vancouver. After "viewing the city," Oleskow and Carstens stayed overnight in Vancouver.

Friday, September 6: Oleskow and Carstens took the "electric car" to New Westminster where the Land Agent took them around and showed them the lands within the railway belt which were open for settlement. Returned to Vancouver at noon, took the boat for Victoria, arriving there in the evening.

Saturday, September 7: In Victoria they were received at the Parliament Buildings by the Minister of Immigration for British Columbia, Colonel Baker. Also present were the Commissioner of Lands, Mr. Martin, and the Provincial Immigration Agent, Mr. Jessup.

Sunday, September 8: Oleskow and Carstens visited Esquimalt, and from there went to Nanaimo to see the coal mines, which were considered the largest in Western Canada.

Monday, September 9: Took the boat to Vancouver, arriving at noon. Boarded the train at 2 P.M. for Sycamous Junction, heading for the Okanagan Valley.

Tuesday, September 10: Changed trains for the Okanagan Branch and arrived in Vernon at 10:00 A.M. Visited Coldstream Valley and viewed farms and ranches, including Lord Aberdeen's farm.

Wednesday, September 11: Boarded the train for Okanagan Landing, spent a few hours inspecting the countryside, and in the afternoon returned by train to Sycamous Junction to join the eastbound train.

Thursday, September 12: Arrived at Banff and spent one day resting after the strenuous days on the Pacific Coast.

Friday, September 13: Left Banff and, without stopping at Calgary, proceeded to Indian Head.

Saturday, September 14: Viewed the large Experimental Farm at Indian Head, collecting information on farming conditions in Assiniboia and Saskatchewan.

Sunday, September 15: Travelled to Winnipeg.

Monday, September 16: Arrived in Winnipeg.

Tuesday, September 17: Left for Morris and Gretna. At Morris, Oleskow and others drove a few miles west and visited Lowe Farm. From there they proceeded to inspect lands east and west of the Red River. At Gretna, Oleskow took a short drive through the Mennonite Reserve to see the villages of Neubergthal and Somerfield.

Wednesday, September 18: Drove through various settlements and viewed land open for homesteading on both sides of the Red River.

Thursday, September 19: Continued inspection of land south of Winnipeg.

Friday, September 20: Returned to Winnipeg at noon, after spending three days viewing the lands south of Winnipeg as far as the United States border.

Saturday, September 21—Monday, September 30: Oleskow spent this time in the United States, on invitation from Reverend Iwan Konstankevych, the editor of *Svoboda* and Reverend Nestor Dmytriw, the parish priest at Mount Carmel, Pennsylvania. Oleskow arrived at Shamokin on September 25. After a few days' stay there and in Mount Carmel, he returned on September 30 to Canada to discuss immigration problems with the Department of the Interior.

Tuesday, Octoberl: Oleskow and Dorundiak returned to Ottawa and stopped over at the Windsor Hotel.

Wednesday, October 2: Oleskow called on the Acting Deputy Minister of the Interior, John R. Hall, and gave him a statement containing proposals in connection with the emigration to Canada of a large number of Ukrainian peasant-settlers' families.

Thursday, October 3: Oleskow was received by T. Mayne Daly, Minister of the Interior.

Friday, October 4: Oleskow and Dorundiak left Ottawa for Montreal to board the S.S. *Parisian* sailing for Europe the next day.

Saturday, October 5: S.S. *Parisian* left Montreal.

Sunday, October 6—Monday, October 14: On board the S.S. *Parisian*. Arrived at Liverpool late in the evening of October 14.

Tuesday, October 15: Oleskow was met by John Dyke of the Canada Government Agency and was invited to see the High Commissioner for Canada in London. He was unable to accept the invitation, however, since he had already overstayed his leave and was anxious to return to Lviw without delay.

SOURCES

Oleskow, Josef. *O emigratsii*/"About Emigration."

——— *Pro vilni zemli*/"About Free Lands."

"Preria"/"The Prairie" Canadian Almanac, 1928.

Public Archives of Canada. Department of the Interior. Immigration files, 1895–1900.
Svoboda, 1895–1903.

PAWLUK, THEODORE (1864–1918)

Theodore Pawluk was born in the village of Zadubrivka, Bukowina, Austria, now Western Ukraine. On April 16, 1899, Pawluk, thirty-five years of age, sailed from Hamburg with his twenty-seven-year-old wife Wasylena (Danyluk) and their two children, Wasyl, seven, and Yustena, two. Ten days later, their ship, the S.S. *Palatia*, arrived in Halifax. Also on board were Mrs. Pawluk's fifty-eight-year-old mother, Maria Danyluk, and her twenty-five-year-old son, George. The group settled on a homestead in the Edna-Star region, in what later became the settlement of Whitford, near Whitford Lake, Alberta. Pawluk became a successful farmer and raised a large family. The other children besides Wasyl and Yustena were George, Alexander, Mary, John, Matthias, Stephen, Florence and Dorothy. Theodore Pawluk died on November 9, 1918, but his wife survived him by some thirty years.

One of Pawluk's sons, Stephen, is the President of the Ukrainian Canadian Research Foundation, and has been the President of the Royal Canadian Legion, Ukrainian Branch No. 360, Toronto, since its formation in 1946. Stephen Pawluk was born in Whitford on February 14, 1910. In 1937 he married Olga Geraimchuk. Before the Second World War, Pawluk served as a Radio Communications Officer with the Merchant Marine, and in 1938, when the possibility of war loomed large, he joined the Royal Air Force in England. In 1944 he transferred to the Royal Canadian Air Force and served with distinction in that branch of the forces until the end of the war in 1945. At present Stephen Pawluk is with the Provincial Government of Ontario in Toronto.

SOURCES
Public Archives of Canada. Sailing Records.
Information obtained from the sons of Theodore Pawluk.

PEDLEY, FRANK (1858–1921)

Frank Pedley was born in St. John's, Newfoundland, the son of Reverend Charles Pedley and Sarah Stowell. He attended McGill University and the Ontario Law School. In August, 1895, he married Helen Louise Hobart of Cobourg, Ontario. Pedley became a barrister in 1890, and practiced law in Toronto until 1897, when he was appointed Superintendent of Immigration in the Department of the Interior, Ottawa, by Clifford Sifton. On November 21, 1902, Pedley was promoted to Deputy Superintendent General of Indian Affairs.

SOURCES
Canadian Annual Review, 1921, 904.
Canadian Men and Women of the Time, 893.
Public Archives of Canada. Department of the Interior. Immigration files, 1897–1900.

PRESTON, WILLIAM THOMAS ROCHESTER (1851–1942)

W. T. R. Preston was born in Ottawa. He became a journalist, and from 1883 to 1893 he was Secretary of the Ontario Liberal Association. In 1893 Preston was appointed Librarian of the Ontario Legislative Library, and in 1899 he became the Inspector of Canadian Immigration Agencies in Europe, with offices in London. During the years that followed, he played an important role in directing the flow of immigration to Canada. In 1902 Preston became Commissioner of Emigration to Canada. He was the author of two books, *The Life and Times of Lord Strathcona* (London, 1914) and *My Generation of Politics and Politicians* (Toronto, 1927). Preston visited Dr. Oleskow in Austria twice during 1899, and produced lengthy reports on both visits. He died at Croydon, Surrey, England, on November 2, 1942.

SOURCES

Canada. Parliament. *Sessional Papers*, XXXIV, No. 10, 1900, Department of the Interior, Paper No. 13, Report No. 2: W. T. R. Preston, Inspector of Agencies in Europe, 12–19.

Canadian Men and Women of the Time.

Encyclopedia Canadiana, VIII, 299.

Public Archives of Canada. Department of the Interior. Immigration files, 1899.

SALISBURY, ROBERT GASCOYNE-CECIL, *3rd Marquis of* (1830–1903)

The Marquis of Salisbury was thrice Prime Minister of Great Britain and four times Secretary of State for Foreign Affairs. Previous to holding these positions he was a Member of Parliament from 1853 until 1868. He is mentioned in Immigration files in connection with Sir Charles Tupper's enquiry of the Austrian authorities concerning Oleskow.

SOURCES

Public Archives of Canada. Department of the Interior. Immigration file, 1896.

Whitaker's Peerage, Baronetage, Knightage and Companionage, London, 1930, 521.

SCHULTZE, EDUARD DANIEL (1825–1916)

Schultze was born in Luebeck, Germany. He came to Canada in 1858, and on May 4, 1860, married Elizabeth Barbara Reinhardt (born in Montreal, September 16, 1837, died June 24, 1925). Schultze was for many years engaged in the wholesale business, and later, in partnership with his son, he became an importer and agent for lines of German manufacture. In 1869, he was appointed Consul for Austria-Hungary in Canada. He was promoted to Consul-General in 1899, and retired in 1901 with the title of Honorary Consul-General. In 1894 he was created a Knight of the Order of Francis Joseph. Schultze was the president of the German Society of Montreal from 1893 until his death in 1916. He was also the president of the German Lutheran Church in 1896.

It was Schultze who issued a letter of introduction for Dr. Oleskow to the Minister of the Interior during the former's visit to Canada in 1895.

Schultze visited Ukrainian settlements in Western Canada several times. He died in Montreal on June 14, 1916, and is buried in Mount Royal Cemetery.

SOURCES

Canadian Men and Women of the Time, 999.

Information provided by Dr. Joachim Brabander, Montreal, President, German Society of Montreal, 1963.

Public Archives of Canada. Department of the Interior. Immigration files, 1895–1900.

SIFTON, SIR CLIFFORD (1861–1929)

Sifton was born in the township of London, Middlesex County, Upper Canada, the son of John Wright Sifton. He was educated at Victoria University, Cobourg (B.A., 1880), and was called to the Manitoba bar in 1882 (Q.C., 1895). Sifton practiced law in Brandon and represented Brandon in the Manitoba Legislature, 1888–96. From 1891 until 1896 he was Attorney-General and Minister of Education. He then entered federal politics and sat for Bandon in the House of Commons, 1896–1911. Sifton served in the Laurier Cabinet as Minister of the Interior and Superintendent General of Indian Affairs from 1896 until 1905. He pursued a vigorous immigration policy. In 1911 he broke with the Liberal Party.

Sifton was knighted in 1915. For some thirty years he was the owner of the *Manitoba Free Press*. Sifton carried on a correspondence with Dr. Oleskow and made him the unofficial Canadian immigration representative in Galicia.

SOURCES

Dafoe, John W. *Clifford Sifton in Relation to his Times.*

Encyclopedia Canadiana, IX, 307 ff.

SMART, JAMES ALLAN (1858–1942)

J. A. Smart was born in Brockville, Ontario, the son of James Smart, sheriff of Leeds and Grenville, Ontario, and Ann (Bogue) Smart. Educated at Brockville and Woodstock, Ontario, he went to Manitoba in 1880. He became an alderman in Brandon, 1882–83, and the Mayor of Brandon in 1885–86, and again 1895–96. Smart sat for Brandon in the Manitoba Legislature, 1886–92. He joined Greenway's administration as Minister of Public Works (1886–92), and was subsequently made Provincial Secretary until 1893. Smart was called to Ottawa by Clifford Sifton in 1897 to become Deputy Minister of the Interior and Deputy Superintendent of Indian Affairs. He resigned from office in December, 1904. James Smart succeeded A. M. Burgess as Deputy Minister of the Interior and took a lively part in the colonization of the West. He also carried on a correspondence with Dr. Oleskow. Smart died in Winnipeg on May 3, 1942, at the age of eighty-four.

SOURCES

Canadian Men and Women of the Time, 1031.

Public Archives of Canada. Department of the Interior. Immigration files, 1897–1900.

Winnipeg Tribune, Obituary, May 4, 1942.

SMITH, HENRY HALL (1846–1928)

H. H. Smith was the Commissioner of Dominion Lands (dealing with matters of immigration) in Winnipeg during the Conservative administration of Sir Mackenzie Bowell and Sir Charles Tupper. He was relieved of his duties in the spring of 1897 when Clifford Sifton created the office of Commissioner of Immigration in Winnipeg and appointed the Mayor of Winnipeg, W. F. McCreary, to that office. Commissioner Smith met Dr. Oleskow when the latter visited Winnipeg in August of 1895.

SOURCES

Canadian Annual Review, 1928, 700.

Public Archives of Canada. Department of the Interior. Immigration files, 1895–1896.

SMITH, SIR DONALD ALEXANDER (1820–1914)

Sir Donald A. Smith was born at Forres, Morayshire, Scotland, the son of Alexander Smith, a tradesman, and Barbara Stuart. The nephew of the Chief Factor of the Hudson's Bay Company, John Stuart (1779–1847), Smith was educated in Scotland; his family was in only modest circumstances, and was unable to support him at university. He entered the service of the Hudson's Bay Company in 1838. From 1838 until 1868 he was stationed in Labrador, and in 1869 he was put in charge of the Company's Montreal office. Gradually he rose in the service of the Company, becoming its Resident Governor and Chief Commissioner in Canada.

Smith entered Canadian politics and represented the Selkirk constituency in the House of Commons from 1870 until 1880, when he resigned due to a disagreement with the Prime Minister's policy. He remained out of Parliament between 1880–87, but in 1887 he re-entered the House of Commons, representing Montreal West, and remained there until 1896, when he was appointed High Commissioner for Canada in London by the government of Sir Charles Tupper. Smith organized the C.P.R. Company in 1887 and was elected president of the Bank of Montreal. In 1897 he was raised to the peerage of the United Kingdom as Baron Strathcona and Mount Royal. Lord Strathcona corresponded with Dr. Oleskow and met him personally in London and on the continent.

SOURCES

Encyclopedia Canadiana, IX, 337.

Preston, W. T. R. *The Life and Times of Lord Strathcona.*

Public Archives of Canada. Department of the Interior. Immigration files, 1896–1900.

SPEERS, C. W.

Unfortunately not much information is available concerning C. W. Speers. He was appointed Dominion Colonization Agent in Winnipeg (later Brandon) in 1897 by Clifford Sifton, Minister of the Interior. Speers' detailed reports on the Ukrainian and other colonies in Manitoba and the Northwest Territories form the basis of the history of the settlement of these colonies.

SOURCES

Public Archives of Canada. Department of the Interior. Immigration files, 1897–1904.

Public Archives of Canada. Sifton Papers, M.G. 2711.D.15, Vol. 33.

TUPPER, SIR CHARLES (1821–1915)

Tupper was born in Amherst, Nova Scotia, the son of the Reverend Charles Tupper and Miriam (Lockhead) Lowe. He was educated at Horton Academy, Wolfville, Nova Scotia, and studied medicine at the University of Edinburgh (M.D., 1843). On his return to Canada, he practiced medicine at Amherst. From 1856 until 1867 he was the Provincial Secretary of Nova Scotia, and served as its premier 1864–67. Tupper played a leading part in the Confederation movement. From 1867 to 1884, he represented Cumberland in the House of Commons (Conservative). In 1870 Tupper entered the Cabinet as President of the Council, and was the Minister of Inland Revenue and Customs, 1872–73. In 1878 he became Minister of Public Works.

As Minister of Railways and Canals (1879–84), Tupper supervised the building of the C.P.R. In 1883, he was appointed High Commissioner for Canada in London, with an interruption of a period of sixteen months (1887–88), when he was Minister of Finance in the Macdonald Cabinet. He remained High Commissioner until 1896, when he returned to Canada in May to take over the post of Prime Minister in Ottawa. On the defeat of the Government, Tupper resumed the leadership of the Conservative opposition until 1900. He was defeated in the general election of 1900, and retired.

Tupper was married to Frances Amelia Morse of Amherst, and had three sons and three daughters. He was made a Baronet of the United Kingdom in 1888. He died at Bexley Heath, Kent, England, in 1915.

Dr. Oleskow met Sir Charles Tupper in London, July 29–31, 1895, when on his way to Canada. The then High Commissioner gave Oleskow a letter of introduction to the Minister of the Interior in Canada and corresponded with him on his return to Europe.

SOURCES

Dictionary of Canadian Biography, II, 674.

Encyclopedia Canadiana, X, 159.

Public Archives of Canada. Department of the Interior. Immigration files, 1895–1896.

Bibliography

THE STUDY is based almost completely on primary source material in the Public Archives of Canada. Copies of some 2,140 documents covering the period between 1895 and 1900 were made, and selected ones are quoted in full or in part. A list of relevant files appears in the section "Explanatory Notes."

PRIMARY SOURCES

CANADIAN GOVERNMENT DOCUMENTS

Department of Citizenship and Immigration, Naturalization Records. (Contained in the files of the Canadian Citizenship Registration Branch, and consulted to verify the spelling of names of persons referred to in reports of the Department of the Interior.)

Department of the Interior (Immigration). *Annual Reports*, 1895–1900. Ottawa: Queen's Printer.

Parliamentary Guide, 1888–1902.

Parliament. House of Commons. *Official Report of Debates* ("Hansard"), 1895–1906. Ottawa: Queen's Printer.

Parliament. *Sessional Papers*, XXXI (1897), XXXII (1898), XXXIII (1899), XXXIV (1900). Ottawa: Queen's Printer.

Public Archives of Canada, 1895–1900. (Documents contained in 19 files of the Department of the Interior dealing directly with the Galician immigration to Canada.)

ALMANACS AND MEMORIAL BOOKS

Illustrated Calendar of the "Ukrainian Voice," Vol. XX. Winnipeg, 1937. (Contains Adamovska, Maria. "Pochatky v Kanadi"/"Beginnings in Canada.")

———, Vol. XXI. Winnipeg, 1938. (Contains Stashyn, Mykhailo. "Moi spohady za sorok lit zhyttia v Kanadi"/"My Memoirs of Forty Years in Canada.")

———, Vol. XXV. Winnipeg, 1942. (Contains Romaniuk, I. M. "Pochatky Nebylivskykh rodyn v Kanadi/"The Beginnings of Nebyliv Families in Canada"; Farion, Anna. "Moi spomyny"/"My Memoirs"; Dalyk, M. "Spomyny pionira"/"Memoirs of a Pioneer.")

"Preria"/"The Prairie" Canadian Almanac. Winnipeg: St. Raphael's Immigrant Welfare Association of Canada,1928. (Contains short biography of Dr. Oleskow by his daughter.)

Propamiatna knyha 1894–1934 vydana z nahody soroklitnioho yuvileyu Ukr. Nar. Soyuzu/"Jubilee Book of the Ukrainian National Association in Commemoration of the Fortieth Anniversary of Its Existence, 1894–1934." Jersey City, N.J.: Svoboda Press. (Contains valuable material on early Ukrainian settlements in Canada and an English section, pp. 460–529.)

Propamiatna knyha Ukrainskoho Narodnoho Domu u Winnipegu/"Memorial Book of the Ukrainian National Home Association in Winnipeg." Material assembled by Semen Kowbel and edited by D. Doroshenko. Winnipeg, 1949. (Contains section written by pioneer settlers, e.g. Romanchych, Dmytro. "Ukrainski kolonii v okruzi Dauphin, Manitoba"/"Ukrainian Colonies in the Dauphin, Manitoba, District; Hryhorczuk, N. "Ukrainska kolonia Ethelbert, Manitoba"/"The Ukrainian Colony of Ethelbert, Manitoba.")

"Providnyk/"The Leader" Illustrated Calendar for Canadian Ukrainians. Winnipeg: St. Raphael's Ukrainian Immigrant Welfare Association of Canada, 1931. (Contains Prodan, C. S. "Okolytsia Stuartburn"/"Stuartburn Settlement"; Yatsiw, Wasyl. "38 lit v Kanadi"/"Thirty-eight Years in Canada"; Banzur, Andriy. "Rozkaz pro sebe"/"About Myself.")

Wachna, Theodosy. Unpublished biography of Theodosy Wachna obtained from his son, Dr. Elias Wachna.

———. "Golden Wedding Anniversary in Honour of Theorosy and Anna Wachna, Stuartburn, Manitoba, July 13, 1947." Private Printing.

Yuvileynyi Almanakh "Svobody" 1893–1953/"Jubilee Almanac of *Svoboda*, 1893–1953." Jersey City, N.J.

OTHER SOURCES

Dmytriw, Reverend Nestor. *Kanadiyska Rus: Podorozhni spomony*/"Canadian Ruthenia: Travel Reminiscences." (Booklet 4.) Mount Carmel, Pa.: *Svoboda* Publishers, 1897.

Mavor, James. *Report of the Board of Trade on the North-West of Canada with Special Reference to Wheat Production for Export.* (Folio VIII-123) London: H.M. Stationery Office, 1905. (Map No. IV, "Map of the North-West of Canada," shows the distribution of the population in 1904 and the racial origins of the immigrants.)

Oleskow, Dr. Josef. *O emigratsii*/"About Emigration." ("Publications of the Michael Kachkowskyi Society," No. 241.) Lviw: December, 1895.

———. *Pro vilni zemli*/"About Free Lands." Lviw: The "Prosvita" ("Enlightenment") Society, 1895.

Preston, W. T. R. *My Generation of Politics and Politicians.* Toronto: D. A. Rose Publishing Co., 1927.

———. *The Life and Times of Lord Strathcona.* London: Eveleigh Nash, 1914.

Secondary Sources

BOOKS, ARTICLES, AND DISSERTATIONS

Abbott, Edith. *Immigration: Select Documents and Case Records.* Chicago: University of Chicago Press, 1924.

Balch, Emily Green. *Our Slavic Fellow Citizens*. New York: Charities Publication Committee, 1910.

Black, Norman Fergus. *History of Saskatchewan and the Old North West*. Regina: North West Historical Company, 1913.

Caro, Leopold. *Wychodztwo Polskie*/"Polish Emigration." Krakow, 1911.

Dafoe, John W. *Clifford Sifton in Relation to his Times*. Toronto: The Macmillan Co., 1931.

Davidson, Gordon A. *The Ukrainians in Canada: A Study in Canadian Immigration*. Montreal, 1947.

Dutkiewicz, Henry J. I. "Main Aspects of the Polish Peasant Immigration to North America from Austrian Poland Between the Years 1863 and 1910." Unpublished Master's thesis, University of Ottawa, 1958.

Handlin, Oscar. *Boston's Immigrants: A Study in Acculturation*. Cambridge, Mass.: Harvard University Press, 1959.

Hurd, W. Burton. *Racial Origins and Nativity of the Canadian People: A Study Based on the Census of 1931 and Supplementary Data*. (Monograph No. 4.) Ottawa: Dominion Bureau of Statistics, 1934.

Kachor, A. *Rola "Prosvity" v ekonomichnomu rozvytku Zakhidnoi Ukrainy*/ " 'Prosvita' in the Economic Development of Western Ukraine." (UVAN Chronicle Series, No. 18.) Winnipeg: Free Academy of Sciences, 1960.

Kohut, Joseph. *Narys istorii Ukrainskoi Katolytskoi Tserkvy sv. Troitsi v Stuartburn, Manitoba: Moi Spomyny*/"A Sketch of the History of the Ukrainian Catholic Holy Trinity Church at Stuartburn, Manitoba: My Memoirs." Yorkton, Saskatchewan: Redeemer's Voice Publishers, 1958.

Makukh, Iwan. *Na narodniy sluzhbi*/"In the Service of the People." Detroit: Ukrainian Free Society of America, 1958.

Ryder, N. B. "The Interpretation of Origin Statistics," *The Canadian Journal of Economics and Political Science*, XXI (November, 1955).

Simpson, G. W. "The Names 'Rus,' 'Russia,' 'Ukraine' and Their Historical Background," *Slavistica* (Winnipeg: Ukrainian Free Academy of Sciences) No. 10 (1951).

Vihorynskyi, Iryney, O.S.B.M. *Ukrainski pereselentsi v Brazylii: Iracema v istorychnomu rozvytku v 1895–1958 r.*/"Ukrainian Settlers in Brazil: Iracema in the Historical Aspect of Its Development during 1895–1958." Iracema: The Brazilian Fathers, Prudentopolis, 1958.

NEWSPAPERS AND PERIODICALS

Edmonton Journal (1948)

London *Times* (1896)

Manitoba Morning Free Press (1896)

Mitteilungen. Institut für Auslandsbeziehungen (Quarterly, Stuttgart, 1957)

Montreal Gazette (1901)

Ottawa Journal (1895)

Svoboda/"Liberty" (Ukrainian weekly, published at Jersey City, N.J., until May 28, 1895, then in Shamokin, Pa., until August 27, 1896, and since then in Mount Carmel, Pa. Years 1895–1900. Contains material written by correspondents from Canada, as well as reprints from the daily *Dilo*/"The Deed," published at Lviw, Galicia.

Toronto Daily Star (1956)
Toronto *Globe* (1898, 1902)
Winnipeg Tribune (1897)

GENERAL REFERENCE BOOKS

Canadian Annual Review of Public Affairs. (Edition of 1904 and later editions.)

Canadian Men and Women of the Time. Edited by H. J. Morgan. Toronto, 1912.

Dictionary of Canadian Biography. Edited by W. Stewart Wallace. Toronto: Macmillan Company, 1945.

Encyclopedia of Ukraine. Paris and New York: Shevchenko Scientific Society, Inc., 1955–1962 (In Ukrainian).

Pioneers and Prominent People of Manitoba. Winnipeg: Canadian Publicity Company, 1925.

Additional Reference Material

GENERAL

Brown, F. J., and Roucek, J. S. (eds.). *One America: The History, Contributions, and Present Problems of Our Racial and National Minorities.* 2nd ed. New York, 1945.

Chumer, Wasyl A. *Spomyny pro perezhyvannia pershykh pereselentsiw v Kanadi*/"Memoirs About the Experiences of the First Ukrainian Settlers in Canada." Edmonton, 1892–1942.

Connor, Ralph. *The Foreigner: A Tale of Saskatchewan.* New York, 1909.

Davie, Maurice A. *World Immigration, With Special Reference to the United States.* New York: Macmillan Co., 1949.

Dawson, C. A., and Younge, E. R. *Group Settlement, Ethnic Communities in Western Canada. Canadian Frontiers of Settlement.* Vol. VII. Toronto: Macmillan Co. of Canada, 1936.

———. *Pioneering in the Prairie Provinces: The Social Side of the Settlement Process.* Vol. VIII. Toronto: Macmillan Co. of Canada, 1936.

England, Robert. *The Central European Immigrant in Canada.* Toronto: Macmillan Co. of Canada, 1929.

———. *The Colonization of Western Canada: A Study of Contemporary Settlement (1896–1934).* London: King and Son, Ltd., 1936.

Gibbon, John Murray. *Canadian Mosaic: The Making of a Northern Nation.* Toronto: McClelland and Stewart, 1938.

Handlin, Oscar. *The Uprooted: The Epic Story of the Great Migrations That Made the American People.* Boston: Atlantic Monthly Press, 1951.

Hansen, Marcus Lee. *The Immigrant in American History.* Cambridge, Mass.: Harvard University Press, 1942.

Kaye, V. J. *Canadians of Recent European Origin: A Survey.* Ottawa: Citizenship Division of the Department of National War Services, 1945.

Kazymyra, Bohdan. *Pershyi Vasylianyn v Kanadi*/"The First Basilian Father in Canada." Toronto: Dobra Knyzhka Publishers, 1961.

Kiriak, Ilia. *Syny zemli*/"The Sons of the Soil." 3 vols. Edmonton, 1939–1945. (A story of the Ukrainian settlers in Canada.)

Krawchuk, Peter. *Na noviy zemli*/"In the New Home." Toronto: Association of United Ukrainian Canadians, 1958. (Life, struggle, and creational work of Canadian Ukrainians.)

Lehman, Heinz. *Das Deutschtum in West Kanada.* Berlin: Junker und Duennhaupt Verlag. 1939. (See especially pp. 73–75.)

Lysenko, Vera. *Men in Sheepskin Coats: A Study in Assimilation.* Toronto: Ryerson Press, 1947.

Mackintosh, Archibald. *Prairie Settlement, the Geographical Setting.* Toronto, 1934.

McWilliams, Margaret. *Manitoba Milestones.* Toronto and London: J. M. Dent, 1928.

Martin, Chester. *"Dominion Lands" Policy.* (*Canadian Frontiers of Settlement,* Vol. II.) Toronto: Macmillan Co. of Canada, 1938.

Morton, A. S. *A History of Prairie Settlement. (Canadian Frontiers of Settlement,* Vol. II.) Toronto: Macmillan Co. of Canada, 1938.

Sisler, W. J. *Peaceful Invasion.* Winnipeg: Ketchen Printing Co., 1944.

Skwarok, J., O.S.B.M. *The Ukrainian Settlers in Canada and Their Schools 1891–1921.* Edmonton, 1958.

Smith, W. F. *Building of the Nation: A Study of some Problems Concerning the Churches' Relation to the Immigrants.* Toronto, 1922. (See especially pp. 107–118.)

Solomon, Barbara M. *Ancestors and Immigrants: A Changing New England Tradition.* Cambridge, Mass.: Harvard University Press, 1956.

Telman, Isaak H. *U dalekiy storoni*/"In the Far-off Country." Kyiv: Radianskyi Pysmennyk, 1956. (Soviet version of the history of Ukrainian emigration. Distorted presentation of facts.—V.J.K.)

Warner, Lloyd, and Srole, Leo. *The Social Systems of American Ethnic Groups.* (*Yankee City Series,* Vol. III.) New Haven: Yale University Press, 1946.

Woodsworth, James S. "Ukrainian Rural Communities: Report of Investigation by the Bureau of Social Research, Governments of Manitoba, Saskatchewan, and Alberta," Mimeographed folio, Winnipeg, January 25, 1917.

———. *Strangers Within Our Gates, Or Coming Canadians.* Toronto: Missionary Society of the Methodist Church of Canada, 1909.

Woznyi, Mykhailo. *Horodnytsia: Propamiatna knyha sela nad Zbruchem v Ukraini*/"Horodnytsia: Memoirs of a Village on the Zbruch River in the Ukraine." Toronto and Oshawa: Horodnytsia Self-reliance Association, 1958. (Contains English résumé and biographies of settlers from the village of Horodnytsia.)

Young, Charles H. *The Ukrainian Canadians: A Study in Assimilation,* ed. Helen R. Y. Reid. Toronto: Thomas Nelson and Sons, 1931.

Young, Donald. *American Minority Peoples: A Study in Racial and Cultural Conflicts in the United States.* New York and London: Harper and Brothers, 1932.

Yuzyk, Paul. *The Ukrainians in Manitoba: A Social History.* Toronto: University of Toronto Press, 1953.

HISTORICAL

Chraplyvyi, Evhen. *Silske hospodarstvo Halytsko-Volynskykh zemel*/"Rural Husbandry of Galician-Volynian Territories." Lviw: "Prosvita" Association, 1936. (Conditions of the peasantry in Poland.)

Hrushevskyi, Mykhailo. *Istoria Ukrainy-Rusy*/"History of Ukraine-Rus," 7 vols. New York, 1955. (Vols. IV–VI contain background on Ukrainian peasantry, burghers, and gentry.)

Kisilewsky, Vladimir J. "Ukrainian National Revival in Austria, 1772–1848." Unpublished Ph.D. dissertation, University of London, 1936. Pp. 145.

Lipinski, Waclaw. *Z dziejów Ukrainiy*/"From the History of the Ukraine," Krakow, 1912. (Contains background history of Ukrainian gentry, many of whose descendants emigrated to Canada.)

Thomas, William J., and Znaniecki, Florian. *The Polish Peasant in Europe and America. Monograph of an Immigrant Group.* 5 vols. Boston: The Gorham Press, 1918–1920.

IMMIGRATION AND ADJUSTMENT OF UKRAINIAN IMMIGRANTS

Byrne, Timothy C. "The Ukrainian Community in North-Central Alberta." Unpublished Master's thesis, University of Alberta, 1937. Pp. 98.

Gold, Norman L. "American Migrations to the Prairie Provinces of Canada 1890–1933." Unpublished Ph.D. dissertation University of California, 1935. Pp. 315.

Mamchur, S. W. "The Economic and Social Adjustment of Slavic Immigrants in Canada with Special Reference to the Ukrainians in Montreal." Unpublished Master's thesis, McGill University, 1935.

ALMANACS AND MEMORIAL BOOKS

Almanakh zolotoho yuvileyu 1905–1955/"The Golden Jubilee Almanac 1905–1955." Winnipeg: Ukrainian Mutual Benefit Association of St. Nicholas, 1957.

Calendar of the "Ukrainian Voice" for the Leap Year 1948. Vol. XXXI. Winnipeg, 1948.

Calendar of the "Ukrainian Voice" for the Jubilee Year 1950. Vol. XXXIII. Winnipeg, 1950.

Farma/"The Farm" Canadian Almanac 1930. Winnipeg: St. Raphael's Ukrainian Immigrant Welfare Association, 1930.

Illustrated Calendar of the "Ukrainian Voice" for the Leap Year 1936. Vol. XIX. Winnipeg, 1936.

Illustrated Calendar of the "Ukrainian Voice" for the Year 1940. Vol. XXIII. Winnipeg, 1940.

Istoria Ukr. Instytutu im. Petra Mohyly v Saskatooni/"Twenty-Five Years of the Petro Mohyla Institute in Saskatoon," ed. by Julian Stechishen. Winnipeg, 1945.

Klynovyi Lystok/"The Maple Leaf" Canadian Almanac. Winnipeg: St. Raphael's Ukrainian Immigrant Welfare Association, 1929.

Nove Pole/"New Field" Canadian Almanac 1927. Winnipeg: St. Raphael's Ukrainian Immigrant Welfare Association, 1927.

Propamiatna knyha poselennia Ukrainskoho Narodu v Kanadi 1891–1941/

"Jubilee Book of the Settlement of Ukrainians in Canada 1891–1941," prepared by the Ukrainian Catholic clergy. Yorkton, 1941.

Providnyk/"The Leader" Illustrated Calendar for Canadian Ukrainians 1930. Winnipeg: St. Raphael's Ukrainian Immigrant Welfare Association, 1930.

Providnyk/"The Leader" Illustrated Calendar for Canadian Ukrainians 1932. Winnipeg: St. Raphael's Ukrainian Immigrant Welfare Association, 1932.

Providnyk/"The Leader" Illustrated Calendar for Canadian Ukrainians 1933. Winnipeg: St. Raphael's Ukrainian Immigrant Welfare Association, 1933.

Providnyk/"The Leader" Canadian Ukrainian Illustrated Calendar 1935. Winnipeg: St. Raphael's Ukrainian Immigrant Welfare Association, 1935.

Providnyk/"The Leader" Canadian Ukrainian Calendar-Almanac 1936. Winnipeg: St. Raphael's Ukrainian Immigrant Welfare Association, 1936.

Yuvileyna knyha Ukraintsiw Katolykiw Saskatchewanu 1905–1955/"Jubilee Book of the Ukrainian Catholics of Saskatchewan 1905–1955." Yorkton: Ukrainian Catholic Council of Saskatchewan, 1955.

Yuvileyna knyha z nahody 30-littia dialnosty Zhinochoho Tovarystva pry Katedri sv. Ivana v Edmontoni/"Thirtieth Anniversary Jubilee Book of the Ukrainian Ladies' Aid of St. John's Ukrainian Orthodox Cathedral in Edmonton." Edmonton, 1957.

Yuvileynyi Almanakh 1894–1944/"Jubilee Almanac 1894–1944," ed. Luke Myshuha. Jersey City, N.J.: Ukrainian National Association, 1944.

Yuvileynyi Almanakh dla vidmichennia 50-littia pratsi Ukrainskoho Holosu/ "Jubilee Almanac to Commemorate the Fiftieth Anniversary of the *Ukrainian Voice* 1910–1960." Winnipeg, 1961.

Yuvileynyi Kalendar Ukrainskoi Rodyny na rik 1941: 1891–1941/"Jubilee Calendar of the Ukrainian Family for the Year 1941: 1891–1941." Mundare, Alta. Basilian Fathers, 1941.

Indexes

I. INDEX OF SURNAMES

NAMES OF SETTLERS were often misspelled in the reports of immigration officers. An attempt was made to correct these mistakes by consulting Naturalization Records and Cummins Directory Maps of 1922–23. The corrected names are listed first, and the misspelled names are placed in brackets. Names contained in the preliminaries and footnotes are not included in this index. Wherever first names or initials were available they have been supplied.

II. INDEX OF PLACE NAMES

Names of places are given in their various transcriptions, as they occur in the text. In the documents quoted in the text, the names of places in Austrian Galicia and Bukowina are, as a rule, spelled in the Polish or German transcription (Lwów, Lemberg), which differs from the Ukrainian spelling that is transcribed phonetically (Lviw).

www.ingramcontent.com/pod-product-compliance
Lightning Source LLC
LaVergne TN
LVHW010447080826
844660LV00027B/1227